"As a life-long educator, I believe that the key to addressing our collective needs and to fostering equity and justice is to harness and develop the power of every individual to fully realize their potential and contribute to the larger community in ways that are grounded in and honor their identities and backgrounds. Inclusive leadership is fundamental to doing this, and this timely volume provides a thorough roadmap. It's a great go-to resource during these turbulent times!"

— *Ana Mari Cauce, PhD, President and Professor of Psychology, University of Washington, USA*

"A powerful new perspective on leadership! Ferdman, Prime, and Riggio's excellent new book provides a crucial tool for inclusive leadership to grow and strengthen your organization. A must read!"

— *Marshall Goldsmith, PhD, USA, Thinkers50 World's Most Influential Thinker, and* New York Times #1 *bestselling author of* Triggers, Mojo, *and* What Got You Here Won't Get You There

"Changing organizations and societies to dismantle the legacy of racial oppression requires new visions and new leadership capacities. This timely volume provides much-needed perspectives and actionable steps to help move us into a more equitable and inclusive future."

— *David M. Porter, Jr., PhD, Chief Diversity, Equity, and Inclusion Officer, Haas School of Business, University of California, Berkeley, USA*

"Inclusive leadership has never been more important, and this timely collection of powerful essays by leading thinkers lays the groundwork for cultivating inclusive leadership that promotes equity, justice and vitality for all types of people, especially those who traditionally hold less power or privilege. An essential resource for anyone who seeks to promote inclusion at all levels of the organization."

— *Laura Morgan Roberts, PhD, Professor of Practice, Darden School of Business, University of Virginia, USA, and co-editor*, Race, Work, and Leadership: New Perspectives on the Black Experience

"Filled with wise and practical insights and suggestions, this book is a must read for leaders who want to build a great organization and win in these extraordinarily challenging times."

— *Steve Reinemund, Retired Chairman and CEO, PepsiCo, and Former Dean, Wake Forest University School of Business, USA*

"Anyone who calls themselves a leader should read this book. Based in the best of practice and science, the thoughtful and expert perspectives woven through each chapter offer crucial insights toward achieving positive change."

*— Eden King, PhD, Diversity and Inclusion Scholar, Lynette S. Autrey Professor of Psychology at Rice University, USA, and Past President, Society of Industrial and Organizational Psychology*

"Now more than ever, workplaces need to be transformed—diverse teams make better decisions than homogeneous ones, and leaders can set the tone from the top. Although the leadership of organizations has become more diverse in recent years, is it enough? How do we ensure that all members of an organization feel they actually belong? Ferdman, Prime, and Riggio provide us a roadmap for how to conceptualize inclusive leadership, why it is important, and how to achieve it. Rooted in social psychology and organizational behavior, this volume belongs on the bookshelves of leaders across all sectors of society."

*— Peter Salovey, PhD, President and Chris Argyris Professor of Psychology, Yale University, USA*

"I'm writing this three weeks after George Floyd was killed, and I'm inundated with calls from organizational leaders who are inspired to advance racial equity, but who're flummoxed as to where to start. In this comprehensive anthology, they will find a bounty of ideas and practices – grounded in theory and research – that address the critical importance of inclusive leadership in fostering diverse, equitable, and inclusive teams, organizations, and societies. A must-read!"

*— Kumea Shorter-Gooden, PhD, Former Chief Diversity Officer, University of Maryland, College Park, USA, and Co-author,* Shifting: The Double Lives of Black Women in America

"The timeliness of this book is commendable. By examining the type of leadership required to cultivate inclusion at a community and societal level, the authors address a real need during the COVID-19 pandemic, when inequalities have become more pronounced. The book contains useful strategies and frameworks for all to benefit from."

*— Nene Molefi, CEO, Mandate Molefi Consultants, South Africa*

"Most organizations talk about the vital importance of diverse perspectives in driving organizational success, however when it comes to creating an inclusive culture for their diverse workforces, they often fall short. What truly drives change is well-grounded information that provides direction for action. This book offers all of that and more."

*— Donna Sharp, Associate Dean, Executive Education, UCLA Anderson School of Management, USA*

"Being an inclusive leader doesn't happen naturally. Inclusive leadership is a skill. It can be learned. And that learning requires studying the views of experts—practitioners, role models, and scholars. The chapter authors in this book have much to offer those who want to be an inclusive leader. And the world needs everyone to be an inclusive leader."

— *Julie O'Mara, Board Chair, The Centre for Global Inclusion, Co-author,* Global D&I Benchmarks: Standards for Organizations Around the World, and *Past-President, American Society for Training and Development (now ATD), USA*

"Now more than ever, organizations need to challenge their dominant leadership paradigms. The future of work lies in fostering inclusive leadership for all of our teams, organizations, and communities. This outstanding volume, which brings together perspectives, insights, and best practices from leading thinkers and practitioners in the field, provides the deep guidance that is needed to help leaders develop these new skills and mindsets."

— *Allan H. Church, PhD, Senior Vice President Global Talent Management, PepsiCo, and Co-editor,* Handbook of Strategic 360 Feedback

"*Inclusive Leadership* is a valuable addition to the field of diversity and inclusion. The collection of perspectives and resources included in the text provides a guidebook for creating and transforming organizational cultures to be more inclusive of all of their employees, customers, and stakeholders. Perhaps the most valuable aspect of the book is its practicality. Any organizational leader will benefit from reading and applying these insights!"

— *Howard Ross, Author of* Everyday Bias and *of* Our Search for Belonging, *USA*

"This book will become the go-to resource for anyone who believes that inclusion is a necessary function of leadership in order to achieve a just and equitable society. It simplifies the complexities and challenges at individual, group, and systemic levels. It also illuminates the hard-won lessons and provides practical tools of brilliant practitioners who have a pragmatic approach to this work."

— *Joe Goldman, President, Democracy Fund, USA*

"If choosing the journey to become an inclusive leader, you will find no better roadmap than this book. You can peruse the landscape for a broad view, or meander into specifics—competencies and practices, tools and tips. For sure, upon reading this book, how and why to become an inclusive leader will not be in doubt."

— *Barbara Deane, Co-founder and Co-director, Institute for Sustainable Diversity and Inclusion, Editor-in-Chief,* DiversityCentral.com, and *Associate Editor*, Diversity at Work: The Practice of Inclusion

"This book on inclusive leadership is a comprehensive and valuable resource for creating and maintaining inclusive leaders, organizations, and societies. Deeply researched by a broad array of voices from various backgrounds, organizations, and cultures, it provides a roadmap for what all leadership should look like."

— *Steven Humerickhouse, Executive Director, The Forum on Workplace Inclusion, Augsburg University, USA*

"Take advantage of this well-crafted volume to deepen your understanding and practice of inclusive leadership. Try exploring its rich perspectives with an inclusive mindset: Pick a chapter that resonates with you—you'll be affirmed and likely inspired by it. Pick another chapter that seems unfamiliar or a bit weird—you'll be stretched and perhaps intrigued by it. Both good outcomes for a diverse world!"

— *Cynthia McCauley, PhD, Senior Fellow, Center for Creative Leadership, USA*

"*Inclusive Leadership* is a *tour de force*, illustrating both the clarity and the complexity of intersectionality and authentic selves in organizations. The remarkable timeliness of this collection, combined with the deep scholarship and thought that underlies it, makes it a 'must-have' for any student or practitioner of leadership who is concerned with equity, social justice, and inclusion."

— *Bill Berman, PhD, CEO, Berman Leadership Development, and Past-President, Society of Consulting Psychology*

"In the world today, leadership often means change. Leading change effectively means involving the people who are expected to bring about the change. Inclusive leadership guarantees this involvement and therefore leads to commitment to change and the generation of ideas that provide creativity. Thanks to Ferdman and his colleagues we have with this exceptional book evidence and stories that support the need for outstanding change leadership."

— *W. Warner Burke, PhD, E. L. Thorndike Professor of Psychology and Education, Teachers College, Columbia University, USA*

"The future will belong to leaders and organizations that can create and maintain a culture of inclusion and respect—in business, political life, and society overall. Bernardo Ferdman is a master at helping individuals and teams learn to do this, and he and his fellow editors have brought the best of scholarship and practice to this book. *Inclusive Leadership* will be a key resource for the enlightened manager."

— *Laurie Dowling, Executive Director, National Utilities Diversity Council*

# Inclusive Leadership

In a time of increasing divisiveness in politics and society there is a desperate need for leaders to bring people together and leverage the power of diversity and inclusion. *Inclusive Leadership: Transforming Diverse Lives, Workplaces, and Societies* provides leaders with guidance and hands-on strategies for fostering inclusion and explains how and why it matters.

*Inclusive Leadership* explores cutting-edge theory, research, practice, and experience on the pivotal role of leadership in promoting inclusion in diverse teams, organizations, and societies. Chapters are authored by leading scholars and practitioners in the fields of leadership, diversity, and inclusion. The book is solidly grounded in research on inclusive leadership development, diversity management, team effectiveness, organization development, and intergroup relations. Alongside the exhaustive scholarship are practical suggestions for making teams, groups, organizations, and the larger society more inclusive and, ultimately, more productive.

Leaders and managers at all levels, HR professionals, and members of diverse teams will find *Inclusive Leadership* invaluable in becoming more effective at cultivating inclusive climates and realizing its many benefits—including innovation, enhanced team and organizational performance, and social justice.

**Bernardo M. Ferdman**, PhD, has worked with leaders and organizations for over three decades to bring inclusion to life. He is an award-winning scholar-practitioner and consultant, distinguished professor emeritus of organizational psychology, and Fellow of SIOP, SCP, APA, and other groups. He has published and presented extensively on inclusion, diversity, and related topics.

**Jeanine Prime**, PhD, is a researcher and advisor who has worked with corporate clients to create inclusive workplaces for over twenty years. She has held research leadership roles at Catalyst and more recently at Gartner. Her expertise includes stereotyping, implicit bias, change management, and inclusive leadership.

**Ronald E. Riggio**, PhD, is the Henry R. Kravis Professor of Leadership and Organizational Psychology at Claremont McKenna College. A social/personality psychologist and leadership scholar, he has published over a dozen authored or edited books and more than 150 articles/book chapters. His research interests are in leadership, team processes, and organizational communication.

**Leadership: Research and Practice Series**
A James MacGregor Burns Academy of Leadership Collaboration

**Series Editors**



**Snapshots of Great Leadership**
Second Edition
*Jon P. Howell and Isaac Wanasika*

**What's Wrong with Leadership? Improving Leadership Research and Practice**
*Edited by Ronald E. Riggio*

**Following Reason: A Theory and Strategy for Rational Leadership**
*Mark Manolopoulos*

**When Leaders Face Personal Crisis: The Human Side of Leadership**
*Gill Robinson Hickman and Laura E. Knouse*

**Leadership and the Ethics of Influence**
*Terry L. Price*

**Becoming a Leader: Nine Elements of Leadership Mastery**
*Al Bolea and Leanne Atwater*

**Inclusive Leadership: Transforming Diverse Lives, Workplaces, and Societies**
*Edited by Bernardo M. Ferdman, Jeanine Prime, and Ronald E. Riggio*

**For more information about this series, please visit: www.routledge.com/psychology/series/LEADERSHIP**

# Inclusive Leadership

## Transforming Diverse Lives, Workplaces, and Societies

Edited by
Bernardo M. Ferdman,
Jeanine Prime, and
Ronald E. Riggio

NEW YORK AND LONDON

First published 2021
by Routledge
52 Vanderbilt Avenue, New York, NY 10017

and by Routledge
2 Park Square, Milton Park, Abingdon, Oxon, OX14 4RN

*Routledge is an imprint of the Taylor & Francis Group, an informa business*



*Library of Congress Cataloging-in-Publication Data*
Names: Ferdman, Bernardo M, editor. | Prime, Jeanine, editor. | Riggio, Ronald E, editor.
Title: Inclusive leadership : transforming diverse lives, workplaces, and societies / edited by Bernardo M Ferdman, Jeanine Prime, Ronald E Riggio.
Description: New York : Routledge, 2020. | Includes bibliographical references and index. |
Identifiers: LCCN 2020015487 (print) | LCCN 2020015488 (ebook) | ISBN 9781138326743 (hardback) | ISBN 9781138326750 (paperback) | ISBN 9780429449673 (ebook)
Subjects: LCSH: Leadership. | Teams in the workplace–Management.
Classification: LCC HD57.7 .I53 2020 (print) | LCC HD57.7 (ebook) | DDC 658.4/092–dc23
LC record available at https://lccn.loc.gov/2020015487
LC ebook record available at https://lccn.loc.gov/2020015488

ISBN: 978-1-138-32674-3 (hbk)
ISBN: 978-1-138-32675-0 (pbk)
ISBN: 978-0-429-44967-3 (ebk)

Typeset in Sabon
by Swales & Willis, Exeter, Devon, UK

# Contents

# The Editors

**Bernardo M. Ferdman**, PhD, is Principal of Ferdman Consulting, focusing on supporting leaders and organizations in bringing inclusion to life, and Distinguished Professor Emeritus of Organizational Psychology at Alliant International University. He is also Faculty Director of the Inclusive Leadership Program at UCLA Anderson Executive Education. Bernardo is passionate about helping to create an inclusive world where more of us can be fully ourselves and accomplish our goals effectively, productively, and authentically, and has worked for over three decades with diverse groups and organizations to increase individual and collective effectiveness and inclusion. Bernardo edited *Diversity at Work: The Practice of Inclusion* (Wiley, 2014) and has published and presented extensively on inclusion, diversity, Latinx identity, and other multicultural issues. A Fellow of the Society for Industrial and Organizational Psychology, the Society of Consulting Psychology (SCP), the American Psychological Association, and various other groups, Bernardo has received various awards, including SCP's 2019 Award for Excellence in Diversity and Inclusion Consulting, and he is the 2020 H. Smith Richardson Jr. Visiting Fellow at the Center for Creative Leadership. He is a past Chair of the Academy of Management's Diversity and Inclusion Theme Committee and of AOM's Gender and Diversity in Organizations Division, and served as President of the Interamerican Society of Psychology and of the Diversity Collegium. Bernardo—a native Spanish speaker who immigrated to the US as a child—earned a PhD in Psychology at Yale University and an AB degree at Princeton University. ORCID 0000-0003-1640-8097.

**Jeanine Prime**, PhD, has 20 years of experience as a researcher and advisor working with corporate clients to create workplaces where all employees can realize their full potential. As a research leader at Gartner she directed studies serving heads of diversity and inclusion, talent management, and total rewards. Prior to that, as Senior Vice President of Research at Catalyst, she headed the organization's research arm, generating breakthrough research and insights on workplace inclusion. Jeanine's expertise includes topics such as gender in organizations, stereotyping, implicit bias, change management, and leadership effectiveness. Her research has been published in scholarly journals and books and has been featured in several business publications, including *Fast Company*, *The Wall Street Journal*, and *Harvard Business Review*. Jeanine holds a Bachelor's degree in Psychology from Spelman College, a PhD in social psychology from Cornell University, and an MBA from the State University of New York at Binghamton.

**Ronald E. Riggio**, PhD, is the Henry R. Kravis Professor of Leadership and Organizational Psychology at the Kravis Leadership Institute at Claremont McKenna College and a Visiting Scholar at Churchill College, Cambridge University. Ron is a leadership scholar with 20 authored or edited books and more than 150 articles/book chapters. His research interests are in leadership, organizational communication, and social skills/competence.

# Contributors

**Nicholas P. Aramovich**, PhD, is an Assistant Professor of Psychology at San Diego Miramar College, San Diego, California, where he teaches coursework in psychology, research methods, and statistics. His scholarly interests involve understanding small group dynamics, team performance, leader effectiveness, and organizational diversity. He has presented his research on these topics at major conferences and published several research papers in top-tier academic journals. In addition to his academic experience, Nick has worked in a variety of internal HR, research, and analyst roles. Nick has a Master of Arts Degree in Industrial/Organizational Psychology from the University of Colorado at Denver and a PhD in Social Psychology from the University of Illinois at Chicago.

**Doyin Atewologun**, PhD, a Chartered Organizational Psychologist, is the Dean of the Rhodes Scholarships at the Rhodes Trust, where she oversees the Rhodes Scholar experience and program in Oxford, providing strategic leadership and management to the Trust's support for Scholars' academic success, well-being, and leadership development. Doyin is also Director of Delta Alpha Psi, a niche leadership and inclusion consultancy. Previously, Doyin was Director of the Gender, Leadership & Inclusion Centre at Cranfield School of Management, UK. Doyin has published in top-tier management journals and has worked with many of the FTSE 100, the UN, the UK National Health Service and the UK Civil Service.

**Monica E. Biggs**, EdD, is a consultant with 30 years of experience assisting organizations in areas of team building and culture change, and assisting leaders in developing the skills needed in the midst of turbulent change. She served as a senior consultant with The Kaleel Jamison Consulting Group for over 20 years and is now retired from the firm. Monica has taught diversity and systems leadership at Russell Sage College of Troy, New York.

**Lize A. E. Booysen**, DBL, is Professor of Leadership and Organizational Behavior at the Graduate School of Leadership and Change, Antioch

University, executive leadership coach at the Center for Creative Leadership, Greensboro, North Carolina, and Professor Extraordinaire at University of Stellenbosch Business School, Cape Town, South Africa. Lize holds a Doctorate in Business Leadership and is an internationally recognized scholar in the field of diversity, race, gender, and cross-cultural leadership.

**Donna Chrobot-Mason**, PhD, is Associate Professor and Director of the Center for Organizational Leadership at the University of Cincinnati (UC), Cincinnati, Ohio. She is Director of UC Women Lead, a ten-month executive leadership program for high potential women at the University of Cincinnati. She is also a Senior Partner for RCSN, an executive recruiting and leadership consulting firm. Her research focuses on leadership across differences and strategies for creating organizational practices, policies, and a climate that supports diversity and fosters intergroup collaboration.

**Stephanie J. Creary**, PhD, is Assistant Professor of Management at The Wharton School, University of Pennsylvania, Philadelphia, Pennsylvania. Her research on identity and diversity in the workplace has been published in leading academic journals and popular press outlets. She earned her PhD degree from the Boston College Carroll School of Management.

**Martin N. Davidson** is the Johnson & Higgins Professor of Business Administration and serves as Senior Associate Dean and Global Chief Diversity Officer at the University of Virginia's Darden School of Business, Charlottesville, Virginia. His thought leadership has changed how global leaders approach inclusion and diversity in their organizations. His scholarly research appears in top academic and practitioner publications and his book, *The End of Diversity as We Know It: Why Diversity Efforts Fail and How Leveraging Difference Can Succeed*, introduces a research-driven roadmap to help leaders effectively create and capitalize on diversity in their organizations.

**Bernadette Dillon** is the co-founder of the 360 Inclusive Leadership Compass and Chalk & Cheese Consulting. Prior to this, Bernadette worked at Deloitte for almost 15 years in both Australia and the UK, where she researched, wrote, and consulted extensively on inclusive leadership, and diversity and inclusion more broadly.

**Nancy DiTomaso**, PhD (University of Wisconsin, Madison), is Distinguished Professor of Management and Global Business at Rutgers Business School—Newark and New Brunswick, New Jersey. Her research addresses issues of diversity, culture, and inequality, as well as the management of knowledge-based organizations and the management of scientists and engineers. Her 2013 book, *The American*

*Non-Dilemma: Racial Inequality without Racism* (Russell Sage) won the C. Wright Mills Award from the Society for the Study of Social Problems.

**David J. G. Dwertmann**, PhD, is Assistant Professor of Management at Rutgers University School of Business-Camden, New Jersey. David is interested in the social and cognitive processes that result in feelings of otherness and how this affects organizations and employees. His work has been published in premier business journals such as the *Academy of Management Journal*, *The Leadership Quarterly*, *Human Resource Management*, and the *Journal of Management* among others, and David has received local, national, and international awards for his work.

**Nurcan Ensari**, PhD, is a social and organizational psychologist who teaches and conducts research in the area of intergroup relations, leadership, and diversity management. She conducts multicultural research with international collaborators from England, India, Turkey, Thailand, Greece, and Hong Kong. She is currently Professor and Program Director in the California School of Professional Psychology at Alliant International University, Alhambra, California.

**Heather Foust-Cummings**, PhD, is the passionate leader of Catalyst's researchers, librarians, and fact-checkers who are thought leaders on building workplaces that work for women. A sought-after speaker, she has consulted for organizations across industries. Heather received her PhD and MA from Emory University and her BS from University of Tennessee at Chattanooga, Tennessee.

**Charlotte Harman** is a Senior Consultant at Kiddy and Partners, who specialize in leadership assessment, development, and strategy. Previously, Charlotte worked for Cubiks, where she developed Cubiks' model of inclusive leadership and development solution with Dr. Doyin Atewologun. She holds an MSc in Organisational Psychology from City University London, UK. Her published research on women's ambition and barriers to female career progression received a BPS excellence award.

**Effenus Henderson** is President and CEO of HenderWorks, Inc. and Co-Director of the Institute for Sustainable Diversity and Inclusion. He served as Chief Diversity Officer for Weyerhaeuser Company, Federal Way, Washington, until his retirement in December 2013.

**Stefanie K. Johnson**, PhD, is Associate Professor of Management at the Leeds School of Business, University of Colorado, Boulder, Colorado. She has published 60 journal articles and book chapters, and is the author of *Inclusify: Harnessing the Power of Uniqueness and Belonging to Build Innovative Teams* (Harper Collins, 2020). She has presented her work at over 170 meetings around the world including at the White House for a 2016 summit on diversity in corporate America.

**Ray Jones**, PhD, is Clinical Professor of Business Administration at the University of Pittsburgh's Katz School of Business, Pittsburgh, Pennsylvania. His research and teaching focuses on ethics and leadership in organizations, with a strong emphasis on corporate social responsibility. He serves as the Director of the David Berg Center for Ethics and Leadership in Pitt Business and is the coordinator of the Certificate Program in Leadership and Ethics (CPLE).

**Judith H. Katz**, EdD, and **Frederick A. Miller** are both recipients of ODN's Lifetime Achievement Award and have helped Fortune 100 companies leverage differences, increase engagement, and transform workplaces for over 35 years. As Executive Vice President and CEO (respectively) of The Kaleel Jamison Consulting Group, Inc., the oldest culture change and diversity and inclusion firm, started in 1970, they have co-authored several books, their latest being *Safe Enough to SOAR: Accelerating Trust, Inclusion, and Collaboration in the Workplace*. Judith serves on the Board of Trustees of Fielding Graduate University. Fred serves on the boards of Day & Zimmermann, Rensselaer Polytechnic Institute's Center for Automated Technology Systems, and Hudson Real Estate Partners.

**Brittany K. Lambert** is a PhD candidate in organizational leadership at the Leeds School of Business, University of Colorado, Boulder, Colorado. Her research focuses on helping people thrive at work, particularly those who are under-studied or marginalized. She has presented her work at major meetings globally, published book chapters, and consulted with organizations in conjunction with her research. Brittany was previously a strategy consultant and manager for the Chief Strategy Officer at Deloitte.

**Lauren A. Lanzo** earned her PhD in industrial-organizational psychology from The George Washington University, Washington, DC. Her research on women in leadership positions and improving team and co-leader effectiveness has been published in peer-reviewed journals and presented at numerous conferences. She currently works as an internal consultant using science-backed approaches and analytics to inform human resource strategies. Although her passion lies in applying science to practice, she continues to be dedicated to pursuing her various research interests.

**Hannes L. Leroy**, PhD, is Academic Director of the Erasmus Centre of Leadership, Rotterdam, The Netherlands. Hannes helps to oversee the quality of leadership development at different levels in Erasmus University (undergraduate, graduate, post-graduate, and executive education).

Furthermore, as steward of the League of Leadership initiative he helps to oversee an international consortium of top business schools across the world with the mission of collectively enhancing quality standards of leadership development. Aligned with these efforts, Hannes has published numerous studies on leadership and its development in top journals, has taught a wide variety of leadership classes, and is principal coordinator of various leadership development curricula.

**Robert W. Livingston**, PhD, is Lecturer of Public Policy at Harvard University's John F. Kennedy School of Government, Cambridge, Massachusetts. Robert's research focuses on diversity, leadership, and social justice. His work has been published in multiple top-tier academic journals. Robert has delivered diversity training and has served as a management consultant for numerous Fortune 500 companies, as well as public-sector agencies/municipalities and non-profit organizations.

**Carolyn J. Lukensmeyer**, PhD, was the first Executive Director of the National Institute for Civil Discourse, an organization that works to reduce political dysfunction and incivility in the political system. As a leader in the field of deliberative democracy, she works to restore our democracy to reflect the intended vision of our founding fathers. Carolyn previously served as Founder and President of AmericaSpeaks, an award-winning nonprofit organization that promoted nonpartisan initiatives to engage citizens and leaders through the development of innovative public policy tools and strategies, and that brought citizens to the table to play their rightful role in public policy decision-making.

**Deborah Meehan** is the Founder and Co-Executive Director of the Leadership Learning Community, a learning network of 4,500 practitioners, funders, and researchers committed to developing the leadership needed to create a more just, equitable, and sustainable society by promoting models of leadership that are more inclusive, networked, and collective.

**Audrey J. Murrell**, PhD, is currently Acting Dean for the University of Pittsburgh Honors College, Professor of Business Administration, and Senior Research Fellow for the David Berg Center for Ethics and Leadership, Pittsburgh, Pennsylvania. She is the author of several books including: *Mentoring Dilemmas: Developmental Relationships within Multicultural Organizations* (with Faye Crosby and Robin Ely); *Intelligent Mentoring: How IBM Creates Value through People, Knowledge and Relationships* (with Sheila Forte-Trummel and Diana Bing); *Mentoring Diverse Leaders: Creating Change for People, Processes and Paradigms* (with Stacy Blake-Beard); and *Diversity Across Disciplines: Research on People, Policy, Process, and Paradigm* (with Jennifer Petrie-Wyman and Abdesalam Soudi).

**Lisa H. Nishii**, PhD, is Vice Provost for Undergraduate Education at Cornell University, Ithaca, New York, and is on the faculty of the Human Resource Studies Department at Cornell's ILR School. Lisa is an expert on inclusion in organizations. Her research focuses on the influence of organizational practices, leadership behaviors, and climate for inclusion on individual- and group-level outcomes. Lisa actively publishes in top-tier journals, including the *Academy of Management Review*, *Academy of Management Journal*, *Journal of Applied Psychology*, *Personnel Psychology*, and *Science*.

**Lynn R. Offermann**, PhD, is Professor of Industrial-Organizational Psychology and of Management at The George Washington University, Washington, DC. Her research focuses on leadership and followership, teams, and diversity in organizations. She is a Fellow of the Society for Industrial and Organizational Psychology, the American Psychological Association, and the Association for Psychological Science. Lynn has extensive experience supporting organizations in developing individual, team, and organizational capabilities and was recognized by the Society of Consulting Psychology with their award for excellence in diversity and inclusion consulting.

**Jennifer Petrie-Wyman**, EdD, is Assistant Director of the David Berg Center for Ethics and Leadership at the University of Pittsburgh, Pittsburgh, Pennsylvania. At the University of Pittsburgh, she researches ethical leadership and international development with attention to women's business development in Africa. Her work has been presented at national and international conferences and published. She is co-editor of the book *Diversity Across Disciplines: Research on People, Policy, Process, and Paradigm* with Audrey J. Murrell and Abdesalam Soudi.

**Ashleigh Shelby Rosette**, PhD, is Professor of Management and Organizations, Senior Associate Dean of Executive Programs, and a Center of Leadership and Ethics scholar at the Fuqua School of Business at Duke University, Durham, North Carolina. She is a Fellow at the Samuel Dubois Cook Center on Social Equity and a leading diversity scholar. Her diversity research focuses on leadership, social inequity, and intersectionality and has been published in top academic journals.

**Sandy Caspi Sable**, PhD, co-founded the 360 Inclusive Leadership Compass and Chalk & Cheese Consulting with Bernadette Dillon. In her time with Deloitte and beyond, she has served as an advisor and executive coach to global leaders and their organizations to enable them to leverage the power of diversity through inclusion.

**Edgar H. Schein**, PhD, is Society of Sloan Fellows Professor of Management Emeritus and Professor Emeritus at the MIT Sloan School of Management. Edgar Schein made a notable mark on the field of organization development. He is well known for his ground-breaking work on the Organizational Culture model. Ed's recent books include *Humble Consulting* (2016), *Organizational Culture and Leadership, 5th Edition* (2017), *Humble Leadership* (2018, co-authored with Peter A. Schein), and *The Corporate Culture Survival Guide, 3rd Edition* (2019, co-authored with Peter A. Schein).

**Peter A. Schein** is a strategy consultant in Silicon Valley. He provides help to start-ups and expansion-phase technology companies. Peter's work draws on 30 years of industry experience in marketing and corporate development for technology pioneers. His recent books include *Humble Leadership* (2018, co-authored with Edgar H. Schein) and *The Corporate Culture Survival Guide, 3rd Edition* (2019, co-authored with Edgar H. Schein).

**Emily Shaffer**, PhD, is a social psychologist focusing on experiences of underrepresented groups in educational and organizational settings. Emily is a go-to expert for Catalyst's inclusion and engaging men research. Emily earned her PhD from Tulane University, her MA from San Diego State University, and her BA from University of Arizona.

**Aarti Shyamsunder**, PhD, is an industrial-organizational psychologist who runs Psymantics Consulting, her own independent consulting practice, out of Mumbai, India. Her work focuses mainly on leadership, gender diversity and inclusion, and assessment. Aarti was recognized as one of India's Future Emerging HR Leaders at the "Are You in the List" Awards.

**Daryl G. Smith**, PhD, is Senior Research Fellow and Professor Emerita of Education and Psychology at Claremont Graduate University, Claremont, California. She is the author of *Diversity's Promise for Higher Education: Making it Work*, *Diversity in Higher Education: Emerging Cross-National Perspectives on Institutional Transformation*, and *Achieving Faculty Diversity: Debunking The Myths*.

**J. Goosby Smith**, PhD, is Associate Professor of Management and Leadership at The Citadel, The Military College of South Carolina, in Charleston, South Carolina. She is Assistant Provost for Diversity, Equity, and Inclusion and director of the campus Truth, Racial Healing, and Transformation Center.

**Tanya Cruz Teller** is a creative leader of systemic change processes founded on principles of personal transformation, collaborative partnerships, whole systems thinking, and appreciative inquiry. Her organization development work is committed to creating a diverse, equitable, and inclusive (DEI) world through building flourishing organizations. As an expert panelist of the *Global Diversity & Inclusion Benchmarks*, Tanya combines international OD and DEI. Prior to consulting independently, as South Africa (SA) Country Director for the Synergos Institute, Tanya brought together government, business, and civil society in partnerships to create a more equitable society in SA and the region. Tanya co-authored the book, *Thriving Women, Thriving World: An Invitation to Dialogue, Healing and Inspired Action* (with Diana Whitney, Marlene Ogawa, Caroline Adams Miller, Jessica Cocciolone, Haesun Moon, Kathryn Britton, Alejandra Leon De La Barra, and Angela Koh).

**Lars Hasselblad Torres** is Executive Director of Artisan's Asylum. Lars is a lifelong artist, educator, entrepreneur, and public scholar with a passion for democratic social change. Lars's experience includes leading Burlington, Vermont's makerspace (The Generator), through a five-fold fundraising and budget increase; founding a creativity sandbox (Local 64) that provides workspace, community, and creative support to Central Vermont's independent and creative workforce; and serving the state's creative economy (Vermont Agency of Commerce and Community Development) by seeking ways to remove barriers to economic growth for independent creatives, startups, and companies.

**Dnika J. Travis**, PhD, is a recognized researcher, educator, and change leader. Dnika's renowned research on emotional tax and having tough conversations across differences has been featured in top-tier media outlets. She earned her PhD from University of Southern California, MSW from University of Michigan, and BA from Hampton University.

**Tara Van Bommel**, PhD, is an expert in stereotyping and prejudice. At Catalyst, Tara is a lead statistician and spearheads research initiatives for Women and the Future of Work. Tara earned her PhD and Master's degrees from Tulane University and her BA from the University of Denver.

**Hans van Dijk**, PhD, is Assistant Professor in the Department of Organization Studies of Tilburg University, Tilburg, The Netherlands. His research focuses on three areas: diversity and inclusion, refugee integration, and meta-science. His work on diversity and inclusion highlights how stereotypes and status attributions shape behavior and performance in and of diverse work groups and has been published in journals such as *Academy of Management Annals* and *Organizational Behavior and Human Decision Processes*. He frequently teaches executives how to create inclusive organizations and has developed an Inclusive Behavior Training that provides participants with insights and tools to be inclusive in their everyday behavior.

**Ilene C. Wasserman**, PhD, is President of ICW Consulting Group, a consultancy that specializes in helping executives and their teams to strengthen their capacity to collaborate by leveraging diversity and inclusion, using action learning, peer coaching, and strengths-based methodologies. Ilene teaches at the graduate level and is a Senior Leadership Fellow at the Wharton School, University of Pennsylvania, Philadelphia, Pennsylvania. She has written several articles and book chapters and has co-authored two books: *Communicating Possibilities: A Brief Introduction to CMM* and *Peer Coaching: Principles and Practices*.

**Michael Welp,** PhD, is a co-founder of White Men as Full Diversity Partners, a leadership development consultancy. Michael is author of *Four Days To Change: 12 Radical Habits to Overcome Bias and Thrive in a Diverse World* and is the host of The Insider Outsider podcast. His TEDx talk is entitled *White Men: Time to Discover Your Cultural Blind Spots*.

**Mary-Frances Winters** is CEO of The Winters Group, Inc., a 36-year-old diversity, equity, and inclusion consulting firm that has worked with hundreds of clients globally. She has served on national not-for-profit, corporate, and university boards, and has received many awards and honors including the ATHENA award, Diversity Pioneer from *Profiles in Diversity Journal*, The Winds of Change from Forum on Workplace Inclusion, and Forbes 10 Diversity Trailblazers. She is the author of five books, including *Inclusive Conversations: Fostering Equity, Empathy and Belonging Across Differences* and *We Can't Talk About That at Work! How to Talk About Race, Religion, Politics and Other Polarizing Topics*.

# Series Foreword

As this book goes to press, there is something unsettling about studying the concept of inclusiveness while being told to "self-isolate" during the coronavirus pandemic. In an era of "shelter-in-place" and "social distancing," how exactly are we supposed to promote inclusivity? A multinational chatroom? Paradoxically, the timing is perfect for this work. We can use this time to reflect and emerge stronger. To deconstruct, reconstruct, reinvent, and reimagine the kind of world we want our children and grandchildren to inherit.

Like other offerings from the Kravis-deRoulet leadership conference series, this remarkable volume benefits from the collective wisdom and learning of top social science scholars and leadership practitioners that grew out of this gathering. So, while there were divergent and creative perspectives presented at the conference, there were also significant insights into how leaders can facilitate a more inclusive workplace. For example, even at a basic level, we're such a "go along to get along" world that often people think we have to "normalize" to be accepted into a group. Yet this strategy often has the opposite effect: isolation and a lack of authenticity. One author, Martin Davidson, suggests that "embracing your weirdness" is a more productive approach. As Series Editor, I loved it, and you will, too. Maybe this is more of an "Onward" than a "Foreword." Enjoy!

*Georgia Sorenson*
*University of Cambridge*

# Preface and Overview

## Inclusive Leadership

*Bernardo M. Ferdman, Jeanine Prime, and Ronald E. Riggio*

As we finalize writing this, the world is in the midst of the novel coronavirus pandemic, with changes happening hourly and uncertainty about the future only increasing. While governments, businesses, NGOs, and every person are challenged with difficult decisions about how to act and what restrictions to put in place to prevent the further spread of a new and dangerous disease—one for which there is yet no vaccine or cure—it has become exceedingly salient how interdependent all people in the world have become. The rush to close borders, to restrict movement, and to practice physical distancing—and the difficulty, insecurity, and pain that this is causing—paradoxically highlight how truly impermeable boundaries no longer exist. Information, ideas, and influence have become truly global, and what happens in a marketplace in Wuhan, a nursing home in Seattle, or a business meeting in Milan—not to mention stock markets, factories, or communities anywhere in the world—quickly can and does reverberate far and wide. The idea that we can simply choose to stay in the comfort zone of working and interacting with people who are just like ourselves is no longer viable. Moreover, as we look to chart the course to address challenges for which there is no precedent or experience that precisely matches what may be needed, the world and our leaders are confronted with the need to stay open to possibilities they may never have considered and voices that they have not been used to tapping and engaging.

From our perspective, the current world situation and its likely aftermath make the subject of this book particularly timely, and also timeless. *Inclusive leadership*—leadership that promotes and facilitates experiences of inclusion for all, across multiple identities, and that supports the development of workgroups, organizations, communities, and even whole societies where diversity is a source of collective advantage; where ideas, contributions, and direction can come from all types of people; and where equity and social justice are focal goals—is clearly needed, not only now but for a future in which collective survival and vitality will require innovation, talent, and engagement from all people, not just from those traditionally in positions of power or privilege or those who have historically been in the "in-group."

Inclusive leadership requires fully engaging and adopting the lens and practice of inclusion (Ferdman & Deane, 2014a) as we live and work together in diverse groups, workplaces, and societies, and transforming our mindsets, behavior, and collective practices, values, and norms so as to more fully engage and mutually benefit from our many differences. Indeed, inclusion provides "a key driver and basis for reaping diversity's potential benefits" (Ferdman & Deane, 2014b, p. xxiv). As Barbara Deane and one of us (Ferdman) have pointed out:

> the concept and practice of inclusion provide a frame to permit addressing the dynamics of diversity in more complex, expansive, and productive ways. Through an inclusion lens, we can continue to incorporate our prior insights regarding diversity and also highlight the practices needed so that individuals, groups, and organizations can truly benefit from that diversity. Through an inclusion lens, we can attend to the complexity of individual experience and identity, without losing sight of intergroup relations, intercultural dynamics, and systemic processes and structures.
>
> (Ferdman & Deane, 2014b, p. xxiv)

This imperative for inclusion and the leadership needed to achieve it—at all levels of system, now and in the future—was the inspiration for the 25th Annual Kravis-deRoulet Leadership Conference, *Inclusive Leadership: Transforming Diverse Lives, Workplaces, and Societies*, held at Claremont McKenna College in Claremont, California, in March, 2017. As the organizers, we brought together a range of researchers and practitioners from different disciplines to discuss and better understand inclusive leadership. The dialogue that began at the conference did not end with its conclusion but continued as the presenters went forward to write about their research and practice in inclusion and inclusive leadership—newly enhanced by the content shared at the conference and in ongoing discussions after it ended. Other experts, who could not be present at the conference, were recruited to round out the topics presented in this volume.

The result is this book, which explores cutting-edge theory, research, practice, and experience on the pivotal role and features of inclusive leadership in diverse organizations and societies. The twenty-nine chapters, written by forty-seven authors, give testament to the power of diverse voices to provide useful insights and solutions. Our authors span five continents, multiple disciplines, and various sectors, industries, roles, and work experiences; together, they provide a unique and necessary in-depth look at the components, manifestations, nuances, and complexities of inclusive leadership across a range of settings and levels of analysis.

## Overview

The titles of the various sections of the book give the outline for the story. The first part sets the stage, in five chapters, with a discussion of key frameworks and perspectives for inclusive leadership. These explore how experiences of both exclusion and inclusion vary based on gender and race (Livingston and Rosette, Chapter 3) as well as culture (Schein and Schein, Chapter 5), and describe the key role of both inclusion and leadership for gaining the benefits of diversity (Johnson and Lambert, Chapter 4). This context frames up the challenges, practices, and importance of inclusive leadership—at the interpersonal, group, organizational, and societal levels (Ferdman, Chapter 1)—and speaks to the urgent need to advance its study and practice as a core part of the field of leadership (Ensari and Riggio, Chapter 2).

The second part—with eight chapters—explores the practice of inclusive leadership at the interpersonal and group levels. From boundary spanning (Chrobot-Mason and Aramovich, Chapter 10) to climate shaping (Nishii and Leroy, Chapter 12), from vulnerability and integrity (Wasserman, Chapter 6) to inclusive everyday behaviors (Atewologun and Harman, Chapter 7), from the need to lead oneself as well as others (van Bommel et al., Chapter 8) to the need to create fairness as well as synergy (Dwertmann and van Dijk, Chapter 11), and from the importance of creating inclusion at the team level (Offermann and Lanzo, Chapter 13) to the importance of "embracing the weird" (Davidson, Chapter 9), our authors identify critical leadership practices for cultivating inclusive interpersonal and group dynamics, as well as the requisite attributes and behaviors leaders need to be successful in implementing these practices. They also identify the critical moments and group processes where these practices must be applied for optimal outcomes.

The third part incorporates five chapters and focuses on the role that inclusive leadership plays in helping to create organizations that respect, foster, and sustain inclusion and leverage the diversity of all their members to positive ends. Authors cover a wide range of practices that help to institutionalize inclusion and create shared responsibility for its realization within organizations. Examples of these practices come from a range of organizational settings and contexts, including the military (Goosby Smith, Chapter 18), and give attention to "responsible inclusive leadership development" (Booysen, Chapter 14), "diversity workspaces" for supporting using differences as a key resource (Creary, Chapter 15), skills and practices for "bold, inclusive conversations" (Winters, Chapter 16), and the need to work both top down and outside in as well as bottom up and inside out to remove barriers to inclusion at the micro, meso, and macro levels (Shyamsunder, Chapter 17).

The fourth part of the book brings together four chapters and goes beyond looking at teams and organizations to examine the type of leadership required to cultivate inclusion at the community and societal level. The authors highlight critical challenges to inclusive societies, including increasing social inequality (DiTomaso, Chapter 19) and political polarization and incivility (Lukensmeyer and Torres, Chapter 21), and suggest ways to address these. From polarity management (Henderson, Chapter 22) to differentiating complex identities (Smith, Chapter 20), these chapters outline frameworks, strategies, and tactics that can contribute to creating more inclusive societies.

The fifth part—comprised of six chapters—provides much-needed strategies, models, and resources for the development of inclusive leadership, across multiple levels of analysis. These contributions lay out how models and approaches such as experiential and service learning (Murrell et al., Chapter 24), appreciative inquiry as an organization development intervention (Cruz Teller, Chapter 27), and 360-feedback focusing on inclusive behavior (Dillon and Caspi Sable, Chapter 26) can be applied to enhancing inclusive leadership for both individuals and organizational systems. Authors describe how inclusion can be made a part of ongoing organizational and leadership practice (Katz et al., Chapter 23) and the importance of considering and addressing broader systemic issues, including White male culture (Welp and Schein, Chapter 25) and systemic racial inequities and oppression (Leadership Learning Community Collaboration, Chapter 28) in the process of developing greater inclusion and the leadership needed to accomplish it. These chapters provide practical case studies and compelling examples of inclusive leadership in practice.

In the concluding section, the three of us (Prime et al., Chapter 29) provide summary reflections on what we learned and why it matters, including what the collection of chapters taught us about inclusion and what it takes to foster and sustain it in groups, organizations, and communities.

We believe that an extensive range of readers will find the contents of this book to be both compelling and practical. Those in positions of authority or leadership, whether in work or community settings—including leaders and managers at all levels, HR professionals, and members of diverse teams—as well as anyone who would like or needs insight and guidance into what it takes to create relationships, workplaces, and societies where diversity is a source of collective benefit and where people can be free to develop and contribute their talents without suppressing or hiding valued identities, will find this volume to be an indispensable handbook. The book will also be helpful to anyone who would like an in-depth understanding of the connections between leadership and inclusion, including HR and OD practitioners, professors and students of leadership, organizational behavior, organizational psychology, management, business, and human resource management, and to those curious about what leadership will look like in the future.

In his concluding comments at the 25th Annual Kravis-deRoulet Leadership Conference, David A. Thomas, at the time Professor at the

Harvard Business School and now President of Morehouse College, and a renowned scholar of diversity and intergroup relations in organizations, said the following:

> This conference has done a job that I have never seen done at any other conference [to illustrate] that inclusion is a multi-level phenomenon—individual, group, organizational, and societal. At the end of the day, it comes back to what are the experiences that we are creating for an individual? If we have all of the right policies and practices in place, but individuals still are not finding that they have the ability to be self-authoring, then something is not working. The implication for those of us who want to pick up this mantle of inclusive leadership—particularly those of us who operate as individual contributors or leaders of teams, or even as leaders of organizations—is that we have to develop comfort in creating what my mentor, Clayton Alderfer, described in a phrase he coined several decades ago as "incongruent embeddedness." That means that there may be a set of dynamics that swirl around my work team in the organization that are not inclusive and that serve to undermine inclusiveness. My job as a leader is to create incongruence in that embeddedness, so that the team that I manage is having a different experience, operating in a way that is incongruent with what may be the dominant patterns around them. I think that this takes courage, and it takes skill.
>
> I [also] found myself thinking about ... what metaphor would capture this word, when we didn't have labels like diversity and inclusion? In 1986, when I finished my dissertation, I was asked, "what is your work really about?" This was when everyone was still doubtful about this kind of work. And I remember I said, it is "liberation work." As I sat here today, I came back to that statement. It is liberation work because it is about liberating the human spirit. It is about altering the patterns in society and organizations that suppress our ability to be self-authoring, our ability to bring our gifts to the table, our ability to connect to each other. Think about what it means not to be free, not have liberty. It does not have to be because you are in shackles, but it could be because of the mind and the human spirit. We are engaged in liberation work, and that is what we, I believe, are taking on.
>
> (Thomas, 2017)

As the stewards of this project, we could not agree more with Thomas. At its core, inclusive leadership is very much about liberation, for each of us and for all of us. We hope and trust that our readers will discover this as well, and will incorporate the mindsets, practices, and systems of inclusive leadership into their own lives, workplaces, and communities, so as to lift up all people and permit all of us to thrive together.

*March 2020*

*Bernardo M. Ferdman*
*San Diego, California*

*Jeanine Prime*
*Washington, District of Columbia*

*Ronald E. Riggio*
*Claremont, California*

## References

Ferdman, B. M. & Deane, B. R. (Eds.). (2014a). *Diversity at work: The practice of inclusion*. San Francisco, CA: Jossey-Bass.

Ferdman, B. M., & Deane, B. R. (2014b). Preface—Diversity at work: The practice of inclusion. In B. M. Ferdman & B. R. Deane (Eds.), *Diversity at work: The practice of inclusion* (pp. xxi–xxxii). San Francisco, CA: Jossey-Bass.

Thomas, D. A. (2017, March 4). *The way forward: Next steps on the path to inclusion* [Conference presentation]. Inclusive Leadership: Transforming Diverse Lives, Workplaces, and Societies, 25th Annual Kravis-deRoulet Conference, Kravis Leadership Institute, Claremont McKenna College, Claremont, CA.

# Acknowledgments

This book would not have been possible without and has greatly benefited from the help and support of many people. In particular, we would like to extend our great appreciation to the chapter authors, who both shared important and necessary perspectives, expertise, and ideas in their contributions, and were also patient and magnanimous in responding to our editorial requests and in staying with us throughout the process.

Our editor at Routledge, Christina Chronister, was enthusiastic about the project from the very beginning, and both supported and prodded us in ways that helped move us forward and make the volume a reality. Danielle Dyal, editorial assistant at Routledge/Taylor & Francis, went above and beyond—and was particularly gracious and kind—as she helped us address final details quickly and productively. Eman Hardaway and Sophia Sung provided us with research and logistical assistance at various points in the project.

The Kravis Leadership Institute at Claremont McKenna College supported the 25th Annual Kravis-deRoulet Leadership Conference and provided both tangible and other assistance throughout the process of creating this volume, with support from a number of Institute staff. We are particularly appreciative of the help given us by Samuel Johnson, student assistant at the Institute, who was instrumental in formatting chapters for submission and cataloguing permissions and other material; Angelica Ferreira, Nancy Flores, and Tiffany Nolasco all were instrumental in supporting us both at the conference and afterwards as we collected materials, communicated with authors, and accomplished needed tasks. We are immensely grateful to all of them!

Particularly in the midst of the uncertain times we are living in at the moment, when we are required to stay and work at home to avoid spreading the novel coronavirus, it is especially salient to each of us how much we appreciate and are grateful to our life partners and our families, who have supported us and this project all along the way, who have helped us to keep our work in proper perspective, and who provide us with grounding and meaning to make our focus on the greater good especially important.

# Part I

# From Exclusion to Inclusion

## The Challenges of Inclusive Leadership

# 1 Inclusive Leadership

## The Fulcrum of Inclusion

*Bernardo M. Ferdman*

The ability to be inclusive and to foster and sustain an inclusive culture in groups, workplaces, and communities is a critical component of 21st-century leadership. Successful and effective leadership in today's organizations and societies and in those of the future requires strong understanding of and skills for creating and catalyzing opportunities to benefit from all types of diversity and to enhance these capacities in oneself and others. Thus, inclusive leadership goes well beyond cultural competence or managing diversity to incorporate creating and fostering the conditions that allow everyone—across and with their differences and without having to subsume or hide valued identities—to be at and to do their best, to see the value in doing so, and to belong and participate in ways that are safe, engaging, appreciated, and fair. In short, inclusive leadership means bringing inclusion to life, whether in an interpersonal relationship, a work group, an organizational system, or a community. Beyond facilitating participation, voice, and belonging without requiring assimilation, inclusive leadership also involves fostering equity and fairness across multiple identities.

In recent years, as the focus on diversity, equity, and inclusion around the world and especially in organizations has expanded, the number of articles, books, blogs, speeches, and other material addressing aspects of inclusive leadership has also grown. These perspectives on inclusive leadership tend to vary in at least three major ways. The first relates to how much explicit and focal attention is given to diversity, intergroup dynamics, and equity. The second has to do with the levels of system that are addressed: intrapersonal, interpersonal, group, organizational, and/or societal. A third aspect of variation—often cross-cutting the other two—involves the degree to which traditional hierarchical structures are assumed, such that leadership is seen as the responsibility of and primarily emanating from those holding particular positions (e.g., executive, manager, supervisor, etc.)—in other words, as being based on a particular role—versus viewing leadership as a social process constructed collectively and relationally and constituted by a set of functions and processes that produce direction, alignment, and commitment (Drath et al., 2008) and that also serve to catalyze adaptive work (Heifetz & Laurie, 1997) by individuals and groups.

In my own work on inclusion and inclusive leadership over the years, both on my own and with colleagues (e.g., Ferdman, 2014b, 2017; Ferdman & Brody, 1996; Gallegos et al., 2020; Holvino et al., 2004; Wasserman et al., 2008), I have sought to integrate these perspectives, proposing a multi-level systemic view of the practice of inclusion (Ferdman, 2014b) and its goals, and highlighting the importance of addressing multiple social identities and cultures as core to inclusion (e.g., Ferdman, 1995). In this chapter, I apply this approach to lay out elements of a broad and integrative framework for inclusive leadership that considers individual and collective effectiveness as well the importance of participation, engagement, safety, voice, and equity in the context of the complexity and intersectionality of multiple social identities, intergroup relations, and their multifaceted organizational and societal manifestations.

I do so in the context of a view of leadership that acknowledges the particular responsibilities of those with authority in a group, organization, or community, but that also recognizes the ways in which anyone in these systems can display acts of leadership—acts that in some way move that system toward adaptive work, greater inclusion, and mutually beneficial processes and outcomes. In particular, I ground this aspect of my approach to inclusive leadership in the work of Heifetz and colleagues (Heifetz, 1994; Heifetz & Laurie, 1997; Heifetz & Linsky, 2002), who describe leadership as an activity, not a set of personality characteristics; for them the core activity of leadership is mobilizing groups and individuals to address adaptive challenges, and helping to create the conditions that make this adaptive work possible.

The central questions that inclusive leadership—and inclusive leaders—address, in this conceptualization, include the following:

1 How can people work and live together, interact, and engage in positive and mutually enhancing ways—productively, effectively, and authentically—in diverse groups, organizations, and communities while maintaining valued identities and cultures and fostering equity and fairness? How can collectives use their differences as a source of benefit for both individual members and the whole?
2 What behavior, mindsets, values, interactions, norms, policies, processes, and systems encourage, support, and incentivize people to work together and interact positively while maintaining their multiple identities, their cultures, and their sense of authenticity? How does the practice of inclusion manifest in a particular group, organization, or community? What do equity and fairness mean in that same collective (and in the larger systems of which it is a part)?

3 How can these goals and the factors that bring them about be clarified, articulated, and implemented so as to catalyze sustainable changes on the part of individuals and collectives?
4 What are the individual qualities, behaviors, and interactions that support finding answers to these questions and implementing them?

The key to inclusive leadership is the way in which it helps people, groups, organizations, and societies find answers to these questions that work, that are sustainable, and that maximize experiences of inclusion, across a range of identities and social positions (Ferdman, 2014b). I refer to inclusive leadership as the *fulcrum of inclusion* because it plays a key role in magnifying inclusion within levels of analysis and transmuting inclusion across levels of analysis—from micro to macro and vice versa. Although specific answers to the questions can and do vary across contexts, depending for example on the particular diversity dimensions and their dynamics relevant in a specific collective, inclusive leadership involves mobilizing people to jointly co-construct the best and most sustainable approaches.

The first question has to do with inclusion—defining and clarifying it, and giving it a prominent role in social collectives—whether a group, an organization, or a whole society. Inclusive leadership both makes this question and the need to address it prominent and also supports the adaptive work needed to address it. The second and third questions have to do with individual and collective change and even transformation, so as to help foster and instill new ways of thinking, behaving, interacting, and engaging across differences in these social collectives. This can often require reassessing and redefining previously held practices, ideas, or values that serve as barriers to inclusion and equity. And the final question has to do with noting and raising up the perspectives, voices, and influence of those most likely to support changes needed to drive and sustain inclusion and equity.

In the rest of this chapter, I provide a frame to help think about these processes that constitute inclusive leadership. First, I define inclusive leadership through the lens of diversity, inclusion, and equity in a multilevel systems perspective. Then I expand on this definition to discuss how inclusive leadership serves a pivotal role as a fulcrum or force multiplier to foster and magnify inclusion at micro and macro levels and to connect micro and macro aspects of inclusion. I conclude by discussing key elements of inclusive leadership and a set of behaviors that leaders can use to increase and facilitate inclusion and that are likely to foster this within- and cross-level reverberation of inclusion.

## Leadership through the Lens of Diversity, Inclusion, and Equity

Inclusion is fundamental for the success of diverse groups, organizations, and societies (Ferdman, 2014b). It supports equity, encourages people's multi-faceted talents and contributions and permits reaping their benefits, and also supports individual development, growth, engagement, and self-determination (Ferdman, 2014b, 2017). In sum, it is the short answer to the first question posed earlier. So, how does each of these concepts—*diversity*, *equity*, *inclusion*—matter for leadership?

### *Diversity and Inclusive Leadership*

*Diversity* is essentially the "representation of multiple identity groups and their cultures in a particular organization or workgroup" (Ferdman, 2014b, p. 3) or in a larger system, such as a community or society. (It is important to highlight that diversity is always an attribute of a collective, and never of a specific individual. There is no such thing as a "diverse person," in spite of frequent use of that term to denote someone different than the dominant group.) Diversity is both simple and complex, which I have previously explained as follows:

> At its most basic level, diversity is simply about difference; people vary in many ways, some based on individual differences and others grounded in the range of social identities and groups that we belong to. At the same time, diversity can be multilayered and complex, because these identities and characteristics combine within each of us, and because there are histories of relationships between groups that also come into play.
>
> When we first hear about diversity, we tend to focus on demographic or identity dimensions, especially the most visible ones (e.g., gender, race, ethnicity, culture, age, national background, sexual orientation, physical ability/disability). At the same time, diversity also involves less visible and more individual dimensions (e.g., personality, abilities, thinking style, values, experiences). In short, diversity involves the differences and similarities among people across many dimensions represented in a particular group or organization. These dimensions combine within individuals, influencing how we approach and experience work and life as well as how we perceive and treat each other.
>
> (Ferdman, 2018, paras 3–4)

Diversity and its dynamics at different levels of system—whether in a group, an organization, or a community—present both challenges and opportunities for leaders. As has become clearer from a growing body of theory, research, and practice, diverse collectives can derive great benefit from their differences, but can also experience tensions related to those same differences. Phillips (2014), for example, compellingly summarized how racial, gender, and other types of diversity in groups can lead to availability of more information, more creativity, greater innovation, and deeper processing. But truly gaining these benefits requires more attention to process and to creating opportunities for the differences to emerge in the service of collective goals (see, e.g., Creary et al., 2019). This also means removing invidious biases, discrimination, and other barriers to diversity in the first place.

Given that diversity is a reality in most human collectives—whether workgroups, organizations, or the larger society—it is also a critical leadership issue. A key aspect of inclusive leadership, then, involves awareness of, attitudes about, and approaches to diversity:

> At both societal and organizational levels, leaders must in some way address diversity and intergroup relations. Doing this requires addressing questions about the proper role of differences in culture and identity at both individual and group levels and about appropriate ways to structure relationships across these differences. It also requires clarifying which differences matter, in what ways, and to whom. Answers to these questions are often grounded in widely divergent values and ideologies regarding diversity.
>
> (Ferdman, 2017, p. 238)

Inclusive leadership requires mindsets and skills for noticing, engaging with, and creating space for multiple dimensions of diversity, as well as the varying ways in which people deal with this diversity. It requires being able to explain how diversity matters, and to help people close the gap between the tendency to avoid, reject, or minimize differences in identities or cultures and the need to move toward approaches that highlight the value of diversity and other positive diversity mindsets (van Knippenberg et al., 2013) that allow for, encourage, and support deriving the mutual benefits of diversity (e.g., Bennett, 2014; Hannum et al., 2010; Miller & Katz, 2007). Thus, inclusive leadership involves noting the identities and associated differences that matter, and providing space and perspectives to help people recognize, appreciate, address, and work with these differences in a positive way (see, e.g., Creary, this volume; Ferdman, 2017; Plaut et al., 2009; Rock et al., 2016), as well as challenging invidious biases and discriminatory beliefs and practices.

A key element for making this happen is inclusion, another core foundation for inclusive leadership and essential for deriving the benefits of diversity (Ferdman & Deane, 2014), which I address in the next section.

### *Inclusion and Inclusive Leadership*

*Inclusion* is a system of "creating and embedding organizational, leadership, and interpersonal practices that result in a sense of safety, full belonging, participation, and voice across the range of diversity dimensions, without requiring assimilation or loss of valued identities" (Ferdman, 2016, para. 4). Inclusion is a fundamental practice—at the individual, group, and organizational levels—for gaining the benefits of diversity and for making it possible for all people to flourish and to contribute at their best and is thus a foundational element of organizational success. At the societal level, it is similar, but perhaps even more complex, given the range of social institutions and settings involved.

The essence of inclusion has to do with how much people feel appreciated, valued, safe, respected, engaged, able to be authentic, and therefore able and willing to provide their full contributions to the collective, whether in work or other settings—both as individuals and as members of multiple identity groups (Ferdman, 2014b); people feel included when they can fully belong without having to subsume their uniqueness or their differences from others (Ferdman, 2010, 2017; Shore et al., 2011). Inclusion—engaging in ways that value and respect human diversity and provide mutually beneficial opportunities for all to contribute and matter—requires shifting individual, group, and societal interactions to leverage, appreciate, and integrate human differences and to disrupt patterns of social inequality and their effects.

Interpersonally and at the group, organizational, and societal levels, inclusion involves behaviors, practices, and policies that result in such experiences of inclusion individually as well as collectively (Ferdman, 2014b), that eliminate invidious discrimination and promote fairness, and that foster climates for inclusion (Nishii & Rich, 2014). Inclusion is therefore a set of related practices and their outcomes that "involve each and all of the following: an individual or group experience; a set of behaviors; an approach to leadership; a set of collective norms and practices; and personal, group, organizational, or social values" (Ferdman, 2014b, p. 4). This is how I have previously defined inclusion:

> Inclusion is an active process in which individuals, groups, organizations, and societies—rather than seeking to foster homogeneity—view and approach diversity as a valued resource. In an inclusive system, we value ourselves and others because of and not despite our differences (or similarities); everyone—across multiple types of differences—should be empowered as a full participant and contributor who feels and is connected to the larger collective without having to give up individual uniqueness, cherished identities, or vital qualities.
>
> On its face, inclusion can be simple and straightforward: it is about presence, participation, safety, voice, authenticity, equity, and equality for more people across multiple identity groups. Yet, at the same time, inclusion is complex and multifaceted. Inclusive systems—through a combination of individual behavior and attitudes, group norms, leadership approaches, and organizational policies and practices [Ferdman, 2014b]—enable each person to flourish and develop,

> providing opportunities to fully connect and engage in ways that are beneficial for both the individual and the collective. . . . Like multiculturalism, inclusion values the coexistence of multiple values, perspectives, styles, and means of accomplishing goals within the same social system. However, it broadens the focal dimensions of difference and more fully addresses their intersectionality. . . . Inclusion provides a lens that reorganizes how we look at and experience identity, interpersonal interactions, group dynamics, intercultural interactions, intergroup relations, and even work itself.
>
> (Ferdman, 2017, pp. 238–239)

Thus, inclusion is a multi-layered construct and process that can and needs to be created at multiple levels of system. Figure 1.1 shows a graphic representation of my multilevel systemic framework for inclusion (Ferdman, 2014b). The idea is that the fundamental criterion as to whether inclusion exists is at the individual level, the *experience of inclusion* (Davidson & Ferdman, 2002; Ferdman, 2014b), and that this can vary from person to person, often in relation to social identities and other factors:

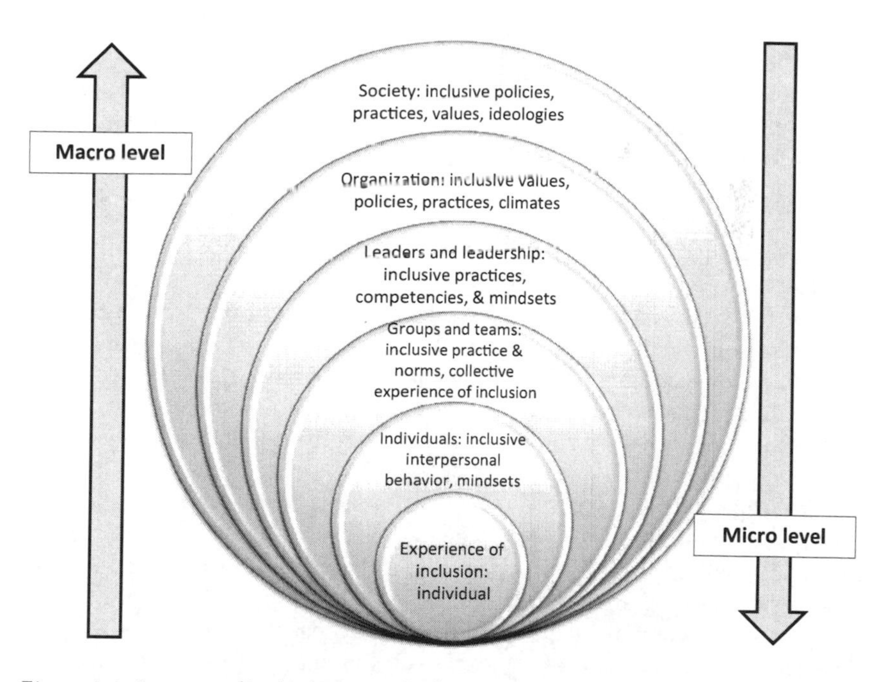


*Figure 1.1* Systems of inclusion: a multi-level analytic framework. Source: adapted from Figure 1.2 in B. M. Ferdman (2014b, p. 17).

> Without the experience of inclusion, people who are different in notable ways from the traditionally represented groups may not feel quite as safe, accepted, or valued and may therefore be less likely to fully engage, participate, and contribute. If their sense of identity is threatened or they do not feel that they can be their authentic self, their talents and full contribution may be diminished or lost. In inclusive workplaces, people can be fully themselves, striving to be their best, without fear or without a sense that they must hide or become someone else.
>
> (Ferdman, 2018, para. 6)

In this model, inclusion is viewed as a practice with manifestations and elements at various levels of system, from micro to macro. It is "an interacting set of structures, values, norms, group and organizational climates, and individual and collective behaviors, all connected with inclusion experiences in a mutually reinforcing and dynamic system" (Ferdman, 2014b, p. 16).

This means that inclusion can be created, strengthened, and sustained at each and all of these levels. And this is why leadership has such a critical role in this process:

> In many ways, inclusive leadership is the linchpin for inclusion at other levels of the multilevel framework; it can facilitate (and perhaps even be considered a key part of) inclusion in groups, organizations, and societies, as well as help translate and spread inclusion across these levels.
>
> (Ferdman, 2014b, p. 19)

Thus, inclusive leadership is leadership for inclusion: the mindsets, practices, and ways of influencing other people and the systems in which we work and live, so as to clarify and support learning about what inclusion is (and can be), to foster inclusion on an ongoing basis (including expecting and rewarding inclusive behavior), to embed inclusive values and processes in how work is done, and to make inclusion sustainable. In other words, inclusive leadership involves helping collectives find meaningful and appropriate answers to the questions I posed earlier, especially that of how to use differences as a source of benefit for both individual members and the whole, and how the practice of inclusion will specifically manifest in the behavior, norms, interactions, and processes of that collective.

A complete view of inclusive leadership needs to consider how change happens at each level of analysis—individual, interpersonal, group, organizational, and societal—and the influence processes, competencies, and interventions that foster more inclusion, both within and across levels. Booysen (2014) combines these elements to define inclusive leadership as

> a respectful relational practice that enables individuals and collectives to be fully part of the whole, such that they are directed, aligned and committed toward shared outcomes, for the common good of all, while retaining a sense of authenticity and uniqueness.
> (p. 322; see also Booysen, this volume)

A key element of inclusive leadership then, involves inspiring and challenging individuals and collectives to develop a vision of inclusion for themselves and each other and to find ways to close the gap between that vision and current reality. Because inclusion is not the same for different people or groups, and because it incorporates a range of paradoxical elements—for example, between belonging/absorption and distinctiveness/uniqueness; between stable, well-defined norms and shifting and open norms; and between comfort and discomfort (see Ferdman, 2017 for details)—inclusive leadership requires the capacity to understand, engage with, and manage these tensions, while challenging self and others to move toward better processes and outcomes.

### *Equity and Inclusive Leadership*

A third and essential construct needed for inclusive leadership is *equity*. Equity is a way of assessing fairness and justice, whether of outcomes (distributive justice) or processes (procedural justice).

A common view of equity in social science focuses on exchanges (Cook & Hegtvedt, 1983) and the appropriate or most fair way of allocating resources or other outcomes (for example pay) as a function of contributions (for example, amount or value of the work). More generally, this has to do with deservingness: who is considered to deserve what or how much, relatively speaking. Essentially, on this view equity is perceived and experienced when outcomes are proportional to relevant inputs or contributions in the same measure across the people or groups we are comparing, and people therefore get what they are thought to deserve.

At a societal level (at this point in history), we would not expect or claim, for example, that only White people should get paid for their work, while people of color should work for free. Nonetheless, we know from much research that there continue to be great racial disparities in earnings in the United States and other societies (see, e.g., https://inequality.org/facts/racial-inequality)—even when comparing within the same type of work; this is one example of a prominent type of inequity. There are also great disparities in wealth in the United States as a function of race. This is cited by many as another example of racial inequity, one that should be addressed with reparations or other ways of making up for the practice of slavery and subsequent oppression that created that wealth gap. Yet, at the same time, others do not necessarily see this gap as inequitable, because they may be thinking about deservingness not in a historical context, but purely in individual terms—with regard to the work or inputs on the part of the specific person or family (see, for more discussion on this, Ferdman, 1997). This also applies to the workplace, for example in assessing fairness or equity in pay. Even though few people would claim that everyone should be paid the same, regardless of the type and amount of work they do, there is no agreement on what degree of inequality or disparity is fair, for example, between a CEO and the other employees in an organization. So, in spite of the general principle, there is no general consensus on what equity or fairness would look like.

A similar view can be applied to processes: processes—for example, those in hiring or promotions, or in how people are treated when they apply for social services, seek health care, or must go to court—are viewed as equitable when how someone is treated, and their experiences in going through the process, are commensurate with general rules or principles for that process. In other words, factors perceived to be irrelevant do not affect those experiences. This is also true at the group level, when comparing across groups. For example, there is ample evidence that people's race can make a great difference in how they experience and are treated by the criminal justice system in the U.S. (see, e.g., https://eji.org). While many people might agree that this is not fair—in other words, that justice should be "blind"—the same people might disagree as to whether the differences in the experience within the justice system of those who can afford to pay for a lawyer versus those who cannot is inequitable.

As illustrated by the examples, a key challenge in determining equity has to do with different views of what constitutes a relevant contribution or factor in assessing fairness (Ferdman, 1997). In the context of diversity and inclusion, it is evident that when factors such as intergroup bias or discrimination determine or affect important outcomes (such as access to particular types of jobs, education, or health care; who gets paid how much; access to housing and other social benefits; who speaks in a meeting, etc.), this is not equitable. Instead, equity involves providing both access to opportunity and to outcomes without invidious bias—whether overt or covert—and making sure that irrelevant factors do not hinder or help particular groups of people.

Indeed, many see equity as a focal goal or result of inclusion. David A. Thomas (2017), in his comments at the conclusion of the 25th Annual Kravis-deRoulet Conference that led to this book, framed it this way:

> What is the result of inclusion? What is it that we see, regardless of what we call it? Some of the things that were said today helped me to start to move toward my own answer. One is this notion that we will know when we have actually made an inclusive society or organization, when there is no correlation between identity group membership and life chances. At a societal level that's about not being able to predict, if you are born Black or born into a particular social class, what the outcomes are that you can achieve in a society, breaking that correlation. Or inside organizations: that that is no longer a predictor of how far you can go, how [far] you are likely to go, and where we will find you working. That means that inclusion doesn't leave behind some of the work that used to fall under other labels, like affirmative action or equal opportunity.

In this sense, then, equity is also about power and access to power. When access to roles with more power—for example membership on corporate boards, or executive positions in corporations, or election to legislative bodies—is associated with membership in identity groups that are societally more dominant—for example, being a White man—then we could say that this is not equitable, especially to the extent that this cannot be explained in other ways.

Inclusive leadership, then, involves noting, calling out, and addressing inequities. It also means challenging groups, organizations, and societies to foster more equitable processes, systems, and outcomes. Inclusive leadership involves noticing and voicing issues of equity and power and addressing them.

To do this, inclusive leadership requires challenging all-too-widely accepted ideas of what is "normal" with regard to access to resources and to their allocation, and holding up a mirror to self and others about our unspoken or taken-for-granted assumptions about both outcomes and processes. Is it fair and equitable that women are paid, on average, only a fraction of what men earn? Is it fair and equitable that these disparities are even greater when race and ethnicity are considered? Is it fair and equitable that people with disabilities have a much harder time finding suitable employment? Is it fair and equitable that new fathers are much less likely to take parental leave, even if offered, or that people who are transgender are much less likely to get the health care they need, or to feel safe when they go to work or even walk down the street? Is it fair and equitable that there are very few women leading major corporations or serving as chief of state around the world?

These are but a few of the most visible examples of the types of distributive and procedural justice issues that inclusive leadership must address. At a more micro level, other issues come up: is someone using up all the airtime in a meeting? Does everyone ignore the person in the wheelchair? Are women paid less than men in the organization? Is the organization only looking for new hires from certain universities and in majors? What are the effects of the organization's policies and practices (and products) in the larger society on different groups of people, when diversity is considered?

Inclusive leadership involves seeing and disrupting patterns of inequality and inequity by raising these types of questions; challenging groups, organizations, communities, and societies to work through the tensions and dilemmas involved to address, mitigate, and ideally eliminate inequities; and to find ways to collaborate to remove barriers to equity and fairness. Simultaneously attention to equity and fairness creates better working conditions, promotes social responsibility and engagement, and fosters more sustainability for organizations and the communities and world around them.

## Inclusive Leadership as the Fulcrum for the Practice of Inclusion

As discussed throughout the prior section, inclusive leadership plays a key role in highlighting diversity in groups, organizations, and communities; in catalyzing inclusive behavior, norms, and values, on the part of members of those collectives; in driving and sustaining inclusive organizational practices and systems; in promoting, fostering, and sustaining inclusive values, perspectives, policies, and systems in communities and societies; and in working to ensure that equity is a focal goal and result. Inclusive leaders help to create a compelling vision of diversity, inclusion, and equity, and challenge themselves and others to work to do what is needed to make that vision a reality (Gallegos, 2014; Gallegos et al., 2020). Inclusive leaders must be stewards and facilitators of an inclusive culture, as they attend to themselves and their effect on others, the groups in which they participate and lead, and the systems in which they play influential roles.

In the context of the systems model described earlier (and depicted in Figure 1.1), inclusive leadership can be seen as the essential fulcrum for the development of an inclusive group, organization, or larger system. In the most general sense, a fulcrum is something that plays a pivotal role in a given activity or situation. More concretely, a fulcrum is the pivot around which a lever turns; by resting on the fulcrum, a lever is able to convert force pushing down at one end into equivalent force pushing up at the other end. In the case of a seesaw, the fulcrum is usually in the middle, at the center of gravity, helping to balance the two sides and create equilibrium. In the case of a lever, the fulcrum can be moved closer to the weight that needs to be raised, so that less force pushing down is needed at the longer end.

Paralleling a physical fulcrum, leadership plays a pivotal role in inclusion in at least two important ways. On the one hand, inclusive leadership gives meaning to and helps to translate societal and/or organizational-level processes, practices, policies, and values into everyday behaviors and relationships, thus fostering inclusive practices and behavior in groups and in interpersonal interactions, and the experience of inclusion at the individual level. In this sense, inclusive leadership translates macro-level inclusion to the micro-level. On the other hand, inclusive leadership can combine what would otherwise be isolated or disparate individual behavior and experiences, interpersonal interactions, and group dynamics, and gives them meaning and visibility that translates them into patterns with larger organizational or societal significance. Inclusive leadership thus also translates micro-level aspects of inclusion to the macro level. In addition to transmuting inclusion across levels of analysis, leadership plays an important role in highlighting and strengthening inclusive practices at each level of analysis. I expand on these three aspects of inclusive leadership in the following sections.

### *From Macro to Micro*

Leadership plays a key role in helping to bring societal and organizational goals, values, and policies related to inclusion to life in everyday behavior and interactions. Nishii and Paluch (2018) described the key implementation behaviors that leaders engage in to create strong HR systems. Fundamentally, these behaviors, including explaining and modeling what is expected of followers, serve to create collective meaning and translate aspects of the organizational system so that they make sense and can be implemented in specific situations. Buengeler et al. (2018) described various ways in which leaders in organizations can respond to human resources diversity practices in particular, and how these responses can affect employees' experiences of inclusion.

In many workplaces, the everyday experience of workers is grounded in the way they are treated by supervisors and managers, and can also be affected by the tone set at higher levels by executives. Organizations may have policies and systems in place designed to foster inclusion, but, ultimately, it is most likely how these are interpreted and implemented, in combination with leader and supervisor behavior, that affects whether or not the organization's members will experience inclusion.

In a related study, for example, Chen (2011) found that respondents who perceived their leaders as displaying more authentic leadership (Avolio & Gardner, 2005) were also more likely to report affective commitment to their organization (r=.59); this relationship was partially and significantly mediated by the experience of inclusion. In my own work (Ferdman, 2014a) with a consulting client on their Global Inclusion Survey, I found that employee ratings of their supervisors' inclusive behavior were highly correlated (r=.64) with how included the employees felt in the company. The overall experience of inclusion was also positively correlated with ratings on items quite connected to leadership, assessing respondents' perception that they were given similar opportunities to others to develop their skills and careers, the degree of comfort they felt expressing their ideas, concerns, and opinions, and their belief that their supervisor made promotion and placement decisions based on performance, skills, and abilities. Buengeler and Den Hartog (2015) found that teams in a multinational company that were diverse in nationality performed better to the extent that the supervisor was perceived as treating the team members fairly, and that this perception was shared among the team. This result highlights the importance not only of how the supervisor behaves, but of how consistently this is experienced across the group. And Travis et al. (2019) reported that, in a multinational sample of 2,164 from 15 companies, 45% of the variance in employee experience of inclusion—how valued, trusted, authentic, and psychologically safe they felt—was predicted by the degree to which their supervisors behaved inclusively.

Beyond modeling and explaining desired behavior, inclusive leaders play an important role in reminding those around them about core values and imperatives at the organizational and societal level. Many organizations have strong value statements, often including diversity and inclusion. But unless these are taken into account in making decisions, in interactions, and in conducting business, they will not have much implication for everyday experience and behavior. Similarly, societies can have policies and values, such as democracy or multiculturalism, that only become real when they affect what happens in specific situations. Inclusive leadership, then, involves serving as the conduit for this macro to micro influence.

### *From Micro to Macro*

Leadership also plays a key role in noting and highlighting micro-level experiences and behavior, recognizing patterns, and giving them life at the organizational and societal levels. People in an organization may very well be individually kind to each other, may collaborate effectively, and may generally be open to differences. However, it is only when these and other manifestations of inclusive behavior become normative and institutionalized, based on the meaning and importance that leaders give to such behavior and on the norms and expectations that they systematically promote and communicate and that they embed into the organization's standard practices, that we can begin to speak of a truly inclusive organization.

As Wasserman et al. (2008) point out, a key responsibility of inclusive leaders is to create a "meta-narrative" that can create and foster a vision of what an inclusive culture is and needs to be. This is more likely to happen when leaders build on values, behaviors, needs, and aspirations that are already present in the organization, at least in some form, and then "connect the dots" among these (see also Wasserman, Chapter 6, this volume, and Cruz Teller, Chapter 27, this volume). Inclusive leaders can weave together various disparate components of inclusion (e.g., O'Mara, 2014) so that the combination can become a notable and persistent feature of the organization as a whole.

In sum, inclusive leaders can tell the story, make meaning, and help to give life to the views, needs, and aspirations of members of the organization, especially those who may have less access to power or visibility. By using the lenses of diversity, equity, and inclusion, inclusive leaders can make it more possible for relevant dynamics to be addressed in systemic ways.

### *Strengthening Within-Level Inclusion*

Inclusive leadership also involves designing, implementing, and sustaining inclusive practices at each level of analysis. To foster inclusion in groups, for example, it is important to co-construct suitable norms, to allow for dialogue about process, to facilitate sometimes difficult conversations that bring differences to light and help to make them work for collective benefit, and to call out and address inequities—whether in participation, treatment, or experience. At the organizational level, inclusive leadership involves keeping issues of diversity, equity, and inclusion at the forefront, and catalyzing systematic and effective ways to address them (see, e.g., O'Mara & Richter, 2017). At the community and societal levels, inclusive leaders must do the same, with the additional challenges of navigating political tensions and, often, strong intergroup conflicts.

## Manifestations of Inclusive Leadership: Qualities and Behaviors

Various authors (e.g., Booysen, 2014; Chrobot-Mason et al., 2013; Gallegos et al., 2020; Wasserman et al., 2008) have listed key components of inclusive leadership, generally speaking, and of its behavioral expressions and features (Gallegos, 2014; Travis et al., 2019), and I provide such a list in this section. But what characterizes leaders who are particularly likely to foster the translation or transmutation between micro and macro levels and are effective in doing so? I believe that such leadership includes, at a minimum, the following key elements:

1 *Self-awareness and authenticity*. Inclusive leaders must not only understand themselves as individuals and as members of multiple identity groups, but they must also be clear about how their role and function serves to magnify or dampen inclusive behavior by

followers on the one hand and to serve as catalysts for organizational change on the other. Inclusive leaders must encourage others to be authentic, must be authentic themselves, and must help create the conditions that permit both of these to happen.

2 *Conceptual and operational clarity and vision.* Inclusive leaders must be clear not only about what inclusion is but also how it operates in an everyday fashion in their organization and among its particular people. At the same time, they must have the capacity to see beyond what currently exists and to hold themselves and the organization's people accountable for new and more far-reaching possibilities.

3 *Capacity for complexity and paradoxical thinking and behavior.* To serve effectively as the fulcrum for inclusion across micro and macro levels, leaders must often simultaneously hold and balance seemingly disparate and even conflicting perspectives and views, as well as behave in ways that can appear to be conflicting. For example, they must be accepting of the organization's people and their styles and behavior, while at the same time catalyzing learning and openness to new possibilities and ways of doing things. They must push the organization to higher standards of fairness and transparency while making sure that existing norms and values are acted on. They must help create a climate in which the organization's people feel valued and included for who they are, yet simultaneously create suitable discomfort with the status quo, thus encouraging and pushing members of the organization to expand their range of behavior and acceptance. The ability to understand, hold, and manage the tensions and paradoxes of inclusion (Ferdman, 2017) is a vital element of inclusive leadership.

In addition to these broad characteristics, inclusive leaders need to display and model inclusive behavior, and encourage it in others. A number of the chapters in this book describe some of these practices. The following is a list of ways in which leaders can build more inclusion at work:

1 Acknowledge and appreciate differences of all types in the group and in the organization.
2 Learn about and be mindful of personal biases; examine and address assumptions about power, voice, competence, and effectiveness, especially how these relate to our different identities.
3 Seek to notice and remove systematic bias and discrimination—whether conscious or inadvertent—and to replace these with more productive and fair ways to work with difference.
4 Model and encourage authenticity.

*Table 1.1* Inclusive behaviors.[1]

| *For Everyone* | *For Leaders* |
| --- | --- |
| (Behaviors that everyone can exhibit to foster inclusion for themselves and others) | (Behaviors that leaders, especially those in positions of authority, can exhibit, in addition to those for everyone, to foster inclusion) |
| 1 **Acknowledge, connect, and engage with others.** Greet them (in culturally appropriate ways). Get to know them.<br>2 **Listen deeply and carefully,** as an ally not a critic. Check for understanding. Develop and use cultural understanding.<br>3 **Engage a broad range of perspectives.** Invite new voices. Provide space for dissent. Have the courage to say what needs to be said. Check whether people feel included.<br>4 **Openly share information; seek clarity and openness.** Share your intent and process.<br>5 **Be curious.** Learn how other people and groups may see and experience the world differently than you and your groups. Identify and share your assumptions.<br>6 **Become comfortable with discomfort.** Find and use your voice (even if different from others). Use discomfort as an opportunity for learning. Openly address disagreements—engage differences.<br>7 **Increase your self-awareness.** Understand your biases, assumptions, cultural background, and areas of privilege. Be aware of how your verbal and nonverbal behavior communicate to others. Recognize that all of us have complex identities; learn more about yours.<br>8 **Be willing to learn and be influenced by others.** Ask others about what they know, think, and | 1 **Hold yourself and others accountable for creating an inclusive culture.** Use your power and position to challenge inequities at the individual, group, and system levels. Create safety for self and others. Question traditional assumptions regarding what performance and performers look like.<br>2 **Invite engagement and dialogue.** Take the time for authentic conversation. Acknowledge and learn from mistakes. Explicitly consider and ask who else needs to be included—continually ask who is missing.<br>3 **Model bringing one's whole self to work and give permission for and encourage others to do so.** Show up authentically. Be vulnerable. Honor the full range of who people are. Be intentional about where you show up and where you are visible.<br>4 **Foster transparent decision-making.** Make it safe for others to express different perspectives. Model not having all the answers. Share data and information to the fullest extent possible.<br>5 **Understand and engage with resistance.** Engage many people in your efforts, especially those who have different views or ideas. Fully hear and respond to people's concerns and ideas. Have a goal of creating the best possible option rather than influencing others to agree. |

(*Continued*)

*Table 1.1* (Cont.)

| *For Everyone* | *For Leaders* |
|---|---|
| feel, especially when their perspective may be different from yours. Remain humble and flexible.<br>9 **Be respectful and demonstrate fairness.** Speak up when others are excluded. Be aware of your impact, not just your intent.<br>10 **Foster interdependence & teamwork.** Move from an "I" to a "we" mindset. Recognize whom you rely on to achieve tasks, and who relies on you. Invite active participation of all team members. | 6 **Understand and talk about how inclusion connects to the mission and vision.** Paint the big picture. Consistently explain why and how inclusion matters. Recognize your critical role in linking the effort to individuals. |

1 Copyright © 2020 by Bernardo M. Ferdman. Used with permission. (This list is an adaptation of Inclusive Behaviors and Practices, Version 1.1, April 2009, by B. M. Ferdman, J. H. Katz, E. Letchinger, and C. Thompson, created for The Institute for Inclusion and presented in Ferdman, B. M., Katz, J. H., Letchinger, E., & Thompson, C. (2009, March 9) Inclusive Behaviors and Practices: Report of the Institute for Inclusion Behavior Task Force. Presentation at the Institute for Inclusion 4th Conference, Arlington, VA).

5 Create opportunities tailored to individuals' special qualities and strengths, seek out unique voices, and highlight both individual uniqueness and collective identity.
6 Give all stakeholders the opportunity to engage in constructing norms and processes for inclusion while holding each other accountable.
7 Learn to be comfortable with discomfort and seek out situations that will result in learning, growing, and collective mutual benefits.

(Ferdman, 2018, para. 8)

In Table 1.1, I provide a detailed list, adapted from a list initially created by Ferdman, et al. (2009); the list is divided into those behaviors that everyone can do, regardless of role and degree of authority, and those that are particularly the responsibility of designated leaders—those holding roles that require overseeing, supervising, or managing others.

## Conclusion

Inclusive leadership can sometimes feel elusive and particularly challenging. In part because of the tensions inherent in inclusion, the seeming lack of clear guideposts or parameters, and the controversial and often polarizing as well as hierarchical aspects of intergroup relations, leaders need to develop this capacity in ways that foster ongoing learning and growth, build on their strengths, and provide safe and helpful ways to experiment, make mistakes, ask difficult questions, and practice new or different ways to engage across differences. Our collective future depends on it!

## References

Avolio, B. J., & Gardner, W. L. (2005). Authentic leadership development: Getting to the root of positive forms of leadership. *The Leadership Quarterly*, *16*, 315–338. https://doi.org/10.1016/j.leaqua.2005.03.001

Bennett, J. (2014). Intercultural competence: Vital perspectives for diversity and inclusion. In B. M. Ferdman & B. R. Deane (Eds.), *Diversity at work: The practice of inclusion* (pp. 155–176). San Francisco, CA: Jossey-Bass.

Booysen, L. (2014). The development of inclusive leadership practice and processes. In B. M. Ferdman & B. R. Deane (Eds.), *Diversity at work: The practice of inclusion* (pp. 296–329). San Francisco: Jossey-Bass. https://doi.org/10.1002/9781118764282.ch10

Buengeler, C., & Den Hartog, D. N. (2015). National diversity and team performance: The moderating role of interactional justice climate. *International Journal of Human Resource Management*, *26*, 831–855. https://doi.org/10.1080/09585192.2014.991345

Buengeler, C., Leroy, H., & De Stobbeleir, K. (2018). How leaders shape the impact of HR's diversity practices on employee inclusion. *Human Resource Management Review*, *28*(3), 289–303. https://doi.org/10.1016/j.hrmr.2018.02.005

Chen, C. (2011). *The mediating effect of employees' experience of inclusion and the moderating effect of individual work values on the relationship of authentic leadership style and organizational commitment.* [Doctoral dissertation, Alliant International University]. ProQuest Dissertations and Theses Database.

Chrobot-Mason, D., Ruderman, M. N., & Nishii, L. H. (2013). Leadership in a diverse workplace. In Q. M. Roberson (Ed.), *The Oxford handbook of diversity and work* (pp. 315–340). New York, NY: Oxford University Press.

Cook, K. S., & Hegtvedt, K. A. (1983). Distributive justice, equity, and equality. *Annual Review of Sociology*, *9*(1), 217–241. https://doi.org/10.1146/annurev.so.09.080183.001245

Creary, S., McDonnell, M.-H., Ghai, S., & Scruggs, J. (2019, March 27). When and why diversity improves your board's performance. *Harvard Business Review Digital Articles*. https://hbr.org/2019/03/when-and-why-diversity-improves-your-boards-performance.

Davidson, M. N., & Ferdman, B. M. (2002). The experience of inclusion. In B. Parker, B. M. Ferdman, & P. Dass, (Chairs), *Inclusive and effective networks: Linking diversity theory and practice* [All-Academy Symposium]. 62nd Annual Meeting of the Academy of Management, Denver.

Drath, W. H., McCauley, C. D., Palus, C. J., Van Velsor, E., O'Connor, P. M. G., & McGuire, J. B. (2008). Direction, alignment, commitment: Toward a more integrative ontology of leadership. *Leadership Quarterly*, *19*(6), 635–653. https://doi.org/10.1016/j.leaqua.2008.09.003

Ferdman, B. M. (1995). Cultural identity and diversity in organizations: Bridging the gap between group differences and individual uniqueness. In M. M. Chemers, S. Oskamp, & M. Costanzo (Eds.), *Diversity in organizations: New perspectives for a changing workplace* (pp. 37–61). Thousand Oaks, CA: Sage.

Ferdman, B. M. (1997). Values about fairness in the ethnically diverse workplace. *Business & the Contemporary World*, *9*, 191–208.

Ferdman, B. M. (2010). Teaching inclusion by example and experience: Creating an inclusive learning environment. In K. M. Hannum, L. Booysen, & B. B. McFeeters (Eds.), *Leading across differences: Cases and perspectives—Facilitator's guide* (pp. 37–50). San Francisco: Pfeiffer.

Ferdman, B. M. (2014a, May 15). Assessing employee inclusion in the workplace: An applied organizational approach. In B. Chung, (Chair), *Moving from diversity to inclusion: New directions in inclusion research* [Symposium]. 29th Annual Conference of the Society for Industrial and Organizational Psychology, Honolulu, HI.

Ferdman, B. M. (2014b). The practice of inclusion in diverse organizations: Toward a systemic and inclusive framework. In B. M. Ferdman & B. R. Deane (Eds.), *Diversity at work: The practice of inclusion* (pp. 3–54). San Francisco, CA: Jossey-Bass. https://doi.org/10.1002/9781118764282.ch1

Ferdman, B. M. (2016). Diversity and organizational change/performance. In J. Stone, R. Dennis, P. Rizova, & A. D. Smith (Eds.), *The Wiley-Blackwell encyclopedia of race, ethnicity, and nationalism*. San Francisco: Wiley. https://doi.com/10.1002/9781118663202.wberen680

Ferdman, B. M. (2017). Paradoxes of inclusion: Understanding and managing the tensions of diversity and multiculturalism. *The Journal of Applied Behavioral Science*, *53*(2), 235–263. https://doi.org/10.1177/0021886317702608

Ferdman, B. M. (2018, October 25). *Inclusion at work*. Society of Consulting Psychology. https://www.societyofconsultingpsychology.org/index.php?option=com_dailyplanetblog&view=entry&year=2018&month=10&day=24&id=25:inclusion-at-work

Ferdman, B. M., & Brody, S. E. (1996). Models of diversity training. In D. Landis & R. S. Bhagat (Eds.), *Handbook of intercultural training* (2nd ed., pp. 282–303). Thousand Oaks, CA: Sage.

Ferdman, B. M., & Deane, B. R. (Eds.). (2014). *Diversity at work: The practice of inclusion*. San Francisco: Jossey-Bass.

Ferdman, B. M., Katz, J. H., Letchinger, E., & Thompson, C. (2009, March 9). *Inclusive behaviors and practices: Report of the Institute for Inclusion Behavior Task Force*. [Presentation]. Institute for Inclusion 4th Conference, Arlington, VA.

Gallegos, P. V. (2014). The work of inclusive leadership: Fostering authentic relationships, modeling courage and humility. In B. M. Ferdman & B. R. Deane (Eds.), *Diversity at work: The practice of inclusion* (pp. 177–202). San Francisco: Jossey-Bass.

Gallegos, P. V., Wasserman, I. C., & Ferdman, B. M. (2020). The dance of inclusion: New ways of moving with resistance. In K. M. Thomas (Ed.), *Diversity resistance in organizations* (2nd ed., pp. 165–177). New York, NY: Taylor & Francis.

Hannum, K., McFeeters, B. B., & Booysen, L. (Eds.). (2010). *Leading across differences: Casebook*. San Francisco: Pfeiffer.

Heifetz, R. A. (1994). *Leadership without easy answers*. Cambridge, MA: Harvard University Press.

Heifetz, R. A., & Laurie, D. L. (1997). The work of leadership. *Harvard Business Review*, *75*(1), 124–134.

Heifetz, R. A., & Linsky, M. (2002). *Leadership on the line: Staying alive through the dangers of leading*. Boston, MA: Harvard Business School Press.

Holvino, E., Ferdman, B. M., & Merrill-Sands, D. (2004). Creating and sustaining diversity and inclusion in organizations: Strategies and approaches. In M. S. Stockdale & F. J. Crosby (Eds.), *The psychology and management of workplace diversity* (pp. 245–276). Malden, MA: Blackwell.

Miller, F. A., & Katz, J. H. (2007). *The path from exclusive club to inclusive organization: A developmental process*. Retrieved from http://blogs.ces.uwex.edu/inclusiveexcellence/files/2011/11/Path-from-Exclusive-Club-to-Inclusive-Organization-Article.pdf.

Nishii, L. H., & Paluch, R. M. (2018). Leaders as HR sensegivers: Four HR implementation behaviors that create strong HR systems. *Human Resource Management Review*, *28*(3), 319–323. https://doi.org/10.1016/j.hrmr.2018.02.007

Nishii, L. H., & Rich, R. E. (2014). Creating inclusive climates in diverse organizations. In B. M. Ferdman & B. R. Deane (Eds.), *Diversity at work: The practice of inclusion* (pp. 330–363). San Francisco: Jossey-Bass.

O'Mara, J. (2014). Global benchmarks for diversity and inclusion. In B. M. Ferdman & B. R. Deane (Eds.), *Diversity at work: The practice of inclusion* (pp. 415–430). San Francisco: Jossey-Bass.

O'Mara, J., & Richter, A., & 95 expert panelists (2017). *Global diversity & inclusion benchmarks: Standards for organizations around the world*. Centre for Global Inclusion. Retrieved from http://centreforglobalinclusion.org/gdib

Phillips, K. W. (2014). How diversity makes us smarter. *Scientific American*, *311*(4). Available online at www.scientificamerican.com/article/how-diversity-makes-us-smarter

Plaut, V. C., Thomas, K. M., & Goren, M. J. (2009). Is multiculturalism or color blindness better for minorities? *Psychological Science*, *20*(4), 444–446. https://doi.org/10.1111/j.1467-9280.2009.02318.x

Rock, D., Halvorson, H. G., & Grey, J. (2016, September 22). Diverse teams feel less comfortable–and that's why they perform better. *Harvard Business Review Digital Articles*. Available at https://hbr.org/2016/09/diverse-teams-feel-less-comfortable-and-thats-why-they-perform-better.

Thomas, D. A. (2017, March 4). *The way forward: Next steps on the path to inclusion* [Presentation]. Inclusive leadership: Transforming diverse lives, workplaces and societies, 25th Annual Kravis-deRoulet Conference, Kravis Leadership Institute, Claremont McKenna College, Claremont, CA.

Travis, D. J., Shaffer, E., & Thorpe-Moscon, J. (2019, November 21). *Getting real about inclusive leadership: Why change starts with you*. Catalyst, Inc., New York, NY. https://www.catalyst.org/research/inclusive-leadership-report

van Knippenberg, D., van Ginkel, W. P., & Homan, A. C. (2013). Diversity mindsets and the performance of diverse teams. *Organizational Behavior and Human Decision Processes*, *121*(2), 183–193. https://doi.org/10.1016/j.obhdp.2013.03.003

Wasserman, I. C., Gallegos, P. V., & Ferdman, B. M. (2008). Dancing with resistance: Leadership challenges in fostering a culture of inclusion. In K. M. Thomas (Ed.), *Diversity resistance in organizations* (pp. 175–200). Mahwah, NJ: Erlbaum.

# 2 Exclusion of Inclusion in Leadership Theories

*Nurcan Ensari and Ronald E. Riggio*

Although the scientific study of leadership is over 100 years old, the focus of leadership theories and research has been quite narrow. It has been more exclusive than inclusive. For the most part, our images of the ideal leader shape our interpretation and evaluation of leader behaviors and factor into our construction of leadership theories and models. As a result, the meaning and importance given to the concept of leadership varies depending on culture (Dorfman et al., 2004; Jung & Avolio, 1999; Wood & Jogulu, 2006). The production of knowledge and research in the field of leadership has been accomplished primarily in the United States and Europe (Yukl, 2012). Leadership researchers, who mainly hail from the U.S. and Europe, primarily studied workplace leaders in corporate settings (Yukl, 1998). The leaders studied were primarily male and primarily White. Moreover, when research was conducted in non-Western countries these studies typically involved the application of Western models and theories (e.g., Gong et al., 2009; Hur et al., 2011; Jung et al., 2009).

A great deal of effort has gone into testing the universality of Western leadership theories across cultures, rather than developing culturally sensitive theories. A good example is the GLOBE project. Although GLOBE studied leadership in dozens of countries and cultures, much of the focus was on identifying universal behaviors and characteristics of leaders across cultures (House et al., 2004). Only later did GLOBE provide descriptive information about what leadership looked like in different cultures, but again, the same Western-centric model of leader characteristics was used (Chhokar et al., 2007). Historically, there has been little attention paid to cultural variations in leadership (although this is slowly changing).

Likewise, much attention has been given to trying to validate Western leadership theories or models across cultures, and this has led to a very ethnocentric view of leadership (Ayman & Korabik, 2010). Little attention has been paid to better understanding the role that stereotypes, unconscious biases, social role expectations, attributional errors, and power and status differentials play in leadership (Ayman & Korabik, 2010). As a result, an *emic* approach (i.e., leadership is studied within a culture) as opposed to an *etic* approach (i.e., leadership theories are validated across cultures) has predominated.

The goal of this chapter is to critique classic and current theories of leadership, pointing out the lack of inclusivity in terms of the applicability of the theories to understanding "real world" leadership. We discuss more inclusive approaches to theory construction, and, finally, provide suggestions and direction for creating more inclusive theories and approaches to studying and practicing leadership.

## Exclusivity in Leadership Theories

As noted, not only were leadership models developed from studying White male leaders in male-dominated organizations, but the theories were developed and studied primarily by men. The earliest theory, often referred to as the "Great Man" theory of leadership, shaped leadership perceptions and led to stereotypes of what effective leaders look like, while focusing on the more masculine behaviors exhibited by these leaders (Borgatta et al., 1954). This led to a biased and incomplete depiction of leadership. In addition, this bias helped limit access to, and success at, leadership positions for women and for people from minority groups. Moreover, the expectations associated with the Great Man theory meant that members of non-dominant groups, including women, were expected and pressured to behave in ways that were consistent with the White male-centric conception of effective leaders. When gender has been studied in leadership research, the focus is primarily on how men and women (or White and non-White) leaders differed in their leadership style, behavior, and effectiveness.

Like the Great Man theory, trait theories of leadership are also exclusive. Trait theories, as well as their more modern versions that focus on leader competencies, suggest that people who possess certain qualities, traits, or competencies are better suited for positions of leadership. The exclusivity in these theories involves the process by which these traits were identified. This was a universalist approach that did not consider variations due to culture, gender, or social category (e.g., race, occupation/sector, etc.). Although a few studies did show cultural variations in traits (e.g., Ayman et al., 2012; Gerstner & Day, 1994; Ling et al., 2000), most research agreed that the key traits of a successful leader are associated with men and masculinity (Ayman-Nolley & Ayman, 2005; Heilman, 2001; Leffler et al., 2006). For example, in exploring extraversion, a trait commonly associated with leadership, Eagly and Carli (2007) found that women scored lower on the assertiveness aspect of extraversion, but they scored higher on the warmth and positive emotion aspects of extraversion. A meta-analysis found that agentic traits such as masculinity and dominance were most characteristic of leadership emergence (Lord et al., 1986). A masculine (i.e., high instrumentality, low expressivity) gender-role orientation was most related to leadership emergence (Goktepe & Schneier, 1989). The real-life consequences have been detrimental for women and their aspirations to attain leadership positions—positions that are developed based on the masculine portrayal of leadership (i.e., more men than women seem to be a "fit" for these leadership positions).

Although there is some evidence that certain leadership traits are universally effective (e.g., acting with consideration, concern for production, and rewarding others, are examples of such traits; Muczyk & Reimann, 1987), two of the most studied traits associated with leader effectiveness, participative and directive behaviors, are associated with a Western ideology. Dorfman and colleagues (1997) found that while directive leadership behaviors are associated with employee satisfaction and commitment in Taiwan and Mexico, participative leadership behaviors only showed a positive impact in the United States and South Korea. Thus, critical traits that Western research has identified as predictive of effective leadership may be differentially effective in different countries and cultures.

More contemporary theories of leadership still suffer from a Western-centric bias. For example, the leader–member exchange (LMX) approach stated that the relationship between the leader and the follower determines leadership perceptions and effectiveness (Graen & Uhl-Bien, 1995). Thus, the quality of the relationship is key to the success of the leader. The exclusivity in this leadership approach is in the lack of understanding of the role of diversity in dyadic relationships. The assessment of the quality of the relationship has not been culturally validated, as LMX has not much been studied with diverse dyads from different cultures or social categories (Ayman & Korabik, 2010; Scandura & Lankau, 1996). A few studies suggest that the quality of LMX is low when the dyads come from different backgrounds (e.g., Green et al., 1996; Vecchio & Brazil, 2007; Vecchio & Bullis, 2001). For example, the quality of LMX is lower when women managers work with men rather than with women subordinates (Ayman et al., 2004; Green et al., 1996). Furthermore, there are cultural variations in how LMX relates to outcomes. For example, LMX was linked to positive outcomes depending on the organizational climate in China (Aryee & Chen, 2006; Chen & Tjosvold, 2007), and depending on the span of supervision in Germany (Schyns et al., 2005). When diverse dyads were examined in China (i.e., an American manager with Chinese subordinates), *guanxi* (personal relationship) had a significant role in the openness of the dyadic interaction (Ayman & Korabik, 2010; Chen & Tjosvold, 2007). Clearly, there is a need for the LMX model to be more inclusive of cross-cultural dyads and inclusive of culturally differing relationships.

The same is true for transformational leadership theory (Bass, 1985, 1996; Bass & Avolio, 1990), which states that certain leadership behaviors (e.g., individualized consideration, intellectual stimulation, idealized influence, and inspirational motivation) evoke desirable follower behaviors. Similar to LMX, this theory also mainly concerns dyadic relationships. The exclusion of the role of the leader in group processes limits the generalizability of the theory to cultures where collective outcomes and intra-group relationships are more focal than individual accomplishments and dyadic relationships (see Yukl, 1999). Furthermore, the transformational leadership behaviors measured by the widely used Multifactor Leadership Questionnaire (MLQ) are based on a Western conception of leadership. For example, inspirational motivation, intellectual stimulation, and individualized consideration are all associated with individualistic and more egalitarian cultures, rather than collectivistic cultures, where direction, delegation, and protection are expected from leaders. Transformational theory does not address how leaders facilitate cooperation within the group, gain trust of the followers, or build collective identity, which are essential values in collectivistic cultures. Followers' commitment and loyalty to the leader create a bi-directional relationship whereby leaders' protection is reciprocated with followers' commitment in collectivistic cultures; however, influence is unidirectional, flowing from the leader to the follower, in transformational leadership theory (Yukl, 1999).

Generalizability of the transformational leadership theory is debatable. Transformational behaviors of women and men leaders are perceived differently by followers (Ayman et al., 2009), and the behaviors defining transformational leadership differ across cultures (e.g., Den Hartog et al., 1997). Although the validity of transformational leadership was shown in many countries (Judge & Piccolo, 2004), there is limited evidence for measurement equivalence of transformational leadership across culture and gender (Yukl, 1999). Thus, due to the lack of inclusivity in transformational leadership theory, certain leader behaviors in various social and cultural groups have not been properly examined in the scholarly research following this theory.

## The Role of Culture in Leadership

Culture shapes our perception of an ideal leader. One of the most popular and comprehensive cross-cultural leadership projects, the GLOBE study (House et al., 2004), attempted to establish a universal model of leadership. However, the results are mixed, and many studies suggested that the universal characteristics and behaviors of leaders are manifested in different ways in different countries due to their distinct cultural norms, values, and philosophical frameworks (Ayman & Korabik, 2010; van Emmerik et al., 2008).

Most Western societies (generally characterized as individualistic and low power distance cultures by Hofstede, 1980) promote leaders who produce greater bottom lines. Therefore, effective leadership in such societies is assessed by financial results, and personal initiatives such as networking and mentoring are seen as imperative stages of leadership development (Jogulu, 2010). The ideal leadership prototype in Western societies is a highly charismatic, autonomous, participative, and team-oriented leader (House et al., 2004). Western societies are shaped by a democratic view on which leadership roles can easily be changed based on individual effort ("anyone can get to the top"), and are mostly seen as involving coordinating and delegating behaviors (Jogulu, 2010). Leadership is seen as participative; leaders value their followers' active participation in the decision-making process (Ashkanasy et al., 2002). The Western approach to business ethics is based on utilitarianism, emphasizing moral responsibilities and the relationship between the individual and the firm (Palazzo, 2002; Steinmann & Löhr, 1992). Western leaders tend to score high on performance orientation and humane orientation (Ashkanasy et al., 2002; House et al., 2004).

On the other hand, in most non-Western societies (generally characterized as collectivistic and high power distance cultures by Hofstede, 1980), long-term organizational goals, protection of followers, loyalty, mutual commitment, and hard work shape the idea of effective leadership (Jogulu, 2010). Effective leadership in these societies is seen as a collective outcome prioritizing collective needs and community engagement (Hofstede, 1980). Leadership roles are directing, and can only be attained based on social status and titles, which prescribe the hierarchical relationships between the leader and the followers (Jogulu, 2010). Most of the East Asian countries are rooted in Confucian philosophy focusing on particularistic ethics, fatalism, and high performance (House et al., 2004; Hwang et al., 2015; Scarborough, 1998).

Considering these cultural variations, globalization trends push organizations toward a better understanding of different cultural values and beliefs, and toward promoting and rewarding culturally sensitive leadership behaviors and approaches. More corporations have been moving operations to subsidiaries located in other countries, and more non-Western corporations are becoming successful in the worldwide market. As a result, new trends in management practices are emerging. Leaders are realizing that the key to success is to understand the cultural characteristics that impact their followers' behavioral and attitudinal preferences (Dorfman et al., 1997; Hofstede, 1980; Hofstede & Minkov, 2010). As Western leadership theories have been transferred across the globe, there is a need for more inclusive leadership theories that are sensitive to cultural, social, and economic differences among countries (Hofstede, 1980).

## Toward More Inclusive Approaches to Leadership

In traditional leadership theories, the key behaviors and approaches primarily focus on the leadership characteristics recognized by the dominant social groups in Western cultures. More inclusive approaches to leadership theory suggest how and why certain individuals become successful leaders while incorporating social and cultural dimensions that shape many aspects of leadership. More specifically, inclusive leadership theories should provide an approach to study (a) social and cultural factors that shape successful leaders and their relationships with others; (b) implications of leader behaviors for individuals from diverse backgrounds; (c) how leaders can be inclusive, as well as effective in fostering inclusion; and (d) integrative perspectives that are sensitive to both majority and minority identities of both followers and leaders. In fostering inclusion, leaders must demonstrate flexibility and acceptance of individual differences and show individualized consideration in guiding, motivating, and directing others (Bass & Riggio, 2006). They should also promote collaboration, shared decision-making, and consensus-building toward career advancement and the well-being of all employees (Sabharwal, 2014). A sense of humanity that accounts for the richness of cultures and expands on diversity is also pivotal to inclusive leadership (Gallegos, 2014).

There are a few contemporary leadership models that have identified certain leadership styles that may be more apt to value an inclusive work culture and climate. Servant leadership, for instance, has been suggested to promote inclusive ideals to thrive in diverse organizations "by helping diverse employees feel empowered and valued, fostering equitable, socially responsible and more humane workplaces, as well as by being more sensitive to various societal expectations" (Gotsis & Grimani, 2016, p. 985). A servant leader prioritizes the growth and success of the followers, promotes social responsibility, advocates for diversity, shows care and genuine concern for followers' needs, and commits to solving issues of exclusion (Ferdman, 2014; Gotsis & Grimani, 2016).

Another leadership theory that is associated with perceptions of inclusion is authentic leadership. Authentic leaders are expected to shape "proximal organizational climates that are more inclusive, caring, engaged, and more oriented toward developing strengths" (Gardner et al., 2005, p. 367). Authentic leadership was associated with higher levels of organizational citizenship behaviors (OCBs) mediated by perceptions of inclusion, which enhanced followers' self-worthiness and pro-social behaviors (Cottrill et al., 2014). Authentic leadership promotes inclusion through role modeling, transmission of relevant information, generation of learning processes, and facilitation of replication of inclusive behaviors by others (Boekhorst, 2015).

How can we develop more inclusive leadership theories? This can only be achieved if there is a fundamental paradigm shift in leadership theorizing (Chin, 2010). Chin (2010, p. 150) framed it this way:

> Inclusive leadership bears multiple connotations involving incorporation of diversity dimensions in leadership theory, explanations of how these dimensions shape our understanding of leadership, as well as investigation of the mechanisms through which diverse followers' perceptions of diverse leaders affect leadership development. Leadership theories should be expanded to address social equality and inclusion issues made salient amidst rapidly changing societal and organizational contexts.

In order to move beyond traditional leadership theories and approaches, researchers should adopt more culturally integrative approaches. Some Western-based leadership styles may fit within an Eastern culture, or vice versa, when applied in a culturally sensitive way. For instance, some researchers have argued that transformational leadership style predicts leadership success in Japan (Yokochi, 1989) and Singapore (Koh, 1990), because leaders' ideology and vision are more readily accepted when there is greater acceptance of authority (Jung & Avolio, 1999). Although, traditionally, more transactional and autocratic leadership styles were adopted in Eastern cultures (Hofstede, 1980), a culturally contingent leadership style in Malaysia (Jogulu, 2010) has been advocated. An integration of transactional and paternalistic leadership would potentially meet collectivistic followers' expectations of a leader as the legitimate authority figure who sets clear expectations of roles and responsibilities but also maintains group harmony, fosters trusting long-term relationships, and protects the well-being of the followers (Jogulu, 2010).

Leadership styles are important in shaping organizational culture and work climate. Future research should try to develop a comprehensive framework for leadership that would guide the field toward understanding how leaders help to shape inclusive work environments. Researchers should analyze the inclusivity of current leadership theories and suggest ways in which these can have greater potential for fostering and supporting inclusiveness in the workplace (Gotsis & Grimani, 2016). Future models should include a shared process of leadership that enhances both individual and collective identities and capacities (Yukl, 1999). In such a collective leadership model, some leadership functions are shared and some are allocated to others, thereby creating a collective identity (Yukl, 1999).

Leadership is not universal. Inclusive leadership theories should go beyond gender and race/ethnicity issues, which are important and have been studied extensively; such theories should delve into how diversity and its various dimensions shape perceptions of leadership and question our conceptualizations of leadership effectiveness. We should explore how leader behaviors shape diversity (Chin & Sanchez-Hucles, 2007). According to Chin and Sanchez-Hucles (2007), "if theories of leadership are to be robust, they should be able to address complexity" (p. 609) and incorporate diverse social categories such as race, gender, sexual orientation, and others.

To develop more inclusive theories of leadership, both emic and etic perspectives (Berry, 1997; Gelfand et al., 2002) need to be included. Studies on gender, culture, and leadership provide support for the influence of intrapsychic processes, social structural processes, and interpersonal processes. Thus, both gender and culture matter because they can affect a leader's style, behavior, emergence, and effectiveness in many complex ways. For example, gender and culture matter because leaders' gender role identities and cultural values can affect the choices they make about the manner in which they will lead. Moreover, the low social status that is attributed to leaders who are women and people of color can result in the devaluation of their accomplishments by others. In addition, when there is a lack of congruence between people's implicit stereotypes of leadership and the traditional roles associated with women and people of color, leaders from these social groups experience a higher level of scrutiny and have more trouble legitimizing their authority (Eagly & Carli, 2007). Thus, future work should focus on understanding the dynamics attributable to sociodemographic gender, gender-role orientation, and their intersection, as well as how the relation between leadership and outcomes is affected by dyadic and group diversity, or by cultural values and assumptions: "Gender and culture should become variables that are incorporated into theory building in leadership" (Ayman & Korabik, 2010, p. 166).

New leadership trends are emerging as more women enter into leadership positions. As globalization increases, as more relationship-oriented leadership styles arise, and as the recognition of the importance of social skills spreads, leadership theories need to adapt. The "feminization" of leadership (e.g., Eagly & Carli, 2003; Rudman & Glick, 2001) led to a more "androgynous conception of leadership" with equal emphasis on task and people skills (Ayman & Korabik, 2010). As Ayman and Korabik (2010) compellingly argue:

> An examination of the effects of gender and culture has the potential to change our definition of what constitutes leadership and what is considered to be effective leadership. This more inclusive conceptualization can expand the vision of leadership to represent all human beings.
>
> (p. 160)

## Conclusions and Moving Forward

Moving forward—in light of the acceleration of globalization, growth in diversity in organizations, and changing practices, organizations, and social environments—means that a positive shift in leadership theories is called for. The shift that we recommend necessitates contemporary leadership theories and practices that recognize the uniqueness of every person's potential and can inspire as many leaders as possible while avoiding exclusion of members of underrepresented, underprivileged social groups. More specifically, leadership theories need to move away from their Western-centric and male-centric origins, and consider more diverse and inclusive theory-building, drawing on research in non-Western cultures and work that takes a more gender-neutral perspective (Johnson & Lacerenza, 2019). At the same time, we must move from more simplistic and leader-centric theories of leadership to complex theories that take into account leaders, followers, context, and culture and how all of these factors come together to co-construct what we consider as leadership. In contrast to attempts to portray the "Great Man" and develop a prototype for the perfect leader, inclusive leadership theories should guide us on how to see the leadership potential in every person, and focus on development of leadership skills across diverse social and cultural groups. They should also focus on how key aspects of inclusive leadership (e.g., participative decision-making regardless of hierarchies, employee engagement and involvement, empowerment, respectful relationships, encouragement for innovation, and mutual support) can be enhanced (Wuffli, 2015).

Finally, leadership research needs to be both interdisciplinary and cross-disciplinary if we are truly to understand the complexity of leadership. Leadership theories serve the purpose of guiding how we think about leadership and they lay down a roadmap for leadership development. If our theories are limited—if they are too simplistic, or if they do not take into account the roles of culture, gender, and diversity of background and thought—then our practice of leadership is also limited.

For practitioners, there is a need to be aware of the limitations of many of the well-known and researched leadership theories. It is important to realize that reliance on these theories to guide practice has the potential to distort the picture when working with leaders and leadership with different groups of people and in different cultures.

What are the implications for the leaders of the future? Bennis (1999) said that "exemplary leadership and organizational change are impossible without the full inclusion, initiatives and cooperation of followers" (p. 74). The leaders of the future must understand the power of diverse talent, embrace inclusion, and become powerful motivators for their diverse followers. In the journey toward inclusion, Ferdman (2007) identified exploration of one's cultural identities, biases, and preferences as the first step. Self-knowledge and acceptance of multiple identities would allow leaders to promote cultural awareness among their followers, and encourage them to bring their authentic self to work (Ferdman, 2007; Ferdman & Roberts, 2014). When personal values are aligned to inclusion, the leader is seen as authentic in this journey. As a next step, inclusive leaders are expected to develop the necessary skills that would allow them to be global communicators, inclusive decision-makers, and multicultural agents. Finally, inclusion must be reflected in leaders' attitudes and behaviors, in searching for diverse talent, in seeing that as a source of competitive advantage, in inspiring others toward a shared vision aligned with multiculturalism, in providing fair opportunities for all employees, in realizing others' potential and in encouraging them to make unique contributions, and in driving organizations toward global collaboration and success.

## References


Aryee, S., & Chen, Z. X. (2006). Leader-member exchange in a Chinese context: Antecedents, the mediating role of psychological empowerment and outcomes. *Journal of Business Research*, *59*(7), 793–801. https://doi.org/10.1016/j.jbusres.2005.03.003

Ashkanasy, N. M., Trevor-Roberts, E., & Earnshaw, L. (2002). The Anglo cluster: Legacy of the British empire. *Journal of World Business*, *37*(1), 28–39. https://doi.org/10.1016/S1090-9516(01)00072-4

Ayman, R., & Korabik, K. (2010). Leadership: Why gender and culture matter. *American Psychologist*, *65*(3), 157–170. https://doi.org/10.1037/a0018806

Ayman, R., Korabik, K., & Morris, S. (2009). Is transformational leadership always perceived as effective? Male subordinates' devaluation of female transformational leaders. *Journal of Applied Social Psychology*, *39*(4), 852–879. https://doi.org/10.1111/j.1559-1816.2009.00463.x

Ayman, R., Mead, A. D., Bassari, A., & Huang, J. (2012). Implicit leadership in Iran: Differences between leader and boss and gender. In S. Turnbull, P. Case, G. Edwards, D. Schedlitzki, & P. Simpson (Eds.), *Worldly leadership* (pp. 135–157). London: Palgrave Macmillan. https://doi.org/10.1177%2F2158244015579727

Ayman, R., Rincbiuso, M., & Korabik, K. (2004, August). *Organizational commitment and job satisfaction in relation to LMX and dyad gender composition* [Paper Presentation]. International Congress of Psychology, Beijing, China.

Ayman-Nolley, S., & Ayman, R. (2005). Children's implicit theory of leadership. In J. R. Meindl & B. Schyns (Eds.), *Implicit leadership theories: Essays and explorations* (pp. 189–233). Greenwich, CT: Information Age. https://doi.org/10.1057/9780230361720_7

Bass, B. M. (1985). *Leadership and performance beyond expectations*. New York: Free Press. https://doi.org/10.1002/hrm.3930250310

Bass, B. M. (1996). *A new paradigm of leadership: An inquiry into transformational leadership*. Alexandria, VA: US Army Research Institute for the Behavioral & Social Sciences.

Bass, B. M., & Avolio, B. J. (1990). Developing transformational leadership: 1992 and beyond. *Journal of European Industrial Training*, *14*(5), 21–27. https://doi.org/10.1108/03090599010135122

Bass, B. M., & Riggio, R. E. (2006). *Transformational leadership* (2nd ed.). Abingdon: Taylor & Francis/Routledge. https://doi.org/10.1080/10887150701451312

Bennis, W. (1999). The end of leadership: Exemplary leadership is impossible without full inclusion, initiatives, and cooperation of followers. *Organizational Dynamics*, *28*(1), 71–80. https://doi.org/10.1016/S0090-2616(00)80008-X

Berry, J. W. (1997). Immigration, acculturation, and adaptation. *Applied Psychology: An International Review*, *46*(1), 5–34. https://doi.org/10.1111/j.1464-0597.1997.tb01087.x

Boekhorst, J. A. (2015). The role of authentic leadership in fostering workplace inclusion: A social information processing perspective. *Human Resource Management*, *54*(2), 241–264. https://doi.org/10.1002/hrm.21669

Borgatta, E., Bales, R., & Couch, A. (1954). Some findings relevant to the Great Man Theory of leadership. *American Sociological Review*, *19*(6), 755–759. https://doi.org/10.2307/2087923

Chen, N. Y., & Tjosvold, D. (2007). Guanxi and leader member relationships between American managers and Chinese employees: Open-minded dialogue as mediator. *Asia Pacific Journal of Management*, *24*(2), 171–189. https://doi.org/10.1007/s10490-006-9029-9

Chhokar, J. S., Brodbeck, F. C., & House, R. J. (2007). *Culture and leadership across the world: A GLOBE report of in-depth studies of the cultures of 25 countries*. Mahwah, NJ: Lawrence Erlbaum.

Chin, J. L. (2010). Introduction to the special issue on diversity and leadership. *American Psychologist*, *65*(3), 150–156. https://doi.org/10.1037/a0018716

Chin, J. L., & Sanchez-Hucles, J. (2007). Diversity and leadership. *American Psychologist*, *62*(6), 608–609. https://doi.org/10.1037/0003-066X62.6.608

Cottrill, K., Lopez, P. D., & Hoffman, C. (2014). How authentic leadership and inclusion benefit organizations. *Equality, Diversity and Inclusion: An International Journal*, *33*(3), 275–292. https://doi.org/10.1108/EDI-05-2012-0041

Den Hartog, D. N., van Muijen, J. J., & Koopman, P. L. (1997). Transactional versus transformational leadership: An analysis of the MLQ. *Journal of Occupational and Organizational Psychology*, *70*(1), 19–34. https://doi.org/10.1111/j.2044-8325.1997.tb00628.x

Dorfman, P. W., Hanges, P. J., & Brodbeck, F. C. (2004). Leadership and cultural variation: Identification of culturally endorsed leadership profiles. In R. J. House, P. J. Hanges, M. Javidan, P. W. Dorfman, & V. Gupta (Eds.), *Culture, leadership, and organizations: The GLOBE study of 62 societies* (pp. 669–719). Thousand Oaks, CA: Sage Publications.

Dorfman, P. W., Howell, J. P., Hibino, S., Lee, J. K., Tate, U., & Bautista, A. (1997). Leadership in Western and Asian countries: Commonalities and differences in effective leadership processes across cultures. *The Leadership Quarterly*, *8*(3), 233–274. https://doi.org/10.1016/S1048-9843(97)90003-5

Eagly, A. H., & Carli, L. L. (2003). The female leadership advantage: An evaluation of the evidence. *The Leadership Quarterly*, *14*(6), 807–834. https://doi.org/10.1016/j.leaqua.2003.09.004

Eagly, A. H., & Carli, L. L. (2007). *Through the labyrinth: The truth about how women become leaders*. Boston, MA: Harvard Business School Press.

Ferdman, B. M. (2007). Self-knowledge and inclusive interactions. *San Diego Psychologist*, *22*(5), 25–26.

Ferdman, B. M. (2014). The practice of inclusion in diverse organizations: Toward a systemic and inclusive framework. In B. M. Ferdman & B. R. Deane (Eds.), *Diversity at work: The practice of inclusion* (pp. 3–54). San Francisco, CA: Jossey-Bass. https://doi.org/10.1002/9781118764282.ch1

Ferdman, B. M., & Roberts, L. M. (2014). Creating inclusion for oneself: Knowing, accepting and expressing one's whole self at work. In B. M. Ferdman & B. R. Deane (Eds.), *Diversity at work: The practice of inclusion* (pp. 93–127). San Francisco, CA: Jossey-Bass. https://doi.org/10.1002/9781118764282.ch3

Gallegos, P. V. (2014). The work of inclusive leadership: Fostering authentic relationships, modeling courage and humility. In B. M. Ferdman & B. R. Deane (Eds.), *Diversity at work: The practice of inclusion* (pp. 177–202). San Francisco, CA: Jossey-Bass.

Gardner, W. L., Avolio, B. J., Luthans, F., May, D. R., & Walumbwa, F. (2005). "Can you see the real me?" A self-based model of authentic leader and follower development. *The Leadership Quarterly*, *16*(3), 343–372. https://doi.org/10.1016/j.leaqua.2005.03.003

Gelfand, M. J., Raver, J. L., & Ehrhart, K. H. (2002). Methodological issues in cross-cultural organizational research. In S. G. Rogelberg (Ed.), *Handbook of research methods in industrial and organizational psychology* (pp. 216–246). Malden, MA: Blackwell Publishing. https://doi.org/10.4135/9781483386874.n94

Gerstner, C. R., & Day, D. V. (1994). Cross-cultural comparison of leadership prototypes. *The Leadership Quarterly*, *5*(2), 121–134. https://doi.org/10.1016/1048-9843(94)90024-8

Goktepe, J. R., & Schneier, C. E. (1989). Role of sex, gender roles, and attraction in predicting emergent leaders. *Journal of Applied Psychology*, *74*(1), 165–167. https://doi.org/10.1037/0021-9010.74.1.165

Gong, Y., Huang, J., & Farh, J. (2009). Employee learning orientation, transformational leadership, and employee creativity: The mediating role of employee creative self-efficacy. *Academy of Management Journal*, *52*(4), 765–778. https://doi.org/10.5465/amj.2009.43670890

Gotsis, G., & Grimani, K. (2016). The role of servant leadership in fostering inclusive organizations. *Journal of Management Development*, *35*(8), 985–1010. https://doi.org/10.1108/JMD-07-2015-0095

Graen, G. B., & Uhl-Bien, M. (1995). Relationship-based approach to leadership: Development of leader-member exchange (LMX) theory of leadership over 25 years: Applying a multi-level multi-domain perspective. *The Leadership Quarterly*, *6*(2), 219–247. https://doi.org/10.1016/1048-9843(95)90036-5

Green, S. G., Anderson, S. E., & Shivers, S. L. (1996). Demographic and organizational influences on leader–member exchange and related work attitudes. *The Leadership Quarterly*, *6*(2), 203–214.

Heilman, M. E. (2001). Description and prescription: How gender stereotypes prevent women's ascent up the organizational ladder. *Journal of Social Issues*, *57*(4), 657–674. https://doi.org/10.1111/0022-4537.00234

Hofstede, G. (1980). Motivation, leadership, and organization: Do American theories apply abroad? *Organizational Dynamics*, *9*(1), 42–63. https://doi.org/10.1016/0090-2616(80)90013-3

Hofstede, G., & Minkov, M. (2010). Long-versus short-term orientation: New perspectives. *Asia Pacific Business Review*, *16*(4), 493–504. https://doi.org/10.1080/13602381003637609

House, R. J., Hanges, P. J., Javidan, M., Dorfman, P. W., & Gupta, V. (2004). *Culture, leadership, and organizations: The GLOBE study of 62 societies*. Thousand Oaks: Sage Publications.

Hur, Y. H., van den Berg, P. T., & Wilderom, C. P. (2011). Transformational leadership as a mediator between emotional intelligence and team outcomes. *The Leadership Quarterly*, *22*(4), 591–603. https://doi.org/10.1016/j.leaqua.2011.05.002

Hwang, S. J., Quast, L. N., Center, B. A., Chung, C. N., Hahn, H., & Wohkittel, J. (2015). The impact of leadership behaviours on leaders' perceived job performance across cultures: Comparing the role of charismatic, directive, participative, and supportive leadership behaviours in the U.S. and four Confucian Asian countries. *Human Resource Development International*, *18*(3), 259–277. https://doi.org/10.1080/13678868.2015.1036226

Jogulu, U. D. (2010). Culturally-linked leadership styles. *Leadership & Organization Development Journal*, *31*(8), 705–719. https://doi.org/10.1108/01437731011094766

Johnson, S. K., & Lacerenza, C. N. (2019). Leadership is male-centric: Gender issues in the study of leadership. In R. E. Riggio (Ed.), *What's wrong with leadership: Improving leadership research and practice* (pp. 121–137). New York: Routledge.

Judge, T. A., & Piccolo, R. F. (2004). Transformational and transactional leadership: A meta-analytic test of their relative validity. *Journal of Applied Psychology*, *89*(5), 755–768. https://doi.org/10.1037/0021-9010.89.5.755

Jung, D., Yammarino, F. J., & Lee, J. K. (2009). Moderating role of subordinates' attitudes on transformational leadership and effectiveness: A multi-cultural and multi level perspective. *The Leadership Quarterly*, *20*(4), 586–603. https://doi.org/10.1016/j.leaqua.2009.04.011

Jung, D. I., & Avolio, B. J. (1999). Effects of leadership style and followers' cultural orientation on performance in group and individual task conditions. *Academy of Management Journal*, *42*(2), 208–218. https://doi.org/10.2307/257093

Koh, W. L. K. (1990). *An empirical validation of the theory of transformational leadership in secondary schools in Singapore*. Ann Arbor, MI: UMI Dissertation Services.

Leffler, H., Ayman, R., & Ayman-Nolley, S. (2006, July). *Do children possess the same stereotypes as adults? An exploration of children's implicit leadership theories* [Paper Presentation]. 26th Congress of Applied Psychology, Athens, Greece.

Ling, W., Chia, R. C., & Fang, L. (2000). Chinese implicit leadership theory. *Journal of Social Psychology*, *140*(6), 729–739. https://doi.org/10.1080/00224540009600513

Lord, R. G., de Vader, C. L., & Alliger, G. M. (1986). A meta-analysis of the relation between personality traits and leadership perceptions: An application of validity generalization procedures. *Journal of Applied Psychology*, *71*(3), 402–410. https://doi.org/10.1037/0021-9010.71.3.402

Muczyk, J. P., & Reimann, B. C. (1987). The case for directive leadership. *Academy of Management Executive*, *1*, 301–311.

Palazzo, B. (2002). U.S.-American and German business ethics: An intercultural comparison. *Journal of Business Ethics*, *41*, 195–216. https://doi.org./10.1023/A:1021239017049

Rudman, L. A., & Glick, P. (2001). Prescriptive gender stereotypes and backlash toward agentic women. *Journal of Social Issues*, *57*(4), 743–762. https://doi.org/10.1111/0022-4537.00239

Sabharwal, M. (2014). Is diversity management sufficient? Organizational inclusion to further performance. *Public Personnel Management*, *43*(2), 197–217. https://doi.org/10.1177%2F0091026014522202

Scandura, T. A., & Lankau, M. J. (1996). Developing diverse leaders: A leader-member exchange approach. *The Leadership Quarterly*, *7*(2), 243–263. https://doi.org/10.1016/S1048-9843(96)90043-0

Scarborough, J. (1998). *The origins of cultural differences and their impact on management*. Westport, CT: Quorum Books.

Schyns, B., Paul, T., Mohr, G., & Blank, H. (2005). Comparing antecedents and consequences of leader–member exchange in a German working context to findings in the US. *European Journal of Work and Organizational Psychology*, *14*(1), 1–22. https://doi.org/10.1080/13594320444000191

Steinmann, H., & Löhr, A. (1992). A survey of business ethics in Germany. *Business Ethics: A European Review*, *1*(2), 139–141. https://doi.org/10.1111/j.1467-8608.1992.tb00196.x

van Emmerik, I. J. H., Euwema, M. C., & Wendt, H. (2008). Leadership behaviors around the world: The relative importance of gender versus cultural background. *International Journal of Cross Cultural Management*, *8*(3), 297–315. https://doi.org/10.1177/1470595808096671

Vecchio, R. P., & Brazil, D. M. (2007). Leadership and sex-similarity: A comparison in a military setting. *Personnel Psychology*, *60*(2), 303–335. https://doi.org/10.1111/j.1744-6570.2007.00075.x

Vecchio, R. P., & Bullis, R. C. (2001). Moderators of the influence of supervisor–subordinate similarity on subordinate outcomes. *Journal of Applied Psychology*, *86*(5), 884–896. https://doi.org/10.1111/j.1744-6570.2007.00075.x

Wood, G. J., & Jogulu, U. D. (2006). Malaysian and Australian male and female middle managers: A cross-cultural comparison of workplace attitudes, aspirations for promotion, and self-rated leadership styles. *International Journal of Knowledge, Culture and Change Management*, *6*(3), 109–120. hdl.handle.net/10536/DRO/DU:30020923

Wuffli, P. A. (2015). *Inclusive leadership: A framework for the global era*. Heidelberg, Germany: Springer-Verlag.

Yokochi, N. (1989). Leadership styles of Japanese business executives and managers: Transformational and transactional [Unpublished doctoral dissertation]. United States International University, San Diego.

Yukl, G. (1999). An evaluation of conceptual weaknesses in transformational and charismatic leadership theories. *The Leadership Quarterly*, *10*(2), 285–305. https://doi.org/10.1016/S1048-9843(99)00013-2

Yukl, G. (2012). Effective leadership behavior: What we know and what questions need more attention. *Academy of Management Perspectives*, *26*(4), 66–85. https://doi.org/10.5465/amp.2012.0088

Yukl, G. A. (1998). *Leadership in organizations* (4th ed.). Upper Saddle River, N.J: Prentice Hall.

# 3 Stigmatization, Subordination, or Marginalization?

## The Complexity of Social Disadvantage across Gender and Race

*Robert W. Livingston and Ashleigh Shelby Rosette*

Individuals who do not fit the prototype of the White male leader can face many hurdles when seeking to attain or maintain leadership roles. A question often posed when examining existing barriers is whether Black men, White women, or Black women face the greatest leadership challenges. This chapter argues that a comparative focus on the *quantity* or severity of social disadvantage across groups is a short-sighted approach that can fail to appreciate the unique experiences of members from various subordinated groups. Instead, a more accurate and useful framework is one that explicates nuanced differences in the *quality* of the challenges facing leaders from distinct under-represented social groups. Building on existing data and theory, we argue that a typology of social disadvantage is created by two orthogonal dimensions—perceived threat and perceived interdependence—that interact to determine whether these groups experience stigmatization (high threat, low interdependence), benevolent subordination (low threat, high interdependence), hostile subordination (high threat, high interdependence), or marginalization (low threat, low interdependence). We further argue that this typology can shed light on the nature of leadership challenges faced by specific intersectional groups—Black men through stigmatization, White women through subordination, and Black women through marginalization. Implications for the challenges faced by leaders from distinct social groups are discussed.

During the 2008 U.S. Presidential campaign, speculation swirled around which of the two non-prototypical candidates, Barack Obama or Hillary Clinton, would secure the Democratic nomination. With relatively few substantive policy differences between the leading contenders, the political discourse frequently turned to a debate involving whether race or gender would yield the most social disadvantage for these two competitors pursuing the most powerful leadership position in the world. Although it is an oversimplification to suggest that the outcome of the 2008 Democratic race was reduced to a referendum on racial versus gender disadvantage, this example does mimic an ongoing clash in social science research that tends to pit one socially disadvantaged group against another (e.g., Levin et al., 2002; Navarrete et al., 2010).

The central assumption of this chapter is that a focus on the comparative degree of hardship among socially disadvantaged groups does little to advance our understanding of the persistence of disadvantage in general, or the ways in which organizations can create greater inclusion for a variety of socially disadvantaged groups. A more productive approach to understanding inclusive leadership involves a nuanced investigation of the distinctions that exist among socially disadvantaged groups (e.g., White women, Black men, Black women), *in addition to* considering the mechanisms that regulate the dynamics between the dominant group (i.e., White men) and the various socially disadvantaged groups that must interact with it to access power and leadership.

To account for the variation in socially disadvantaged groups, examinations of the leadership gap must adopt an intersectional lens. Although we acknowledge the various forms of intersectionality, as well as the continuum within social categories, the current chapter focuses on the intersectionality of binary gender and dichotomous Black-White racial categories. We argue that the three socially disadvantaged groups that result from race × gender intersectionality (i.e., Black men, White women, and Black women) face qualitatively different challenges, not differential degrees of the same challenge. Specifically, we argue that Black men struggle against stigmatization, White women struggle against subordination, and Black women struggle against marginalization. In the sections that follow, we first describe the theoretical basis of our typology, which derives from an integration of intersectional theories with a White hegemonic patriarchal perspective. We then elaborate on the differences between stigmatization, subordination, and marginalization, and how each affects leaders from different intersectional groups. Finally, we offer suggestions to help remedy the numerous barriers that members of socially disadvantaged groups encounter as they aspire to attain top leader positions.

## An Intersectional Lens

Historically, the study of systems of privilege have focused on a single subordinate identity at a time—the disadvantage of "women" (e.g., Eagly & Karau, 2002; Heilman et al., 1989; Schein, 1973) or the absence of "racial minorities" in leadership roles (e.g., Carton & Rosette, 2011; Zapata et al., 2016)—but not the consideration of multiple subordinate identities simultaneously (e.g., Black women; see Sanchez-Hucles & Davis, 2010; Eagly & Chin, 2010; Livingston et al., 2012, for exceptions).

Although research on subordinate identities in isolation has led to a great deal of understanding about access to leadership roles and leadership dynamics in those roles, the experience of racial disadvantage, for example, is not independent of the (dis)advantage that can come about because of one's gender or a host of other ascribed or achieved status markers (Beale, 1970; Collins, 2015; Crenshaw, 1989). Similarly, the experience of gender discrimination and subordination is not independent of the biases in favor or against one's racial group (Beale, 1970; Collins, 2015; Crenshaw, 1989), especially in a leadership context (Rosette et al., 2016). Each subordinate and/or dominant identity is inextricably linked to the other, and this interconnected consideration is needed in order to fully understand the social disadvantage experienced by White women, Black women, and Black men in a leadership context.

Among those theoretical perspectives that have advocated for an intersectional lens, many have chosen to pit one socially disadvantaged group against another. These existing frameworks formulate arguments for a hierarchy of oppression among the socially disadvantaged. For example, the ethnic-prominence hypothesis suggests that ethnic minority women are more influenced by expectations of ethnic rather than gender discrimination (Levin et al., 2002). However, the subordinate male target hypothesis argues ethnic discrimination is more strongly directed toward ethnic minority men compared with ethnic minority women (Navarrete et al., 2010). Although these perspectives (and others not mentioned here) present valid arguments for their respective points of view, they tend to emphasize quantitative rather than qualitative comparisons. We adopt an alternative approach that strives to better understand how each subordinate group's experience is *distinct* from each other relative to the socially advantaged group—White men.

## A Typology of Social Disadvantage

One of the most enduring findings in the study of leadership is that a concentration of advantage resides with White men as they occupy the vast majority of CEO positions, senior executive positions, and board of director positions in organizations (Catalyst, 2017, 2018). White men occupy well over 90% of all CEO positions, account for upwards of 72% of corporate leadership at many of these companies (Jones, 2017), and, since the country's founding, have held the U.S. presidency for all but two terms. As a result, one would classify White men as socially advantaged in the vast majority of leadership contexts in the United States. The magnitude of power differences between White men and any socially disadvantaged group overshadows any lateral comparisons of power differences between socially disadvantaged groups (Rosette et al., 2008). Therefore, our analysis is grounded in the relationship between the most socially advantaged group —White men—and three socially disadvantaged groups.

To gain a deeper understanding of social disadvantage, one must assess its meaning within a specific social context and in relation to social advantage (Dean & Platt, 2016; Festinger, 1954). The relational dynamics between the advantaged group and socially disadvantaged groups are critically relevant, from both a theoretical and practical perspective. Thus, our focus shifts from a less relevant (though still important) horizontal comparison of socially disadvantaged groups at the bottom of the organizational hierarchy to a vertical comparison of dynamics between the dominant group and socially disadvantaged groups. Given this vertical focus within the social hierarchy pyramid, which compares the apex (i.e., White men) to the base (e.g., White women, Black women, and Black men), we integrate our intersectional framework with a White hegemonic patriarchal perspective to propose a novel typology of social disadvantage in the leadership domain.

We propose that two intergroup dynamics—threat and interdependence (both perceived from the White male perspective)—interact to determine the nature of the challenges that socially disadvantaged groups face when interacting with White men to acquire power. As a result of this integrative framework, we argue that Black men struggle against stigmatization (high threat, low interdependence), White women struggle against hostile (high threat, high interdependence) or benevolent subordination (low threat, high interdependence), and Black women battle against marginalization (low threat, low interdependence). Our typology of social disadvantage is presented in Figure 3.1.

We define interdependence as the degree to which the dominant group *perceives* the outgroup as being necessary or important from a social, biological, or practical standpoint. This definition is consistent with the White hegemonic patriarchal perspective (Sidanius & Pratto, 1999) and is often linked to the interest or survival of the dominant group (Buss,

| | | Perceived Interdependence | |
|---|---|---|---|
| | | Low | High |
| Perceived Threat | Low | Marginalization | Subordination I (Benevolent) |
| | High | Stigmatization | Subordination II (Hostile) |

*Figure 3.1* Typology of social disadvantage.

1990; Eisenberger et al., 2003; Glick & Fiske, 1996). At the core of this dimension is whether or not there is common fate or some level of cooperation necessary between two groups in order for either to function or exist.

We also define threat from the White hegemonic patriarchal perspective (Sidanius & Pratto, 1999) as the degree to which the dominant group perceives the outgroup as being a threat to its power and privileged position atop the social hierarchy. Is the group perceived as having the motivation and/or ability to challenge or undermine the power of the dominant group? If so, the group could be seen as a threat, regardless of whether the intention, motivation, or ability is real or imagined. We draw this definition, in part, from realistic conflict theory, which emphasizes the conflict and discrimination that can occur between groups who are in competition for the same resources (Sherif, 1961).

The interdependence/threat distinction shares similarities with the classic communality/agency or warmth/competence dichotomy, which plays a prominent role in social psychology research on person perception (e.g., Abele et al., 2008) and leader perceptions in organizational behavior (e.g., Eagly & Karau, 2002; Rudman et al. 2012). Like communality (and related dimensions such as "warmth" in the Stereotype Content Model; Fiske et al., 2002), interdependence implicates interpersonal relationships (Bakan, 1966). However, interdependence differs from communality/warmth in important ways. Interdependence requires a functional reliance on another whereas communality/warmth does not. The latter is more related to cooperation and common purpose rather than a functional need or dependency of one group on another group.

Likewise, our threat dimension is similar to, yet distinct from, agency/competence. Both agency and threat can be described as asserting the self or possessing a baseline level of capability (Bakan, 1966). However, threat also entails the perception of a *negative* capability (and intent, perhaps) to challenge or harm the ingroup. This assumption is missing from both agency and competence, which can both be perceived as positive traits that complement or enhance the goals of the ingroup. In Intergroup Image Theory (IIT), this would be the difference between the "ally" image and the "enemy" image (Alexander et al., 2005). Both the ally and the enemy can possess comparable levels of competence and agency. The only difference is whether this capacity is perceived as going in favor of or against the interests of the ingroup.

We represent these two dimensions—threat and interdependence—as orthogonal, such that an outgroup can be high or low on either dimension (see Figure 3.1). When considered in tandem, four quadrants emerge. We label the quadrants: Stigmatization, Subordination I (benevolent), Subordination II (hostile), and Marginalization.

## Stigmatization

*Stigmatization* is produced by the combination of low interdependence and high threat. Consistent with the etymology of the word, stigmatized individuals are "marked" by society (Goffman, 1963). Although stigmatized groups are socially devalued and negatively evaluated (Crocker et al., 1998), they are also "visible" rather than hidden, which leads to high levels of vigilance and monitoring from outgroups (Alexander et al., 2005). For example, IIT distinguishes between two types of low status or socially devalued groups depending on the level of power they are seen as possessing (Alexander et al., 2005). Low status without power produces the "dependent" image, whereas low status with power produces the "barbarian" image. Based on our current conceptualization, only the barbarian image would represent stigma because the combination of low status with high power (and low compatibility) produces the threat that is necessary to satisfy our construal of stigmatization.[1] To use a historical example, Romans could not completely ignore the barbarian tribes who lived in close proximity to them because these tribes represented a real threat to the empire (Heather, 2006). Therefore, they were ever-watchful and vigilant of the barbarians despite the "primitive" and, in general, negative perceptions that they held of these groups (Ferris, 2004).

## Subordination

On the opposite diagonal, the combination of high interdependence and low threat produces *subordination*. Subordinate groups often serve an important or essential role in the lives of dominant group members (Glick & Fiske, 1996; Sidanius & Pratto, 1999). Subordinated groups are not viewed in a categorically negative manner; rather, these groups (e.g., children) can and do elicit positive beliefs and emotions, especially when the dominant group believes that its position of power is not threatened. For example, research on ambivalent sexism has shown that men hold generally positive emotions toward women who accept subordinate roles but have negative emotions toward women who resist subordination in search of equality, power, and opportunity (Glick & Fiske, 1996). Glick et al. (2000) state that "men's dependence on women fosters benevolent sexism—subjectively positive attitudes that put women on a pedestal but reinforce their subordination" (p. 763).

Borrowing from ambivalent sexism theory (Glick & Fiske, 1996), we refer to the high interdependence/low threat condition as *benevolent subordination*. Unlike stigmatization, the hallmark of benevolent subordination is not that the group is marked in a negative way—only that the group be deemed unworthy of power and authority. However, when these subordinated groups resist the dominance and authority of the hegemonic patriarchy, thereby presenting a high threat rather than a low threat, then affection and protection can quickly morph into anger and resentment. When this takes place, the orientation toward the subordinated group shifts from affection to aggression. Accordingly, we label this high threat quadrant as *hostile subordination*. Research has shown that, across cultures, women choose to conform to traditional gender roles as a means of receiving benevolent sexism *instead of* hostile sexism, particularly in cultures with highly misogynist attitudes toward women (Glick et al., 2000). Thus, although benevolent sexism seems to be a kinder and gentler form of subordination, data clearly show that both hostile and benevolent sexism serve a similar function—the disempowerment and subordination of women (see Glick & Fiske, 2001, for discussion).

## Marginalization

Finally, the combination of low threat and low interdependence produces *marginalization*. One definition of the verb *to marginalize* is "to treat someone or something as if they are not important" (Cambridge Dictionary). Unlike subordinated groups, marginalized groups are not seen as being necessary or relevant to the dominant group (Frable, 1993). And unlike stigmatized groups, marginalized groups are not seen as a formidable threat to the power or position of the dominant group (Alexander et al., 2005). Instead, marginalized groups barely register in the dominant group's consciousness. Because marginalization is characterized by low scrutiny and high invisibility, individuals occupying this quadrant experience both unique advantages and disadvantages (Purdie-Vaughns & Eibach, 2008) compared with stigmatized and subordinated individuals who are both visible (albeit for different reasons).[2]

It is important to recognize that this proposed typology of social disadvantage is fluid and context-dependent, such that individuals or entire social groups can move from one quadrant to another depending on the interpersonal, social, or historical context. For example, an individual woman can quickly shift from benevolent subordination to hostile subordination as a function of the level of threat that she activates via her decision to conform to prescribed gender stereotypes or not (Glick & Fiske, 1996). Historically, Blacks have shifted from subordination (both benevolent and hostile) to stigmatization as a function of the perceived increase in Black power as well as the reduced interdependence between Blacks and Whites in the colonial South compared with today (see also "paternalistic racism," Sidanius & Pratto, 1999, or "dependent" versus "barbaric" image, Alexander et al., 2005, for further discussion). Finally, the social disadvantage of Native Americans has shifted from stigmatization (in colonial America when they were seen as a realistic threat) to marginalization as a function of decimation and the resulting invisibility of the Native population, which contributed to a reduction in perceived threat (Alexander et al., 2005). In the next section we explore the implications of this model for understanding the unique and distinct challenges facing different leaders who are not White men.

## Implications for Leadership: An Intersectional Approach

We believe that our proposed typology has implications for socially disadvantaged group members striving to attain or maintain leadership positions. As stated in the last section, the typology is framed from the perspective of White male patriarchy, which holds control over, and perhaps feels subjective entitlement to, leadership roles. Given White men's hyper-representation they also become the de facto gatekeepers of leadership accessibility for socially disadvantaged individuals who aspire to positions of power and authority. Therefore, the relevant questions become: How does the White patriarchal establishment perceive individuals from socially disadvantaged groups who aspire to hold leader roles? How does the nature of these leadership challenges differ from group to group? Finally, what are the strategies that enable otherwise socially disadvantaged group members to succeed in their quest for leadership (i.e., leader emergence) and what are the constraints put on them, if any, once they attain these roles (i.e., with regard to leader behavior)?

We believe that our typology can help to identify and parsimoniously characterize the distinct challenges that face would-be and extant leaders from socially disadvantaged groups by providing a lens for how their diffuse social group is perceived. For example, because *stigmatized groups* are visible, negative, and threatening, we reason that aspiring leaders from stigmatized groups would have to undermine the perception of threat facing their group before they would be allowed into leadership positions by the White hegemonic patriarchy. Similarly, because the default for (role-consistent) *subordinate groups* is warmth combined with the perception that they are unsuitable for leadership because they lack authority, their challenge is to demonstrate that they are capable of leadership positions—while also not appearing too discrepant from the tight norms around warmth and cooperation that are applied to them. Finally, because *marginalized groups* are not surveilled or policed the way that stigmatized and subordinated groups are, we believe that the norms will be looser for them at the same time that leadership hurdles are higher for them—both of these effects due to marginalization.

Returning to our intersectional lens, we argue that Black men, White women, and Black women are stigmatized, subordinated, and marginalized, respectively. Therefore, the challenges facing actual and aspiring leaders from these social groups should conform more or less to the strategies and challenges outlined above. Specifically, the primary challenge of Black male leaders is to reduce the amount of threat, fear, and negativity that is associated with them (Livingston & Pearce, 2009). The primary challenge of White female leaders is to show that they are able to break out of subordinated roles to effectively function in leadership positions. Paradoxically, once they demonstrate this it places them in the "threat" category because they now stand in violation of traditional gender roles. Therefore, their challenge is to walk a tightrope between being docile and authoritative (Williams et al., 2014). Finally, the challenge for Black women—as a group that does not present the same threat to White men that Black men do (Navarrete et al., 2010), nor holds the same relevance for White men that White women do (Beale, 1970; Glick & Fiske, 2001)—is simply garnering enough visibility to appear on the radar (Crenshaw, 1989; Purdie-Vaughns & Eibach, 2008). However, if they do manage to make it into these roles, we argue that their marginalized status will confer less restrictive norms for how they behave, which ironically gives them a wider range of leader behaviors than either Black male leaders or White female leaders. In the paragraphs to follow, we present data in support of this formulation and then end the chapter with a set of recommendations for both individuals and organizations.

## Black Men and Stigmatization

We posit that the primary dimension of social disadvantage facing Black men in contemporary American society is stigmatization. There are multiple sociological indicators that Black men are marked and socially devalued by the dominant culture, including police shootings and mass incarceration (Alexander, 2010). Moreover, social dominance theory argues that men from socially disadvantaged outgroups (e.g., Black males) receive a particularly high level of scrutiny and oppression from the dominant group compared with women from subordinate outgroups. The subordinate-male-target-hypothesis (SMTH) maintains that inter-racial conflict is primarily a male-on-male phenomenon because the men from the outgroup represent the biggest threat to the hierarchical structure (Navarrete et al., 2010; Sidanius et al., 2018). It stands to reason, then, that Black male leaders would be punished for showing too much dominance, confidence, or agency because it only exacerbates the threat that is experienced by the White male patriarchy. On the other hand, Black male leaders should benefit from traits or behaviors that make them appear more docile, harmless, and controllable.

Consistent with our proposition, our data indicate that Black male leaders who behave in a dominant manner were perceived significantly less positively than White male leaders who engaged in identical behavior; however, Black male leaders who behaved in a more docile manner were not perceived less positively than docile White leaders (Livingston et al., 2012). In addition to advantages conferred to Black leaders with docile behaviors, Black men with a docile *appearance* have an advantage in leader accessibility compared with Black men who do not possess a docile appearance. For example, Livingston and Pearce (2009) found that "babyfaceness" was beneficial to Black male leaders because it functioned as a "disarming mechanism" that rendered them more docile and affable in appearance, and therefore less threatening to White males in power—a phenomenon that has been labeled "The Teddy Bear Effect." Black Fortune 500 CEOs were significantly more babyfaced than White Fortune 500 CEOs, even though no difference in babyfaceness between Black men and White men exists in the general population. In addition, the more babyfaced a Black male CEO was, the larger his corporation and salary tended to be. The opposite pattern of findings was obtained for White male CEOs. That is, more babyfaced White CEOs tended to earn less money and run smaller companies than mature-faced White CEOs.

Taken together, these findings strongly suggest that disarming mechanisms (e.g., babyfaced appearance, docile behaviors) benefit Black male leaders whereas they do not benefit White male leaders, and, if anything, undermine the authority of White male leaders—who, by virtue of their dominant status, are entitled to power and do not need to be disarmed. Overall, these findings support the notion that Black male leaders are stigmatized, and, as such, benefit from any signals that attenuate the level of threat that is associated with them. This general finding of stigmatization does not appear to be confined to leadership positions. In fact, Hall and Livingston (2012) found evidence that even Black professional athletes face similar challenges. Our archival data indicate that Black NFL players are more likely to be penalized for celebrating after touchdowns compared with White NFL players. Furthermore, experimental data show that Black men who celebrate are penalized because they are seen as arrogant. White NFL players who celebrate are also perceived as arrogant, but they are not penalized for it. Finally, there was no difference in perceptions or salary recommendations for humble Black versus White NFL players (i.e., those who did not celebrate after a touchdown, but instead returned the ball to the referee). In summary, Black men benefit from traits and behaviors that render them more docile or impotent because this undermines the perception of threat that is associated with them.

Returning to the Barack Obama example, there are many aspects of his appearance and his behavior that can be perceived as disarming. He has an ectomorphic (i.e., lanky) build, which is both prototypically boyish and western European (Zebrowitz & Collins, 1997). He is also bi-racial and therefore lower in racial phenotypicality. Many lines of research have shown that Blacks with lighter skin or lower phenotypicality are rated more favorably by Whites (Blair et al., 2004; Livingston & Brewer, 2002; Maddox, 2004). With regard to his behavior, Barack Obama always upheld standards of "respectability," almost never showing anger, raising his voice, or behaving boorishly. White men do not have to subscribe to these standards of respectability, whether as President, Senator, Supreme Court Justice, or in any other position of leadership. In fact, research has shown that anger and incivility can benefit White men by making them seem powerful (Brescoll & Uhlmann, 2008; Tiedens, 2001), even though the same behaviors are detrimental to women and people of color (Brescoll & Uhlmann, 2008; Livingston et al., 2012). Finally, Obama has been criticized by some Black intellectuals for not challenging White hegemonic patriarchy in a way that would produce "real" change (West, 2017), or for not standing up for Blacks who did challenge White hegemonic patriarchy (e.g., Rev. Jeremiah Wright). In short, the goal here is not to criticize Obama's competence, values, or performance, but rather to point out that Black men in positions of power are constrained in their behaviors. In order to successfully function in positions of power in White-dominated contexts, Black men often have to "disarm" themselves.[3]

## White Women and Subordination

We propose a different mechanism to explain the subordination of White women leaders. Because (benevolent) subordination is characterized by interdependence and low threat, White women are already disarmed by virtue of their gender. That is, women are inextricably linked to subordination because they are conferred low status relative to White men in the gender hierarchy (Rudman et al., 2012). Therefore, what can benefit them in leadership positions is being "armed" rather than "disarmed." In other words, the default challenge of White women leaders is to demonstrate that they are capable of assuming high power roles. Thus, all else being equal, women leaders should benefit from features that signal capacity (Rosette & Tost, 2010).

Livingston and Pearce (2009) included faces of (White) women CEOs as well as Black men and White men in their research. Although the results indicate that babyfaceness benefitted Black male leaders, babyfaceness was a detriment for White female leaders. That is, White women CEOs were much *lower* in babyfaceness than either White men CEOs or Black men CEOs, despite the fact that women in the general population tend to be more babyfaced than men (Zebrowitz, 2001). The implication here is that White women are not threatening in the way that Black men are, and therefore they don't need disarming mechanisms like a baby face. On the contrary, women CEOs need to be "armed" with extreme maturefaceness to signal that they are competent enough to do the job.

As previously mentioned, White women who display too much dominance run the risk of creating threat because the default hierarchical relationship between men and women is transformed into a competitive relationship. Competition (rather than cooperation) is a violation of *prescribed* gender stereotypes, or notions of how women "should" behave (Rudman & Fairchild, 2004). A well-documented effect implicated in the underrepresentation of women in leadership positions is *agentic backlash*, which refers to penalties that (White) women, even those who are leaders, face for appearing too assertive, self-promoting, bossy, or angry (Brescoll & Uhlmann, 2008; Eagly & Carli, 2007; Eagly & Karau, 1991; Livingston et al., 2012; Okimoto & Brescoll, 2010; Rudman, 1998; Rudman & Fairchild, 2004). These penalties do not apply to White men. For instance, a meta-analysis by Eagly and Johnson (1990) showed that women who adopted an autocratic style of leadership (i.e., making executive decisions without permission or approval from others) were evaluated less favorably than men who adopted an autocratic style of leadership. However, no difference in evaluation emerged between White men and White women who adopted a more democratic style of leadership (i.e., eliciting approval and buy-in from others before making decisions).

In fact, some studies have shown that White male leaders are often *rewarded* for displaying agentic emotions (i.e., anger) and behaviors (Brescoll & Uhlmann, 2008; Tiedens, 2001) whereas women leaders are punished for demonstrating the same behaviors (Brescoll & Uhlmann, 2008). The mechanism purported to underlie these discrepant effects for men versus women is the confirmation versus violation of *prescriptive* gender stereotypes (Rudman & Fairchild, 2004). Men are "supposed" to be tough, confident, dominant, power-seeking, and competitive (unless you are a man of color), whereas (White) women are "supposed" to be passive, humble, submissive, self-deprecating, and cooperative. Men and women who conform to or violate these normative standards are rewarded or punished accordingly.

In summary, White women's social disadvantage relative to White men is due to high levels of interdependence, which creates stringent norms and expectations for behavior that will facilitate a "peaceful" co-existence (if peace requires not challenging the power of the dominant group, which is often the case). It is also due to low levels of threat, which is reflected by traits such as cooperation, nurturance, and docility, which present no challenge to the existing patriarchal power structure. However, becoming a leader is, in itself, an act of sedition for White women. Therefore, they benefit from behaviors that simultaneously confirm their ability to function in the role and demonstrate their adherence to prescribed gender norms. Therefore, their challenge is walking a tightrope that puts them somewhere between benevolent subordination (where they are liked but not respected) and hostile subordination (where they are possibly respected but certainly not liked).

Returning to the Hillary Clinton example, there are few doubts about Hillary Clinton's agency or competence. Almost universally, she is perceived as a smart and tough woman who can handle all of the demands of a leadership role. Her overwhelming challenge is the perceived threat that her gender-inconsistent behavior creates—which leads people to dislike her, despite the fact that they respect her ability. What might increase liking and, consequently, support? More gender-consistent behavior, of course, which is exactly what she did when she cried in New Hampshire during the primaries and witnessed a subsequent boost in her polling numbers as a result.

## Black Women and Marginalization

It is important to note that nearly all of the research looking at agentic backlash against women leaders has focused exclusively on White women. Will Black women, for example, incur the same agency penalties that White women face—perhaps even more so? Or will Black women be immune to agency penalties due to a different set of norms, stereotypes, expectations, and perceptions than those of White women?

Two dominant theoretical perspectives in the literature make opposite predictions. On the one hand, the double jeopardy perspective argues that Black women might face double the penalty of White women because, in addition to the penalty associated with their gender, there is an added penalty associated with race (Bell & Nkomo, 2001; Settles, 2006). On the other hand, the intersectional invisibility perspective maintains that Black women are not the additive combination of Black + woman, but rather a complex combination resulting in a unique experience that can sometimes result in advantageous rather than disadvantageous outcomes (Purdie-Vaughns & Eibach, 2008). Therefore, Black women can suffer either more or less penalty than Black men or White women, depending on the context.

We have obtained data that support both perspectives. For example, Livingston et al. (2012) found that Black male leaders and White female leaders were evaluated more negatively when they behaved in a dominant manner rather than a more docile manner. Consistent with previous research, White male leaders were not evaluated more negatively when they behaved in a dominant manner. However, our results revealed that Black female leaders were also not penalized for behaving in a more dominant manner compared with when they behaved in a more docile manner. These data suggest that Black women are not subject to the same agency penalties as Black male leaders and White female leaders, paradoxically giving them more freedom to exhibit a range of leadership behaviors.

We argue that this "free pass" that Black women receive is the result of marginality. Because the dominant group is neither dependent on nor threatened by Black women, this leads to looser norms around acceptable behavior for Black women leaders, compared with Black men or White women. Consistent with this idea, past research has shown that the prescriptive stereotypes of Black women are less stringent. Whereas dominance is proscribed for both Black men and White women (Hall & Phillips, 2012), there are not strong norms against dominance for Black women (Ghavami & Peplau, 2013; Hall & Phillips, 2012; Rosette et al., 2016). This is consistent with other research showing that Black women are perceived as more masculine than White women (Goff et al., 2008; Sesko & Biernat, 2010). Therefore agentic behaviors do not contradict norms or expectations to the same degree that they do for White women.

If Black women have the same latitude and freedom as White men to behave assertively in leadership roles, then why are there not more Black women leaders? Black women are conspicuously absent from many top leadership roles, occupying 0% of Fortune 500 CEO positions compared with roughly 1% and 5% for Black men and White women, respectively. Rosette and Livingston (2012) found that Black women leaders do indeed face double jeopardy when their competence is called into question. Specifically, we found that when Black female leaders made a mistake on the job, their competence was more likely to be called into question compared with Black male leaders or White female leaders who made a mistake (who themselves suffered a penalty relative to White male leaders). This effect was also due to marginality. That is, we found that the excessive penalty against Black women leaders was mediated by leader typicality, or the perception that they were two degrees removed from the White male leadership prototype. Black men and White women were only one degree removed because they possessed either maleness or Whiteness, respectively.

In summary, there is a complicated set of findings for Black women leaders which is consistent with the theoretical notion that invisibility or marginalization provides both advantages and disadvantages (Purdie-Vaughns & Eibach, 2008). On the one hand, being marginalized appears to lead to more freedom for Black women to exhibit leadership behaviors that would not be tolerated from a Black man or a White woman. On the other hand, being marginalized means that Black women leaders are the first to be dismissed if any doubts around competence arise because they are outside of the periphery of the leadership prototype.

The former CEO of Xerox, Ann Mulcahy, a White woman, served as a mentor and sponsor to Ursula Burns, a Black woman, who eventually became her successor. During their exchanges, Ms. Mulcahy encouraged Ms. Burns to have more of a poker face, since according to Ms. Burns "on my face, you could tell everything in 30 seconds. You could tell exasperation. You could tell fed-up-ness" (Bryant, 2010). Undoubtedly,

Ms. Mulcahy was giving Ms. Burns earnest and heartfelt advice, perhaps based on her own experience. But she may have failed to realize that Black women leaders may have more latitude to express agentic emotions than White women leaders—particularly when they are performing at a very high level of competence, which was the case for Ursula Burns.

## Recommendations for Overcoming Challenges

The primary purpose of this chapter is to provide a parsimonious framework for understanding qualitative differences in the nature of social disadvantage, and to raise awareness of the unique challenges that different groups face when they occupy leadership roles. A natural reaction that we get to this research, particularly from White women and people of color is: what should I do to advance professionally? Because people differ widely with regard to their values, needs, and goals, it is difficult to offer universal recommendations. Some individuals are concerned primarily about individual advancement, whereas others are deeply concerned about social justice more broadly. Recommendations for what to do might be quite different for two such individuals. Moreover, the burden of "what to do" should not fall on the people who have the least amount of social power. Therefore, we will offer some recommendations for what organizations and White male allies can do to increase the representation and inclusion of White women and people of color in leadership roles.

### *Flip the Script*

The systemic continuation of favoritism toward White male leadership should be explicitly acknowledged and recognized. The usual way in which to frame the racial and gender disparity in leadership positions is to focus on the low proportion of racial minorities and women who occupy these positions. This focus mutes the disproportionate privileges and advantages that accrue to White male leaders. We suggest that when defining the leadership gap as a problem, it is just as important for organizations to examine reasons underlying the overrepresentation of White men in these roles (e.g., cronyism, sponsorship, lower standards for "potential," etc.) as it is to understand why racial minorities and White women are not represented. People often believe that women and racial minorities have an advantage based on preferential hiring and promotion policies (e.g., affirmative action), but they fail to see the invisible, built-in system of affirmative action for White male leaders, which is often much more potent than organizational structures and policies designed to benefit women and minorities. The holistic focus may help to remedy the disparities and foster more inclusive organizations.

### *Become a Champion*

Stand up for socially disadvantaged group members. Becoming a champion or advocate for Black women, White women, and Black men can potentially alter the trajectory of their careers. Having someone to help shepherd them through persistent structural, systemic, and personal biases against them is likely paramount to them in attaining leader roles. Women report receiving less organizational support than men (Ibarra et al., 2013; Kossek et al., 2017; McDonald & Westphal, 2013). Black and Asian women often report lack of role models and lack of access to crucial social networks (Bell & Nkomo, 2001; Liang & Peters-Hawkins, 2017). As a result, feelings of isolation and disconnection from the organization are common (Bell & Nkomo, 2001; Turner, 2002). Advocating on behalf of those who may not feel as though they can promote themselves helps to facilitate feelings of inclusiveness.

### *Build a Diverse Posse*

People are often drawn to others who look, think, and behave similarly to themselves. This *homophily* can promote exclusivity rather than inclusiveness. Purposely reaching past one's comfort level to embrace discomfort and opening one's circle to individuals who are different can help remedy the effects of the homophily, or similarity-attraction, paradigm. Undoubtedly racial minorities and White women can initiate their own relationships, but it can often be more difficult for them to do so than for dominant group members in organizations. Perhaps an organizational program or policy can help facilitate such interactions.

### *Recognize that Intersectionality Matters*

It can be somewhat easy to categorize racial minorities and women and the varying combination of these social categories as a monolithic or uniform group relative to White men. However, interlocking systems of power and privilege affect each socially disadvantaged group differently (e.g., Hill Collins & Bilge, 2016) and these distinctions should be acknowledged when attempting to develop an inclusive organization. An intersectional framework can shed light on how overlapping identities interact and combine to form distinct experiences. For example, what a Black male associate may need to be successful may be distinct from those tools needed to assist a White female associate at the same level. It is incumbent upon the organization to provide a space to explore these nuanced experiences of the socially disadvantaged in their organization.

## Notes

1 The group or individual with low status and low power might fall into the category of what we label *marginalization* (to be discussed shortly), especially if the group is not relevant or essential to the functioning of the dominant group.
2 We recognize that much of the research on stigma has included visibility or concealability as a dimension of how the stigmatized (and stigmatizer) experience and copes with stigma (e.g., Deaux et al., 1995; Frable, 1993; Kleck & Strenta, 1980; Jones et al., 1984). Consistent with these theoretical perspectives, we concur that visibility of the stigmatized individual or group has a dramatic impact on the way in which social disadvantage is experienced, as well as on coping mechanisms. The only difference is that we refer to relatively invisible groups (as a function of low threat rather than invisible indicators of group membership) as marginalized rather than stigmatized to highlight the important differences in their experiences as socially devalued individuals.
3 Al Sharpton and Jesse Jackson, for example, are not as constrained and do not need to be as docile because their primary leadership contexts and constituents are Black. However, some would argue that this is why they are also less palatable to "mainstream" (i.e., White) audiences. Indeed, both have waged unsuccessful bids for President of the United States.

## References

Abele, A., Cuddy, A., Judd, C., & Yzerbyt, V. (2008). Fundamental dimensions of social judgment. *European Journal of Social Psychology, 38*(7), 1063–1065. https://doi.org/10.1002/ejsp.574

Alexander, M. G., Brewer, M. B., & Livingston, R. W. (2005). Putting stereotype content in context: Image theory and interethnic stereotypes. *Personality and Social Psychology Bulletin, 31*(6), 781–794. https://doi.org/10.1177/0146167204271550

Alexander, M. (2010). *The new Jim Crow: Mass incarceration in the age of colorblindness*. New York, NY: New Press.

Bakan, D. (1966). *The duality of human existence: An essay on psychology and religion*. Chicago, IL: Rand McNally.

Beale, F. (1970). Double jeopardy: To be Black and female. In T. C. Bambara (Ed.), *The Black woman: An anthology* (pp. 90–100). New York: Signet.

Bell, E. L., & Nkomo, S. M. (2001). *Our separate ways: Black and White women and the struggle for professional identity*. Boston, MA: Harvard Business Review Press.

Blair, I. V., Judd, C. M., & Chapleau, K. M. (2004). The influence of Afrocentric facial features in criminal sentencing. *Psychological Science, 15*(10), 674–679. https://doi.org/10.1111/j.0956-7976.2004.00739.x

Brescoll, V. L., & Uhlmann, E. L. (2008). Can an angry woman get ahead? Status conferral, gender, and expression of emotion in the workplace. *Psychological Science, 19*(3), 268–275. https://doi.org/10.1111/j.1467-9280.2008.02079.x

Bryant, A. (2010, February 20). Xerox's new chief tries to redefine its culture. *The New York Times*, BU1.

Buss, D. M. (1990). The evolution of anxiety and social exclusion. *Journal of Social and Clinical Psychology, 9*, 196–201. https://doi.org/10.1521/jscp.1990.9.2.196

Carton, A., & Rosette, A. S. (2011). Explaining bias against black leaders: Integrating theory on information processing and goal-based stereotyping. *Academy of Management Journal*, *54*(6), 1141–1158. https://doi.org/10.5465/amj.2009.0745

Catalyst. (2017). *Missing pieces report: The 2016 board diversity census of women and minorities on Fortune 500 Boards*. New York: Author. https://www.catalyst.org/system/files/2016_board_diversity_census_deloitte_abd.pdf.

Catalyst. (2018, January 9). *Women CEOs of the S&P 500*. New York: Author. https://www.catalyst.org/knowledge/women-ceos-sp-500.

Collins, P. H. (2015). Intersectionality's definitional dilemmas. *Annual Review of Sociology*, *41*, 1–20. https://doi.org/10.1146/annurev-soc-073014-112142

Crenshaw, K. (1989). Demarginalizing the intersection of race and sex: A Black feminist critique of antidiscrimination doctrine, feminist theory and antiracist politics. *University of Chicago Legal Forum*, *1989*(1), 139–167.

Crocker, J., Major, B., & Steele, C. (1998). Social stigma. In D. T. Gilbert, S. T. Fiske, & G. Lindzey (Eds.), *The handbook of social psychology* (pp. 504–553). New York, NY: McGraw-Hill.

Deaux, K., Reid, A., Mizrahi, K., & Ethier, K. A. (1995). Parameters of social identity. *Journal of Personality and Social Psychology*, *68*(2), 280–291. https://doi.org/10.1037/0022-3514.68.2.280

Dean, H., & Platt, L. (Eds.). (2016). *Social advantage and disadvantage*. Oxford, UK: Oxford University Press.

Eagly, A. H., & Carli, L. L. (2007). *Through the labyrinth: The truth about how women become leaders*. Boston, MA: Harvard Business School Press.

Eagly, A. H., & Chin, J. L. (2010). Diversity and leadership in a changing world. *American Psychologist*, *65*(3), 216–224. https://doi.org/10.1037/a0018957

Eagly, A. H., & Karau, S. J. (1991). Gender and the emergence of leaders: A meta-analysis. *Journal of Personality and Social Psychology*, *60*(5), 685–710. https://doi.org/10.1037/0022-3514.60.5.685

Eagly, A. H., & Karau, S. J. (2002). Role congruity theory of prejudice toward female leaders. *Psychological Review*, *109*(3), 573–598. https://doi.org/10.1037/0033-295X.109.3.573

Eagly, A. H., & Johnson, B. T. (1990). Gender and leadership style: A meta-analysis. *Psychological Bulletin*, *108*(2), 233–256. https://doi.org/10.1037/0033-2909.108.2.233

Ibarra, H., Ely, R., & Kolb, D. (2013). Women rising: The unseen barriers. *Harvard Business Review*, *91*(9), 60–66.

Eisenberger, N., Lieberman, M. D., & Williams, K. D. (2003). Does rejection hurt? An fMRI study of social exclusion. *Science*, *302*, 290–292. https://doi.org/10.1126/science.1089134

Frable, D. E. (1993). Being and feeling unique: Statistical deviance and psychological marginality. *Journal of Personality*, *61*(1), 85–110. https://doi.org/10.1111/j.1467-6494.1993.tb00280.x

Ferris, I. M. (2004). *Enemies of Rome: Barbarians through Roman eyes*. New York, NY: The History Press.

Festinger, L. (1954). A theory of social comparison processes. *Human Relations*, 7, 117–140.

Fiske, S. T., Cuddy, A. J. C., Glick, P., & Xu, J. (2002). A model of (often mixed) stereotype content: Competence and warmth respectively follow from perceived status and competition. *Journal of Personality and Social Psychology, 82*, 878–902. https://doi.org/10.1037/0022-3514.82.6.878

Ghavami, N., & Peplau, L. A. (2013). An intersectional analysis of gender and ethnic stereotypes: Testing three hypotheses. *Psychology of Women Quarterly, 37*(1), 113–127. https://doi.org/10.1177/0361684312464203

Goffman, E. (1963). *Stigma: Notes on the management of spoiled identity*. New York, NY: Simon & Schuster.

Glick, P., & Fiske, S. T. (1996). The Ambivalent Sexism Inventory: Differentiating hostile and benevolent sexism. *Journal of Personality and Social Psychology, 70*, 491–512. https://doi.org/10.1037/0022-3514.70.3.491

Glick, P., & Fiske, S. T. (2001). An ambivalent alliance: Hostile and benevolent sexism as complementary justifications for gender inequality. *American Psychologist, 56*, 109–118. https://doi.org/10.1037/0003-066X.56.2.109

Glick, P., Fiske, S. T., Mladinic, A., Saiz, J. L., Abrams, D., Masser, B., ... López, W. L. (2000). Beyond prejudice as simple antipathy: Hostile and benevolent sexism across cultures. *Journal of Personality and Social Psychology, 79*, 763–775. https://doi.org/10.1037/0022-3514.79.5.763

Goff, P. A., Thomas, M. A., & Jackson, M. C. (2008). "Aint I a woman?": Towards an intersectional approach to person perception and group-based harms. *Sex Roles, 59*, 392–403. https://doi.org/10.1007/s11199-008-9505-4

Hall, E. V., & Phillips, K. W. (2012). Optimal masculinity: Feminine races or genders attenuate sanctions for domineering behavior. *Academy of Management Proceedings, 2012*(1), 16134. https://doi.org/10.5465/AMBPP.2012.287

Hall, E. V., & Livingston, R. W. (2012). The hubris penalty: Biased responses to "celebration" displays of Black football players. *Journal of Experimental Social Psychology, 48*(4), 899–904. https://doi.org/10.1016/j.jesp.2012.02.004

Heather, P. (2006). *The fall of the Roman Empire: A new history of Rome and the barbarians*. New York, NY: Oxford University Press.

Heilman, M. E., Block, C., Martell, R., & Simon, M. (1989). Has anything changed? Current characterizations of men, women, and managers. *Journal of Applied Psychology, 74*(6), 935–942. https://doi.org/10.1037/0021-9010.74.6.935

Hill Collins, P., & Bilge, S. (2016). *Intersectionality*. Cambridge, UK: Polity Press.

Jones, E. E., Farina, A., Hastorf, A. H., Markus, H., Miller, D. T., & Scott, R. A. (1984). *Social stigma: The psychology of marked relationships*. New York, NY: W. H. Freeman & Company.

Jones, S. (2017, June 9). White Men account for 72% of corporate leadership at 16 of the Fortune 500 Companies. *Fortune*. https://fortune.com/2017/06/09/white-men-senior-executives-fortune-500-companies-diversity-data

Kleck, R. E., & Strenta, A. (1980). Perceptions of the impact of negatively valued physical characteristics on social interaction. *Journal of Personality and Social Psychology, 39*(5), 861–873.

Kossek, E. E., Su, R., & Wu, L. (2017). "Opting out" or "pushed out"? Integrating perspectives on women's career equality for gender inclusion and interventions. *Journal of Management, 43*(1), 228–254. https://doi.org/10.1177/0149206316671582

Levin, S., Sinclair, S., Veniegas, R. C., & Taylor, P. L. (2002). Perceived discrimination in the context of multiple group memberships. *Psychological Science, 13*(6), 557–560. https://doi.org/10.1111/1467-9280.00498

Liang, J. G., & Peters-Hawkins, A. L. (2017). "I am more than what I look alike": Asian American women in public school administration. *Educational Administration Quarterly*, *53*(1), 40–69. https://doi.org/10.1177/0013161X16652219

Livingston, R. W., & Brewer, M. B. (2002). What are we really priming? Cue-based versus category-based processing of facial stimuli. *Journal of Personality and Social Psychology*, *82*(1), 5–18.

Livingston, R. W., & Pearce, N. (2009). The teddy bear effect: Does having a baby face benefit Black chief executive officers? *Psychological Science*, *20*, 1229–1236. https://doi.org/10.1111/j.1467-9280.2009.02431.x

Livingston, R. W., Rosette, A. S., & Washington, E. F. (2012). Can an agentic Black woman get ahead? The impact of race and agentic emotional expression on female leader status. *Psychological Science*, *23*(4), 354–358. https://doi.org/10.1177/0956797611428079

Maddox, K. B. (2004). Perspectives on racial phenotypicality bias. *Personality and Social Psychology Review*, *8*(4), 383–401. https://doi.org/10.1207/s15327957 pspr0804_4

McDonald, M. L., & Westphal, J. D. (2013). Access denied: Low mentoring of women and minority first-time directors and its negative effects on appointments to additional boards. *Academy of Management Journal*, *56*(4), 1169–1198. https://doi.org/10.5465/amj.2011.0230

Navarrete, C. D., McDonald, M. M., Molina, L. E., & Sidanius, J. (2010). Prejudice at the nexus of race and gender: An outgroup male target hypothesis. *Journal of Personality and Social Psychology*, *98*, 933–945. https://doi.org/10.1037/a0017931

Okimoto, T. G., & Brescoll, V. L. (2010). The price of power: Power-seeking and backlash against female politicians. *Personality and Social Psychology Bulletin*, *36*, 923–936. https://doi.org/10.1177/0146167210371949

Purdie-Vaughns, V., & Eibach, R. P. (2008). Intersectional invisibility: The distinctive advantages and disadvantages of multiple subordinate-group identities. *Sex Roles*, *59*, 377–391. https://doi.org/10.1007/s11199-008-9424-4

Rosette, A. S., Koval, C., Ma, A., & Livingston, R. W. (2016). Race matters for women leaders: Intersectional effects on agentic deficiencies and penalties. *The Leadership Quarterly*, 27, 429–445. https://doi.org/10.1016/j.leaqua.2016.01.008

Rosette, A. S., Leonardelli, G. J., & Phillips, K. W. (2008). The White standard: Racial bias in leader categorization. *Journal of Applied Psychology*, *93*, 758–777. https://doi.org/10.1037/0021-9010.93.4.758

Rosette, A. S., & Livingston, R. W. (2012). Failure is not an option for Black women: Effects of organizational performance on leaders with single versus dual-subordinate identities. *Journal of Experimental Social Psychology*, *48*(5), 1162–1167. https://doi.org/10.1016/j.jesp.2012.05.002

Rosette, A. S., & Tost, L. P. (2010). Agentic women and communal leadership: How role prescriptions confer advantage to top women leaders. *Journal of Applied Psychology*, *95*(2), 221–235. https://doi.org/10.1037/a0018204

Rudman, L. A. (1998). Self-promotion as a risk factor for women: The costs and benefits of counterstereotypical impression management. *Journal of Personality and Social Psychology*, *74*, 629–645. https://doi.org/10.1037//0022-3514.74.3.629

Rudman, L. A., & Fairchild, K. (2004). Reactions to counterstereotypic behavior: The role of backlash in cultural stereotype maintenance. *Journal of*

*Personality and Social Psychology*, *87*, 157–176. https://doi.org/10.1037/0022-3514.87.2.157

Rudman, L., Moss-Racusin, C. A., Phelan, J. E., & Nauts, S. (2012). Status incongruity and backlash effects: Defending the gender hierarchy motives prejudice against female leaders. *Journal of Experimental Social Psychology*, *48*, 165–179. https://doi.org/10.1016/j.jesp.2011.10.008

Sanchez-Hucles, J. V., & Davis, D. D. (2010). Women and women of color in leadership: Complexity, identity, and intersectionality. *American Psychologist*, *65*(3), 171–181. https://doi.org/10.1037/a0017459

Schein, V. E. (1973). The relationship between sex role stereotypes and requisite management characteristics. *Journal of Applied Psychology*, *57*(2), 95–100. https://doi.org/10.1037/h0037128

Settles, I. H. (2006). Use of an intersectional framework to understand Black women's racial and gender identities. *Sex Roles*, *54*(9-10), 589–601. https://doi.org/10.1007/s11199-006-9029-8

Sesko, A. K., & Biernat, M. (2010). Prototypes of race and gender: The invisibility of Black women. *Journal of Experimental Social Psychology*, *46*(2), 356–360. https://doi.org/10.1016/j.jesp.2009.10.016

Sherif, M. (1961). *Intergroup conflict and cooperation: The Robbers Cave experiment* (Revised Edition). Norman, OK: University Book Exchange.

Sidanius, J., Hudson, S. T. J., Davis, G., & Bergh, R. (2018). The theory of gendered prejudice: A social dominance and intersectionalist perspective. In A. Mintz & L. Terris (Eds.), *The Oxford handbook of behavioral political science*. https://doi.org/10.1093/oxfordhb/9780190634131.013.11

Sidanius, J., & Pratto, F. (1999). *Social dominance: An intergroup theory of social hierarchy and oppression*. Cambridge, UK: Cambridge University Press.

Tiedens, L. Z. (2001). Anger and advancement versus sadness and subjugation: The effect of negative emotion expressions on social status conferral. *Journal of Personality and Social Psychology*, *80*, 86–94. https://doi.org/10.1037/0022-3514.80.1.86

Turner, C. S. V. (2002). Women of color in academe: Living with multiple marginality. *The Journal of Higher Education*, *73*(1), 74–93. https://doi.org/10.1080/00221546.2002.11777131

West, C. (2017, January 9). Pity the sad legacy of Barack Obama. *The Guardian*. https://www.theguardian.com/commentisfree/2017/jan/09/barack-obama-legacy-presidency

Williams, J. C., Phillips, K. W., & Hall, E. V. (2014). *Double jeopardy: Gender bias against women of color in science*. Center for Work-Life Law, UC Hastings College of the Law, University of California. https://worklifelaw.org/publications/Double-Jeopardy-Report_v6_full_web-sm.pdf

Zapata, C. P., Carton, A. M., & Liu, J. T. (2016). When justice promotes injustice: Why minority leaders experience bias when they adhere to interpersonal justice rules. *Academy of Management Journal*, *59*(4), 1150–1173. https://doi.org/10.5465/amj.2014.0275

Zebrowitz, L. A., & Collins, M. A. (1997). Accurate social perception at zero acquaintance: The affordances of a Gibsonian approach. *Personality and Social Psychology Review*, *1*(3), 204–223. https://doi.org/10.1207/s15327957pspr0103_2

# 4 Why Diversity Needs Inclusion and How Leaders Make It Happen

*Stefanie K. Johnson and Brittany K. Lambert*

There is clearly a business case for diversity (Credit Suisse, 2012; Dezsö & Ross, 2012; Hunt et al., 2015; Huddleston, 2015; Morgan Stanley, 2016; Noland et al., 2016). But to achieve its full benefits, leaders must actually buy in to diversity and then stoke it with inclusion. For example, Nishii (2013) showed that teams with greater gender diversity had lower turnover and absenteeism but only if the teams had an inclusive climate. In this chapter we explain why companies cannot harness the full benefits of diversity without leaders who are committed to inclusion. Finally, we frame our discussion on inclusive leadership around eight key behaviors derived from 158 interviews with workplace leaders.

Leaders trying to figure out how to build high quality, inclusive relationships in their work environments can take cues from Shore and her colleagues (2011). These scholars break inclusion into two key elements: making employees believe that they are respected and valued for their unique perspectives (uniqueness) and ensuring they feel that they fully belong to the group (belongingness) (Shore et al., 2011). Shore's theory is rooted in optimal distinctiveness theory that highlights these two basic needs to belong, but as one's unique self (Brewer, 1991), making it distinct from other conceptualizations of inclusion.

For the purposes of this chapter we adopt Shore et al.'s framework of uniqueness and belonging to theorize about some key behaviors that might increase feelings of uniqueness (the belief that one is valued and respected for one's unique perspective) and belonging (the belief that one is a critical and valued member of the team). We specifically focus on behaviors because psychology research suggests that our behaviors influence our cognitions and emotions (Beck, 1979), thus behaving inclusively may also positively impact thoughts and emotions related to inclusion. To build our theory, we conducted a qualitative analysis of data from 158 interviews focused on diversity and inclusion in their workplace from the perspective of leaders and followers. The sample included CEOs, executives, managers, and their followers from a variety of industries including technology, finance, healthcare, and retail. More than one person conducted the interviews and all were professionally transcribed. We looked for instances in which leaders and followers identify behaviors that create inclusion—or behaviors that, when absent, diminish inclusion. We frame these inclusive behaviors as either increasing uniqueness or increasing belonging.

### *Uniqueness*

The value of uniqueness in the workplace is a tension-filled paradox. On the one hand, scholars acknowledge that differences among workers (absent inclusive leadership) may increase conflict (Nishii & Mayer, 2009). On the other hand, difference is also a protecting factor against blind spots that come from homogeneity (Apfelbaum, 2014). Regardless, the shift in our society toward individualism will make it a leadership imperative to acknowledge, value, and navigate differences. Bob Chapman, CEO of Barry-Wehmiller, has a radical perspective on uniqueness called "Truly Human Leadership." He and his company take a platform that each individual at work should be valued in the same way a parent values their child. In other words, each worker matters. It seems to be working for Barry-Wehmiller as the company has grown from $20M to $3B under Chapman's helm.

Accordingly, we identified four leader behaviors that work to increase a follower's belief that their uniqueness (distinct identity) is recognized and valued (Fromkin & Snyder, 1980). Our theory asserts these behaviors both (1) bring in and encourage new perspectives and (2) support diversity and equitable employment practices. We draw support for our theory from other scholarly work on inclusion in the work place. First, several new theoretical models of inclusive leadership point toward the value of new perspectives in enhancing work (Randel et al., 2018). Randel and colleagues put it this way: "By paying special attention to soliciting different points of view and approaches, inclusive leaders are able to support perspectives and orientations that are not the norm but that contribute to performance" (p. 193). We find a similar pattern in our data, but specifically operationalize these behaviors as (1) displaying empathy toward followers (listening to their emotional point of view) and (2) trying to learn from followers (listening to their added cognitive perspective to inform workplace decisions).

Second, fair employment practices are part of Nishii's (2013) model of inclusive climate, and we extend this dimension to leader behaviors. Specifically, we argue that from the perspective of a minority group member it is not possible to feel that your unique perspective is valued if you concurrently experience unfair treatment by your boss or you do not believe your boss supports diversity and inclusion. Moreover, Leslie (2019) theorizes that even diversity practices with the best of intentions can backfire as a result of unintended signals that are sent by the organization. Therefore, leadership behaviors fostering uniqueness include (3) actively and publicly supporting diversity and inclusion and (4) ensuring fairness in employment practices.

### *Show Public Support for Diversity and Inclusion*

Leaders must actively and publicly support diversity. This looks like both weaving diversity into everyday conversations and in the overarching goals and purpose of the team. One of our interviewees told us: "I think some of the most effective leaders, when it comes to more diverse teams, set the tone from the start. And, they explain the reason and the purpose for those who are participating." Alternatively, day-to-day conversations are just as important. Openly discussing stigmatized topics ensures questions and concerns do not turn into biases. As one leader told us: "Fundamentally, it's just actually talking about [diversity and inclusion]. Actually engaging with their teams in the importance of diversity and inclusion."

On the flip side, leaders who did not exhibit public support for diversity and inclusion pointed out how that sends a different message to the team:

> I was thinking about certain leaders that really don't talk about it. It doesn't mean that they're against it, they just don't embrace bringing it into their strategy or even minor conversations, then it doesn't get into the fabric of the team.

Respondents indicated that leaders who do both of these things positively impact the trajectory of careers. For example, one participant discusses how important other women supporting her was to her career: "Madeleine Albright says, 'There's a special place in hell for women that don't support other women' . . . there's absolutely no way I would be where I am today without the support of mentors and people, both men and women."

### *Ensure Fairness in Employment Practices*

Of course, it is quite difficult to feel that your unique background is valued if you concurrently believe you are being discriminated against. Leaders who were successful at promoting diversity and inclusion often discussed fairness in regard to hiring: "We are close on our metrics and our diversity numbers at all levels of management. I try to assure that we have fair and equitable hiring processes or promotion processes so that people aren't overlooked." Opportunities to practice fairness also came up around promotion and pay. For example, one follower said:

> [Leadership] looks at who gets merit raises, they look carefully at salaries and they cut the data by race and ethnicity, they cut it by gender, to really make sure that staff are receiving fair compensation and that there's not the dynamic of racism or sexism that's impeding in how compensation or promotion opportunities occur.

Less obvious forms of practicing fairness include assigning tasks equitably, without letting biases about gender roles have an influence. One follower told a story about women of color being asked to complete extra office "housework" in the form of bringing food to meetings and how this showed she was not being valued for her unique perspective but was, instead, being saddled with extra busy work. The follower explained that she felt less valued as a woman when:

> The boss said, "Oh yeah, it'd be great if you had food at this new meeting to make sure that we're all fed," and that … [was] really shocking to me, because I just felt like it was inappropriate comment. Like, I don't think that person's responsibility is to feed us.

### *Have Empathy for Followers*

Empathy emerged as a key leader behavior for effectively creating uniqueness because having empathy allowed for more authentic connections between people. Empathy looks like taking the time to understand what is going on for someone and validating their experience. Fostering these connections is particularly critical to reaching individuals with invisible and stigmatized forms of diversity, such as neurodiversity. One leader said, "You think about the culture, about creating a warm, welcoming environment, a culture of compassion and empathy for people. The desire to create this experience that is this safe place for people to connect." Another leader talked about taking a stand on issues that were important to his followers. He said, "I think a lot of it was because my employees were emailing me. And that's important. So I just had an empathetic response to my employees and did something about it."

Conversely, many followers pointed out how a lack of empathy can hurt their individual identity, in that it can inadvertently create polarization among employees. Importantly, this theme came from as many White men as it did from women and people of color. One interviewee told us:

> The older White males, they live in a climate, I think some of them are afraid. The organizational leaders will have candid conversations about [diversity and inclusion] and there's no empathy on either

side. I've heard them say, "This is where we're going. Get over it [in reference to creating more diversity]," which is not an empathetic statement to make, right?

### *Demonstrate a Desire to Learn from Others*

Nearly all of the leaders we interviewed who were champions for diversity and inclusion expressed a clear desire to learn from diverse perspectives. Taking a posture of learning looks like being open to hearing different perspectives to inform your own. It includes listening and asking questions and importantly reflecting what you learn in decision making. One leader said:

> I think that's where there is an opportunity for all of us is to continue to learn those cultural differences that exist with people whether they're from different countries or different ethnic backgrounds. I do think men and women process things differently generally ... and I think ... continuing to educate everybody on those differences is helpful.

Another leader said, "You want to give people [of all races and genders] the opportunity to share and educate you so that you are making the right decision." Conversely, followers complained that their opinions were not heard so they did not feel as if their unique perspectives were valued. One woman said simply, "I'm asked for my opinion, but in the end my opinion never matters."

## ***Belonging***

Belonging is also equally important and was recently dubbed by LinkedIn to be a top trend in workplace diversity and inclusion efforts in 2019 (Kabel, 2019). Shore and her colleagues (Shore et al., 2011) describe the belonging component of inclusion as people feeling integrated, like an insider, unified, or similar. Brené Brown, Research Professor at the University of Houston, Endowed Chair at the Graduate College of Social Work, and author of five #1 *New York Times* bestsellers, emphasizes the importance of belonging in a recent book and stream of research. In a recent interview with *Forbes*, Brown offers that we have a "crisis of disconnection in our society" (i.e., we are more separated and lonely than ever before) and that belonging happens when we recognize we are tied together by something greater than us (Schawbel, 2017). In agreement with Brown, Pat Wadors, Senior Vice President of Global Talent at LinkedIn, says belonging is such an innate human need that some argue it is more important than pay, that we are hardwired for it, and in fact "belonging and attachment to a group of coworkers is a better motivator for some employees than money" (Wadors, 2016, para. 10). Applied to the workplace, belongingness centers on having strong human connections and feeling like part of the team.

In view of these findings, we offer four leadership behaviors that foster belongingness. Our findings suggest that, first, leaders should help followers feel like insiders by (1) being transparent and (2) empowering followers to make decisions. Second, leaders should make diversity and inclusion a cultural ethos by (3) aligning majority group members with diversity and inclusion and (4) motivating cultural change toward inclusion through celebrations and visioning. Our qualitative findings lend support to recent scholarly models of inclusive leadership. Specifically, we mirror Randel et al. (2018) in our conclusions that ensuring followers are supported (i.e., feel like insiders) is critical to belonging. However, we diverge from this model to offer evidence that leaders should intentionally elicit and ensure participation and alignment from majority group members, namely White men. We also make a distinction between what might be thought of as distributive fairness, what we argue is needed to encourage uniqueness, and procedural (or informational) fairness, what we refer to as transparency and find to encourage belonging. We describe each of the four behaviors with insights from our interviews below.

### *Be Transparent*

To create this insider feeling, leaders talked about the importance of transparency. Specifically, transparency looks like acknowledging truth and reality, regardless of how that might disrupt an ideal image. As a result, transparency distributes power to employees. One leader said in relation to being transparent about diversity:

> I think it's transparency. We're having success or we're not. I think it's okay to challenge everyone to think differently. I think it certainly has an impact with the rest of the organization and while some might be uncomfortable with it, or not understand why it's important, I think as leaders it's our responsibility to make sure it's out there, it's transparent, we're honest with ourselves.

Another leader said, "Transparency is one of the things that I think we neglect to acknowledge. Even if it's embarrassing or whatever. People need to know." In contrast, non-inclusive leaders were described as, "holding onto decision making so that you're again maintaining your position of power at the cost of not being transparent or collaborative."

### *Empower People*

A second theme that emerged was the importance of empowering people so they feel trusted and like essential members of the team. Empowering people looks like delegating responsibility and trusting people to follow through. A leader said, "It's empowering (others), whether you're a manager or a director, it's empowering your staff, as we work in that space, to continue to push that work forward." A follower said, "That feeling of empowerment, I think has to be an experience that people have in an inclusive environment. They have to feel empowered. They can't just be told they're empowered. They have to feel empowered at some point in time." On the flip side, others talked about not empowering their teams. One leader explained:

> We had a paternalistic culture in the organization. There was a kind of complacency that developed over generations. The "take care of me" and not enough self-responsibility. So, we wanted to help nurture the culture in a new way. This is one of many ways in which we were doing it. You find this mostly in the corporate world, too. With this whole notion about having self-responsibility, about maturing, particularly young people first joining the workforce. Demonstrating that maturity about their career ambitions and their career development.

### *Align Allies*

As leaders seek to foster inclusion, it is easy to take majority group members for granted. However, it is critical that leaders take action to rally majority group members, namely White men, around inclusion and diversity. Leaders we interviewed practiced aligning White male employees to diversity and inclusion efforts by doing things like bystander intervention training. One leader said:

> We've done bystander intervention training as well so that when you see things occur, you have the tools to kind of like call them out, or be confronting them in a way that's not shameful, but moves the work forward or advances equity that way.

Another leader explained why aligning allies was so important, "I know a lot of people view [diversity and inclusion efforts] as reverse discrimination. I think there's always that risk. I tend to look at goals as having some flexibility and still doing the right thing." Bringing White men in as allies through methods such as bystander intervention training shows them that they are part of the solution, rather than accusing them of being part of the problem. This changes the narrative.

*Motivate Cultural Change*

Finally, to really connect people to diversity and inclusion, it involves motivating others. This looks like celebrating diversity and inclusion and incorporating it into the culture. Many of the leaders who were successful at increasing diversity and inclusion said that they made it part of the rites and rituals (the mission, vision, and values) of the organization. As one leader said, "It's about always recognizing small wins ... Having a plan in place and celebrating those steps along the way, that will help you reach those even bigger outcomes. Because that also helps you keep the momentum going." Another leader said:

> Basically, team activities, celebrations. I'm real big about taking the team out either for happy hour so celebrations when we achieve certain goals ... like if it's the holidays, holiday parties, holiday happy hours. And we just celebrate ourselves when we have big goals that we must achieve and we make sure that we recognize those, and we recognize those individuals also when they achieve big things.

There was also a large focus on making diversity and inclusion part of the core values:

> Diversity and inclusion is one of our core values, and it has been for many, many years ... That speaks volumes for potential applicants and candidates to see on our job descriptions when they apply. Our core values are spelled out and their definition.

Conversely, when leaders don't take it to that level of making diversity and inclusion part of the organization's values or culture it can hinder success. One follower said that her organization was not successful at diversity and inclusion because of "the absence of vision and values around equity and justice."

## Summary

So, what makes diversity and inclusion so difficult? At its heart, despite the benefits of diversity that we read about every day, many leaders still do not believe deeply that diversity is good. Even if leaders buy in to diversity in theory, unconscious biases, pressing demands from company performance standards, and the hard work required to navigate differences in a work team can undermine a leader's diversity efforts. Furthermore, in order to see the benefit of diversity, leaders must be dedicated to leading inclusively, that is, ensuring their people uniquely belong (Shore et al., 2011). Inclusive leaders are the key ingredient to the power of diverse thinking (Nishii & Mayer, 2009).

## Practical Advice for Leaders

### *Support Uniqueness*

1. Show public support for diversity and inclusion by speaking up and making your commitment known to others.
2. Ensure fairness in employment practices including selection, promotion, and pay.
3. Have empathy for followers by trying to understand their perspective.
4. Demonstrate a desire to learn from different perspectives by hiring people who differ from the norm and designing more inclusive meetings.

### *Support Belonging*

1. Be transparent, particularly around diversity and inclusion issues.
2. Empower people to be successful by setting high expectations for others and utilizing self-managed work teams.
3. Align allies by ensuring that White men are involved in the diversity and inclusion process.
4. Motivate continued commitment to diversity and inclusion by making it part of the fabric of the organization and celebrating successes.

## References

Apfelbaum, E. (2014, March 7). *There's a case against diversity in the workplace—but the alternative is even scarier*. Quartz. https://qz.com/185131/theres-a-case-against-diversity-in-the-workplace-but-the-alternative-is-even-scarier

Beck, A. T. (1979). *Cognitive therapy and the emotional disorders*. New York, NY: Penguin.

Brewer, M. B. (1991). The social self: On being the same and different at the same time. *Personality and Social Psychology Bulletin*, *17*(5), 475–482. https://doi.org/10.1177/0146167291175001

Credit Suisse. (2012, July 31). *Large-cap companies with at least one woman on the board have outperformed their peer group with no women on the-board by 26% over the last six years, according to a report by Credit Suisse Research Institute*. https://www.credit-suisse.com/about-us-news/en/articles/media-releases/42035-201207.html

Dezsö, C. L., & Ross, D. G. (2012). Does female representation in top management improve firm performance? A panel data investigation. *Strategic Management Journal*, *33*(9), 1072–1089. https://doi.org/10.1002/smj.1955

Huddleston, J. T. (2015, December 7). You'd be smart to buy stock in companies with women on their boards. *Fortune*. http://fortune.com/2015/12/07/female-board-directors-returns

Hunt, V., Layton, D., & Prince, S. (2015, February). *Diversity matters*. McKinsey & Company. https://www.mckinsey.com/~/media/mckinsey/business%20functions/organization/our%20insights/why%20diversity%20matters/diversity%20matters.ashx

Kabel, A. (2019, January 7). *Eight top trends in diversity & inclusion for 2019* [Post]. LinkedIn. https://www.linkedin.com/pulse/eight-top-trends-diversity-inclusion-2019-amir-kabel

Leslie, L. M. (2019). Diversity initiative effectiveness: A typological theory of unintended consequences. *Academy of Management Review*, *44*(3), 538–563. https://doi.org/10.5465/amr.2017.0087

Morgan Stanley (2016, May 11). *Why it pays to invest in gender diversity*. https://www.morganstanley.com/ideas/gender-diversity-investment-framework

Nishii, L. H. (2013). The benefits of climate for inclusion for gender diverse groups. *Academy of Management Journal*, *56*(6), 1754–1774. https://doi.org/10.5465/amj.2009.0823

Nishii, L. H., & Mayer, D. (2009). Do inclusive leaders help to reduce turnover in diverse groups? The moderating role of leader-member exchange in the diversity to performance relationship. *Journal of Applied Psychology*, *94*(6), 1412–1426. https://doi.org/10.1037/a0017190

Noland, M., Moran, T., & Kotschwar, B. (2016, February 8). *New Peterson Institute research on over 21,000 companies globally finds women in corporate leadership can significantly increase profitability*. Petersen Institute for International Economics. https://piie.com/newsroom/press-releases/new-peterson-institute-research-over-21000-companies-globally-finds-women

Northouse, P. G. (2018). *Leadership: Theory and practice*. Thousand Oaks, CA: Sage.

Randel, A. E., Galvin, B. M., Shore, L. M., Ehrhart, K. H., Chung, B. G., Dean, M. A., & Kedharnath, U. (2018). Inclusive leadership: Realizing positive outcomes through belongingness and being valued for uniqueness. *Human Resource Management Review*, *28*(2), 190–203. https://doi.org/10.1016/j.hrmr.2017.07.002

Schawbel, D. (2017, September 12). Brené Brown: Why human connection will bring us closer together. *Forbes*. https://www.forbes.com/sites/danschawbel/2017/09/12/brene-brown-why-human-connection-will-bring-us-closer-together

Shore, L. M., Randel, A. E., Chung, B. G., Dean, M. A., Holcombe Ehrhart, K., & Singh, G. (2011). Inclusion and diversity in work groups: A review and model for future research. *Journal of Management*, *37*(4), 1262–1289. https://doi.org/10.1177/0149206310385943

Wadors, P. (2016, August 10). Diversity efforts fall short unless employees feel that they belong, *Harvard Business Review Digital Articles*. https://hbr.org/2016/08/diversity-efforts-fall-short-unless-employees-feel-that-they-belong

# 5 The Problem of Inclusion from a Multicultural Perspective[1]

*Edgar H. Schein and Peter A. Schein*

This chapter focuses on what inclusion means in different cultural contexts and how these meanings have powerful implications for how organizations and their leaders should approach their diversity and inclusion programs. We provide several examples of underinclusion and overinclusion, and the implications of the misunderstandings that can arise from this. The concept of *cultural islands* is described as one way to deal with potential cultural differences.

## Cultural Variation in Human Societies

One of the central findings of anthropology is that all societies are stratified in some way or other, leading to castes, hereditary classes, and status-based echelons—which in Western societies claim to be meritocracies based on individual achievement. What defines a given echelon is the members' perception of "us" versus "them" by the members of that echelon and their consequent building of actual barriers to reduce the inclusion of non-members.

It is a general process to define ourselves as a group or tribe based on similar background (genetic and/or cultural), similar network of acquaintances, or similar patterns of personal achievement such as level of education, organizational rank, or wealth. Viewing this from a broad cultural perspective it is important to think carefully about the question of how the members of an organization may define *their* sense of who they are, who is in, who is not, what efforts are to be devoted not only to increase inclusion but also to define clearly who is excluded and why. U.S. society is in a phase of valuing diversity of talent and is therefore actively creating programs that will not only bring in such talent but will, in that process, ignore other criteria that may define who is "us" and who is "them."

**Story 1: An Example of Societal Organizational Self-Definition**

I (Ed) was having lunch with a colleague who had just spent a two-week holiday in Morocco. We are both deeply interested in the problems of leadership in complex organizations, so he told me what he learned when he met various managers in several large Moroccan organizations.

One particular conversation was quite representative of what he learned in all of them. He asked his informant about career advancement and was told that this depended entirely on whom you know and especially on family connections. Promotions went primarily to family members, and if they did not perform well, they would be sidelined with some face-saving lateral move but under no circumstances would they be fired. If one wanted to be promoted and was not a member of the family it was essential to build close friendships with those members of the family who were perceived to have power and status. One's only chance was to ride in on the coattails of others who were being promoted.

It was well understood that the criteria for inclusion were to be a member of the founding or currently owning family or at least to be a good friend of such a member. It was asserted that most organizations operated by these exclusionary criteria.

In Ed's own experience as a consultant in various other cultures he found this pattern to be far more common than the U.S.-espoused value of meritocratic promotion on the basis of achievement typical in U.S. business. We see U.S. organizations trying to be uncompromising on performance criteria relevant to the task and preferring not to consider hiring people who might help meet diversity goals but may also marginally underperform other members of the candidate pool or work group. We rarely assume the posture that the job of a leader is to take *any group* with widely mixed talents and find a way to develop it into an effective organization as some leaders in other cultures might do when faced with a large collective of varying talents. Opting for the "best" person for the job is a common default position, even if the "right" person for the job comes from an under-represented cultural background.

Many U.S. companies do recognize, to varying degrees, that inclusion often requires additional education and training, accept that responsibility, and, therefore, benefit ultimately from a broader and more innovative workforce. But we also have hierarchy- and status-based echelons that function as closed tribes, even as the U.S. meritocratic ideology trends to eschew tribal membership connections in favor of demonstrable talent and achievement. In the multicultural multinational context, however, we may find that most organizations are as tribal as the Moroccan ones in the above example. In the U.S., when we see such a system, we may espouse moral outrage, point out how performance is undermined by nepotism, and end up ignoring correlated cultural factors that explain why an organization might actually prefer such nepotism on the rationale that relatives can be trusted more than outside employees.

This last point was well illustrated within the U.S. in the story of a California aerospace company plant that had been built in a racially diverse community that happened to be home to many friends and relatives of some of the early leaders of this plant. They were extremely proud of their superior production and safety record and attributed it primarily to the high level of familiarity, open communication, and high trust levels that resulted from the history of neighborly belonging if not nepotism. This point is frequently reinforced by the argument that you can count on friends and relatives being more trustworthy and reliable than even supremely qualified strangers hired through highly inclusive recruiting practices.

This California plant's story had an unfortunate end. Several plants in other companies had been found by the Department of Defense to have falsified some employment records and therefore collected more money for wages than was appropriate. This discovery led the Department of Defense to insist that, from that point on, all plants would install time clocks and very tight supervision and inspection procedures by outsiders. The morale of the plant plummeted and, worse, both performance and safety declined. The plant inevitably became more diverse, but it did so at the expense of what had been a very effective tribal culture. One important lesson is that the bases on which we trust people are derived from the occupational culture of management which is often based on the principle that one cannot trust anyone and therefore requires rules and mechanisms like time clocks that may unwittingly override the efforts to be more diverse.

In U.S. business culture, we have tended to equate efficiency with success, which, taken to the logical extreme, equates the moral high roads of meritocracy and inclusiveness with efficiency, even at the risk of ignoring exceptional cases where organizational effectiveness may derive from other designs that do not conform to meritocratic or even democratic ideals. Effectiveness is elusive and complex, drawing from work relationship histories as well as inclusive futures. The challenge is to add the right mix of talents and points of view into the historical substrate so that what we consider right is both efficient and effective. The point is that inclusiveness as a value can compete with other conflicting values in organizations that must be profitable and grow in order to survive. It remains an open question whether we should ever accept that another value can supersede inclusiveness.

## Levels of Relationship

The members of different echelons or "tribes" distinguish themselves by where they live, where they work, how they dress, how and what they speak, who they associate with, and through various other markers that make it possible to maintain their identity. Such markers can create clear physical boundaries such as 'hoods, enclaves, gated communities, or social boundaries that influence who members seek to associate with in public, and perhaps most profoundly, distinctions in the level of inclusion or intimacy that members will seek and/or tolerate in a relationship.

Therefore, to best contextualize *inclusion*, we have to recognize that societies differentiate "levels of relationships" between individuals based on the purpose of the relationship (Schein, 2016; Schein & Schein, 2017, 2018). Such levels are visible in all cultures even though the same purpose for a given relationship may be expressed differently by different echelons and the boundaries between levels will vary by cultural rules and norms (see Table 5.1).

*Table 5.1* Four levels of relationship in society.

**Level Minus 1—Denying Personhood: Coercion and Exploitation**
Examples: Prisoners, POWs, slaves, sometimes members of extremely different cultures or ones we consider underdeveloped, sometimes very old or very emotionally ill people, the victims or "marks" for criminals or con men, sometimes the employees in a coercive organization. Trust and openness are at a minimum across the hierarchic boundaries, but we recognize, of course, that inside the coerced groups intense self-protective relationships form.

**Level 1—Acknowledging the Person in a Role: Transactional Relationships**
Examples: Strangers on the street, seatmates on trains and planes, service people whose help we need which includes professional helpers of all sorts whose behavior is governed by the defined role definitions in the culture, fellow employees, bosses, and direct reports whom we know formally and in terms of their official roles or ranks.

We treat each other as fellow humans whom we trust to a certain degree not to harm us and with whom we have polite levels of openness in conversation, but we do not "know" each other except in our various roles and statuses. What we say and what we promise is limited by cultural rules and the degree to which we feel psychologically safe. Professional helpers such as doctors fall into this category because their role definition requires them to maintain "professional distance."

**Level 2—Seeing the Whole Person Above and Beyond their Role or Status**
Examples: Casual friendships, others whom we know as unique individuals, members of working teams, people whom we have gotten to know through

(*Continued*)

*Table 5.1* (Cont.)

common work or educational experiences, bosses, employees, clients, or helpers with whom we have developed personal but not intimate relationships.

This kind of relationship implies a deeper level of trust and openness in terms of 1) making and honoring commitments and promises to each other; 2) agreeing to not undermine each other or harm what we have agreed to do; and 3) agreeing not to lie to each other or withhold information relevant to our task.

**Level 3—Emotional Intimacy, Close Friendships, and Love**
Examples: Relationships where stronger positive emotions and intimate physical contact are involved. This kind of relationship is usually viewed as undesirable in work or helping situations. Trust here goes one step beyond level 2 in that the participants not only agree not to harm each other but assume that they will actively support each other when possible or when needed.

The members of any given echelon have a clear sense of what level of relationship they will want and/or tolerate with others who either clearly fit into a different category or are unknown and therefore "unsafe" if the relationship gets too close. The next example suggests these complex relationship dynamics.

### Story 2: Ed's Disappointing Sabbatical

In the mid-1970s I was invited to take a sabbatical semester at the C.E.I. (Centre d'Etudes Industrielle) in Geneva. My wife and I were given a very nice apartment in Veriez just a half-mile from the school. I had a relatively light teaching load, so we expected to meet other faculty and get involved in the school's social life. We met a lot of these people at an initial welcoming party, but to our dismay were not subsequently invited to anything other than one dinner with our official host. Exploring Geneva was gratifying, but after five weeks was not sufficiently involving, and we had not gotten to know anyone, so we found ourselves leaving Geneva and shifting to a month in Paris and then a month in London for the rest of the sabbatical. I commuted into Geneva to teach my classes.

In discussing all of this with our host, an expatriate American professor, we learned that the Swiss, German, and French faculty all had the view that making friends with visiting Americans was not worth the emotional effort because Americans would only get involved superficially (i.e., Level 1) and would quickly forget any friends they might have made in Geneva. The Europeans viewed the building of a friendship as a Level 2 process and would be very disappointed when their new American friends forgot them once they were back in the U.S. They had had enough painful past experiences to lead them to not go out of their way to get close with American visitors!

This experience aligned well with the stereotypical national character model that had been developed in contrasting Europeans and Americans. The famous social psychologist Kurt Lewin (1947) noted that the person can be seen, like an onion, as having many layers, some of which are harder to penetrate. He described Americans as having a very permeable outer barrier, in our terms able to make Level 1 relationships quickly and easily, yet found it much harder to make what we call Level 2 commitments to others because this would restrict their very American sense of freedom and independence. Europeans, on the other hand, had a much thicker outer layer, but once one penetrated it, one could create Level 2 relationships and their concomitant obligations very quickly. Europeans were often misled by the easy informality of the Americans and misjudged the degree to which this meant a more personal commitment. The colleagues in Geneva felt that Americans are very friendly, but often saw it as not really authentic, and they were not sure whether they could trust or count on them in other contexts.

This story highlights how complex the word *inclusion* is, in that our Geneva friends believed they had included us as much as they felt they needed to and had no idea that we felt shunned to such a degree that we left Geneva. Expats or digital nomads may experience just such a level of difference, of distance, even indifference in places that are demonstrably welcoming and even respectful of the visiting "other." There may be no issue with inclusion but there is a clear distinction between the levels of relationship that may be expected by the hosts and by the visitors. Level 2 open and trusting relationships are always in the context of cultural overlays as powerful drivers of degrees of inclusion and degrees of bias, regardless of the official Level 1 relationship norms.

Taking this one step further, the U.S. casual concept of inclusion based on friendliness in the workplace can, paradoxically, also create what one might call "overinclusion" for someone from another culture, as is illustrated in the next story.

### Story 3: The Dilemma of a South Asian Woman in Silicon Valley

This story is about a complaint that Ed heard from a woman from India about her workgroup's efforts to be informal and more inclusive. The group consisted primarily of Americans who would get together at lunch and at breaks and talk about their daily adventures which included lengthy stories about their spouses, their kids, and their various networks of relationships.

The coworkers clearly expected this woman to share information about her family, which made her extremely uncomfortable because in her social circles at home in India this kind of information was considered private and not to be shared in the work setting. She not only was unable to participate at this level, but the easy informality made it difficult for her to point out to the others how in her culture this kind of conversation was not considered appropriate in the work setting.

Her choice was to begin to avoid informal gatherings with her coworkers which they misunderstood as her not wanting to be included. They dropped to a more formal Level 1 relationship with her, she became less engaged, and the group sacrificed effectiveness as it lost some of the contributions she could have made to the group. Even worse, others noticing this distancing incorrectly assumed that the group was excluding her, and the group was beginning to be perceived as racially biased!

One question this story raises is whether efforts to include can become de facto invasions of privacy, and worse, the victim's feelings become suppressed and not discussable according to norms of the native or first culture. This raised the critical reflection and the question "who could have done something to ameliorate this problem and what might they have been able to do?" The easy American answer is: "Well, why didn't she just speak up and tell the group she was uncomfortable?" Unfortunately, all this seemingly simple question would reveal is our own naiveté if not ethnocentricity about how organizational relationships in other cultures actually work. All too often we are surprised to learn after the fact that what in the U.S. we might consider to be "normal" may be viewed as rude or an invasion of privacy, even in adjacent cultures that share many common assumptions (as may be the case with South Asian cultures in Silicon Valley).

Our U.S. business pragmatism and achievement orientation provide us with a powerful rationale for increasing diversity. Many leaders see the inherent inefficiency, unfairness, and dysfunctionality of *exclusion* and therefore strive to include when they can. We may even try to overcome our latent unconscious biases toward other "tribes," but then quite innocently project our own cultural informality onto members from other cultures without considering what their expectations about level of inclusion and relationship boundaries might be.

In some contexts, inclusion at Level 1, giving others the same basic rights of citizenship and opportunities for personal development, may be sufficient and appropriate. For many leaders in the U.S. there is a distinct need to analyze carefully what level of involvement is needed in the work situation and what level of inclusion is required for the best work to be done.

For example, suppose a surgeon from another culture is leading a U.S. operating team on a new complex procedure. Will this doctor be expected to relate to the rest of the team at least at Level 2 openness and trustworthiness, as might be the norm for the equivalent U.S.-based surgeon? This is a tricky context, fraught with a tough combination of limited time, unknown and unseen expectations of a diverse team, and a real likelihood of complications that may stretch the team in unexpected directions. Inevitably it is the senior surgeon's responsibility to build the openness and trust required to adapt to unknowns in a very compressed time frame.

One socio-technical approach has been described as the eye-contact checklist, in which the surgeon leads the team through the technical procedural drill while using it as a safe space in which to establish more personal connection to the rest of the team. Such an approach may take some time, yet benefits by bringing people to the table, eye to eye, rather than allowing critical participants to just stay in their roles. The goal is to open communication channels quickly so that the team can adapt and information can flow quickly. The cultural overlay, the potentially widened distance between multiple cultures—not just multiple roles—clearly complicates that matter further. Socio-technical "tools" such as the person-to-person checklisting process may help shrink distances rapidly by providing an immediate sense of psychological safety to "speak up," particularly if there is an awareness a priori that such cultural and role distinctions tend to challenge this psychological safety. When medical teams are highly interdependent, it is sometimes essential that they voluntarily undergo joint teambuilding to reach Level 2 relationships before the pressures of unanticipated events in the real work create problems (Edmondson, 2012).

## Cultural Islands as Inclusion Mechanisms

Cultural misunderstanding that leads to distance and exclusion is unfortunately all too common, as has been documented in many studies of cross-national joint ventures. One thing that leaders can do to ameliorate such problems is to create special events at culturally neutral locations at which cultural biases and habits can be shared, examined, and accepted (Salk, 1997; Schein, 2016; Schein & Schein, 2017, 2018).

For example, in Ed's MIT classrooms, if he had students from several different cultures, he set aside a special evening event designed to explore each other's cultures around some specific questions that would make a difference to a manager. For example, he asked each student to tell what he or she would do or did do on the occasion of a boss doing something incorrect. Would they speak up? If not, why not? The discussion revealed important cultural norms that could easily get in the way of teamwork. Finding differences in what they would do might make them feel excluded, but the sharing of their stories and listening to each other was the more important activity to make them feel included. The essence of the cultural island is the norm that we can tell each other our stories and count on each other to listen and try to understand. In the process we may also discover the limits of what we can and should talk about, and, more importantly, where are the areas of interdependence in our work where we need to develop norms of mutual trust. If our South Asian woman in the example above had been in a safe space, had the chance to explain the cultural difference in a work-neutral context, might this misunderstanding gap have been bridged if not clarified for the shared benefit of the group when "back at work?"

With an MIT class of Sloan Fellows that included managers from as many as ten different countries, an evening seminar brought in volunteers who wanted to explore cultural differences by breaking up into pairs across nationalities and agreeing in this safe temporary environment to "ask each other the questions they never dared to ask." It was amazing how more intense conversation took place when psychological safety was shared in which to explore each other's cultures. The important lesson on inclusion was that with the six Japanese Sloan Fellows, we found out that even though they had been with the class for six months and had done social things together, they had not really gotten to know each other very well at all. They were included but only at a very superficial social level. If this had been a company in which they actually had to work together, we would have had to do the above exercise in which everyone was invited to share how they dealt with trust issues in hierarchical relationships.

Creating cultural islands requires leadership insight as to when and how, and either leadership group skills or the presence of a group-oriented facilitator. In the U.S. context we have so marginalized the field of group dynamics that most people in leadership positions lack the skills of setting up and managing meetings or building teams. Inclusion is a group process, so insight into group dynamics and training in managing cross-cultural groups is perhaps the most important activity to focus on as we contemplate a future of multicultural work.

## Conclusion

We have pointed out in this chapter some of the problems associated with the cultural norms surrounding relationships and what it takes to feel included or excluded. We have not discussed the impact of these various programs on performance, but we of course recognize that groups and organizations are sociotechnical systems that have to both perform the tasks necessary for their survival and create a social culture that permits the members to be comfortable with each other in fulfilling the task.

"Cultural island" exercises are invariably valuable in building bridges that can develop into effective Level 2 relationships and create comfort. Such exercises represent another socio-technical scheme that starts with a technical objective and so often yields a powerful socio-benefit. The challenge for leaders is to answer the diversity and inclusion call for improved task performance as well, taking into account the cultural variations in how inclusion is defined and experienced. It is a relatively easy technical task to adjust staffing and workforce composition to fit modern norms of gender and racial diversity. This can bring the potential multiplicative effects of new perspectives, new approaches, and new ways of working in groups. If such inclusiveness nets higher paced innovation, it would certainly appear that accomplishing the technical goal (for instance meeting a diversity goal) increases efficiency.

Still, it is critical to remain focused on the socio goal. When meeting diversity goals is coupled with exercises in cross-cultural exchange, with "cultural island" exercises, and with safe spaces to explore different norms and assumptions, the Level 2 trust and openness that develops can become the substrate for deeper and more resilient organizational effectiveness. A leader embracing an attitude of cultural relativism by requiring group exercises in cultural openness has a great opportunity to expand on the efficiencies gained with a diverse workforce by nurturing the Level 2 relationships that turn cultural diversity into cultural synergy.

## Note

1 Copyright © Edgar H. Schein & Peter A. Schein, Reflections on Diversity and Inclusion, January 18, 2019.

## References

Edmondson, A. C. (2012). *Teaming: How organizations learn, innovate, and, compete in the knowledge economy*. Hoboken, NJ: John Wiley & Sons.

Lewin, K. (1947). Group decision and social change. In T. N. Newcomb & E. L. Hartley (Eds.), *Readings in social psychology* (pp. 197–211). New York: Holt, Rinehart & Winston.

Salk, J. (1997). Partners and other strangers: Cultural boundaries and cross-cultural encounters in international joint venture teams. *International Studies of Management and Organizations*, *26*(4), 48–72. https://doi.org/10.1080/00208825.1996.11656694

Schein, E. H. (2016). *Humble consulting: How to provide real help faster*. Oakland, CA: Berrett-Koehler.

Schein, E. H., & Schein, P. A. (2017). *Organizational culture and leadership* (5th ed.) Hoboken, NJ: John Wiley & Sons.

Schein, E. H., & Schein, P. A. (2018). *Humble leadership: The power of relationships, openness, and trust*. Oakland, CA: Berrett-Koehler.

# Part II

# Leadership Practices for Fostering and Benefiting from Inclusive Interpersonal and Team Dynamics

# 6 Inclusive Leadership in Complex Times

## Leading with Vulnerability and Integrity

*Ilene C. Wasserman*

This chapter takes a relational communication perspective on two critical qualities of inclusive leadership in complex times: vulnerability and integrity. There are many characterizations of our current social context as being complex, including the description of a VUCA (volatile, uncertain, complex, ambiguous) culture, wicked problems (Buchanan, 1992), permanent white water (Vaill, 1996), or just times of uncertainty, risk, and emotional exposure (Brown, 2012). The challenges to leading in complex times are less about the technical challenges, which trained specialists can address. The greater challenges are the adaptive ones, which involve situations in which there is no clear answer and issues that require experimentation and improvisation (Heifetz & Laurie, 1997; Heifetz & Linsky, 2002; Heifetz et al., 2009). Adaptive challenges most often involve values, beliefs, roles, relationships, and are best addressed not by any one of us, but by bringing together different perspectives. The process of leading inclusively involves creating the conditions that increase the likelihood that differences will be noticed, sought out, and valued. It also involves shaping cultures that secure the scaffolding that supports those conditions.

The relational communication perspective suggests that inclusive leadership is something we create in relationships—in the rhythm of relational practices—to foster the conditions for engaging the strengths and full capacity of all people in the organization (McCauley et al., 2010; McNamee, 2016; Uhl-Bien, 2006). Doing this requires both vulnerability and integrity. *Vulnerability* is the "willingness, in a particular moment, to let go of knowing and certainty—freeing oneself from normal habits of … grasping for guarantees and for knowledge as a possession" (Pearce, 2014, p. 4). *Integrity* is the commitment to the expression of honesty in alignment with one's moral principles. Both are qualities produced in relational processes between and among leaders and members of the organization that support more inclusive cultures.

After introducing the key concepts of inclusive leadership in times of complexity, of vulnerability, and of integrity, I share two stories that exemplify vulnerability and integrity as critical expressions of inclusive leadership. One story is from the 25th Kravis-deRoulet Leadership Conference, *Inclusive Leadership: Transforming Diverse Lives, Workplaces, and Societies*, which took place in March 2017 at Claremont McKenna College (and on which this volume is based), and the second is a composite story from my work as an executive coach with senior leaders who are committed to developing their capacity for leading inclusively.

## Leading Inclusively: Being Vulnerable with Integrity

The contemporary business landscapes of organizations have been characterized by complexity, ambiguity, uncertainty, and interdependence (Wasserman & Blake-Beard, 2010). This characterization builds on that of VUCA, which stands for volatility, uncertainty, complexity, and ambiguity, a term grounded in work by Bennis and Nanus (1985) and initially developed by the U.S. military (Kinsinger & Walch, 2012).

So, what are the conditions of complexity? Information is generating at an accelerated pace. The people we encounter and work with are different from us on many dimensions of diversity (including race, age/generation, nationality, culture, faith orientation, profession, function, social class, lifestyle and family structure, political ideology, and perhaps many others). The requirements of leaders to process information, make decisions, and make the most of tangible and relational resources at hand are significant (Ruderman & Chrobot-Mason, 2010; Ruderman et al., 2010). The process of meaning-making in each moment is shaped and influenced by the people and context in which we are engaging (Gergen, 2009) and there are many contexts in which to contend.

Complex issues are adaptive challenges, challenges for which there are not simple right answers (Heifetz & Linsky, 2002). Such issues are unpredictable and unknowable. Under such conditions, small actions can have big impacts and causes and effects are not clearly linked (Snowden & Boone, 2007). Robert Johansen (2012) suggests that surviving and thriving in this chaotic environment calls for a different VUCA response: vision, understanding, clarity, and agility.

Inclusive leadership extends our thinking beyond assimilation strategies or organizational demography to empowerment and participation of all, by removing obstacles that cause exclusion and marginalization. This involves skills and competencies for relational practice, collaboration, building inclusion for others, partnerships and consensus building, and true engagement of all (Ferdman, 2010; Mor Barak & Travis, 2010). Ferdman (2010) makes the important link between leadership and creating cultures of inclusion when he suggests that attention to inclusion pushes the envelope for leaders, because the required skill set involves an increasing capacity for complexity.

This kind of response likens to the qualities of inclusive leadership. Booysen (2014) defines inclusive leadership as:

> an ongoing cycle of learning through collaborative and respectful relational practice that enables individuals and collectives to be fully part of the whole such that they are directed, aligned and committed toward the shared outcomes for the common good of all while retaining a sense of authenticity and uniqueness.
>
> (Booysen, 2014, p. 306)

Additionally, we are interdependent. Our interdependence means that leaders need to shift their approach from directing and driving to framing, inviting, exploring, reflecting, synthesizing, and incorporating other perspectives and new ways of making meaning in relation to those perspectives (Booysen, 2014; Wasserman & Blake-Beard, 2010). This shift engenders a sense of vulnerability—letting go of being the one with the answers—to literally and metaphorically recognizing and inviting the wisdom in the room. Instilling the conditions for an inclusive culture calls for both creating a sense of vulnerability and taking a stance of integrity.

Leaders, as the shapers of the organization's culture, need to be the voice of a unified meta-narrative that supports a vision of an inclusive culture (Wasserman et al., 2008). The challenges to leading with vulnerability and integrity are especially evident when the need for a unified meta-narrative is in tension with forces that pull us to simplistic categorizations and polarizations.

In the next section I elaborate on these tensions and explore these skills and competencies from the standpoint of how, by engaging with vulnerability and integrity, we can create inclusive leadership in relationship with each other.

## Leading Inclusively: The Capacity for Complexity

If we consider inclusive leadership to be a relational construct—one that is determined, communicated, and negotiated in relationships—how do we know, as Ferdman (2014) asks, "whether a particular organizational practice or individual behavior is inclusive?" (p. 15). He goes on to assert that, "ultimately, [this determination] should be based on whether those affected by the practice or behavior feel and are included. At the core, and particularly from a psychological perspective, inclusion needs to be conceptualized phenomenologically—in other words, in terms of people's perceptions and interpretations" (p. 15).

This raises the question as to whether inclusive leadership is a *something* that exists independently of a relationship, or whether instead, inclusive leadership, by design, is only present and affirmed if it is both experienced as such by others and it helps to create an inclusive culture. In this regard, Gergen (2009) proposes that all meaning results from coordinated action:

> In all that we say and do, we manifest conditions of relationship. In whatever we think, remember, create, and feel—in all that is meaningful to us—we participate in relationship. The word "I" does not index an origin of action, but a relational achievement.
>
> (Gergen, 2009, p. 133)

Inclusive leaders demonstrate self and relational awareness, seek out multiple voices and perspectives, and listen deeply (Gallegos, 2014). Doing so requires involving a sense of vulnerability to suspend what one knows and the way one knows, as well as a degree of agility and a capacity for engaging complexity (Wasserman & Durishin, 2014). As already stated, these capacities are especially critical at times when our public discourse is characterized by polarized narratives of what is valued, who is valued, and what constitutes social justice.

At the interpersonal level, agility and the capacity for complexity are aspects of adult development (Kegan, 1994). At the group, team, and organizational levels, these capacities both require and create cultures that accommodate and encourage vulnerability, humility, and inquiry. Vulnerability and humility are traits that expand the leader's stance from one of being all knowing to that of seeing opportunities to perceive lessons to be learned from others (Gallegos, 2014; Wasserman & Gallegos, 2009).

Kegan (1994) created a model of adult development that describes level of consciousness as the increasing capacity for complexity. The conditions of our social worlds require a degree of capacity to be able to stand apart from and observe how we are engaging, while, at the same time, determining what to do next. This process requires a degree of self-awareness and relational awareness, to notice what might be our reactive or taken-for-granted response, and to pause, to critically evaluate what we may have culturally inherited or may have framed from our experiences, and to include and incorporate other considerations (Wasserman, 2014). As already stated, these capacities are especially critical at times when our public discourse is characterized by polarized narratives of what is valued and who is valued. The capacity to hold one's stance with integrity while considering other, potentially competing perspectives is a more sophisticated understanding of how self, relationships, and large social systems function systemically and mutually influence each other.

Pearce (2014) describes the shift to this level of self-awareness as a miracle because it opens vistas for how we can go on together. At this level of self and relational awareness, we have our beliefs rather than our beliefs having us. Having the agility to be ourselves while being able to see ourselves, we are poised to change, to evolve, and, potentially, to make things better.

In the next section I introduce the NOREN model (Wasserman & Fisher-Yoshida, 2017) as a process for critical self-reflection in relationship.

## The Systemic Practice of Inclusive Leadership: The NOREN Model

The NOREN Model (Wasserman & Fisher-Yoshida, 2017; see Figure 6.1)—named for an acronym that stands for notice, observe, reflect, engage, and notice again—outlines a process of refection-in-action for observing oneself at the same time as one engages with others. Leading inclusively with vulnerability and integrity requires the capacity to notice what one is doing and to hold a stance of inquiry with the social world one is simultaneously creating with others in the process of engaging in communicative acts. The relational communication perspective focuses our attention to the patterns we are making together in relationships—be they interpersonal, team, or organizational.

For some, the challenge of noticing is to strengthen their capacity to be the observer. For others, the challenge is more about self-authorizing and valuing one's voice, or, as described in the NOREN process, engaging. As noted by hooks (1989), for some, owning one's voice and the value one has to offer in speaking up is a process, not a one-time accomplishment. The recursive processes of engaging and observing and engaging again are intentional enactments of inclusive leadership.

As leaders navigate increasingly diverse contexts, they will need to be in touch not only with what they know but also the way they know. In looking at how they know, inclusive leaders need to notice their so-

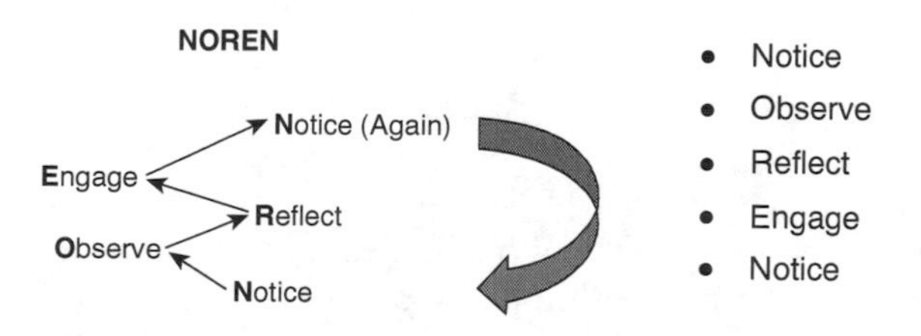


*Figure 6.1* NOREN: Notice; Observe; Reflect; Engage; Notice again. (Wasserman & Fisher-Yoshida, 2017, p. 80)

called taken-for-granted assumptions, and how these affect how they show up with others and what they do in those interactions. Reflective tools such as the NOREN process support critical self-reflection and the capacity for transformative learning and transforming relationships (Mezirow, 1991, 2000).

In the next section I offer two examples of reflecting on leading inclusively. One example is from an activity that my colleague Laura Morgan Roberts and I facilitated to engage the group of attendees—faculty, students, and practitioners—at the 25th Kravis-deRoulet Leadership Conference (the event where initial versions of many of the chapters in this volume were first presented). The second example is a composite from a coaching context related to developing the skills of leading inclusively.

## Leading Inclusively: Articulating the Principles through Shared Storytelling and Reflection

> I can tell you that what I've tried to do since I started ... is communicate the notion that America is a critical actor and leader on the world stage ... but that we exercise our leadership best when we are listening; when we recognize the world is a complicated place ... when we lead by example; when we show some element of humility and recognize that we may not always have the best answer, but we can always encourage ... and support the best answer.
>
> (President Barack Obama, G-20, 2009)

### *Discovering the Qualities of Inclusive Leadership in a Group Setting*

Complex adaptive issues benefit from bringing together all voices and intentionally mining the ongoing meaning that is negotiated and perpetuated in the interaction such that people in relationships can influence one another. My colleague, Laura Morgan Roberts, and I were invited to design and facilitate an interactive session at the 25th Kravis-deRoulet Leadership Conference, *Inclusive Leadership: Transforming Diverse Lives, Workplaces, and Societies*, in March 2017 at Claremont McKenna College. As Obama states, we exercise our leadership best when we are listening and when we recognize that the world is a complicated place. We based our approach in part on this perspective.

Roberts and I designed and facilitated a process that honored the wisdom in the room by inviting participants to define inclusive leadership through a process of reflecting on times or episodes when they experienced it, and mining those stories to articulate what it means to be an inclusive leader. The design outlined in the appendix (at the end of this chapter) was grounded in the theoretical frameworks of appreciative inquiry (Cooperrider et al., 2005; Whitney & Trosten-Bloom, 2013) and the relational communication perspective. Both appreciative inquiry and the relational communication perspective are based on the theory that we actively create meaning in our social interactions. The relational communication perspective invites us to look at how we coordinate meaning together, and to see that as continuously emerging in each turn of our communicative acts. It is in these acts that we are continuously making and shaping identity, relationships, organizations, communities, and cultures through arguments, collaboration, conflict, and relationships (Pearce, 2007; Wasserman & Fisher-Yoshida, 2017). We do so through telling *stories* (Pearce & Cronen, 1980). The principles of appreciative inquiry invite conversations to elevate the stories of the positive core of what people already know, to imagine what is possible, to define what could be, and then determine what to do to make that come to life. Because there are multiple ways of telling stories as well as of interpreting them, it is important to develop the skill and capacity to look at what stories we choose to tell, how we are telling them, and how we are making sense of them in the emerging moments we create together.

From the relational communication perspective, inclusive leadership is something we are doing and creating together in the rhythm of leading and following in support of inclusion (Hollander, 2009). It shifts the construct of communication from seeing it as moving information from one mind to another to the idea that communication performs meaning. For leaders, the associated skills include:

- recognizing the limitations of one's individual perspective;
- valuing the wider possibilities created by engaging diverse perspectives;
- seeing reality as continuously emerging in communicative processes among people;
- listening to the unique needs of others to support their voice; and
- noticing and opening to the humility and vulnerability of *not knowing*.

Thus, what constitutes inclusive leadership from a personal, positional, cultural, and systemic perspective is something we can discover by mining our stories of our experiences.

At the conference, after people engaged at their tables, we invited them to share highlights from their conversations. The themes we heard about the qualities of inclusive leaders are paraphrased and synthesized as follows:

- An inclusive leader is not necessarily the person who has the title, but one who inspires people to enter the circle.
- Inclusion is more than the ability to flex; it is the capacity to see more in others than they see in themselves.

- Inclusive leaders invite others in; they are connectors to opportunities and share their leadership with others, and do so with humility.
- Inclusive leadership emphasizes commonality and unique contributions, doing so without creating hierarchy.
- Inclusive leadership requires a dynamic approach to hearing different perspectives—to listening—with empathy and to being willing to engage the messiness of unfolding meaning.

The very qualities that participants identified from exploring their own affirmative experiences with inclusive leadership aligned with what we read in the literature. We then asked: what are the conditions that support inclusive leadership? We heard responses focusing on personal qualities, structure, and processes, captured by the following themes:

- Create conditions for people to know and understand each other, such as face-to-face opportunities. It is easier to be civil with people when you are with them in person.
- Put in place structural rules to invite, attend to, and listen to the counter point of view, particularly the perspectives of outliers or those in the minority. This involves doing what is needed to support a sense of safety (Edmondson, 1999).
- Civility needs rules for engagement, paradoxically allowing us to engage in our different ways while keeping some things out of bounds. We need to consider how what you need interferes with my boundaries, and vice versa, for example.

Enacting or performing inclusive leadership with vulnerability and integrity requires the capacity to notice what one is doing to hold a stance of inquiry with the social world one is simultaneously creating with others in the process of engaging in communicative acts. The relational communication perspective focuses our attention to the patterns we are making together in relationships—be they interpersonal, team, or organizational.

### *Discovering the Challenges and Opportunities of Becoming a More Inclusive Leader*

The second example comes from my coaching experience, and is grounded in Kegan and Lahey's (2001, 2009) immunity to change (ITC) model. The ITC model supports self-reflection, self-awareness, and insight, particularly when addressing improvement goals that address adaptive challenges, goals that are deeply challenged by competing commitments. Here I offer a mapping of a composite of clients who were seeking to develop their capacity for leading inclusively, as well as for embracing and modeling vulnerability.

In one instance, my client aspired to be a more inclusive leader, yet was struggling to let others take on more responsibility. He wanted to delegate and include more and do less "micro-managing." Table 6.1 outlines the process we used to address this goal.

Another client highlights the other side of the continuum. The feedback she gets from those who work with and for her is that her commitment to humility and modesty short-changes the visibility of her team. Table 6.2 outlines the process we worked on to support her in speaking up more, thereby elevating the voices of the team and supporting their fullest contribution.

As we learned from the participants at the conference described earlier, an inclusive leader is not necessarily the person who has the title, but one who inspires people to enter the circle, who institutionalizes vulnerability and authenticity in service of expanding capabilities and growing together.

*Table 6.1* Delegating and including more; micro-managing less.

| *Improvement goal* | *Behaviors that interfere* | *Hidden competing commitments* | *Big assumptions or fears* |
|---|---|---|---|
| Delegating and including more; micro-managing less | I am involved in everything and every meeting.<br>I double check everything I delegate.<br>People need to prove that they can deliver superior outcomes before I trust them. | I am responsible for the success of the business and want to make sure it is perfect.<br>I want to be valued and seen as the person delivering results. | If I am not involved, the business will fail.<br>If I delegate, I give up power and prestige and risk my social standing. |

*Table 6.2* Promoting the achievements of the team.

| *Improvement goal* | *Behaviors that interfere* | *Hidden competing commitments* | *Big assumptions or fears* |
|---|---|---|---|
| Promoting the achievements of the team by speaking up. | I wait until I think I have enough information.<br>I wait for an invitation to speak. | I want to be certain I have done my research and that what I say is valued.<br>I value giving others credit and not being self-aggrandizing. | If I initiate speaking up I will be seen as boastful and self-serving. |

Inclusive leadership requires practicing vulnerability with integrity. Building on the ITC model, Kegan and Lahey (2016), along with colleagues, encourage using the model as a systemic practice to create what they call an *everyone culture*. They encourage leadership teams and teams throughout the organization to develop and share their ITC map with others on their teams. In doing so, they enact a sense of vulnerability, humility, and integrity with each other, and engender support for each other in their commitments to ongoing development for themselves and others around them.

## Conclusion

Complex times create adaptive challenges. Inclusive leadership may be less about having a definable list of attributes and more about how we create the conditions for including, such that all people, even those who typically feel marginalized, are actively engaged. Providing relational leadership in today's diverse organizations is anything but simple, as I and a co-author noted elsewhere:

> Our interdependence means that leaders need to shift their focus from themselves as creating and transmitting leadership to being a leader who invites, considers, and incorporates other perspectives and new ways of making meaning in relation to those perspectives. These are the essential ingredients for leading well in today's complex organizational reality.
>
> (Wasserman & Blake-Beard, 2010, p. 206)

We feel a culture of inclusion when there is the presence of a set of conditions and processes that invite conversation and explore shared meaning in order to resolve the most complex problems. As we learned from Ernst and Yip (2009), "solutions to adaptive challenges reside not in the executive suite but in the collective intelligence of employees at all levels, who need to use one another as resources, often across boundaries, and learn their way to those solutions" (p. 124). Complex times require more flexible structures and the skills to extend the invitation for people to fully engage, not necessarily as individuals but in multiple configurations to spark new ways of thinking and engaging. President Obama spoke to this at the G-20 meetings in 2016:

> The complicated challenges of the 21st century cannot be met without coordinated and collective action. Agreement is not always easy, and results do not always come quickly. Respecting different points of view; forging consensus instead of dictating terms—that can sometimes be frustrating. But it is how progress has been won and how it will be won in the future.
>
> (Obama, 2016)

The qualities, performances, conditions, and structures that create inclusive leadership in complex times, are, at the core, the capacity to be vulnerable, to suspend being all-knowing, and to be truly curious and open to possibilities that may not otherwise be anticipated. This sense of vulnerability is based on a sense of trust and also creates trusting conditions that both model and invite conversations that explore differences. Leading inclusively manifests in integrity, using personal experiences strategically. Further, inclusive leadership is aligned and supported by the culture of the organization with policies and everyday practices (Holvino et al., 2004; Nishii & Rich, 2014).

Leaders, as the shapers of the organization's culture, need to be the voice of a unified meta-narrative that supports a vision of an inclusive culture (Wasserman et al., 2008). As my colleagues and I have pointed out, "[c]reating and maintaining an inclusive culture is a complex and ongoing process that requires continuous self-examination and thoughtful reflection by leaders and all members of the organization" (Wasserman et al., 2008, p. 181). Specifically, we elaborate on four things leaders must do to foster cultures of inclusion:

> 1 Explicitly define (and redefine) the boundaries and rules for acceptable behavior.
> 2 Create the conditions for conversations to explore differences.
> 3 Model and communicate an understanding of and valuing of (and comfort with) diversity.
> 4 Be authentic and use personal experiences strategically.
>
> (pp. 186–187)

As we experienced at the 2017 Kravis-deRoulet conference, *Inclusive Leadership: Transforming Diverse Lives, Workplaces, and Societies*, the definition of what inclusive leadership looks like is a continuous exploration that deepens and expands when explored in dialogue. Further, we continue to learn more about the conditions and processes that support the ongoing engagement of people, from the margins to the center, when we invite the conversation and shared meaning-making. The invitation to vulnerability and integrity involved in engaging with inquiry feeds the continuous exploration and institutionalization of the leadership behaviors, process and social network characteristics, and actions that foster inclusive leadership and inclusive cultures.

## References

Bennis, W., & Nanus, B. (1985). *Leaders: The strategies for taking charge.* New York, NY: Harper & Row.

Booysen, L. (2014). The development of inclusive leadership practices and processes. In B. M. Ferdman & B. R. Deane (Eds.), *Diversity at work: The practice of inclusion* (pp. 296–329). San Francisco, CA: Jossey-Bass. https://doi.org/10.1002/9781118764282.ch10

Brown, B. (2012). *Daring greatly: How the courage to be vulnerable transforms the way we live, love, parent and lead.* New York, NY: Gotham Books.

Buchanan, R. (1992). Wicked problems in design thinking. *Design Issues, 8* (2), 5–21.

Cooperrider, D. L., Sorenson, P., Yaeger, T., & Whitney, D. (2005). *Appreciative inquiry: Foundations in positive organization development.* Chicago, IL: Stipes Publishing.

Edmondson, A. (1999). Psychological safety and learning behavior in work teams. *Administrative Science Quarterly, 44*, 350–383. https://doi.org/10.2307/2666999

Ernst, C., & Yip, J. (2009). Boundary spanning leadership: Tactics to bridge social identity groups in organizations. In T. L. Pittinsky (Ed.), *Crossing the divide: Intergroup leadership in a world of difference* (pp. 89–99). Boston, MA: Harvard Business School Press.

Ferdman, B. M. (2010). Teaching inclusion by example and experience: Creating an inclusive learning environment. In B. B. McFeeters, K. M. Hannum, & L. Booysen (Eds.), *Leading across differences: Cases and perspectives—Facilitator's guide* (pp. 37–50). San Francisco, CA: Pfeiffer.

Ferdman, B. M. (2014). The practice of inclusion in diverse organizations: Toward a systemic and inclusive framework. In B. M. Ferdman & B. R. Deane (Eds.), *Diversity at work: The practice of inclusion* (pp. 3–54). San Francisco, CA: Jossey-Bass. https://doi.org/10.1002/9781118764282.ch1

Gallegos, P. (2014). The work of inclusive leadership: Fostering authentic relationships, modeling courage and humility. In B. M. Ferdman & B. R. Deane (Eds.), *Diversity at work: The practice of inclusion* (pp. 177–202). San Francisco: Jossey-Bass. https://doi.org/10.1002/9781118764282.ch6

Gergen, K. (2009). *Relational beings: Beyond self and community.* New York, NY: Oxford University Press.

Heifetz, R. A., & Laurie, D. L. (1997). The work of leadership. *Harvard Business Review, 75*(1), 124–134.

Heifetz, R. A., & Linsky, M. (2002). *Leadership on the line: Staying alive through the dangers of leading.* Boston, MA: Harvard Business School Press.

Heifetz, R. A., Linsky, M., & Alexander, G. (2009). *The practice of adaptive leadership: Tools and tactics for changing your organization and the world.* Boston, MA: Harvard Business School Press.

Hollander, E. P. (2009). *Inclusive leadership: The essential leader-follower relationship.* New York, NY: Routledge.

Holvino, E., Ferdman, B. M., & Merrill-Sands, D. (2004). Creating and sustaining diversity and inclusion in organizations: Strategies and approaches. In M. S. Stockdale & F. J. Crosby (Eds.), *The psychology and management of workplace diversity* (pp. 245–276). Malden, MA: Blackwell.

hooks, b. (1989). When I was a young soldier for the revolution: Coming to voice. In b. hooks, (Ed.). *Talking back: Thinking feminist, thinking Black* (pp. 10–18). Boston, MA: South End Press.

Johansen, B. (2012). *Leaders make the future.* San Francisco, CA: Berrett-Koehler.

Kegan, R. (1994). *In over our heads: The mental demands of modern life.* Cambridge, MA: Harvard University Press.

Kegan, R., & Lahey, L. (2001). *How the way we talk can change the way we work: Seven languages for transformation*. San Francisco, CA: Jossey-Bass.
Kegan, R., & Lahey, L. (2009). *Immunity to change: How to overcome it and unlock the potential in yourself and your organization*. Boston, MA: Harvard Business School Press.
Kegan, R., & Lahey, L. (2016). *An everyone culture: Becoming a deliberately developmental organization*. Boston, MA: Harvard Business Review Press.
Kinsinger, P. & Walch, K. (2012, July 9). *Living and leading in a VUCA world*. Thunderbird School of Global Management Knowledge Network. https://web.archive.org/web/20120809043242/http://knowledgenetwork.thunderbird.edu/research/2012/07/09/kinsinger-walch-vuca
McCauley, C., van Velsor, E., & Ruderman, M. (2010). Introduction: Our view of leadership development. In E. van Velsor, C. McCauley, & M. Ruderman (Eds.), *The Center for Creative Leadership handbook of leadership development* (3rd ed., pp. 1–22). San Francisco, CA: Jossey-Bass.
McNamee, S. (2016). The ethics of relational process: John Shotter's radical presence. In T. Corcoran & J. Cromby (Eds.), *Joint action: Essays in honor of John Shotter* (pp. 128–146). London, England: Routledge.
Mezirow, J. A. (1991). *Transformative dimensions of adult learning*. San Francisco, CA: Jossey-Bass.
Mezirow, J. A. (2000). *Learning as transformation: Critical perspectives on a theory in progress*. San Francisco. CA: Jossey-Bass.
Mor Barak, M. E., & Travis, D. J. (2010). Diversity and organizational performance. In Y. Hasenfeld (Ed.), *Human services as complex organizations* (2nd ed., pp. 341–378). Thousand Oaks, CA: Sage.
Nishii, L. H., & Rich, R. E. (2014). Creating inclusive climates in diverse organizations. In B. M. Ferdman & B. R. Deane (Eds.), *Diversity at work: The practice of inclusion* (pp. 330–363). San Francisco, CA: Jossey-Bass. https://doi.org/10.1002/9781118764282.ch11
Obama, B. H. (2009). G-20 Speech [www.politics.co.uk/feature/foreign-policy/london-g20-summit-obama-takes-the-world-stage.htm]
Obama, B. H. (2016). G-20 Speech [https://obamawhitehouse.archivesgov/the-press-office/2016/09/05/press-conference-president-obama-after-g20-summit]
Pearce, W. B. (2007). *Making social worlds: A communication perspective*. Malden, MA: Blackwell.
Pearce, W. B. (2014). At home in the universe with miracles and horizons. In S. Littlejohn & S. McNamee (Eds.), *The coordinated management of meaning: A festschrift in honor of W. Barnett Pearce* (pp. 1–48). Madison, NJ: Fairleigh Dickinson University Press.
Pearce, W. B., & Cronen, V. (1980). *Communication, action and meaning*. New York, NY: Praeger.
Ruderman, M. N., & Chrobot-Mason, D. (2010). Triggers of social identity conflict. In K. Hannum, B. B. McFeeters, & L. Booysen (Eds.), *Leading across differences: Cases and perspectives* (pp. 81–86). San Francisco, CA: Pfeiffer.
Ruderman, M. N., Glover, S., Chrobot-Mason, D., & Ernst, C. (2010). Leadership practices across social identity groups. In K. Hannum, B. B. McFeeters, & L. Booysen (Eds.), *Leading across differences: Cases and perspectives* (pp. 95–114). San Francisco, CA: Pfeiffer.

Snowden, D. J., & Boone, M. E. (2007). A leader's framework for decision-making. *Harvard Business Review, 85*(11), 69–76.

Uhl-Bien, M. (2006). Relational leadership theory: Exploring the social processes of leadership and organizing. *Leadership Quarterly, 17*(6), 645–676. https://doi.org/10.1016/j.leaqua.2006.10.007

Vaill, P. B. (1996). *Learning as a way of being: Strategies for survival in a world of permanent white water*. San Francisco, CA: Jossey-Bass.

Wasserman, I. C. (2014). Strengthening interpersonal awareness and fostering relational eloquence. In B. M. Ferdman & B. R. Deane (Eds.), *Diversity at work: The practice of inclusion* (pp. 128–154). San Francisco, CA: Jossey-Bass. https://doi.org/10.1002/9781118764282.ch4

Wasserman, I. C., & Blake-Beard, S. (2010). Leading inclusively: Mind- sets, skills and actions for a diverse, complex world. In K. Bunker, T. Hall, & K. Kram (Eds.), *Extraordinary leadership: Addressing the gaps in senior executive development* (pp. 197–212). San Francisco: Jossey-Bass.

Wasserman, I. C., & Durishin, L. (2014). Culture change and strategic conversations: Adaptive leadership in action. *International Journal of Appreciative Inquiry, 16*(1), 37–41. https://doi.org/10.12781/978-1-907549-18-2-7

Wasserman, I. C., & Fisher-Yoshida, B. (2017). *Communicating possibilities: A brief introduction to the Coordinated Management of Meaning*. Taos Institute Press.

Wasserman, I. C., & Gallegos, P. V. (2009). Engaging diversity: Disorienting dilemmas that transform relationships. In B. Fisher-Yoshida, K. D. Geller, & S. A. Schapiro (Eds.), *Innovations in transformative learning: Space, culture, and the arts* (pp. 155–175). New York, NY: Peter Lang.

Wasserman, I. C., Gallegos, P. V., & Ferdman, B. M. (2008). Dancing with resistance: Leadership challenges in fostering a culture of inclusion. In K. M. Thomas (Ed.), *Diversity resistance in organizations* (pp. 175–200). Mahwah, NJ: Erlbaum.

Whitney, D., & Trosten-Bloom, A. (2013). *The power of appreciative inquiry*. San Francisco, CA: Berrett Kohler.

# Appendix to Chapter 6
## What is Inclusive Leadership?

### Invitation

Please pair up with one other person in the room—preferably someone you do not know and someone who is different from you in some way—generationally, racially, culturally, etc. In these pairs you will engage in an inclusive leadership discovery. You will take turns being the interviewer and the storyteller, and will have the opportunity to share with your partner about an experience of inclusive leadership.

In times like these, the notion of inclusion seems to be challenged in the public sphere. Broadcast journalism and blog posts report some discourse around who doesn't fit and who shouldn't be allowed. On a daily basis, some people are less included than others, and some people are less valued.

*And yet*, there are many places where the value of inclusive leadership is evident; where leaders are stepping up and being ever bolder about embracing and welcoming the richness of diversity.

### Inclusive Leadership Discovery: Part 1

Think about a time when you experienced inclusive leadership/leading. You may be the subject, or it may be someone you admired for their ability to notice and engage others—particularly those who, often, experience themselves to be on the margin. What was it about the person, the group, and/or the organization that created that sense of inclusive leadership? *Make some notes to yourself.*

### Inclusive Leadership Discovery: Part 2

Join with two other pairs. With your group:

Mine each story for what we can learn about the conditions, qualities, etc. that foster inclusive leadership in relationships. Identify common themes across stories, as well as key distinctions in how you think about and experience inclusive leadership. As a group, develop a list of "inclusive leadership catalysts."

## Proactive Inclusive Leadership

As you plan to take a more proactive role in facilitating inclusive leadership in your workplace, school, or community: what *capabilities* have you developed through your experiences of counteracting marginalization and exclusion, while promoting inclusion (your own or others)? What *insights* have you developed through your experiences of counteracting marginalization and exclusion, while promoting inclusion (your own or others)? What *relationships* have you cultivated through your experiences of counteracting marginalization and exclusion, while promoting inclusion (your own or others)?

Opening activity at *Inclusive Leadership: Transforming Diverse Lives, Workplaces, and Societies*, 25th Kravis-deRoulet Leadership Conference, created by I. C. Wasserman & L. M. Roberts, 2017.

# 7 Inclusive Leadership Practices

## The Power of Microbehaviors[1]

*Doyin Atewologun and Charlotte Harman*

This chapter contributes to understanding how leadership practices can help build inclusive organizations through the power of everyday behaviors. Specifically, we examine how everyday encounters between individuals who occupy varying levels of socially ascribed privilege result in feelings of inclusion or non-inclusion.

First, we shed light on inclusion as understood from the lived experience of minority-status organizational members in everyday encounters. Second, we demonstrate how overtly positive (i.e., inclusive) or negative (i.e., exclusionary) practices can be complex and may not be necessarily interpreted as mutually exclusive categories of positive/inclusive and nonpositive/exclusionary experiences. Individuals who are the "targets" of such practices are not passive in response to these experiences; they actively engage with and try to negotiate their perceptions of, and responses to, these practices of inclusion and exclusion (Lofland, Snow, Anderson, & Lofland, 2005). Thus, we discuss the importance of understanding how others who may have inclusive leadership "done" to them observe, understand, and also proactively manage or reconstruct experiences relating to inclusive leadership.

We also discuss practical implications, including the idea that the responsibility for sustaining inclusive work cultures rests beyond formal leadership positions, and that this challenges organizational members—line managers and team leaders alike—to demonstrate relationship-based, "other-focused" leadership by learning about the ubiquitous nature of everyday behaviors and other powerful, yet subtle, approaches for cultivating inclusive cultures.

### What is Inclusive Leadership?

Inclusive leadership is the extent to which individuals in positions of organizational privilege and power enable others' access to information, resources, and participation in decision-making by being open and available to less powerful others (Nembhard & Edmondson, 2006; Roberson, 2006; Ryan, 2006). It is associated with outcomes such as empowerment (Hollander, 2009), the creation of psychologically safe environments in which individuals feel comfortable being themselves (Edmondson, 1999), and subsequent improved learning and performance (Hirak, Peng, Carmeli, & Schaubroeck, 2012).

Inclusive leadership helps to explain the impact leaders can have on individuals who differ in their access, involvement, and organizational influence (for example, minority-status group members such as White women or women and men from minority ethnic backgrounds). When inclusive leaders share access and power with multiple team members (i.e., have high-quality leader–member exchange relationships), this attenuates the relationship between diversity and turnover (Nishii & Mayer, 2009). Although explicit research into inclusive leadership behavior and socio-demographic identity (e.g., gender, ethnicity, religion) is lacking, broader leadership research acknowledges the privilege inherent in leadership positions. This chapter therefore seeks to further enhance understanding of the nature of inclusive leadership, its impact on minority-status organizational members (i.e., individuals outside of the norm/majority group), and the practical implications for organizations, leaders, and individuals who may be on the receiving end of exclusionary or inclusive everyday leadership practices.

Focusing on all levels of analysis—intrapersonal, interpersonal, contextual, and structural—is important for meaningful understanding of inclusion, diversity, and inequalities at work (Ferdman, 2014; Syed & Özbilgin, 2009). This is because people's emotions, behaviors, actions, and interactions with colleagues, the organizational culture, and how society is organized, all contribute to explaining unequal outcomes in society. Power differentials between people, due to their membership in various social identity groups, are present at every one of these levels, "from identities and self-concepts, to interpersonal interactions, to the operation of firms, to the organization of economic and legal systems" (Browne & Misra, 2003, p. 490).

Power is a key process through which subtle acts legitimize some, and not other, individuals in organizations (Van Laer & Janssens, 2011). Theorists and empirical researchers (e.g., Atewologun et al., 2016; Cortina, 2008; Kenny & Briner, 2007; Van Laer & Janssens, 2011; Zanoni et al., 2010) emphasize the significance of everyday *micro-behaviors* featuring in the experiences of minority and less privileged individuals in society. Seemingly momentary ("micro") interactions can have a powerful impact on the behavior and engagement levels of minority status—demographically atypical or less powerful—organizational members. A focus on these micro-level interactions between privileged and less privileged others can contribute to understanding the nature of inclusive leader behaviors and, potentially, how minority members may anticipate, interpret, or respond to these behaviors at work.

Micro-behaviors are everyday acts that reinforce inclusion of similar others (positive micro-affirmations) and/or sustain exclusion of those who are different (negative micro-inequities) (Rowe, 2008). They are small, ephemeral, often unconscious acts, which, over time, result in including and affirming people (typically those with whom one is familiar and likes), while excluding others, typically those perceived as different (Rowe, 2008). In contrast to overt traditional expressions of racism and discrimination, such as aggressive acts, name calling or physical abuse, everyday racism is reproduced through routine and taken-for-granted practices and procedures in everyday life (Essed, 1991). Although some work has been conducted to understand micro-experiences of difference at work through everyday discrimination (e.g., Van Laer & Janssens, 2011) and workplace incivilities (Cortina, 2008), further research is required on micro-experiences of inclusion in organizations (Nishii & Mayer, 2009).

### *How is Inclusive Leadership Experienced?*

Research (e.g., Atewologun et al., 2016) indicates that minority status members face everyday encounters that signal their identities as minority status members. Minority status can be signaled based on one's social identity membership (e.g., female rather than male gender; Asian over White ethnicity) or formal rank or professional relationship. In the workplace, higher status individuals will regularly engage in actions that signal inclusion, enabling minority status colleagues' access to information, resources, and participation in decision-making, or demonstrate openness and availability to them. Some of these encounters can be interpersonal interactive experiences; they will occur during routine/familiar encounters (e.g., team meetings) as well as non-routine/unfamiliar contexts (e.g., new client meetings). Additionally, interactions can occur between parties who have relatively clear and structured role relationships (e.g., consultant to client, line manager to subordinate) as well as more fluid, emergent role relationships (e.g., during group discussions or networking events). Thus, experiences of inclusive leadership can happen across a broad range of contexts and within a wide definition of privilege, power, and status, rather than only in formal or more prescriptive (e.g., manager–subordinate/leader–follower) relationships.

### *Inclusive and Non-Inclusive Leadership Practices*

Similar to what has been found in clinical studies on how tiny everyday encounters with individuals can signal micro-aggressions (Sue et al., 2007), organizational experiences are also replete with cues signaling individuals' inclusion or exclusion, as illustrated in Table 7.1. The table draws attention to the everyday nature of these behaviors, experienced through colleagues' talk (i.e., verbal cues), colleagues' action (i.e., behavioral cues), and the physical spaces in which work occurs (i.e., environmental cues).

*Table 7.1* Illustrative forms of everyday inclusive and non-inclusive practices

| *Episodes* | *Verbal cues* | *Behavioral cues* | *Environmental cues* |
|---|---|---|---|
| Inclusive | Being greeted by name by a senior leader. Being invited to join the conversation when quiet or on the outskirts of the group. Being thanked for sharing a different view that is outside of that of the norm. | Being copied into a series of important decision-making email exchanges. Eye contact and nodding to encourage, even during halting or hesitant speech. Being greeted with a smile and warmth. | Observing wide demographic diversity in the room of a senior leader. Pictures of a diverse range of customers or icons hung around the office. Observing an office layout where individuals are seated in groups with mixed demographics/levels rather than in groups of similar individuals. |
| Non-inclusive | Absent offers of refreshments from dominant status group colleagues, signaling one's invisibility. Anglicizing a name (e.g., calling Juanpa "John") without the person's say-so. Talking over someone or taking credit for their comment in a high stakes meeting. | A client's limp handshake or facial expression, signaling disappointment or surprise when walking into the room. Not attending to, or disregarding someone's remarks because they were delivered in an unfamiliar accent and so were not understood. "High-fiving" male members but not female members of a team for fear the latter is inappropriate. | Observing an image of a homogeneous group titled "a high-performing team" in a PowerPoint presentation at a teambuilding event. Physical adjustments have not been made to a work station, disabling someone from doing their job. Informal relationship building only happens in the pub after work, when some individuals (e.g., working mothers or those who do not drink) have limited access to those settings. |

### *Inclusive and Exclusionary Leadership Practices*

Building on the table above, examples of inclusive leadership behaviors include sending messages of belonging through personal introductions, directed attention during high-stakes meetings, and involvement in critical decision-making. These inclusive leadership behaviors can be experienced through both formal and informal organizational processes and interactions.

One example of formal processes that can trigger inclusive leadership behavior is setting an organizational strategy that clearly encourages the contribution of different social identities to decisions, thus advocating the value of diverse perspectives to the organization. When nationality or ethnicity (e.g., Indian, Chinese, Japanese) is perceived as a tangible asset and valuable, an individual's minority status becomes more apparent as it is called out explicitly. This can lead to experiences that signal inclusion, which in turn can have a strong affirming impact on minority status employees. However, critics (e.g., Noon, 2010; Thomas & Ely, 1996) may challenge this approach to embracing diversity because making minority group status explicit heightens awareness of differences in status and may create a further gulf between majority and minority status groups. In addition, it may raise negative implications for those who are in a "minority group" but cannot contribute to the organization's strategy in a meaningful way. For example, what are the implications for individuals of minority sexual orientation or minority ethnic individuals who have culturally assimilated and do not self-identify as culturally different from the majority White group? What about employees from cultures considered irrelevant to prevailing business strategy (e.g., the Caribbean)? Or junior minority employees who may have limited access to high profile international clients/projects? Such individuals may have limited obvious cultural value to offer the business.

In contrast to these formal inclusive behaviors, other practices can be more informal, spontaneous, and less prescribed by business outcomes. Such "small" actions by significant others can range from ephemeral encounters (such as being recognized and called by name in passing in a corridor) to more direct acts of inclusion (such as when a dominant status colleague calls out observations of others being interrupted or others' ideas being co-opted). These small actions, repeated over time, eventually become normal practice and embedded into team and organizational cultures, signaling to newcomers that this is "the way we do things around here." This indicates that bottom-up and informal approaches to inclusion can supplement formal top-down approaches discussed in the previous paragraph.

Many leadership models (e.g., visionary, servant, authentic models) celebrate the positive and exemplary behaviors expected to be manifested by leaders. Thus, it may come as a surprise that behaviors enacted (or missed opportunities to act) by leaders, or those otherwise occupying varying levels of socially ascribed privilege, may be experienced as exclusionary by some colleagues. Even if unintentional, everyday cues can trigger a sense of exclusion that has long-term well-being implications (Deitch et al., 2003; Van Laer & Janssens, 2011).

Attention should be paid even to subtle contextual or environmental cues; for example, what images are projected and what do these mean? Attending a team-building workshop and projecting a homogeneous "high-performing team" image of all White men is perhaps deemed merely illustrative by the facilitator, but can serve as a cue that prevents colleagues who do not see themselves in this image from aspiring to be part of a "high-performing team."

Of course, individuals are not just passive targets of inclusive or exclusionary leadership practices. Indeed, much research demonstrates that minority-status individuals engage in agentic behavior to respond to this behavior by reconstructing and reaffirming themselves despite their subordinated status in organizational and social systems. Individuals could see themselves as resilient under stress, as agile across cultures or contexts, or as having complex and hybrid identities (e.g., Atewologun et al., 2016; Van Laer & Janssens, 2014). These coping responses suggest individuals are aware of the importance of having to assert oneself in the context of being marginalized (however inadvertently) due to one's social group membership.

Overall, employees tend to hold their leaders to higher standards. It is likely that those in hierarchically privileged/powerful positions (i.e., organizational leaders) will be expected to "know better" by avoiding inadvertent negative micro-behaviors. Further, it is likely that when there are formal and top down inclusion strategies, employees would expect that senior leaders are spearheading this change, and are, in fact, visible role models for inclusion. So, we join with other scholars (e.g., Brief et al., 2000) to highlight the role that those in authority have in sustaining micro-discriminatory practices against minority groups, and underscore the significant impact of organizational leaders in creating and challenging inclusive cultures. Thus, leaders need to translate inclusion as strategy into their everyday practice, and to be aware that their behaviors are likely to be even more scrutinized by minority and majority status employees looking up to them as role models for inclusive culture change.

## Implications

This chapter has highlighted how micro-behaviors can signal access, or the lack thereof, to resources, decision-making, and contact with socially privileged colleagues. Privileged others therefore have an important ongoing role to sustain or challenge non-inclusive workplace practices.

By examining interpersonal encounters between more and less privileged/powerful individuals, the chapter integrates thinking on leader inclusion/exclusion and micro-behaviors (micro-inequities and micro affirmations). However, there is certainly scope for ongoing empirical and theoretical development of some of the topics raised. Specific questions to be answered include: how do minority status individuals adopt dynamic responses to non-inclusive behaviors by privileged others (e.g., how do they challenge organizational leaders? How do they refute exclusionary practices directed at them?). Also, how can we increase awareness in instigators who may not be cognizant of the impact of exclusionary everyday behaviors? How do we increase awareness for observers and what are the best interventions to turn observers into active bystanders for inclusion?

### *Practical Implications*

The chapter draws attention to situations that may hamper the ability of minority status individuals (including demographically atypical individuals) to fully engage and connect with colleagues, while also offering pointers for leaders seeking to create affirming cultures in talk (verbal cues), action (behavioral cues), and in the physical work spaces they create (environmental cues). Some responsibility for inclusion rests beyond formal leadership positions on anyone perceived as having the authority to speak to these issues (e.g., HR, diversity & inclusion professionals, diversity champions, members of minority groups and networks). Studies have found that minority status individuals report one notable identity-salient encounter a week; that is, an encounter that makes them feel like an outsider (Atewologun et al., 2016). When colleagues, line managers, and team leaders who are dominant group members are aware of the frequency and normality of encounters that trigger awareness of difference—positively and negatively—they will be less likely to underestimate the impact of their talk, behavior, and the spaces they create on the lived experience of their minority status colleagues.

The findings also provide practical implications for improving workplace inclusion. When implementing inclusive leadership interventions, leaders should venture first to understand the concept of inclusive leadership and why it is important to them and their organization. This is particularly important because inclusive leadership behaviors may be experienced as disruptive and different when compared with stereotypical, traditional leadership behaviors that are more assertive and hierarchical in nature.

We have been working on developing such an intervention suite that includes inclusive leadership familiarization workshops and an inclusive leadership feedback tool (similar to a 360-degree feedback questionnaire). This intervention is designed to help leaders consider and receive feedback on the extent to which they are acting inclusively and give them insight into the everyday behaviors that they may not be consciously aware affect others. When taking part in the inclusive leadership feedback tool, it is very possible that leaders might receive negative ratings on these behaviors, yet typically receive positive feedback on other, traditional "leadership" competencies/behaviors. Not being used to this feedback, it would be easy for these leaders to reject the feedback or fail to engage fully with the findings, disregarding them as unimportant or irrelevant to good leadership. Therefore, it is important to socialize the concept upfront through workshops and other forms of communication (advocating what inclusive leadership means, what it looks like and feels like at the level of everyday experience, and why it is important), and follow up any interventions with structured coaching or development programs.

Further, we propose that in order to maximize buy-in from majority group members, it is important not to label everyday inclusive leadership practices as behaviors to improve "female" or "minority ethnic" outcomes. Doing so runs the risk of further exacerbating the in-group versus out-group relationship between social groups. Instead, organizations and inclusive leadership consultants should focus on how increasing inclusive leadership practices and reducing exclusionary (even if inadvertent) practices will benefit the entire workforce, by making it a more collaborative and facilitative environment for everyone involved. For a topic which can otherwise be quite conceptual, attention to micro-behaviors can provide a powerful way to translate inclusive leadership into meaningful everyday behavior for individuals to understand (both when socializing the topic and encouraging others to provide feedback on their leaders).

With regard to training on being more inclusive, learning about micro-behaviors may also offer insight into some of the subtle (and low effort) methods of promoting affirming and inclusive cultures. It is important to go beyond a traditional focus on addressing individual stereotypes and assumptions to highlighting and training managers on the differential impact of their everyday actions (Nishii & Mayer, 2009). Similarly, focus on inclusive leadership behavior helps shift away from awareness that comes from understanding that one is unconsciously biased (e.g., Kandola, 2009) to thinking about what one can actively do about it. It could provide a more positive message to help individuals understand what they can do rather than what they need to stop doing or what they cannot do, an approach typical of the compliance approach to diversity in organizations.

From the perspective of helping individuals on the receiving end of micro-behaviors in the workplace, one practical implication could be to hold workshops where these individuals come together to share their experiences. Providing such forums and facilitation could provide further examples of what exclusive and inclusive behaviors look like and how they can be addressed, and provide an opportunity for these individuals to generate solutions or learn from others around how best to actively manage exclusion. Such an intervention could help to tackle exclusive behavior in the workplace actively and on an ongoing basis.

## Concluding Remarks

Although we focus on increasing everyday inclusive practices, we note that true inclusion is about changing the system rather than assimilation or integration, and involves deep reflection on one's privileged status (Ryan, 2006) rather than a check list of inclusive leader behaviors to follow. Additionally, a focus on the micro level does not mean we ignore the powerful effect of contextual and structural influences in reinforcing difference and inequality in organizations. Undoubtedly, a multitude of factors at the macro level (e.g., history, legislation), meso level (e.g., organizational policy) and micro level (individual agency) influence issues of diversity, and ethnicity within it (Syed & Özbilgin, 2009). It is thus important to remain cognizant of both agency and structural dimensions, even if one chooses to focus on one.

In conclusion, it is important to pay attention to informal micro-behaviors because they sustain exclusion and encourage inclusion of certain groups at work. Inclusive leadership behaviors can be formal and informal, and exclusionary experiences can be refuted by targets of these practices. With this chapter we hope to help advance understanding of inclusive leadership, specifically the nature of cues that may signal belonging and leaders' responsibility to manage employees' experiences of these cues.

### Actions Leaders Can Take to Remodel and Institutionalize Inclusive Micro-Behaviors

Responsibility for inclusion rests beyond formal leadership positions with anyone perceived as having the authority to speak to these issues. Here, we list some actions that a wide range of people can take (e.g., HR, diversity & inclusion professionals, diversity champions, members of minority groups and networks as well as employees occupying varying levels of socially ascribed privilege).

- Leaders should seek to understand what inclusive leadership means in their context.
    - Inclusive leadership behaviors may be experienced as quite disruptive and different when compared with stereotypical, traditional leadership behaviors.
    - Organizational leaders should socialize the concept upfront, advocate what inclusive leadership means, what it looks like and feels like at the level of everyday experience, and why it is important, and follow up any interventions with structured coaching or development programs to develop inclusive leaders throughout the organization.

- Leaders should communicate how increasing inclusive leadership practices and reducing exclusionary practices will benefit the entire workforce, for example, by making it a more collaborative and facilitative environment for everyone involved.
- Leaders should draw attention to micro-behaviors as inclusive leadership practice:
    - Help translate inclusive leadership into meaningful everyday behavior for individuals.
    - Offer insight into some of the subtle (and low effort) methods of promoting affirming and inclusive cultures.
    - Help shift away from awareness of unconscious biases to thinking about what individuals can actively do about it.
- Leaders (with assistance from external consultants where necessary) could hold workshops where potential targets of inclusive and exclusionary leadership practices come together to share their experiences. This helps to provide further examples of what exclusive and inclusive behaviors look like in a given organizational context, discuss how they can be addressed, and generate solutions or learn from others around how best to actively manage exclusion

## Note

1 This chapter was developed from a conference research paper presented at the 2012 Equality, Diversity, & Inclusion conference by Doyin Atewologun called "The Nature and Impact of Inclusive and Non-Inclusive Micro-Behaviours on Minority Ethnic Organisational Members."

## References

Atewologun, D., Sealy, R., & Vinnicombe, S. (2016). Revealing intersectional dynamics in organizations: Introducing 'intersectional identity work'. *Gender, Work & Organization*, *23*(3), 223–247. https://doi.org/10.1111/gwao.12082

Brief, A. P., Dietz, J., Cohen, R. R., Pugh, S. D., & Vaslow, J. B. (2000). Just doing business: Modern racism and obedience to authority as explanations for employment discrimination. *Organizational Behavior and Human Decision Processes*, *81*(1), 72–97. https://doi.org/10.1006/obhd.1999.2867

Browne, I., & Misra, J. (2003). The intersection of gender and race in the labor market. *Annual Review of Sociology*, *29*(1), 487–513. https://doi.org/10.1146/annurev.soc.29.010202.100016

Cortina, L. M. (2008). Unseen injustice: Incivility as modern discrimination in organizations. *Academy of Management Review*, *33*(1), 55–75. https://doi.org/10.2307/20159376

Deitch, E. A., Barsky, A., Butz, R. M., Chan, S., Brief, A. P., & Bradley, J. C. (2003). Subtle yet significant: The existence and impact of everyday racial discrimination in the workplace. *Human Relations*, *56*(11), 1299–1324. https://doi.org/10.1177/00187267035611002

Edmondson, A. C. (1999). Psychological safety and learning behavior in work teams. *Administrative Science Quarterly*, *44*(2), 350–383. https://doi.org/10.2307/2666999

Essed, P. (1991). *Understanding everyday racism: An interdisciplinary theory* (Vol. 2). Newbury Park, CA: Sage.

Ferdman, B. M. (2014). The practice of inclusion in diverse organizations: Toward a systemic and inclusive framework. In B. M. Ferdman & B. R. Deane (Eds.), *Diversity at work: The practice of inclusion* (pp. 3–54). San Francisco, CA: Wiley. https://doi.org/10.1002/9781118764282.ch1

Hirak, R., Peng, A. C., Carmeli, A., & Schaubroeck, J. M. (2012). Linking leader inclusiveness to work unit performance: The importance of psychological safety and learning from failures. *The Leadership Quarterly*, *23*(1), 107–117. https://doi.org/10.1016/j.leaqua.2011.11.009

Hollander, E. (2009). *Inclusive leadership: The essential leader-follower relationship*. New York, NY: Routledge.

Kandola, B. (2009). *The value of difference: Eliminating bias in organisations*. Oxford, UK: Pearn Kandola.

Kenny, E. J., & Briner, R. B. (2007). Ethnicity and behavior in organizations: A review of British research. *Journal of Occupational and Organizational Psychology*, *80*(3), 437–457. https://doi.org/10.1348/096317906X156313

Lofland, J., Snow, D., Anderson, L., & Lofland, L. H. (2005). *Analyzing social settings: A guide to qualitative observation and analysis* (4th ed.). Belmont, CA: Wadsworth.

Nembhard, I. M., & Edmondson, A. C. (2006). Making it safe: The effects of leader inclusiveness and professional status on psychological safety and improvement efforts in health care teams. *Journal of Organizational Behavior*, *27*(7), 941–966. https://doi.org/10.1002/job.413

Nishii, L. H., & Mayer, D. M. (2009). Do inclusive leaders help reduce turnover in diverse groups? The moderating role of leader-member exchange in the diversity to turnover relationship. *Journal of Applied Psychology*, *94*(6), 1412–1426. https://doi.org/10.1037/a0017190

Noon, M. (2010). The shackled runner: Time to rethink positive discrimination? *Work, Employment and Society*, *24*(4), 728–739. https://doi.org/10.1177/0950017010380648

Roberson, Q. M. (2006). Disentangling the meanings of diversity and inclusion in organizations. *Group & Organization Management*, *31*(2), 212–236. https://doi.org/10.1177/1059601104273064

Rowe, M. (2008). Micro-affirmations and micro-inequities. *Journal of the International Ombudsman Association*, *1*(1), 45–48.

Ryan, J. (2006). Inclusive leadership and social justice for schools. *Leadership and Policy in Schools*, *5*(1), 3–17. https://doi.org/10.1080/15700760500483995

Sue, D. W., Capodilupo, C. M., Torino, G. C., Bucceri, J. M., Holder, A., Nadal, K. L., & Esquilin, M. (2007). Racial microaggressions in everyday life: Implications for clinical practice. *American Psychologist*, *62*(4), 271–286. https://doi.org/10.1037/0003-066X.62.4.271

Syed, J., & Özbilgin, M. (2009). A relational framework for international transfer of diversity management practices. *The International Journal of Human Resource Management*, *20*(12), 2435–2453. https://doi.org/10.1080/09585190903363755

Thomas, D. A., & Ely, R. J. (1996). Making differences matter: A new paradigm for managing diversity. *Harvard Business Review*, *74*(5), 79–90.

Van Laer, K., & Janssens, M. (2011). Ethnic minority professionals' experiences with subtle discrimination in the workplace. *Human Relations*, *64*(9), 1203–1227. https://doi.org/10.1177/0018726711409263

Van Laer, K., & Janssens, M. (2014). Between the devil and the deep blue sea: Exploring the hybrid identity narratives of ethnic minority professionals. *Scandinavian Journal of Management*, *30*(2), 186–196. https://doi.org/10.1016/j.scaman.2013.08.004

Zanoni, P., Janssens, M., Benschop, Y., & Nkomo, S. (2010). Unpacking diversity, grasping inequality: Rethinking difference through critical perspectives. *Organization*, *17*(1), 9–29. https://doi.org/10.1177/1350508409350344

# 8 Inclusive Leadership from the Inside Out

*Tara Van Bommel, Emily Shaffer, Dnika J. Travis, and Heather Foust-Cummings*

Creating an inclusive workplace is not simply an idealistic goal; it can be the crux of smart organizations. Unfortunately, our workplaces are not immune to societal inequities and challenges that stifle our ability to connect, learn, or bridge divides. Sexism, racism, ageism, ableism, and heterosexism—and their unique intersections—are examples of tough issues with long histories that are painfully challenging to combat. Experiences of prejudice, discrimination, and privilege shape who we are as individuals, and who we are as individuals shapes who we are at work (Geiger & Jordan, 2014; Nugent et al., 2016). Early efforts to address these inequities tended to focus on surface-level diversity (e.g., Chatman et al., 1998; Mor Barak et al., 1998), yet much of the literature on the outcomes of diverse workplaces is mixed, at best (Ely & Thomas, 2001; Ferdman, 2014; Kochan et al., 2003). Some research has shown that more diverse teams are more productive (Gomez & Bernet, 2019) and are adept at problem-solving (Hong & Page, 2004). On the other hand, diversity may lead to conflict and higher rates of turnover (Jehn et al., 1999; Mannix & Neale, 2005; Pelled et al., 1999). What does seem clear is that the benefits of diversity do not emerge solely or simply by having a mix of demographically diverse groups. Rather, enhancing diversity *and* intentionally building an inclusive workplace culture are key (Ferdman, 2014).

The dysfunctions that arise amid diversity without inclusion reflect the larger challenge at hand: diversity and inclusion are really two sides of the same coin (Ferdman, 2017)—trying to cultivate either/or is like trying to split the coin and derive the same value. The heart of the challenge is to embrace and cultivate the contradictions that are central to experiences of inclusion. Ferdman (2017) argues for cultivating a "both/and" approach (Smith et al., 2016) whereby seemingly opposite forces can exist in the same space—and the resultant discomfort is a catalyst for growth rather than a point of conflict. For example, a paradox that Ferdman cites as a challenge for diversity and inclusion is the balance of belonging and uniqueness. On the surface, these two qualities appear to represent opposing forces, but research has indicated that both are requisite to experiences of inclusion (Prime & Salib, 2014). Indeed, experiences of workplace inclusion were found to be dependent upon the dual experience of belonging and uniqueness, not on either feeling alone (Prime & Salib, 2014). Thus, inclusive workplaces can be understood as the "atmosphere where people can belong, contribute, and thrive," all while feeling valued for their unique qualities and contributions (Travis et al., 2019), and inclusive leadership is a cornerstone of facilitating this experience.

But how exactly can leaders and organizations foster workplaces that accommodate the duality of a "both/and" approach to inclusive leadership? The answer lies, in part, in acknowledging the multi-level nature of this problem (Ferdman & Davidson, 2002) and addressing the individual-, interpersonal-, and organizational-level components of diversity and inclusion. When we take this approach as given, the imperative becomes clear: organizations must be deliberate about developing leaders' skills when it comes to ensuring that employees are treated fairly, respected, valued, and honored for their unique attributes, and allowing employees to contribute to decision-making (Ferdman, 2014; Mor Barak, 2000; Prime & Salib, 2014; Shore et al., 2011; Travis et al., 2019). Yet taking this essential step is often easier said than done. To illustrate, let's consider the following scenario:

Harper has enjoyed leading a geographically dispersed team of programmers for over three years. She is proud of her accomplishments in both enhancing the ethnic and gender diversity of the team and creating more opportunities for team members to take ownership of their work. Despite these team gains, Harper struggles to build a safe space for team members to express dissenting or alternate viewpoints. She just received feedback that some people feel uncomfortable offering new or different ideas, even though everyone seemingly works well enough together to meet quarterly goals. She is disheartened and doesn't know what to do. Perhaps Harper needs to rethink her leadership strategy beyond her outward behaviors—building accountability systems and providing visibility to the team. A trusted colleague advises Harper to look inward at her own behaviors—to be curious about sticking points when problems arise; to self-reflect on mistakes made, as well as her openness to sharing learnings from those missteps with her team; and to look deeply at whose voices are being heard and whose are not.

As this vignette shows, both outward leadership and inward behaviors are central to inclusive leadership. Harper's colleague identifies the importance of cultivating a "both/and" leadership style: simply leading outward *or* leading inward won't necessarily make you an inclusive leader. Rather, the combination of *both* elicits an outcome greater than the sum of its parts. What are core skills that help leaders treat their team members fairly? What is the impact of inclusive leadership on employees' experiences in the workplace? In this chapter we review the evolution of Catalyst's research and the implications for practice, which, taken together, get at the very heart of the challenges and opportunities for embracing a "both/and" style of inclusive leadership.

## The Beginnings of Inclusive Leadership Research at Catalyst

Catalyst's foundational study of inclusive leadership surveyed 1,512 employees in six countries to better understand employees' perceptions of their managers. Prime and Salib (2014) uncovered four cross-cutting managerial behaviors that predict whether employees feel like they belong and are valued for their uniqueness. Leaders help their direct reports realize feelings of *empowerment* toward their career development and performance. Displays of *humility* occur when leaders acknowledge their mistakes and limitations, and take a learning approach to self-improvement, which involves learning from criticism and alternate viewpoints. *Courageous* leaders do the right thing, and act on their convictions and principles, regardless of any potential negative repercussions. *Accountability* is present when employees are trusted to manage their own projects and performance. These four inclusive leadership behaviors were shown to significantly predict inclusion (Prime & Salib, 2014). In this study, the authors defined inclusion as the dual experience of feeling belongingness and being valued for one's unique qualities. This definition of inclusion drew from seminal work documenting the universal human need for connection and belonging (Baumeister & Leary, 1995). In fact, because team productivity and team success flourish when inclusion is present (Salib & Shi, 2017), an inclusive leadership style indirectly benefits managers and leaders. Thus, the collective outcome of inclusive experiences for employees at all levels is just as, if not more, important to organizational outcomes as the bottom line.

## Revising and Refining What it Means to Lead Inclusively

Inclusive leadership is the future of work and of business, and it requires that we pinpoint an action framework that can generate more inclusive workplaces. Catalyst's second study of inclusive leadership aimed to address this necessary framework by asking people to focus more attention and effort inward—on one's own ability to self-reflect, lead with curiosity, and learn from others and one's own missteps. Additionally, the framework focuses on outward actions that can be integrated into one's daily life, emphasizing the need for the "both/and" approach. The Leading Outward/Leading Inward inclusive leadership model builds upon the research of Prime and Salib (2014), as well as inclusion frameworks (Ferdman, 2014; Mor Barak, 2000; Shore et al., 2011), effective leadership models (Brimhall et al., 2017; Cottrill et al., 2014; Nishii & Mayer, 2009; Randel et al., 2018), and theories of human and organizational behavioral change (Stone et al., 2009). The Leading Outward/ Leading Inward model highlights two conceptually distinct ways in which managers can lead inclusively.

- Most intuitively, managers can **lead outward** by creating an atmosphere where their employees can be treated fairly and have the ability to flourish. The outward focus is on "doing" through accountability, helping employees take ownership of their jobs, and allyship.
- At the same time, managers can **lead inward** by taking a hard look at who they are and developing attributes that make people want to work for and with them. These behaviors focus on "being"—curiosity, courage, and humility.

This doing + being approach is a call to action for organizations and leaders that provides tangible steps individuals can take to lead inclusively. With this framework in mind, Catalyst tested six core behaviors that comprise inclusive leadership and found that these behaviors accounted for 45% of the variance in employees' experience of inclusion (Travis et al., 2019).

## Leading Outward

Catalyst's foundational study of inclusive leadership authored by Prime and Salib (2014) featured empowerment in the model. One major extension to that model was to break down the concept of empowerment. The concept of empowerment can be vague, and is often interpreted in a way that, ironically, can be disempowering. Some contend that programs meant to empower employees inadvertently create scenarios where there is more control over employees, and, moreover, managers can view the empowerment of their employees as a loss of their own power or control (Spreitzer, 2007). Instead of thinking of empowerment as something that can be given—and thus taken away—leaders should focus on creating an atmosphere where employees can be empowered. Although the nuance may be subtle, by leading outward, leaders create a climate where employees can garner their own empowerment instead of it being contingent on others.

### *Accountability*

Inclusive leaders set expectations for their employees to achieve their goals, and to grow and develop their skills. Setting clear expectations allows employees to understand what they need to achieve to be successful. In doing so, employees can develop their own goals and create a plan to achieve them. Providing regular feedback is key to leading effectively (Karakowsky & Mann, 2008). Leaders can only hold their employees accountable if strengths and areas for opportunity are discussed.

### *Ownership*

Similarly, it is essential that leaders enable employees to develop a sense of ownership over their work. When expectations and larger goals are clear, employees can work autonomously and create their own path toward achieving those goals. Inclusive leaders do not need to delineate each step of a process for their employees; they only need to set the course and provide guidance when needed. Importantly, employees' sense of autonomy has been linked to less burnout (Gilbert et al., 2017).

### *Allyship*

Visibly advocating for members of underrepresented groups is key to inclusive leadership. The first step toward being an ally is to educate yourself. Challenge yourself to learn about and consider the historical and societal issues that influence the experience of employees who belong to underrepresented groups (Travis et al., 2019). Consider the structural inequalities and power imbalances in society that inevitably pervade the workplace. Use your knowledge to recognize and critically evaluate your own biases and behavior. Unconscious bias exists within all of us and within the workplace, and inclusive leaders take the first step by holding themselves accountable for recognizing it (Catalyst, 2014). When leaders acknowledge undesired behavior, it sets a norm within a team and encourages others to speak out when something isn't right. Setting these norms within a team can have lasting effects (Zitek & Hebl, 2007).

## Leading Inward

Leading inclusively has as much to do with who you are as it does with what you do. Those who lead inward take an honest look at who they are and do not shy away from the difficult, and often uncomfortable, work that it takes to critically evaluate one's strengths and weaknesses.

These leaders understand that change starts with them. They set the pace and role model the behaviors they wish to see in their employees. Those who lead inward demonstrate curiosity, humility, and courage.

### *Curiosity*

Curious leaders seek to understand the different points of view and experiences of their colleagues. Taking a learning-centric approach conveys to employees that a leader is motivated to understand and consider team members' thoughts and approaches toward getting work done. Leaders who approach their work with a desire to learn feel more efficacious in their ability to lead (Hendricks & Payne, 2007). The positive impact of curiosity not only has positive outcomes for leaders, it impacts their employees as well. Leaders focused on learning inspire this mindset in their employees by showing that sharing new and different ideas is welcomed and encouraged (Garvin et al., 2008).

### *Humility*

Savvy and inclusive leaders do not think they have all the answers. Leaders who demonstrate humility role model the way that mistakes should be handled by admitting when mistakes are made and using them as an opportunity for learning. When leaders exercise humility, employees are more satisfied with their jobs, are more engaged, and are less likely to leave (Owens et al., 2013). It is important to acknowledge that admitting mistakes or limitations may feel risky for some. In fact, younger leaders and female leaders have expressed that being humble may put them at risk for being seen as incompetent (Hekman, 2012). Despite these risks, employees whose leaders demonstrate humility often feel as though developing skills, instead of having mastered them, is accepted, and that they do not have to cover up their own mistakes (Hekman, 2012). Let's face it: mistakes are bound to happen, but the way leaders handle them influences the way employees respond.

### *Courage*

Courageous leaders act on their principles. They understand that doing so may be uncomfortable or even risky, but they know it's important to speak out when something isn't right and to lead in ways consistent with their values. Leaders who demonstrate courage can be trusted by others because their actions align with their stated values (Wong et al., 2007), and leaders who demonstrate courage inspire courage in others (Hannah et al., 2011). Although employees may find it difficult to speak up at work, having a leader who role models this behavior sets the example for the group, and may signal to employees that they're able to do the same.

It is important to note that, across the markets and countries Catalyst studied, these inclusive leadership attributes remained relevant to predicting employee experiences of inclusion (Prime & Salib, 2014; Travis et al., 2019). In our globalized economy, leaders need not put on a new leadership hat in each country or location in which they operate. Instead, leaders can focus on these core behaviors to enable employee inclusivity across the board.

## The Benefits of an Inclusive Workplace

Inclusive leadership behaviors are powerful predictors of employees' experience of inclusion. In Catalyst's Leading Outward/Leading Inward study, inclusive leadership predicted over 45% of this employee experience (Travis et al., 2019). Specifically, the six core inclusive leadership behaviors significantly predicted employees' experience of inclusion such that, as inclusive leadership increased by one standard deviation, employees' experience of inclusion increased by two-thirds of a standard deviation.

Yet what are these experiences of inclusion? It's important that employees feel *valued* for what makes them unique. A sense of *trust* is cultivated when employees are involved in the decision-making process and feel as though they are crucial members of the team. People also experience inclusion when they can be and can express their *authentic* self in the workplace. Psychological safety is also critical to an employee's experience of inclusion.

Compellingly, in Catalyst's second-phase study of inclusive leadership, Travis and colleagues (2019) found psychological safety expressed itself in two distinct ways (Travis et al., 2019). As a broader concept, psychological safety encompasses the cognitive and behavioral experiences that define environments where employees can make mistakes and take risks without being penalized. The authors contend that *psychological safety: latitude* represents the cognitive component, which is feeling safe to express divergent viewpoints and make mistakes without fear of reprisal. *Psychological safety: risk-taking* emerged as the behavioral component—the sense of safety that enables employees to act on addressing tough issues at work, ask for help, or take a risk.

## Why Employee Experiences of Inclusion Matter

Employee experiences of inclusion should be central to organizations' operating models—not just because inclusion predicts a long list of relevant business outcomes, but because of its positive impact on employees. Put simply, employees who feel included are more satisfied, more engaged, and want to stay at their organizations. In a study of Canadian professionals, among those experiencing high levels of inclusion at work, as defined by the co-occurrence of belongingness and uniqueness, more than 75% reported satisfaction with their overall work and advancement (Thorpe-Moscon, 2015). Inclusion had a large influence on employee satisfaction with their supervisor: 86% of employees who perceived high inclusion reported satisfaction with their supervisor, but when inclusion was low, only 23% had satisfactory supervisory experiences (Thorpe-Moscon, 2015). Similarly, employees who feel included report being more engaged and dedicated to their organization's mission (Travis et al., 2019).

Travis and colleagues (2019) also found that employees' overall experience of inclusion (defined by feeling valued, feeling trusted, able to be authentic, and feeling a sense of psychological safety: latitude and risk-taking) explained 35% of employee engagement, 49% of team problem-solving, 20% of employee intent to stay, and 18% of employee innovation. Among the many factors that can explain why employees feel engaged, inclusion alone contributes over one-third of the reason why employees are invested in their work. Additionally, the study found that the more included employees feel, the less likely they are to report intent to leave their positions (Travis et al., 2019). Moreover, inclusion impacts retention: experiences of inclusion are associated with a weak intent to leave, and conversely, a lack of inclusion is associated with a strong intent to leave (Thorpe-Moscon, 2015). Indeed, 20% of an employee's intent to stay at their organization can be explained by inclusion (Travis et al., 2019). As a result, organizations with inclusive cultures already are a step ahead of those without.

Inclusion has particularly beneficial effects for women and men of color, who are more likely to suffer the negative effects of exclusion. Specifically, inclusion has been shown to buffer against the negative impacts of emotional tax for women and men of color (Travis et al., 2016). A series of studies on emotional tax found that, among Asian, Black, and Latinx professionals who were experiencing emotional tax, feeling included was associated with a lower intent to leave the organization, greater creativity, a higher likelihood of speaking up about important or difficult issues at work, and greater feelings of psychological safety (Travis & Thorpe-Moscon, 2018).

Inclusion predicts the performance of individuals and work teams. High levels of inclusion are associated with greater innovation and cooperation (Salib & Shi, 2017). Salib and Shi (2017) found that when women feel included, they are twice as likely to engage in innovative behaviors, such as suggesting new products or processes. Further, women and men who reported high levels of inclusion, compared with those who reported the least, exhibited 74% more cooperation and 81% more innovation. Inclusive environments also foster team citizenship behaviors; for example, team members will be willing to go beyond their job requirements to help team members achieve objectives for the greater good of the workgroup (Prime & Salib, 2014). And almost half of a team's ability to problem solve—the ability to work together constructively to find solutions to problems—can be explained by inclusion (Travis et al., 2019).

## Toward a Future of Inclusive Leadership: Actions That Organizations, Managers, and Teams Can Take to Lead Inclusively

Even with the bounty of conveniences and advances that technology has lent to the human experience, the core of what makes us successful now—our ability to connect and understand one another—will continue to define our success in the future. Inclusive leadership can be cultivated at all levels of an organization. Below are actions that organizations, managers, and teams can take to begin or continue their inclusive leadership journey. We humans are constantly evolving and must cultivate inclusion and inclusive leadership at every turn. Otherwise, people can fall back to old habits, ways of working, and norms that reinforce the status quo (Azjen, 1991).

### *Organizations*

- **Invest in your leaders.** Make it a priority to budget for internal or external leadership training. Ensure that managers are able and encouraged to take the time to develop their skill sets. Keep in mind that there is no finish line. The commitment toward an inclusive workplace must be ongoing because diverse organizations only succeed when everyone experiences inclusion.
- **Incentivize inclusive leadership.** Tie promotion and compensation to employee evaluations of their managers. Reward those who go the extra mile to create an inclusive environment for their direct reports. Work with leaders at your organization using the Leading Outward/Leading Inward framework above to assess progress toward leading inclusively, and how these behaviors can be carried out in your unique workplace. Make these principles and their link to the incentives clear so leaders can begin to develop or refine these skills.

### *Managers*

- **Take your employees' perspective.** Make it a priority to understand the point of view of your employees. Make sure they know you understand and appreciate these perspectives, even if you don't always agree. Not only does it convey that you are genuinely interested in their ideas, you might also develop solutions that you otherwise may not have considered. Decades of research show just how important perspective-taking can be. Perspective-taking allows you to see similarities between yourself and others that you may not have noticed otherwise, and this has even been shown to reduce the likelihood that stereotypes are brought to mind (Galinsky & Moskowitz, 2000; Moskowitz et al., 1999). As a result, taking the time to consider things from your employees' point of view will help make you less biased, which may help build stronger relationships with your team, making it a group in which ideas can be safely shared and considered.

- **Let employees know what is expected of them.** Employees can only create and reach their own goals if they know what they are striving for. Make sure to link current projects and tasks back to your team's or the organization's larger goals and hold employees accountable for their work toward this broader purpose. This helps employees cultivate autonomy and have a sense of ownership over their work.
- **Lead by example.** Don't overlook your role in setting the tone of your team culture. If you say, "We value honesty," speak your truth and demonstrate those behaviors. Or if you say, "We can solve any problem together," you must schedule time to debrief on work-related projects, issues, and sticking points, and have strategies in place to address conflict. Those who lead inward understand that "who they are" plays just as big a role in leading inclusively as "what they do."
- **Don't be afraid to fail—as long as you keep learning.** Being an inclusive leader does not mean you have all the answers or will do everything right all the time. When things do not go as planned, resist the urge to cover it up or explain it away. Though it may be uncomfortable, let employees know when a mistake has been made, and plan for how it can be remedied. Treating your mistakes as learning opportunities will encourage and inspire your employees to do the same.

### *Teams*

- **We each can be an inclusive leader.** It's not only those in managerial positions who can be inclusive leaders or work to develop these skills. All employees and individual contributors can help to make their workplaces more inclusive ones. Start by having conversations and inviting others into the conversation as well. Some people may be less likely to voice their thoughts and ideas, but that does not mean they don't have something to contribute. Make sure everyone gets a say when working to solve problems (Catalyst, 2019).

- **Be curious and practice active listening.** Make it a priority to learn more about your colleagues and their point of view. Ask them about their experiences (Thorpe-Moscon et al., 2019). Oftentimes, we automatically start thinking about our reply or get defensive, even before others finish speaking. Be aware and actively listen to what your team members are saying, and instead of trying to understand that person through your own experiences, try to take their perspective.

## References

Azjen, I. (1991). The theory of planned behavior. *Organizational Behavior and Human Decision Making Processes*, *50*(2), 179–211. https://doi.org/10.1016/0749-5978(91)90020-T

Baumeister, R. F., & Leary, M. R. (1995). The need to belong: Desire for interpersonal attachments as a fundamental human motivation. *Psychological Bulletin*, *117*(3), 497–529. https://doi.org/10.1037/0033-2909.117.3.497

Brimhall, K. C., Mor Barak, M. E., Hurlburt, M., McArdle, J. J., Palinkas, L., & Henwood, B. (2017). Increasing workplace inclusion: The promise of leader-member exchange. *Human Service Organizations: Management, Leadership & Governance*, *41*(3), 222–239. https://doi.org/10.1080/23303131.2016.1251522

Catalyst. (2014, December 11). *How to combat unconscious bias as a leader in your organization.* https://www.catalyst.org/research/infographic-how-to-combat-unconscious-bias-as-a-leader-in-your-organization

Catalyst. (2019). *Conversation roadblocks and how to surmount them.* https://www.catalyst.org/wp-content/uploads/2019/10/Conversation-Roadblocks-Infographic-Print.pdf

Chatman, J. A., Polzer, J. T., Barsade, S. G., & Neale, M. A. (1998). Being different yet feeling similar: The influence of demographic composition and organizational culture on work processes and outcomes. *Administrative Science Quarterly*, *43*(4), 749–780. https://doi.org/10.2307/2393615

Cottrill, K., Lopez, P. D., & Hoffman, C. C. (2014). How authentic leadership and inclusion benefit organizations. *Equality, Diversity, and Inclusion*, *33*(3), 275–292. https://doi.org/10.1108/EDI-05-2012-0041

Ely, R. J., & Thomas, D. A. (2001). Cultural diversity at work: The effects of diversity perspectives on work group processes and outcomes. *Administrative Science Quarterly*, *46*(2), 229–273. https://doi.org/10.2307/2667087

Ferdman, B. M., & Davidson, M. N. (2002). Inclusion: What can I and my organization do about it. *The Industrial-Organizational Psychologist*, *39*(4), 80–85.

Ferdman, B. M. (2014). The practice of inclusion in diverse organizations: Toward a systemic and inclusive framework. In B. M. Ferdman & B. R. Deane (Eds.), *Diversity at work: The practice of inclusion* (pp. 3–54). San Francisco, CA: Jossey-Bass. https://doi.org/10.1002/9781118764282.ch1

Ferdman, B. M. (2017). Paradoxes of inclusion: Understanding and managing the tensions of diversity and multiculturalism. *The Journal of Applied Behavioral Science*, *53*(2), 235–263. https://doi.org/10.1177/0021886317702608

Galinsky, A. D., & Moskowitz, G. B. (2000). Perspective-taking: Decreasing stereotype expression, stereotype accessibility, and in-group favoritism. *Journal of Personality and Social Psychology*, *78*(4), 708–724. https://doi.org/10.1037/0022-3514.78.4.708

Garvin, D. A., Edmondson, A. C., & Gino, F. (2008). Is yours a learning organization? *Harvard Business Review*, *86*(3), 109–116.

Geiger, K. A., & Jordan, C. (2014). The role of societal privilege in the definitions and practices of inclusion. *Equality, Diversity and Inclusion: An International Journal*, *33*(3), 261–274. https://doi.org/10.1108/EDI-12-2013-0115

Gilbert, M.-H., Dagenais-Desmarais, V., & St-Hilare, F. (2017). Transformational leadership and autonomy support management behaviors: The role of specificity in predicting employees' psychological health. *Leadership & Organization Development Journal*, *38*(2), 320–332. https://doi.org/10.1108/LODJ-08-2015-0173

Gomez, L. E., & Bernet, P. (2019). Diversity improves performance and outcomes. *Journal of the National Medical Association*, *111*(4), 383–392. https://doi.org/10.1016/j.jnma.2019.01.006

Hannah, S. T., Avolio, B. J., & Walumbwa, F. O. (2011). Relationships between authentic leadership, moral courage, and ethical and pro-social behaviors. *Business Ethics Quarterly*, *21*(4), 555–578. https://doi.org/10.5840/beq201121436

Hekman, D. R. (2012). Modeling how to grow: An inductive examination of humble leader behaviors, outcomes, and contingencies. *Academy of Management Journal*, *55*(4), 787–818. https://doi.org/10.5465/amj.2010.044

Hendricks, J. W., & Payne, S. C. (2007). Beyond the big five: Leader goal orientation as a predictor of leadership effectiveness. *Human Performance*, *20*(4), 317–343. https://doi.org/10.1080/08959280701521983

Hong, L., & Page, S. E. (2004). Groups of diverse problem solvers can outperform groups of high-ability problem solvers. *Proceedings of the National Academy of Sciences*, *101*(46), 16385–16389. https://doi.org/10.1073/pnas.0403723101

Jehn, K. A., Northcraft, G. B., & Neale, M. A. (1999). Why differences make a difference: A field study of diversity, conflict and performance in workgroups. *Administrative Science Quarterly*, *44*(4), 741–763. https://doi.org/10.2307/2667054

Karakowsky, L., & Mann, S. L. (2008). Setting goals and taking ownership: Understanding the implications of participatively set goals from a causal attribution perspective. *Journal of Leadership & Organizational Studies*, *14*(3), 260–270. https://doi.org/10.1177/1071791907308047

Kochan, T., Bezrukova, K., Ely, R., Jackson, S., Joshi, A., Jehn, K., . . . Thomas, D. (2003). The effects of diversity on business performance: Report of the diversity research network. *Human Resource Management*, *42*(1), 3–21. https://doi.org/10.1002/hrm.10061

Mannix, E., & Neale, M. A. (2005). What differences make a difference? The promise and reality of diverse teams in organizations. *Psychological Science in the Public Interest*, *6*(2), 31–55. https://doi.org/10.1111/j.1529-1006.2005.00022.x

Mor Barak, M. E. (2000). The inclusive workplace: An ecosystems approach to diversity management. *Social Work*, *45*(4), 339–353. https://doi.org/10.1093/sw/45.4.339

Mor Barak, M. E., Cherin, D. A., & Berkman, S. (1998). Organizational and personal dimensions in diversity climate: Ethnic and gender differences in employee perceptions. *The Journal of Applied Behavioral Science*, *34*(1), 82–104. https://doi.org/10.1177/0021886398341006

Moskowitz, G. B., Skurnik, I., & Galinsky, A. D. (1999). The history of dual-process notions, and the future of preconscious control. In S. Chaiken & Y. Trope (Eds.) *Dual-process theories in social psychology* (pp. 12–36). New York, NY: Guilford Press.

Nishii, L. H., & Mayer, D. M. (2009). Do inclusive leaders help to reduce turnover in diverse groups? The moderating role of leader–member exchange in the diversity to turnover relationship. *Journal of Applied Psychology*, *94*, 1412–1426. https://doi.org/10.1037/a0017190

Nugent, J. S., Pollack, A., & Travis, D. J. (2016). *The day-to-day experiences of workplace inclusion and exclusion*. Catalyst. https://www.catalyst.org/wp-content/uploads/2019/01/the_day_to_day_experiences_of_workplace_inclusion_and_exclusion.pdf

Owens, B. P., Johnson, M. D., & Mitchell, T. R. (2013). Expressed humility in organizations: Implications for performance, teams, and leadership. *Organization Science*, *24*(5), 1517–1538. https://doi.org/10.1287/orsc.1120.0795

Pelled, L. H., Eisenhardt, K. M., & Xin, K. R. (1999). Exploring the black box: An analysis of work group diversity, conflict, and performance. *Administrative Science Quarterly*, *44*(1), 1–28. https://doi.org/10.2307/2667029

Prime, J., & Salib, E. R. (2014). *Inclusive leadership: The view from six countries*. Catalyst. https://www.catalyst.org/wp-content/uploads/2019/01/inclusive_leadership_the_view_from_six_countries_0.pdf

Randel, A. E., Galvin, B. M., Shore, L. M., Holcombe Ehrhart, K., Chung, B. G., Dean, M. A., & Kedharnath, U. (2018). Inclusive leadership: Realizing positive outcomes through belongingness and being valued for uniqueness. *Human Resource Management Review*, *28*(2), 190–203. https://doi.org/10.1016/j.hrmr.2017.07.002

Salib, E. R., & Shi, Y. (2017). *The journey to inclusion: Building workplaces that work for women in Japan*. Catalyst. https://www.catalyst.org/wp-content/uploads/2019/01/journeytoinclusion_english_10-11-17_final.pdf

Shore, L. M., Randel, A. E., Chung, B. G., Dean, M. A., Ehrhart, K. H., & Singh, G. (2011). Inclusion and diversity in work groups: A review and model for future research. *Journal of Management*, *37*(4), 1262–1289. https://doi.org/10.1177/0149206310385943

Smith, W. K., Lewis, M. W., & Tushman, M. L. (2016, May). "Both/and" leadership: Don't worry so much about being consistent. *Harvard Business Review*, pp. 63–70.

Spreitzer, G. (2007). Taking stock: A review of more than twenty years of research on empowerment at work. In J. Barling & C. L. Cooper (Eds.), *The SAGE handbook of organizational behavior: Volume I – micro approaches* (pp. 54–72). London, UK: Sage Publications. https://doi.org/10.4135/9781849200448.n4

Stone, D. N., Deci, E. L., & Ryan, R. M. (2009). Beyond talk: Creating autonomous motivation through self-determination theory. *Journal of General Management*, *34*, 75–91. https://doi.org/10.1177/030630700903400305

Thorpe-Moscon, J. (2015). *Inclusion is key to keeping Canadian high potentials*. Catalyst. https://www.catalyst.org/wp-content/uploads/2019/01/inclusion_is_key_to_keeping_canadian_high_potentials.pdf

Thorpe-Moscon, J., Pollack, P., & OluLafe, O. (2019). *Empowering workplaces combat emotional tax for people of colour in Canada*. Catalyst. https://www.catalyst.org/wp-content/uploads/2019/06/Emotional-Tax-Canada-2019.pdf

Travis, D. J., Shaffer, E. S., & Thorpe-Moscon, J. (2019). *Getting real about inclusive leadership: Why change starts with you*. Catalyst. https://www.catalyst.org/wp-content/uploads/2020/03/Getting-Real-About-Inclusive-Leadership-Report-2020update.pdf

Travis, D.J., & Thorpe-Moscon, J. (2018). *Day-to-day experiences of emotional tax among women and men of color in the workplace*. Catalyst, Inc. https://www.catalyst.org/wp-content/uploads/2019/02/emotionaltax.pdf

Travis, D. J., Thorpe-Moscon, J., & McCluney, C. (2016). *Emotional tax: How Black women and men pay more at work and how leaders can take action*. Catalyst. https://www.catalyst.org/wp-content/uploads/2019/01/emotional_tax_how_black_women_and_men_pay_more.pdf

Wong, P. T., Davey, D., & Church, F. B. (2007, July). *Best practices in servant leadership* [Paper]. Servant Leadership Research Roundtable, School of Global Leadership and Entrepreneurship, Regent University. https://www.regent.edu/acad/global/publications/sl_proceedings/2007/wong-davey.pdf

Zitek, E. M., & Hebl, M. (2007). The role of social norm clarity in the influenced expression of prejudice over time. *Journal of Experimental Social Psychology*, *43*, 867–876. https://doi.org/10.1016/j.jesp.2006.10.010

# 9 Embracing the Weird

## Developing Inclusive Leadership Competency by Leveraging Uniqueness

*Martin N. Davidson*

All leaders confront the ongoing challenge of developing work cultures that promote high employee engagement and performance (Christian et al., 2011; Harter et al., 2002). This task is even more daunting as the increasing diversity of domestic and global workforces introduces all-too-familiar tensions and faultlines among members of the organization (Lau & Murnighan, 1998). Inclusive leadership—the practice of creating work climates and cultures that foster the highest levels of engagement and productivity from diverse employees—is a critical resource in navigating this terrain. Skillful inclusive leaders master core competencies such as being curious about difference, learning about their biases, and cultivating global business acumen (Davidson, 2011). However, a less well-articulated catalyst to developing an effective practice of inclusive leadership is the ability to explore and learn from one's experience of being marginal, of operating from outside the norm (Ibarra & Obodaru, 2016). Highly effective inclusive leaders connect with their own experience of liminality, providing both an empathic pathway to followers who are also marginal and modeling ways of connecting for those who are not marginal. In this chapter I examine how the ability to internalize and learn from experiences of deviating from cultural norms or social convention allows leaders to develop inclusive leadership competency. Put another way, I map out how embracing one's weirdness—the unique set of attributes and experiences that a person internalizes to motivate herself to think, feel, and behave in counternormative ways—helps individuals become better inclusive leaders. Indeed, a goal of this chapter is to illuminate one pathway by which leaders demonstrate Quinn and Quinn's definition of leadership as that which "occurs when people choose to follow someone who deviates from an accepted cultural norm or social convention" (Quinn & Quinn, 2015, pp. 8–9).

### It's Hard to Create an Inclusive Workplace

Inclusive workplaces embody a collective commitment to integrating diverse cultural identities as a source of insight and skill that contributes to getting real work done (Davidson, 2011; Ely & Thomas, 2001). However, these inclusive environments are not commoditized spaces that a leader can acquire from a top-notch consulting firm. Rather, inclusive environments are the product of leaders and organization members enacting inclusive practices (Ferdman & Davidson, 2002; Ferdman, 2014). Inclusive practices create environments in which a broader range of people can feel safe, accepted, valued, and able to contribute their talents and perspectives for the benefit of the collective (Ferdman & Roberts, 2014). These practices promote resilient high quality connections across difference among colleagues (Davidson & James, 2007), imbue an ethos of transparency and fairness throughout the organization, and instill a value for collaborative decision-making that incorporates diverse perspectives (Nishii, 2013).

The problem is that the everyday pressures of leadership frequently hinder one's ability to practice inclusion. Leaders juggle complexity, ambiguity, and competing strategic demands in their organizations: do they need to foster greater collaboration or greater independence among business units? In the global marketplace, how do they maintain control and consistency across national/cultural boundaries? How do they access the data they need to make effective decisions when gatekeepers frequently limit information flow upward? In my conversations with C-level executives, these business challenges are but a few of the issues that keep them awake at night—and that divert mindshare from the practice of inclusion. Confronting the overwhelming presence of these challenges frequently leaves leaders throwing up their hands and extolling "I just don't have time to be sensitive to everybody."

This understandable frustration underscores the need to address the most formidable barriers leaders face in attempting to enact inclusive leadership practice: their own skill gaps. Leaders often do not know how to support individuals as group members, ensure justice and equity within the group, and promote individuals' diverse and unique contributions to the work of the group (Randel et al., 2018). Studies also highlight the importance for inclusion of showing respect and empathy, recognizing the other as different but equal, showing appreciation for different voices by listening actively to them, trying to understand disparate viewpoints and opinions, and integrating different voices into the ongoing cultural discourse (Pless & Maak, 2004). Ongoing research is likely to reveal additional critical competencies for inclusive leadership. But whatever the requisite collection of skills, far too many leaders fail to master it. The good news is that there may be an untapped accelerator for learning these essential leadership competencies.

## Knowing Yourself Helps You Lead Inclusively

Individuals who are self-aware—who understand their own identities and experience—begin to tap into that accelerant. They are more likely to develop leadership practices that are supportive and energizing for others (Avolio & Gardner, 2005). The idea that the awareness of one's myriad social identities creates greater facility in self-management and leadership is not new (Ferdman & Roberts, 2014). Indeed, such leaders are more apt to have higher quality relationships with others and more likely to experience well-being (Sedlovskaya et al., 2013). Moreover, they are more likely to demonstrate courage and resilience in the face of challenges (Detert & Burris, 2007).

Developing this personal insight, however, requires traveling along two parallel paths. On one path, a leader uncovers characteristics and attributes that highlight strengths the individual possesses and can use as resources for superior leadership (Roberts, 2013). A variety of tools that help individuals identify these generative attributes aid in the development of that facet of self-insight (Rath, 2007; Roberts, 2013). However, there is also a "dark side" of personal insight in which we explore not just weaknesses in our portfolio of skills, but more fundamental characteristics and attributes toward which we typically have considerable aversion.[1] This is the path of exploring one's weirdness.

## Why Weirdness Matters

There is an apocryphal story of Michelangelo in which he offered the following response to the inquiry of how he sculpted the famed statue of David: "You just chip away at everything that doesn't look like David." This approach to sculpting can also be applied to the inclusive leader's self-development. Frequently, emerging leaders—often identified for development because they show some distinctive talent—cultivate a persona they believe will allow them to be successful in their professional environments. They mimic any variety of counterproductive behaviors and practices, incorrectly assuming those actions will make them successful leaders. These leaders fail because in making themselves over, they learn to conceal the strengths and attributes that made them emergent leaders. They have unwittingly internalized messages—real and inferred—that many of their unique attributes would be liabilities to their success in the future.

Several years ago, my colleague Heather Wishik and I conducted research that potentially refuted that assumption (Wishik & Davidson, 2004). We asked senior executives of Fortune 500 companies to identify their most effective cross-cultural managers. We interviewed these managers to understand what made them exceptional. A number of insights emerged, but we were struck by an observation we had made about many U.S. leaders in the 1990s and early 2000s who were more skillful in leading diverse workgroups. These leaders frequently had some experience of social identity marginality in their life experience. In the sample of managers we interviewed in our global study, the experience was frequently that of living in a country or culture that was not native to the person and experiencing some hardship as a result. Some were children of expatriates and had followed their parents to different cultures. Among U.S. managers we observed anecdotally that many White male leaders came from a lower socio-economic class and, while on their rags to riches journey, frequently experienced challenging episodes of being discounted or excluded because of their class origins. As they moved up, they no longer belonged to their culture of origin, but they also did not fit, at least initially, into their more affluent environments (Martin & Côté, 2019). These are but a few of the conditions that might cause one to feel "weird." Yet, these managers' success was the result, in part, of their ability to capitalize on these experiences that, at first glance, were seen as impediments.

## The Experience of Weirdness

While the *Oxford English Dictionary* definition of weirdness as "the quality of being very strange" is illuminating, weirdness has a more specific meaning for our purposes. One's weirdness derives from a unique set of attributes and experiences that a person internalizes to motivate her or him to think, feel, and behave in counternormative ways. Moreover, weirdness also captures a valence of experience that is frequently aversive or unpleasant—indeed even painful—to the individual. This contrasts with the experience some have of weirdness as uniquely eccentric and ego enhancing, as captured by the city motto of Austin, Texas: "Get Weird!"

Consider two facets of weirdness. At a descriptive level, the elements that define a person as weird make that person differ substantively from his or her colleagues. In exploratory interviews with weird people in different corporate settings, our research team identified individuals who, by the convergent assessment of their colleagues, were deemed as outliers within the team. We did not define for the team members what makes one an outlier; we simply captured the team's global assessment. We interviewed those outliers to learn more about their experience of being weird. They described the ways in which they saw the world differently from their colleagues for many reasons.

Capturing the first facet of weirdness, some thought differently, seeing the world and approaching problems in unusual ways. One respondent commented:

> [I] kind of do the traffic control thing and look at like where there is [*sic*] like small fires starting and then just come in and pour some fuel on it.
>
> (L.M.)

Another respondent expressed it this way:

> I drive more from my gut than my head. More from my heart than my head, and Company X is an excruciatingly rational and literal place and that is not something that I fit into.
>
> (S.P.)

Others, by virtue of their social identity and group membership, reported feeling weird because they saw the world in ways consistent with their cultural identity, but different from the majority of their colleagues. This was especially true when the environment was more culturally homogeneous. The experiences of many people of color or White women who were the first and only of their identity group included the feeling of being weird (if not always labeled that way).

The second facet of weirdness was more poignant. An almost universal experience of these individuals was one of isolation and alienation. They frequently discussed their outlier experience in dispirited tones, even as they recounted the praise they received for their uniquely diverse perspectives and contributions. They rarely escaped some sense of suffering connected with being outside the norm. Interestingly, this was true even for individuals who received praise and encouragement for being different. It seemed that the core experience of weirdness was often accompanied by anxiety about the capacity to belong. There also seemed to be a concern that the weirdness was stable. One respondent captured a kind of resignation to being on the outside this way:

> I feel badly because … I will continue to think on it but I'll be honest, like I feel like my job is to like be the voice in the wind that's telling people where to go … If my voice is in the wind pushing people in this direction, I definitely have people that are like trying to fight the wind.
>
> (J.S.)

These initial interviews reveal that weirdness creates a shadow. Because it is unpleasant and stigmatizing, individuals may work to downplay or "cover" that which they experience as weird (Yoshino & Smith, 2014). However, this concealment and aversion has costs. Individuals expend energy to avoid appearing and feeling weird. Moreover, they work to distance themselves from contexts and people who are likely to stimulate their weird feelings and behaviors. As such, they limit their opportunities for building critical professional and personal relationships and for undertaking "stretch" experiences, each of which is critical in order to learn and grow.

## Embracing the Weird: The Fundamental Inclusive Leadership Practice

If insight into one's marginal experiences is truly a resource for effective inclusive leadership, those aspiring to develop their competence in this domain may benefit from exploring and experimenting with *their* experiences of weirdness. In doing so, they are better positioned to see their experience of otherness as a foundation for building networks and for learning. They can use their weirdness as an opportunity to differentiate themselves from others, thereby providing opportunities to see old problems and challenges in new ways. These efforts are especially generative in environments that include people of many different backgrounds, identities, and experiences. Drawing on Ferdman's (2014) inclusive leadership framework (see also Chapter 1, this volume), leaders can leverage their weirdness in multiple ways.

### *How to Embrace Intrapersonally*

Exploring weirdness in oneself begins with identifying traits or interests one possesses *and* dislikes. This requires the challenging practice of examining weaknesses, frailties, and vulnerabilities that we typically hide from others. A fruitful way to begin this exploration might be identifying blind spots in one's behavioral repertoire or observing habitual internal dialogue that includes self-denigration. Mindfulness practices that encourage one to remain present while reflecting on unappealing aspects of oneself can also be a helpful skill to cultivate. In particular, the practice of noting—but not judging—oneself when reflecting on those aspects diminishes the impulse to avoid exploring them. On the face of it, this way of looking at one's "warts" may not be the most energizing practice to undertake. However, it is a powerful way to prepare an inclusive leader to undertake the actions outlined below.

### *How to Embrace Interpersonally*

Seek out people you typically avoid or find unappealing. Frequently, we avoid other people for good reasons: for example, we experience them as unsavory or noxious in some way. There is nothing wrong with this discernment. The problem is that once the aversion to weirdness becomes a habit, it is far too easy to dismiss the very people with whom we most need to connect. These other people may be valuable in achieving completion of a task. They may be people from whom we can learn. Or they may just be people we find likeable. The experiment of embracing problematic others can help one become aware of the weird—yet valuable—people who frequently become invisible in organizations.

Once these people have been identified, a useful skill for connecting with them is exploring differences, rather than similarities. Typically, people meet and bond with others by discovering commonalities, such as favorite dishes or hobbies, that reinforce a feeling of closeness. However, another powerful way to connect is to explore ways in which we differ from another person. The key is to cultivate a stance of curiosity. Inquire about background information or interests and learn about aspects of the person's experience that may feel foreign or even uncomfortable to discuss. Through this process of connection, one can build more robust and resilient professional relationships across difference that enhance collaboration and individual well-being (Davidson & James, 2007; Dutton & Heaphy, 2003).

### *How to Embrace in Groups*

Seek out the outliers in a team. Frequently, there is a team member about whom teammates say, "if only she wasn't part of the team, we would be great!" While that may ultimately prove to be true, the reflexive avoidance of that which is weird to us can shield us from the value that outliers can provide to a team. Approaching weird teammates with curiosity—as opposed to isolating them—may surface perspectives, ideas, and innovation (Hewlett et al., 2013). Moreover, when a leader models the behavior of exploring the weird in a team, she or he may encourage other team members to do the same. The surfacing and valuing of diverse input in teams enhances team performance and increases the likelihood that the team can maintain that performance over time (e.g., Nederveen Pieterse et al., 2013).

### *How to Embrace Organizationally*

Our research interviews revealed that the dynamic of weirdness also manifests at the organizational level. Interdepartmental tension and dysfunction often result when one unit engages in countercultural practices or policies. This is particularly evident in highly decentralized organizational structures. Leaders can reinforce the value of doing things differently, particularly when the counternormative practices create valuable output. Highlighting the value of experimentation and failure—key in any organizational learning process—can also instill norms of embracing the weirdness in the organization (Davidson, 2011; Garvin et al., 2008). Creating collaborative structures that support knowledge transfer can also foster organizational learning from the weirdness (Barley et al., 2018).

## The Opportunity of Weirdness

Some try to overcome their weirdness by "overwriting" it—replacing it with mindsets, behaviors, and social networks that approximate the local norms. In essence, they work to eliminate the weird parts of themselves and try to blend in with "normal" people. For these people, marginality and weirdness is a liability that disrupts the individual's progress and must be excised in order to achieve professional goals. One implication of this choice is a greater risk of alienation from key organizational members: other weird people. A core objective of leadership is to bring into alignment people from differing identities, backgrounds, and perspectives to better serve the organization's mission and goals. One of the most powerful levers a leader has to accomplish this is the quality of relationships the leader creates with those individuals and their networks (Dutton & Heaphy, 2003). Adopting a habit of screening out weird people—the consequence of choosing to excise it in oneself—risks excluding the very people who possess the novel ideas and talents the leader may need most to achieve his or her goals. And there's an additional risk: the leader's aversion to weirdness likely sends a message to the larger organization that exclusion of others—and the negative effects associated with it—are sanctioned.

The practice of embracing weirdness creates a multitude of opportunities. It helps us come to terms with both our best selves and our internalized ideas of our worst selves. When we embrace our weirdness, we gain greater control over the fears and anxieties that cause us to act from egoistic, self-focused motives rather than generative mission-focused motives. This self-control better positions us to make choices that lead to efficacious outcomes in our professional and personal lives.

The capacity to discern wise choices from foolish ones matters in many ways. But it is especially important in the actual practice of embracing weirdness. Not all weird is good. Some of it is particularly destructive and should rightly be eschewed. In an iterative way, we become better at sorting our productive weirdness from our destructive weirdness. The more we explore weirdness, the more we understand how to free it up so that it enhances our organizations and our lives.

Embracing weirdness is embracing freedom. The more we stop hiding, the more we are free to be who we need to be in the contexts in which we work and live.

## Note

1 This aversion typically results from internally held images of ourselves that we reject. Those images are, of course, also informed by social interaction.

## References

Avolio, B. J., & Gardner, W. L. (2005). Authentic leadership development: Getting to the root of positive forms of leadership. *The Leadership Quarterly*, *16*(3), 315–338. https://doi.org/10.1016/j.leaqua.2005.03.001

Barley, W. C., Treem, J. W., & Kuhn, T. (2018). Valuing multiple trajectories of knowledge: A critical review and agenda for knowledge management research. *Academy of Management Annals*, *12*(1), 278–317. https://doi.org/10.5465/annals.2016.0041

Christian, M. S., Garza, A. S., & Slaughter, J. E. (2011). Work engagement: A quantitative review and test of its relations with task and contextual performance. *Personnel Psychology*, *64*(1), 89–136. https://doi.org/10.1111/j.1744-6570.2010.01203.x

Davidson, M. N. (2011). *The end of diversity as we know it: Why diversity efforts fail and how leveraging difference can succeed*. San Francisco, CA: Berrett-Koehler Publishers.

Davidson, M. N., & James, E. H. (2007). The engines of positive relationships across difference: Conflict and learning. In J. Dutton & B. R. Ragins (Eds.), *Exploring positive relationships at work: Building a theoretical and research foundation* (pp. 137–158). Hillsdale, NJ: Lawrence Erlbaum Associates.

Detert, J. R., & Burris, E. R. (2007). Leadership behavior and employee voice: Is the door really open? *Academy of Management Journal*, *50*(4), 869–884. https://doi.org/10.5465/AMJ.2007.26279183

Dutton, J., & Heaphy, E. (2003). The power of high quality connections. In K. Cameron, J. Dutton, & R. Quinn (Eds.), *Positive organizational scholarship* (pp. 263–278). San Francisco, CA: Berrett-Koehler.

Ely, R. J., & Thomas, D. A. (2001). Cultural diversity at work: The effects of diversity perspectives on work group processes and outcomes. *Administrative Science Quarterly*, *46*(2), 229–273. https://doi.org/10.2307/2667087

Ferdman, B. M. (2014). The practice of inclusion in diverse organizations: Toward a systemic and inclusive framework. In B. M. Ferdman & B. R. Deane (Eds) *Diversity at work: The practice of inclusion* (pp. 3–54). San Francisco, CA: Jossey-Bass. https://doi.org/10.1002/9781118764282.ch1

Ferdman, B. M. & Davidson, M. N. (2002). Inclusion: What can I and my organization do about it? *The Industrial-Organizational Psychologist*, *39*(4), 80–85.

Ferdman, B. M., & Roberts, L. M. (2014). Creating inclusion for oneself: Knowing, accepting, and expressing one's whole self at work. In B. M. Ferdman & B. R. Deane (Eds) *Diversity at work: The practice of inclusion* (pp. 93–127). San Francisco, CA: Jossey-Bass. https://doi.org/10.1002/9781118764282.ch3

Garvin, D. A., Edmondson, A. C., & Gino, F. (2008). Is yours a learning organization? *Harvard Business Review*, *86*(3), 109–116.

Harter, J. K., Schmidt, F. L., & Hayes, T. L. (2002). Business-unit-level relationship between employee satisfaction, employee engagement, and business outcomes: A meta-analysis. *Journal of Applied Psychology*, *87*(2), 268–279. https://doi.org/10.1037/0021-9010.87.2.268

Hewlett, S. A., Marshall, M., & Sherbin, L. (2013). How diversity can drive innovation. *Harvard Business Review*, *91*(12), 30.

Ibarra, H., & Obodaru, O. (2016). Betwixt and between identities: Liminal experience in contemporary careers. *Research in Organizational Behavior*, *36*, 47–64. https://doi.org/10.1016/j.riob.2016.11.003

Lau, D. C., & Murnighan, J. K. (1998). Demographic diversity and faultlines: The compositional dynamics of organizational groups. *Academy of Management Review*, *23*(2), 325–340. https://doi.org/10.5465/amr.1998.533229

Martin, S. R., & Côté, S. (2019). Social class transitioners: Their cultural abilities and organizational importance. *Academy of Management Review*. https://doi.org/10.5465/amr.2017.0065

Nederveen Pieterse, A., van Knippenberg, D., & van Dierendonck, D. (2013). Cultural diversity and team performance: The role of team member goal orientation. *Academy of Management Journal*, *56*(3), 782–804. https://doi.org/10.5465/amj.2010.0992

Nishii, L. H. (2013). The benefits of climate for inclusion for gender-diverse groups. *Academy of Management Journal*, *56*(6), 1754–1774. https://doi.org/10.5465/amj.2009.0823

Pless, N. M., & Maak, T. (2004). Building an inclusive diversity culture: Principles, processes, and practice. *Journal of Business Ethics*, *54*(2), 129–147. https://doi.org/ 10.1007/s10551-004-9465-8

Quinn, R. W., & Quinn, R. E. (2015). *Lift: The fundamental state of leadership* (2nd ed.). San Francisco, CA: Berrett-Koehler.

Randel, A. E., Galvin, B. M., Shore, L. M., Ehrhart, K. H., Chung, B. G., Dean, M. A., & Kedharnath, U. (2018). Inclusive leadership: Realizing positive outcomes through belongingness and being valued for uniqueness. *Human Resource Management Review*, *28*(2), 190–203. https://doi.org/10.1016/j.hrmr.2017.07.002

Rath, T. (2007). *Strengths finder 2.0*. New York, NY: Gallup Press.

Roberts, L. M. (2013). Reflected best self engagement at work: Positive identity, alignment, and the pursuit of vitality and value creation. In S. A. David, I. Boniwell, & A. Conley Ayers (Eds), *The Oxford handbook of happiness* (pp. 767–782). New York, NY: Oxford University Press. https://doi.org/10.1093/oxfordhb/9780199557257.013.0056

Sedlovskaya, A., Purdie-Vaughns, V., Eibach, R. P., LaFrance, M., Romero-Canyas, R., & Camp, N. P. (2013). Internalizing the closet: Concealment heightens the cognitive distinction between public and private selves. *Journal of Personality and Social Psychology*, *104*(4), 695–715. https://doi.org/10.1037/a0031179

Wishik, H. R., & Davidson, M. N. (2004). *Three core approaches to global leadership and its complexities*. Charlottesville, VA: Darden Graduate School of Business Working Paper Series.

Yoshino, K., & Smith, C. (2014). Fear of being different stifles talent. *Harvard Business Review*, *92*(3), 28.

# 10 Boundary-Spanning Leadership

## Strategies to Create a More Inclusive and Effective Network

*Donna Chrobot-Mason and Nicholas P. Aramovich*

The greatest challenges we face today know no boundaries. Disease, poverty, climate change, and natural disasters have no regard for national, cultural, or economic differences. And yet the organizations we create to tackle such challenges operate within a context in which geographic, demographic, and organizational boundaries not only exist, but make collaboration difficult and complex. The responsibility to overcome such barriers to collaboration rests largely upon the shoulders of today's organizational leaders. Yet, our traditional individual-focused definition of leadership, in which leadership resides within an individual who holds a leadership title, fails to provide sufficient insight into the leadership needed during today's turbulent times. Complex challenges require not just a single leader, but rather a network of leaders collaborating to share ideas, best practices, and resources.

The traditional image of leader as hero, savior, or white knight is being replaced with a new image: that of a collective group of people exerting influence and taking action (Yukl, 1999). Various labels have been applied to emerging leadership practices, including relational, collective, shared, and interdependent. In plural forms of leadership, rather than accomplishing tasks organized by a hierarchy of authority, tasks are achieved through networks of influence relationships (Fletcher, 2004) and boundary spanning (Ernst & Chrobot-Mason, 2010). Thus, the role of leaders is changing from a romantic savior to that of a boundary spanner or connector, requiring key behaviors designed to create an inclusive and collaborative network.

In this chapter we examine the important role that leaders play in spanning boundaries between individuals, teams, divisions, and organizations. We explain what a boundary-spanning mindset is and how leaders can begin to adopt this mindset. We then identify the types of behaviors that leaders must engage in to span boundaries effectively. Next, we focus on connecting and networking behavior and the importance of developing an inclusive network to more effectively span boundaries. As part of this, we lead readers through an activity to map their own network and identify opportunities for improvement.

## The Challenge of Intergroup Collaboration

Leadership may be defined as the creation of direction, alignment, and commitment (McCauley et al., 2010). In order to achieve their goals, leaders must foster collaboration both within and across groups. Yet, such collaboration is often fraught with significant barriers as diverse groups attempt to work together. According to social identity theory, the organizational groups we belong to are an important part of our personal identity. Yet, at the same time, the way we define ourselves and the groups we belong to create divisions in the workplace that demarcate the boundaries between "us" and "them" (e.g., Hogg et al., 2012; Lau & Murnighan, 1998). Differences based on demographics (age, gender, race, sexual orientation, etc.), geography, organizational hierarchy, and area of expertise are just some of the many barriers or boundaries that leaders must span to accomplish their mission. Unfortunately, hundreds of studies using the minimal groups paradigm show that the very existence of social categories engenders a competitive and ethnocentric orientation toward the other side (Hogg, 2015). Research also finds that intergroup relations are characterized by much more mistrust, competition, and conflict than relationships between individuals (Wildschut et al., 2003).

One might assume that the best approach to fostering intergroup collaboration is to minimize the boundaries between groups and focus on creating a shared identity through establishing superordinate goals. Indeed, classic social psychological research shows that intergroup cooperation is encouraged when two groups adopt the same overarching goal, and understand that neither group can achieve it without the help of the other (Hogg, 2015; Sherif, 1966). Importantly, however, research and theory suggest that if establishing superordinate goals comes at the expense of eroding existing group boundaries, intergroup conflict rather than cooperation is likely to occur (Hogg & Terry, 2000; Hornsey & Hogg, 2000). The key to understanding this apparent paradox is informed by optimal distinctiveness theory, which suggests that humans strive for the optimal balance between two fundamental but opposing needs—the need for belonging, validation, and similarity on the one hand, and the need for uniqueness and individuation on the other (Brewer, 1991). According to the theory, individuals meet their need for belonging and similarity through relationships with in-group members, and meet their need for uniqueness through comparisons with out-groups (Brewer, 1991).

The implication for organizational leaders is that employees and work groups will be most satisfied when they are made to feel a part of the organization's broader mission, but also recognized for their unique expertise and contributions (Ernst & Chrobot-Mason, 2010). In contrast, when leaders focus only on shared identity and purpose, and minimize group differences, employees from different groups may view this as an assimilation strategy that threatens their unique identities (e.g., Roberts & Creary, 2013). When this happens, group members may react negatively, for example by derogating their leader who is seen as the source of their identity threat (Petriglieri, 2011). Indeed, research indicates that applying a colorblind perspective (i.e., ignoring differences as opposed to valuing diversity) is negatively related to employees' trust in their organization (Purdie-Vaughns et al., 2008). Similarly, minority group members distance themselves from their groups and experience more relationship conflict when group leaders support colorblindness, but report feeling more accepted when leaders endorse multiculturalism (Meeussen et al., 2014). Furthermore, research shows that when leaders believe in the performance benefits of diversity, the negative effects of socio-demographic faultlines on group cohesion are mitigated (Schölmerich et al., 2016).

Thus, to overcome the challenges often inherent in attempts at intergroup collaboration, leaders must first adopt a boundary-spanning mindset. Then, leaders must engage in boundary-spanning behaviors that foster inclusion and collaboration by balancing organizational members' paradoxical needs for both belonging and uniqueness.

## Boundary Spanning: Changing Your Mindset

The appreciation for and willingness to integrate both similarities and differences across groups is a key feature of adopting a *boundary-spanning mindset.* The basis of this mindset is the recognition that collaboration between two or more diverse groups—including harnessing the unique ideas, perspectives, and contributions of each—is necessary to achieve certain organizational goals (Chrobot-Mason et al., 2016). Additionally, however, leaders who adopt a boundary-spanning mindset have an understanding and appreciation of the importance that group memberships have for personal identity. Accordingly, they recognize that emphasizing similarities and common goals as well as differences and unique perspectives across groups is necessary to avoid intergroup conflict stemming from social identity threat.

Therefore, we propose that leaders who seek to encourage and facilitate intergroup collaboration should create a sense of belonging by focusing on a common, shared, or inclusive goal or mission that diverse groups are all working to achieve. At the same time however, boundary-spanning leaders must send the message that individuals and groups are valued for the unique perspectives, experiences, opinions, priorities, and expertise that they bring to that common mission.

## Boundary Spanning: Leading across Difference

In our view, adopting a boundary-spanning mindset is a necessary precursor to being a boundary-spanning leader, as it provides the motivation to enact three broad classes of behaviors. Specifically, based on the work of Ernst and Chrobot-Mason (2010) and a review of the literature, we suggest that boundary-spanning leaders engage in three high-level boundary-spanning practices: 1) managing group boundaries, 2) identifying common ground, and 3) leveraging differences. In the sections that follow, we describe these high-level practices as well as specific leadership behaviors for each.

### *Managing Group Boundaries*

As previously mentioned, rather than eliminate group boundaries, leaders should instead focus on a strategy to carefully manage existing group boundaries. In our experience, leaders are often surprised to learn that successful boundary spanning requires activities that serve to strengthen team boundaries (Dey & Ganesh, 2017). Specifically, *boundary reinforcement* involves leaders working with different teams or subgroups to make members more aware of team boundaries, focus energy and commitment on the central team task, and encourage the team to develop a clear and distinct team identity (e.g., Cross et al., 2000; Faraj & Yan, 2009). Specific activities may include involving group members in shaping or re-shaping their mission, vision, and goals; creating team-specific language, symbols, or artifacts to reinforce their mission/vision, honoring "homegrown" cultural practices (for example celebrating successes), and adapting information and communication technology to fit the needs of the team (e.g., Faraj & Yan, 2009).

The complementary practice of *buffering* involves shielding group members from external demands, pressure, or interference so that they can focus on their central tasks, as well as developing and maintaining a clear group identity (Dey & Ganesh, 2017; Ernst & Chrobot-Mason, 2010; Faraj & Yan, 2009). Specific leader activities include working with team members to create formal and informal procedures as well as norms for managing external requests. Research finds that leaders who are skilled at buffering their teams from external demands are perceived to have strong political skills (e.g., Benoliel & Somech, 2015), which is understandable as buffering and guarding activities may be perceived negatively by external stakeholders (Ancona & Caldwell, 1988). However, both buffering and boundary reinforcement are important practices for boundary-spanning leaders because they are related to important team outcomes, including psychological safety and team performance (for a review, see Dey & Ganesh, 2017).

Finally, boundary management requires leaders to encourage members to identify both the differences and similarities between groups and to help each one understand the identities of the other groups. The goal is to help group members understand and appreciate their counterparts' values, priorities, expertise, roles, and needs. Specific activities may involve encouraging members of some groups to attend meetings of the other groups, or to read postings on their intranet site (Ernst & Chrobot-Mason, 2011). In sum, these boundary-management behaviors overcome threats to group members' unique identities by maintaining positive distinctiveness (Fiol et al., 2009) and identity clarity (Ernst & Chrobot-Mason, 2011; Rothman & Chrobot-Mason, 2012).

### *Identifying Common Ground*

By managing boundaries and maintaining positive distinctiveness between groups, leaders set the stage for identifying common ground. Their next goal is to encourage members from different groups to develop personal connections by "stepping outside" of group boundaries into a neutral zone where people can interact as individuals rather than as members of separate identity groups (Ernst & Chrobot-Mason, 2011). This leadership strategy was derived from research based on social identity theory, which suggests that the conflict stemming from group-based identity differences can be mitigated by emphasizing one-on -one personal interactions rather than group-based interactions (Brewer & Miller, 1984). It is also consistent with research that emphasizes leadership as a relational process (Hogg, 2001).

If such connecting is sustained over time and new relationships are built, the boundaries that created rigid borders between groups become more porous and intergroup trust will grow. Researchers, however, caution the need to create boundaries that are porous enough to allow resources and information in, yet not so porous as to undermine the boundary management work described earlier by creating uncertainty about who is on the team and who may be accountable for specific team outcomes (Faraj & Yan, 2009; Hackman, 2002). One example of connecting is when leaders create "attractor" or larger open-air workspaces that encourage informal interaction and can temporarily eliminate the physical boundaries that separate groups by job function or supervisory level (Ernst & Chrobot-Mason, 2011). In creating attractor spaces, it is important that leaders maintain some physical boundaries as research shows that open office plans actually decrease productivity and employee well-being (Davis et al., 2011). Yet it is important for leaders to create opportunities for employees to interact and develop relationships with one another. This builds on the work done earlier by the leaders encouraging group members to prioritize getting to know one another and understand others' values, priorities, expertise, roles, and needs. These activities encourage people to individuate others by empathizing with them or taking their perspective and avoids some of the negative effects of social categorization, such as stereotyping (Hogg, 2015).

Once relationships have been developed and trust built between groups, leaders can then begin the work of creating a common mission, vision, or set of goals (Ernst & Chrobot-Mason, 2011). In doing so, the goal is to create an intergroup relational identity (Hogg, 2015; Hogg et al., 2012) in which each group's distinct and unique roles in the service of contributing to a common, superordinate goal are identified. By engaging groups in crafting and co-creating a superordinate goal, leaders encourage groups to transcend their smaller group identity and create a new and larger identity (Dovidio et al., 2001; Sherif, 1958).

One type of leadership practice to foster a common mission is for leaders to narrate stories as a way to express common purpose and identity (Ernst & Chrobot-Mason, 2011). Examples include sharing anecdotes of previous success within the company, case studies of industry leaders, or even important historic events in which multiple groups needed to come together to achieve a common mission. According to Ernst and Chrobot-Mason (2011), these types of narratives transmit values to guide and instruct behavior and encourage disparate groups to work together as members of a shared community in pursuit of some transcendent purpose. In addition, some of our own research involving interviews with leaders suggests that many leaders use the tactic of convening key stakeholders from different groups and constituencies to share information, brainstorm ideas, and engage in collective problem-solving around shared issues. In doing so, these leaders involve others in the co-creation of common purpose. However common purpose is achieved, when members of different groups share a superordinate identity, much research from social psychology suggests that past conflicts are overcome and competitive intergroup relationships are transformed into cooperative ones (Hogg, 2015). For example, research by Kane (2010) shows that when different subgroups shared a superordinate identity, the knowledge from one was more likely to be considered and used by the other.

### *Leveraging Differences*

Once common goals and shared collective identity are established, a leader's role is to leverage the unique capabilities of all individuals and groups to the fullest extent (Chrobot-Mason & Aramovich, 2013; Kochan et al., 2003; Page, 2007). It is, however, important to note that managing boundaries in which differences are emphasized is a critical first step. If the leader attempts to build a superordinate identity without first meeting group members' needs for uniqueness by valuing differences, this will likely lead to intergroup polarization (Gaertner et al., 1993; Gaertner et al., 1999). Research and theory on subcategorization (Haslam & Ellemers, 2005; Hewstone & Brown, 1986) and cross-cutting roles and identities (Brewer, 1995) has shown that when groups have distinct but complementary roles to contribute toward a common goal, both differences and commonalities are emphasized, leading to more positive intergroup attitudes and work outcomes (Eggins et al., 2002; Haslam et al., 2003). In summary, leaders who can effectively span boundaries and meet group member needs for both uniqueness and belonging will be best able to leverage the value that diversity can bring.

## Becoming a Boundary-Spanning Leader: Start with Connecting

One way to begin the work of developing your boundary-spanning leadership skills is to map your existing network to identify opportunities for leveraging differences. There are three main reasons leaders should attempt to maximize the effectiveness of their network. First, leaders who are able to cultivate a network of diverse relationships will be more aware of the unique capabilities of different groups in their networks. Armed with this awareness, they can identify which groups, inside or outside of their organization, are particularly important or well-suited for involvement in a specific collaborative effort. Second, it models this important behavior for others. Third, creating an effective network ensures that when the leader is faced with a novel or particularly difficult problem, they are better equipped to enlist the help of others—especially other leaders—and develop intergroup collaborations to gain access to resources or expertise that will be helpful (Hogg, 2015).

Mapping your network need not be complex. You can gain a basic understanding of the effectiveness of your network by following the steps below. To participate in this activity, all you will need is a blank piece of paper, a pencil, and a highlighter or marker. These are the steps:

1. On a blank piece of paper, draw a small circle in the middle of the page with your name in the middle.
2. Identify individuals or organizations that are part of your leadership network—those most critical to your success.
3. For this next set of instructions, read the following (3a–3c) through once before drawing on your piece of paper.

    a. Draw squares with the names of those individuals or organizations inside the square and draw arrows from you (in the circle) to each of these squares.

b The arrows will indicate relationships. For a strong relationship (e.g., someone you interact with frequently, trust and know well, rely on, etc.) use a solid line. For a weak relationship, draw a dashed line.

c Finally, draw arrows (solid or dashed to indicate the strength of relationship) between all the individuals and organizations displayed in your network. In other words, if two people in your network have a weak relationship (e.g., know of one another but have not collaborated), then you may wish to draw a dashed line between those two people. If no relationship exists between individuals or organizations in your network, this will be illustrated with no line drawn between them.

4 Consider the individuals and organizations in your network with respect to diversity. It may be the case that most of the people and organizations in your network are a lot like you in terms of expertise, demographics, perspectives, values, etc. However, highlight those that you feel are quite different from you in some meaningful way.

5 Now, examine your network by looking at what you have drawn. Note any initial reactions or observations you have before reading further.

There are three main factors to consider when evaluating your network. Effective networks are open, deep, and diverse (Cullen-Lester et al., 2016). First, an *open network* is one in which not all individuals and organizations are connected to one another. A closed network, in contrast, is one in which members of the network share information and resources. Leaders who have open networks are boundary spanners or "brokers," in that they serve to connect individuals or groups to one another who would otherwise not know or have access to one another. In this way, leaders are able to facilitate the sharing of unique expertise and resources (Burt, 1992). Second, a *deep network* involves strong ties or deep relationships characterized by trust, mutual disclosure, and a level of intimacy (Tortoriello et al., 2012). This of course suggests that more is not always better when it comes to evaluating members of one's network. Developing and maintaining deep relationships requires time and energy. Although it may seem advantageous to develop as large a network as possible, quantity, of course, comes at the expense of quality. Rather than create a large network filled with superficial relationships or weak ties, research suggests that leaders benefit more from nurturing fewer but deeper relationships (Cross & Thomas, 2011), particularly with sponsors and key stakeholders (Ibarra & Hunter, 2007).

Finally, leaders should strive to create a *diverse network*. This may be the most difficult to achieve: decades of research suggest that we as human beings are drawn to and interact most with people we consider to be most like us (Byrne, 1971; McPherson et al., 2001). And yet, as we have argued throughout this chapter, to be effective in today's turbulent and complex workplace, leaders can no longer rely only on themselves or the knowledge and resources to which those like them have access. Rather, today's effective leader knows how to leverage the diverse expertise, background, experiences, and ideas of many different individuals, groups, and organizations. A diverse network is one in which members of the network cross hierarchical, organizational, functional, geographic, and demographic lines (Cross & Cummings, 2004). Such relationships result in greater learning, less bias in decision making, and greater personal growth (Cross & Thomas, 2011).

## Building a More Inclusive Network

As you consider the extent to which your network is open, deep, and diverse, you may wish to ask yourself questions such as the following:

1 What connections should I actively attempt to make going forward?
2 What can I do to deepen key relationships in my network?
3 Are there some connections in my network that I should step back from to focus on fewer but more in-depth ties?
4 What blind spots exist in my network (with regard to, for example, areas of expertise, demographic differences, etc.)?
5 What can I do to create a more diverse and inclusive network?

Cullen-Lester et al. (2016) identify four strategies for improving one's network: building a new connection, maintaining or deepening a relationship, leveraging a contact, and transitioning (or weakening) a relationship. Naturally, individuals tend to utilize and feel more comfortable with some strategies over others. For instance, some may find meeting and talking to new people at networking events to be exciting while others find it draining. Some may be very comfortable asking a contact to recommend them for a promotion or valued opportunity, while others shy away from such an approach that they perceive to be opportunistic. However, it is important to note that all four are effective strategies to enhance one's network (Cullen-Lester et al., 2016) and therefore should be utilized at different times depending on one's professional and networking goals and needs.

Indeed, it is important to evaluate one's network on a regular basis and consider over- and under-utilization of these four strategies, particularly during times of transition. For example, while it may be useful to conduct a network diagnosis to identify blind spots and potential opportunities to improve effectiveness in one's current role, it may be even more useful to evaluate one's network from the perspective of a future role. Examining one's network through the lens of obtaining a promotion, making a significant career transition, or tackling a new grand challenge allows one to identify key individuals, groups, or organizations that will be critical to one's success and then begin to find opportunities to make those connections.

Perhaps the most important thing to consider when attempting to create a more inclusive network is to recognize that building such a network requires effort and thoughtful attention (Burt & Ronchi, 2007). If we fail to pay attention to the type of network we are creating, we will more than likely build a network of people much like ourselves with relational ties to others much like ourselves. It is only through ongoing evaluation and adaption of our networking strategies as well as a boundary-spanning mindset that we are able to span across boundaries to create a more inclusive and thus a more effective network.

## Conclusion

In conclusion, solving the world's most significant challenges requires organizations and the people within them to collaborate across boundaries. However, collaborating across boundaries is difficult—not only practically, but psychologically as well. Indeed, national, geographic, cultural, and demographic boundaries form the bases of our social identities, and collaborating with diverse others is often fraught with conflict. We suggest that leaders are more effective leading across boundaries when they adopt a boundary-spanning mindset and engage in three high-level boundary-spanning practices: 1) managing group boundaries, 2) identifying common ground, and 3) leveraging differences. Additionally, one way for leaders to begin to develop their boundary-spanning leadership skills is to start by mapping and strengthening their existing networks. Mapping their networks allows leaders to gain an awareness of the unique capabilities of different individuals and groups in their networks, so that they know who to call on when opportunities for collaboration arise. Finally, strengthening their networks by forming connections to others ensures that when leaders are faced with particularly novel or difficult problems, they are better equipped to enlist the help of others—especially other leaders—to develop the necessary intergroup collaborations to solve these problems across boundaries.

## References

Ancona, D. G., & Caldwell, D. F. (1988). Beyond task and maintenance: Defining external functions in groups. *Group & Organization Management*, *13*, 468–494. https://doi.org/10.1177/105960118801300405

Benoliel, P., & Somech, A. (2015). The role of leader boundary activities in enhancing interdisciplinary team effectiveness. *Small Group Research*, *46*, 83–124. https://doi.org/10.1177/1046496414560028

Brewer, M. B. (1991). The social self: On being the same and different at the same time. *Personality and Social Psychology Bulletin*, *17*, 475–482. https://doi.org/10.1177/0146167291175001

Brewer, M. B., & Miller, N. (Eds.). (1984). *Groups in contact: The psychology of desegregation*. Orlando, FL: Academic Press.

Brewer, M. B. (1995). Managing diversity: The role of social identities. In S. E. Jackson, & M. N. Ruderman's (Eds.), *Diversity in work teams: Research paradigms for a changing workplace* (pp. 47–68). Washington, DC: American Psychological Association. https://doi.org/10.1037/10189-002

Burt, R. S. (1992). *Structural holes: The social structure of competition*. Cambridge, MA: Harvard University Press.

Burt, R. S., & Ronchi, D. (2007). Teaching executives to see social capital: Results from a field experiment. *Social Science Research*, *36*(3), 1156–1183. https://doi.org/10.1016/j.ssresearch.2006.09.005

Byrne, D. E. (1971). *The attraction paradigm*. New York, NY: Academic Press.

Chrobot-Mason, D., & Aramovich, N. (2013). The psychological benefits of creating an affirming climate for workplace diversity. *Group and Organization Management*, *38*(6), 659–689. https://doi.org/10.1177/1059601113509835

Chrobot-Mason, D., Yip, J., & Yu, A. (2016). Leading beyond we: The nature and consequences of a boundary spanning mindset. In L. M. Roberts, L. P. Wooten, & M. N. Davidson (Eds.), *Positive organizing in a global society: Understanding and engaging differences for capacity-building and inclusion* (pp. 105–109). New York, NY: Taylor & Francis.

Cross, R., & Cummings, J. N. (2004). Tie and network correlates of individual performance in knowledge-intensive work. *Academy of Management Journal*, *47*(6), 928–937. https://doi.org/10.2307/20159632

Cross, R., & Thomas, R. J. (2011). A smarter way to network. *Harvard Business Review*, *89*(7–8), 149–153.

Cross, R. L., Yan, A., & Louis, M. R. (2000). Boundary activities in 'boundaryless' organizations: A case study of a transformation to a team-based structure. *Human Relations*, *53*, 841–868. https://doi.org/10.1177/0018726700536004

Cullen-Lester, K. L., Woehler, M. L., & Willburn, P. (2016). Network-based leadership development: A guiding framework and resources for management educators. *Journal of Management Education*, *40(3)*, 321–358. https://doi.org/10.1177/1052562915624124

Davis, M. C., Leach, D., & Clegg, C. (2011). The physical environment of the office: Contemporary and emerging issues. In G. P. Hodgkinson & J. K. Ford (Eds.), *International review of industrial and organizational psychology* (Vol. 26, pp. 193–237). Chichester, UK: Wiley. https://doi.org/10.1002/9781119992592.ch6

Dey, C., & Ganesh, M. P. (2017). Team boundary activity: A review and directions for future research. *Team Performance Management: An International Journal*, *23*, 273–292. https://doi.org/10.1108/TPM-06-2016-0029

Dovidio, J. F., Gaertner, S. L., Niemann, Y. F., & Snider, K. (2001). Racial, ethnic, and cultural differences in responding to distinctiveness and discrimination on campus: Stigma and common group identity. *Journal of Social Issues*, *57*(1), 167–188. https://doi.org/10.1111/0022-4537.00207

Eggins, R. A., Haslam, S. A., & Reynolds, K. J. (2002). Social identity and negotiation: Subgroup representation and superordinate consensus. *Personality and Social Psychology Bulletin*, *28*, 887–899. https://doi.org/10.1177/014616720202800703

Ernst, C., & Chrobot-Mason, D. (2010). *Boundary spanning leadership: Six practices for solving problems, driving innovation, and transforming organizations*. New York, NY: McGraw-Hill.

Ernst, C., & Chrobot-Mason, D. (2011). Flat world, hard boundaries: How to lead across them. *MIT Sloan Management Review*, *52*(3), 81–88.

Faraj, S., & Yan, A. (2009). Boundary work in knowledge teams. *Journal of Applied Psychology*, *94*, 604–617. https://doi.org/10.1037/a0014367

Fiol, C. M., Pratt, M. G., & O'Connor, E. J. (2009). Managing intractable identity conflicts. *Academy of Management Review*, *34*, 32–55. https://doi.org/10.5465/AMR.2009.35713276

Fletcher, J. K. (2004). The paradox of postheroic leadership: An essay on gender, power, and transformational change. *The Leadership Quarterly*, *15*, 647–661. https://doi.org/10.1016/j.leaqua.2004.07.004

Gaertner, S. L., Dovidio, J. F., Anastasio, P. A., Bachman, B. A., & Rust, M. C. (1993). The common ingroup identity model: Recategorisation and the reduction of inter-group bias. *European Review of Social Psychology*, *4*, 3–24. https://doi.org/10.1080/14792779343000004

Gaertner, S. L., Dovidio, J. F., Rust, M. C., Nier, J. A., Bankers, B. S., Ward, C. M., . . . Houlette, M. (1999). Reducing intergroup bias: Elements of intergroup cooperation. *Journal of Personality and Social Psychology*, *76*, 388–402. https://doi.org/10.1037/0022-3514.76.3.388

Hackman, J. R. (2002). *Leading teams: Setting the stage for great performances*. Boston, MA: Harvard Business School Press.

Haslam, S. A., Eggins, R. A., & Reynolds, K. J. (2003). The ASPIRe model: Actualizing social and personal identity resources to enhance organizational outcomes. *Journal of Occupational and Organizational Psychology*, *76*, 83–113. https://doi.org/10.1348/096317903321208907

Haslam, S. A., & Ellemers, N. (2005). Social identity in industrial and organizational psychology: Concepts, controversies, and contributions. In G. P. Hodgkinson & J. K. Ford (Eds.), *International review of industrial and organizational psychology* (Vol. 20, pp. 39–118). Chichester, UK: John Wiley & Sons, Ltd. https://doi.org/10.1002/0470029307.ch2

Hewstone, M., & Brown, R. (1986). Contact is not enough: An intergroup perspective on the contact hypothesis. In M. Hewstone & R. Brown (Eds.), *Contact and conflict in intergroup encounters* (pp. 1–44). Oxford, UK: Blackwell.

Hogg, M. A. (2001). A social identity theory of leadership. *Personality and Social Psychology Review*, *5*, 184–200. https://doi.org/10.1207/S15327957PSPR0503_1

Hogg, M. A. (2015). Constructive leadership across groups: How leaders can combat prejudice and conflict between subgroups. *Advances in Group Processes*, *32*, 177–207. https://doi.org/10.1108/s0882–614520150000032007

Hogg, M. A., & Terry, D. I. (2000). Social identity and self-categorization processes in organizational contexts. *Academy of Management Review*, *25*, 121–140. https://doi.org/10.2307/259266

Hogg, M. A., van Knippenberg, D., & Rast, D. E. (2012). Intergroup leadership in organizations: Leading across group and organizational boundaries. *Academy of Management Review*, *37*, 232–255. https://doi.org/10.5465/amr.2010.0221

Hornsey, M. J., & Hogg, M. A. (2000). Assimilation and diversity: An integrative model of subgroup relations. *Personality and Social Psychology Review*, *4*(2), 143–156. https://doi.org/10.1207/S15327957PSPR0402_03

Ibarra, H., & Hunter, M. (2007). How leaders create and use networks. *Harvard Business Review*, *85*(1), 40–47.

Kane, A. A. (2010). Unlocking knowledge transfer potential: Knowledge demonstrability and superordinate social identity. *Organization Science*, *21*, 643–660. https://doi.org/10.1287/orsc.1090.0469

Kochan, T., Bezrukova, K., Ely, R., Jackson, S., Joshi, A., Jehn, K., . . . Thomas, D. (2003). The effects of diversity on business performance: Report of the Diversity Research Network. *Human Resource Management*, *42*, 3–21. https://doi.org/10.1002/hrm.10061

Lau, D. C., & Murnighan, J. K. (1998). Demographic diversity and faultlines: The compositional dynamics of organizational groups. *Academy of Management Review*, *23*, 325–340. https://doi.org/10.5465/amr.1998.533229

McCauley, C. D., Van Velsor, E., & Ruderman, M. N. (2010). Introduction: Our view of leadership development. In E. Van Velsor, C. McCauley, & M. N. Ruderman (Eds.), *Handbook of leadership development* (pp. 1–26). San Francisco, CA: John Wiley & Sons Inc.

McPherson, M., Smith-Lovin, L., & Cook, J. M. (2001). Birds of a feather: Homophily in social networks. *Annual Review of Sociology*, *27*, 415–444. https://doi.org/10.1146/annurev.soc.27.1.415

Meeussen, L., Otten, S., & Phalet, K. (2014). Managing diversity: How leaders' multiculturalism and colorblindness affect work group functioning. *Group Processes & Intergroup Relations*, *17*, 629–644. https://doi.org/10.1177/1368430214525809

Page, S. E. (2007). Making the difference: Applying a logic of diversity. *Academy of Management Perspectives*, *21*(4), 6–20. https://doi.org/10.5465/amp.2007.27895335

Petriglieri, J. L. (2011). Under threat: Responses to and the consequences of threats to individuals' identities. *Academy of Management Review*, *36*, 641–662. https://doi.org/10.5465/amr.2009.0087

Purdie-Vaughns, V., Steele, C. M., Davies, P. G., Ditlmann, R., & Crosby, J. R. (2008). Social identity contingencies: How diversity cues signal threat or safety for African Americans in mainstream institutions. *Journal of Personality and Social Psychology*, *94*, 615–630. https://doi.org/10.1037/0022-3514.94.4.615

Roberts, L. M., & Creary, S. J. (2013). Navigating the self in diverse work contexts. In Q. M. Roberson (Ed.), *The Oxford handbook of diversity and work* (pp. 73–97). New York, NY: Oxford University Press. https://doi.org/10.1093/oxfordhb/9780199736355.013.0005

Rothman, J., & Chrobot-Mason, D. (2012). Intrapersonal and interpersonal ARIA process. In J. Rothman (Ed.), *From identity-based conflict to identity-based cooperation* (pp. 35–50). New York, NY: Springer.

Schölmerich, F., Schermuly, C. C., & Deller, J. (2016). How leaders' diversity beliefs alter the impact of faultlines on team functioning. *Small Group Research*, *47*(2), 177–206. https://doi.org/10.1177/1046496416630960

Sherif, M. (1958). Superordinate goals in the reduction of intergroup conflict. *American Journal of Sociology*, *63*(4), 349–356. https://doi.org/10.1086/222258

Sherif, M. (1966). *In common predicament: Social psychology of intergroup conflict and cooperation*. Boston, MA: Houghton Mifflin.

Tortoriello, M., Reagans, R., & McEvily, B. (2012). Bridging the knowledge gap: The influence of strong ties, network cohesion, and network range on the transfer of knowledge between organizational units. *Organization Science*, *223*(4), 1024–1039. https://doi.org/10.1287/orsc.1110.0688

Wildschut, T., Pinter, B., Vevea, J. L., Insko, C. A., & Schopler, J. (2003). Beyond the group mind: A quantitative review of the interindividual-intergroup discontinuity effect. *Psychological Bulletin*, *129*, 698–722. https://doi.org/10.1037/0033-2909.129.5.698

Yukl, G. (1999). An evaluative essay on current conceptions of effective leadership. *European Journal of Work and Organizational Psychology*, *8*, 33–48. https://doi.org/10.1080/135943299398429

# 11 A Leader's Guide to Fostering Inclusion by Creating a Positive Diversity Climate

*David J. G. Dwertmann and Hans van Dijk*

## Introduction

The interest of academics and practitioners in inclusive leadership has increased significantly over recent years. Reasons for this are an increasingly diverse workforce, encompassing individuals from different backgrounds, cultures, genders, age groups, etc., and the continued challenge to prevent negative consequences such as discrimination and sub-group formation while fostering positive outcomes such as creativity, innovation, and enhanced problem-solving capabilities (van Knippenberg & Schippers, 2007). Recent developments such as the Black Lives Matter protests, the #MeToo movement, Brexit, Trump's immigrant ban, the persecution of Rohingyas, and strengthened right-wing parties in elections show how fragile and important inclusion is. Leaders all over the world are in prime positions to shape the conditions that allow individuals from all backgrounds to feel included. Yet, while such inclusive leadership is a hot topic, there is surprisingly little guidance on how to lead inclusively. Therefore, in this chapter, we provide practical guidance on the behaviors that help leaders prevent the negative and foster the positive effects of diversity in teams and organizations. We understand leadership here as a broad range of behaviors and actions encompassing all organizational levels (from one-on-one interactions to organizational policies implemented by the CEO and board), but, where relevant, we distinguish between behaviors from individual leaders versus actions from the organizational leadership. Diversity simply captures the distribution of a characteristic in question across members of a unit. Inclusion exists when individuals from all backgrounds feel like they belong to a unit without having to behave in a certain way to be accepted.

In order to provide leaders with concrete measures to foster feelings of inclusion, we build on a recent review of the diversity climate literature by Dwertmann et al. (2016). In this article, the authors define diversity climate as "employees' perceptions about the extent to which their organization values diversity as evident in the organization's formal structure, informal values, and social integration of underrepresented employees" (p. 1137). Diversity climate thus represents the implicit norms regarding which behavior is expected and rewarded in the workplace and we describe its fairness & discrimination and synergy components in more detail below. We argue that a major way via which inclusive leadership shapes feelings of inclusion—employees' joint perception of belongingness and uniqueness/authenticity (Jansen et al., 2014; Shore et al., 2011)—is by setting and establishing such norms.

Employees are known to learn norms through attaching meaning to the interactions and events they observe around them (Schneider & Reichers, 1983). For example, if employees observe that minority group members in their work unit are regularly marginalized by colleagues without any negative repercussions, they will come to understand such behavior as legitimized and appropriate. One of the most critical sources of this information is the leader or manager (Schneider et al., 2017), who, based on a position of power, is able to legitimize or sanction actions in the workplace. In addition, leaders represent one of the prime role models due to the visibility of their actions, thereby also affecting employees' understanding of normatively appropriate behavior (Brown et al., 2005; Dwertmann & Boehm, 2016).

In this chapter we first describe the construct of diversity climate in more detail and introduce its fairness & discrimination and synergy components. Second, we indicate why and how inclusive leadership shapes both components of diversity climate. Finally, we provide specific measures or action items that leaders and organizations can implement to create more positive diversity climates and hence a more inclusive workplace.

## The Fairness & Discrimination and Synergy Components of Diversity Climate

Dwertmann et al. (2016) propose in their review that a diversity climate consists of two components: fairness & discrimination and synergy. The fairness & discrimination component is defined as

> shared perceptions about the extent to which the organization and/or workgroup successfully promotes fairness and the elimination of discrimination through the fair implementation of personnel practices, the adoption of diversity-specific practices aimed at improving employment outcomes for underrepresented employees, and/or strong norms for fair interpersonal treatment.
>
> (p. 1151)

It thus indicates to what extent employees of all backgrounds are likely to be recruited and promoted, and do not feel excluded. Teams and organizations that do well on this fairness & discrimination component are less likely to suffer from the potential negative consequences of diversity. Psychological research has shown that individuals are drawn to others who are similar to themselves, because similar others are more likely to share interests and views (Byrne, 1971). Leaders therefore tend to recruit and promote people similar to themselves, which comes at the expense of the often required variety to achieve creative and innovative outcomes. Furthermore, in diverse teams and organizations the preference for similar others increases the likelihood that majority members form a subgroup and that members from traditionally underrepresented groups are and feel excluded. Such experiences and feelings reduce trust, cohesion, and communication, which is detrimental for performance (Hinds et al., 2000; van Knippenberg et al., 2004). Because such exclusion tendencies are due to people's innate preference for similar others, norms are needed that help employees to act more inclusively. The fairness & discrimination component of a diversity climate provides such norms.

The synergy component of a diversity climate refers to "the extent to which employees jointly perceive their organization and/or workgroup to promote the expression of, listening to, active valuing of, and integration of diverse perspectives for the purpose of enhancing collective learning and performance" (Dwertmann et al., 2016, p. 1151). As such, it primarily taps into the potential of diversity to leverage innovation and performance. Research in diversity indicates that diverse teams and organizations thrive when they are able to mobilize and integrate the cognitive variety present in diverse groups (van Knippenberg et al., 2004). Moreover, by understanding the potential value of diversity, teams and organizations may be better able to recognize the qualities of people from traditionally underrepresented groups, value their input more, and allow them to perform at their best level. Employees working in climates that score high on the synergy component of a diversity climate thus are more open to divergent and dissenting input, which makes teams and organizations more efficient and less likely to fall prey to groupthink or related causes of sub-optimal decision-making (van Dijk et al., 2017).

The fairness & discrimination and the synergy components of diversity climate are complementary, such that only teams and organizations that score relatively high on both components will be perceived as inclusive. Existing theoretical research suggests that two needs must be met to allow individuals to feel included: the need to belong (i.e., be an accepted member of the group) and the need for uniqueness/authenticity (i.e., to be valued for being oneself; Jansen et al., 2014; Shore et al., 2011). Even though empirical support for this conceptualization is still necessary, it suggests that employees working in diversity climates that are characterized by a strong discrimination & fairness component but a weak focus on the synergy component are likely to have their need for belongingness satisfied, given that norms suggest to treat everyone fairly. However, their need for uniqueness/authenticity is less likely to be met, given that team or organizational norms do not necessarily foster and value authenticity and divergent perspectives (Puritty et al., 2017). In contrast, employees working in diversity climates that emphasize the synergy component but not the discrimination & fairness component are likely to have their need for uniqueness/authenticity satisfied, given that others recognize and value their individual expertise and input. However, they are likely to be treated unfairly and as outsiders which will likely not meet their need to belong.

Note that aside from the group as a whole, minority members in particular are likely to suffer from a weak diversity climate. The situation is easier for employees who are part of the majority group because they are surrounded by similar others and may actually benefit individually from the exclusion of minority members. However, feelings of inclusion are important regardless of demographic background and, over the course of their life, everyone will be in situations in which they are in the minority (e.g., in terms of age). Moreover, employees who belong to the majority on one dimension of diversity (e.g., men) may belong to the minority on another dimension of diversity (e.g., foreigner). Such so-called intersectionalities suggest that all employees are likely to belong to a minority group on some dimension of diversity, which only further underscores the importance of establishing a positive diversity climate.

Accordingly, in order to promote feelings of inclusiveness and realize the potential benefits of diversity while mitigating its potential negative effects, it is important for teams and organizations to foster the discrimination & fairness *as well as* the synergy components of diversity climate (see Figure 11.1). The bad news is that this does not happen automatically but requires purpose and effort. Based on long-established research on similarity-attraction and social identity effects (Byrne, 1971), the default appears to be that employees huddle together with people similar to themselves and shun away from interacting with those different from them, which not only inhibits minority employees' need to belong, but also hampers the extent to which employees are able to recognize and value minority members' qualities (van Dijk et al., 2017), and hence the extent to which teams and organizations can benefit from synergistic performance outcomes. Fortunately, there are many ways in which team and organizational climates can be influenced and, hence, managed. In particular, leaders tend to have a strong influence on the work climate of a team or organization (Kozlowski & Doherty, 1989). We therefore propose that to be inclusive, leaders should seek to establish a diversity climate that is characterized by high levels of its fairness & discrimination as well as its synergy components. Behaviors that influence one component do not automatically impact the other. In what follows, we therefore first outline the behaviors that shape the fairness & discrimination component of a diversity climate, and subsequently indicate how leaders can develop the synergy component of a diversity climate.

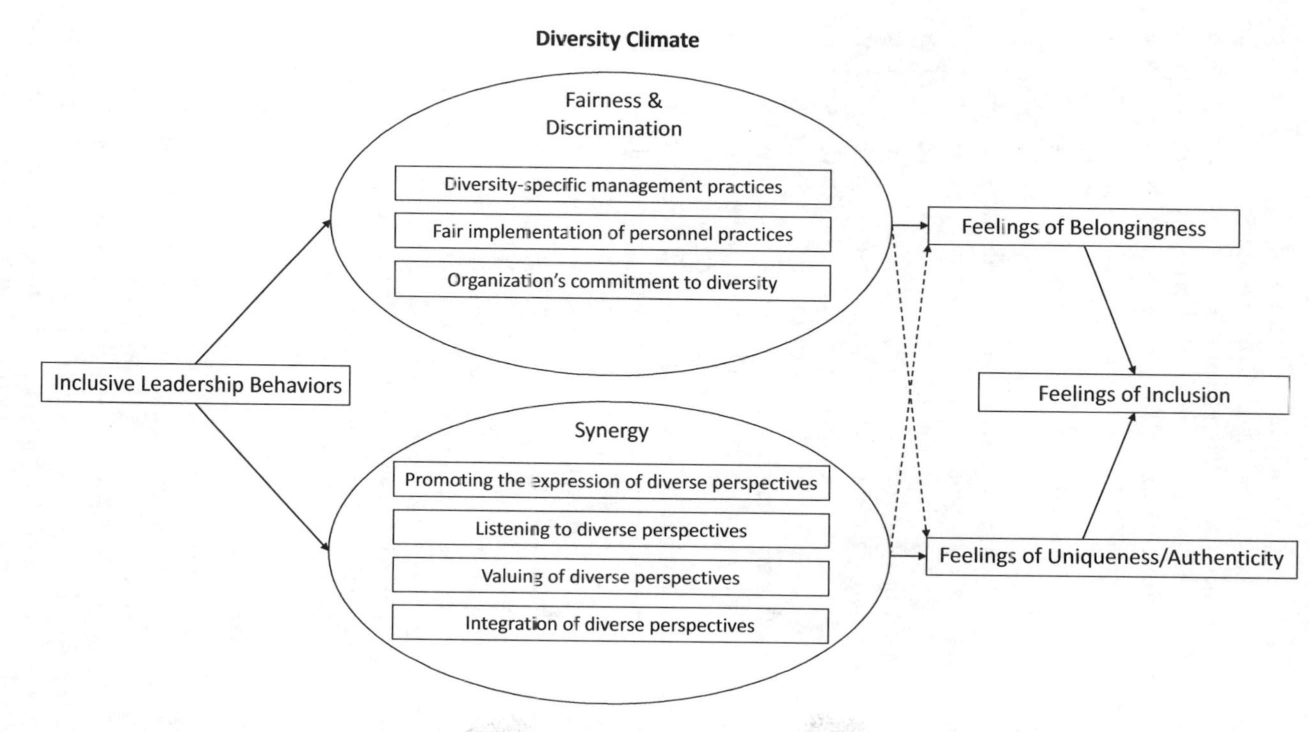


*Figure 11.1* A conceptual model linking inclusive leadership behaviors, diversity climate, and feelings of inclusion.
*Note*: solid lines represent stronger effects, dashed lines weaker effects. We focus on the former rather than the latter in this chapter.

## Leadership Behaviors that Influence the Fairness & Discrimination Component of Diversity Climate

The fairness & discrimination component focuses on the elimination of interpersonal biases, stereotypes, and stigmatization. We outline the exemplary leadership behaviors that will influence the various parts of the fairness & discrimination component of diversity climate: commitment to diversity, implementation of fair personnel practices, and creation of diversity-specific practices.

### *Commitment to Diversity*

Creating a climate that is free of discrimination and offers fair opportunities for all employees starts with a leader's attitude toward diversity. The leader's commitment to diversity should be unquestioned. If leaders say that they support diversity but their behavior reveals otherwise (e.g., through favoritism, stereotyping, or microaggressions; Puritty et al., 2017; van Dijk et al., 2017), any initiative aimed at facilitating diversity is likely to fail. The promotion of diversity in such an environment is likely to lead to diversity skepticism (van Dijk et al., 2012), where members share a disbelief in the pro-diversity claims and consider diversity initiatives as little more than window-dressing to protect company image and avoid lawsuits (Dwertmann et al., 2016; Ely & Thomas, 2001). By showing an unwavering commitment to diversity in their walk as well as their talk, leaders establish a solid foundation for the employment of other initiatives, and signal to employees that diversity is valued. Crucial here is that leaders do not differentiate relationship quality with employees based on demographic similarity. One way to check this is to regularly write down the names of direct reports in order of the quality of relationship with them. Next, leaders should add demographic information for everyone (age, gender, race, etc.). The final step is to check whether the ranking of relationship quality aligns with the demographic similarity with the leader. This easy exercise can make an implicit personal bias explicit and help leaders to reconsider their actions.

### *Implement Fair Personnel Practices*

Leaders should ensure that processes and procedures related to hiring, employment, and promotion of employees are designed such that they provide equal chances for minority compared with majority group members and that they are really aimed at identifying and rewarding the most competent and best performing individuals. By implementing various practices specifically aimed at eliminating discrimination and securing fairness in recruitment, selection, and performance management, leaders indicate that they shun away from favoritism and via their personnel practices aim to hire the best person for every job and promote the best performing employees, irrespective of demographic backgrounds. Training aimed at mitigating bias (e.g., Lieberman et al., 2014; Vinkenburg, 2017) is likely to help leaders achieve that aim.

### *Diversity-Specific Practices*

Once fair personnel practices are in place, leaders can assess their effectiveness and evaluate whether additional measures are needed. To do so, it is helpful to track the representation of minority employees by recording the proportion of employees of a particular background for each job category and hierarchical level. By comparing this with the proportion of individuals with particular backgrounds in the area and sector, leaders have an indication of whether the inclusive practices translate into outcomes in terms of representation, or whether they need to intervene and/or adjust specific personnel practices. It would also be helpful if leaders track whether minority employees are equally likely to get a promotion throughout all ranks compared with majority employees. In case such data shows that there are fewer applications from members of particular minority groups, leaders could consider more explicitly targeting these groups in their recruitment (Avery & McKay, 2006). If such data shows that there are ample applications but that members of particular minority groups are less likely to be selected or promoted, leaders may actively approach the hiring managers and consider using more affirmative selection approaches (e.g., threshold selection; Noon, 2012).

At the organizational leadership level, it is important that the leaders who are responsible for such practices are held accountable. Rewarding leaders for showing unbiased personnel decisions motivates and reinforces the desired behavior (van Dijk et al., 2017). Moreover, Dobbin and Kalev (2016) show that to guarantee accountability, leaders at the top levels of organizations would do well to assign a diversity manager that is tasked with the overall responsibility for creating an inclusive workplace. Ideally, such a diversity manager is of a high rank, given that a recent study suggests that, in the United States, the hierarchical rank of the person certifying the company's required federal Equal Employment Opportunity-1 report is directly related to a better representation of diverse employees at higher levels (Graham et al., 2017). Furthermore, given that promotion in organizations often hinges on finding mentors and sponsors (Ng et al., 2005) and that majority members tend to find mentors more easily on their own than minority members, leaders would do well to set up or at least stimulate mentoring programs for minority employees, for example by encouraging seasoned employees to become a mentor of minority employees (Dobbin & Kalev, 2016).

## Leadership Behaviors that Influence the Synergy Component of Diversity Climate

The synergy component focuses on leveraging the heterogeneity of cognitive resources (i.e., different knowledge, experiences, and perceptions) in diverse units. Leadership behaviors that influence the different parts of the synergy component are: promoting the expression of diverse perspectives, listening to diverse perspectives, valuing of diverse perspectives, and, finally, integrating diverse perspectives into decision making. In all of this, the main challenge for leaders is the existence of status differentials in diverse teams. Social status is defined as "the extent to which an individual or group is respected or admired by others" (Magee & Galinsky, 2008, p. 359). Different demographic backgrounds are often associated with status differences such that members of minority groups hold lower status than majority group members (Konrad & Gutek, 1987). These demography-based status differentials often prevent minority team members from voicing their opinions and majority members from acknowledging and valuing the ideas of lower-status members. Thus, a key goal for leaders should be the reduction of status differences that are based on demographics instead of competence and performance.

### *Promoting the Expression of Diverse Perspectives*

There are multiple ways in which leaders can promote the expression of diverse perspectives. One way is to clearly communicate the expectation that everyone participates during team meetings. Leaders can actively ask members who have not participated in a discussion for their opinion. This requires leaders to keep track of individual contributions. Importantly, past research has shown that the order of contributions is critical (Janis, 1972). Leaders should not voice their opinion or support for certain ideas during early stages of meetings. If they do, it is unlikely that employees will voice divergent opinions. People often do not want to disagree with the boss. Therefore, leaders should keep a position of neutrality until all team members have contributed their opinion.

### *Listening to Diverse Perspectives*

Contributions from high-status team members are often given more consideration than those of low-status members (Correll & Ridgeway, 2003). This is why it is important for leaders to actively acknowledge contributions from all team members. However, since voicing their preferences might not be enough, leaders might apply another strategy, diffusing the source of ideas during team meetings. One way that this can be achieved is by using the nominal group technique (Delbecq & van de Ven, 1971). Nominal groups are groups in which individuals work independently but in each other's presence (Faure, 2004). For the nominal group technique, a question or problem is posed and all employees individually write their ideas on index cards. Next, either a moderator or facilitator presents all ideas to the team or the cards are shuffled and the team members present the ideas (without knowing the source of the idea). This disconnect between ideas and sources prevents teams from consciously or unconsciously paying more attention to the suggestions of high-status members. Thus, every voice should be heard. Anonymous votes to pick the best idea should further increase individuals' comfort with expressing their opinion.

### *Valuing of Diverse Perspectives*

In order to create an environment in which diverse perspectives are being valued, leaders should acknowledge and openly discuss new and unconventional ideas. Otherwise, new members are less likely to constructively criticize existing work processes and team members are unlikely to search for better ways to do things, which hinders innovation. Voicing this understanding of expected behaviors is important (Hülsheger et al., 2009). If leaders shut down new ideas, employees are less likely to speak up in the future, other employees are less likely to listen to the diverse perspectives of their colleagues, and diverse perspectives will not be given much attention. One way through which leaders can emphasize the importance of building on each other's ideas is by creating situations in which solutions can only be achieved as a team (e.g., through team training). Such situations can foster awareness that the whole can be more than the sum of its parts. A more structural practice that leaders can implement to promote the valuing of diverse perspectives is establishing the norm that each reaction to a new idea should start with an acknowledgment of and elaboration on the potential value of the idea before discussing its potential caveats.

### *Integration of Diverse Perspectives*

Leaders can act as role models for building on the ideas of others (Bandura, 1986). During meetings, leaders can ask questions such as "How can we combine both of these ideas?" Challenging employees to come up with solutions and the use of incentives can be effective in fostering innovation (Hülsheger et al., 2009). Successes should get showcased and celebrated to reinforce the outlined norms and increase members' identification with the team at large.

## Summary and Conclusion

Recent developments across the globe (e.g., Black Lives Matter protests, #MeToo movement, Brexit, Trump's immigrant ban, the persecution of Rohingyas, strengthened right-wing parties in elections) have highlighted the importance and fragility of inclusion. Leaders in government, institutions, and organizations are in prime positions to exert their influence and create the boundary conditions that foster inclusion. Diversity climate is one of the key factors in this regard and this chapter has highlighted a number of pathways through which leaders can take action. The fairness & discrimination component is a necessary but insufficient condition for inclusion. A focus on synergy will help organizations revamp the potential performance benefits of a diverse workforce and allow all individuals to feel like they can fully contribute. In outlining the specific leadership behaviors that shape the fairness & discrimination and synergy components of diversity climate, we provide a practical guide for leaders to foster feelings of inclusion. We summarize key leadership behaviors in the action items listed next.

## Action Items

### *Fairness and Discrimination Component*

#### *Commitment to Diversity*

- Show an unwavering commitment to diversity in walk and talk.
- Do not differentiate the quality of relationships with employees based on demographics.

#### *Implement Fair Personnel Practices*

- Implement practices that secure fairness in recruitment, selection, and performance management.
- Follow with training that helps to mitigate biases.

#### *Diversity-Specific Practices*

- Record and monitor the proportion of employees in different demographic groups for each job category and hierarchical level and their progress. Correct where necessary via specific interventions (e.g., targeted recruitment, threshold selection).
- Reward employees for showing unbiased personnel decisions.
- Task a (high-level) manager with the overall responsibility for creating an inclusive workplace.

- Provide mentoring opportunities for all employees, particularly minorities.

### *Synergy Component*

#### *Promoting the Expression of Diverse Perspectives*

- Clearly communicate the expectation that everyone participates during team meetings.
- Actively ask members who have not participated in a discussion for their opinion.
- Maintain a position of neutrality until all team members have contributed their opinion.

#### *Listening to Diverse Perspectives*

- Actively acknowledge contributions from all team members.
- Diffuse the source of ideas during team meetings through the use of the nominal group technique and other decision-making tools.
- Consider anonymous votes to pick the best idea.

#### *Valuing of Diverse Perspectives*

- Acknowledge and openly discuss new and unconventional ideas.
- Create situations in which solutions can only be achieved as a team (e.g., team training).
- Establish the norm that each reaction to a new idea should start with an acknowledgment of and elaboration on the potential value of the idea before discussing its potential caveats.

#### *Integration of Diverse Perspectives*

- Challenge employees to come up with solutions that combine aspects of different ideas.
- Use incentives to foster innovation.
- Showcase and celebrate innovative successes.

## References

Avery, D. R., & McKay, P. F. (2006). Target practice: An organizational impression management approach to attracting minority and female job applicants. *Personnel Psychology*, *59*(1), 157–187. https://doi.org/10.1111/j.1744-6570.2006.00807.x

Bandura, A. (1986). *Social foundations of thought and action: A social cognitive perspective*. Englewood Cliffs, NJ: Prentice-Hall.

Brown, M. E., Treviño, L. K., & Harrison, D. A. (2005). Ethical leadership: A social learning perspective for construct development and testing. *Organizational Behavior and Human Decision Processes*, *97*(2), 117–134. https://doi.org/10.1016/j.obhdp.2005.03.002

Byrne, D. E. (1971). *The attraction paradigm*. New York, NY: Academic Press.

Correll, S. J., & Ridgeway, C. L. (2003). Expectation states theory. In J. Delamater (Ed.), *Handbook of social psychology* (Vol. 35, pp. 29–51). New York, NY: Kluwer Academic Press.

Delbecq, A. L., & van de Ven, A. H. (1971). A group process model for problem identification and program planning. *The Journal of Applied Behavioral Science*, *7*(4), 466–492. https://doi.org/10.1177/002188637100700404

Dobbin, F., & Kalev, A. (2016). Why diversity programs fail. *Harvard Business Review*, *94*(7), 52–60.

Dwertmann, D. J. G., & Boehm, S. A. (2016). Status matters: The asymmetric effects of supervisor-subordinate disability incongruence and climate for inclusion. *Academy of Management Journal*, *59*(1), 44–64. https://doi.org/10.5465/amj.2014.0093

Dwertmann, D. J. G., Nishii, L. H., & van Knippenberg, D. (2016). Disentangling the fairness & discrimination and synergy perspectives on diversity climate: Moving the field forward. *Journal of Management*, *42*(5), 1136–1168. https://doi.org/10.1177/0149206316630380

Ely, R. J., & Thomas, D. A. (2001). Cultural diversity at work: The effects of diversity perspectives on work group processes and outcomes. *Administrative Science Quarterly*, *46*(2), 229–273. https://doi.org/10.2307/2667087

Faure, C. (2004). Beyond brainstorming: Effects of different group procedures on selection of ideas and satisfaction with the process. *Journal of Creative Behavior*, *38*(1), 13–34. https://doi.org/10.1002/j.2162-6057.2004.tb01229.x

Graham, M. E., Belliveau, M. A., & Hotchkiss, J. L. (2017). The view at the top or signing at the bottom? Workplace diversity responsibility and women's representation in management. *ILR Review*, *70*(1), 223–258. https://doi.org/10.1177/0019793916668879

Hinds, P. J., Carley, K. M., Krackhardt, D., & Wholey, D. (2000). Choosing work group members: Balancing similarity, competence, and familiarity. *Organizational Behavior and Human Decision Processes*, *81*(2), 226–251. https://doi.org/10.1006/obhd.1999.2875

Hülsheger, U. R., Anderson, N., & Salgado, J. F. (2009). Team-level predictors of innovation at work: A comprehensive meta-analysis spanning three decades of research. *Journal of Applied Psychology*, *94*(5), 1128–1145. https://doi.org/10.1037/a0015978

Janis, I. L. (1972). *Victims of groupthink: A psychological study of foreign-policy decisions and fiascoes*. Boston, MA: Houghton Mifflin.

Jansen, W. S., Otten, S., van der Zee, K. I., & Jans, L. (2014). Inclusion: Conceptualization and measurement. *European Journal of Social Psychology*, *44*, 370–385. https://doi.org/10.1002/ejsp.2011

Konrad, A. M., & Gutek, B. A. (1987). Theory and research on group composition: Applications to the status of women and ethnic minorities. In S. Oskamp & S. Spacapan (Eds.), *Interpersonal processes: The Claremont Symposium on Applied Social Psychology* (pp. 85–121). Newbury Park, CA: Sage.

Kozlowski, S. W. J., & Doherty, M. L. (1989). Integration of climate and leadership: Examination of a neglected issue. *Journal of Applied Psychology*, *74*(4), 546–553.

Lieberman, M. D., Rock, D., & Cox, C. L. (2014). Breaking bias. *Neuro Leadership Journal*, *5*, 1–17.

Magee, J. C., & Galinsky, A. D. (2008). Social hierarchy: The self-reinforcing nature of power and status. *Academy of Management Annals*, *2*(1), 351–398. https://doi.org/10.1080/19416520802211628

Ng, T. W. H., Eby, L. T., Sorensen, K. L., & Feldman, D. C. (2005). Predictors of objective and subjective career success: A meta-analysis. *Personnel Psychology*, *58*(2), 367–408. https://doi.org/10.1111/j.1744-6570.2005.00515.x

Noon, M. (2012). Simply the best? The case for using "threshold selection" in hiring decisions. *Human Resource Management Journal*, *22*(1), 76–88. https://doi.org/10.1111/j.1748-8583.2011.00168.x

Puritty, C., Strickland, L. R., Alia, E., Blonder, B., Klein, E., Kohl, M. T., . . . Gerber, L. R. (2017). Without inclusion, diversity initiatives may not be enough. *Science*, *357*(6356), 1101–1102. https://doi.org/10.1126/science.aai9054

Schneider, B., González-Romá, V., Ostroff, C., & West, M. A. (2017). Organizational climate and culture: Reflections on the history of the constructs in the Journal of Applied Psychology. *Journal of Applied Psychology*, *102*(3), 468–482. https://doi.org/10.1037/apl0000090

Schneider, B., & Reichers, A. E. (1983). On the etiology of climates. *Personnel Psychology*, *36*(1), 19–39. https://doi.org/10.1111/j.1744-6570.1983.tb00500.x

Shore, L. M., Randel, A. E., Chung, B. G., Dean, M. A., Holcombe Ehrhart, K., & Singh, G. (2011). Inclusion and diversity in work groups: A review and model for future research. *Journal of Management*, *37*(4), 1262–1289. https://doi.org/10.1177/0149206310385943

van Dijk, H., Meyer, B., van Engen, M. L., & Lewin Loyd, D. (2017). Microdynamics in diverse teams: A review and integration of the diversity and stereotyping literatures. *Academy of Management Annals*, *11*(1), 517–557. https://doi.org/10.5465/annals.2014.0046

van Dijk, H., van Engen, M., & Paauwe, J. (2012). Reframing the business case for diversity: A values and virtues perspective. *Journal of Business Ethics*, *111*(1), 73–84. https://doi.org/10.1007/s10551-012-1434-z

van Knippenberg, D., De Dreu, C. K. W., & Homan, A. C. (2004). Work group diversity and group performance: An integrative model and research agenda. *Journal of Applied Psychology*, *89*(6), 1008–1022. https://doi.org/10.1037/0021-9010.89.6.1008

van Knippenberg, D., & Schippers, M. C. (2007). Work group diversity. *Annual Review of Psychology*, *58*, 515–541. https://doi.org/10.1146/annurev.psych.58.110405.085546

Vinkenburg, C. J. (2017). Engaging gatekeepers, optimizing decision making, and mitigating bias: Design specifications for systemic diversity interventions. *The Journal of Applied Behavioral Science*, *53*(2), 212–234. https://doi.org/10.1177/0021886317703292

# 12 Inclusive Leadership

## Leaders as Architects of Inclusive Workgroup Climates

*Lisa H. Nishii and Hannes L. Leroy*

### Introduction

According to the most commonly adopted definition of inclusion in the research literature, inclusion is comprised of the simultaneous experience of belonging and having one's uniqueness valued by others (Shore et al., 2011). We adopt a more specific version of this definition in our work: in order to realize the positive performance benefits of diversity and inclusion, it is essential that individuals experience belonging and uniqueness not just in their social interactions at work, but also within the context of decision-making and idea generation. The latter involves experiencing belonging within important decision-making conversations and having one's competencies and unique perspectives valued such that one is fully included in information integration processes. The most critical context for determining experiences of inclusion is arguably one's local workgroup, in particular the group processes and interpersonal relationships to which people are most often exposed, and rely on most, in their day-to-day work. Thus, the focus of our chapter is on the leader behaviors that shape the workgroup context—more specifically, the workgroup climate for inclusion—in ways that promote experiences of inclusion for employees.

Workgroup climate refers to employees' shared perceptions about the behaviors that are expected and rewarded, and it represents one of the most powerful determinants of employee behavior, and therefore experiences, within organizations (Mischel, 1977; Schneider et al., 2017). Whereas, in practice, people tend to think of organizations as having *a* culture or climate, researchers distinguish between types of organizational climate based on the strategic focus of interest—for example, climate for service versus climate for safety or climate for diversity (Ehrhart et al., 2014)—because each one of these strategic foci necessitates different employee behaviors to achieve success. Most research on organizational climate as it relates to diversity and inclusion has focused on diversity climate (Dwertmann et al., 2016), or the conditions needed to reduce discrimination and enhance fairness such that organizations are more successful at increasing their demographic diversity throughout their organizations. This mirrors the dominant focus of diversity and management practices (e.g., pay equity initiatives; targeted recruiting and leadership development programs) in both research and practice, which has been on equal employment opportunity (Nishii et al., 2018).

However, promoting social and informational/decisional inclusion requires more than preventing discrimination. Equal employment practices strengthen relationships between members of historically marginalized identity groups and their organization (i.e., stronger attraction, sense of being invested in and supported for individual success), but typically do not speak directly to the key challenges that must be addressed in order for synergistic performance outcomes to emerge through inclusion (Ely & Thomas, 2001; Nishii, 2013). Even when diversity management practices successfully improve equal employment opportunity or a unit is characterized as having a positive diversity climate, individuals can still experience forms of interpersonal incivility and informational exclusion that thwart inclusion. This is because diversity management practices and conceptualizations of diversity climate that are narrowly focused on reducing discrimination and enhancing fairness do not pay sufficient attention to the social environment in which diversity effects play out (Roberson et al., 2016). Facilitating inclusion requires more than preventing bias; leaders need to proactively create workgroup norms that counteract intergroup tensions that commonly arise in diverse groups to enable and motivate group members to leverage cognitive diversity effectively.

Therefore, compared with diversity climate, climate for inclusion is less focused on employees' perceptions about the extent to which the workgroup promotes equal employment opportunity and more on perceptions about the extent to which the workgroup promotes the integration of diverse identities and perspectives (Dwertmann et al., 2016). Given that the inclusiveness of a workgroup's climate is a determining factor in employees' experiences of inclusion, we build on research that has established that leaders play a foundational role in shaping workgroup climate (Schneider et al., 2017) in defining inclusive leadership as the leader behaviors that create inclusive climates.

As we describe more below, it is up to workgroup leaders to develop shared motivations, norms, and accountability structures that clarify for employees what inclusion means, how they stand to benefit from it, and the role they play in co-creating their own and others' experiences of inclusion. They do this based on the critical incidents and other organizational cues to which they systematically attend and react, and the employee behaviors that they reward and sanction (Nishii & Paluch, 2018; Zohar & Luria, 2004).

## Inclusive Workgroup Climates

At the individual level, inclusion involves experiencing a sense of belonging to the collective while simultaneously feeling that one's individuality or uniqueness is valued by others (Ferdman, 2014; Shore et al., 2011). The concept of inclusion has been intertwined with that of learning and performance because unless individuals feel connected to the collective without having to hide aspects of their identity, their capacity to contribute added value is diminished (Ferdman, 2017). The workgroup conditions that encourage and make possible the expression, valuing, and integration of diverse perspectives for the purpose of enhancing collective learning and performance are what define inclusive climates (Dwertmann et al., 2016). The three foundational dimensions of inclusive climates—perceived fairness, cultural integration of differences, and inclusive decision-making—as established in prior empirical research (Nishii, 2013), mirror the conditions required for positive intergroup contact (Allport, 1954). The first involves *Perceived Fairness* in the implementation of practices and distribution of opportunities and resources such that arbitrary status differences are delegitimized within the local context. The second involves an emphasis on the *Cultural Integration of Differences*, made possible through proactive investments in developing personalized understandings of the ways in which coworkers' perspectives and experiences are both similar and different. Doing so helps people to blur surface-level distinctions and move beyond overly simplistic, stereotype-based, we-versus-them assumptions. The last dimension involves *Inclusive Decision-Making*, which requires the adoption of interaction norms that facilitate the expression and integration of diverse perspectives.

Research conducted across a range of organizations—including federal and private, large and small, as well as global and domestic—has confirmed the expectation that employees indeed report significantly better experiences when they work in units with inclusive climates, regardless of their demographic background (Nishii, 2020). More specifically, because individuals are better understood for who they are in inclusive climates, they experience higher levels of fit with their coworkers as well as between their skills and the demands of the job, and are less likely to report experiences of harassment and discrimination. They also report higher levels of engagement and perceived support from their organization and their managers, receive higher performance ratings, and are less likely to turn over. Moreover, commonly observed identity-group differences in the favorability of workplace experiences such as perceived organizational support, quality of interpersonal relationships, fit with one's job and workgroup, and even engagement tend to be drastically reduced or even disappear in inclusive climates (Nishii, 2011). Given the emphasis that is placed in inclusive climates on developing personalized understandings of coworkers, it comes as no surprise that research also shows that members of workgroups with inclusive climates develop more positive and fewer negative relationships with coworkers from different demographic backgrounds. Corresponding levels of information integration and cohesion among group members fuel higher unit performance (Nishii & McAlpine, 2018).

These consistently positive individual- and group-level benefits of inclusive climates led us to seek to understand what accounts for the variability in the inclusiveness of climates across groups. It is important to note that in the same way that organizations can be thought of as differing in their level of inclusiveness, workgroups within a single organization can also vary in how inclusive they are. Several decades of research on climate have clearly documented that experiences and perceptions of climate are a product of leadership, work, and other situational factors, and as a result tend to revolve around the workgroup level of analysis (Schneider et al., 2017). Workgroup managers in particular serve as powerful "climate engineers" (Rentsch, 1990; Zohar, 2002) because they have legitimacy in the eyes of their subordinates, can exercise discretion in the way they communicate about and implement organizational practices, and their daily proximity to employees makes them the most qualified to reward and sanction employee behavior in ways that yield desired performance. Indeed, employees pay careful attention to the words and actions of their managers in an effort to interpret what is expected of them (Pfeffer, 1981).

## Leaders as Climate Shapers

We describe our efforts to understand the specific characteristics and behaviors of unit leaders that make them more successful at shaping inclusive workgroup climates in two related sections below. In line with more traditional approaches to examining leader-related predictors of climate (Lewin, Lippitt, & White, 1939), we begin by sharing the results of what is known as an individual differences approach that is focused on identifying trait- or personality-based markers that differentiate leaders of workgroups with highly inclusive climates from those of workgroups lacking inclusive climates. We then reframe what we learned from that research into what we view as a more useful framework that describes the fundamental *process* behaviors through which leaders construct inclusive workgroup climates.

## Leader Traits

The question of interest here has to do with the types of people who are more likely to engage in behaviors that promote inclusive climates. Building on research on a wide range of topics in the organizational sciences that has established personality as an important determinant of work-related behavior (Barrick & Mount, 1991; Judge et al., 2003; Mayer et al., 2007), we explored how unit leaders' scores on the Big Five personality dimensions relate to the inclusiveness of their unit climate, as reported by their followers. The five dimensions of personality are 1) openness to experience (i.e., intellectual, curious); 2) extraversion (i.e., sociable and warm); 3) agreeableness (i.e., sensitive, sympathetic, kind); 4) conscientiousness (i.e., dependable, detail-oriented); and 5) neuroticism (i.e., anxious, moody, stressed, self-focused) (Costa & McCrae, 1992).

Of the five dimensions, we expected leader openness, extraversion, and agreeableness to be more strongly associated with inclusive climates than conscientiousness, and leader neuroticism to be negatively associated with inclusive climates. We outline our rationale in the rest of this paragraph. Leaders who score high on openness to experience should be more curious about the different ideas and perspectives held by diverse employees, and therefore more naturally build relationships with different others and listen actively to diverse perspectives. Because they are more talkative, positive, and sociable (Costa & McCrae, 1992; Goodstein & Lanyon, 1999), extraverted leaders are more likely to create work environments in which people voice their opinions and engage in lively discussions (Avery, 2003). Compared with individuals who score low on agreeableness and are antagonistic and argumentative, highly agreeable individuals are sympathetic and trustworthy. As such, leaders high on agreeableness are more likely to shape inclusive climates by being sensitive to and respectful of diverse others. Conscientiousness refers to the tendency to be prepared, dutiful, and detail-oriented (Costa & McCrae, 1992). Although it is highly predictive of task performance and could make leaders more likely to implement practices consistently and fairly across employees, because its interpersonal implications are less obvious than those of the first three dimensions described above, we did not expect conscientiousness to be as strongly associated with the inclusiveness of a leader's unit climate. Finally, neurotic individuals tend to be anxious, moody, self-focused, and fearful, and they react emotionally to unexpected or difficult situations. Therefore, we expected that leaders high on neuroticism would be less in tune with employees (particularly those who are dissimilar to the leader) and more easily upset by employee input, thereby being much less likely to shape inclusive climates.

Beyond the big five personality dimensions, we also expected that how learning goal-oriented leaders are would influence how they respond to the challenge of learning and adopting the skills, behaviors, and perspectives required for effectively managing diversity-related dynamics within their teams (Dweck & Leggett, 1988; McCauley et al., 1994). Individuals with a "performance goal orientation" are motivated to defend their self-image by either *avoiding* failure or *proving* their competence, and therefore may view the management of diversity as threatening because of the inherent unpredictability introduced by diversity (Crocker & Canevello, 2008; Dweck, 1986). They also tend to view others as competition (Dragoni, 2005), and thus performance-goal-oriented leaders are likely to respond more negatively to followers who express dissenting perspectives, tempted to approach conflict with the goal of "winning" rather than integrating diverse perspectives. In comparison, those with a "learning goal orientation" are motivated to develop new skills and master challenging tasks or situations even when doing so may require taking risks (Dweck, 1986; VandeWalle, 1997). Thus, the core premise of inclusive climates as being environments in which diverse individuals embrace learning from diverse others in order to enhance their collective cultural competence and performance (Ely & Thomas, 2001) should be attractive rather than threatening to leaders high in learning goal orientation. Accordingly, we expected leaders' learning goal orientation to be positively related and leaders' performance (proving and avoiding) goal orientation to be negatively related to the climate for inclusion in their units.

To test these hypotheses, we collected data from 2,266 employees nested within 319 work units of a national wholesale distribution company about the inclusiveness of their unit climates, and then matched their data to five-factor personality and achievement goal orientation data provided by the leaders of those units (Nishii & Langevin, 2009). Controlling for the level of gender, racial, and age diversity within groups, we found that the personality dimension with the strongest positive relationship with unit climate for inclusion was extraversion, followed by openness to experience. Leader neuroticism was negatively associated with the inclusiveness of unit climate, and conscientiousness and agreeableness were unrelated. As expected, followers who worked for leaders who scored high on learning goal orientation were more likely to characterize their unit climate as inclusive, while the opposite was true of leaders with high performance goal orientation. Examining both the big five personality factors and dimensions of goal orientation simultaneously revealed that learning goal orientation and openness overlap, or are somewhat redundant, in their predictive value.

## Leadership as a Process of Climate Engineering

The main limitation of an individual differences approach to understanding the impact that leaders have on the development of inclusive climates is that the practical implications of these findings for organizations are rather limiting: either select for desired personality traits when hiring, or assign leaders with the desired personality profile to manage units that lack inclusive climates in the hope that they will be able to make a positive difference. Yet, in reality, only a subset of an organization's managers will be highly extraverted, open to experience, agreeable, and learning-goal-oriented. What can be done with the rest? Will simply directing them to engage in more inclusive leadership behaviors do the trick? We think that is unlikely, unfortunately.

Instead, what is required is to teach leaders at all levels of the organization about the process through which they can become purposeful architects of inclusive climates (Rentsch, 1990; Zohar, 2002). Although an organization's diversity and inclusion strategy may be developed and communicated by senior leaders, the reality is that the policies and practices as articulated by senior leaders are usually too abstract to provide clarity to employees about what they mean for the behaviors that are expected of them on a day-to-day basis. This is certainly true of all strategic objectives espoused by senior leaders—they need to be translated into clear and compelling messages about how employees should align their behaviors with those strategic objectives (Boswell, 2006)—but perhaps even more so for espoused diversity and inclusion strategies, since they can be notoriously decoupled from practice (Nishii et al., 2018). It is easy for espoused inclusion strategies to be perceived as representing symbolic window-dressing because: a) employees can easily attribute their adoption to external, regulatory pressures (Edelman et al., 2001) rather than to genuine internal motivations on the part of senior leaders to enhance inclusion; and b) while inclusion is touted as being important by almost all organizations, clear guidance about how to create environments where employees experience inclusion is rare.

Thus, the ultimate effectiveness of inclusion initiatives—and the strength of a unit's inclusive climate—depends on the clarity and consistency of "sense-giving" that managers provide for those initiatives (Green, 2004). Managers shape employees' climate perceptions based on the critical events, organizational activities, and pieces of communication that they systematically bring to the attention of their followers, discuss, and react to; employee behaviors that they assess, control, and reward; and the way they allocate scarce resources such as rewards and time (Schein, 2017; Wood & Bandura, 1989; Zohar, 2002; Zohar & Luria, 2004; Zohar & Polachek, 2014). There are four interrelated climate engineering behaviors that we describe more below: (1) articulating what inclusion means, why it is important, and the employee behaviors that are expected of employees to co-produce it; (2) role modeling inclusive behaviors; (3) reinforcing inclusive behaviors; and (4) assessing followers' climate perceptions. Together, these mutually reinforcing leadership behaviors reduce ambiguity about the behaviors that are expected of employees to promote inclusion and enhance felt accountability for aligning one's behaviors with those expectations.

*Articulating* what inclusion means as well as its importance involves connecting broad, espoused organizational messages about inclusion with more micro, task-based goals (Boswell, 2006). Employees first need to understand why inclusion goals are important for the organization and the workgroup, and by extension also for the individual employee. Team leaders must convey key lessons from the influential work of Piaget (1971, 1975), according to which interactions with dissimilar others introduce people to discrepant views that create a state of "disequilibrium" that accelerates cognitive growth. When people confront experiences or ideas that do not easily fit within their existing understanding of the world, they are pushed to reexamine their views in an effort to reconcile the discrepancy (Nemeth, 1986); because doing so involves deeper-level cognitive processing, it tends to have a more profound effect on learning and growth (Gurin et al., 2002). Without an understanding of the collective benefits that derive from successfully capitalizing on and integrating the unique contributions of each member of the team, employees are less likely to internalize inclusion goals (Ely & Thomas, 2001). Employees also need to understand *how* to contribute to inclusion goals in order to be able to do so effectively, for example by distributing voice opportunities across group members, suspending judgment, and building informational bridges.

One of the paradoxes of inclusion is whether group members can simultaneously develop a strong collective identity by emphasizing the ways in which they are similar to others while also maintaining their individuality (Ferdman, 2017; Shore et al., 2011). The answer to this depends on the values and norms that the group leader articulates as being the essence of the group's shared identity. It is important for the leader to differentiate between conformity to a standard that reflects the dominant majority (i.e., assimilation) from conformity to shared expectations about valuing diversity. To the extent that group members see themselves reflected in the "hybrid" group culture that is co-created through true dialogue, the less likely it is that they will experience pressure to assimilate (Earley & Mosakowski, 2000). Key to this is for the leader to articulate not just that empathic perspective-taking is critical for promoting inclusion, but explaining why—that is, because it catalyzes interpersonal understanding (i.e., individualization) and helps the person being listened to feel cared for and accepted (i.e., belonging) without necessarily requiring that the listener express agreement or hide one's own perspectives (i.e., again preserving individualization; McCormick, 1999).

*Role modeling* espoused values related to inclusion is essential; otherwise, employees interpret staged espousals as superficial rather than legitimate (Zajac & Westphal, 1994). In order for leaders to be seen as "walking the talk," they must be willing to suspend judgment and even their authority in order to participate as co-learners within the team. They need to role model perspective taking by stretching the way they think about or see something in order to see it from a group member's point of view. They need to invite the contributions of group members by demonstrating their openness to new ideas, willingly admitting to not knowing all the answers, expressing non-judgmental curiosity about the assumptions underlying the different views expressed, and being aware of whether their nonverbal behaviors appropriately reinforce their intentions. It is important to point out here the clear link between the behaviors that leaders need to role model to shape inclusive climates and the personality dimensions that we found to predict inclusive climates. These dispositional traits matter because they increase the likelihood that individuals naturally engage in these desired behaviors. The ability to model intercultural openness is also likely to be higher among leaders who have had developmental experiences in multicultural contexts that pushed them to understand that people often have different evaluations of the same experience (Chrobot-Mason et al., 2013).

In addition, in order for the message of inclusion to match the method, it is important for the group leader to involve group members in shaping the process rules that govern when and how group members should engage in inclusive decision-making processes. Team chartering represents an effective process for collaboratively developing team agreements or rules about *how* team members will work together toward common goals, for example how dissent can be expressed productively, work tasks delegated, and disagreements resolved (Mathieu & Rapp, 2009). Once these rules are determined based on everyone's input, the expectation is that group members will hold each other accountable for upholding the agreements so that the team can function inclusively according to plan. It is good practice to also come to agreement about the circumstances under which the group should consider renegotiating its agreements so that otherwise group members can focus on their work and develop trust in the group's system for protecting inclusion.

*Reinforcing*. It is one thing for employees to accurately perceive the desired behaviors being role modeled by their manager, and another to contribute to the inclusiveness of the workgroup climate by successfully engaging in inclusive behaviors themselves. The latter requires that managers consistently—across situations and employees—provide feedback so that employees know how to modify their behavior to meet expectations. This process helps group members to develop crisp behavior-outcome contingencies, and in particular to distinguish between what might be considered constructive and destructive expressions of deviance (Kelley, 1993). This includes both verbally acknowledging positive behaviors and sanctioning undesirable behaviors by calling attention to them and also by refusing to prop up employees who are repeat offenders. When star performers are rewarded or promoted despite being known to engage in micro-aggressions towards coworkers, employees receive the message that engaging in inclusive behaviors may not be so important after all, thereby diluting the strength of their inclusive climate perceptions.

*Assessing* followers' understanding of the inclusive behaviors that are expected is critical for being able to make adjustments to the way that expectations are articulated, role modeled, and reinforced in order to yield desired outcomes. Assessment also requires soliciting direct feedback as well as perceiving more subtle cues from group members in an effort to understand why something that was intended has not been accomplished. Even in the face of clearly articulated expectations for how to engage one another's diverse perspectives and strengths, group leaders need to be attuned to the possibility that pre-existing dynamics that stem from societal systems of privilege and oppression may pose greater psychological obstacles to inclusion for some members than others. As such, group leaders must skillfully assess when neutrality could actually perpetuate the status-quo and engage instead in "multi-partiality," in which they challenge dominant ideologies in order to provide the structural equality that is needed to allow for more complete dialogue involving group members who might otherwise feel silenced by identity threats. In other words, sometimes a neutral stance towards valuing the coexistence and expression of multiple perspectives may not successfully cultivate inclusion for all members because individuals enter the social context of the group from varying levels of societally determined status.

## Conclusion

As we have demonstrated above, developing strong, inclusive climates necessitates that leaders be very intentional about enacting a series of interconnected behaviors that together send a clear message about what inclusion means, why it is important, and how organizational members co-create it through their interaction patterns. We hope to have illustrated how organizational-level policies and practices alone are usually insufficient for promoting inclusion. Instead, workgroup leaders need to be equipped with the knowledge and coaching required to shape and reinforce inclusive workgroup norms. There is no single or easy formula for accomplishing this important goal, which is why it remains elusive in so many workplaces. The specific behaviors that are needed will be shaped by the organizational and workgroup context, including the extent to which organizational practices and rhetoric reinforce a commitment to inclusion, the pre-existing positive interaction patterns that can be leveraged and the negative ones that must be undone, the nature of the team's work, the demography of the workgroup and organization, and the receptiveness of employees. With that said, there are a number of climate engineering behaviors that can be thought of as uniformly valuable across circumstances. We provide concrete examples as a practical guide to managers in Table 12.1.

*Table 12.1* Examples of climate engineering behaviors.

| | |
|---|---|
| Articulating | *Articulate what inclusion means and why it is important*<br>• Communicate shared goals and vision in a way that can be easily understood and to which workgroup members can align their own goals.<br>• Translate broader organizational messages about inclusion into tangible behavioral guidelines that employees can apply to the way they approach their work. Provide examples of situations when a lack of inclusion negatively impacted results and examples that illustrate business benefits of developing an inclusive climate.<br>• Communicate the value of diversity in a way that is visible, understandable, and unambiguous; explain how inclusion promotes workgroup success and is relevant for all workgroup members.<br>• Help workgroup members to see how diversity of perspectives, expertise, and strengths promotes the attainment of strategic objectives. Share examples of good decisions and/or innovations that have been made possible by the integration of cognitive diversity, as well as examples of poor decisions that resulted from homogeneous thinking.<br>*Articulate "rules of engagement" that promote inclusion (i.e., how)*<br>• Explain not just what behaviors are expected—for example "rules" for how to engage inclusively during workgroup interactions—but also why they are important.<br>• Utilize team chartering as a tool for collectively articulating group process rules (e.g., about information sharing, listening, decision-making, shared roles, accountability). |
| Role modeling | *Invest time and space for individuals to develop positive relationships across difference; prioritize inclusive interactions*<br>• Invest time and space necessary for team members to learn about one another as individuals, for example by emphasizing one-on-one personal interactions and assigning tasks to rotating pairs (e.g., pair A with B and C with D, then A with C and B with D, etc.).<br>• Role model behaviors that go beyond the absence of negative treatment and instead develop high-trust relationships by consistently paying attention to others.<br>• Treat each interaction with workgroup members as having important ramifications for the future of the relationship.<br>• Be consistent—across situations and people—about prioritizing inclusion. If there are situations when inclusive |

(*Continued*)

rules of engagement can or should be suspended, provide a transparent rationale.

- Communicate openly, honestly, and often; engage in personal self-disclosure.
- Continuously attend to how one is coordinating meaning with others in the relationship.
- Identify behaviors that contradict the message of inclusion and stop doing them.

*Demonstrate what it means to value diverse perspectives; adopt team practices that facilitate integration of diverse perspectives*

- Recognize one's own mistakes so that workgroup members don't become preoccupied with avoiding mistakes rather than learning from them.
- Rather than avoid conflicts that arise from identity differences, engage with the intent to understand the many factors at play to enable those involved to learn from differences; help workgroup members to reflect on the conflict, capture the learning that took place, and consider how it can be applied to improve future interactions.
- Crowdsource ideas to inform decision-making.
- De-correlate errors and protect against groupthink by collecting independent input from group members prior to a group discussion.
- Encourage the least expert or newest members of the workgroup to voice their perspective first.
- Conduct "after-action reviews" to collectively identify factors that lead the workgroup astray from effectively leveraging diverse perspectives. After an event or project completion, ask the following questions: What was supposed to happen? What actually happened? What explains the differences (what worked and what didn't)? What should be done differently next time?
- Utilize premortem discussions to legitimize doubts and encourage more imaginative and thorough discussion. Right before proceeding with a decision, ask the group, "imagine we go down this path and a year from now it turns out to be a disaster. Provide a narrative about why."

*Demonstrate commitment to fair treatment as being an essential foundation for inclusion*

- Make competence visible, particularly of group members who belong to lower-status identity groups or are considered "role incongruent."

(*Continued*)

*Table 12.1* (Cont.)

| | |
|---|---|
| | • Respond to employee mistakes and performance deficits with similar levels of differentiated feedback and coaching.<br>• Rotate informal leadership opportunities across work-group members so that patterns in how leadership is claimed and granted within the group do not perpetuate status hierarchies.<br>• Cross workgroup roles with social identity group membership.<br>• Question assumptions about competence and be vigilant about basing evaluations or interpretations on observable facts.<br>• Avoid inconsistent treatment by making exceptions or "idiosyncratic deals" for some members but not others.<br>• Invest in developing high-quality, high-trust relationships with each workgroup member rather than privileging a select few (based on potential or similarity/familiarity). |
| Reinforcing | *Reinforce inclusion-oriented behaviors and discourage exclusion-oriented behaviors*<br>• Reward learning-oriented behaviors; provide (and accept) constructive feedback that encourages workgroup members to be more open to learning from interactions with coworkers.<br>• Provide verbal praise and formal incentives to reinforce desired inclusive behaviors.<br>• Avoid the temptation to sidestep problematic behaviors; show disapproval in response to undesired behaviors immediately following the behavior so that employees are able to clearly link behavior to outcomes.<br>• Be consistent in reactions to positive and negative behaviors; allowing undesirable behaviors to slide for some workgroup members undermines climate strength.<br>• Attend to and interrupt common status dynamics (e.g., when higher-status group members speak first, talk over others, or otherwise dominate workgroup conversations). |
| Assessing | *Assess and increase awareness of how inclusion and exclusion are at play in your workplace*<br>• Be vigilant about observing group dynamics—look for power dynamics (e.g., micro-aggressions), evidence of shifting standards, and detrimental assumption-driven behavior.<br>• Ask workgroup members for feedback about what is and is not working. |

(*Continued*)

*Table 12.1* (Cont.)

| |
|---|
| • Engage in dialogue to understand others' experiences, unearth deep-rooted assumptions, and identify adaptations that need to be made to strengthen the workgroup climate.<br>• Where available, utilize employee survey data to prompt dialogue about what the data show and the actions that can be taken to improve employee experiences.<br>• Recognize that organizations are not gender, racially, or culturally neutral; develop awareness of how one's own social identity context and that of others impacts perceptions of, and reactions to, workplace experiences. |

## References

Allport, G. W. (1954). *The nature of prejudice*. Reading, MA: Addison-Wesley. https://doi.org/10.2307/3791349

Avery, D. R. (2003). Personality as a predictor of the value of voice. *The Journal of Psychology*, *137*, 435–446. https://doi.org/10.1080/00223980309600626

Barrick, M. R., & Mount, M. K. (1991). The big five personality dimensions and job performance: A meta-analysis. *Personnel Psychology*, *44*, 1–26. https://doi.org/10.1111/j.1744-6570.1991.tb00688.x

Boswell, W. (2006). Aligning employees with the organization's strategic objectives: Out of "line of sight," out of mind. *International Journal of Human Research Management*, *17*(9), 1489–1511. https://doi.org/10.1080/09585190600878071

Chrobot-Mason, D., Ruderman, M., & Nishii, L. H. (2013). Leadership in a diverse workplace. In Q. M. Roberson (Ed.), *The Oxford handbook of diversity and work*, (pp. 315–340). Oxford, UK: Oxford University Press. https://doi.org/10.1093/oxfordhb/9780199736355.013.0018

Costa, P. T., & McCrae, R. R. (1992). *Revised NEO Personality Inventory (NEO-PIR): Professional manual*. Odessa, FL: Psychological Assessment Resources, Inc.

Crocker, J., & Canevello, A. (2008). Creating and undermining social support in communal relationships: The role of compassionate and self-image goals. *Journal of Personality and Social Psychology*, *95*, 555–575. https://doi.org/10.1037/0022-3514.95.3.555

Dragoni, L. (2005). Understanding the emergence of state goal orientation in organizational work groups: The role of leadership and multilevel climate perceptions. *Journal of Applied Psychology*, *90*, 1084–1095. https://doi.org/10.1037/0021-9010.90.6.1084

Dweck, C. S. (1986). Motivational processes affecting learning. *American Psychologist*, *41*, 1040–1048. https://doi.org/10.1037/0003-066X.41.10.1040

Dweck, C. S., & Leggett, E. L. (1988). A social cognitive approach to motivation and personality. *Psychological Review*, *95*, 256–273. https://doi.org/10.1037/0033-295X.95.2.256

Dwertmann, D., Nishii, L. H., & van Knippenberg, D. (2016). Disentangling the fairness & discrimination and synergy perspectives on diversity climate: Moving the field forward. *Journal of Management*, *42*(5), 1136–1168. https://doi.org/10.1177/0149206316630380

Earley, P. C., & Mosakowski, E. (2000). Creating hybrid team cultures: An empirical test of transnational team functioning. *Academy of Management Journal*, *43*(1), 26–49. https://doi.org/10.5465/1556384

Edelman, L. B., Fuller, S. R., & Mara-Drita, I. (2001). Diversity rhetoric and the managerialization of law. *American Journal of Sociology*, *106*(6), 1589–1641. https://doi.org/10.1086/321303

Ehrhart, M. G., Schneider, B., & Macey, W. H. (2014). *Organizational climate and culture: An introduction to theory, research, and practice*. New York, NY: Routledge. https://doi.org/10.4324/9781315857664

Ely, R. J., & Thomas, D. A. (2001). Cultural diversity at work: The effects of diversity perspectives on work group processes and outcomes. *Administrative Science Quarterly*, *46*, 229–273. https://doi.org/10.2307/2667087

Ferdman, B. M. (2014). The practice of inclusion in diverse organizations: Toward a systemic and inclusive framework. In B. M. Ferdman & B. R. Deane (Eds.), *Diversity at work: The practice of inclusion* (pp. 3–54). San Francisco, CA: Jossey-Bass. https://doi.org/10.1002/9781118764282.ch1

Ferdman, B. M. (2017). Paradoxes of inclusion: Understanding and managing the tensions of diversity and multiculturalism. *The Journal of Applied Behavioral Science*, *53*(2), 235–263. https://doi.org/10.1177/0021886317702608

Goodstein, L. D., & Lanyon, L. D. (1999). Applications of personality assessment to the workplace: A review. *Journal of Business and Psychology*, *18*, 533–553. https://doi.org/10.1023/A:1022941331649

Green, S. E. (2004). A rhetorical theory of diffusion. *Academy of Management Review*, *29*, 653–669. https://doi.org/10.5465/amr.2004.14497653

Gurin, P., Dey, E. L., Hurtado, S., & Furin, G. (2002). Diversity and higher education: Theory and impact on educational outcomes. *Harvard Educational Review*, *72*(3), 330–366. https://doi.org/10.17763/haer.72.3.01151786u134n051

Judge, T. A., Erez, A., Bono, J. E., & Thoresen, C. J. (2003). The core self-evaluations scale: Development of a measure. *Personnel Psychology*, *56*, 303–331. https://doi.org/10.1111/j.1744-6570.2003.tb00152.x

Kelley, S. W. (1993). Discretion and the service employee. *Journal of Retailing*, *69* (1), 104–126. https://doi.org/10.1016/S0022-4359(05)80005-3

Lewin, K., Lippitt, R., & White, R. K. (1939). Patterns of aggressive behavior in experimentally created "social climates." *Journal of Social Psychology*, *22*, 272–280. https://doi.org/10.1080/00224545.1939.9713366

Mathieu, J. E., & Rapp, T. L. (2009). Laying the foundation for successful team performance trajectories: The roles of team charters and performance strategies. *Journal of Applied Psychology*, *94*(1), 90–103. https://doi.org/10.1037/a0013257

Mayer, D. M., Nishii, L. H., Schneider, B., & Goldstein, H. (2007). The precursors and products of justice climates: Group leader antecedents and employee attitudinal consequences. *Personnel Psychology*, *60*(4), 929–963. https://doi.org/10.1111/j.1744-6570.2007.00096.x

McCauley, C. D., Ruderman, M. N., Ohlott, P. J., & Morrow, J. E. (1994). Assessing the developmental components of managerial jobs. *Journal of Applied Psychology*, *79*, 544–560. https://doi.org/10.1037/0021-9010.79.4.544

McCormick, D. W. (1999). Listening with empathy: Taking the other person's perspective. In A. Cooke, A. Craig, B. Greig, & M. Brazzel (Eds.), *Reading book for human relations training* (pp. 57–60). Arlington, VA: NTL Institute.

Mischel, W. (1977). The interaction of person and situation. In D. Magnusson & N. S. Endler (Eds.), *Personality at the crossroads* (pp. 333–352). Hillsdale, NJ: Erlbaum.

Nemeth, C. J. (1986). Differential contributions of majority and minority influence. *Psychological Review*, *93*(1), 23–32. https://doi.org/10.1037/0033-295X.93.1.23

Nishii, L. H. (2011, August). *Eliminating the experiential differences that divide diverse groups through climate for inclusion* [Paper Presentation]. Annual Conference of the Academy of Management, San Antonio, TX.

Nishii, L. H. (2013). The benefits of climate for inclusion for gender diverse groups. *Academy of Management Journal*, *56*(6), 1754–1774. https://doi.org/10.5465/amj.2009.0823

Nishii, L. H. (2020). The role of inclusive climates in closing the gender gap. In E. Kossek (Ed.), *Creating gender-inclusive organizations: Lessons from research and practice to advance women leaders* (pp. 15–25). Toronto, Canada: University of Toronto Press.

Nishii, L. H., Khattab, J., Shemla, M., & Paluch, R. (2018). A multi-level process model for understanding diversity practice effectiveness. *Academy of Management Annals*, *21*(1), 37–82. https://doi.org/10.5465/annals.2016.0044

Nishii, L. H., & Langevin, A. (2009, August 11). *Climate for inclusion: Unit predictors and outcomes* [Paper Presentation]. Annual Conference of the Academy of Management, Chicago, IL.

Nishii, L. H., & McAlpine, K. L. (2018, August 13). *A social networks lens to understanding the relationship between inclusive climates and outcomes* [Paper Presentation]. Annual Conference on the Academy of Management, Chicago, IL.

Nishii, L. H., & Paluch, R. (2018, August 13). Leaders as HR sensegivers: Four HR implementation behaviors that create strong HR systems. *Human Resource Management Review*, *28*(3), 319–323. https://doi.org/10.1016/j.hrmr.2018.02.007

Pfeffer, J. (1981). *Power in organizations.* Marshfield, MA: Pitman Publishing Corp.

Piaget, J. (1971). The theory of stages in cognitive development. In D. R. Green, M. P. Ford, & G. B. Flamer (Eds.), *Measurement and Piaget* (pp. 1–111). New York, NY: McGraw-Hill.

Piaget, J. (1975). *The equilibration of cognitive structures: The central problem of intellectual development*. Chicago, IL: University of Chicago Press.

Rentsch, J. R. (1990). Climate and culture: Interaction and qualitative differences in organizational meanings. *Journal of Applied Psychology*, *75*(6), 668–681. https://doi.org/10.1037/0021-9010.75.6.668

Roberson, Q., Holmes IV, O., & Perry, J. L. (2016). Transforming research on diversity and firm performance: A dynamic capabilities perspective. *Academy of Management Annals*, *11*, 189–216. https://doi.org/10.5465/annals.2014.0019

Schein, E. H. (2017). *Organizational culture and leadership* (5th ed.). Hoboken, NJ: John Wiley & Sons, Inc.

Schneider, B., González-Romá, C., Ostroff, C., & West, M. (2017). Organizational climate and culture: Reflections on the history of the constructs. *Journal of Applied Psychology*, *102*(3), 468–482. https://doi.org/10.1037/apl0000090

Shore, L. M., Randel, A. E., Chung, B. G., Dean, M. A., Ehrhart, K. H., & Singh, G. (2011). Inclusion and diversity in work groups: A review and model for future research. *Journal of Management*, *37*, 1262–1289. https://doi.org/10.1177/0149206310385943

VandeWalle, D. (1997). Development and validation of a work domain goal orientation instrument. *Educational and Psychological Measurement*, *57*(6), 995–1015. https://doi.org/10.1177/0013164497057006009

Wood, R., & Bandura, A. (1989). Social cognitive theory of organizational management. *Academy of Management Review*, *14*(3), 361–384. https://doi.org/10.5465/amr.1989.4279067

Zajac, E. J., & Westphal, J. D. (1994). The costs and benefits of managerial incentives and monitoring in large U.S. corporations: When is more not better? *Strategic Management Journal*, *15*, 121–142. https://doi.org/10.1002/smj.4250150909

Zohar, D. (2002). Modifying supervisory practices to improve subunit safety: A leadership-based intervention. *Journal of Applied Psychology*, *87*, 156–163. https://doi.org/10.1037/0021-9010.87.1.156

Zohar, D., & Luria, G. (2004). Climate as a social-cognitive construction of supervisory safety practices: Scripts as proxy for behavioral patterns. *Journal of Applied Psychology*, *89*, 322–333. https://doi.org/10.1037/0021-9010.89.2.322

Zohar, D., & Polachek, T. (2014). Discourse-based intervention for modifying supervisory communication as leverage for safety climate and performance improvement: A randomized field study. *Journal of Applied Psychology*, *99*(1), 113–124. https://doi.org/10.1037/a0034096

# 13 Team Inclusion Over Time

## The Case for Early Intervention

*Lynn R. Offermann and Lauren A. Lanzo*

Though the importance of fostering diversity has been and continues to be recognized by most organizations, the current focus on diversity has widened to include the concept of inclusiveness. There is an increasing awareness of the fact that simply achieving a heterogeneous body of employees is insufficient to reap the benefits of diversity (Ferdman, 2014; Pless & Maak, 2004). Diversity in and of itself has no intrinsic value for an organization (Giovannini, 2004). Instead, the potential positive or negative effects of a diverse workforce stem from the way in which the talents of these diverse individuals are used. Specifically, the degree to which all individuals feel included, accepted, and valued should influence their ultimate effectiveness, satisfaction, and willingness to stay.

The concept of inclusiveness overlaps with that of diversity, but it is still a distinct construct (Chavez & Weisinger, 2008; Ferdman, 2014; Roberson, 2006). To be diverse, a workforce must be composed of members with differing characteristics. To be inclusive, an organization must ensure that all of these different members "are allowed to participate and are enabled to contribute fully" (Miller, 1998, p. 151). As a commonly cited maxim by consultant Vernā Myers goes, "Diversity is being invited to the party; inclusion is being asked to dance" (https://youtu.be/9gS2VPUkB3M). Thus, an organization's inclusiveness may be influenced by a number of factors, such as the degree to which all employees can access resources, influence decisions, become involved in organizational processes, and feel accepted by their peers and supervisors (Mor Barak & Cherin, 1998; Roberson, 2006).

Research provides strong support for the importance of inclusion. For instance, Ibarra (1993) notes that "one of the most frequently reported problems faced by women and racial minorities in organizational settings is limited access to or exclusion from informal interaction networks" (p. 56). More recent work by Acquavita et al. (2009) found that perceptions of inclusion and exclusion, organizational diversity, and supervisory support were significant predictors of job satisfaction among social workers. Nishii and Rich (2014) note the value of creating climates of inclusion in work units and teams, finding that such inclusive units report higher commitment and less likelihood of leaving their unit —benefits that accrue to both majority and minority group members. These units also evidenced increased levels of innovation and profit.

To date, most examinations of inclusion have focused on individual perceptions independent of the units and teams in which people work. We view this as an unfortunate omission, since perceptions of inclusion in an organization are likely to be highly dependent on perceptions of one's team or work unit. A manager may preach inclusion, but if your teammates don't value you and exclude you from professional and social contact, the manager's words will ring hollow. In this chapter we address the construct of team inclusiveness—what it is, how it can be measured, why measuring it accurately is important, and how measurement can change its meaning. We also present an example of measuring inclusion over time from our own study of project teams over several months, which demonstrates how inclusion may, or may not, change over time, and the effects it may have on team performance. Specifically, we provide evidence for the importance of developing inclusion early in a team's lifecycle, rather than assuming that inclusion will necessarily increase with time and contact. Based on our own research and practice as well as that of others, we include implications for organizational practice throughout the chapter as to how to develop inclusive teams, with a particular focus on recommendations for leaders charged with ensuring that all staff feel valued and included in the teams on which they labor. Although all team members should be encouraged to be inclusive, we believe that ensuring inclusion is now a major leadership responsibility in order for organizations to realize the individual and organizational benefits that accrue to those units embracing inclusion.

## Team Inclusion: Meaning and Measurement

Many definitions of inclusion refer to a state in which individuals perceive themselves as being part of something larger than themselves, usually a group, team, and/or organization. Still, inclusion is often conceptualized at the individual level. Talking about inclusive teams, then, presents an interesting issue as to how to best aggregate what is often thought of as an individual perception to the team level of analysis. What does it mean to have an inclusive team? And how do we measure that? Accurate measurement of inclusion as an emergent team phenomenon, as opposed to an individual perception, is necessary to understand and develop tools to create and maintain feelings of inclusion within a team, group, or organization.

It is particularly important to consider how best to conceptualize and measure team inclusion because the manner in which we measure psychological constructs at different levels (i.e., individual versus team) can impact the inferences we draw from the analysis, and in turn, the practical implications the findings have for an organization. For example, most emergent phenomena of interest in research on teams, groups, or organizations are considered multilevel and dynamic; if measured at the individual level and at one point in time, all inferences would be made under the assumption that the construct of interest is specific to each individual and unchanging over time (i.e., static rather than dynamic). Given that inclusion can be conceptualized as a collective team or group feeling that does or does not develop over time, individual-level, static measurement of inclusion may result in a loss of information and understanding about how collective feelings of inclusion develop, function over time, and ultimately impact team effectiveness.

In a discussion on diversity and inclusion in organizations, DeNisi (2014) suggests that industrial-organizational psychologists are well positioned to make invaluable contributions to the study of inclusion through the field's expertise in measuring psychological constructs. One challenge is becoming more knowledgeable and skilled at addressing how to measure and model dynamic, multilevel constructs. Taking the multilevel nature of team inclusion into consideration when conceptualizing and measuring these feelings is important, specifically because different composition models can alter the interpretation of the construct at different levels.

Chan (1998) put forth several composition models and explained how the conceptualization of a construct can change based on the different models. His categories of models include (a) the *additive model*, which is a summation or averaging of lower level scores and does not consider agreement or variance in scores, (b) the *direct consensus model*, which measures within-group agreement and conceptualizes the higher-level construct as consensus among the lower-level, (c) the *referent-shift model*, which also measures within-group agreement but changes the referent (e.g., from individual-level referent "I" to team-level referent "the team"), (d) the *dispersion model*, which measures the amount of within-group variance of the higher-level construct, and (e) the *process model*, which accounts for changes in behavior and conceptualizes the higher-level construct as dynamic rather than static.

It is important to understand how different conceptualizations of multilevel constructs can change based on which of these composition models is employed. Individual feelings of inclusion are conceptually different from those at the team or organization level, or the "collective experience of inclusion" (as labeled by Ferdman et al., 2010). These higher-level inclusion constructs can be further delineated depending on which composition model is used (see Chan, 1998, for an in-depth review and examples). Research on inclusion can best serve organizations when the composition model conceptually matches the issue or research question. For example, if an organization is interested in determining whether minority employees feel included within their workgroup, an individual-level model is appropriate. However, when conceptualizing inclusion at a higher, group or organization level, different composition models can answer different questions.

The commonly used additive model (i.e., summation or average of individual perceptions) may not be as informative as a direct consensus or dispersion model, which refers to "the shared assignment of meaning" of inclusion and the variance in perceptions of inclusion, respectively (Chan, 1998, p. 237). Determining the shared meaning of inclusion and the variance in perceptions of inclusion can be useful when assessing the level and strength of a group or organization's climate of inclusion. Identifying groups with both high and low variance may be important because it is an indication of whether some individuals feel included and others do not, and in turn, the strength of the collective feelings of inclusion (e.g., high variation in team members' perceptions may indicate low inclusive climate strength). Ferdman (2014) argues this point by emphasizing these differences in theory and practice within an organization. He notes that one member of a group may feel included or excluded but that alone does not tell us whether this is a shared feeling among group members or whether the group or organization as a whole values inclusion, and thus has an inclusive climate.

Referent-shift and process models can also provide key information on feelings of inclusion by changing the measured referent from "I" to "the team, group, or organization." Shifting the referent from "I" (as in "I feel included in this team") to "the team, group, or unit" ("my team is committed to working through disagreements") changes the meaning of the perception of inclusion to individual perceptions about how the team (or group, or organization) perceives inclusion. For example, this can answer the question of whether individuals perceive inclusion as a shared value within their group. This can be useful in understanding why individuals do or do not behave in an inclusive manner given that individuals tend to engage in behaviors that are congruent with the norms and values within their group (Fishbein & Ajzen, 1975). Indeed, recent research has found that leader use of more implicitly inclusive language ("we" references) was associated with greater voice behaviors (sharing suggestions, opinions, problems, and doubts) in team members (Weiss et al., 2018).

Lastly, a process model is a powerful way to measure changes in individual- or team-level constructs that are not static phenomena. This model may be of particular use to the study of team inclusion by incorporating time in order to gain a better understanding of the emergence and changes in perceptions of inclusion. Leaders who assume that inclusion is static will miss changes in inclusion over time resulting from experiences working together. Time is a key element in much organizational research but is especially important to consider when investigating inclusion as it relates to emergent phenomena and temporal dynamics within a team (Bell & Kozlowski, 2012). Previous research defines a construct as emergent "when it originates in the cognition, affect, behaviors, or other characteristics of individuals, is amplified by their interactions, and manifests as a higher-level, collective phenomenon" (Kozlowski & Klein, 2000, p. 55). In a practical sense, leaders seeking to measure and increase inclusion should consider that many team context constructs such as inclusion emerge based on the dynamic interactions that team members have over time (Bell & Kozlowski, 2012), thus highlighting the importance of including time in our models.

The most recent conceptualization of team process models is the input-mediator-ouput-input model (IMOI; Ilgen, Hollenbeck, Johnson, & Jundt, 2005), which argues for the cyclical or episodic nature of team functioning. In this model, team outputs (such as performance or attainment of valued emergent states such as feelings of inclusion or collective efficacy) are also considered inputs that denote a cyclical causal feedback loop. This suggests that attainment or lack of attainment of feelings of inclusion becomes a predictor of future team processes and outcomes. Lastly, teams are often fluid because members may enter and leave over a team's life course. Time is an essential component to fully understand how a team's fluidity and membership changes impact team processes and emergent states. These time-related factors suggest that one-time leader actions to develop inclusivity may not be sufficient to reinforce a climate of inclusion; rather, as teams move through different tasks, performance episodes, or changes in membership, additional leader attention to inclusion issues is needed.

Despite suggestions that team inclusion, like many team processes, is dynamic and not a one-time achievement (Ferdman, 2014), much of the current body of literature treats team inclusion as static and either present or absent. This is likely because much of the research on team inclusion has been cross-sectional. In an effort to leverage our research on inclusion and create evidence-based recommendations for practice, we need to be confident that the conclusions we draw from research are based on a full understanding of the multilevel, dynamic nature of inclusion.

Considering the dynamics of how inclusion does or does not emerge over time is not only crucial to our understanding of the construct and how to effectively foster it within organizational settings, but it will also improve prediction of key individual and organizational outcomes. Outcomes such as team member satisfaction and viability are commonly measured as individual attitudes (e.g., "I would work with this team again in the future," Tesluk & Mathieu, 1999), while outcomes such as team or organizational performance are measured at higher levels. Klein et al. (1994) note that relationships between predictor and outcome are stronger when the referent is consistent across both, supporting the argument for improved measurement of feelings of inclusion. In other words, when assessing the link between team inclusion and relevant organizational outcomes, prediction is improved when team inclusion is paired with team-level outcomes (e.g., team performance, team commitment), as opposed to individual outcomes (e.g., job satisfaction), which are better predicted by individual feelings of inclusion. In the next section we provide an example of how we measured team-level inclusion over time and discuss the practical implications of our findings in understanding the development of team inclusion.

## Studying Team Inclusion Over Time

Despite greater awareness of the value of inclusion in organizations and work teams, information on the dynamics of inclusion is limited. As noted above, the literature often treats inclusion as something that is either present or absent, oblivious to the prospect that, as with many team constructs, it may well change over time. As Ferdman (2014) has noted, inclusion is not a static one-time accomplishment, but is rather a dynamic set of processes. Unfortunately, longitudinal work examining patterns of perceived inclusion over the course of team life is lacking, a major gap that we addressed in a study of college project teams over the course of a semester. In a recent study (Lanzo & Offermann, 2016), we examined team inclusion over the life of both diverse and homogeneous student project teams. Management students were randomly assigned to teams and tasked to complete a class project over the course of the semester. At the end of the semester, teams gave a class presentation in the form of a skit in which each member was required to play a role. The end product was designed to ensure that team coordination and contributions from all members were required for effective performance.

In order to assess inclusion over time, students completed online surveys at five time points throughout the semester. Team inclusion, as well as additional team process variables (e.g., communication) and emergent states (e.g., cohesion and trust), were assessed at times 2, 3, and 4 throughout the semester. Team inclusion was measured using Ferdman et al.'s (2009) 23-item inclusion scale, a measure framed from the individual referent point of view (i.e., "I feel like an outsider on my team"). Using a direct consensus model, ratings from all team members were aggregated. We justified aggregation by calculating the proportion of total variance accounted for by group membership and the reliability of group level means (*ICC*(1) and *ICC*(2)) as well as interrater agreement ($r_{wg}$; James, Demaree, & Wolf, 1984). At the end of the semester, team effectiveness was assessed through external ratings of performance (a consensus rating from five graduate teaching assistants' individual ratings) and by team member ratings for perceived team productivity, member satisfaction, and viability.

Results of this study demonstrate both the value of high inclusion for team processes as well as the importance of team inclusion early in a team's life. When team inclusion was high, all teams benefitted from better team processes (e.g., trust, cohesion, reduced relationship conflict, and increased time spent meeting face to face). In terms of effectiveness, inclusion was predictive of internal measures of effectiveness, including perceived productivity, satisfaction, and viability. These results support the value of inclusion found in previous work cited above. Interestingly, the teams' external rating of effectiveness (the presentation grade) was not affected by inclusion. It is possible that in teams with lower inclusion, a few team members who were most concerned about their grade were able to step up and put in additional work to ensure a better end product comparable to that produced by more inclusive teams. Thus, while the externally assessed presentation grade was not affected, internal feelings about the group and the desire to work together again were negatively affected.

Although low inclusion was not detrimental to the team grade, it likely represented a decreased amount of member engagement that would have more negative effects in a longer-term team. In situations where individuals have the opportunity to leave (either the team or the organization), the internal impact of low inclusion may drive people to seek work elsewhere, decreasing retention. Additionally, these relationships were not moderated by gender or ethnic diversity, demonstrating the importance of team inclusion regardless of the amount of diversity within a team.

Of greatest interest was that inclusion did not increase over time; rather, inclusion at time 1 was predictive of internal team outcomes at all subsequent time points. Practically, this suggests the importance of establishing team inclusion early in a team's life. Perhaps ironically, despite its stability over time, this finding also highlights the importance of measuring inclusion as a dynamic construct. If inclusion had only been measured at time 1 (or at any other one point in the semester), we would not have determined the importance of early inclusion and the necessity to address lack of inclusion early in a team's lifecycle rather than hope inclusion would increase with increasing contact within the team.

Although inclusion did not develop over time in this study, this does not suggest that team inclusion is necessarily static. One reason team inclusion did not increase over the course of the team's time together may be that there needs to be an environment through which inclusion can be fostered if it does not initially unfold. Our teams lacked formal leadership, and an astute leader may be able to help put teams on a good path to inclusion and encourage more inclusive practices as the team evolves. The fact that inclusion did not develop over time in our study is important in and of itself because it highlights the need to identify what *does* increase feelings of inclusion over a team's life course and how leaders and team members can best develop and maintain inclusion.

## Implications for Practice

The study described above provides evidence that inclusion or exclusion was established quickly in project teams and held fairly constant across the team's life, accruing multiple benefits to those teams able to achieve it. Teams benefited from increased inclusion in terms of better team processes (higher levels of trust and cohesion, lower levels of task and relationship conflict), better individual outcomes (higher satisfaction and willingness to work together in the future), and higher self-rated productivity. Our work also shows that inclusion at the get-go predicted later inclusion—perceptions of inclusion did not grow over time as many have naively hoped. Thus, it is vitally important that those leaders overseeing organizational teams, as well as team leaders themselves, help teams to get off on the right foot in establishing inclusive practices. We suggest the following strategies and actions for leaders to take to promote team inclusion.

### *Monitor Behaviors Associated with High Reported Inclusion*

Sherbin and Rashid (2017) suggest that inclusive leadership is comprised of six behaviors:

1 ensuring that team members speak up and are heard;
2 making it safe to propose novel ideas;
3 empowering team members to make decisions by asking for input from each member when making decisions;
4 taking advice and implementing feedback;
5 giving actionable feedback; and
6 sharing credit for team success.

These authors claim that workers with team leaders who exhibit at least three of these behaviors are more likely to feel welcome and included, freer to express their opinions, and more likely to perceive that their ideas are heard than workers with team leaders who exhibit none of these behaviors. They also claim that employees with inclusive leaders are 1.3 times more likely to feel that they can be innovative.

These behaviors are not inherently difficult if incorporated into normal operating procedures. For example, when running meetings, leaders can make it a habit to consciously attend to who is speaking and who is not, and encourage those more reluctant to participate by asking for their ideas. They can take care to ensure that members respond to each other's ideas respectfully and with an open mind, establish clear guidelines for civility and respect even in the face of disagreement, and model that behavior. Do not tolerate bullying or those who would dominate conversation, keeping the discussion flowing to all parties present. Engage all team members in making decisions, and use their ideas whenever possible, giving credit for their contributions.

These behaviors are concrete and measurable and can be monitored through discussion and survey along with other summary assessments of how people feel in their teams. Using 360-degree feedback to team leaders can be a way to assess leader effectiveness in making everyone feel they can bring their best to the team and rewarding those team leaders who are able to create climates of inclusion.

### *Train Team Leaders to Develop Inclusive Behaviors before the Team Starts Its Work*

Rather than wait for potential feelings of exclusion to take place, spend time with team leaders to help them consider how they will initially bring their group together before the group forms. Train team leaders on key inclusive behaviors and help them consider what has made them feel included or excluded in other teams in which they have participated. Support kick-off meetings, initial team retreats, and other ways that team leaders can bring their team members together and ensure that everyone has the opportunity to participate. Some people will naturally talk more than others, but all should feel comfortable participating.

### *Mitigate Unconscious Bias*

Most of us have some forms of implicit bias, unconscious associations that we make between certain groups of people and stereotypes about those groups. These implicit biases may do as much damage as more blatant discrimination, and are likely far more pervasive (Sue, 2010). Research shows that countering such implicit biases begins by being aware that you have them. As a result, a number of organizations have undertaken implicit bias training. For example, the U.S. Department of Justice is training over 28,000 of its employees to recognize and address their own implicit biases in the hope of mitigating biases (U.S. Department of Justice, 2016). Interviews with chief diversity officers in organizations noted for their success in achieving inclusive climates conducted by Offermann and Basford (2014) similarly showed that these organizations were spending substantial training time in confronting issues of more subtle forms of exclusion and have reported positive results for their efforts. Including ratings of inclusion by team members in evaluations of team leaders, managers, and senior leaders can help determine the success of these efforts.

### *Ensure that Commitment to Inclusion Starts at the Top*

"CEOs who have abdicated responsibility for this issue to the CHRO or Chief Diversity Officer must now take ownership and hold business leaders accountable at all levels" (Bourke et al., 2017, para. 6). Although we believe that holding all levels of leaders responsible for inclusion is vitally important, we would also add that there is no substitute for CEOs modeling inclusion in terms of who is on their own executive team, and how much they themselves are seen as displaying inclusive behaviors. Psychologists have long known that even as children, we model behavior rather than words. In the organizational context, previous research has demonstrated a "trickle down" effect when it comes to employees modeling behaviors exhibited by top leadership (Mawritz et al., 2012). Setting a positive example at the middle and upper management level can have a large impact on how employees behave within the organization. Preaching inclusion while surrounding oneself with only those who look, sound, and act like you sends a powerful message throughout the organization that is directly counter to creating a truly inclusive organization.

These strategies can all help generate more inclusive teams in which all members can make their best contributions. We maintain that leaders need to step up to the challenges of ensuring that teams are inclusive, and that they are effectively using the talents of all employees. Our work suggests that such leader efforts are best deployed at the start of team life to establish the norms and climate that will continue as time passes, and that leaders should actively monitor team perceptions over a team's life to ensure that all members continue to feel included. The leader efforts required to do this are not overwhelming or difficult, primarily requiring attention and awareness. Yet the payoff in terms of team commitment, satisfaction, and retention may be truly great.

## Summary of Practical Suggestions for Developing and Sustaining Team Inclusion

### *Understand the Differences Between Individual Feelings of Inclusion and Collective Team Perceptions, Values, and Inclusive Behaviors*

Team inclusion is a collective and dynamic construct, not simply a combination of individual feelings of inclusion. Understanding this is key to diagnosing issues and implementing interventions to increase collective feelings of inclusion. Averages can hide the exclusion of a member amid the high scores of the rest of the team; look at variability across members to identify cliques and outsiders.

### *Train Team Leaders to Develop Inclusive Behaviors before the Team Starts Its Work*

The more that leaders, both formal and informal, demonstrate inclusive behaviors at the start of a team's lifecycle, the more likely the team will successfully develop a climate of inclusion. Do not assume inclusion will get better over time based simply on increased contact.

### *Recognize that Establishing Inclusion is not a One-Time Effort*

Understanding that team inclusion can change over time can help ensure that leaders regularly monitor behaviors associated with higher reported inclusion such as:

- Ensuring that team members speak up and are heard.
- Making it safe to propose novel ideas.
- Empowering team members to make decisions.
- Taking advice and implementing feedback.
- Giving actionable feedback.
- Sharing credit for team success.

### *Mitigate Unconscious Bias within the Team*

Regular monitoring of perceived team or unit inclusion with feedback to managers can help, along with offering coaching to those leaders and team members perceived as lacking in inclusive behaviors.

### *Get the Visible and Public Commitment of Leadership to Creating a Culture of Inclusion*

Inclusion begins at the top and flows down to all levels of the organization. When leading a team at any level, publicly demonstrate commitment to inclusion, model inclusive behaviors, and hold all members accountable to supporting a positive and inclusive team culture.

## References

Acquavita, S. P., Pittman, J., Gibbons, M., & Castellanos-Brown, K. (2009). Personal and organizational diversity factors' impact on social workers' job satisfaction: Results from a national internet-based survey. *Administration in Social Work*, *33*(2), 151–166. https://doi.org/10.1080/03643100902768824

Bell, B. S., & Kozlowski, S. W. (2012). Three conceptual themes for future research on teams. *Industrial and Organizational Psychology*, *5*(1), 45–48. https://doi.org/10.1111/j.1754-9434.2011.01403.x

Bourke, J., Garr, S., van Berkel, A., & Wong, J. (2017). *Diversity and inclusion: The reality gap*. Deloitte Insights, Deloitte. https://www2.deloitte.com/us/en/insights/focus/human-capital-trends/2017/diversity-and-inclusion-at-the-workplace.html

Chan, D. (1998). Functional relations among constructs in the same content domain at different levels of analysis: A typology of composition models. *Journal of Applied Psychology*, *83*(2), 234–246. https://doi.org/10.1037/0021-9010.83.2.234

Chavez, C. I., & Weisinger, J. Y. (2008). Beyond diversity training: A social infusion for cultural inclusion. *Human Resource Management*, *47*(2), 331–350. https://doi.org/10.1002/hrm.20215

DeNisi, A. S. (2014). An I/O psychologist's perspective on diversity and inclusion in the workplace. In B. M. Ferdman & B. R. Deane (Eds.), *Diversity at work: The practice of inclusion* (pp. 564–579). San Francisco, CA: Jossey-Bass. https://doi.org/10.1002/9781118764282.ch21

Ferdman, B. M. (2014). The practice of inclusion in diverse organizations: Toward a systemic and inclusive framework. In B. M. Ferdman & B. R. Deane (Eds.), *Diversity at work: The practice of inclusion* (pp. 3–54). San Francisco, CA: Jossey-Bass. psycnet.apa.org/doi/10.1002/9781118764282.ch1

Ferdman, B. M., Avigdor, A., Braun, D., Konkin, J., & Kuzmycz, D. (2010). Collective experience of inclusion, diversity, and performance in work groups. *Revista De Administração Mackenzie*, *11*(3), 6–26. https://doi.org/10.1590/S1678–69712010000300003

Ferdman, B. M., Barrera, V., Allen, A., & Vuong, V. (2009, August). Inclusive behaviors and the experience of inclusion. In B. G. Chung (Chair), *Inclusion in organizations: Measures, HR practices, and climate* [Symposium]. 69th Annual Meeting of the Academy of Management, Chicago, IL.

Fishbein, M., & Ajzen, I. (1975). *Belief, attitude, intention, and behavior: An introduction to theory and research*. Reading, MA: Addison-Wesley.

Giovannini, M. (2004). What gets measured gets done: Achieving results through diversity and inclusion. *Journal for Quality and Participation*, *27*(4), 21–27.

Ibarra, H. (1993). Personal networks of women and minorities in management: A conceptual framework. *Academy of Management Review*, *18*(1), 56–87. https://doi.org/10.2307/258823

Ilgen, D. R., Hollenbeck, J. R., Johnson, M., & Jundt, D. (2005). Teams in organizations: From input-process-output models to IMOI models. *Annual Review of Psychology*, *56*(1), 517–543. https://doi.org/10.1146/annurev.psych.56.091103.070250

James, L. R., Demaree, R. G., & Wolf, G. (1984). Estimating within-group interrater reliability with and without response bias. *Journal of Applied Psychology*, *69*(1), 85–98. psycnet.apa.org/doi/10.1037/0021-9010.69.1.85

Klein, K. J., Dansereau, F., & Hall, R. J. (1994). Levels issues in theory development, data collection, and analysis. *Academy of Management Review*, *19*(2), 195–229. https://doi.org/10.5465/amr.1994.9410210745

Kozlowski, S. W. J., & Klein, K. J. (2000). A multilevel approach to theory and research in organizations: Contextual, temporal, and emergent processes. In K. J. Klein & S. W. J. Kozlowski (Eds.), *Multilevel theory, research, and methods in organizations: Foundations, extensions, and new directions* (pp. 3–90). San Francisco, CA: Jossey-Bass.

Lanzo, L. A., & Offermann, L. R. (2016, April 15). *Team inclusion over time: Patterns and outcomes* [Poster Presentation]. 31st Annual Conference of the Society for Industrial and Organizational Psychology, Anaheim, CA.

Mawritz, M. B., Mayer, D. M., Hoobler, J. M., Wayne, S. J., & Marinova, S. V. (2012). A trickle-down model of abusive supervision. *Personnel Psychology*, *65*(2), 325–357. https://doi.org/10.1111/j.1744-6570.2012.01246.x

Miller, F. A. (1998). Strategic culture change: The door to achieving high performance and inclusion. *Public Personnel Management*, *27*(2), 151–160. https://doi.org/10.1177%2F009102609802700203

Mor Barak, M. E., & Cherin, D. (1998). A tool to expand organizational understanding of workforce diversity. *Administration in Social Work*, *22*(1), 47–64. https://doi.org/10.1300/J147v22n01_04

Nishii, L., & Rich, R. (2014). Creating inclusive climates in diverse organizations. In B. M. Ferdman & B. R. Deane (Eds.), *Diversity at work: The practice of inclusion* (pp. 330–363). San Francisco, CA: Jossey-Bass. https://doi.org/10.1002/9781118764282.ch11

Offermann, L. R., & Basford, T. E. (2014). Inclusive human resource management: Best practices and the changing role of human resources. In B. M. Ferdman & B. R. Deane (Eds.), *Diversity at work: The practice of inclusion* (pp. 229–259). San Francisco, CA: Jossey-Bass. https://doi.org/10.1002/9781118764282.ch8

Pless, N. M., & Maak, T. (2004). Building an inclusive diversity culture: Principles, processes, and practice. *Journal of Business Ethics*, *54*(2), 129–147. https://doi.org/10.1007/s10551-004-9465-8

Roberson, Q. M. (2006). Disentangling the meanings of diversity and inclusion in organizations. *Group & Organization Management*, *31*(2), 212–236. https://doi.org/10.1177%2F1059601104273064

Sherbin, L., & Rashid, R. (2017, May 23). Diversity doesn't stick without inclusion. *Harvard Business Review Digital Articles*. https://hbr.org/2017/02/diversity-doesnt-stick-without-inclusion

Sue, D. W. (2010). *Microaggressions in everyday life: Race, gender, and sexual orientation*. Hoboken, NJ: Wiley.

Tesluk, P. E., & Mathieu, J. E. (1999). Overcoming roadblocks to effectiveness: Incorporating management of performance barriers into models of work group effectiveness. *Journal of Applied Psychology*, *84*(2), 200–217. https://doi.org/10.1037/0021-9010.84.2.200

U.S. Department of Justice. (2016). *Department of Justice announces new department-wide implicit bias training for personnel*. https://www.justice.gov/opa/pr/department-justice-announces-new-department-wide-implicit-bias-training-personnel

Weiss, M., Kolbe, M., Grote, G., Spahn, D. R., & Grande, B. (2018). We can do it! Inclusive leader language promotes voice behavior in multi-professional teams. *The Leadership Quarterly*, *29*, 389–402. https://doi.org/10.1016/j.leaqua.2017.09.002

# Part III

# Leadership Practices for Building Inclusive Organizations

# 14 Responsible Inclusive Leadership

## A Whole System Collective Process Outcome

*Lize A. E. Booysen*

There are a number of distinctive aspects to 21st-century workplaces that call for different ways of leading. This chapter highlights four of these aspects that necessitate responsible and inclusive leadership practice.

First, workplaces operate in contexts characterized by high levels of volatility, uncertainty, complexity, and ambiguity (VUCA). This VUCA world leads to decreased levels of knowing, predictability, and certainty and calls for adaptive and innovative capabilities in organizations (Hazy & Uhl-Bien, 2015).

Second, there is a trend toward the democratization of workplaces, involving less hierarchical structures and more networked systems. In these workplaces, leadership is more distributed and decision-making is pushed toward lower levels in the organizational structures (Jackson & Parry, 2018).

Third, the dominant implicit leadership mental model in most workplaces is changing from the great man leadership model—a view of leaders as usually men who heroically take charge and decide on everything in autocratic, directive, and controlling ways of leading—to more networked, shared, and relational ways of leading, in which empowerment and equal partnerships are valued and leadership is co-created (Booysen, 2014). The view that leadership resides in a single person or in an elite group is losing traction. In its place, the notion that leadership resides in the collective—in both formal leaders and followers—and should be dispersed throughout the organizational system is gaining traction (Denis et al., 2015).

Last, general disillusionment with the rise of irresponsible and destructive leadership has given way to a counter-narrative that questions the ethical nature of leadership and asks the critical question, "leadership for what?" (Maak & Pless, 2006, p. 102). This counter-narrative calls for more responsible and sustainable leadership, with a focus on the triple bottom line (profit, people, and the planet) (Miska & Mendenhall, 2018).

These four changes—(1) our VUCA world, (2) the democratization of workplaces, (3) relational and shared leadership, and (4) responsible leadership—call for a different way of leading, one that is responsible and inclusive and is based on inclusive democratic workplaces, social justice, and fairness for all involved.

In the rest of this chapter I unpack the reasons why a combination of responsible and inclusive leadership is particularly suitable and a good fit for our current workplaces, first by discussing my view of what *responsible inclusive leadership* is and what makes it good leadership practice. Second, I discuss the relational, emergent, and collective nature of responsible inclusive leadership practice. Finally, I provide a practical framework and examples to illustrate how responsible inclusive leadership is produced in joint collective relational practice dispersed throughout the whole organizational system.

## Responsible Inclusive Leadership as Good Practice

> When "I" is replaced with "we" even illness becomes wellness—
>
> Malcom X

In previous work (Booysen, 2014) I surmised that inclusive workplaces are based on collaborative, pluralistic, co-constructed, and coevolving value frames that rely on mutual respect, equal contribution, and valuing of difference, which is different than exclusive workplaces where conformity to pre-established mainstream ways of doing is expected. In that chapter I argued that inclusive leadership removes impediments that cause marginalization and exclusion and extends our thinking beyond assimilation strategies and organizational demography toward empowerment and participation of all. I also pointed out that inclusive leadership involves particular skills and competencies for relational practice, collaboration, creating inclusive work cultures, partnerships, consensus building, and true engagement. I concluded that inclusive leadership is good practice, and that in truly inclusive workplaces all people will feel valued, respected, and recognized. I defined inclusive leadership as:

> respectful relational practice, that enables individuals and collectives to be fully part of the whole, directed, aligned, and committed toward shared outcomes, for the common good of all, while retaining a sense of authenticity and uniqueness.
>
> (Booysen, 2014, p. 306)

Somewhat similar to my definition of inclusive leadership, responsible leadership can be defined "as a relational and ethical phenomenon, which occurs in social processes of interaction with those who affect or are affected by leadership and have a stake in the purpose and vision of the leadership relationship" (Maak & Pless, 2006, p. 103).

Over the past 10 to 15 years, we have seen discussions around the concepts of responsibility and leadership expand from social responsibility (leaders being responsible mainly for shareholder wealth), to corporate social responsibility (CSR) (focusing on ethical, economic, and legal aspects of sustainable organizational practices), to responsible leadership (as defined in the previous paragraph), and finally to global responsible leadership (focusing on a multitude of local and global domains of sustainable organizational practices) (Miska & Mendenhall, 2018).

These shifts resulted in broadening the focus of responsible leadership from agent views, which see managers as agents of shareholders securing maximum profits—"doing well" for the shareholders (aligned with a social responsible view)—to converging views, which see managers as reconciling making maximum profit for shareholders with other stakeholder considerations—"doing well" (for shareholders) by also "doing good" (for stakeholders, including the community, more aligned with CSR). The next turn in focus was toward normative stakeholder views that focused on relational and ethical considerations of a broader stakeholder base including employees, customers, suppliers, communities, and shareholders and of the triple bottom line: doing well by doing good and avoiding harm for all stakeholders in the community: responsible leadership (Maak & Pless, 2006). The current focus is on multi-domain stakeholder views in global responsible leadership. This is aligned with a transnational CSR approach that includes ethical and triple-bottom-line responsibility and sustainability both in a local and global context: "creating sustainable enterprises that not only reconcile economic, environmental, and social bottom lines, but enhances all of them at the same time" (Stahl et al., 2018, p. 9).

This broader base of inclusion of contributors essentially speaks to inclusive practices. In my view, the intersection between inclusive leadership and responsible leadership indeed lies on the normative stakeholder level (doing well by doing good and avoiding harm for all stakeholders in the community) that broadens agency and inclusion.

Inclusion functions on a micro level inside the organization, encompassing individuals (internal micro), groups (internal meso), and organizational processes (internal macro level). Inclusion also operates on a larger external macro level outside the organization, involving other stakeholders, communities, societies, nations, and the planet (Ferdman, 2014).

Responsible leadership—with its focus on broad-based inclusion of stakeholders, on justice and fairness, and on relational practice and ethical aspects—can be seen as an expansion of inclusive leadership. While there is substantial overlap between these perspectives (both emphasize inclusion, justice, fairness, and the common good of all), the difference lies in the emphasis on the *levels* of inclusion.

I would argue that inclusive leadership generally foregrounds the internal organizational level (micro, meso, and macro) and relational practices, with some emphasis on the immediate external macro level, while responsible leadership generally foregrounds a broader stakeholder external view and ethical practices, with some emphasis on the internal organizational level. For example, inclusive leadership tends to emphasize inclusion of individuals and collectives on cross-functional and internal organizational levels with a focus on obtaining organizational goals, while responsible leadership tends to emphasize a broader base of inclusion, by focusing on collaboration between organizations and the communities they serve, between private and public enterprises, and a more active role of the citizenry towards triple-bottom-line sustainability (also see Figure 14.1).

That is why I propose the combined terminology of *responsible inclusive leadership*, leadership that equally emphasizes the internal organizational and the external macro levels of inclusion on the one hand, and relational, ethical, and sustainable practices on the other hand.

In the next section I illustrate how responsible inclusive leadership is relational, emergent, and collective in nature.

## The Relational, Emergent, and Collective Nature of Responsible Inclusive Leadership Practice

There is tension in leadership theory between leader- or entity-focused theories, which are mostly psychological, and relational and collective theories, which are mainly sociological (Jackson & Parry, 2018). The more dominant entity-based theories explain individual, group, and organizational performance outcomes primarily by identifying and examining specific leader behaviors, like traits and styles, and shared assumptions. The general assumption of these theories is that leaders will be successful if they have certain traits and understand and adapt to shared values and follower expectations.

The basic assumption of relational theories is that both leadership and contexts are products of social interactions between all involved; leadership is relational and socially constructed by the collective. Relational-based perspectives focus on how reciprocal social interactions between everyone in the (organizational) system emerge and evolve, and are co-constructed and sustained in interpersonal, group, and collective relationships and collaboration. From this view, effective leadership is not within the control of any individual. Instead, leadership happens and is the product of social interaction of all individuals in a specific context (which is also co-constructed, fluid, and emergent). From a relational-based perspective, leadership resides in interactions and is a function of interactions (Uhl-Bien, 2006). It is collective in nature and functions in

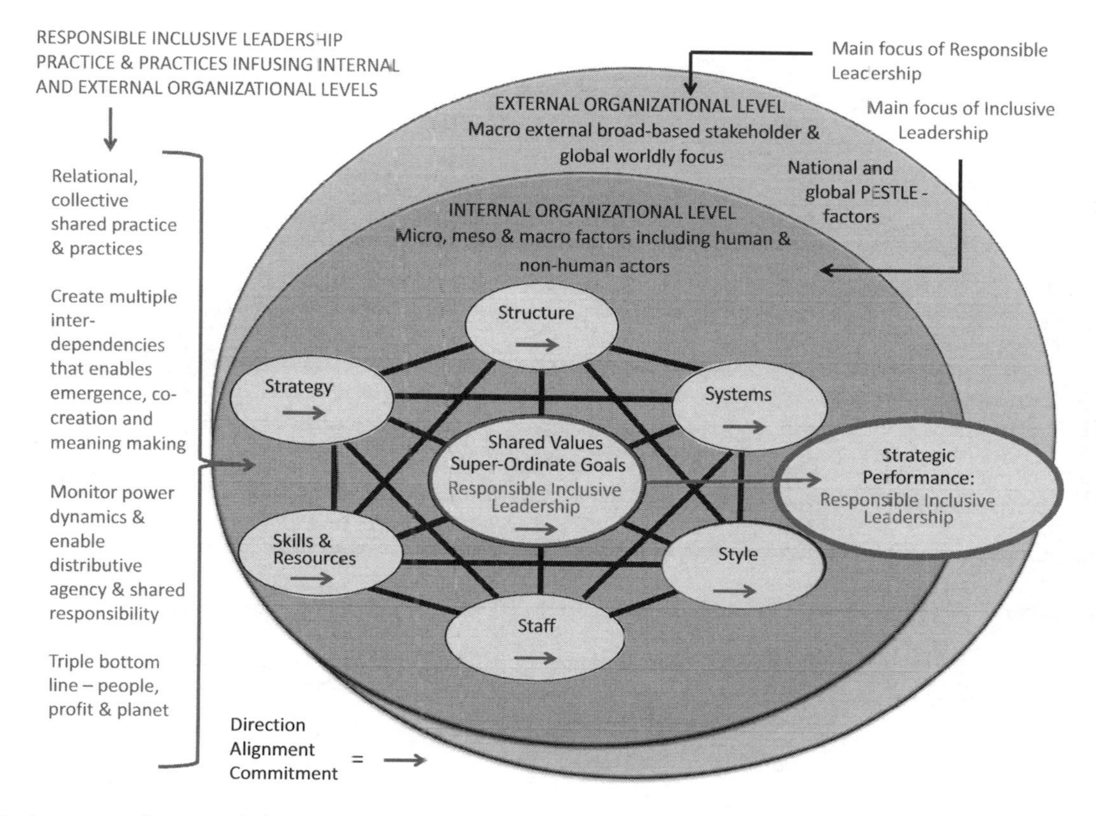

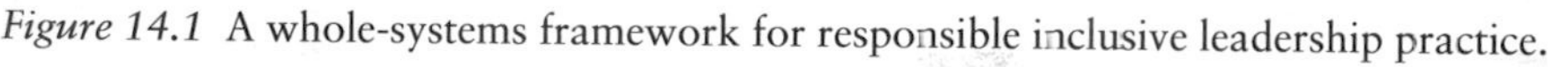

*Figure 14.1* A whole-systems framework for responsible inclusive leadership practice.

the plural, not only in positional leadership or an elite few (Denis et al., 2015), and it is a way-of-being in the world that emphasizes speaking "with" others rather than "to" others, or "living well with others" (Cunliffe & Eriksen, 2011, p. 1439).

Table 14.1 captures the key differences between more traditional less inclusive entity-based practices of leadership and more inclusive relational-based views that can be applied in practice.

*Table 14.1* Differences between traditional entity-based and inclusive relational-based leadership practice (source: adapted from Booysen, 2014, pp. 304–305,[1] in Ferdman and Deane, 2014)

| *Traditional Entity-Based Leadership* | *Inclusive Relational-Based Leadership* |
|---|---|
| **Focus of the leader:** | **Focus of leader practices:** |
| • Entity (individual reality) perspective, subject–object understanding of leadership—human capital focus.<br>• Leader centered—focus on follower–leader exchanges of the leadership process.<br>• Focus on me, us, and them.<br>• Focus on difference, similarity, and common ground.<br>• Orient to outcomes and business processes. | • Relationships (multiple reality) perspective of leadership—understanding throughout organization—social capital focus.<br>• Relational context and process centered—focus on various forms of relationships and networks of reciprocal social interactions—social constructions made in a process.<br>• Focus on we and all.<br>• Value and pursue diversity and multiple viewpoints.<br>• Orient to outcomes, social processes, context, and business processes. |
| **The use of power:** | **The use of power:** |
| • Power is seen as a commodity, a leadership tool, concentrated in certain individuals.<br>• Forceful and controlling.<br>• Smooth things over.<br>• Hierarchical and positional. | • Power is seen as distributed throughout the system—focus on mutual enabling practices, i.e., collaboration, power sharing, and empowerment.<br>• Thoughtful, reflective, transparent, participating, and inclusive.<br>• Co-create courageous expectations.<br>• Networked and "in place." |
| **Decision-making processes:** | **Decision-making processes:** |
| • Direct, tell, and sell.<br>• Give marching orders.<br>• Make decisions. | • Elicit and facilitate, create space for dialogue.<br>• Set boundaries and frame the intention. |

(*Continued*)

*Table 14.1* (Cont.)

| *Traditional Entity-Based Leadership* | *Inclusive Relational-Based Leadership* |
|---|---|
| • Engage in directing and controlling. | • Create a process for engagement, decision-making, and leading as learning.<br>• Engage in meaning making and opportunity creating, agency and partnerships. |
| **The role of leadership:** | **The role (activity) of leadership:** |
| • Leadership is seen as a formal role that drives organizational process.<br>• Entity-based process of leading.<br>• Positional, formal, and informal.<br>• Input based. | • Leadership is seen as generated in social dynamics.<br>• Collective consensual process of leading and enabling mutual commitment.<br>• Community and collectives of leaders, and leaders in place, formal and informal.<br>• Emergent and processual. |
| **The role of the leader:** | **The role of leadership practices:** |
| • Create and enforce rules and regulations.<br>• Take control and solve problems.<br>• Honoring responsibility and engagement.<br>• Focus on similarity and common ground. | • Question dominant and normative practices. Focus on fairness, equity, civil dissent, distributed agency.<br>• Create a holding space for followers to solve problems.<br>• Honor relational responsibility and integrity, and mindful engagement.<br>• Value and pursue diversity, multiple viewpoints, and mutuality. |

In summary, relational leadership practice is a collective and distributive process. It focuses on we and all (based on social capital or relationships) and not only on me, us, or them (based on human capital or entities). Relational practice also links back to responsible leadership's broad-based multiple stakeholder view and a shared responsibility of living well with others, while doing no harm. Responsible inclusive leadership rests on relational practices as one of its main underpinnings: honoring collective relational responsibility, distributive agency, mindful engagement, and individual accountability.

Leadership involves both *practices* (workplace task activities, routines, and standard operating procedures to get the job done) and *practice* (coordinative effort) to keep the process of leadership and emergence going. In spite of the collective shared process, leadership may arise from the actions or practices of individuals due to organizational structural conditions, positional placements, access to information and expertise, or proximity that will enable meaning making (Shotter, 2016; Simpson, 2016). This makes leadership the shared responsibility of the collective, and each and every individual in the collective (Ford, 2016). *This means that while leadership does not belong to anyone in particular, it is the shared responsibility of everyone in the system.*

Moreover, leadership does not only reside in the people; the whole organizational system is involved. The vision, mission, shared values, rules, conventions, technologies, procedures, and the artifacts of the organizational system are all embedded in the leadership process. It is a shape-shifting social phenomenon produced through collective relational practice distributed throughout the whole system (Ford, 2016).

Aligned with the above, the Center for Creative Leadership defined leadership as "a process by which people with shared values and work collectively create direction, alignment and commitment (DAC) utilizing all parts of the organizational systems, within a culture of collaboration and cooperation" (Drath et al., 2008, p. 636), thus tapping into the energy of the whole system to produce leadership.

*Direction* refers to widespread agreement in a collective on overall goals, aims, and mission (agreement on goals). *Alignment* refers to the organization and coordination of knowledge, work, systems, and processes in a collective (coordination of work). *Commitment* refers to the willingness of members of a collective to subsume their own interests and benefit within the collective interest and benefit (giving extra effort). People can intentionally engage and establish enabling practices in their organizations through direction, alignment, and commitment for emergence and leadership to happen (Boekhorst, 2015; Ford, 2016; Gotsis & Grimanai, 2016; Hazy & Uhl-Bien, 2015).

The practice of leadership, then, does not reside in a person, nor is it dependent on any particular person to lead, mobilize, or take action on behalf of others; it is inherently relational, shared, distributed, collective, and co-created. Consequently, leadership can happen within teams, workgroups, task forces, divisions, communities, and whole organizations, stakeholders in the external macro context, across teams, levels, and functions, and organizations, and it can be formal (positional) and informal (in place).

From the above discussion leadership can be framed as a process outcome that exists and emerges in relational, collective, and distributed practice and practices in context, dispersed throughout the whole system (Raelin, 2016, p. 3).

## The Production of Responsible Inclusive Leadership in the Whole Organizational System

Leadership does not take place in a vacuum, but rather in specific organizational contexts (systems) that are directed by vision, mission, shared values, and superordinate goals and that lead to strategic outcomes. Internal cross-functional organizational factors (or spheres of influence) that play a role in the leadership production process are strategy, structure, systems, style, staff, skills, or resources (Higgins, 2005, based on McKinsey's 7-S framework of strategy implementation). These internal organizational factors are used in tandem as levers in the leadership process to attain the organization's envisioned strategic outcomes, based on its shared values and superordinate goals. Therefore, if responsible inclusive leadership is a superordinate goal and shared value of an organization it should be embedded in and aligned with all its cross-functional organizational factors (see Figure 14.1 and Table 14.2).

Figure 14.1 presents a practice-based framework for understanding how responsible inclusive leadership can be produced by direction, alignment, and commitment throughout the organizational system and the context in which it operates. This framework conceptualizes responsible inclusive leadership as occurring on the micro, meso, and macro levels and highlights the different main foci of responsible and inclusive leadership.

This framework highlights that leadership gets produced through direction, alignment, and commitment across all the internal cross-functional organizational factors or six spheres of influence (strategy, structure, systems, style, staff, and skills/resources) that are driven by its superordinate goals (Higgins, 2005).

The superordinate goals and shared values in Figure 14.1 drive the strategic performance of the organization. The strategic performance of the organization ultimately depends on the collective alignment of strategy, structure, systems, style, staff, and skills/resources with its shared goals. Consequently, if responsible inclusive leadership is valued and seen as a superordinate goal of the organization, all the other spheres of influence (strategy, structure, systems, style, staff, skills/resources) need to be deliberately aligned to enable responsible inclusive leadership practice (as shown in Figure 14.1). This means the leadership process includes not only collective human action, but also the internal processes, policies, procedures (operations), rituals, and artifacts (climate and culture) of the organization, as well as the external organizational context. Table 14.2 highlights examples of such enabling practices that can be institutionalized across the functional spheres of influence in the organization to produce responsible inclusive leadership.

Lastly, while responsible inclusive leadership is a collective organizational system-wide process, we still need to take a critical look at how

*Table 14.2* Responsible inclusive leadership practices

| *Cross-Functional Spheres of Influence* | *Goals* | *Responsible Inclusive Practices* |
|---|---|---|
| **Strategy:**<br>How we do, what we do. | To do what we do in an inclusive and responsible way, valuing the collective. | Co-create a shared understanding of inclusive and responsible practice in organizational context and include it as a shared value and a super-ordinate goal.<br>Treat inclusive and responsible practice as a strategic imperative to be mainstreamed across all functional areas.<br>Hold everyone accountable to principles of responsible leadership, especially positional leaders, by, for instance, building it into their performance contracts. |
| **Structure:**<br>How people and work are organized. Organization structures, roles, and responsibilities, how people are organized to work together, division of labor. | To optimize networking and enhance collaboration through enabling organizational structures to be sensitive to historical and political systemic hegemonic practices and counteract these through systems and policies. | Maximize role and task interdependencies to enhance cooperation and compromise.<br>Create enabling decision making and reporting structures and distributed power-sharing possibilities in order for people to take up agency by creating flatter and flexible networked organization structures with permeable boundaries.<br>Create fluid roles and responsibilities (aligned with mission clarity) to enhance shared responsibilities and organic job enrichment and enlargement.<br>Fix responsibility to uphold responsible and inclusive practices, and hold everyone accountable.<br>Create physical shared safe (third) spaces for dialogue and participation.<br>Distribute work and responsibility fairly and equitably in a consultative manner, break down fault-lines and deliberately create maximum mix diverse work groups. |

| | | |
|---|---|---|
| **Systems:** Systems, processes, and information that link people together. | To create a climate of inclusion in everyday practice.<br>To build a culture of inclusion that is empowering and enabling in nature. | Socialize the expectation of respectful engagement, trust, sharing, honest giving and receiving of feedback, and civil dissent.<br>Build values of responsible inclusive leadership into performance management systems, and management systems and processes to ensure a match between enacted and espoused values.<br>Audit and diagnose processes for unequal power dynamics and exclusion and marginalization and instill corrective practices, for instance, work–life integration and effectiveness policies and practices, flexible work arrangements.<br>Make sure there is free flow of information and equal access to information, and open communication that enables equal voice and choice for all.<br>Monitor systems and processes and assess climate (atmosphere of respect, equity, fairness, safe environment for brave, authentic, and transparent dialogue to take place) and culture (practices, systems, and processes based on shared assumptions and values to enhance responsible practices and inclusion) for continuous improvement. |
| **Style:**<br>Leadership discourse, tools, concepts, implicit leadership models (also see Table 14.1). | To make responsible inclusive leadership a strategic key performance area and part of the performance appraisal process for everyone in the organization. | Build high trust and quality relationships, be supportive and reflective, practice humility, “not knowing,” and curious inquiry, be willing to fail and support others who have failed, apologize when needed.<br>Enact responsible inclusive leadership values, and be vocal about valuing difference, and keep others accountable to do the same, honor relational responsibility and integrity, and mindful engagement, and engage in power sharing, collaborative, participative, and enabling practices.<br>Question dominant and normative practices, focus on fairness, equity, distributed agency, and voice and choice for all. Create holding environments for open dialogue and civil dissent. |

(*Continued*)

*Table 14.2* (Cont.)

| *Cross-Functional Spheres of Influence* | *Goals* | *Responsible Inclusive Practices* |
| --- | --- | --- |
| | | Engage in community building by focusing on shared goals and aspirations, focus on collective creativity, mutual commitments, and shared responsibility.<br>Take up the responsibility of being leaders in place and create space for others to do the same.<br>Be a good, brave, and courageous citizen of the collective, speak up and call out exclusive practice through authentic respectful engagement and relational transparency, speak truth to power, be courageous "leaders" and "followers." |
| **Staff:**<br>People, agents or actors, leaders, followers. | To recruit, appoint, and maintain diverse people who will thrive in responsible inclusive organizations. | Advertise widely, use inclusive recruitment processes to ensure heterogeneity exists in the workplace. Set targets to deliberately include individuals from marginalized groups.<br>Constitute heterogeneous selection panels representing diverse views and all stakeholders.<br>Intentionally recruit, select, and appoint people who are triple-bottom-line driven and committed to principles of social justice, fairness, and inclusion.<br>Make high levels or the potential to develop high levels of relational integrity (living well with everyone) a requirement for appointment.<br>Socialize appointees into the ethos of responsible inclusive leadership practice, through buddy-ship, mentorship, role-modeling, coaching, and formal training and development.<br>Continuously develop relational practice and responsible inclusive leadership capabilities across the organization on all levels through leadership development and training. |

| | | |
|---|---|---|
| **Skills/Resources:** Dominant competencies and capabilities, skills technology, money. | To value a diverse set of skills, capabilities, competencies, and worldviews.<br>To allocate and distribute resources in a fair and equitable manner. | Focus on the importance and strengths of appreciating difference, different ways of knowing, and different worldviews.<br>Put systems and processes in place that ensure fair distribution of resource allocation, and that all have access to shared resources, for instance broad-based stakeholder input and shared decision-making on how resources should be allocated, distributed, and shared.<br>Incentivize responsible and inclusive practices, use resources to showcase individual and collective responsible and inclusive practices.<br>Provide resources for deliberate co-creation, emergence, and innovation. |

power with others and agency might play out in organizational structures and cultures. Agency in this collective process is still governed by pre-established and existing rules based on the system's socio-historical-cultural-political context that results in power dynamics that create inequalities in the system (Schedlitzki & Edwards, 2014). Consequently, certain people and groups have *power to*, power to act on behalf of others, or *power over* others, where power can be used to punish, incentivize, marginalize, or empower others. Responsible inclusive leadership creates spaces where power is distributive and seen as *power with*, which emphasizes mutuality and co-creation (Ford, 2016). For example, creating flatter and flexible networked organization structures with permeable boundaries enables people to cooperate, collaborate, share, and co-create, because it breaks down silo behavior and opens up power-sharing opportunities, rather than concentrating power and decision-making in certain individuals who then have power over others.

To be more inclusive, we thus need to acknowledge that power dynamics also permeate participatory spaces, and can still marginalize disenfranchised groups while privileging dominant groups by accepting them as the norm. It is therefore crucial to continuously monitor that agency is distributed throughout the organization system to optimize its inclusive capacity. One way to do this, for example, is to deliberately break down fault lines in creating teams and departments with maximum-mix diverse work groups.

## Conclusion

This chapter showed that responsible inclusive leadership is shared by the whole collective; it does not "belong" to anyone in particular, and it is distributed throughout all aspects of and co-created within the organizational system. This also means that—even though leadership does not belong to anyone in particular—it is the shared responsibility of everyone in the system!

I conclude with an initial definition of responsible inclusive leadership as

> an emergent process of co-creative meaning-making through collaborative and respectful relational practice that enables individuals and collectives to be fully part of the whole through authentic voice and unique choice, and to be directed, aligned, and committed toward shared sustainable outcomes for the common good of all, including the planet.

I also leave the reader with the following question: are you tapping into the energy of the whole organization through responsible, inclusive, collaborative, and shared practice, empowering all, or are you still practicing exclusive entity-based practices by trying to be in control, hold the answers, and do things autonomously?

To tap into the energy of the whole system in a responsible and inclusive manner, leaders need to cultivate high quality connections, question dominant and normative practices, and have a "both/and" perspective, rather than a binary "either/or" perspective. Leaders also need to frame leadership as a collective, shared, networked, interdependent process, and use metaphors such as Partnership of Equals, Confluence of Agendas, Communities of Practice, or Webs of Inclusion for the common good of all.

## Note

1 Based on Anderson and Ackerman-Anderson (2001); Booysen (2001); Ferdman and Brody (1996); Heifetz, Linsky, and Alexander (2009); Komives and Wagner (2009); McCauley et al. (2010); Pless and Maak (2004); Riggio (2008); Uhl-Bien (2006); Wasserman et al. (2008).

## References

Anderson, D., & Ackerman-Anderson, L. S. (2001). *Beyond change management: Advanced strategies for today's transformational leaders*. San Francisco, CA: Jossey-Bass/Pfeiffer.

Boekhorst, J. A. (2015). The role of authentic leadership in fostering workplace inclusion: A social information processing perspective. *Human Resource Management*, *54*(2), 241–264. https://doi.org/10.1002/hrm.21669

Booysen, L. (2001). The duality in South African leadership: Afrocentric or Eurocentric. *South African Journal of Labour Relations*, *25*(3&4), 36–64.

Booysen, L. A. E. (2014). The development of inclusive leadership practice and processes. In B. M. Ferdman & B. R. Deane (Eds.), *Diversity at work: The practice of inclusion* (pp. 296–329). San Francisco, CA: Jossey-Bass. https://doi.org/10.1002/9781118764282.ch10

Cunliffe, A. L., & Eriksen, M. (2011). Relational leadership. *Human Relations*, *64*(11), 1425–1449. https://doi.org/10.1177/0018726711418388

Denis, J.-L., Langley, A., & Sergi, V. (2015). Leadership in the plural. *Academy of Management Annals*, *6*(1), 211–283. https://doi.org/10.1080/19416520.2012.667612

Drath, W. H., Mccauley, C. D., Palus, C. J., Velsor, E. V., Oconnor, P. M., & Mcguire, J. B. (2008). Direction, alignment, commitment: Toward a more integrative ontology of leadership. *The Leadership Quarterly*, *19*(6), 635–653. https://doi.org/10.1016/j.leaqua.2008.09.003

Ferdman, B. M. (2014). The practice of inclusion in diverse organizations: Toward a systemic and inclusive framework. In B. M. Ferdman & B. R. Deane (Eds.), *Diversity at work: The practice of inclusion* (pp. 3–53). San Francisco, CA: Jossey-Bass. https://doi.org/10.1002/9781118764282.ch1

Ferdman, B. M., & Brody, S. E. (1996). Models of diversity training. In D. Landis & R. Bhagat (Eds.), *Handbook of intercultural training* (2nd ed., pp. 282–303). Thousand Oaks, CA: Sage.

Ferdman, B. M., & Deane, B. R. (2014). *Diversity at work: The practice of inclusion.* San Fransciso, CA: Jossey Bass. https://doi.org/10.1002/9781118764282

Ford, J. (2016). Gendered relationships and the problem of diversity in leadership-as-practice. In J. A. Raelin (Ed.), *Leadership-as-practice: Theory and application* (pp. 223–243). New York, NY: Taylor & Francis.

Gotsis, G., & Grimanai, K. (2016). The role of servant leadership in fostering inclusive organizations. *Journal of Management Development*, *35*(8), 985–1010. https://doi.org/10.1108/JMD-07-2015-0095

Hazy, J. K., & Uhl-Bien, M. (2015). Towards operationalizing complexity leadership: How generative, administrative and community-building leadership practices enact organizational outcomes. *Leadership*, *11*(1), 79–104. https://doi.org/10.1177%2F1742715013511483

Heifetz, R. A., Linsky, M., & Alexander, G. (2009). *The practice of adaptive leadership: Tools and tactics for changing your organization and the world.* Boston, MA: Harvard Business Press.

Higgins, J. M. (2005). The eight 'S's of successful strategy execution. *Journal of Change Management*, *5*(1), 3–13. https://doi.org/10.1080/14697010500036064

Jackson, B., & Parry, K. (2018). *A very short, interesting, and reasonably cheap book about studying leadership*. Thousand Oaks, CA: Sage.

Komives, S. R., & Wagner, W. (Eds.). (2009). *Leadership for a better world: Understanding the social change model of leadership development.* San Francisco, CA: Jossey-Bass.

Maak, T., & Pless, N. (2006). Responsible leadership in a stakeholder society: A relational perspective. *Journal of Business Ethics*, *66*, 99–115. https://doi.org/10.1007/s10551-006-90472

McCauley, C., van Velsor, E., & Ruderman, M. (2010). Introduction: Our view of leadership development. In E. van Velsor, C. McCauley, & M. Ruderman (Eds.), *The Center for Creative Leadership handbook of leadership development* (3rd ed., pp. 1–22). San Francisco, CA: Jossey-Bass.

Miska, C., & Mendenhall, M. (2018). Responsible leadership: A mapping of extant research and future directions. *Journal of Business Ethics*, *148*, 117–134. https://doi.org/10.1007/s10551-015-2999-0

Pless, N. M., & Maak, T. (2004). Building an inclusive diversity culture: Principles, processes, and practice. *Journal of Business Ethics*, *54*(2), 129–147. https://doi.org/10.1007/s10551-004-9465-8

Raelin, J. A. (Ed.). (2016). *Leadership-as-practice: Theory and application.* New York, NY: Taylor & Francis.

Riggio, R. E. (2008). Leadership development: Current state and future expectations. *Consulting Psychology Journal: Practice and Research*, *60*(4), 383–392. https://doi.org/10.1037/1065-9293.60.4.383

Schedlitzki, D., & Edwards, G. (2014). *Studying leadership: Traditional and critical approaches*. Thousand Oaks, CA: Sage.

Shotter, J. (2016). Turning leadership inside-out and back-to-front: A dialogical–hermeneutical account. In J. A. Raelin (Ed.), *Leadership-as-practice: Theory and application* (pp. 132–154). New York, NY: Taylor & Francis.

Simpson, B. (2016). Where's the agency in leadership as practice. In J. A. Raelin (Ed.), *Leadership-as-practice: Theory and application* (pp. 159–177). New York, NY: Taylor & Francis.

Stahl, G. K., Pless, N. M., Maak, T., & Miska, C. (2018). Responsible global leadership. In M. E. Mendenhall, J. S. Osland, A. Bird, G. R. Oddou, M. J. Stevens, M. L. Maznevski, & G. K. Stahl (Eds.), *Global leadership: Research, practice, and development* (3rd ed., pp. 363–388). New York, NY: Routledge.

Uhl-Bien, M. (2006). Relational leadership theory: Exploring the social processes of leadership and organizing. *Leadership Quarterly, 18*(4), 645–676. https://doi.org/10.1016/j.leaqua.2006.10.00

Wasserman, I. C., Gallegos, P. V., & Ferdman, B. M. (2008). Dancing with resistance: Leadership challenges in fostering a culture of inclusion. In K. M. Thomas (Ed.), *Diversity resistance in organizations* (pp. 175–200). New York, NY: Taylor and Francis.

# 15 Diversity Workspaces

## Pathways for Cultivating Inclusion in Diverse Organizations

*Stephanie J. Creary*

Importantly, individuals' experiences of inclusion are influenced by the groups with which they interact most frequently at work (Boehm et al., 2014; Ely & Thomas, 2001; Kramer, 1991). For instance, work group members may feel valued and respected when their primary workgroup views their cultural differences as a resource for learning and growth, and feel disrespected and devalued when their differences are viewed as the basis for discrimination (Ely & Thomas, 2001). To this end, primary work groups play a key role in individuals' experiences of inclusion and their support for and engagement in inclusive practices at work. Yet, insights from both academic scholarship (Ferdman, 2014, 2017; Roberson, 2013; Shore et al., 2010) and the popular and business press (Wittenberg-Cox, 2017; Yoshino & Smith, 2013) also suggest the value of *inclusive leaders*; that is, leaders who create pathways that enable individuals to "feel safe, trusted, accepted, respected, supported, valued, fulfilled, engaged, and authentic" at work (Ferdman, 2014, p. 18).

In this chapter I discuss a pathway that inclusive leaders can create to foster inclusion in diverse organizations: *diversity workspaces*. A diversity workspace is a physical, social, and psychological holding environment that supports individuals and groups in engaging their differences as valued resources at work and in organizations more broadly (cf. identity workspaces; Petriglieri & Petriglieri, 2010). Inclusive leaders can create two types of diversity workspaces: personal diversity workspaces and organizational diversity workspaces. The first engages individuals with a shared demographic identity in becoming more effective leaders. The second enlists individuals with either shared or different demographic identities in creating more effective organizations. Each diversity workspace has the capacity to promote inclusion in different ways (see Table 15.1). Hereafter, I examine and discuss each of these diversity workspaces in more detail.

### Personal Diversity Workspaces

Inclusive leaders can create *personal diversity workspaces* or those that expand members' capacities to be effective in their leadership roles

*Table 15.1* Diversity workspaces as pathways for inclusion in diverse organizations

<table>
<tr><th></th><th>Personal Diversity Workspaces</th><th>Organizational Diversity Workspaces</th></tr>
<tr><td>Purpose</td><td>Expand the capacity of individuals with a common social identity to be effective in their leadership roles.</td><td>Grow social capital among individuals with different and potentially complementary social identities that can expand the organization's capacity to be effective.</td></tr>
<tr><td>Workspace Characteristics</td><td>Personal Engagement<br>Individuals invest in, relate to, and identify with this workspace, their roles, and each other because they share a common background and goals.</td><td>Personal Engagement<br>Individuals invest in, relate to, and identify with this workspace, their roles, and each other because they share common goals.</td></tr>
<tr><td></td><td>Resource Mobilization<br>Individuals receive and provide career and social support from people with a similar social identity in this workspace.</td><td>Resource Mobilization<br>Individuals engage their different experiences and perspectives as resources for expanding the organization's capacity for collective work in this workspace.</td></tr>
<tr><td>Effects on Inclusion</td><td colspan="2">Sense of Inclusion<br>Individuals feel a sense of belonging and uniqueness in both types of workspaces.</td></tr>
<tr><td></td><td colspan="2">Inclusive Interpersonal Behavior<br>Individuals seek the opinions of and are curious about similar others, and treat them with respect in both types of workspaces.</td></tr>
<tr><td></td><td>Group-Level Inclusion<br>Individuals abide by norms for treating everyone in this workspace with respect and giving everyone a voice.</td><td>Group-Level Inclusion<br>Individuals with different social identities abide by norms for treating everyone in this workspace with respect, giving everyone a voice, collaboration, and working through conflicts productively and authentically.</td></tr>
<tr><td></td><td>Inclusive Organization<br>This workspace provides the container in which individuals can interact and interpret their experiences, which can lead them to advocate for more inclusive organizational policies and practices.</td><td>Inclusive Organization<br>This workspace provides the container in which individuals can interact and interpret their different experiences, which can enable them to develop more inclusive organizational policies and practices.</td></tr>
</table>

in order to enhance member retention and promotion rates, sense of belonging, engagement, commitment, and well-being at work. To achieve these outcomes, personal diversity workspaces emphasize both leader and leadership development. Leader development involves "enhancing individual human capacity (that is, knowledge, skills, attitudes)" while leadership development promotes "growth of social capital (such as relationships and networks) between individuals" (Booysen, 2014, p. 300; see also Day et al., 2008). Examples of personal diversity workspaces include women's leadership development programs, diversity recruitment and development programs, and employee network groups. In these workspaces, individuals with a shared demographic identity discover who they are and who they are becoming as leaders and the challenges they may face in light of their demographic identities. For instance, leadership programs designed specifically for women can help women to understand the gender dynamics that can make it difficult for them to advance into senior leadership roles, including few role models for women, gendered career paths and gendered work, women's lack of access to networks and sponsors, and women leaders' heightened visibility (Ely et al., 2011). To help members navigate these challenges, leaders who create these workspaces focus on 360-degree feedback, networking, negotiations, leading change, and managing career transitions.

Inclusive leaders create personal diversity workspaces to facilitate members' personal engagement in their leadership roles. Personal engagement occurs when "people employ and express themselves physically, cognitively, and emotionally during role performances" (Kahn, 1990, p. 694). Specifically, members learn to invest in, relate to, and identify with this workspace and their leadership roles because they share a common set of experiences and goals. They also learn to practice respectful engagement in their interactions with other members. Respectful engagement describes interactions between people that convey verbally and non-verbally that they are psychologically available and receptive to conversation, they speak and react from a genuine and honest place; they affirm others' situations and value; they recognize others' contributions and demonstrate genuine interest in their feelings, thoughts, or actions; they value others' time; they engage in active listening; and they use supportive communication (Dutton, 2003). Thus, the combination of similarity (Byrne, 1971) and mutual respect (Miller & Stiver, 1997) helps members of personal diversity workspaces internalize their leadership roles.

Inclusive leaders also create personal diversity workspaces to mobilize resources that strengthen and support workspace members. Specifically, workspace members learn to receive and provide support to people with a similar demographic identity. For example, minority development programs such as EY Unplugged bring together minority professionals to network and connect with minority executives during their first four months of employment at EY (Hewlett, 2017). Mobilizing resources in this way helps members of these workspaces to feel more efficacious at work.

By facilitating personal engagement and resource mobilization, personal diversity workspaces cultivate inclusion at multiple levels. First, they create a sense of belonging and uniqueness among members by recognizing the different challenges and opportunities that they face as people with a shared social identity while also strengthening their relationships with one another. These workspaces also foster inclusive interpersonal behavior by encouraging members to seek the opinions of and be curious about other members while treating them with respect. They promote group-level inclusion by encouraging members to abide by shared norms for respect and giving everyone a voice. Finally, they facilitate a more inclusive organization by providing the container in which all members can interact and interpret their experiences, which can lead them to advocate for more inclusive organizational policies and practices for their social identity group.

Yet, there can be downsides to personal diversity workspaces. First, those who are not invited to participate in them may feel excluded, which may lead them to devalue these workspaces. Second, members of these workspaces may find it difficult to transfer their learning to their day-to-day workplace experiences. To mitigate these issues, inclusive leaders can sponsor and provide support for the development and implementation of these workspaces while providing clarity on their purpose. For instance, leaders can invite non-members to participate in different workspace events as guest attendees or mentors. In this role, non-members can be charged with helping to translate key workspace lessons to real-world scenarios through role-playing, simulation, or other coaching opportunities. Leaders can also establish criteria for effectiveness and success. These criteria may include greater retention and promotion rates, sense of belonging, engagement, commitment, and well-being of employees who have participated in these workspaces relative to demographically similar peers who have not.

## Organizational Diversity Workspaces

Inclusive leaders also create *organizational diversity workspaces* or those that build individuals' skills for inclusion and motivate them to improve their organization's capacity to foster inclusion. Demographic identities among members of these workspaces may either be shared or different. Examples include some women's leadership development programs, diversity recruitment and development programs, employee network groups, and diversity councils. When effective, organizational diversity workspaces can enhance retention and promotion rates, a sense of belonging, engagement, commitment, and well-being at work for a wide range of organizational members. They can also enhance product and service innovation. For example, members of PepsiCo's employee network groups engage minority group members as strategists and consultants for developing products and business initiatives that support their communities' and the organization's effectiveness (Creary, 2008). The Adelante group, in particular, helped the company to create a variety of new Frito-Lay products and increase the company's sales (PepsiCo, 2012). In contrast, members of diversity councils whose demographic identities differ from one another combine and leverage their different experiences and perspectives as sources of new insight for their organizations. For instance, Deloitte's Inclusion Council brings together employees with different demographic identities to work on diversity issues, with the goal of generating a broader pool of allies, advocates, and sponsors across social identity groups (Green, 2017).

Similar to personal diversity workspaces, inclusive leaders create organizational diversity workspaces to facilitate members' personal engagement in their leadership roles. Members similarly invest in, relate to, and identify with this workspace and their leadership roles because of their common work-related goals (i.e., improve work-based tasks, processes, or business initiatives). They also learn to practice respectful engagement in their interactions with one another (Dutton, 2003). As such, the combination of similarity in work-related goals (Byrne, 1971) and mutual respect (Miller & Stiver, 1997) helps members of these workspaces to internalize their leadership roles.

Inclusive leaders also create organizational diversity workspaces to mobilize resources that can expand the organization's capacity for collective work (Creary et al., 2015; Ely & Thomas, 2001). For example, Cisco's employee resource groups enable members to contribute insights on the organization's talent management processes, which fosters their engagement at work (Creary, 2010). Mobilizing resources in this way helps members of these workspaces to feel more efficacious at work and that they can contribute to their organization in organizationally meaningful ways.

By facilitating personal engagement and resource mobilization, organizational diversity workspaces also cultivate inclusion at multiple levels. First, they can create a sense of belonging and uniqueness for members by allowing them to recognize and employ their experiences as sources of collective value in organizations. These workspaces can also foster inclusive interpersonal behavior by encouraging members to seek the opinions of and be curious about others in the workspace while treating them with respect. They can also promote group-level inclusion by encouraging members to abide by shared norms for treating everyone in the workspace with respect, giving everyone a voice, and instilling collaboration among members as they focus on using their experiences to improve work-based tasks, processes, and initiatives. Finally, they can facilitate a more inclusive organization by providing the container in which members can interact and interpret their experiences and the value they bring to the workplace, which enables them to develop more inclusive organizational policies and practices.

There can also be downsides to organizational diversity workspaces, however. First, members may feel that these workspaces are peripheral to the main work of their organizations and may limit their participation in them. Second, the focus on organizational effectiveness in these workspaces may feel at odds with the types of personal development promoted in other diversity workspaces. To mitigate these issues, inclusive leaders can link members' performance feedback, bonus compensation, and eligibility for other developmental opportunities to their participation in these workspaces. They can also establish criteria for effectiveness and success, which may include greater retention and promotion rates, sense of belonging, engagement, commitment, well-being of employees, and products or service innovation stemming from workspace contributions.

## Conclusion

Creating more inclusive workplaces is important for realizing the benefits of diversity in organizations. Yet, I contend that leaders must purposefully create workspaces that can enable this outcome. My goal in conceptualizing two types of diversity workspaces is not to suggest that one form is better or more effective than another for cultivating inclusion in diverse organizations. Rather, I contend that each workspace can play a significant role in developing the capacity to cultivate inclusion in organizations. I suggest that implementing both types of workspaces in organizations has the potential to have an additive effect on inclusion (see Figure 15.1). That is, I propose that a greater sense of inclusion, more inclusive interpersonal behavior, greater group-level inclusion, and a more inclusive organization can emerge in organizations that are committed to implementing both personal and organizational diversity workspaces.

## Practical Insights and Action Items for Implementing Diversity Workspaces

- In order for diversity workspaces to cultivate inclusion, top leaders must *sponsor and provide support for their development and implementation.* Top leaders should also be held accountable for ensuring their effectiveness and success.
- When developing and implementing diversity workspaces, leaders should *be clear on their purpose.* Different workspaces have different intended goals, whether those are to enhance leader effectiveness or organizational effectiveness. Leaders should identify their pressing diversity needs and align diversity workspaces with those needs.

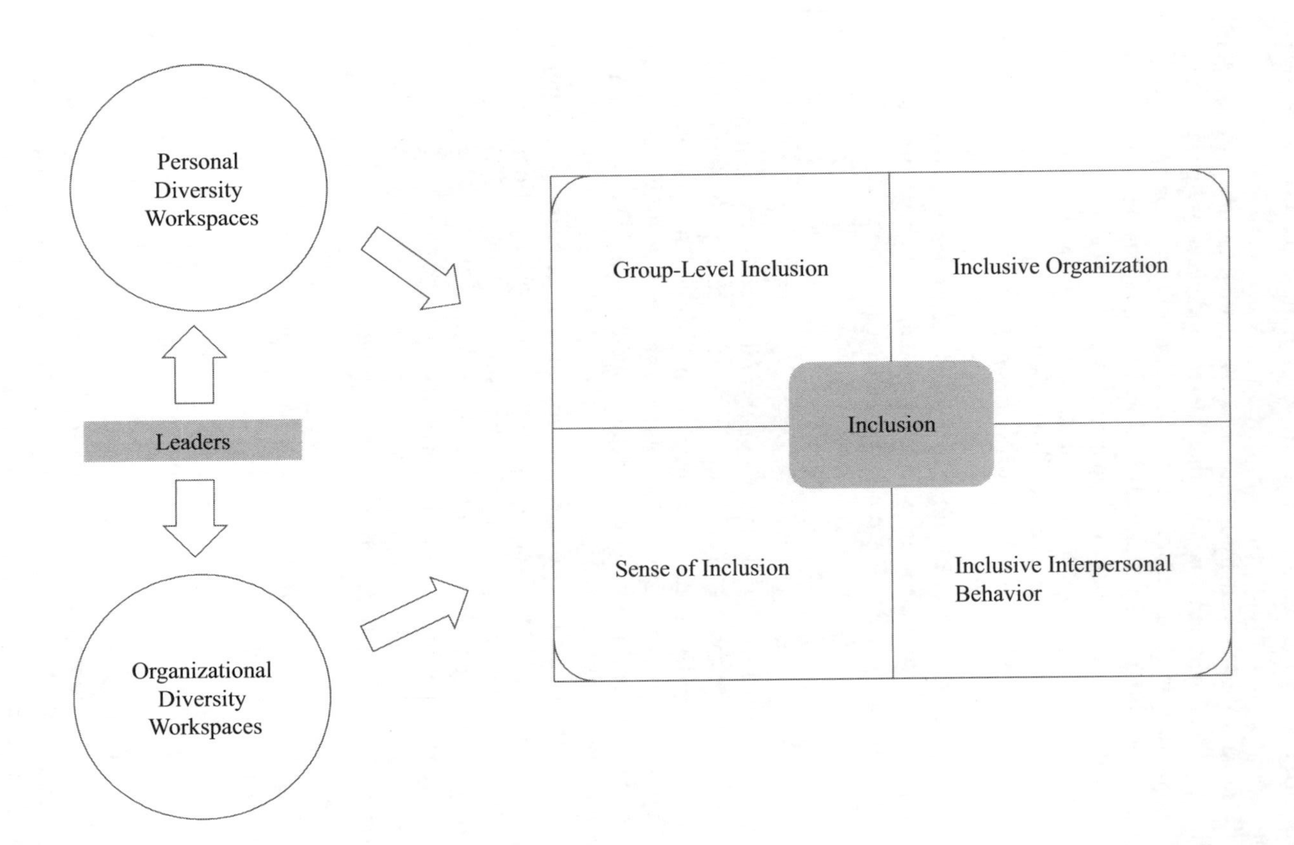


*Figure 15.1* Cultivating inclusion through diversity workspaces.

- *Creating and maintaining a sense of psychological safety* in diversity workspaces should be a goal that is transparent to participating members. Individuals should be encouraged to seek support from and provide support to other members including those who are both similar to and different from them in some way. To that end, mentoring and exercises in fostering respectful engagement should be considered central components of diversity workspaces since they can enable members to feel more comfortable in expressing their identity similarities and differences and relating those to their experiences at work.
- Diversity workspaces should *emphasize leader and leadership development* in order to feel integral to the organization and the way work is done. Thus, these workspaces should focus on creating mechanisms for incorporating identity-based insights in their activities and, potentially, work-based tasks, processes, and initiatives.

## References

Boehm, S. A., Dwertmann, D. J., Kunze, F., Michaelis, B., Parks, K. M., & McDonald, D. P. (2014). Expanding insights on the diversity climate–performance link: The role of workgroup discrimination and group size. *Human Resource Management, 53*(3), 379–402. https://doi.org/10.1002/hrm.21589

Booysen, L. (2014). The development of inclusive leadership practice and processes. In B. M. Ferdman & B. R. Deane (Eds.), *Diversity at work: The practice of inclusion* (pp. 296–329). San Francisco, CA: Jossey-Bass. https://doi.org/10.1002/9781118764282.ch10

Byrne, D. E. (1971). *The attraction paradigm*. New York: Academic Press.

Creary, S. J. (2008). *Leadership, governance, and accountability: A pathway to a diverse and inclusive organization*. New York, NY: The Conference Board.

Creary, S. J. (2010). *Is age really just a number? Investigating approaches to employee engagement*. New York, NY: The Conference Board.

Creary, S. J., Caza, B. B., & Roberts, L. M. (2015). Out of the box? How managing a subordinate's multiple identities affects the quality of a manager-subordinate relationship. *Academy of Management Review, 40*(4), 538–562. https://doi.org/10.5465/amr.2013.0101

Day, D. V., Harrison, M. M., & Halpin, S. M. (2008). *An integrative approach to leader development: Connecting adult development, identity, and expertise*. New York, NY: Routledge. https://doi.org/10.4324/9780203809525

Dutton, J. E. (2003). *Energize your workplace: How to create and sustain high-quality connections at work*. San Francisco, CA: John Wiley & Sons.

Ely, R., Ibarra, H., & Kolb, D. (2011). Taking gender into account: Theory and design for women's leadership development programs. *Academy of Management Learning & Education, 10*(3), 474–493. https://doi.org/10.5465/amle.2010.0046

Ely, R. J., & Thomas, D. A. (2001). Cultural diversity at work: The effects of diversity perspectives on work group processes and outcomes. *Administrative Science Quarterly, 46*(2), 229–273. https://doi.org/10.2307/2667087

Ferdman, B. M. (2014). The practice of inclusion in diverse organizations: Toward a systemic and inclusive framework. In B. M. Ferdman & B. R. Deane (Eds.), *Diversity at work: The practice of inclusion* (pp. 3–54). San Francisco, CA: Jossey-Bass. https://doi.org/10.1002/9781118764282.ch1

Ferdman, B. M. (2017). Paradoxes of inclusion: Understanding and managing the tensions of diversity and multiculturalism. *The Journal of Applied Behavioral Science*, *53*(2), 235–263. https://doi.org/10.1177/0021886317702608

Green, J. (2017, July 19). Deloitte thinks diversity groups are passé. *Bloomberg Businessweek*. https://www.bloomberg.com/news/articles/2017-07-19/deloitte-thinks-diversity-groups-are-pass

Hewlett, S. A. (2017, September 29). Advancing Latino talent in the workplace. *Huffington Post*. https://www.huffpost.com/entry/advancing-latino-talent-in-the-workplace_b_59ce780be4b034ae778d4a15

Kahn, W. A. (1990). Psychological conditions of personal engagement and disengagement at work. *Academy of Management Journal*, *33*, 692–724. https://doi.org/10.5465/256287

Kramer, R. M. (1991). Intergroup relations and organizational dilemmas: The role of categorization processes. *Research in Organizational Behavior*, *13*, 191–228.

Miller, J. B., & Stiver, I. P. (1997). *The healing connection*. Boston, MA: Beacon Press.

PepsiCo. (2012). *PepsiCo's Adelante named 2011 Employee Resource Group of the Year at LATINA Style 50 Awards*. https://www.hispanicprblog.com/pepsico-adelante

Petriglieri, G., & Petriglieri, J. L. (2010). Identity workspaces: The case of business schools. *Academy of Management Learning and Education (AMLE)*, *9*(1), 44–60. https://doi.org/10.5465/AMLE.2010.48661190

Roberson, Q. M. (Ed.). (2013). *The Oxford handbook of diversity and work*. New York, NY: Oxford University Press. https://doi.org/10.1093/oxfordhb/9780199736355.001.0001

Shore, L. M., Randel, A. E., Chung, B. G., Dean, M. A., Ehrhart, K. H., & Singh, G. (2010). Inclusion and diversity in work groups: A review and model for future research. *Journal of Management*, *37*(4), 1262–1289. https://doi.org/10.1177/0149206310385943

Wittenberg-Cox, A. (2017, August 3). Deloitte's radical attempt to reframe diversity. *Harvard Business Review Digital Articles*. https://hbr.org/2017/08/deloittes-radical-attempt-to-reframe-diversity

Yoshino, K., & Smith, C. (2013). *Uncovering talent: A new model of inclusion*. Deloitte. https://www2.deloitte.com/content/dam/Deloitte/us/Documents/about-deloitte/us-about-deloitte-uncovering-talent-a-new-model-of-inclusion.pdf

# 16 Engaging in *Bold, Inclusive Conversations*[1]

## A Developmental Approach

*Mary-Frances Winters*

> For too many of us it's become safer to retreat into our own bubbles, whether in our neighborhoods, or on college campuses, or places of worship, or especially our social media feeds, surrounded by people who look like us and share the same political outlook and never challenge our assumptions. . . . All of us have more work to do. . . . Hearts must change. . . . But without some common baseline of facts, without a willingness to admit new information and concede that your opponent might be making a fair point . . . then we're going to keep talking past each other.
>
> President Barack H. Obama, 44th President United States of America
> Farewell Address, January 10, 2017

### Introduction

There is a growing body of research (Alon et al., 2016; Hewlett et al., 2013) suggesting that innovation tends to increase in work environments where employees feel safe, comfortable in bringing their full selves to work, and believe they can speak up. Needless to say, innovation is an important driving force for organizational success and sustainability.

In inclusive organizations, employees feel they can bring their full, whole, authentic selves to work. Inclusive leaders understand that employees bring with them identity-based stresses and concerns from the external world, such as racial tensions, disagreements over immigration issues, gender-identity debates, religious intolerance, and many others. These issues are front and center in employees' hearts and minds and can negatively impact their ability to do their best work. They can also lead to increased workplace conflict and misunderstandings. Because of that, leaders need not only the skills and competencies to address such conflicts effectively, but they also must help create brave spaces for dialogue around these issues.

The adage "don't talk about politics, religion, or other polarizing topics at work" used to be the rule. However, the current sociopolitical climate, coupled with immediate access and consumption of news via social media, has made this widely held tenet impossible to abide by. The contentious political and social climate around the world and the multitude of values and beliefs in today's increasingly diverse workplaces compel leaders to understand how these differences can impede productivity and innovation if they are not identified and addressed.

Because many of us have been taught not to talk about polarizing topics, especially at work, chances are we lack the skills to do so effectively. Learning to effectively engage in bold, inclusive conversations is hard work and requires a developmental approach that "meets people where they are" relative to their understanding of cultural differences and how these differences influence employee worldviews.

This chapter provides a blueprint for increasing leader capacity to effectively engage in and facilitate inclusive conversations around potentially difficult diversity and inclusion issues. In the chapter the following questions are explored:

- What is the business case for engaging in bold, inclusive conversations?
- What is the roadmap for engaging in bold, inclusive conversations? What do you need to know and be able to do as a leader?
- What are some best-practice examples of organizations whose members have mastered the skills for engaging in bold, inclusive conversations?

## The Business Case for Engaging in Bold, Inclusive Conversations

It may seem counterproductive to encourage employees to talk about polarizing topics that, on the surface, do not seem to be related to getting the work done. However, research shows that building employees' capacity to effectively engage in dialogue across polarizing topics does enhance productivity, engagement, retention, and innovation. This is no easy task, though, and some of the challenges you can expect are outlined here.

First, as the workforce becomes more diverse—in terms of race and ethnicity, religious and political affiliations, sexual orientations, disability statuses, and many other aspects—so do employees' issues and emotions. Events of the past few years, such as videotaped and widely disseminated instances of police brutality, religious intolerance against Muslims and Jews, polarized views about transgender rights, and extreme political divisions, make it impossible for many *not* to bring strong emotions about these issues into the workplace. Social scientists (e.g., Kaplan et al., 2016) contend that the more we feel threatened, the greater our tendency to polarize. Today, many people believe that their way of life is being threatened, which only engenders more fear of the "other." When people are fearful, they will not be able to be at their best and do their best work. It is therefore incumbent on leaders to learn how to effectively address the myriad of concerns employees are bringing to the workplace.

Second, leaders need to recognize the impact of polarized views on employees' attitudes, behaviors, and perceptions. In a 2016 survey (Radio One, Inc., 2016) that explored the state of race relations in the United States, only 44% of Whites, compared with 77% of Blacks, were very concerned about the killings of Black people at the hands of police. However, when asked about the killings of police officers in Dallas, over 75% of *both* Blacks and Whites were very concerned. Likewise, a 2015 poll (Cooper, Cox, Lienesch, & Jones, 2015) showed that 56% of Americans feel that Muslim values are at odds with U.S. values. Yet, 68% indicated that they had never or seldom talked to a Muslim. These polarized views will impact employees' attitudes, perceptions, and perhaps behaviors in the workplace. For example, according to Lakhani (2017), Muslims continue to make up a disproportionate amount of the EEOC's religion-based discrimination charges, hovering at over 20%.

Third, polarization is the antithesis of inclusion in that it fosters an "us and them" environment. Organizations today are striving to create inclusive cultures because inclusion drives engagement and innovation. In fact, a 2013 Gallup study showed that inclusion and engagement are highly correlated. In the study, the most engaged employees rated their company high on diversity and inclusion. The least engaged employees, on the other hand, rated their company very low.

Fourth, today's divisive, sociopolitical climate also impacts workplace productivity. My consulting firm, The Winters Group, has conducted dialogue sessions for a variety of different clients to support them in effectively addressing the aftermath of recent traumatic events and the associated polarized views. The first question we asked was: "describe how you are feeling in one word." Responses ranged from depressed, despondent, frustrated, angry, helpless, hopeless, to encouraged, energized, hopeful, and optimistic. The majority of the emotions expressed, though, were negative.

According to a 2014 report by SAMHSA (Substance Abuse and Mental Health Services Administration), an agency within the U.S. Department of Human Services, some individuals may display symptoms associated with posttraumatic stress disorder (PTSD) when exposed to traumatic events, be it one-time, multiple, or repetitive events: "Emotional reactions to trauma can vary greatly and are significantly influenced by the individual's sociocultural history. Beyond the initial emotional reactions during the event, those most likely to surface include anger, fear, sadness, and shame" (2014, p. 62).

Research also shows that diverse ethnic, racial, and cultural groups are more likely to experience adverse effects from various traumas and to meet criteria for posttraumatic stress (Bell, 2011). The same goes for LGBT individuals who, in addition to experiencing trauma associated with their sexual orientation, also have to deal with lack of legal protection and laws of exclusion (Brown, 2008). The bottom line is that, in many workplaces today, you find Black men fearful that they will be wrongly targeted by police, Muslim women who wear a hijab afraid they will be the subject of bullying or worse, and transgender employees afraid to use the bathroom corresponding to their gender identity. These individuals may be less engaged and productive as a result.

Lastly, leaders must be aware that their silence is often interpreted as "you don't care." During The Winters Group's virtual learning sessions we asked: what is the impact when your manager and your company are silent about what is going on in the external world? The most common response was "we don't think they care." One of the key drivers of engagement, according to Gallup's Q12 Engagement Survey (Gallup, Inc, 2013), is the feeling that "somebody cares about me at work." Employees who are impacted by outside events, either directly or indirectly, are looking for their companies to say and do something. Progressive organizations are creating intentional strategies and actions for engaging in difficult dialogue during these polarizing times. Later in the chapter I provide examples of what best-practice organizations are doing in this regard.

## The Roadmap for Engaging in Bold, Inclusive Conversations

Honing our skills to engage in bold, inclusive conversations is a developmental process that starts with self-exploration. Depending on our level of cross-cultural competence, we may each be at a different level of capability. Figure 16.1 summarizes the model; this section describes its various components.

### *Understand Your Cultural Self*

Investing time to understand your cultural self is the first step. Our identity is core to who we are and how we see the world. Whether it is our race, ethnicity, gender, sexual orientation, religion, veteran status, or roles as parents, these aspects of our identity shape our worldview. In fact, they influence how we view and respond to current events, what we interpret as right or wrong, and what we stand for or against. As leaders, it is important you understand why you believe what you believe, and why you disagree with those things you disagree with, including the cultural sources for those beliefs. Your ability to effectively engage and facilitate difficult conversations is directly connected

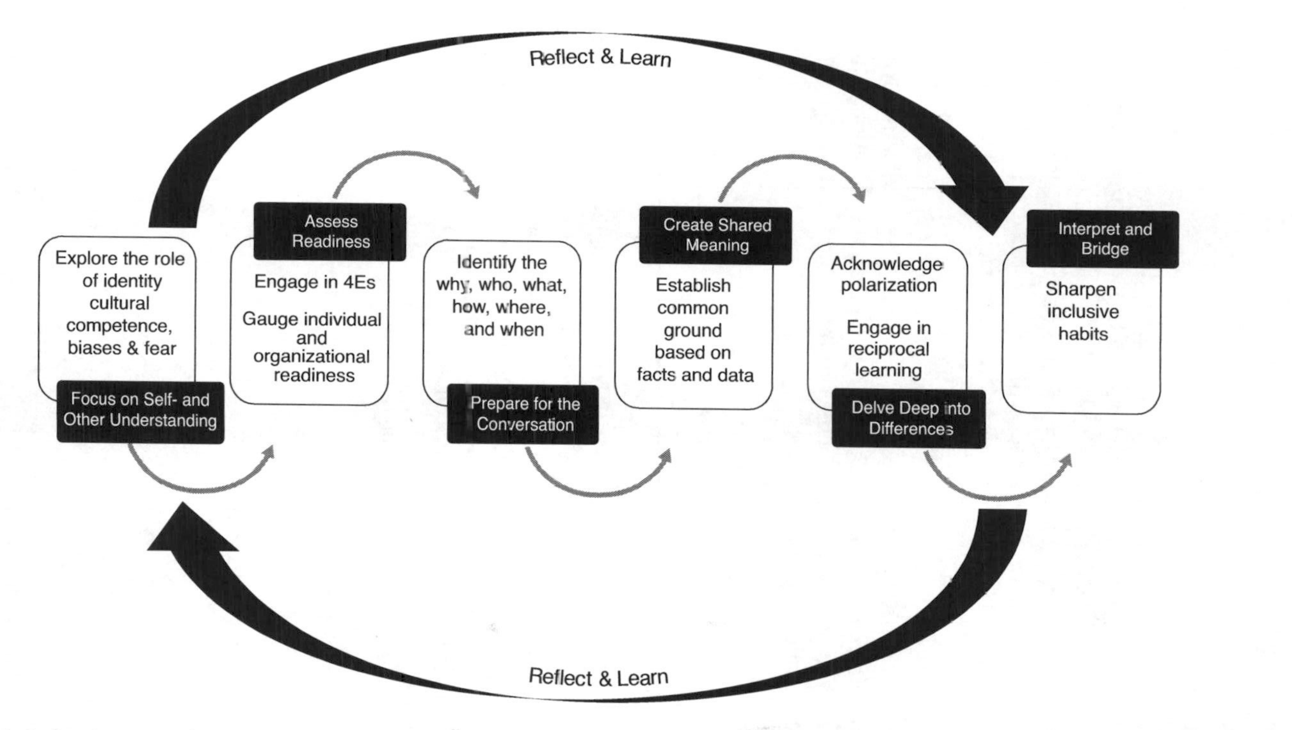


*Figure 16.1* A developmental approach to engaging in bold, inclusive conversations. Reprinted from *We Can't Talk About That at Work: How to Talk About Race, Religion and Politics and Other Polarizing Topics* (p. xiv), by M.-F. Winters, 2017, Oakland, CA: Berrett-Koehler. Copyright 2017 by Mary-Frances Winters. Reprinted with permission.

to your degree of self-awareness. Table 16.1 lists the questions you need to ask yourself in your journey toward cultural self-awareness.

### *Understand Others*

It is impossible to have effective conversations across differences if you have not taken the time to learn about those who are culturally different from you. You cannot converse effectively about that which you do not know. For example, how could you possibly know what it is like to be Muslim, gay, or millennial, if you have never interacted with, or informed yourself about those identities? Table 16.2 lists questions that can facilitate your understanding of others.

The 4 E model™ (Winters, 2017)—comprised of exposure, experience, education, and empathy—can also serve as a guide to improve your understanding of others. To gain knowledge about those who are different from you, you need to focus on these four different areas, described in the following sub-sections.

*Table 16.1* Questions that facilitate self-awareness

- Who am I culturally?
- Where did I grow up? What was the culture of my community growing up?
- What did I learn about right/wrong, good/bad growing up?
- What are my values and beliefs and how have they changed over time?
- If I had to describe a cultural community to which I belong, what would I say?
- Have I explored my unconscious and conscious biases? Am I managing them?
- Do I understand the power and privilege I might be bringing to the conversation?

*Table 16.2* Questions that facilitate other-awareness

- Do I know the history of the other group from their perspective?
- Do I understand the underlying systems that impact outcomes for the group(s)?
- What do I know in general about cultural differences between the group and my group (e.g., direct versus indirect communication styles, individualistic versus group-oriented cultures, how power is displayed, etc.)?
- What do I know about the group's typical values and beliefs and how and why they were shaped as they are (e.g., millennials have had a very different experience with technology than baby boomers, which shapes their worldview)? How much do I know about diversity within the group?

### *Exposure*

Ask yourself: who is in my world? The less exposure you have to people who are different than you, the less likely you will be ready to engage in bold, inclusive conversations.

### *Experience*

This takes exposure a step further. Experience is about engaging with those who are different from you in ways that are cross-culturally enriching. If you are White, just declaring "one of my best friends is Black" is not sufficient. What kinds of meaningful conversations do you have about their different lived experiences? Or do you not talk about race because it is uncomfortable? Or perhaps you do not think it is necessary because you assume your friend is just like you?

As an example of the difference between exposure and experience, AT&T's CEO Randall Stephenson (as cited in Shinneman, 2016) made a public statement at an employee meeting about Black Lives Matter. When sharing his story, Stephenson stated that one of his long-time friends, who happens to be African American, provided an "aha" experience for him. Stephenson said that he learned only recently that his friend's life as an African American male doctor is fraught with being called negative names, being mistaken for the server in restaurants, and needing to always carry his ID, even in his own neighborhood, because of experiences with law enforcement. Stephenson told his employees that he was embarrassed that he had known this man for many years, had shared intimate moments, and counted him as one of his best friends, yet he had no idea of his daily struggles as a Black man in America. Stephenson had exposure to difference in this case; however, he did not have experience.

### *Education*

Experience and exposure should be complemented with formal education. This may include workplace training, continuing education, research, visiting museums, reading books, watching documentaries, or other systematic or focused approaches to learning.

### *Empathy*

The first three Es provide the capacity for the fourth E: empathy. This means having the capacity to understand the perspective of others, which is essential when engaging in bold, inclusive conversations. Empathy is not possible if I know nothing about you.

### *Engage in Reciprocal Learning*

One way to expand your experience with others is to engage in reciprocal learning. The Winters Group offers a program called *Cross-Cultural Learning Partners* in which we pair individuals who are different in some way (e.g., race, gender, sexual orientation, religion) and invite them to go on a guided journey of learning about each other. The program includes short lessons with reflective questions and recommendations for experiences that participants can share such as engage with each other's faith community or visit a cultural museum together.

### *Assess Organizational Readiness*

So far, I have advised you to enhance your understanding of your own and other cultural norms. Understanding the organizational culture is also key in assessing readiness to engage in bold, inclusive conversations. Table 16.3 lists the questions you need to answer about your own organization so you can ascertain its readiness to tackle bold, inclusive conversations.

*Table 16.3* Questions to gauge your organization's readiness to embark on bold, inclusive conversations

- Is inclusion explicitly articulated as one of the organization's values?
- Does the organization demonstrate that it values inclusion through actions by all leaders in the organization?
- Are there formal programs in place promoting inclusion (e.g., employee network groups, mentoring, training, recruitment of diverse talent, etc.)?
- Does the organization celebrate diversity with different company-sponsored events?
- Does the organization actively support philanthropic causes of diverse groups?
- Is there visible evidence of employee diversity?
- Are leaders evaluated on their inclusion practices?
- Is it a culture of risk taking or risk aversion?
- Is it common to call out the "elephants in the room" or does the organization tend not to tackle tough subjects?
- Would you characterize the culture as passive-aggressive?
- Does leadership show they care about all employees?
- Is it a closed (i.e., few people allowed in the inner circle) or open culture?
- Are leaders well trained to support employee development and address relevant personal concerns?
- What is the level of trust of leadership?

### *Build Cross-Cultural Trust*

Although all of the questions in Table 16.3 are important, the most critical inquiry in assessing organizational readiness is the level of trust within the organization, especially the level of trust placed in the leadership. People will not talk honestly and openly when there is little or no trust. To build trust, you need to consistently practice the 4 Es outlined above. There are many reasons why historically marginalized groups do not trust dominant groups. Centuries of legal systemic racism, exclusion, and inequities may make it particularly difficult to build trust. Therefore, leaders need to understand the history and recognize that building trust may take longer than building trust between and among dominant groups.

Zak (2017), in an article on the neuroscience of trust, describes a study that compared individuals at low-trust companies with those in high-trust companies. In high-trust companies, employees reported over twice as much energy at work, 76% more engagement, 29% more satisfaction with their lives, and 50% more productivity. They also reported experiencing 74% less stress, 13% fewer sick days, and 40% less burnout. Investigators found, through brain studies and other research, that there are eight management behaviors that foster trust. The four described here are particularly pertinent to fostering bold, inclusive conversations.

#### *Sharing of Information Broadly*

If you do not have the whole picture, it is impossible to have effective dialogue.

#### *Intentional Relationship Building*

As mentioned earlier, exposure and experience with difference are critical components of bold, inclusive conversations. In other words, the better I know you, the more I can trust you.

#### *Vulnerability*

The willingness on the part of leaders to admit when they do not know something builds credibility and trust. It may be more difficult to admit ignorance on topics like race and religion due to the fear of how you will be perceived. Managers may feel like they should know more than they do and the historically marginalized employee may feel the same. However, when a manager genuinely shows interest and honestly admits not knowing something, it will likely engender more trust.

*Facilitation of Whole-Person Growth*

We often define inclusion as the ability of individuals to bring their whole selves to work. Zak (2017) contends that assessing personal growth with discussions about work–life integration and family, as well as allowing time for recreation and reflection, does have a powerful effect on trust, which, in turn, improves employees' engagement and retention.

### *Preparing for the Conversation*

Given the complexity of engaging in bold, inclusive conversations, making sure to plan and prepare is critical. Table 16.4 includes a series of questions to consider when preparing for such conversations. In addition, you need to ensure the following is in place.

*Establish a Brave Zone*

A brave zone takes the idea of a safe zone further. It makes it okay to bring up topics that may make people uncomfortable.

*Ensure Confidentiality*

It is critical that people in the conversation believe that what they say will be held in confidence and not shared with others who are not in the room.

*Listen for Understanding*

Listening is a key skill for engaging effectively in difficult dialogue. We often listen to respond and not necessarily to understand. Also, understand that there may need to be more than one session and that the first one might only have the goal of listening to each other with no debate allowed. After the listening meeting, it is important to reflect and think about what you have learned. Do you now have a greater understanding of the other's perspective?

*Table 16.4* What to consider in preparation for conducting bold, inclusive conversations

- Why are we having the conversation?
- Who should be part of the dialogue, and why?
- What is the desired outcome?
- How should the conversation be conducted?
- Where should the conversation be held?
- When will the conversation take place?
- What are the ground rules?

### *Expect Non-Closure*

It is human nature to want to "wrap things up" and bring closure. These topics are complex and may need a number of sessions to foster greater understanding. Be comfortable with the idea that sessions may end without closure.

### *Reflect and Learn*

John Dewey, American philosopher and educator, said that we do not learn from our experiences, but rather, we learn from reflecting on our experiences (Goodreads, n.d.). Reflecting on why you felt the way you did during the discussion and why someone else may have had a different interpretation is paramount for learning and developing empathy.

### ***"Cut Each Other Some Slack" and Assume Positive Intent***

As we learn, we make mistakes. Bold, inclusive conversations are only possible if we assume that "we don't know what we don't know" and we did not intend harm. There is a tendency to want to punish people, especially public figures, when they say something that offends a particular group. Punishment for those who intended to offend is warranted. Punishing those who do not understand the context may have the effect of shutting down the possibility of conversations about polarizing topics. The fear of offending and the fear of not knowing enough can loom large in these situations. So, we must learn to be patient and recognize that we are all developmentally at different places of understanding.

### ***Create Shared Meaning and Find Common Ground***

It is difficult to convince someone to change what they believe; this should not be the goal of engaging in these conversations. However, reaching a point of mutual understanding should be the goal. Initial conversations about a polarizing topic should be focused on finding out what you agree on. For example: we all care about safety; we all want to be treated fairly; we all want to be able to trust our leaders. Achieving common ground is not necessarily easy and may take several conversations where you do not have closure and you leave each with the goal of learning and reflecting more.

### ***Delving into Differences***

It is only after you have reached some areas of agreement that you are ready to delve into your different perspectives. It is in those brave spaces that we will be challenged to go deeper in our understanding of differences. Table 16.5 lists a series of strategies you need to consider when engaging in dialogue around differences.

*Table 16.5* Strategies to consider when engaging in dialogue around differences

- Acknowledge the polarization.
- Distinguish interpretations and clarify definitions. Even "universal" terms and values can be interpreted differently across cultures. What do terms like *fairness*, *safety*, and *trust* mean to those involved in the dialogue? Discuss those differences.
- Uncover your different perspectives and listen with an open mind. Tell your story.
- Know when to "press pause." Set aside time to reflect. Be okay with non-closure.
- Strive for reciprocal empathy. There is no official "end game" in engaging in these conversations. But if we can get to the point of reciprocal empathy (i.e., the ability to know what it is like to be the "other"), we increase the likelihood of generating new ways to engage with each other.

## Best Practices in Implementing Bold, Inclusive Conversations

There are a number of organizations where bold, inclusive conversations are taking place. The success of these organizations in these initiatives stems from their intentionality in connecting their inclusion goals with their vision, mission, and values. They are also benefiting from increased engagement, productivity, and retention. Here, I offer three examples of best practices of companies that are effectively holding employee dialogues.

### *Sodexo*

Sodexo, a company that is routinely heralded for its progressive inclusive practices (for example, Sodexo has been number 1 on *DiversityInc*'s Top 50 list several times, and has won a number of other awards for diversity and inclusion), is also taking a proactive approach in supporting employees to navigate the current social and political environment. The company has issued several statements letting employees know that it cares and advising them on where they can seek support internally.

The Winters Group has designed several virtual learning labs for Sodexo's inclusion community, including human resources and employee network group leaders, to provide tools and tips for engaging in bold conversations. The 90-minute learning sessions, entitled *Affirming Inclusion: Meaningful Dialogue Across Difference*, explore strategies for maintaining inclusive environments after tragedies. In addition, Sodexo trained 20 of its employee business resource group leaders to facilitate authentic leadership workshops that include content on engaging in inclusive conversations.

### *NASA: Goddard*

NASA Goddard has been conducting dialogues on difficult subjects since 2010, including on generations, gender, religion, sexual orientation, disabilities, and race. The format used involves groups of 15 to 17 people from different functional areas who come together face to face for two to three and one-half hours every other week for four to six months. They explore identity, unconscious bias, micro-triggers, and power and privilege, among other topics. The process includes reflection, action planning, journaling, top-of-mind observations and, of course, dialogue. Unlike traditional training classes, participants sit in a circle with no tables to foster community and trust. The purpose of these sessions is to align with Goddard's mission. Goddard measures effectiveness with a variety of internal surveys and has found that the return on investment is higher levels of engagement and retention.

### *Booz Allen Hamilton*

Booz Allen Hamilton (BAH) responded to the polarized sociopolitical climate by first initiating a series of dialogue sessions with different employee affinity groups (e.g., African American, Asian and Middle Eastern, Latino). As part of what they call Bridging Differences Series: Inclusive Conversations Empowered by You, they are continuing to expand the dialogues to be open to all employees. Taking a phased approach that includes other related initiatives, the two-hour sessions allow BAH leadership to reaffirm their commitment to inclusion and to link to their values, to provide employees with an opportunity to share how the external environment is impacting their ability to be fully present at work, and, lastly and most importantly, to provide them with skills for engaging in difficult conversations. Employees share that allowing these dialogue sessions reassures them that leadership cares and wants to understand their unique perspectives.

## Conclusion

As a leader seeking to create an inclusive environment in your organization, learning to engage in inclusive conversations on polarizing topics is essential. The tips offered in Table 16.6 are based on the list of "inclusive habits to live by" outlined in *We Can't Talk About That at Work* (Winters, 2017, pp. 119–121) and should be useful guidance for the learning journey.

It is not easy being a leader in today's fast-changing world. Leadership competencies continue to evolve. Issues that 20 years ago would not have been included on the list of required skills are now integral to effective leadership. Learning how to effectively engage in polarizing conversations is one of them.

*Table 16.6* Key practices for leading bold, inclusive conversations

| | |
|---|---|
| **Acknowledge** | You don't know everything; there is always something to learn. |
| **Legitimize** | Other perspectives are just as valid as yours and should be listened to for understanding, not necessarily agreement. |
| **Listen** | Listen to understand. Listen for your own cultural assumptions, perceptions, and expectations. |
| **Reflect** | Spend more time reflecting on your own values and beliefs. Why do you believe what you believe? Why would someone believe the opposite? Can you respect the beliefs of others even when you don't agree? |
| **Describe** | Learn to describe behaviors from a neutral perspective before providing your interpretation and expand the number of interpretations you consider. |
| **Contextualize** | Consider the circumstances, conditions, and history of the topic for which you are having a bold, inclusive conversation. Provide the proper context for the conversation. |
| **Pause** | Take a deep breath. Think about what you are going to say. Pause to be more patient as well. Be patient of mistakes. |
| **Accept** | Accepting does not mean agreeing. You are accepting that there are myriad worldviews and it is important to learn more about them. |
| **Question** | Show genuine interest in others. Be curious, not judgmental about their experiences. |
| **Respect** | Respect the dignity of every person even when you don't agree with them. Separate the person from the position. Practice the platinum rule: treat others the way they want to be treated. |
| **Apologize** | If you say something that offends someone else, genuinely apologize. The impact on the other person may be very different than your intent. Do not defend your comment; simply say, "I am sorry; please help me understand why that was offensive." Consider it a teaching moment. |
| **Connect** | Making meaningful connections across difference is one sure way of breaking down barriers and enhancing our capacity for empathy and shared understanding. |
| **Empathize** | Sympathy leads to patronization and pity. Empathy allows you to see the situation from the perspective of the other person. |

## Note

1 *Bold, Inclusive Conversations* is a registered service mark of The Winters Group, Inc.

## References


Alon, A., Elron, D., & Jackson, L. (2016). *Innovation: Clear vision, cloudy execution.* https://www.accenture.com/t20180705t112257z__w__/us-en/_acnmedia/pdf-10/accenture-innovation-research-execsummary.pdf

Bell, C. C. (2011). Trauma, culture, and resiliency. In S. M. Southwick, B. T. Litz, D. Charney, & M. J. Friedman (Eds.), *Resilience and mental health: Challenges across the lifespan* (pp. 176–187). New York, NY: Cambridge University Press.

Brown, L. S. (2008). Feminist therapy. In J. L. Lebow (Ed.), *Twenty-first century psychotherapies: Contemporary approaches to theory and practice* (pp. 277–306). Hoboken, NJ: John Wiley & Sons.

Cooper, B., Cox, D., Lienesch, R., & Jones, R. P. (2015). *Anxiety, nostalgia, and mistrust: Findings from the 2015 American values survey.* Public Religion Research Institute. https://www.prri.org/research/survey-anxiety-nostalgia-and-mistrust-findings-from-the-2015-american-values-survey

Gallup, Inc. (2013). *State of the American workplace.* https://www.gallup.com/workplace/238085/state-american-workplace-report-2017.aspx

Goodreads (n.d.) John Dewey quotes. https://www.goodreads.com/author/quotes/42738.John_Dewey

Hewlett, S. A., Marshall, M., & Sherbin, L. (2013). *Innovation, diversity, and market growth.* New York, NY: Center for Talent Innovation.

Kaplan, J., Gimbel, S. I., & Harris, S. (2016). Neural correlates of maintaining one's political beliefs in the face of counterevidence. *Scientific Reports*, *6*(39589). https://doi.org/10.1038/srep39589

Lakhani, K. (2017, February 15). Workplace discrimination against Muslims. *onlabor: Workers, Unions, Politics.* https://onlabor.org/workplace-discrimination-against-muslims

Radio One, Inc. (2016). *Black, white and blue: A spotlight on race in America.* Edison Research Survey Results. https://www.edisonresearch.com/wp-content/uploads/2016/08/Radio-One-Edison-Research-Report-2016-Spotlight-on-Race-in-America.pdf

Shinneman, S. (2016, October 3). 'Tolerance is for cowards' ... AT&T CEO Randall Stephenson speaks on racial tension and Black Lives Matter. *Dallas Business Journal.* https://www.bizjournals.com/dallas/blog/techflash/2016/10/tolerance-is-for-cowards-at-t-ceo-randall.html

Substance Abuse and Mental Health Services Administration. (2014). *Trauma-informed care in behavioral health services.* Treatment Improvement Protocol (TIP) Series 57. HHS Publication No. (SMA) 13-4801. Rockville, MD: Author.

Winters, M. F. (2017). *We can't talk about that at work! How to talk about race, religion, politics, and other polarizing topics.* Oakland, CA: Berrett-Koehler.

Zak, P. J. (2017). The neuroscience of trust. *Harvard Business Review*, *95*(1), 84–90. https://hbr.org/2017/01/the-neuroscience-of-trust

# 17 Inclusive Leadership

## Driving Multilevel Organizational Change

*Aarti Shyamsunder*

## Introduction

One of the broadest and indeed most inclusive descriptions of inclusion—the one that I adopt in this chapter—comes from Davidson and Ferdman (2002, p. 1), who suggest that

> experiences of inclusion result when policies, structures, practices, and norms of behavior are aligned in such a way that every member of a given collective (community, organization, or network) has a fair and equal opportunity to access the joint resources of that collective.

To drive change, many diversity and inclusion researchers and practitioners have focused on a *bottom-up* approach, one that involves changing mindsets and behaviors one at a time: one person, one group, one unfair rule, and one HR policy at a time. Although this strategy might result in incremental changes, and those small changes may have ripple effects that extend beyond one individual or group, their effects can be disparate, fleeting, and may not necessarily amount to large-scale, lasting, and sustained change. The *systemic or top-down* approach, in contrast, involves challenging the ecosystems that currently validate and perpetuate bias and inequality; this approach focuses on changing behavior and interactions by changing the contexts and systems in which they take place. The former approach lacks the scale and scope often needed for sustainable systemic change, while the latter approach lacks the nuance and agility that can make for quick impact.

This tension between the bottom-up and top-down perspectives is reminiscent of the recurrent and unsolved debate in institutional change theories (Al Saidi, 2019) between agency and structure as drivers of change. While neither approach alone is sufficient, both are necessary. For organizations, communities, and societies to embrace inclusion more wholeheartedly, both bottom-up efforts *and* systemic top-down changes are required. The role of inclusive leaders in this conceptualization is to create the conditions and take the courageous steps required for more bold, systemic action that harnesses both individual agency and the power of structural change.

This chapter touches on some ways in which current conceptualizations of work and of efforts to make workplaces more inclusive may be failing. Further, it positions inclusive leaders as key *change agents* who can foster inclusion and impact macro (organizational and societal) factors as well as meso (relational) and micro (individual) factors (Ferdman, 2014a, 2014b). Macro-level impact in this chapter refers to systemic, structural, and overarching organizational or societal changes. Micro-level impact more directly involves individual actions, biases, and choices (referred to in this chapter as *individual ABCs*). The meso level straddles the two others, shaping narratives and leveraging narratives to serve as the bridge between the individual (micro) and the institutional (macro) levels.

## From Individual Actions, Biases, and Choices to System Change

In order to catalyze large-scale change and create more diverse and inclusive workplaces and societies, inclusive leaders must consider factors beyond the narrow ones of individual *actions*, individual *biases*, and individual *choices* (i.e., the individual "ABCs" that constitute the currently prevalent paradigm of inclusion). To understand why the focus on the individual ABCs (that is, the micro level) is insufficient, it is important to understand how this focus emerged and how it has not made enough of an impact. Over time, as the equality agenda has drifted toward the agenda of managing diversity and encouraging inclusion at work, the *individual* has taken prominence over the *collective* as the unit and object of study and intervention. A lot of research on diversity and inclusion, work–life issues, and related topics has focused on the individual over the collective (for example, studying individual struggles and coping mechanisms for balancing work and family demands, more than exploring new norms of work and family roles). This has also shifted the responsibility for success or failure to individual actions, biases, and choices. Thus, systemic failures at the more macro levels, such as organizational-level processes and operations and societal-level norms, then get explained away as being a result of individual actions, biases, and choices, especially those ABCs of the disadvantaged, the excluded, and the "diverse" few. As Tressie McMillan-Cottom (2019) puts it, "we look for ways to assign personal responsibility for structural injustices to bodies we collectively do not value." This powerful quote reinforces the idea that currently dominant macro-level systems seek to maintain current inequities, exclusion, and even oppression, in part, by furthering the focus on the micro-level ABCs. Looking beyond these ABCs will minimize assignment of blame and responsibility unfairly to the very people who are most disadvantaged and excluded, and help inclusive leaders to enact better solutions by better understanding the root causes of exclusion and inequality.

The following sections describe ways in which this focus on the individual ABCs has resulted in an understanding of work and inclusion that is incomplete, unsustainable, and unfair. The final section enumerates ideas and examples of how inclusive leadership can make a difference in shifting defaults and tapping into both individual ABCs and structural/systemic change.

## Work Today is Not Inclusive

Despite long-term focus on issues of equality, diversity, and inclusion in the realm of work, several forms of inequality, discrimination, and exclusion persist and mark the experience of employees everywhere, across their work and careers (Özbilgin, 2009). Scholars (e.g., Saini, 2017) have contended that scientific discourse itself is saturated with processes of othering and therefore science itself has been limited due to the biased perspectives of scientists. Our current understanding of "work"—especially in research and scholarship—involves seeing the ideal worker as one who spends most of his (not usually her!) time at work, sacrificing personal and family time to demonstrate loyalty to his employer, and prioritizing work and career needs above most others. When it comes to defining ideal leadership qualities, this ideal worker prototype gets further distilled into notions of a "boss," "manager," and "leader" that overlap more with agentic and masculine stereotypes (e.g., dominant, confident, decisive, independent) than with communal and feminine stereotypes (e.g., nurturing, collaborative, humble, team-focused) (Schein & Davidson, 1993). Finally, the idea of finding success at work through merit-based systems itself has been questioned by scholars. For instance, Haney and Hurtado (1994) linked racial disparities in income and employment in the U.S. to the concept of "merit" implied in the use of standardized tests and the nature of legal doctrine around these, which have undermined efforts to address structural causes of racial discrimination. Others find evidence of the so-called "paradox of meritocracy" (e.g., Castilla & Benard, 2010, p. 543), whereby current ideas of merit end up ascribing superior qualities to dominant group members, which in turn further increases bias. Together, these ideal worker and ideal leader norms shape our definitions of merit, and imply that the easier path to the top is for those who conform. Currently prevalent work norms reward some people (mostly men with certain socioeconomic and demographic privileges) and make it harder for others (such as minority women from lower socioeconomic backgrounds) to succeed and thrive.

Critical accounts of the work in the field of EDI (equality, diversity, and inclusion; e.g., Özbilgin, 2009) have argued that the current emphasis on individually driven, voluntary efforts toward anti-discrimination as well as equality and diversity has had a checkered history of success. It is rare to see leaders who risk upsetting these cherished statuses and identities from which they themselves often benefit in favor of more inclusive (if uncomfortable at first) and flexible norms of work. The task for inclusive leaders, therefore, is to replace current notions and systems of work that benefit specific individuals or demographic groups with more equitable and inclusive notions, ones within which everyone has equal chances of benefitting.

## Current "ABC"-Focused Efforts are Limited

In this section I highlight three areas that focus on changing individual "ABCs" (actions, biases, and choices) in the quest for enhanced diversity, equity, and inclusion but have fallen short of truly redefining and restructuring work and workplaces.

To start with, practitioners and even researchers are often asked to provide *a business case* to invest in diversity efforts. This focus on the business case has not been sufficient for accelerating progress on inclusion (Kim, 2018). Relying on the business case (e.g., proving that diversity and inclusion impact financial success, employer branding, talent supply, etc.) to make change and emphasizing the instrumental and bottom-line benefits of diversity can be a cold and individualistic strategy, and detracts from ideas of equality, equal opportunities, and their allied emotive and emancipatory tone for those who are excluded (Özbilgin, 2009).

Second, organizations rely on *diversity and inclusion programs* that have a mixed record of success (Bezrukova et al., 2016). For instance, the highly popular application of unconscious bias training (which usually focuses on making people aware of the ways in which most human beings are biased, even if unintentionally) may be little more than a fashion based on unproven suppositions—and doomed to fail without structural changes (i.e., macro-level, institutional changes) to complement it (Noon, 2018). Other approaches (such as mentoring, training, and networking) are often criticized because their objective is to fix "other" (non-dominant group) employees instead of fixing the system (e.g., Benschop et al., 2015; Ely & Meyerson, 2000). At their very best, all these efforts seeking to change the ABCs of individual managers and employees are likely to have limited impact in the long term, not because of their methods and content, but because, by definition, their scope is limited.

A third set of change efforts that rely more on shifting individual ABCs and less on structures that perpetuate exclusion involve using *HR policies or work–life integration measures* to enhance employee inclusion, often viewing these as a type of accommodation for non-dominant employee groups. A recent review (Williams et al., 2016) concluded that work–family conflict is at an all-time high. Recognizing that "[v]iewing work-family balance as an individual-level problem borders on victim blaming" (Grzywacz & Carlson, 2007, p. 458), inclusive leaders must redefine work norms and find pragmatic ways of integrating these roles that are currently mostly viewed as being incompatible or conflicting with each other and straining on our limited resources of time, attention, energy, and abilities.

## Inclusive Leadership Requires a Multi-Level Approach

Changing times and changing needs of a changing workforce call for massive changes in entire systems. They call for new social norms to be promoted and for proactive disruption of the status quo. Organizational leaders thus have a potentially powerful role to play: as Robin Zheng puts it, referring to the power of individuals in specific roles to shape the collective, "roles are the site where structure meets agency" (Zheng, 2018, p. 870). Scholars and practitioners (e.g., Ferdman, 2014a, 2014b) agree that inclusive leaders must flex between shaping the meaning of social and collective forces to help individuals make meaning, and amplifying individual needs and efforts to inform and influence sustainable, structural, and systemic changes. Inclusive leaders must focus on the macro, top-down changes, as well as the short-term, micro-level changes that might have been prioritized until now. Inclusive leaders must therefore use a balanced approach: changing individuals' ABCs by focusing on behavioral or relational interventions for employees and decision makers (micro- and meso-level changes), and also working to make structural and systemic changes at the macro organizational and even societal levels. The following sections illustrate how inclusive leaders can effect such changes by changing their own approaches, changing others, and changing systems altogether.

## Inclusive Leaders Lead by Example

Although some issues (such as gender gaps and race discrimination) have persisted for a very long time, more recent forces (such as mass migration, the climate crisis, and terrorism) are shaping and dividing the global workforce in new ways. These issues are complex, bigger than any one organization or individual, and therefore need correspondingly big and bold action that is proactive, multipronged, and complex. One example of such action comes from the Tata Group in India, which embarked in 2007 on an agenda of affirmative action (AA) for members of India's Dalit[1] and tribal communities. Over the years, the Tata Affirmative Action Programme (TAAP) (Tata Business Excellence Group, n.d.) has focused on various aspects of social inclusion, including education, employability, employment, entrepreneurship, and "essential enablers" focusing on needs specific to the caste/tribe communities and provision of health care and essential amenities. This is done in the absence of government-mandated or legal requirements, in a country where social norms and history are stacked up against the communities targeted by the TAAP—an example of visionary and socially responsible inclusive leadership. This example of proactive, multipronged, and complex action demonstrates that organizations can be a source of social change and it is perhaps time for organizational leaders to see society as not just a market or a source of talent, but as an important beneficiary as well.

## Inclusive Leaders Empower Others

As Paulo Freire (1970) noted, social change might suffer from either verbalism (excessive reflection and little action) or activism (abundant action but little reflection). For inclusive leaders, therefore, striking the right balance between verbalism and activism, individual agency and imposed structural change, individualistic versus collectivistic notions, and business case and social justice case seems to be key. Inclusive leaders, therefore, must strive to amplify individual voices and empower others to be change agents.

A great example of such an effort comes from Hindustan Unilever (HUL), one of India's leading organizations. Almost 20 years ago, HUL launched Project Shakti (Mahajan, 2018; Rural Marketing, 2018), which involved selecting women from lower socioeconomic backgrounds in India's smaller villages to promote and sell household and hygiene products. With some initial investment, the project eventually took off to the point where these *Shakti Ammas* (Powerful Mothers/Women)—and eventually their male counterparts, *Shaktimaans* (Powerful Men), who started selling products on their cycles to nearby villages—contribute 20% or more in rural sales for HUL and above-average incomes for the Shakti workers. This bold step has led to greater empowerment of rural women, narrowed gender and income gaps for those from economically disadvantaged backgrounds, and improved health and hygiene in rural India, at the same time that it has significantly contributed to the organization's bottom line.

## Inclusive Leaders Find Hidden Strengths in Everyone

In addition to leaders with formal authority, it is important to recognize others who have power and influence. For instance, studies have identified the role of gatekeepers, decision makers in organizational positions of power who shape careers by selecting, promoting, and supporting organizational members (Bosley et al., 2009; Van den Brink & Benschop, 2014). The people who lead massive change efforts might not all have job titles such as CEO or even manager; many of these leaders might in fact be shareholders, community members, or individual employees who master the balance between individual agency and rallying collectives for change. One such model comes from the Change.org Foundation's She Creates Change fellowship program (2019; https://changefoundation.org/she-creates-change). Over the last couple of years, this program has brought together more than 150 Indian women (including me) as a community of leaders for social change in an effort to amplify our voices, arm us with advocacy and campaigning skills, and nurture connections with each other. The campaigns run the gamut, from fighting against misogyny in Bollywood, to lobbying the government for better parental leave for employees, to providing access to electricity in poverty-stricken tribal villages. The community of women changemakers has organically developed different types of leadership roles in the process, which has helped these efforts grow, sustain, and generate multiplicative impact across the country. The emerging roles include those of Champions (leading the change effort), Connectors (influencers who can make introductions, provide referrals, or connect changemakers to relevant media, government, or business contacts), Experts (researchers and social media navigators), and Buddies (to provide moral support, physical and online presence when it counts, and a sounding board for ideas) (Change.org Foundation, 2019). Inclusive leaders are those who take on these roles at various times, as needed, and also recognize the importance of driving change through these different changemakers as the situation demands.

## Inclusive Leaders Question Defaults

Since macro forces (e.g., affirmative action policies) shape individual choices at work (e.g., hiring someone from an underrepresented group) and micro efforts (e.g., individuals protesting a system) can impact social change (e.g., fairer wages or vacation policies), inclusive leaders recognize which defaults and assumptions to question at these different levels to make change. Thus, the best approach for the inclusive leader to adopt is a simultaneous application of both forces: bottom up—such as the "small wins" strategy that creates change through diagnosis, dialogue, and experimentation (Meyerson & Fletcher, 2000)—and the top-down strategy of shifting architectures to nudge individual shifts in behaviors and choices, as described by behavioral economists (e.g., Bohnet, 2016), or even the radical intervention of positive discrimination (e.g., Noon, 2010). Inclusive leaders therefore must practice exercising influence on various aspects of organizational life at all levels: micro (individual), meso (relational), and macro (institutional) (Ferdman, 2014a, 2014b).

A powerful example of how such a multi-level concerted effort that focuses on questioning and addressing defaults can pay off in rich dividends comes from Procter and Gamble (P&G) India. In 2014, when P&G broke ground on a new factory in Hyderabad, one of P&G's largest plants in Asia, its leaders were determined to do it right from the beginning (Procter & Gamble, 2014). India has strict laws regarding shift-work in factories forbidding women to work at night. The P&G Hyderabad plant leaders actively lobbied lawmakers to change the law locally so that women could work all shifts—an example of institutional or macro change. Working simultaneously on micro-level changes (e.g., educating local families on gender and employment issues as questions came up) and macro-level changes (such as changing the law and instituting new safety norms) meant that 30% of the workforce on day one were women—a rare feat, especially in the Indian manufacturing sector. Moreover, these plant employees have been engaging in relationship building with the community (meso-level changes), partnering with local social programs including medical camps, blood donation drives, and school-building activities in more rural areas around Hyderabad to touch lives in those surrounding communities. This powerful example not only shows the power of questioning and addressing defaults, but also demonstrates that the impact of visionary inclusive leadership extends beyond the organization.

## Conclusion: The Role of Inclusive Leaders in Driving Change

The study of inclusion must include a critical assessment of "how the way in which we design, operate and change organizations fundamentally and collectively advantages some members and disadvantages others" (Hinings & Greenwood, 2002, p. 419). With this recognition, then, even for advocates of interventions such as positive discrimination or coercive actions, the role of agency is clear, especially with respect to managers and leaders. These are the change agents who perform the critical functions of translator, sensemaker, catalyst, and oftentimes initiator of change. Popular conceptualizations of inclusive leaders involve descriptions of their attributes (e.g., Prime & Salib, 2014: empowerment, accountability, courage, and humility), traits (e.g., Bourke & Dillon, 2016: commitment, courage, cognizance of bias, curiosity, cultural intelligence, and collaboration) or qualities needed to manage diverse workforces (e.g., Chrobot-Mason et al., 2013: developing quality relationships, cultivating an inclusive climate, spanning boundaries, and framing of diversity initiatives). My conceptualization here is closer to Ferdman's (2014a; see also Chapter 1, this volume) idea of inclusive leaders as the "fulcrum" connecting micro and macro strategies by taking bold steps, constructing narratives of inclusion, and rewarding inclusive behavior. Inclusive leaders are those who are able to transcend dichotomies and use more sophisticated and inclusive repertoires of equality and diversity. Inclusive leaders are ultimately more effective in engaging significant organizational actors and are better positioned to mobilize organizational resources for transformational change (Özbilgin, 2009).

## Action Steps

In this chapter I have highlighted the crucial role that organizational leaders can play to become bolder, more impactful—and more inclusive. The following action ideas building on key themes that follow from the preceding pages are intended to provide leaders with ideas to go from intent to action, from individual ABCs to systemic change.

### *Engage Hearts and Minds—Not Just Brains or Budgets*

Infect your efforts with emotion and empathy, not just the business case and bottom lines. As described earlier, the business case is insufficient and might even distract us from what is needed. Communicate clearly and often, with empathy and humility, about your vision for inclusion.

### *Everyday Action Must Be Matched with Bold, Systemic, Long-Term Changes*

Institutionalize desired changes, whether through government regulations or legal changes, through organizational policy and programs, or—at the unit or team level—through different meeting norms or habits of working. Check the individual (ABC) level as well as system-level impact of each change you bring in.

### *Make Change Easy, Accessible, and Attractive*

Use behavioral economics principles such as nudges or reminders to modify the choice architectures around you, to make inclusion easier and exclusion hard (e.g., Bohnet, 2016). For instance, build in system checks and balances so that no single person alone can make decisions that have to do with people (e.g., hiring, firing, developing others). This leverages people in the system to make better ABC decisions, which in turn impacts the system.

### *Engage on the Ground (and Sometimes This Can Mean in Social Media)*

Identify decision makers and influencers; sometimes this is not the same as the persons in positions of authority. Impacting the system might require impacting influential nodes (people with relationships and impact on several others), which can have multiplicative effects, compared with changing people one ABC at a time.

### *Measure, Plan, Measure*

Continuously and periodically evaluating the outcomes of your efforts can motivate and exponentially impact further efforts and also cause you to change tracks nimbly as needed. Measuring impact at multiple levels—at the individual level (ABCs) as well as the systemic level (changes in aggregate targets)—is critical.

### *There is a Role for Everyone to Play Here*

*Find yours!* Just like the Changemakers from the She Creates Change program found, you may find that there are different roles to be played ... you may choose to be the champion of change or the supporter (by being an expert, a connector, or a buddy).

## Note

1 Dalits are members of India's lowest castes. The caste system has persisted for centuries and continues to impact Indians today, despite caste-based discrimination being outlawed in 1948.

## References

Al Saidi, M. (2019). Institutional change and sustainable development. In W. Leal Filho (Ed.), *Encyclopedia of sustainability in higher education*. Cham, Switzerland: Springer. https://doi.org/10.1007/978-3-319-63951-2_477-1

Benschop, Y., Holgersson, C., van den Brink, M., & Wahl, A. (2015). Future challenges for practices of diversity management in organizations. In R. Bendl, I. Bleijenbergh, E. Henttonen, & A. Mills (Eds.), *The Oxford handbook of diversity in organizations* (pp. 553–574). Oxford, UK: Oxford University Press. https://doi.org/10.1093/oxfordhb/9780199679805.013.24

Bezrukova, K., Spell, C. S., Perry, J. L., & Jehn, K. A. (2016). A meta-analytical integration of over 40 years of research on diversity training evaluation. *Psychological Bulletin*, *11*, 1227–1274. https://doi.org/10.1037/bul0000067

Bohnet, I. (2016). *What works: Gender equality by design*. Cambridge, MA: Harvard University Press.

Bosley, S. L. C., Arnold, J. M., & Cohen, L. (2009). How other people shape our careers: A typology drawn from career narratives. *Human Relations*, *62*(10), 1487–1520. https://doi.org/10.1177%2F0018726709334492

Bourke, J., & Dillon, B. (2016). *Six signature traits of inclusive leadership*. Deloitte Insights, Deloitte. https://www2.deloitte.com/us/en/insights/topics/talent/six-signature-traits-of-inclusive-leadership.html

Castilla, E. J., & Benard, S. (2010). The paradox of meritocracy in organizations. *Administrative Science Quarterly*, *55*, 543–576. https://doi.org/10.2189%2Fasqu.2010. 55.4.543

Change.org Foundation. (2019). *Diverse leadership roles for driving change*. https://womendeliver.org/2019/diverse-leadership-roles-for-driving-change

Chrobot-Mason, D., Ruderman, M. N., & Nishii, L. H. (2013). Leadership in a diverse workplace. In Q. M. Roberson (Ed.), *The Oxford handbook of diversity and work* (pp. 315–340). Oxford, UK: Oxford University Press. https://doi.org/10.1093/oxfordhb/9780199736355.013.0018

Davidson, M. N., & Ferdman, B. M. (2002, August 14). The experience of inclusion. In B. Parker, B. M. Ferdman, & P. Dass, (Chairs), *Inclusive and effective networks: Linking diversity theory and practice* [All Academy Symposium]. 62nd Annual Meeting of the Academy of Management, Denver, CO.

Ely, R. J., & Meyerson, D. E. (2000). Advancing gender equity in organizations: The challenge and importance of maintaining a gender narrative. *Organization*, 7(4), 589–608. https://doi.org/10.1177%2F135050840074005

Ferdman, B. M. (2014a, August 5). Leadership as the fulcrum of inclusion in organizations. In J. Prime, Chair, *The nature and consequences of inclusive leadership* [Symposium]. 74th Annual Meeting of the Academy of Management, Philadelphia, PA.

Ferdman, B. (2014b). The practice of inclusion in diverse organizations: Toward a systemic and inclusive framework. In B. M. Ferdman & B. R. Deane (Eds.), *Diversity at work: The practice of inclusion* (pp. 3–54). San Francisco, CA: Jossey-Bass. https://doi.org/10.1002/9781118764282.ch1

Freire, P. (1970). *Pedagogy of the oppressed*. New York, NY: Herder & Herder.

Grzywacz, J. G., & Carlson, D. S. (2007). Conceptualizing work-family balance: Implications for practice and research. *Advances in Developing Human Resources*, *9*(4), 455–471. https://doi.org/10.1177/1523422307305487

Haney, C., & Hurtado, A. (1994). The jurisprudence of race and meritocracy: Standardized testing and "race-neutral" racism in the workplace. *Law and Human Behavior*, *18*(3), 223–248. https://doi.org/10.1007/BF01499586

Hinings, C. R., & Greenwood, R. (2002). Disconnects and consequences in organization theory? *Administrative Science Quarterly*, *47*(3), 411–421. https://doi.org/10.2307%2F3094844

Kim, M. (2018, March 29). Why focusing on the "business case" for diversity is a red flag. *Quartz at Work*. https://qz.com/work/1240213/focusing-on-the-business-case-for-diversity-is-a-red-flag

Mahajan, V. (2016, December 14). How Unilever reaches rural consumers in emerging markets. *Harvard Business Review Digital Articles*. https://hbr.org/2016/12/how-unilever-reaches-rural-consumers-in-emerging-markets

McMillan-Cottom, T. (2019). In "Thick," Tressie McMillan Cottom looks at beauty, power, and Black womanhood in America. WBUR *On Point*. https://www.wbur.org/onpoint/2019/05/27/thick-tressie-mcmillan-cottom

Meyerson, D. E., & Fletcher, J. K. (2000). A modest manifesto for shattering the glass ceiling. *Harvard Business Review*, *78*(1), 126–136.

Noon, M. (2010). The shackled runner: Time to rethink positive discrimination? *Work, Employment and Society*, *24*(4), 728–739. https://doi.org/10.1177%2F09500 17010380648

Noon, M. (2018). Pointless diversity training: Unconscious bias, new racism, and agency. *Work, Employment and Society*, *32*(1), 198–209. https://doi.org/10.1177%2F0950017017719841

Özbilgin, M. F. (2009). Equality, diversity and inclusion at work: Yesterday, today and tomorrow. In M. F. Özbilgin (Ed.), *Equality, diversity, and inclusion at work: A research companion* (pp. 1–13). Cheltenham, and Northampton, UK: Edward Elgar.

Prime, J., & Salib, E. R. (2014). *Inclusive leadership: The view from six countries*. New York, NY: Catalyst. https://www.catalyst.org/wp-content/uploads/2019/01/inclusive_leadership_the_view_from_six_countries_0.pdf

Procter & Gamble (2014). Our Hyderabad plant is off to a remarkable start. https://us.pg.com/blogs/hyderabad/

Rural Marketing (2018). Project Shakti: More power to rural women. https://ruralmarketing.in/industry/advertising-marketing/project-shakti-more-power-to-rural-women

Saini, A. (2017). *Inferior: How science got women wrong and the new research that's rewriting the story*. Boston, MA: Beacon Press.

Schein, V., & Davidson, M. (1993). Think manager, think male. *Management Development Review*, 6(3), 24–28. https://doi.org/10.1002/(SICI)1099-1379(199601)17:1%3C33::AID-JOB778%3E3.0.CO;2-F

Tata Business Excellence Group. (n.d.). *TAAP Assessment*. https://www.tatabex.com/assessment/taap-assessment

Van den Brink, M., & Benschop, Y. (2014). Gender in academic networking: The role of gatekeepers in professorial recruitment. *Journal of Management Studies*, *51*, 460–492. https://doi.org/10.1111/joms.12060

Williams, J. C., Berdahl, J. L., & Vandello, J. A. (2016). Beyond work-life integration. *Annual Review of Psychology*, *67*, 515–539. https://doi.org/10.1146/annurev-psych-122414-033710

Zheng, R. (2018). What is my role in changing the system? A new model of responsibility for structural injustice. *Ethical Theory and Moral Practice*, *21*(4), 869–885. https://doi.org/10.1007/s10677-018-9892-8

# 18 Peak Moments of Inclusion Among Brothers and Sisters in Arms

*J. Goosby Smith*

## Leadership in a Military Context

While both management and leadership are necessary in all organizations—neither, on its own, being sufficient—in war-fighting organizations superb leadership has direct consequences for mission readiness. In war-fighting organizations, the effectiveness of leadership often has life and death consequences. The importance of leadership is evidenced by the mission statements of the service academies, senior military colleges, and military junior colleges. Every U.S. Service Academy has leadership foremost in its mission. All eight Senior Military Colleges except Norwich University and Virginia Tech explicitly list leadership or leadership development as a key aspect of their institution's existence. Of the four Military Junior Colleges, only Georgia Military College does not list leadership as a key mission element. Since university accreditation, curriculum, co-curriculum, and organizational culture are ideally intentionally aligned with institutional mission statements, the centrality of leadership to most of these esteemed institutions' missions is deliberate. Without consistently effective leadership, a military organization will not be successful.

While both are equally needed in organizations, the acts of "leadership" and "management" are fundamentally different. Managers are primarily concerned with managing processes, measuring performance, and ensuring certainty and predictability; leadership embraces uncertainty, creates change, and envisions moving into the future (Kotter, 2013). Decades ago, Kotter used a military analogy to explain this difference:

> A peacetime army can usually survive with good administration and management up and down the hierarchy, coupled with good leadership concentrated at the very top. A wartime army, however, needs competent leadership at all levels. No one yet has figured out how to manage people effectively into battle; they must be led.
>
> (Kotter, 1990, p. 104)

Effective leadership is important at every level: from the company to the battalion.

Service members and veterans have become increasingly prominent and influential in U.S. culture, politics, and policy. Their relevance escalated after the terrorist attack on New York's World Trade Center Towers on the morning of September 11, 2001. However, this critically important dimension of diversity often has been neglected by contemporary management scholars in the mainstream disciplinary research. For example, a keyword search of the word "military" in the *Academy of Management Journal* yields 41 articles. When "military" is searched for in the abstract or article summary (which indicates that it is a pertinent part of the research), the number of articles decreases to 13, as follows by decade: 1950s (1), 1960s (5), 1970s (3), 1980s (1), 1990s (0), 2000s (2), and 2010s (1). While many important topics were discussed in these articles, none of the 13 articles discussed inclusion. This is not because inclusion is irrelevant; it is because scholarly research is traditionally segregated by discipline.

Despite the applicability of many civilian-derived management and leadership theories, scholars focus mainly on civilian organizations. There is an opportunity for researchers interested in military populations to extend and test management disciplinary theories in military contexts and with personnel from those contexts. Not doing so results in missed opportunities to study these populations, apply theories that support military performance and mission readiness, and apply lessons and relevant findings to organizations and their people, writ large.

The purpose of this chapter is to examine the relevance of a model of inclusion that I helped to derive (Smith & Lindsay, 2014) for understanding how active duty military service members experience inclusion. After briefly discussing diversity, inclusion, and inclusive leadership, the research study and the participants are introduced, followed by the results.

## Diversity, Inclusion, and Inclusive Leadership in a Military Context

### *Diversity*

Historically, the U.S. armed forces have led the U.S. in terms of integrating service members from different identity groups (Smith, 2013). For example, they were among the first U.S. institutions to desegregate and accept Blacks in the mid-20th century. Over time, the four Department of Defense (DoD) branches of the U.S. military have become more racially and ethnically diverse than most large civilian organizations, particularly at the leadership level. In 2015 the racial demographics of the U.S. Total Force (2015 Demographics) were roughly proportional to those of the United States according to the U.S. Census as a whole (U.S. Census Bureau, 2016) as of July 1, 2016. However, with respect to gender, the Total Force of the U.S. military lagged behind many civilian organizations, with its composition of 16.8% female and 83.2% male. Please see the appendix (at the end of this chapter) for details of U.S. Total Force demographics.

## *A Guiding Metaphor*

I have found the metaphor of a garden useful in clarifying the differences between diversity and inclusion (Smith, 2017). Leaders have a better chance of improving their teams and organizations when they have a clear focus on what they are trying to impact. The *garden* refers to the organization (i.e., the squad, platoon, company, battalion, etc.) that the leader is trying to impact. The leaders (i.e., the Non-Commissioned Officers (NCOs), Senior Non-Commissioned Officers (SNCOs), and Officers) are the *gardeners*; they are the ones who delegate where seeds will be planted and they are responsible for nurturing them to a point where they bear fruit. The gardeners (leaders) use different *tools* to lead effectively including, but not limited to, tools of organizational design (i.e., strategy, processes, etc.) (Galbraith et al., 2002). Diversity refers to the *mix of vegetation* in the garden (i.e., meaningful types of diversity of the armed services in terms of race, ethnicity, gender, rank, specialty, etc.). The *soil* in which all vegetation in the garden grows is the organizational culture: the folklore, jargon, stories, and traditions of the garden. The *wider ecological environment* refers to the wider organizational context (i.e., other military organizations, national geopolitics, international conflict, etc.). The *fertilizer* refers to inclusion, which I define as the attitudes, behaviors, and circumstances within which people consistently are willing and able to bring the best of themselves to increase mission readiness, bear good fruit, and achieve the objective.

Although diversity and inclusion are different issues, the metaphor above makes it clear that these two distinct constructs can mutually impact each other. For example, the dimensions of diversity taking center stage in current events at the time of the writing of this chapter are the recent participation of women in combat job specialties (though women have been in war zones for decades), service members' sexual orientations, and transgender service members. These phenomena refer to diversity. However, such diversity-related events likely impact how included service members feel in their units. For example, now that women are allowed to serve in combat, how do their perceptions of inclusion compare with those of their male colleagues? Do transgender service members feel fully integrated into their units? In sum, while diversity and inclusion are different issues, they clearly are interrelated in organizations.

## Inclusion and Inclusive Leadership

### *Inclusion*

Management scholars study inclusion in terms of leader–member exchange (Brimhall et al., 2014), which refers to the individual relationships that leaders build with followers. Their interactions are considered "exchanges," thus the label *leader–member exchange*. When perceiving inclusion in terms of leader–member exchange, the focus is upon the interaction between the leader and the follower. A number of scholars focus upon inclusion at the level of teams or work groups, organizational policies, and leadership practices, including Mor Barak (2013), Ferdman and Davidson (2002), Ferdman and Roberts (2014), Nkomo (2014), and Smith and Lindsay (2014). As these scholars have demonstrated, inclusion is a multi-level phenomenon that impacts (and is impacted by) both formal and informal organizational processes (Brimhall et al., 2014). In this chapter I have chosen to examine inclusion from the perspective of active duty service members.

Inclusion occurs when organizational members feel "valued and appreciated as themselves and as integrated and complex—with their full range of differences and similarities from and with each other" (Ferdman, 2014, p. 5) and with leaders and other organizational stakeholders. Inclusion has been conceptualized as having three dimensions: access to information and resources, involvement in work groups, and ability to influence the decision-making process (Mor Barak & Cherin, 1998). Scholars use the term referring to employee empowerment and organizational participation (Roberson, 2006). Others found that when employees feel a sense of inclusion (or a lack thereof), there are consequences for turnover (Nishii & Mayer, 2009), attitudes and job satisfaction (Miller & Terborg, 1979), job performance, organizational commitment, and citizenship (Wayne et al., 2002), and sense of well-being (Ruggieri et al., 2013). Later, inclusion was defined as having eight dimensions (Person et al., 2015): common purpose, trust, appreciation of individual attributes, sense of belonging, access to opportunity, equitable reward and recognition, cultural competence, and respect.

### *Ubuntic Inclusion*

At the time that we developed the model of Ubuntic inclusion (Smith & Lindsay, 2014), the extant models of inclusion were not based directly on the lived experiences of individuals in organizations. We saw an opportunity to get as close as possible to where individuals experience workplace inclusion: their workplaces. Immediately after doing that research, I got an opportunity to replicate the study on a smaller scale with active duty service members. Below is a summary of how we developed the model and why I find it highly appropriate for studying the experiences of service members.

In an effort to understand what makes people feel included at work (i.e., to understand the "ingredients of the fertilizer"), over the course of roughly a decade, my consulting partner Josie Lindsay and I invited our clients in three large organizations to share their peak moments of inclusion at work. With informed consent and with organizational permission, we collected data from nearly 7,000 people in three organizations: a multinational bank, a multinational retailer, and a large public university. We collected these data through interviews, focus groups, and internet-based open-ended surveys. After engaging a third researcher in content analysis and insisting on 100% agreement, we came up with eight themes and we named our model *Ubuntic Inclusion*. We named the model after the African philosophy of *Ubuntu*, which is a way of living that privileges the collective over the individual. When individuals "have *Ubuntu*," they are said to live their lives in a way that deeply honors the other. Some have defined *Ubuntu* as a sense of deep and inextricable interconnectedness with each other (Tutu, 1999). A white paper that was commissioned by then South-African President Nelson Mandela defines *Ubuntu* in the following way:

> [Ubuntu is] the principle of caring for each other's wellbeing ... and a spirit of mutual support. Each individual's humanity is ideally expressed through his or her relationship with others and theirs in turn through recognition of the individual's humanity. Ubuntu means that people are people through other people. It also acknowledges both the rights and responsibilities of every citizen in promoting individual and societal wellbeing.
>
> (Hailey 2008, p. 3)

*Ubuntu* is often defined as "I am because you are," which means that we *only* exist within the relationships that we have with the other. In the thousands of stories that we analyzed, we saw "flashes" of *Ubuntu*, of high moments of interconnectedness, charity, and interdependence. When we developed the model, the African concept of *Ubuntu* was not the philosophical basis underlying other models of inclusion. Another unique aspect about this model was that it was derived inductively from analyzing qualitative responses of thousands of individuals. In developing the model, unlike the models of our colleagues, we did not privilege existing theory or the well-reasoned opinions of subject-matter experts at the outset; we privileged the people who reported experiencing inclusion. Only after we determined reliable themes in their peak experiences of inclusion did we engage existing theory to better understand the results.

The following eight themes or dimensions of Ubuntic inclusion are each relevant to creating an inclusive unit and war-fighting organization (Smith & Lindsay, 2014, pp. 29–32):

1 *Connection*, feeling a sense of kinship with leaders, peers, the organization, and a larger purpose;
2 *Communication*, being informed about relevant information in a conducive manner in a safe environment;
3 *Care*, being appreciated, assisted, and understood by others;
4 *Intrapersonal Inclusion*, engaging in self-talk about being included (or excluded);
5 *Fairness*, perceiving a sense of equity in the organization and being hired and rewarded with respect to the merit of one's contributions;
6 *Trust*, having confidence in one's peers and the organization and feeling that other stakeholders hold oneself in the same esteem;
7 *Visibility and Reward*, having one's accomplishments seen and celebrated by others and by organizational incentives;
8 *Mentoring and Coaching*, having someone to guide one's organizational success and being that guide for others.

Anecdotally, this model of Ubuntic inclusion quickly gains traction in corporate, military, and not-for-profit organizations when I use it. I was curious to know if these same dimensions held in high-stakes military organizations, so I replicated with active duty service members the questions asked in the 2014 research. Because the large sample we used to derive the model was diverse along multiple dimensions (i.e., veterans, including diverse status, sex, nationality, race, sexual orientation, educational level, role, and a host of other demographic categories), I was optimistic that it would at least be partially applicable. I also chose this model because it is based upon the African philosophy of *Ubuntu*, whose central premise is that we are all connected and only exist in relation to each other (Lewis, 2010). This philosophy is highly compatible with the ethos of military organizations, as evidenced by the common saying, "One fight, one team" (de Bruijn, 2006). My goal in this chapter is to examine the peak moments of inclusion of active duty service members using the model of Ubuntic inclusion to see how the model's dimensions manifest in a military context. (For more detail on the derivation of the model, the research methodology, and the theoretical support of the dimensions, please see Smith & Lindsay, 2014, pp. 17–29.)

### *Inclusive Leadership*

Inclusive leadership is grounded in the relationship between leaders and those in their charge. According to Carmeli et al. (2010, p. 250), inclusive leaders are those "leaders who exhibit openness, accessibility, and availability in their interactions with followers." Hollander (2009) also viewed inclusive leadership as relationship-based, with a focus on the leader meeting employees' needs and employees perceiving that their leaders were available. Choi et al. (2015) found that inclusive leadership is an important factor in employee engagement.

Inclusive leadership refers to the set of self-talk, relationships, and actions that enable organizational members to feel included and willing and able to bring their best selves to the accomplishment of the mission or organizational goal. As mentioned above, there is research that defines and shows the benefits of inclusive leadership. However, what is often missing is a micro-level focus on leadership behaviour: what precisely can a leader do tomorrow to start infusing a sense of inclusion in his or her team? Our model of Ubuntic inclusion (Smith & Lindsay, 2014) answers this question by showing, at an individual behavioral level, the specific things that leaders do and say that make people feel included at work. It is important to note that inclusive leadership is not tied to one's level on an organizational chart. As the reader will see in the following examples, informal leaders and peers, and not just formal leaders, can be agents of inclusion.

## Focus Group Interviews

I got the opportunity to collect data to test this model as part of my research during my Office of Naval Research Faculty Summer Research Fellow Grant, which sponsored this research. For ten weeks I conducted onsite focus group research in a joint services educational entity at a U.S. Air Force base to understand what inclusion looked like in a military context.

During that summer, 16 participants attended my focus group sessions. I asked them to think of a time during their military careers when they experienced a high level of inclusion—a time when they really felt that they belonged and that they mattered. I then asked three follow-up questions: What happened during this experience? What made this experience memorable? Why does this moment stand out as a peak experience of belongingness? After giving participants about ten minutes to record their answers on a handout, I invited each person to share the experience that they documented as I took notes. After I completed the focus groups, I sought the assistance of a retired U.S. Army Equal Opportunity Advisor to help me understand the military environment, the training program the service members were attending, the rank structure, and proper protocols for communicating with and addressing military personnel at the base. This was invaluable in helping me to interact confidently and appropriately with service members.

## The Service Members

The service members with whom I spoke represented several U.S. service branches: Army (USA), Army Reserve (USAR), Navy (USN), Marines (USMC), Army National Guard (ANG), Air Force Reserve (AFR), Coast Guard (USCG). Please see the appendix (at the end of this chapter) for participant demographics. Fourteen were enlisted, one was a junior officer, and one refused to disclose student number so branch and rank are listed as "ANON" for anonymous. My sample was skewed in comparison with the demographics of the total force in that I had more representatives from the Army and the Air Force Reserve. Also, all but one of the participants were enlisted service members.

After analyzing the data, I gave each service member a pseudonym to aid readability. So that I could stay true to their conceptualizations of themselves, I gave participants an open-ended survey to report what *they* most identified with in terms of race and ethnicity and I use their terminology in this chapter. For example, while many refer to Americans of African descent as "African Americans," the participants in these focus groups defined themselves as "Black Americans," "Americans," and "Blacks."

## Analysis

Because the purpose of this study was to explore the applicability of the largely civilian-derived model of Ubuntic inclusion (Smith & Lindsay, 2014), service members' peak moments of inclusion were content-analyzed and coded by the eight dimensions of that model. To review, those eight dimensions were: Connection, Communication, Care, Intrapersonal Inclusion, Trust, Fairness, Mentoring and Coaching, and Visibility and Reward.

## Service Member Experiences of Inclusion

While the purpose of the chapter is to explore the application of the model of Ubuntic inclusion (Smith & Lindsay, 2014) to active duty military service members, each service member is a human being. Toward that end, their stories remain a central part of capturing their experiences of inclusion in their military environments. The stories also serve to contextualize their reflections.

In the following sections, each dimension of the model is defined in detail, followed by examples from research participants that demonstrate how that dimension can manifest in a military environment.

***Connection***

People experience a sense of connection when they: 1) feel connected to a larger purpose, 2) experience a sense of community within their work group, 3) connect through "breaking bread" or eating together, 4) feel a bond or sense of identity with the organization itself, 5) perceive a filial bond with leaders, co-workers, and other individuals throughout the organization, 6) perceive a connection with their team or smaller unit as a whole, 7) have fun with each other in activities such as softball games, retreats, and parties.

Chris identified as Black, but did not supply a student number on the completed questionnaire. As a result, Chris's role and service branch data could not be retrieved from the database. Chris did, however, share that gender was the most salient aspect of identity that impacted him or her. Because of this, it is reasonable to hypothesize that Chris is female because no males said their gender was the most career-impacting identity group membership. Said Chris, "I felt a great deal of inclusion in Korea due to geographical location and closeness at the unit." This "close" level of *Connection* to *Colleagues/Peers* in the unit led to Chris finding this experience so memorable. The "geographical location" was what made this experience so memorable to Chris, though Chris did not elaborate on what aspects of the location contributed to this memory.

Adam, who is a First Lieutenant in the Air Force Reserve, was the only officer in the group. This was because the training course from which service members were selected was largely designed for enlisted (versus officer) personnel. He identified himself a man of "Mixed" race with an ethnicity of Pacific Islander. The dimension of Adam's identity that has most impacted him in his career has been being Hawaiian, "b/c of how isolated the islands are and how unique the people are," because the "local people are proud of their state more than any other state." Adam's peak moment of inclusion came "During [an] Exercise w/Joint Forces" when his "unit really pulled together. We were able to accomplish the mission as a whole and not individually. Even when doing bad, we did it as a team." The salient dimension of inclusion in this moment was *Connection* (*with Colleagues/Peers*). What made this experience so memorable was that "it was w/people that I grew up with and who I regularly spend time w/. Local Hawaiian state pride of just representing," which further reinforces the sense of local *Connection* that he felt. Adam said what made this moment stand out as a moment of belongingness was that he and his colleagues "accomplished the task w/high standards. We stood out as a state more than anything else." This sense of *Visibility and Reward*, specifically *Conquering a Challenge* and having *Internal Visibility* within the organization contributed to what made him feel included.

### *Communication*

The dimension of communication was very broad. The model lists the following indicators as situations and behaviors that create a sense of inclusion: 1) being included in formal communication from the leader or from the organization, 2) enjoying a free communication flow "downward" from one's superior in order to stay up to date on pertinent information, 3) having free "upward" communication with one's supervisor or manager, 4) being included in the informal or "water cooler" conversations (which are often as important as formal communication), 5) having meaningful one-on-one communication with others, 6) being able to be transparent in communication and having leaders speak transparently with them, 7) being made aware of opportunities for career development when they occur, 8) being communicated with in a way of communication that is effective for the message, 9) receiving feedback from leaders, 10) having a "safe space" for communication in which one can be honest without fear of reprisal, and, 11) being in an organization that has multilingual communication that facilitates inclusion of people whose first language was not English.

Mary is an Asian woman whose ethnicity is Filipino. She serves in the Air Force as a Technical Sergeant. Mary's peak moment of inclusion in the military came when she was promoted. Of the promotion, she said "I feel that I have a voice [and] I can make a difference." Interestingly, when asked what made that moment stand out as a peak moment of belongingness, Mary said "because I feel like I belong to a group." *Communication*, specifically the increased ability to use her voice to make an impact (that her promotion provided) impacted her *Intrapersonal* sense of inclusion.

Martha is a woman who defines her race as "Other" and her ethnicity as Cuban-American. She serves as a Sergeant First Class in the Army. Being female is the identity group that has most impacted her in her military career because "it is the easiest to relate to." Martha says that the following three situations constituted her peak moments of inclusion:

> [1] Basic Training—prayed & encouraged each other nightly. [2] Fort Sam Houston with the NCOs of our MT Group we were starting from ground up as being reactivated—[3] Naples—My SI shop—we worked together, PT together and spent a lot of time together outside the unit.

In all of these situations *Connection* to *Colleagues/Peers* was apparent. The dimension of *Care* was also clearly present because she and her comrades helped each other personally and took the time to get to know each other during all of the time they spent together. What made this memorable to Martha was: "graduating together" (*Visibility & Reward, Celebrating Performance with Others*), "Focus on mission" (*Connection to a Larger Purpose*), and "Cooking with [name], the Mud Run, and good PT [Physical Training]," *Connection to Colleagues/Peers*. The moment stands out as a peak experience because of her *Accomplishment*.

Bill is a White male Sergeant First Class in the Army who responded "?" when asked to share his ethnicity. However, if most readers looked at him, they would say he is White. When asked which of his identity groups had been most impactful during his career, he responded "I don't know." What was very clear, though, was Bill's peak moment of inclusion which he emotionally shared. "It was graduation from Marine Corps boot camp" which "was the first time that I was associated with a group and it was a result of individual effort & teamwork." What made this experience so memorable for him was that "it was the first time in my life that I was a part of something bigger than myself [that] had value." This provided Bill with a "sense of pride & accomplishment." The *Connection* that he felt *to a Larger Purpose* and *with Colleagues and Peers* was what made him feel so included. Additionally, he felt a sense of *Visibility and Reward* as a result of conquering the challenge of boot camp with his comrades.

### *Care*

In our research, we found that people feel cared for when 1) someone helps them personally or professionally, 2) people, especially leaders, take the time to get to know them, and show authentic care in their thoughts and feelings, 3) peers, and especially leaders, say "thank you" to them, especially when they have gone above and beyond the call of duty, and 4) when people in the organization, especially leaders, acknowledge them by speaking to them and even calling them by name.

Care appeared less frequently in this military sample than it does in corporate and higher educational samples. Care appeared in the stories of two Sergeants First Class. Lisa experienced care when she reported feeling "appreciated" by her team for her high level of cultural awareness. Martha reporting experiencing care during Basic Training when her unit "prayed & encouraged each other nightly." It is worth exploring in the next round of this research if care continues to be a less frequent aspect of service members' peak moments of inclusion. On the one hand, one could argue, in an organization that requires all of its members to commit to obedience and allegiance, that care is not extremely prevalent. On the other hand, anyone who has been in military environments sees the high levels of cohesiveness, sense of team, and mutual help that frequently is displayed in most military units. This is the dimension that seems to manifest differently in military versus civilian contexts.

### *Intrapersonal Inclusion*

This dimension is different from the others because it exists not interpersonally, but within individuals' hearts and minds. It consists of self-talk about whether or not one will be included or excluded (and whether or not one will intentionally include or exclude oneself). Themes include, 1) expecting to be included, 2) initiating inclusion, for example, introducing oneself, 3) feeling included because the organization told them so, 4) realizing that they need to be flexible in order to be included, 5) feeling the need to exhibit a high degree of self-control at work, 6) feeling that it takes double the effort to only get half of the recognition that they see majority-group members in the organization receive with the same, or often less, effort, 7) feeling the constant pressure to keep proving themselves as valuable assets to their organizations and teams, 8) making the decision to "check out" and essentially give up on being included, 9) managing the impressions that co-workers have of them in an effort to be included, and seeing value in participating in organizational affinity groups that reaffirm their identities, and 11) "leaning toward" inclusion optimistically by being open to inclusive behaviors by others.

Kara is a Black female Master Sergeant in the Army Reserve. The identity membership that has had the greatest impact upon her career is her gender. She says that this is because women in the military "are outnumbered 10 to 1. The majority of these males [are White], leaving Black female[s] having to be smarter, wiser and have *thick skin* [emphasis by author]." This comment is an indicator of the *Intrapersonal Inclusion* dimension's behaviors of having to put in double the effort … and persist in proving oneself.

Jamie, an American male who is an E5 in the Air Force, also experienced the *Intrapersonal* dimension of inclusion. While he identifies his race as Asian, with a specific connection to Korean culture, the aspect of Jamie's identity that has most impacted his career is his "career field" itself. His peak moment of inclusion occurred while he was "getting to [his] first assignment and being accepted." This experience was so memorable because he said he was "nervous about not [being] accepted in [his] first assignment." The dimension of *Intrapersonal Inclusion*, specifically about whether or not it was realistic to expect inclusion, was salient in this situation. This moment stands out for Jamie, as he put it, because "I did not know what to think or expect but going through that first experience helped me get through the rest of my career."

Beth is a White female of Scottish-Irish American ethnicity. She is an E7 in the Army National Guard. When asked which of her identity group memberships has most impacted her military career, her response was "can't say" because she has "had different cultural experiences." Beth's peak moment of inclusion happened when she was "a junior enlisted—lower rank E-1—E-3" and she "felt more like [she] belonged with the group." She had a strong sense of *Intrapersonal Inclusion*, in that she was expecting inclusion. Beth lamented that this moment stood out as a peak experience because "as you go up in rank [you are] more alone."

### *Fairness*

This dimension is centered in actual and perceived equity. Being treated fairly is one of the dimensions that is a necessary foundation for inclusion. People simply don't feel included when they don't think they are being treated fairly. Several indicators existed for our fairness dimension including, 1) fair and legal recruiting and hiring processes in which all qualified candidates have an equal chance to be selected, 2) fair opportunities to participate in professional development that can help their careers, 3) being fairly compensated for their work, in both an absolute sense (industry salary standards) and a relative sense (in comparison with other colleagues), 4) having a fair chance to be promoted if their performance is excellent and they are well-prepared for a new available challenge, 5) perceiving the presence of fair policies and norms that are interpreted and enforced in the same manner regardless of employee status or identity-group memberships, 6) being treated fairly by leaders and peers, and 7) experiencing a culture that has enough flexibility to provide a fair work–life balance.

Michelle is a female Black American who serves as a Sergeant First Class in the Army. She opined that her most impactful identity group(s) are "Gender/Race" because "There are many gender stereotypes still in place/practice in the military. Also, black females have a 'special' stigma in general." For Michelle, it was the intersectionality of race and gender that created the most professional impact. She shared that she felt most included when "My 1st line leader looked at everyone's ability. Gender was not a big factor. This approach enabled all involved to thrive." The sense of *Fairness* in terms of her line leader's treatment made Michelle feel included. She remembers this experience so much because of "the camaraderie" or *Connection* to her *Colleagues/Peers*. This situation stood out to her as a peak experience of belongingness because "It was a professional milestone for me personally. I experienced a lot of success and also fostered some lasting friendships/relationships." Michelle's long-lasting *Connection* with others and her feelings of accomplishment led her to feel most included.

*Trust*, like the dimension *Fairness* above, is also a fundamental requirement for instilling a genuine sense of inclusion in a collective. Some trust behaviors were bidirectional, meaning that respondents felt included when they could trust others and when they were trusted by others. This dimension was unique because it was the only dimension from our original research in which participants consistently identified a specific organizational function in their comments: Human Resources. We found that the following actions and situations make individuals feel included: 1) trusting in the organization's strategy and vision, 2) trusting individuals and processes in Human Resources, 3) having faith and trust in organizational processes such as hiring, termination, discipline, and promotion, 4) being able to trust one's leaders, 5) being trusted by one's leaders, and 6) being able to trust and being trusted by one's coworkers.

Tom is a Filipino male who is a Sergeant in the Army National Guard. When reflecting upon his different identity groups, he said that he was a "Navy brat" born and raised in various countries in Asia. He was exposed to diversity "growing up as 'Americans'" because it allowed him "to be open and social in and out of the workplace." He felt that he had been "valued as an individual" regardless of his rank. Tom's peak moment of inclusion in the service occurred when he was a Staff Sergeant in the Air Force and "[he] was asked based on trust and expertise, to write a policy letter from [the] wing commander." This experience was memorable because "As an Airman, [he was] trusted and valued for [his] opinion." Tom explicitly said that he felt included because he experienced *Trust (being trusted by leaders)*. When asked why this moment stood out as a peak experience, he said that his Commander "could of [sic] asked the MED officer for the [task]. Since then, [he has] been asked for [his] 'guidance' based on his 'expertise'."

### *Visibility and Reward*

This dimension took many forms. At its essence, this dimension refers to all of the ways that people felt visible and celebrated for their contributions in the organization. Organizational members felt included when 1) their work was recognized and acknowledged among their peers, 2) their being rewarded reinforced notions of fairness and meritocracy, 3) they were recognized for conquering a challenge, 4) they had the opportunity to celebrate their performance accomplishments with others, 5) they had a deep level of enjoyment for the reward itself, 6) they were publicly recognized or rewarded for their contributions and sacrifices, 7) they felt that a superior or a colleague saw the hard work that they did and the individual showed their appreciation, 8) they are promoted to a new position based upon being valued, and 9) their leaders or colleagues allowed them to have increased internal visibility in the organization or increased external visibility in the community at large.

Lisa is a Black female whose ethnicity is Jamaican. She serves as a Sergeant First Class in the Army. Of her peak moment of inclusion, Lisa recalled:

> I was exposed to vast ethnic diversity and challenged to influence such groups to become a team. This experience made me feel like

> I belong because being a black female from . . . a culture outside the U.S. not only [allowed] me to relate to diversity but to learn and understand other people's culture, [and] struggles.

This was the one story for which Rater 1 and Rater 2 did not reach convergence. One rater saw Lisa's experience as an example of *Visibility and Reward* because she said that others "appreciated [her] awareness of other cultures."

Leticia is a Black female Sergeant First Class in the Army whose ethnicity is Trinidadian. The aspect of her identity that has most impacted her career is being female because, she said, "it has given me the opportunity to express myself in roles outside of the standard female roles." Her peak moment of inclusion occurred when she was "in basic training where [she was working together]." This *Connection* to her *Colleagues/Peers* was what made Leticia feel included. She continued on to say that what made the experience memorable was "when [they] accomplished the task. The words of congrats, [and] praise [helped me] know the fact [sic] it was appreciated for our hard work." This *Visibility and Reward* of being recognized/acknowledged among peers made the experience memorable. This moment stood out as a peak experience of *Connection* because before joining the military she said, "most of my experience was with my family. Being able to work with others that are not related to you and accomplish something was great for me."

Jack is a White male whose ethnicity is American; he serves as an E7 in the Army. He shared that "graduation from jumpmaster school" was his peak moment of inclusion because "it was the accomplishment of a goal. Being a paratrooper was a childhood dream and after airborne school my next goal as a paratrooper was to be jumpmaster qualified." For Jack, the accomplishment of this goal provided him a sense of *Visibility & Reward*, specifically the intrinsic enjoyment of the reward. He says this moment stands out to him so much because "It's said that paratroopers volunteer twice: once to serve in the military [and] again to be a paratrooper. Jumpmasters are an even smaller, tighter community and I felt like everyone looked at me in a different light once I graduated." The moment was so impactful because of the way others "looked at him in a different light," which provided *Visibility & Reward*. This is also an example of *Intrapersonal Inclusion* because Jack began expecting inclusion once he made this accomplishment.

### *Mentoring and Coaching*

The presence of a guide for one's organizational and career success made people feel included. Like the Trust dimension above, mentoring and coaching were bidirectional in that individuals reported feeling included at work both when they had access to active mentors or coaches and when they, themselves, had the opportunity to mentor or coach others. More specifically, the behaviors and situations that made people feel included for this dimension were 1) having a mentor or a coach who looked out for them, 2) having their desperate need for a mentor or coach fulfilled, 3) benefiting from actively engaged mentors, 4) having a diverse set of mentors, 5) engaging in well-designed formal mentoring programs, 6) having informal mentors who took them under their wing, 7) gaining exposure or getting sponsorship from someone in the organization, 8) having the opportunity to develop their skills and engage in career development activities, and 9) being a mentor or coach for someone else.

Sara is a Hispanic woman of Mexican ethnicity who serves as a Staff Sergeant (E5) in the Air Force Reserve. The aspect of her identity that has most impacted her career is social class.

> I was always in a lower class from birth to about 16 years old. There was always a lack for something; money and food for example. I wanted to be able to provide for myself and pay for college on my own.

Her socioeconomic background serves as a motivation for Sara to achieve her professional goals. She felt most included:

> Right after basic & tech school, when I started working with my unit at the time. I had the chance to be a part of an airman's council in which I could be a voice for other airmen in my shop, TMO [Transportation Management Office] at the time.

Sara said that this *Connection* to her *Colleagues/Peers* was memorable because:

> The opportunity that was given to me helped me want to be better at my job and helped me look for ways to help others and make sure that I could make another person be heard about ideas, concerns, suggestions, and more.

Her ability to serve as "a voice for other airmen" was evidence of the role that *Mentoring and Coaching* plays in making service members feel included. Not only was she able to use her voice, she also experienced inclusion *through being a mentor* by helping others' ideas and concerns get *exposure* within the organization. Sara said this moment stood out so much to her because "I felt like I was being considered."

Kevin is an Asian man with Chinese ethnicity. He is an E7 in the United States Marine Corps. When asked which aspect of his identity most impacted his career, he responded, "Can't think of any." Kevin shared his peak inclusive moment as being "When I was on the inspector general inspection team. I was the inspector chief and

I coordinate[d] the team and [led] the team to mentor [and] inspect many units within the command." This *Mentoring & Coaching* of his team made him feel included because he was *Trusted* by his boss. "My supervisor [gave] full support with what I do and [took] suggestions and recommendations from the field. And [he got] support from higher headquarters." Kevin had open two-way *Communication* with his supervisor, those further up his chain of command, and his peers in the field. This moment stands out as a peak experience because of "support, unit morale, mentorship, and leadership." In sum, *Communication* and *Mentoring & Coaching* were the main ingredients that made Kevin feel included.

## "Take Aways" for Becoming a More Inclusive Leader

Several suggestions for military leaders who want to foster inclusion in their units emerged from this study. Many of the suggestions can be adapted, or even taken literally, by civilian leaders seeking to be more inclusive. Although the organizational context of the military differs, human beings all have similar needs, inclusion (i.e., belongingness) being a basic one (Maslow, 1943).

- CARE:
  - **Be sensitive to dynamics of citizenship status.** All service members are not yet U.S. citizens. This creates a difference in the types of jobs that they can have since non-citizens cannot get a security clearance. Also, there are limitations on how long non-citizens can serve without pursuing citizenship. These and other differences, such as language, can result in these service members feeling a sense of alienation. This is particularly salient for Latinos/Latinas and Asian/Pacific Islanders who report hearing significantly more racioethnic jokes than White service members (Smith & Lindsay, 2014).
  - **Build your team.** Strong teams don't just occur, they are built. When possible, take advantage of informal team-building activities. Creating a highly connected and high-performing team is not a one-time task; it is an action that needs to be reinforced. This can be done by having lunch together, hosting a potluck event, bowling together, or various other sanctioned activities. Other more organized team-building activities can include ropes exercises or escape room activities during down time. The team that plays together performs together.

- CONNECT:
  - **Encourage occasional team collaboration after hours.** Consider having teams volunteer for local events such as 5k runs and

walks that support universally accepted causes (e.g., Susan G. Komen Race for the Cure 5k). The time that team members spend together away from work increases group cohesion if all participate.

- **Take advantage of professional development opportunities to do your own identity-related "work" to increase the empathy and understanding you have for your team.** People have different self-conceptualizations of themselves with respect to their various identity group memberships. Some identities are stronger, or more salient while others are less prominent to how one thinks of oneself. In the focus groups, male participants did not list gender as an impactful identity. Similarly, the White participants did not list race; in fact, they either said "I don't know" or left the question blank. When one is in the majority with respect to *any* dimension of diversity, one tends not to critically analyze that dimension unless led to do so, or unless one is placed in the numeric minority. This lack of critical examination and embrace of one's own various identities creates a blind spot regarding understanding diversity-related dynamics of team members. As a leader, if I don't see how my race or gender impacts my career, I am not likely to see how race and gender impacts *your* career. Such a blind spot can be extremely detrimental for leaders seeking to create an inclusive climate because it negatively impacts their ability to care, connect, mentor, and coach: all dimensions of the Ubuntic inclusion model used in this chapter. This is a lifelong process, so be patient.

- COMMUNICATION:
  - **Be mindful about infusing inclusion into employees' in-processing or on-boarding experiences.** The initial stage of organizational socialization is a unique and nonreplicable opportunity to create a sense of inclusion (Smith & Lindsay, 2014), so special attention should be paid to this stage. This is an area where military organizations far surpass most civilian organizations. There just needs to be assurance that *all* new service members or employees, regardless of identity self-concept or outer manifestation, experience this sense of inclusion. One way to do this is to ensure that each new organizational member attends and successfully completes a well-curated on-boarding process that conveys the organization's values, builds camaraderie, a strong sense of belonging and organizational pride, and a powerful sense of agency: a boot camp. The importance of communicating a sense of inclusion during onboarding cannot be overestimated, as evidenced by the stories of Bill and Jamie. It was during their Marine Basic Training

and first assignment, respectively, that their peak moment of inclusion in their military careers occurred. If your organization does not presently have an on-boarding process, consider creating one that communicates the importance and existence of relevant dimensions of inclusion discussed in this chapter.

- **Listen.** Military leaders, like all leaders, spend much of their time communicating. They regularly attend meetings with their superiors and conduct meetings with their direct reports who depend upon them for information. However, the value of listening cannot be overstated. When service members felt heard and that they had a voice, they perceived a high sense of inclusion. So, whether formally or informally, make it a point to listen to each of your service members each week. Make a schedule if you need to if you have a large unit.
- **Engage in dialogue; do not assume.** As a leader, it is your job to create a working environment that allows anyone in your unit to contribute their best knowledge, skills, and abilities in service of the unit's or the team's mission. This means that people need to be seen for who they are. Therefore, do not assume that you know how (or whether) various diversity dimensions are impacting them. For example, your good intentions behind adjusting things for a female service member *solely* based upon what you think "women" would want may not achieve the positive impact you are seeking. Such assumptions made about people based solely on our assumptions about their identity group is called stereotyping. Leaders are well-advised to remember the saying, "when in doubt, talk it out." Before making adjustments in new areas, ask service members what operational, procedural, or facilities improvements you should be prioritizing.
- **You only get one chance to make a first impression.** One of the things that military organizations get right is their focus on uniformity of the on-boarding experience. For many of the service members whom I interviewed, basic training or their first assignments were the context of their peak moments of inclusion. This means that military leaders have a chance to impact service members' perceptions of inclusion when they assume a new command or when new service members come into their units. In situations like this in which first impressions can be made, leaders should have a concise inclusion plan that reminds them to be intentional about creating and sustaining a sense of inclusion. *This inclusion plan would include explaining why team members were chosen for the team.* For example, mention the person's prior relevant experience or accomplishments. When leaders add someone from a typically underrepresented group to the team and fail to do this, it makes it easier

for existing group members to overlook what the person is bringing to the table and focus solely on their group memberships. Said differently, when leaders don't make a habit of communicating what *every* team member recruited brings to the table, people start to say things like, "S/he was only recruited to fill a quota." While starting this new habit won't completely eliminate these behaviors, it can sure provide countering data to help employees understand that people are hired based upon what they bring to the table in service of achieving the group's goals.

- MENTORING AND COACHING:
  - **Diversity training and education are key.** One pattern that emerged from service members' stories was that those in underrepresented groups were more likely to state that their race or gender impacted their career. Because race and gender impact *all* of our careers (whether or not we are in the majority or minority), this may be a developmental area for service members. Those who are in the majority with respect to any dimension of diversity rarely consider that dimension's impact. For example, if you are reading this book chapter, you likely have not considered how "reader friendly" this text is to a person who experiences blindness or a learning disability. You also may not have thought about how the language in this chapter translates into a different language. It is a common occurrence for those in a majority group to think less about their majority status. Such status is taken for granted, much as a fish takes water for granted (Smith, 2002). Similarly, education is needed to help those who are in the minority understand some of the thought patterns and experiences of those in the majority. Education and training are key for *all* organizational stakeholders because everyone needs to understand everyone better in order for the organization to function as a cohesive and productive unit.
  - **Realize that team members from underrepresented groups will feel more strain as they climb the organizational ladder.** Maintaining a sense of inclusion for females and other service members from underrepresented groups (e.g., minority ethnicities, different social classes) as they climb the organizational ladder is also important. While "it's lonely at the top" is an oft-repeated adage, it may be even truer for such service members. For example, Beth (an E7) said that she felt more of a sense of inclusion when she was a junior enlisted officer. Without a critical mass of individuals with whom one can identify,

promotion can be a double-edged sword. It is therefore important for leaders to help such newly promoted employees to develop networks at higher levels and integrate into new social and professional groups where they can start to build relationships with people who inhabit their new roles.

- **Leaders create more leaders, not followers.** Wherever possible, seek to develop each service member in your charge. Even if it's a brief conversation, discuss the service member's potential career trajectory with him or her. While asking the service member about their career goals is advisable, this may not be enough. Sometimes service members may not even know what is possible, or they may not have the confidence to "dream big." Either encouraging the service member to mentor others or finding that service member a mentor will go a long way to creating a leader who will contribute long-term to the success of the organization. This mentoring is particularly important as service members with identities underrepresented among leadership are promoted. The saying *it is lonely at the top* takes on new meaning as females, African Americans, Asians, Native Americans, and Latinas and Latinos break into senior NCO, Warrant Officer, and field grade officer ranks. It is also worth noting that mentoring doesn't just occur downward, it occurs upward. Senior non-commissioned officers (SNCOs) with more experience need to take newer ones under their wings and provide advice and camaraderie. Most officers will agree that SNCOs mentor junior officers, not the other way around. In sum, mentoring needs to occur formally, informally, upward, downward, and laterally. No one learns to lead in isolation.

- VISIBILITY AND REWARD:
  - **Civilian leaders can borrow from the military's traditions of recognizing team members for achieving goals.** Visibility and reward are important for military service members. Many of the stories of service members took place with respect to a sense of accomplishment (Martha), successfully writing a policy letter (Tom), delivering a staff briefing (Kara), graduating from Marine boot camp (Bill), accomplishing the mission as a whole (Adam), experiencing success (Michelle), accomplishing the goal of completing jumpmaster school (Jack), accomplishing tasks (Leticia). In sum, of the 16 focus group members, 8 (50%) of their peak moments of inclusion came within the context of accomplishing a goal. Given the mission-based ethos of military organizations, this makes sense. As such, the direct and indirect

impacts of collective success are worth further study—possibly for consideration as an independent dimension of inclusion. Because civilian leaders often find themselves in highly individualistic organizations, it would be worthwhile to determine the best ways to recognize team members' individual and collective successes. While civilian organizations do occasionally recognize achievements, the recognition and documentation of that recognition pale in comparison with military organizations. For example, in military organizations, service members are awarded ribbons for certain accomplishments which are then displayed on their uniforms daily. In a civilian organization, few even realize who has earned what certifications. Similarly, in military organizations, the list of who has earned the right to be "promotable" is publicly published. In civilian organizations, the potential for upward mobility is not celebrated as visibly.

- **Give service members a chance to shine.** Several focus group participants experienced the strongest feelings of inclusion in their career when they were given an opportunity to draft important correspondence or give presentations to other groups. Be on the lookout for a diverse group of junior service members with strong skills and find opportunities to let them shine. The group should include White males, Latinas, those from the United States, those in various specialties, younger people, and a variety of other people. The advice to be intentional about focusing on a diverse group is to ensure that you do not just choose the same type of service member to showcase out of habit.
- **Be eager to celebrate team members' special accomplishments.** Give team members the respect that they deserve and truly celebrate their accomplishments. The workplace doesn't need more insecure leaders who are threatened by their own people's successes. Foster a spirit of celebration in your team.

- TRUST:

  - **Train and then trust your people to deliver.** Inexperienced and immature service members or employees can cause immense damage: injury, loss of life, or destruction of costly equipment. However, nearly everyone can be trusted to do *something*. Make sure to trust people as early as possible with the small things. Once they show that they can be trusted with small things, systematically endeavor to trust them with incrementally larger tasks. Being able to trust their colleagues and knowing that you trust them makes service members feel included. The experience of being trusted for one's expertise early in one's career (Tom, Lisa, Sara, and Kevin) also resulted in a peak moment of inclusion among my interviewees. As in any career, new organizational members may be discounted because of their lack of seniority or experience. However, in a military organization that, by the nature of its work, has high human and equipment costs for mistakes, being trusted at every stage of one's career is an important ingredient for feeling included.

- **Ask your people what they think . . . and trust what they say.** While your people may not be privy to the high-level strategic information that you and other leaders have, one thing is fairly certain—they are usually closer to the day-to-day work than you are. This gives them a valuable perspective to share when you need to address process gaps, inefficiencies, or solve tactical problems.

- INTRAPERSONAL INCLUSION:
  - **"Do you" first.** Leaders who seek to make their units more inclusive are committed to creating inclusive environments that develop and value service members (regardless of the unique combination of diversity dimensions that comprise their identities and how they manifest themselves socially). It is far more effective to champion inclusion when you have explored your own implicit biases, worked to decrease your diversity- and inclusion-related blind spots, explored your own leadership behaviors and values, and created your own professional development plan to be a stronger, more diversity-savvy, and more inclusive leader. By "doing you" first, you will lead from the front by modeling the inclusive behaviors that you seek to instill in your team.
  - **Tell them why you hired them.** While the intrapersonal dimension of inclusion is internal to employees, leaders' verbal and nonverbal communication greatly influences their members' self-talk. This is seldom more true than when they first join your team. When you add a new team member, be explicit in sharing your assessment of what value they all add to the group. This will let the team members rest assured that they were selected because of the value they bring to the team and to the organization.

- FAIRNESS:
  - **Be fair (equitable).** No one feels included when they perceive that they are being treated unfairly. You will get the best out of people when they perceive a direct correlation between their performance and their rewards. As much as is possible, treat everyone equitably: giving them what they need to be successful. It is also critically important to base rewards on performance.
  - **Be as transparent as possible.** You may be treating people fairly, yet, if they don't perceive that you are treating them fairly, they

will not feel included. Sometimes this is a result of leaders doing a poor job communicating transparently. For instance, if someone doesn't get a promotion and the leader has not explained to the employee the criteria for promotion, the employee may feel "cheated." Like many organizational issues, accurate, consistent, and transparent leadership communication goes a long way toward slowing rumors and creating a sense of inclusion. On the other hand, sometimes you may have to make a decision that is, in the short term, not going to be perceived as fair. Where possible, in these instances, make sure to communicate your decision-making process *and your plans for restoring equity*. Otherwise, you will irrevocably lose the trust of your unit.

## Study Limitations

All studies have limitations and this one is no exception. The chief limitation of this study is its small sample size which prevents generalizability. Focus groups allow researchers to probe deeply into subjective phenomena experienced by research participants. However, this method is not used to create generalizable theory unless it is done over time and with extremely large sample sizes. Future study on the experience of inclusion in military contexts should explore a larger sample size. Another weakness is that these focus groups came from the same program at the same time. Future research should not only cover additional cohorts of this program, it should collect input from service members in both Continental United States (CONUS) and Outside of the Continental United States (OCONUS) locations. Most of the experiences shared in service members' stories did not occur during their experiences in active combat. Though difficult, it would be beneficial to collect peak moments of inclusion from service members during combat—which, is, after all the raison d'être of warfighting organizations.

## References

Brimhall, K. C., Lizano, E. L., & Mor Barak, M. E. (2014). The mediating role of inclusion: A longitudinal study of the effects of leader-member exchange and diversity climate on job satisfaction and intention to leave among child welfare workers. *Children and Youth Services Review*, *40*, 79–88. https://doi.org/10.1016/j.childyouth.2014.03.003

Carmeli, A., Reiter-Palmon, R., & Ziv, E. (2010). Inclusive leadership and employee involvement in creative tasks in the workplace: The mediating role of psychological safety. *Creativity Research Journal*, *22*, 250–260. https://doi.org/10.1080/10400419.2010.504654

Choi, S. B., Tran, T. B. H., & Park, B. I. (2015). Inclusive leadership and work engagement: Mediating roles of affective organizational commitment and

creativity. *Social Behavior and Personality: An International Journal*, *43*(6), 931–943. https://doi.org/10.2224/sbp.2015.43.6.931
de Bruijn, H. (2006). One fight, one team: The 9/11 commission report on intelligence, fragmentation and information. *Public Administration*, *84*(2), 267–287. https://doi.org/10.1111/j.1467-9299.2006.00002.x
Ferdman, B. M. (2014). The practice of inclusion in diverse organizations: Toward a systemic and inclusive framework. In B. M. Ferdman & B. R. Deane (Eds.), *Diversity at work: The practice of inclusion* (pp. 3–54). San Francisco, CA: Jossey-Bass. https://doi.org/10.1002/9781118764282.ch1
Ferdman, B. M., & Davidson, M. N. (2002). Inclusion: What can I and my organization do about it? *The Industrial-Organizational Psychologist*, *39*(4), 80–85.
Ferdman, B. M., & Roberts, L. M. (2014). Creating inclusion for oneself: Knowing, accepting, and expressing one's whole self at work. In B. M. Ferdman & B. R. Deane (Eds.), *Diversity at work: The practice of inclusion* (pp. 93–127). San Francisco, CA: Jossey-Bass. https://doi.org/10.1002/9781118764282.ch3
Galbraith, J., Downey, D., & Kates, A. (2002). *Designing dynamic organizations: A hands-on guide for leaders at all levels*. New York, NY: AMACOM.
Hailey, J. (2008). *Ubuntu: A literature review* [Unpublished Paper]. Tutu Foundation. http://citeseerx.ist.psu.edu/viewdoc/download?doi=10.1.1.459.6489&rep=rep1&type=pdf.
Hollander, E. P. (2009). *Inclusive leadership: The essential leader-follower relationship*. New York, NY: Routledge.
Kotter, J. P. (1990). What leaders really do. *Harvard Business Review*, *68*(3), 103–111.
Kotter, J. P. (2013, January 9). Management is (still) not leadership. *Harvard Business Review Digital Articles*. https://hbr.org/2013/01/management-is-still-not-leadership
Lewis, B. (2010). Forging an understanding of Black humanity through relationship: An Ubuntu perspective. *Black Theology: An International Journal*, *8*(1), 69–85. https://doi.org/10.1558/blth.v8i1.69
Maslow, A. H. (1943). A theory of human motivation. *Psychological Review*, *50*(4), 370–396. https://doi.org/10.1037/h0054346
Miller, H. E., & Terborg, J. R. (1979). Job attitudes of part-time and full-time employees, *Journal of Applied Psychology*, *64*(4), 380–386. https://doi.org/10.1037/0021-9010.64.4.380
Barak, M. E. (2013). *Managing diversity. Toward a globally inclusive workplace* (3rd Ed.). Thousand Oaks, CA: Sage Publications.
Mor Barak, M. E., & Cherin, D. A. (1998). A tool to expand organizational understanding of workforce diversity. *Administration in Social Work*, *22*, 47–64. https://doi.org/10.1300/J147v22n01
Nishii, L. H., & Mayer, D. M. (2009). Do inclusive leaders help to reduce turnover in diverse groups? The moderating role of leader–member exchange in the diversity to turnover relationship. *Journal of Applied Psychology*, *94*(6), 1412–1426. https://doi.org/10.1037/a0017190
Nkomo, S. M. (2014). Inclusion: Old wine in new bottles? In B. M. Ferdman & B. R. Deane (Eds.), *Diversity at work: The practice of inclusion* (pp. 580–592). San Francisco, CA: Jossey-Bass. https://doi.org/10.1002/9781118764282.ch22

Person, S. D., Jordan, C. G., Allison, J. J., Fink Ogawa, L. M., Castillo-Page, L., Conrad, S., ... Plummer, D. L. (2015). Measuring diversity and inclusion in academic medicine: The Diversity Engagement Survey. *Academic Medicine*, *90*(12), 1675–1683. https://doi.org/10.1097/ACM.0000000000000921

Roberson, Q. (2006, April). Disentangling the meanings of diversity and inclusion in organizations. *Group & Organization Management*, *31*(2), 212–236. https://doi.org/10.1177/1059601104273064

Ruggieri, S., Bendixen, M., Gabriel, U., & Alsaker, F. (2013). Cyberball: The impact of ostracism on early adolescents' well-being. *Swiss Journal of Psychology*, 72(2), 103–109. https://doi.org/10.1024/1421-0185/a000103

Smith, J.-E. G. (2002). *From black and white to shades of gray: Exploring differences in diversity learning and development between Black and White graduate students*. [Unpublished Doctoral Dissertation, Case Western Reserve University]. Cleveland, OH. Case Western Reserve University, Cleveland, OH.

Smith, J. G. (2013). *No laughing matter: Interracial and intra - ethnic patterns in "off color" jokes* (Technical Report No. 11–13). Defense Equal Opportunity Management Institute. https://www.deomi.org/DownloadableFiles/research/documents/No-Laughing-Matter-11-13.pdf

Smith, J. G. (2017). The garden: An organismic metaphor for distinguishing inclusion from diversity. *Graziadio Business Review*, *20*(2). https://gbr.pepperdine.edu/2017/08/the-garden-an-organismic-metaphor-for-distinguishing-inclusion-from-diversity

Smith, J. G., & Lindsay, J. B. (2014). *Beyond inclusion: Worklife interconnectedness, energy, and resilience in organizations*. New York, NY: Palgrave Macmillan. https://doi.org/10.1057/9781137385420

Tutu, D. (1999). *No future without forgiveness: A personal overview of South Africa's truth and reconciliation commission*. London, UK: Rider.

U.S. Census Bureau. (2016b). *Annual estimates of the resident population by sex, race, and Hispanic origin for the United States, States, and Counties: April 1, 2010 to July 1, 2016*. U.S. Census Bureau. https://census.gov

U.S. Department of Defense (2015). *2015 demographics: Profile of the military community*. https://download.militaryonesource.mil/12038/MOS/Reports/2015-Demographics-Report.pdf

Wayne, S. J., Shore, L. M., Bommer, W. H., & Tetrick, L. E. (2002). The role of fair treatment and rewards in perceptions of organizational support and leader-member exchange. *Journal of Applied Psychology*, *87*(3), 590–598. https://doi.org/10.1037/0021-9010.87.3.590

# Appendix to Chapter 18

Sample Service Branch Demographics Compared with Total Force Demographics (U.S. Department of Defense, 2015)

| *Category* | *Sample* | *Total Force* |
|---|---|---|
| USA | 37.5% | 20% |
| USAR | 6.25% | 12.6% |
| ANG | 12.5% | 14.4% |
| NAVY | 6.25% | 13.2% |
| USMC | 6.25% | 7.5% |
| USAF | 12.5% | 12.6% |
| AFR | 12.5% | 4.3% |
| Anonymous Branch | 6.25% | 0% |
| Enlisted | 87.5% | 83% |
| Officer | 6.25% | 17% |
| Anonymous | 6.25% | 0% |
| Male | 50% | 83.2% |
| Female | 43.75% | 16.8% |
| Anonymous | 6.25% | 0% |

Demographic Description of Focus Group Participants

| *Pseudonym* | *Gender* | *Ethnicity-1* | *Ethnicity-2* | *Race* | *Most Impactful Identity Group* | *Branch* | *Rank* |
|---|---|---|---|---|---|---|---|
| Tom | Male | Filipino | Japan and Philippines | Asian | Filipino | ANG | E5 |
| Kara | Female | Black | | Black | Female and Black | USAR | E8 |
| Bill | Male | ? | Haiti, Suriname | White | I do not know. | USA | E7 |
| Adam | Male | Pacific Islander | | Mixed | Hawaii | AFR | O2 |
| Jamie | Male | American | Korean | Asian | Career field | USAF | E5 |
| Lisa | Female | Jamaica | Jamaica | Black | | USA | E7 |
| Sara | Female | Mexican | Mexican | Hispanic | Social Class | AFR | E5 |
| Mary | Female | Filipino | Philippines | Asian | | USAF | E6 |
| Beth | Female | Scottish-Irish American | Germany | White | Can't say | ANG | E7 |
| Michelle | Female | American | | Black | Gender/ Race | USA | E7 |
| Jack | Male | American | | White | | USA | E7 |
| Martha | Female | Cuban-American | Germany | Other | Female | USA | E7 |
| Shawn | Male | Black American | | Black | | USN | E7 |
| Leticia | Female | Trinidadian | Trinidad | Black | Female | USA | E7 |
| Kevin | Male | Chinese | China | Asian | Can't think of any | USMC | E7 |
| Chris | | Black | | Black | Gender | ANON | ANON |

# Part IV

# Leadership Practices for Fostering Inclusive Societies

# 19 Inclusion in a Multicultural Society

*Nancy DiTomaso*

Differences among people make a difference when group membership defines life chances, that is, when diversity is overlaid with inequality. Leaders who want to foster inclusiveness at the societal level, therefore, must address intergroup inequality. In other words, leaders who want to contribute to an inclusive society must necessarily engage challenging issues that are at the very foundation of democracy, namely, the relations between majorities and minorities and between dominant and subordinate groups. Viewing diversity as a "valued resource" in which "we value people because of and not despite our differences" (Ferdman, 2017, p. 238) therefore, is a tall order that requires careful understanding of how differences arise, what sustains them, and the points of leverage for successful change.

Research in social psychology has found that once we categorize people into separate groups, we also rank them (Dovidio et al., 2009). Therefore, diversity always involves inequality (DiTomaso et al., 2007), which means that there is often conflict and even violence when group membership is overlaid on social, political, and economic inequality. Because historically the U.S. was both a slave and a settler society, the country has had deep divisions within the population over its history that have invoked substantial scholarship to address issues of how groups can get along with each other (Alba & Nee, 1997; Gordon, 1964; Park, 1930; Waters & Jiménez, 2005). The U.S. addressed its slave past only after fighting a brutal civil war and then experiencing a long struggle for civil rights that is still underway. The country has addressed its settler past, through many waves of immigration that required each new immigrant group to go through stages of incorporation into the society. For newer immigrant groups, incorporation is still a work in progress and a challenging one. In the intergroup relations both around civil rights and immigration, the processes of incorporation into the society are incomplete to the extent that inequality is still group-based.

In earlier conceptualizations about how to overcome intergroup inequality, most analysts have focused on three sets of indicators to determine the degree of progress and the areas for targeted policy: culture, structure, and identification with the society (Alba & Nee, 2003; Gordon, 1964).

Alba and Nee (1997, p. 836) argue that the end goal of intergroup relations should be one where the group to which one belongs does not determine one's place within society, in terms of all forms of participation. Earlier conceptualizations of immigrant incorporation into the larger society defined outcomes in terms of "assimilation," by which was meant that each new immigrant group should ultimately adopt the ways of the dominant group (Gordon, 1964; Park, 1930). This conceptualization was criticized for its encouragement of "Anglo-conformity," which raised questions about whether immigrant groups needed to give up their own cultures to accept and take on that of the dominant group (Alba & Nee, 1997). Most analyses of immigrant histories in the U.S. suggest that despite pressure, including sometimes explicit policy, toward assimilation, most immigrant groups retained symbolic ties to their heritage cultures and the outcome of their participation in U.S. life has been one of blending, more than assimilation as such (Alba, 1999; Kazal, 1995; Waters & Jiménez, 2005; Williams & Ortega, 1990). In a civil rights context, the focus has been on integration more than assimilation, meaning the ability of Blacks to become full participants with Whites; but the concept of integration too has been criticized, among other things because of its failure to sufficiently address the power differences between Whites and Blacks and the gaps in accessibility that have continued with regard to social, political, and economic resources (Chapman, 2014; Glazer, 1993; Handlin, 1966; powell, 2008).

If we assume that inclusiveness requires relative equality in terms of culture, structure, and identification, then we need to consider how each of these might be conceived in a truly inclusive society. Cultural inclusiveness in this context would mean the ability to participate as desired in the patterns of living and to retain symbolic ties to the group of one's origin, without these posing as obstacles to achievement and rewards. The goal, as it is often stated, is for everyone to be able to "bring their whole selves to work" while still being able to work together and without becoming homogeneous by conformity to a dominant group culture. Structural inclusiveness would mean greater equality across groups, with group membership not affecting the ability to achieve leadership positions and to benefit from rewards. In other words, structural inclusiveness requires material inclusion in terms of income and wealth, jobs and education, and organizational position and authority, not just symbolic inclusion. Identificational inclusiveness would involve a sense of common identity across groups and a commitment to common civic engagement. It represents a sense of common fate and working together, perhaps through a superordinate identity, but without erasing or denationalizing the history and social identity of the groups that make up the whole (Park & Burgess, 1921).

This vision of inclusion requires mutual accommodation across group differences, the transformation of thinking and behaving within each group, and a feeling that a common good arises from the interactions and mutual collaboration of those from different backgrounds. In order for inclusiveness in this form to develop, all groups must be represented by and participate in leadership of social institutions that support and regulate society. Ultimately, inclusion must encompass culture, structure, and identity across groups in ways that reduce or eliminate intergroup inequality.

## The Challenges of Inclusive Societies

Such a vision of inclusiveness underlines the point made by Mor Barak (2005) that inclusion is not only about the workplace but must be addressed within the society as a whole and even with regard to the global environment (DiTomaso, 1996). Further, inclusiveness must address not only perspectives, understandings, attitudes, and values, but also representation in key positions, access to resources, and legal rights to make claims on government and to be protected from exploitation. When inequality is group-based and long term, dominant groups are able to codify in law and customs systems that support and reproduce inequality among groups marked as different in terms of race, ethnicity, language, religion, country of origin, and other aspects of difference (Carmichael & Hamilton, 1967; Tilly, 1998). Dominant groups can shape institutions in which the rules of the game favor them whenever challenges arise or whenever disputes require adjudication. Rules of citizenship, civic participation, arrangements for living and working, rights to vote, payment of taxes, the role of churches, access to schools, investments in public works, and control over law enforcement all favor dominant groups, often at the expense of those who are considered as "other." In systems of long-term inequality, the group to which one belongs determines the opportunity to get ahead, receive rewards, and hold leadership positions from one generation to the next (DiTomaso, 2013). When inequality is overlaid with diversity, dominant group members control the most important decision-making positions, wealth, income, and favorable life situations. Further, the institutions built by dominant groups embed logics of action that contribute to the reproduction of privilege for dominant groups and disadvantage for others. As defined by Thorton et al. (2012), logics of action are the "socially constructed, historical patterns of cultural symbols and material practices, including assumptions, values, and beliefs, by which [groups] provide meaning to their daily activity, organize time and space, and reproduce their lives and experiences" (p. 2). Once embedded in institutions, they no longer depend on individual decision-making, because the everyday practices and rules of the game move things in ways that reproduce existing inequality.

To the extent that dominant groups can reproduce their inequality over the long term, then they also take on the role of a normative ingroup for whom cognitive schema associate their members with competence, worthiness, likability, and leadership (Cuddy et al., 2008; Fiske, 2002; Haslam et al., 1999; Hogg & Terry, 2001). Social psychological research has shown that when others observe dominant group members in positions of leadership and authority, and when those members control greater social resources, it reinforces automatic cognitive assumptions that lead to expectations that those who hold such positions are the ones who deserve them (Ridgeway, 2001; Ridgeway et al., 1998). Such cognitive schema become unconscious (or implicit), and they influence decisions about whom to hire, promote, reward, and honor (Banaji et al., 2003; Jost et al., 2009). Importantly, the research on these processes demonstrates that both dominant and subordinate groups inculcate the same lessons about who is competent and worthy, making change even more difficult (Ridgeway, 2001). Challenges to group-based inequality, therefore, require consciousness-raising social movements that support changes in laws and everyday practices (Tajfel & Turner, 1986). Social change almost always requires social movements to question the status quo and bring lawsuits to challenge decision-making. Unless there are social movements to challenge the status quo, dominant group members develop a sense of entitlement and subordinate group members may support things as they are as a process of system justification and belief in a just world, even when it is to their disadvantage (Jost et al., 2004; Lerner, 1980).

Perhaps the greatest challenge to changing intergroup inequality is establishing the legitimacy for doing so. In the history of nation-building in Western Europe, many nation-states were formed from the incorporation of separate groups that had previously been autonomous (Tilly, 1975). As each group was forcibly or voluntarily made part of the nation-state, a homogeneous culture was often enforced as a way to mark nationality (Tilly, 1975). Homogeneous culture helped define citizens of nation-states, and citizenship became a key marker of those who could make claims on the state. Citizenship often carried with it both rights and benefits that were extended as a trade-off for loyalty to the state, including for paying taxes and supporting the military. As Tilly (1975, pp. 24–25) describes it:

> Indeed, building substantial states in much of Europe meant absorbing numerous political units which already exercised significant claims to sovereignty-free cities, principalities, bishoprics, and a variety of other entities. The European state-makers engaged in the work of combining, consolidating, neutralizing, manipulating a tough, complicated, and well-set web of political relations.

According to Malinowski (1941), as long as the tribe-nation (i.e., the ethnic make-up and identification) was coincident with the tribe-state (i.e., the political entity that defined the boundaries of state), conflict would be lessened. But conflict has always arisen along with political instability when the nation-state incorporates multiple groups who do not all have the rights of citizenship and/or who do not share the same cultural expectations and practices. Such circumstances have arisen historically when national boundaries were often drawn by others in geo-political conflict and also have been prevalent when states attempt to extend their boundaries to new territories and groups. But such conflict arises as well when new groups move to existing nation-states, either by choice or by force, when the nation-state includes both citizens and non-citizens, and when there are multiple groups with disparate cultures (Malinowski, 1941; Tilly, 1975).

In the United States, the long history of slavery created a large group of people who were not extended citizenship rights, and, even after emancipation from slavery, their claims to citizenship rights were often limited, questioned, or suppressed. At the same time, immigrants who came as part of the settler society also made claims to citizenship rights and entitlements, leading to frequent periods of conflict with native-born minorities. Thus, the legal status of competing groups comes into play in intergroup relations, and group claims are often contested in both law and practice. Of course, many other societies have faced similar issues, especially as globalization has created greater interdependencies across countries, and as disruptions of many types have led to flows of population across political boundaries into countries for which they have no or limited citizenship claims.

Because different groups within a given society often benefit differentially from the entry of new immigrants, their incorporation is frequently contested in the political arena. Often the attitudes of citizens to immigrants and refugees will depend on the size of the newcomer groups (Blalock, 1967), the extent of the flow (Alba & Nee, 1997; Waters & Jiménez, 2005), and the sense of distance from the cultures of the new groups from those of the groups who are already part of the country (Koopmans, 2013). For example, when the pace of change is slow, group boundaries are relatively stable, and there are gaps in the flow that enable some blending of cultures, then there is likely to be less conflict in intergroup relations. But when change is more rapid, immigrants or refugees become a larger proportion of the population, and there is a constant flow of groups that are very different in their practices and beliefs from the existing population, then conflict is more likely and efforts to forestall incorporation, especially with regard to rights and benefits, become more vigorous. Some research has suggested that settler societies, such as the U.S., Canada, and Australia, have had an easier time incorporating new entrants than countries where populations have been in place for much longer periods of time, although these countries have also had difficulties incorporating immigrant populations (Koopmans, 2013). Further, especially when there are wider differences between the cultures of existing populations and new entrants, then conflict is also more likely. For example, European countries have experienced a much larger proportion of Muslims among migrants to their largely Christian countries than has been the case for the U.S. and other settler societies (Koopmans, 2013). The ability to build inclusive societies becomes more challenging when the legal status of newcomers or those who differ from the dominant group is uncertain, when the populations are larger and constantly growing, and when the cultural distinctiveness of new populations is greater. There are always challenges for leaders who want to facilitate and support inclusiveness in societies, but sometimes those challenges are especially difficult to address.

## The Role of Leaders in an Inclusive Society

Leaders, whether political, civic, or business, have a responsibility to help create an inclusive society through their own attitudes and behaviors, in the pursuit of goals and strategies on behalf of their organizations, and in terms of their roles as influential citizens of the larger society. Inclusive leaders need to be concerned with how their direct actions affect others and also be attentive to the externalities created by the actions of their organizations. Because the conditions for creating an inclusive society require encouragement and support of greater equality among groups, inclusive leadership is a political task as well as a managerial one. Inclusive leadership requires, therefore, skills in "adaptive problems, process orientation, political engagement, and creating and changing structures" (DiTomaso & Hooijberg, 1996, p. 182).

Societies have become more diverse because immigrants fill important roles in a global economy. As countries have become more interdependent in their economic activities, they are of necessity more interdependent as well in terms of government policy with regard to trade, the environment, military threats and alliances, monetary systems, and in many other ways. Each of these factors contributes to the movement of people escaping threats and seeking opportunities, and in doing so, the countries they leave and those they seek out become more tightly interconnected. Although sometimes people are driven out of their countries of origin because of political strife, environmental disaster, or poor economic prospects, they are also sometimes enticed to move to new host countries who need their labor, their talents, and their services. Further, in a period of slow demographic growth in developed countries, immigrants provide a customer base, support aggregate demand, take jobs that would otherwise not be filled, and contribute to innovation. For organizations to thrive, however, they need more than workers and customers; they also need a civic life that is strong and stable, in which conflict between groups does not interfere with learning from and working with others. Inclusive leaders have an important role in bringing about inclusive societies, which can benefit them as citizens, benefit their organizations, and benefit the society, if the challenges of intergroup inequality and potential intergroup conflict can be mitigated. Whether through personal actions, organizational roles, or as citizens, inclusive leaders must be cognizant of their responsibilities to support inclusiveness.

Inclusive leaders also need to model inclusive behavior in their interactions with others and in their decision-making. They need to be inclusive with their own staff members, by facilitating the growth in skills and capacities of all team members and not just favorites who might share the leader's background and characteristics. Inclusive leaders need to offer fair and living wages when they are in positions of authority to make such decisions, and they need to support such decisions on the part of others. Inclusive leaders need to practice tolerance, because it does not necessarily come naturally, and they need to encourage tolerance and acceptance in others. Inclusive leaders need to encourage mutual learning and create opportunities for sharing innovative ideas and facilitating their implementation. Finally, inclusive leaders need to share their voice and use their influence with others in their organizations, in their neighborhoods and communities, in the public square, and by joining social movements that support inclusive goals.

Perhaps most important, inclusive leaders must recognize the challenges that they face in support of inclusive societies, because in the context of long-term inequality that is group-based, there are many entrenched interests who do not want to see resources and power redistributed nor greater openness in access to opportunities. To facilitate a change of heart and change of direction, inclusive leaders must make clear why diversity is a benefit for the society as a whole. As noted, immigrants serve as customers, which supports aggregate demand and prevents economic woes; they provide a labor force, good neighbors, and stable communities; and they contribute to innovation as they start businesses and bring to work new ways of doing things and new ways of thinking. The presence of immigrants also creates cosmopolitan places for people to live, which tends to draw people with a more global perspective and with it more amenities in neighborhoods and communities. To derive such benefits, inclusive leaders must take on a political role to encourage immigration, especially in societies with a declining birth rate in the native population, which is true of most developed countries. In addition to the support of public policies that open the country to immigration, inclusive leaders should also support organizations of and on behalf of immigrants to help them to become full participants in the societies in which they live. Inclusive leaders also need to support legislation that makes the incorporation of immigrants easier and less costly. A further and very important aspect of inclusive leadership is to fight against the exploitation of immigrants. And inclusive leaders can play an important role to help communicate how opening up the society to refugees contributes not only to humanitarian goals, but also to alleviating explosive situations that can reverberate in adverse ways back to the countries that try to keep refugees out.

The ultimate criteria for inclusion is when group membership is no longer correlated with life chances. Inclusiveness means that everyone from whatever group has the opportunity to achieve and prosper, both as members of groups with distinctive histories and holding on to the value of their own heritage as well as being members of a larger society of which they feel a part and in which they participate as equals. Both Park (1930) and Gordon (1964) argued that such inclusiveness would lead to an inevitable, albeit slow, movement toward a common culture, and indeed, there is some evidence to support such predictions (Kuran & Sandholm, 2008). In other words, perhaps, as Weber (1968, p. 932) suggested, inclusiveness in all its dimensions encourages participants from all backgrounds to "dance together."

## References

Alba, R. (1999). Immigration and the American realities of assimilation and multiculturalism. *Sociological Forum*, *14*(1), 3–25. https://doi.org/10.1023/A:1021632626811

Alba, R., & Nee, V. (1997). Rethinking assimilation theory for a new era of immigration. *International Migration Review*, *31*(4), 826–874. https://doi.org/10.1177%2F019791839703100403

Alba, R., & Nee, V. (2003). *Remaking the American mainstream: Assimilation and contemporary immigration*. Cambridge, MA: Harvard University Press.

Banaji, M. R., Bazerman, M. H., & Chugh, D. (2003, December). How (un)ethical are you? *Harvard Business Review*, *81*(12), 56–64.

Blalock, H. M. (1967). *Toward a theory of minority-group relations*. New York, NY: Wiley.

Carmichael, S., & Hamilton, C. V. (1967). *Black power: The politics of liberation*. New York, NY: Vintage Books.

Chapman, T. K. (2014). Is integration a dream deferred? Students of color in majority White suburban schools. *The Journal of Negro Education*, *83*(3), 311–326. https://doi.org/10.7709/jnegroeducation.83.3.0311

Cuddy, A. J. C., Fiske, S. T., & Glick, P. (2008). Warmth and competence as universal dimensions of social perception: The stereotype content model and the bias map. *Advances in Experimental Social Psychology*, *40*, 61–137. https://doi.org/10.1016/S0065-2601(07)00002-0

DiTomaso, N. & Hooijberg, R. (1996). Diversity and the demands of leadership. *The Leadership Quarterly*, *7*(2), 163–187. https://doi.org/10.1016/S1048-9843(96)90039-9

DiTomaso, N. (2013). *The American non-dilemma: Racial inequality without racism*. New York, NY: Russell Sage Foundation.

DiTomaso, N., Post, C., & Parks-Yancy, R. (2007). Workforce diversity and inequality: Power, status, and numbers. *Annual Review of Sociology*, *33*(1), 473–501. https://doi.org/10.1146/annurev.soc.33.040406.131805

Dovidio, J. F., Gaertner, S. L., & Saguy, T. (2009). Commonality and the complexity of "we": Social attitudes and social change. *Personality and Social Psychology Review*, *13*(1), 3–20. https://doi.org/10.1177%2F1088868308326751

Ferdman, B. M. (2017). Paradoxes of inclusion: Understanding and managing the tensions of diversity and multiculturalism. *The Journal of Applied Behavioral Science*, *53*(2), 235–263. https://doi.org/10.1177%2F0021886317702608

Fiske, S. T. (2002). What we know now about bias and intergroup conflict, the problem of the century. *Current Directions in Psychological Science*, *11*(4), 123–128. https://doi.org/10.1111%2F1467-8721.00183

Glazer, N. (1993). Is assimilation dead? *The Annals of the American Academy of Social and Political Sciences*, *530*, 122–136. https://doi.org/10.1177%2F000271629 3530001009

Gordon, M. (1964). *Assimilation in American life*. New York, NY: Oxford University Press.

Handlin, O. (1966). The goals of integration. *Daedalus*, *95*(1), 268–286.

Haslam, S. A., Oakes, P., Reynolds, K. J., & Turner, J. C. (1999). Social identity salience and the emergence of stereotype consensus. *Personality and Social Psychology Bulletin*, *25*, 809–818. https://doi.org/10.1177%2F0146167299025007004

Hogg, M. A., & Terry, D. J. (2001). *Social identity processes in organizational contexts*. Philadelphia, PA: Psychology Press.

Jost, J. T., Banaji, M. R., & Nosek, B. A. (2004). A decade of system justification theory: Accumulated evidence of conscious and unconscious bolstering of the status quo. *Political Psychology*, *25*(6), 881–919. https://doi.org/10.1111/j.1467-9221.2004.00402.x

Jost, J. T., Rudman, L. A., Blair, I. V., Carney, D. R., Dasgupta, N., Glaser, J., & Hardin, C. D. (2009). The existence of implicit bias is beyond reasonable doubt: A refutation of ideological and methodological objections and executive summary of ten studies that no manager should ignore. *Research in Organizational Behavior*, *29*, 39–69. https://doi.org/10.1016/j.riob.2009.10.001

Kazal, R. (1995). Revisiting assimilation: The rise, fall, and reappraisal of a concept in American ethnic history. *American Historical Review*, *100*, 437–472. https://doi.org/10.1086/ahr/100.2.437

Koopmans, R. (2013). Multiculturalism and immigration: A contested field in cross-national comparison. *Annual Review of Sociology*, *39*, 147–169. https://doi.org/10.1146/annurev-soc-071312-145630

Kuran, T., & Sandholm, W. H. (2008). Cultural integration and its discontents. *The Review of Economic Studies*, *75*(1), 201–228. https://doi.org/10.1111/j.1467-937X.2007.00469.x

Lerner, M. J. (1980). *The belief in a just world: A fundamental delusion*. New York, NY: Plenum.

Malinowski, B. (1941). An anthropological analysis of war. *American Journal of Sociology*, *46*, 521–550. https://doi.org/10.1086/218697

Mor Barak, M. E. (2005). *Managing diversity: Toward a globally inclusive workplace*. Thousand Oaks, CA: Sage.

Park, R. E. (1930). Assimilation, social. In E. Seligman & A. Johnson (Eds.), *Encyclopedia of the social sciences* (Vol. 2, pp. 281–283). New York, NY: Macmillan.

Park, R. E., & Burgess, E. W. (1921). *Introduction to the science of sociology*. Chicago, IL: University of Chicago Press.

powell, j. a. (2008). Is integration possible? *Race, Poverty & the Environment, 15*(2), 42–44.

Ridgeway, C. L. (2001). The emergence of status beliefs: From structural inequality to legitimizing ideology. In J. T. Jost & B. Major (Eds.), *The psychology of legitimacy* (pp. 257–277). Cambridge, UK: Cambridge University Press.

Ridgeway, C. L., Boyle, E. H., Kuipers, K. J., & Robinson, D. T. (1998). How do status beliefs develop? The role of resources and interactional experiences. *American Sociological Review*, *63*(3), 331–350. https://doi.org/10.2307/2657553

Tajfel, H., & Turner, J. C. (1986). The social identity theory of intergroup behavior. In S. A. Worchel & W. G. Austin (Ed.), *The social psychology of intergroup relations* (pp. 7–24). Chicago, IL: Nelson Hall.

Thorton, P. H., Ocasio, W., & Lounsbury, M. (2012). *The institutional logics perspective: A new approach to culture, structure, and processes*. Oxford, UK: Oxford University Press.

Tilly, C. (Ed.). (1975). *The formation of nation states in Western Europe*. Princeton, NJ: Princeton University Press.

Tilly, C. (1998). *Durable inequality*. Berkeley, CA: University of California Press.

Waters, M. C., & Jiménez, T. R. (2005). Assessing immigrant assimilation: New empirical and theoretical challenges. *Annual Review of Sociology*, *31*, 105–125. https://doi.org/10.1146/annurev.soc.29.010202.100026

Weber, M. (1968). *Economy and society* (G. Roth & C. Wittich, Trans.). New York, NY: Bedminister Press.

Williams, J. A., Jr., & Ortega, S. T. (1990). Dimensions of ethnic assimilation: An empirical appraisal of Gordon's typology. *Social Science Quarterly*, *71*(4), 697–710.

# 20 Leadership Excellence in a Pluralistic Society

## The Role of Identity and Inclusive Leadership

*Daryl G. Smith*

The phrase *inclusive leadership* can suggest that leaders disregard difference and simply "include" everyone, regardless of their identities. What we are now learning, in a way that can seem paradoxical, is that inclusive leadership requires attending to the diversity of identities in institutional contexts. When done well, emphasizing identities in the ways described in this chapter actually facilitates healthy communities. But this requires addressing the role of identity quite intentionally. Technology changes over the last decades have required that leaders, community members, and institutions pay attention to building their capacity to accommodate the increasing role of technology. Leadership development in this area requires constant learning and the recognition that fundamental changes will be required. Similarly, creating inclusive institutions also requires intentional and ongoing capacity building. Yet much of the past literature on leadership has paid little attention to what capacity building might require. Some authors have paid attention to women's leadership, or adding "diverse" leaders. Implicit bias research (e.g., Greenwald, 2008) has focused on the challenges of identifying talent from a diversity perspective as well as illuminating the embedded ways in which bias is present regardless of an individual's own identity. In this chapter I focus on the emerging work on identity and its implications for leaders, communities, and institutions. While largely conceptual in nature, understanding the role of identity in general and one's own identity in the context of the group or institution is critical for creating inclusive environments (Smith, 2020).

In addition to the focus on race and gender, most institutions today have a growing list of identities meant to represent inclusiveness. These include ethnicity, sexual orientation, ability, class, and national origin. National events and international crises have elevated attention to immigrants, undocumented students, and religion, and, as we better understand the complexities of gender, increased attention to gender identity.

In contrast, much of the literature on leadership refers to leaders generically without much attention to their identities. And even in the growing literature on inclusion, less attention is paid to how individual and institutional identities impact strategies for change. Thus, neither a laundry list of relevant identities or a generic approach to change will suffice as individuals and institutions grapple with creating thriving communities in increasingly pluralistic contexts. How do we need to think about the complexity and dynamic quality of identity and what implications might this have for leadership and the development of inclusive leaders?

One very obvious question is whether attending to diversity contradicts efforts to create inclusive environments. Is an emphasis on diversity necessarily divisive? Would it be better to downplay identity groupings based on culture and religion? Would it be better to minimize ascribed identities such as race, gender, and ethnicity? As identity gets more multifaceted and complex, one can understand why some think we should not pay attention to identity at the societal level. This is the appeal of color blindness. We are happy to appreciate and celebrate the diversity of individuals and groups as long as at the institutional or societal level things are "neutral" (Markus et al., 2002; Yoshino, 2006). Unfortunately, continuing inequities in society make serious discussion of neutrality with respect to identity much more problematic (Eagly et al., 2004; Wise, 2006). As Gutman (2003, pp. 133, 137) points out: "Socially salient parts of people's identities, such as their color, gender and physical disabilities, shape their interests and their interests in turn shape their identities." She notes, further, that, "the fewer the alternative means of representation available to disadvantaged individuals, the more powerful an ascriptive association is." In other words, until there is significant diversity, identity will remain salient.

Diversity can be divisive when societies and institutions do not attempt to create the conditions for inclusive and equitable institutions. Current research suggests that rather than downplaying identity, a more powerful strategy for society and institutions would be to build on the multiplicities of identities and allow individuals to look at the similarities and differences across them as well as the social context in which identities emerge (Brewer, 2000; Crisp & Hewstone, 2007). To do that requires building institutions that signal and manifest diversity in its culture. For leaders, framing diversity in such a way as to acknowledge salient identities and to build healthy communities is an important component of building capacity for excellence.

## How Particular Identities Emerge as Salient in National Contexts

One of the first concepts to understand is how particular identities emerge as salient. Human diversity takes many forms—personality, points of view, part of the country, appearance, to name but a few. However, the focus of identities in the context of diversity and inclusion is the social, political, and historical context in which they emerge (Chin & Sanchez-Hucles, 2007; Crisp & Hewstone, 2007). As Cole (2009) notes: "Categories such as race, gender, social class and sexuality do not simply describe groups that may be different or similar; they encapsulate historical and continuing relations of political, material social inequality and stigma" (p. 173). Inclusive leadership requires understanding the historical, political, and structural elements of identity because these will have significance for a leader's ability to establish credibility and also to contribute to the professional development of one's constituents.

## Multiple and Intersecting Identities Create Opportunities for Building Healthy Groups

Though early literature in psychology emphasized the development of identity as a single coherent concept, the scholarship in ethnic and women's studies, especially, began to emphasize the multiplicity of identities (Ali, 2003; Anzaldúa, 2002; Cole, 2009; Collins, 2000; Espiritu, 1997; Hull et al., 1982; Omi, 2001; Torres et al., 2003). The study of intersectionality emerged in the literature on international human rights (Crenshaw, 1994) and is now understood to be critical for understanding the interrelationships among identities for both theoretical and practical reasons. In being asked to separate the salience of race from gender, Higginbotham (1993) complained "race only comes up when we talk about African Americans and other people of color. Gender only comes up when we talk about women, and class only comes up when we talk about the poor and working class" (p. 14). Moreover, as Hall (1996) has noted, "The essential issues of race always appear historically in articulation, in a formation, with other categories and divisions and are constantly crossed and re crossed by categories of class, of gender, and ethnicity" (p. 144).

Clearly, then, while current discourse on diversity suggests identities are static, they are not. The concept of identity becomes dynamic and complex when taking into account the interplay of context, multiplicity, and inequity. As Symington (2004) suggests, "people live multiple, layered identities derived from social relations, history, and the operation of structures of power. People are members of more than one community at the same time, and, can simultaneously experience oppression and privilege" (p. 2). Moreover, experiencing both privilege and inequity can lead to behaviors that are contradictory. Frankenberg (1993), for example, describes the ways in which White women in the U.S. experience gender, and then do or do not address race. The inability or unwillingness to learn from inequity through the lens of one identity and create alliances across identities can create greater distrust and divisiveness and inhibit the creation of a strong institutional identity around the mission. Inclusive leadership requires understanding this complexity within and between groups and also creates opportunities to build healthy communities in which this complexity is emphasized, not erased.

## Being Inclusive Requires Understanding that Issues of Identity Must Also Be Differentiated

The list of salient identities that emerge from discussions of inclusion often results in another form of generic discussions where work on comfortable issues seems to suggest progress on "diversity and inclusion." What is critical to understand is that the issues and structural concerns that emerge from each identity might overlap but are also distinctive. Discussions about gender identity often focus on access to bathrooms, changing names, and climate. Inclusive leaders have to be able to address each and all while at the same time making sure that the unfinished business of race in terms of access, hiring, selection for leadership, and culture and climate is not lost.

## Identities Reflect Asymmetrical Power Structures

Another significant concept in the study of identity is asymmetry. A person in a subordinate position experiences identity quite differently than a person in a dominant position. The experience of identity, when it intersects with privilege or inequity, is likely to be *asymmetrical* depending on where one is positioned socially. Holland et al. (1998) describe this positionality from the following perspective: "Social position has to do with entitlement to social and material resources and so to the higher deference, respect, and legitimacy accorded to those genders, races, ethnic groups, castes, and sexualities privileged by society" (p. 271). Although one may experience power in the context of one aspect of one's identity, one may experience inequity in another. The complexity of being a man or woman of color as CEO, for example, reflects this complexity. Leaders who, themselves, are members of underrepresented groups are positioned differently than a White man or even a White woman.

## Comprehensiveness

In addition to multiplicity, intersectionality, and asymmetry, the literature on identity emphasizes that, for any given individual, single—or multiple—sets of identities are not *comprehensive* descriptors for the person. In addressing concepts of identity, one has to be careful not to *essentialize* the identity—to attribute to the individual the general descriptions associated with the group. Assuming all women are caring, empathetic, and collaborative is an example of essentializing. This distinction is important both for the language used in writing about identity and also for avoiding the tendency to stereotype individuals, even when it is well intentioned.

The concept of identity today is a paradox. As it grows in complexity, the meaning of any single identity becomes less clear. At the same time, identity has powerful meaning because of its social salience. Fried (1995) aptly describes the paradox with respect to race: "Biologically race is an illusion. Sociologically it is a pervasive phenomenon" (p. 6). Thus, the personal meaning of identity may be highly individualized at the same time that the social salience of race, gender, sexuality, emerges for groups as very significant (e.g., Mukhopadhyay et al., 2007; Smedley & Smedley, 2005). Communicating one's own recognition of identity without suggesting that a leader "knows" the individual is a critical skill in recognizing the salience of identity.

## Institutions Also Have Embedded Identities that Leaders Will Need to Navigate

Institutionally, identity is not simply a matter of the current membership of the institution and access to the institution. As with individuals and groups described in the prior sections, identity in institutions has many sources, takes multiple forms, is not comprehensive in capturing all characteristics of the institution, and is very much shaped by context. Institutions reflect the cultures, norms, values, and practices of the people in the institution and from the historical and social circumstances in which institutions emerge. Thus, they also reflect the stratification and values of the larger society. Institutional patterns in particular can be shaped by history, by location, and by mission. The art, architecture, accessibility, statements of mission, descriptions of history, and values all contribute to how institutions are seen and perceived.

## Institutional Culture

Institutional culture represents one of the deepest and most important elements of how institutions admit, value, and reward people, and even how institutions are designed. Thus, institutional transformation inevitably requires elements of culture change. As with individuals and groups, the questions an institution asks often reflect deeply held values: *How is excellence defined? Who does our institution serve? What defines "merit?" How should selection be practiced? What defines a family? What kind of knowledge is important? What do different forms of expression mean and what is appropriate? How do we engage with our history?*

For individual leaders or groups whose identities align significantly with the cultural identity of the institution, there is commonly a lack of awareness of certain salient features of institutional culture that appear to exclude. Institutional and societal norms become *invisible*. The institution can appear to be a neutral, cultureless place whose values and practices are, simply, the way "one does business," and where "individuals are treated as individuals." Inevitably, then, these practices are translated into definitions of excellence that reward some groups and not others. Acceptable ways of working, dressing, talking, and even wearing one's hair, are translated from cultural norms to acceptable work norms quite easily. In some institutions, to be successful, people must align with dominant ways of speaking and language choice, must come from certain schools, or must even conform to how emotions are expressed. Bertrand and Mullainathan's (2004) research on hiring in the U.S. suggests that a name that is "too Black" or "too ethnic" can impact search processes. The research on hiring practices demonstrates that most people in an institution tend to hire people like themselves and, significantly, perceive that those most like themselves are the most qualified (Elliott & Smith, 2004).

Moreover, the recent attention to the long histories of harassment and pay gaps for women suggest how deeply these issues go. Early airbags were developed around design assumptions that presumed passengers to be the height of the average man, an assumption that led to airbags being a danger, rather than a safeguard, for many women and children and, of course, to smaller men. These devices were developed in institutional contexts focused on engineering and design. Yet, without attention to the diversity of passengers, one could hardly call these designs excellent. Even today, science is associated with a culture of maleness that continues to be an impediment to opening science up for women at all levels (Rees, 2005; Tobin & Roth, 2007; Valian, 2000, 2005). Inclusive leadership requires an openness to these issues, and a willingness to learn how the institution is experienced. For increasing numbers of companies, identity interest groups become a source of valuable information and perspectives. Surrounding oneself with diverse groups will help ensure that blindness to embedded assumptions and values that might not serve the institution would be minimized.

Deciding what is essential to fulfill institutional purposes is a necessary part of any institution. What makes something a form of institutional *inequity* is when it limits access, success, or participation by individuals or groups who would otherwise be successful. How to navigate often competing mandates from communities and groups is an essential component of inclusive leadership and requires deep understanding of the underlying issues and history.

## Experiencing Institutions

The literature on the experiences of individuals and groups that have been historically marginalized in institutions, or, more accurately, find themselves in institutional cultures where their identities are marginalized, covers a number of areas. The first is being in what are perceived to be hostile or threatening environments. There are many examples, large and small, where even in spite of inclusive rhetoric, people experience their identity as not welcomed or valued and where efforts to participate may be invalidated. A robust body of literature addresses the experience of *stigma*, often associated with exclusion, harassment, and denial of resources (Beatty & Kirby, 2006; Konrad, 2003; Van der Vegt et al., 2006). Being stigmatized can have powerful implications for identity, for relationships with others, and for feelings of competence and even for performance (Davies et al., 2002; Inzlicht & Good, 2006; Levin & van Laar, 2006).

Depending on the environment and history of the institution, there may even be the perception of threat. For instance, to be gay or lesbian in sports may be to experience a constant fear of discovery. To be a Muslim post-9/11 is to wonder how one is seen. To be sure, many African Americans move through their days with heightened vigilance in institutions where racist incidents are common or where there are few people from diverse backgrounds. Threat can also take the form of wondering whether the institution with its cultural norms and practices truly welcomes the perspective of someone from the outside. Is it really okay to criticize the assumptions behind a dress code? Can a gay man put pictures of his husband on his desk? Will a person be viewed negatively if she or he reports racist incidents? Why is there a common understanding among women of the times when one speaks and no one seems to listen?

The large body of literature that describes patterns of response to stigma would probably resonate with most people who are part of stigmatized groups. These include vigilance, stifling complaints, withdrawal, and if the stigmatized identity is concealable, concealment. As Crocker and Garcia (2006, p. 288) note, "The stigmatized often feel caught between two alternatives—confront or overlook prejudice—each of which has undesirable consequences."

The growing literature on *microaggressions* suggests that many of the experiences associated with discrimination do not take the form of major affronts. Rather they are smaller incidents that occur, perhaps unconsciously on the part of the other person, but which are experienced by minorities as insulting, degrading, or potentially threatening. A 2007 review of the literature in the *American Psychologist* reflects the growing importance and patterns of interaction related to microaggressions (Sue et al., 2007).

Identity is particularly relevant when an individual is a token, one of a few in an organization with a particular identity that is salient (Agars, 2004; Kanter, 1977; Yoder, 2002). A central tenet of tokenism is that a person becomes visible as a representative of the group but invisible as an individual. That is why diversity in composition is so critical. Those in token positions may experience a limitation of roles and a restricted range of acceptable behaviors: increased pressure to perform, threats to performance, lack of access to important informational and social networks, and stereotypes (Inzlicht & Good, 2006; Kanter, 1977). The paradox of being in senior leadership and being a token requires complex skills of navigation. The first Black man to lead a historically White university is highly visible racially and as such he will be studied and watched. Consequently, his successes and failures will often be attributed to the salience of race. However, the fact that he is an individual who carries with him the same range of strengths, weaknesses, and characteristics that others carry, irrespective of race, will be considered far less often. As a result, his failure or success will take on huge significance for the group (i.e., African Americans) while placing an extra burden on him as an individual. Sweeping generalizations and conclusions are not made about White males from privileged backgrounds because their sheer number in the upper echelons allows any one individual to be just that—an individual White man who possesses individual strengths and weaknesses. The complexity of position and identity is reflected in this example. As the literature suggests, simply being a CEO from a non-dominant group does not eradicate the issues addressed here. Navigating identity, addressing institutional fears about change, challenging institutional culture, implicit bias, assumptions about competence, and expectations from one's community that change will occur faster than it can, require a clear sense of one's own identity, strong and diverse networks of support, and clear ability to communicate mission and values in ways that resonate.

Being the token can occur for anyone—a White man in nursing for example. However, Yoder and Schleicher (1996) have found that the impact on the individual and the dynamics in the organization vary considerably with gender role violations and are asymmetrical. A man's experience in a woman's field is asymmetrical to a woman in a man's field. Here the status of the field and gender interact. Their research results suggest a much more positive experience for a man in nursing than for a woman in engineering. In one study, for example, women in engineering were seen as less likeable, less attractive, and, significantly, more distanced from colleagues. In nursing, in contrast, men experienced less hostility and were more accepted as a "nontraditional person." Thus, while being "the only one" could apply to anyone, the dynamics vary and are asymmetrical depending on social norms, status, and expectations in society (Fagenson, 1993; Richard, 2000; Richard et al., 2002; Riordan & Shore 1997; Yoder, 2002). This perspective alone has implications for the studies of leadership and the situation of tokens in leadership positions.

Part of the challenge of change in institutional culture is to be able to differentiate between those things that should remain and those things that should change to provide greater inclusivity. The inclusive leadership challenge is to lead a process in which the institution can discern what should change and what should not. In addition, when institutions make changes that seem to address particular identity groups, it has often turned out to improve institutional environments more generally.

Family-friendly policies that were originally introduced as "women's issues" have actually been positive for men as well. It appears that unless institutions understand these investments as being in the best interests of the institution, there will be considerable resistance to making significant changes.

Amartya Sen (2006, p. xiv), a Nobel-Prize-winning economist, notes:

> The hope of harmony in the contemporary world lies in a clearer understanding of the pluralities of human identity, and in the appreciation that they cut across each other and work against a sharp separation along one single hardened line of impenetrable division.

A complex understanding of identity, then, is essential not only for creating excellent institutions that work but also for developing an adequate knowledge base for framing research, policy, and practice related to diversity and institutional transformation. Developing the capacity for inclusive leadership in pluralistic societies will need to be developed intentionally with recognition that who we are, how we are seen, and the context in which we lead will require the development of skills to cross borders, the ability to bring people together, and the skills to create diverse teams that trust and engage with one another for the sake of institutional excellence.

## Implications for Practice

The implications for leaders and for leadership development center on building competency, experience, and knowledge related to inclusion. Each of these items relate to the understanding of identity and its relationship to the practice of inclusive leadership.

1. The ability to navigate the complexity of identity and to understand the significance of one's own identity in a particular context and the salience of identities for institutional mission is critical. A White male may need to establish trust with respect to a commitment to diversity and inclusion. At the same time, the first woman of color appointed to a leadership position may find that she is constrained and has to be strategic about creating change for inclusion using networks, establishing trust, creating diverse teams, and linking mission and excellence to diversity and inclusion.
2. As with understanding one's own identity and its implications, leaders must be willing to understand the institutional context—the history of the institution, its culture and mission in relation to diversity. We see today that fields like technology are having to grapple with cultures, practices, and values that place excellence at risk because of patterns that have not been interrupted.
3. Leaders must help make sure that institutional practices with respect to inclusion are directly linked to its mission, viability, credibility,

and excellence. For such institutions, diversity and inclusion, like technology, must be viewed as imperatives and as critical to the success of the institution for everyone. Practices for identifying talent from diverse groups cannot be seen as a bureaucratic practice or a legalistic one, for example.

4 As with any other critical dimension of leadership, leaders have to be able to establish where progress has been made and where more progress is needed. Intelligent metrics that can illuminate patterns in hiring, promotion, retention, and satisfaction for different identity groups, for example, are essential for creating change. This means focusing not just on representation (though it is critical) but also on culture, climate, and capacity building at all levels of the institution. While revealing the truth about the status of diversity and inclusion can be difficult, honest communication by leaders sets a tone and creates expectations throughout the institution.
5 Building trust and creating leadership teams throughout the institution where difficult dialogues can occur is essential. Too many teams today lack diversity of perspectives or fail to empower people to contribute in ways that in the end produce less than satisfactory decisions.
6 Facilitating communication across and within identity groups is important. Many institutions today have formed identity-based groups not only to support individuals but also to provide feedback to leaders. Engaging with and empowering such groups can be essential for effective communication and also for much needed perspectives.

Developing the ability to cross boundaries requires understanding the role of identities, the ability to understand one's context, and the knowledge of the impact of one's own identities. Developing leaders in and for a pluralistic society will require intentional capacity building that is deep, embedded, and continual.

## References

Agars, M. D. (2004). Reconsidering the impact of gender stereotypes for the advancement of women in organizations. *Psychology of Women Quarterly*, *28*(2), 103–111. https://doi.org/10.1111%2Fj.1471-6402.2004.00127.x

Ali, S. (2003). *Mixed-race, post-race: Gender, new ethnicities and cultural practices*. Oxford, UK: Berg Publishers.

Anzaldúa, G. E. (2002, October 11). Beyond traditional notions of identity. *Chronicle of Higher Education*, *49*(7), B11.

Beatty, J. E., & Kirby, S. L. (2006). Beyond the legal environment: How stigma influences invisible identity groups in the workplace. *Employee Responsibilities and Rights Journal*, *18*(1), 29–44. https://doi.org/10.1007/s10672-005-9003-6

Bertrand, M., & Mullainathan, S. (2004). Are Emily and Greg more employable than Lakisha and Jamal? A field experiment on labor market discrimination. *American Economic Review*, *94*(4), 991–1013. https://doi.org/10.3386/w9873

Brewer, M. B. (2000). Reducing prejudice through cross categorization: Effects of multiple social identities. In S. Oskamp (Ed.), *Reducing prejudice and discrimination* (pp. 165–184). Mahlwah, NJ: Erlbaum.

Chin, J. L., & Sanchez-Hucles, J. (2007). Diversity and leadership. *American Psychologist*, *62*(6), 608–609.

Cole, E. R. (2009). Intersectionality and research in psychology. *American Psychologist*, *64*(3), 170–180. https://doi.org/10.1037/a0014564

Collins, P. H. (2000). Toward a new vision: Race, class and gender as categories of analysis and connection. In M. Adams, W. J. Blumenfeld, C. Castañeda, H. W. Hackman, M. L. Peters, & X. Zúñiga (Eds.), *Readings for diversity and social justice: An anthology on racism, antisemitism, sexism, heterosexism, ableism, and classism* (pp. 457–462). New York, NY: Routledge.

Crenshaw, K. W. (1994). Mapping the margins: Intersectionality, identity politics, and violence against women of color. In M. A. Fineman & R. Mykitiuk (Eds.), *The public nature of private violence: The discovery of domestic abuse* (pp. 93–118). New York, NY: Routledge.

Crisp, R. J., & Hewstone, M. (2007). Multiple social categorization. In M. P. Zanna (Ed.), *Advances in experimental social psychology* (Vol. 39, pp. 163–254). Orlando, FL: Academic Press. https://doi.org/10.1016/S0065-2601(06)39004-1

Crocker, J. & Garcia, J. A. (2006). Stigma and the social basis of the self: A synthesis. In S. Levin & C. van Laar (Eds.), *Stigma and group inequality* (pp. 287–308). Mahwah, NJ: Erlbaum.

Davies, P. G., Spencer, S. J., Quinn, D. M., & Gerhardstein, R. (2002). Consuming images: How television commercials that elicit stereotype threat can restrain women academically and professionally. *Personality and Social Psychology Bulletin*, *28*, 1615–1628. https://doi.org/10.1177/014616702237644

Eagly, A. H., Baron, R. M., & Hamilton, V. L. (Eds.). (2004). *The social psychology of group identity and social conflict*. Washington, DC: American Psychological Association.

Elliott, J. R., & Smith, R. A. (2004). Race, gender, and workplace power. *American Sociological Review*, *69*(3), 365–386. https://doi.org/10.1177/000312240406900303

Espiritu,Y. L. (1997). *Asian American women and men: Labor, laws, and love*. Thousand Oaks, CA: Sage.

Fagenson E. A. (1993). Is what's good for the goose also good for the gander? On being White and male in a diverse workforce. *Academy of Management Executive*, 7(4), 80–82. https://doi.org/10.5465/ame.1993.9503103236

Frankenberg, R. (1993). *White women, race matters: The social construction of whiteness*. Minneapolis, MN: University of Minnesota Press.

Fried, J. (1995). *Shifting paradigms for student affairs: Culture, context, teaching, and learning*. Alexandria, VA: American College Personnel Association.

Greenwald, A. G. (2008). Understanding and using the Implicit Association Test: III. Meta-analysis of predictive validity. *Journal of Personality and Social Psychology*, *97*(1), 17–41.

Gutman, A. (2003). *Identity in democracy*. Princeton, NJ: Princeton University Press.

Hall, S. (1996). New ethnicities. In D. Morley, & K.-H. Chen (Eds.), *Stuart Hall: Critical dialogues in cultural studies* (pp. 441–449). New York, NY: Routledge.

Higginbotham, E. (1993). Sociology and the multicultural curriculum: The challenges of the 1990s and beyond. *Race, Sex, and Class, 1*, 13–24.

Holland, D., Lachicotte, Q., Jr., Skinner, D., & Cain, C. (1998). *Identity and agency in cultural worlds*. Cambridge, MA: Harvard University Press.

Hull, G. T., Scott, P. B., & Smith, B. (Eds). (1982). *All the women are White, all the Blacks are men but some of us are brave: Black women's studies*. New York, NY: Feminist Press.

Inzlicht, M., & Good, C. (2006). How environments can threaten academic performance, self knowledge, and sense of belonging. In S. Levin & C. V. van Laar (Eds.), *Stigma and group inequality* (pp. 129–150). Mahwah, NJ: Lawrence Erlbaum.

Kanter, R. M. (1977). Some effects of proportions on group life: Skewed sex ratios and responses to token women. *American Journal of Sociology, 5*, 965–990. https://doi.org/10.1086/226425

Konrad, A. (2003). Defining the domain of workplace diversity scholarship. *Group and Organization Management, 28*(1), 4–17. https://doi.org/10.1177%2F1059601102250013

Levin, S., & van Laar, C. (Eds.). (2006). *Stigma and group inequality*. Mahwah, NJ: Erlbaum.

Markus, H. R., Steele, C. M., & Steele, D. M. (2002). Colorblindness as a barrier to inclusion: Assimilation and nonimmigrant minorities. In R. A. Shweder, M. Minow, & H. R. Markus (Eds.), *Engaging cultural differences: The multicultural challenge in liberal democracies* (pp. 453–472). New York, NY: Russell Sage Foundation.

Mukhopadhyay, C. C., Henze, R., & Moses, Y. T. (2007). *Race, culture, and biology: An educator's sourcebook*. New York, NY: Rowman and Littlefield.

Omi, M. A. (2001). The changing meaning of race. In N. J. Smelser, W. J. Wilson, & F. Mitchell (Eds.), *America becoming: Racial trends and their consequences* (Vol. 1, pp. 243–263). Washington, DC: National Academy Press.

Rees, T. (2005). Pushing the gender equality agenda forward in the European Union. In M. Sagaria (Ed.), *Women, universities, and change: Gender equality in the European Union and the United States* (pp. 7–22). New York, NY: Palgrave Macmillan.

Richard, O. C. (2000). Racial diversity, business strategy, and firm performance: A resource-based review. *Academy of Management Journal, 43*(2), 164–177. https://doi.org/10.5465/1556374

Richard, O. C., Kochan, T. C., & McMillan-Capehart, A. (2002). The impact of visible diversity on organizational effectiveness: Disclosing the contents in Pandora's black box. *Journal of Business and Management, 8*(3), 1–26.

Riordan, C. M., & Shore, L. M. (1997). Demographic diversity and employee attitudes: An empirical examination of relational demography within work units. *Journal of Appplied Psychology, 82*, 342–358. https://doi.org/10.1037/0021-9010.82.3.342

Sen, A. F. (2006). *Identity and violence: The illusion of destiny*. New York, NY: W.W. Norton.

Smedley, A., & Smedley, B. (2005). Race as biology is fiction: Racism as social problem is real. *American Psychologist, 60*(1), 16–26. https://doi.org/10.1037/0003-066X.60.1.16

Smith, D. G. (2020). *Diversity's promise for higher education: Making it work* (3rd ed.). Baltimore, MD: The Johns Hopkins University Press.

Sue, D. W., Capodilupo, C. M., Torino, G. C., Bucceri, J. M., Holder, A. M. B., Nadal, K. L., & Esquilin, M. (2007). Racial microaggressions in everyday life: Implications for clinical practice. *American Psychologist*, *62*(4), 271–286. https://doi.org/10.1037/0003-066X.62.4.271

Symington, A. (2004, August). Intersectionality: A tool for gender and economic justice. *Women's Rights & Economic Change* (No. 9), Association for Women in Development. https://www.awid.org/sites/default/files/atoms/files/intersectionality_a_tool_for_gender_and_economic_justice.pdf

Tobin, K., & Roth, W. M. (Eds). (2007). *The culture of science education. New directions in mathematics and science education*. Rotterdam, The Netherlands: Sense Publishers.

Torres, V., Howard-Hamilton, M. F., & Cooper, D. L. (2003). Identity development of diverse populations: Implications for teaching and administration in higher education. *ASHE-ERIC Higher Education Report*, *29*(6).

Valian, V. (2000). *Why so slow? The advancement of women*. Cambridge, MA: MIT Press.

Valian, V. (2005). Beyond gender schemas: Improving the advancement of women in academia. *Hypatia*, *20*(3), 198–213. https://doi.org/10.1111/j.1527-2001.2005.tb00495.x

Van der Vegt, G. S., Bunderson, J. S., & Oosterhof, A. (2006). Expertness diversity and interpersonal helping in teams: Why those who need the most help end up getting it least. *Academy of Management Journal*, *49*(5), 877–893. https://doi.org/10.5465/amj.2006.22798169

Wise, T. (2006). Whites swim in racial preferences. In C. W. Hartman (Ed.), *Poverty and race in America: The emerging agendas* (pp. 3–6). Langham, MD: Lexington.

Yoder, J. D. (2002). Context matters: Understanding tokenism processes and their impact on women's work. *Psychology of Women Quarterly*, *26*, 1–8. https://doi.org/10.1111%2F1471-6402.00038

Yoder, J. D., & Schleicher, T. L. (1996). Undergraduates regard deviation from occupational gender stereotypes as costly for women. *Sex Roles*, *35*, 389–400. https://doi.org/10.1007/BF01544294

Yoshino, K. (2006). *Covering: The hidden assault on our civil rights*. New York, NY: Random House.

# 21 Inclusive Leadership

## Essential to Reviving Civil Discourse in a Healthy Democracy

*Carolyn J. Lukensmeyer and Lars Hasselblad Torres*

We live in an extraordinary time, a time that has a collective leadership challenge more urgent to our survival than most of us have known in our lifetimes. Our moment is that much more remarkable for the infectious degradation of political language at the precise time when the words we speak to one another could be the most powerful force to unite us as we confront the challenges we face together.

This chapter summarizes insights from the research and practice of the National Institute for Civil Discourse (NICD) to define and support inclusive leadership through healthy political and public discourse. Discourse that unites communities and nations alike is expansive, it is inclusive in its ability to reach each one of us as human beings, and it is specific enough to direct us toward common goals and common action. Our political language can be the currency with which bonds of trust and cooperation are built; it can equally be the tool that chips away at our mutual ties and sense of purpose as a people.

Stepping back, how would you assess the health of democracy where you live? Would it be the caliber of your nation's or your community's top public servants? The effectiveness of government bureaucracy? Perhaps an important consideration is an effective balance of executive, legislative, and judiciary powers. One often overlooked measure that we study at the NICD is, simply put, the quality of political talk.

That quality, by many accounts, is in decline. The annual Weber Shadwick poll on Civility in America (2019) finds that, for the third straight year, the vast majority of Americans—nearly 70%—feel that we have a serious problem with civility. At NICD we have been particularly interested in the ways that these views impact the quality of governance. Among the top three contributors to incivility in the 2019 poll were the White House and politicians in general. It is no surprise that social media and news outlets are ranked alongside in the top four reasons Americans give for the rise of incivility across the nation.

## The Health of Democracy

Broadly speaking, most Americans live with a "just below the surface" anxiety about the health of our democracy. Since mid-2009 a majority of respondents told pollsters that our country is on the "wrong track" (www.realclearpolitics.com/epolls/other/direction_of_country-902.html). The most recent poll findings suggest that there is a –22% difference between "wrong track" and "right track" respondents despite low unemployment and inflation. Another tool to measure the health of our democratic union is The Edelman Annual Trust Barometer (www.edelman.com/news-awards/2018-edelman-trust-barometer-reveals-record-breaking-drop-trust-in-the-us), which finds that the United States is going through "a record-breaking drop in trust in the U.S."

This collapse of trust in our system of governance is driven by what the Edelman Trust Barometer (2018) calls, "a staggering lack of faith in government ... among the general population, and ... the informed public."

And yet, in the work of NICD across the country—from towns of 3,000 to cities of 300,000—we have found that most Americans experience a longing to be connected. At its root, this is a sense of belonging—to feel known and cared for by others, and to have the chance to know and to care for others. The reality is that the structures and institutions that exercise some of the greatest influence on our lives—government, the media, emerging technology companies—do not allow most of us to connect in ways that foster inclusion; they are far more likely to drive us apart by slivers of disposition and razor-thin margins of preference.

Most of us now experience the daily outpouring of confrontational politics that inhibits our ability to engage with people who think differently. There is very little analysis of the complexity of the "other" side—from our political leaders, social media, and the popular news. It is easier than ever to remain uninformed and dismissive of the ideas and the claims of opponents without taking the time to evaluate the origins and merits of their views.

Consider the gap between how most people respond to incivility and how they would like to respond to incivility. In the most recent Weber Shadwick poll (Civility in America, 2019), when asked how they respond to incivility, Americans' top responses were that they either "ignored the person or people acting uncivilly" (49%) or they "removed themselves from the situation" (47%).

At NICD we see this gap as an indication of the significant appetite to create alternative spaces and experiences for respectful, engaging, and authentic political discussion. And we believe inclusive leaders have an important role to play in building those spaces. We'll get there. First, let's look at how we got where we are today.

## Long History of Uncivil Discourse and Low Civic Engagement

We know that trust in government and uncivil attitudes in American discourse are not a new phenomenon. During the 19th century, the Congressional slavery debate sparked a brawl between congressmen that occurred on the House of Representatives' floor ("The Most Infamous," 1858). The last 50 years were also dominated by bouts of incivility and citizen disengagement. These began with attacks on civil rights protesters and continued with assassinations of beloved leaders, urban riots, prolonged involvement in a very unpopular war, and the resignation of a scandal-ridden president.

All of these periods of conflict saw an increase of citizens' rancor toward one another, cultivating a cumulative climate of mistrust that includes a dramatic decline in Americans' trust in government. Interest in civic life declined and this included the political arena.

And yet citizen engagement in governance is essential to the health of democracy; democratic nations are founded on the idea that government is the trustee of citizens' views and that they remain an important factor in government decisions. If citizens and residents have authentic opportunities to participate in debates about choices that affect our lives, the results will more likely reflect our interests. Without this collective citizen voice (or citizen engagement) it is very difficult for elected leaders and government officials to make tough choices necessary to meet the serious challenges facing our nation (Lukensmeyer, 2013). Conversely, uncivil debate disrupts or discourages the connection of citizens to government officials. Such isolated officials are more likely to cater their decisions to benefit special economic, political, or ideological interests rather than benefit everyday Americans.

Incivility exacerbates the massive gulf between what Americans believe about their government, and what government actually does (Lukensmeyer, 2017). President Jimmy Carter presciently described how the lack of civility alienated citizens and reduced civic engagement as part of his infamous 1979 "malaise" speech (Klein, 2013). Carter (1979) warned that:

> Our people are losing that faith, not only in government itself but in the ability as citizens to serve as the ultimate rulers and shapers of our democracy. As you know, there is a growing disrespect for government and for churches and for schools, the news media, and other institutions. You see too often . . . a system of government that seems incapable of action. You see a Congress twisted and pulled in every direction by hundreds of well-financed and powerful special interests. You see every extreme position defended to the last vote, almost to the last breath by one unyielding group or another.

President Ronald Reagan (1981) reinforced this view in his first inaugural address, after he defeated President Carter. He proclaimed that "in this present crisis, government is not the solution to our problem; government is the problem." This and similar attacks on the efficacy of government have convinced a growing number of citizens that engagement is futile, encouraging withdrawal from participation in decisions that affect our lives.

Americans are sophisticated in their assessment of the impact of incivility on the politics and governance of the nation. The 2019 Weber Shadwick poll finds that Americans largely agree that incivility leads to political gridlock (73%), lessens political involvement (71%), and can lead to fewer people attracted to public office (61%).

## An Extraordinarily Uncivil Presidential Campaign

In 2016, the national primary process left us in a position to experience one of the most uncivil spectacles of popular politics in modern history. The 2016 presidential election significantly increased the crisis of incivility affecting our nation. During the presidential campaign, senior surrogates of the Trump campaign provoked convention crowds to heap ridicule and wrath on a completely legitimate presidential candidate, leading to chants of "lock her up" ("Retired general . . .", 2016). The most important political arena of a nation once the beacon of democracy had, seemingly overnight, become as divisive and empty of substance as daytime television entertainment.

A post-2016 election public opinion poll by the Weber Shandwick public relations firm ("Poll finds ...", 2017) found that "a record high 69 percent of Americans believe that the U.S. has a major civility problem." The poll found that Hillary Clinton voters "named politicians as the group most responsible for the decline in civility." Donald Trump voters, in contrast, "blamed the news media . . . demonstrators/ protestors . . . and the Internet/social media."

The same Weber Shandwick poll also shows that four of five Americans "found the election uncivil." Andy Polansky, CEO of Weber Shandwick, noted that "we have seen a steady increase over that time in the recognition of how civility is a major problem facing Americans. Without a doubt, public discourse was challenged in the 2016 U.S. presidential campaign" ("Poll finds ...", 2017).

The divisions and the anger exposed during the 2016 campaign lives with us today. The top two discussion topics that Americans—Republicans, Democrats, and Independents alike—fear will lead to incivility are President Trump and politics; the only real difference is which answer each group ranks as its first (Civility in America, 2019).

The Weber-Shandwick poll reinforces other findings that show a majority of Americans think our country is on the wrong track (e.g., RCP Poll Average, Direction of the Country, https://www.realclearpolitics.com/epolls/other/direction_of_country-902.html). This decline in civility has exacted a toll on American democracy, according to an annual assessment by Freedom House, a global democracy watchdog organization. Freedom House conducts an "annual global report on political rights and civil liberties, composed of numerical ratings and descriptive texts for each country" (https://freedomhouse.org/reports/freedom-world/freedom-world-research-methodology). Their 2017 "assessment of democracy" in the United States found that:

> Democratic norms erode[d] within the United States .... The past year brought further, faster erosion of America's own democratic standards than at any other time in memory .... The United States has experienced a series of setbacks in the conduct of elections ... under leadership from both major political parties—but in 2017 its core institutions were attacked by an administration that rejects established norms of ethical conduct across many fields of activity.
>
> (Abramowitz, 2018, para. 16–17)

## A Civic Engagement Increase is Visible

At the National Institute for Civil Discourse, we are fortunate to have both a birds-eye and a ground-level view of the opportunity at hand. Weber Shandwick data suggests that in 2019, for the first time in five years, we saw a decline in Americans' negative attitudes toward civility. And where we have indicated that there is evidence of a rising appetite for civil engagement in communities across the country, we see new models of entrepreneurial civic leadership. In cafes and workplaces, in bars, and in "makeshift" spaces across the country, ordinary Americans are taking charge and are creating the right context, structure, and process for healthy, civil political discourse.

These are the inclusive leaders who inspire us, who give us hope that despite a decade of decline in civility there are tender shoots of hope growing in our public square. It is these citizen leaders who are working against the cynicism of political operatives, under the weight of government gridlock, and beneath a cloud of mistrust to weave together a fabric of civil renewal. Some leaders are taking a page from community organizing manuals and others are striking out on their own. We are seeing GenZ seeking their political footing using astute mainstream media practices backed by smart social media strategy and mass organizing. A new generation of millennial leaders is winning elections by tapping the power of technology to bring diverse coalitions together. And boomers are doubling down, using traditional community infrastructure to call the conversation on inclusion, justice, and politics. And, most hearteningly, there is a tremendous amount of experimentation by every generation.

## Best Practices for Civil Engagement

The case for civil discourse that leads to citizen engagement is as strong as the experience is inspiring. The question is whether and how we nurture and expand both the case and the experience to form a new infrastructure for democratic politics.

At AmericaSpeaks, the organization one of us (Carolyn) founded in 1995 and led for 18 years, we committed to pursuing and researching the best practices to bring people with widely different points of view together to build trust, foster empathy, and forge agreement across our differences. We learned that, to be successful, inclusive leaders of civility and engagement efforts must account for the following seven core design principles:

1. Participants must be informed, establishing a baseline of shared facts.
2. Leaders must know the context in which they are inviting participation.
3. Discussion must have an authentic link to decision makers.
4. Every conversation must ensure diverse participants.
5. Leaders are responsible for creating a safe space for engagement.
6. The process must lead to the discovery of shared priorities.
7. There must be a plan to sustain citizens' engagement over time.

(Lukensmeyer, 2013, p. 83)

Taken together, these principles are a powerful formula for a new and essential form of democratic engagement. We have continued to apply these design principles in all of the National Institute for Civil Discourse's initiatives, whether we are working with the public, with elected officials, or with journalists. Here is how we think they must play out at any scale, from community conversations to national civic engagements.

### *Shared Fact Base*

This is the first essential principle of inclusive leadership. Although anyone is entitled to their own opinions, as the saying goes, no one is entitled to their own set of facts. Citizens and residents who discuss the substance of decisions that will affect their lives—and the lives of others—must have in-depth information that is accessible, neutral, and factual (Lukensmeyer, 2013). This principle is a specific challenge in our time because of pervasive editorialization of the news in mainstream media and the ready availability of blatantly false information on the internet. Civil discussion begins with a generally shared set of facts that can be used as a basis for healthy discussion of interpretation and the underlying values and preferences that give rise to our policy choices.

Today, too many of us cling to our own set of facts. We consume information from slanted sources that cater to our views of how the world should be according to a value base, rather than how it is in fact. Known examples include mainstream outlets like Fox News, pseudo factual outlets like Alex Jones' InfoWars, and many of the "Antifa" websites that have emboldened far-right groups in the U.S. (Is there an "Alt-Left?", 2017). Today's social media platforms also enable people to distribute information, often from unqualified sources, between millions of users with limited to no fact-checking or validity requirement (Allcott & Gentzkow, 2017).

We are now seeing an increase of senior public officials freely disregarding fact or falsely misleading the public to build and harden support for their policy proposals. Ad hominem attacks are also used to discredit persons and information that undermine the agendas of extremist politicians. A new standard practice in this discursive environment is to repeatedly undermine factual information with the label "fake news" as a tactic to discredit the people and the entities providing this information.

Establishing a "false equivalency" is another increasingly common disinformation tool that undermines civil discourse and civic engagement. It occurs when both sides of a debate receive equal media coverage or decision makers' attention, even when a scientific or other credible consensus overwhelmingly favors one viewpoint. The false equivalency conveys that the facts are unsettled so that more analysis is necessary before addressing the problem. The political scientists Thomas Mann and Norman Ornstein (2012) have noted that, "a balanced treatment of an unbalanced phenomenon is a distortion of reality, and a disservice" (p. 194) to citizens.

### *Context*

It is critical to know the context in which people are asked to participate. Participants must watch for any shifts in demographics, geography, leadership, or other circumstances that could have a direct impact on whether a citizen involvement process produces actionable results (Lukensmeyer, 2013). It is essential to include all affected groups at the beginning of the decision-making process so that the final outcome clearly reflects views of a broad group of people rather than a narrow one. It is also useful to study the recent history of the community where the engagement will be held in order to have a sensitivity for the way change impacts daily life, the nuance of prominent attitudes, and individuals' disposition toward future change.

### *Link to Decision Makers*

Any discussion of policy change organized by inclusive leaders must ensure that citizens have an authentic link to decision makers. Without a meaningful connection between discussion and impact, it is too easy for government decision makers to ignore public input (Lukensmeyer, 2013). The inclusive leader must negotiate a commitment to concrete action by government officials, steps designed to provide thoughtful commitments in response to citizens' concerns, rather than prepared remarks or canned talking points.

### *Diverse Participants*

Civil engagement forums that are built around diverse participants and different points of view will provide decision makers with the necessary breadth of representation to adopt the group's recommendations. In other words, the outcomes of a diverse forum are far more likely to be politically palatable than outcomes that are not the result of diverse thought and experience. Diverse participation also builds trust among local leaders and other citizens. The involvement of diverse voices tends to reduce the potential for future political roadblocks by including divergent points of view in the process (Lukensmeyer, 2013).

### *Create Safe Spaces*

It is essential to create a safe space where people feel comfortable expressing themselves without fear of retribution or exile (Lukensmeyer, 2013). Discussions that occur in neutral public or historical places can create such an environment. The internet, however, can be an *unsafe* place for engagement—principally because it enables participants to level hurtful insults, vicious claims, or dangerous threats without accountability. Furthermore, the poisonous discursive cultures of "trolling" and "doxing" are difficult if not impossible to control on the internet, generating polarized interpretations of "safety." Nameless attacks on people involved in civic engagement decreases their participation as they want to protect themselves from future attacks online.

### *Uncover Common Ground*

Engagement through civil discourse is most effective when citizens participate in a deliberative process that yields commonly held perspectives and values between participants with divergent views. When these shared priorities have been revealed, citizens and residents provide far more consensus guidance for decision makers' action—often stronger and more durable insights than public opinion polls, "listening sessions," and other common input mechanisms can provide. Shared priorities also pave the way for the public support and engagement necessary for implementation of a shared decision (Lukensmeyer, 2013).

Among the lost arts of governance today is compromise; instead we have governing bodies faced with rancor, division, and gridlock. By contrast, inclusive leaders recognize that the possibility of compromise is central to civil discourse; it is an acceptable outcome to any engagement. For citizens to have an impact on governance, decision makers must hear the consensus recommendations of civil public advisory groups instead of divided or opposing viewpoints. Our mechanisms of civil discourse must design new kinds of public engagement opportunities that focus on sharing views and building agreement rather than highlighting differences, which fosters stalemate, inaction, and alienation (Lukensmeyer, 2013).

### *Sustainable Mechanisms*

Sustaining citizen engagement requires regular, ongoing opportunities for authentic participation. These mechanisms must be creative and innovative in seeking new ways to motivate and sustain measurable increases in citizens' commitment to and systematic embrace of participation with decision makers. Without such enduring mechanisms, civic engagement efforts will erode over time (Lukensmeyer, 2013).

The next generation of inclusive leaders are going to be entrepreneurs in civil discourse and civic engagement (Lukensmeyer, 2013). Each of you will be restless in your search for the means to renew and sustain healthy civic engagement and political discourse—whether that is through community-based institutions, local political party apparatus, higher office—even online mechanisms that safeguard free speech while preserving decency and respect among people. And, most importantly, the new inclusive leadership will identify promising pathways to embed these mechanisms in governance, ensuring that, with time, they cultivate new habits of civic participation in democratic life.

## The Next Steps for Inclusive Leadership

For inclusive leaders, the future state of our democracy must be a conscious priority. Therefore, being intentional about our vision of sustained mechanisms for civil discourse is essential. Inclusive leaders can connect with local institutions to provide training for participants, teaching techniques to improve engagement over time while empowering participants to teach others.

Inclusive leaders will also recognize the importance of celebrating success—particularly early accomplishments that lay the foundation for tone, quality, and impact of engagement. Such celebrations reward participants for their emotional investment, affirm for participants that their efforts are worthwhile, and energize the momentum to remain engaged (Lukensmeyer, 2017).

Finally, and perhaps most important, as inclusive leaders we must seek ways to embed civil discussion and civic engagement in governance at all levels—municipal, state, and national. This should be considered as critical "infrastructure" to sustain civil discourse and civic engagement in a democracy. This infrastructure is comprised of seven fundamental components (Lukensmeyer, 2013):

1 A legislative mandate for participation.
2 Safe, accessible physical spaces.
3 Broader access to communications technology.
4 Skilled facilitators to moderate discussions.
5 An organizational infrastructure.
6 Trustworthy, fact-based media.
7 Robust civic education.

These components provide the structure necessary for ongoing civic engagement rather than one-time discussions that leave issues undecided and participants discouraged.

## Conclusion

Most of us see the signs that something has dramatically changed in the way we conduct our democratic affairs in the United States. We have arrived at an extraordinary moment when each of us can—indeed we must—play a transformative role in discursive politics. The challenges of reviving civility, deepening civil discourse, and reinvigorating civic engagement provide inclusive leaders with the opportunity to engage with three core constituencies as collaborators: elected officials who ensure that their engagement strategy is responsive to the public's business, managers in government who embrace high standards of civil engagement practice in their work, and a public that asserts their place at the table, actively participating in debates on the issues and policies that affect our lives (Lukensmeyer, 2017).

After nearly a decade of working to revive civility and respect in our political and public discourse, the National Institute for Civil Discourse has distilled the essence of our work in five principles (Lukensmeyer, 2017), in fact foundational truths, that we invite inclusive leaders in every sector to bring into their work. These are as follows:

1 Today the American people are better than our current politics would suggest.
2 Americans come alive and thrive when we have the opportunity to talk with and listen to people with differing views.
3 Elected officials must heed the consensus recommendations from groups of civilly engaged diverse citizens and residents.
4 People who are bought into and own the outcomes of policy discussions are more committed to participate in their implementation.
5 A willing and able public outreach capacity is in place across the country to bring people together across our differences, and we

know how to design processes that will enable them to see one another's humanity and find common ground.

In addition to approaching engagement under these circumstances, the NICD has identified three important elements to the revival of civility. We believe these are concrete actions around which inclusive leaders can rally communities and new allies. First, it is vital to respond rapidly to uncivil language or behavior shown to the public via the media. Second, form a local "Citizens for Civility" network or committee that can nimbly turn ideas into action. Finally, hold candidates and elected officials accountable for their civil or uncivil conduct (Lukensmeyer, 2017). Again, remember to celebrate success and hold low standards to account. It is particularly important to publicly praise or otherwise reward officials who do the right thing so that they know we are watching and care. These are the north stars on our journey toward democratic renewal.

The essence of inclusive leadership today is to bring us all into the search for the political will to strengthen our institutions and redesign our mechanisms of governance. It is up to each one of us to change the quality of public discourse in our democracy. Every single one of us has the capacity and capability to do that. Our task as inclusive leaders is to nurture confident and well-tempered citizens and to support receptive public officials; each interaction that occurs among everyday Americans who can talk with each other across our differences begins to reweave the patchwork pattern of our threadbare body politic. Each step and each stitch draws us closer together as a nation, into that essential framework that has held us together for so long, our democratic union.

## References

Abramowitz, M. J. (2018). *Democracy in crisis*. Freedom House. https://freedomhouse.org/report/freedom-world/2018/democracy-crisis

Allcott, H., & Gentzkow, M. (2017, Spring). Social media and fake news in the 2016 election. *Journal of Economic Perspectives*, *31*(2), 211–236. https://doi.org/10.1257/jep.31.2.211

Carter, J. (1979, July 15). *Address to the nation on energy and national goals*. The American Presidency Project. https://www.presidency.ucsb.edu/ws/?pid=32596

Civility in America. (2019). *Solutions for tomorrow*. https://www.webershandwick.com/wp-content/uploads/2019/06/CivilityIn America2019SolutionsforTomorrow.pdf

*2018 Edelman trust barometer*. (2018, January 21). https://www.edelman.com/research/2018-edelman-trust-barometer

Is there an "Alt-Left?" (2017, August 17). *Snopes.com* https://www.snopes.com/2017/08/17/is-the-alt-left-a-real-thing

Klein, E. (2013, August, 9). Jimmy Carter's "malaise" speech was popular! *Washington Post*. https://www.washingtonpost.com/news/wonk/wp/2013/08/09/jimmy-carters-malaise-speech-was-popular

Lukensmeyer, C. J. (2013). *Bringing citizen voices to the table: A guide for public managers*. San Francisco, CA: Jossey-Bass.

Lukensmeyer, C. J. (2017, March 3). *Then and now: How do we respond to the sea-change in our political and public discourse?* [Keynote Presentation]. Inclusive Leadership: Transforming Diverse Lives, Workplaces, and Societies, 25th Annual Kravis-de Roulet Conference. Claremont McKenna College, Claremont, CA.

Mann, T. E., & Ornstein, N. J. (2012). *It's even worse than it looks: How the American constitutional system collided with the new politics of extremism*. New York, NY: Basic Books.

Poll finds Americans united in seeing an uncivil nation divided about causes and civility of presidential candidates. (2017, January 23). *Weber Shandwick Poll*. https://www.webershandwick.com/news/article/poll-finds-americans-united-in-seeing-an-uncivil-nation-divided-about-cause

Reagan, R. (1981, January 20). *Inaugural address*. https://www.reaganlibrary.gov/research/speeches/inaugural-address-january-20-1981

Retired general and senior Trump campaign advisor Michael Flynn "led a 'lock her up' chant at the Republican convention," (2017, December 1). *Time*, http://time.com/5044847/michael-flynn-hillary-clinton-republican-convention-lock-her-up

The most infamous floor brawl in the history of the U.S. House of Representatives. (1858, February 6). *History, Art & Archives*, United States House of Representatives. https://history.house.gov/Historical-Highlights/1851-1900/The-most-infamous-floor-brawl-in-the-history-of-the-U-S–House-of-Representatives/

# 22 The Practice of Inclusive Leadership in Disruptive and Polarizing Times

*Effenus Henderson*

The practice of leadership is undergoing profound change. Traditional management practices are no longer effective in leading a multicultural, globally diverse, and technically savvy workforce. Leaders must develop inclusive skills in an era of growing polarities about diversity and inclusion. They must consider that some people doubt the value of tackling oppressive

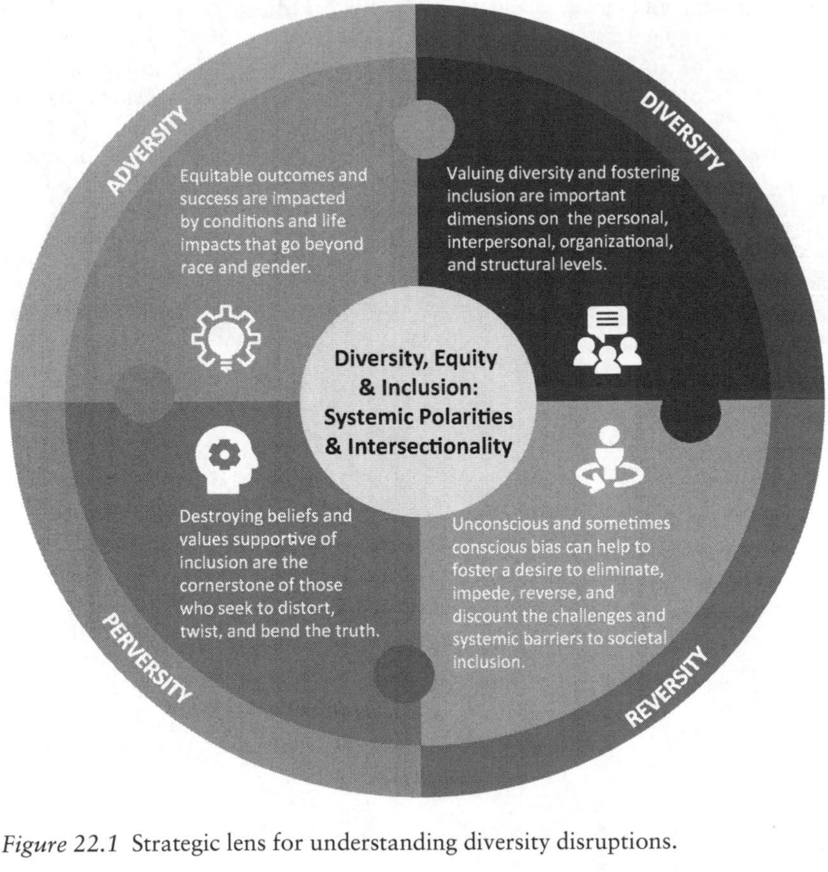

*Figure 22.1* Strategic lens for understanding diversity disruptions.

systems, discrimination, and bias, and are skeptical of embarking on initiatives to foster respect and civility in the workplace.

Historically, diversity work has been facilitated by small departments of practitioners who owned the work. Organizational leaders did not fully embrace diversity, equity, and inclusion as their work and, as a result, were not fully participating in diversity conversations or outcomes. As we move toward 2025, leaders must recognize that a growing number of people, especially rural working-class Whites, do not agree with the diversity equation, have opposite and non-approving views of a multicultural society, and want to reverse efforts designed to build a diverse and inclusive workplace. As this opposition grows, the practice of inclusive leadership must be strengthened to respond to these growing threats and challenges.

In this chapter I examine this emerging context and discuss three disruptive platforms (reversity, adversity, and perversity)—sometimes competing with each other—that create cultural clashes and that impact the practice of inclusive leadership. I provide a framework for pursuing diversity, equity, and inclusion initiatives in a more systemic and sustainable way. Along with these concepts, I explore polarity management, a useful tool for helping bridge the upsides and downsides of each concept. By understanding these concepts and growing polarities, more inclusive, sustainable, and resilient change efforts can be pursued in today's disruptive and polarizing times.

## The Context

There is an emerging social construct in global human capital management shaping the way business leaders, human resource professionals, diversity and inclusion practitioners, management coaches, and forward-looking change agents must view their work. This new construct, *the new normal*, will influence the way employees, investors, activists, government leaders, and civil society assess how organizations manage their human capital practices and corporate social responsibility (CSR). The management of human capital is being shaped by profound demographic change as well as a new wave of technology, artificial intelligence, data management, and social media considerations. Indeed, reporting on diversity, equity, and inclusion efforts will be a required part of CSR practice in the future.

This "new normal" is taking place in an era of growing polarities and ideological differences, especially around issues of race, immigration, religion, sexual orientation, and citizenship. As these dynamics emerge, relationships (on and off the job) will be influenced and driven by the new wave of available technology and social media that help to shape bias and embolden perspectives about those that are different. Sophisticated software with enhanced artificial intelligence capabilities will be used to persuade and amplify emotional responses to diversity and inclusion. Social media is becoming a primary venue for such amplification.

Diversity and inclusion efforts have evolved over the past four decades and the change in practice has been a result of some of these trends. Early efforts were focused on meeting regulatory and compliance requirements resulting from various equal opportunity laws and regulations, which required organizations to make good faith efforts to improve the diversity of their workforces. The United States Department of Labor's Office of Federal Contract Compliance Programs (OFCCP) has been monitoring the practices of companies holding federal contracts by reviewing their organizational affirmative action programs. When contractors are found to be in violation of regulations, they are required to make voluntary adjustments in their programs, processes, systems, and practices through conciliation agreements.

As diversity, equity, and inclusion (DEI) practices have matured, organizational strategies have shifted to plans and initiatives that seek to "monetize the value of diversity and inclusion practices" (*ROI of Diversity*, Diversity Best Practices) through more strategic approaches and systemic frameworks linked to business strategies, and that focus on action plans covering relationships with stakeholders, including employees, customers, suppliers, investors, community leaders, and government regulators. Many of these stakeholders are demanding more transparency in reporting and are monitoring the practices of organizations.

Corporate social responsibility indices are adding workforce diversity to their reporting requirements as it is seen as key to productivity, innovation, and profitability. There is growing evidence that more diverse and inclusive organizations outperform, are more innovative, and have higher levels of customer satisfaction than less diverse and inclusive organizations (Hunt et al., 2018).

In recent years there has been growing activism by external stakeholders challenging organizational practices. While the practice of inclusion has been improving inside of organizations, stakeholders are becoming more active in challenging non-inclusive organizational practices at board meetings, on social media, and in the community. The Business Roundtable (2019) has updated its statement on the purpose of the corporation to incorporate some of these emerging social issues and opportunities.

## Changing Societal Tensions Impacting Diversity, Equity, and Inclusion Efforts

Diversity, equity, and inclusion initiatives are being influenced by a growing clash of ideologies, perspectives, and beliefs about the role of such efforts in society (Krupa, 2018). Efforts are being challenged, disrupted, and in some instances reversed by a growing number of conservative and nationalist activists. For diversity, equity, and inclusion initiatives to be sustainable, they will require committed leadership, laser-focused strategies, and thoughtful response strategies to anti-diversity activists and their counter-disruptive narratives and tactics (Dempsey & Brafman, 2018).

Diversity practitioners and organizational leaders charged with advancing diversity, equity, and inclusion initiatives and practices must be aware that the landscape is changing dramatically. Adversaries of such initiatives are introducing new methods, tools, and narratives to counter these progressive changes. They are identifying preexisting fractures in ideology, preferences, and mindsets and introducing strategies to reverse public support, negate empirical data and fact-based approaches, amplify fear and emotional responses, and exploit deeply held biases.

## Three Disruptive Platforms

There are three distinct and polarizing concepts that leaders should understand in order to manage forward-looking and sustainable diversity, equity, and inclusion (DEI) change during disruptive times. Adversaries of diversity and inclusion are using strategies framed around three concepts I have researched over the past two decades: *reversity*, *perversity*, and *adversity*. These concepts are part of the new strategic lens that should be considered when leaders are assessing resistance to successful forward-looking change processes. Too often, diversity and inclusion change agents have not paid enough attention to these forces of resistance. Historical efforts have focused on mitigating disparities and inequities (problems that need to be solved) in workforce representation but have not focused adequate attention to growing polarities. As a result, diversity practitioners and organizational leaders are not well equipped to assess the negative forces working against diversity, equity, and inclusion. Leaders do not fully appreciate how the current national climate of hate and bigotry impacts the lived experience of diverse employees within their organizations. Inclusive leaders must develop sustainable and forward-looking ways of responding to these growing threats.

### *Reversity*

*Reversity*, a term I coined in the early 1990s, refers to the growing opposition and organized political action focused on the reversal of affirmative action, diversity, equity, and inclusion efforts in both industry and civil society. It is designed to "fracture commitment" and "pit" identity groups against one another (Henderson, 2019). I recently applied the term *fractionality* to refer to "the process of separating people by their diversity dimensions for the purpose of leveraging their biases, stereotypes of others, and their worldview to craft a targeted emotional response and strategic outcome based on fear" (Henderson,

2019) to targeted audiences. Such efforts are now being organized and scaled using technology.

In some communities and groups, the movement has been pushed by conservative groups, most noticeably the religious right and Tea Party groups, and its momentum has been accelerated by emerging Alt-Right groups. Some supporters base their rationale on biblical and very narrow fundamentalist Christian values and growing White nationalist ideologies. The changing demographic composition of the United States has created fear and trepidation at the thought of the country becoming a majority-minority one. White nationalists fear the loss of White privilege and superiority in such an environment and see such efforts as a form of "White genocide" (see: www.adl.org/education/references/hate-symbols/diversity-white-genocide). Education reform and the teaching of "soft skills" courses in diversity, equity, and inclusion are increasingly coming under attack from these sources.

In the late 1990s and early 2000s, the goal of anti-diversity activists was to oppose diversity and affirmative action. These efforts were largely local and grassroots-oriented. The attacks were centered on concepts such as multiculturalism, group-based identity, and qualifications for jobs. A key part of the strategy was to link efforts at valuing diversity with mediocrity. More recently, efforts have moved from the grassroots to the national platform with public policy actions designed to eliminate, impede, or reverse programs that support diversity and to negate data-based accounts of the challenges and systemic barriers to societal inclusion. A pivotal part of this national strategy currently focuses on the appointment of conservative judges.

In 2017, Brian Resnick published an article, "White Fear of Demographic Change is a Powerful Psychological Force," suggesting that increasing diversity could make America a more hostile place. Resnick pointed to a study by social psychologist Jennifer Richeson suggesting that:

> when people are in the majority, the sense of their race is dormant. But the prospect of being in the minority can suddenly make white identity—and all the historical privilege that comes with it—salient. And, she guessed, the prospect of losing majority status was likely to make people (perhaps unconsciously) uneasy.
>
> (Resnick, 2017, para. 4)

To counter diversity and inclusion efforts, White nationalist extremists are working to turn back the clock on affirmative action and diversity and are working to prevent diverse views from being heard or considered (Hassan, 2019).

Overall, this reversity dynamic has important implications, most notably:

- Insurgents and anarchists opposed to inclusivity are becoming more vocal and insensitive.
- Their fear-based actions are designed to destabilize progressive beliefs, patterns, and values.
- Their emphasis is on a perceived and growing sense of loss by an increasing number of White citizens.
- The impact of demographic change, particularly the increasing proportion of minority children, especially those born to Hispanic immigrants, and dramatic changes in migration patterns, is creating hostility toward refugees and immigrants.
- The resulting resentment toward minorities and immigrants is leading to a heightened sense of intolerance to programs such as Deferred Action for Childhood Arrivals (DACA), an Obama-era program that allows undocumented immigrants brought to the U.S. as minors to legally remain in the country to study or work.

### *Perversity*

*Perversity* is a term I have applied to new and powerful narratives and story-telling that seeks to persuade people to back away from diversity and inclusion, which are considered to be threats. This is seen, for example, among commentators who disparage advocates for social justice and diversity. Perversity focuses on creating narratives at the local and national levels to attack diversity, equity, and inclusion agendas, initiatives, champions, and allies by distorting, twisting, and misrepresenting the truth using fear and disparagement tactics (Henderson, 2017). I believe the target is White working-class people who feel they are losing out because of DEI programs.

Narratives and stories target newspapers and the internet and use fake articles, editorials, and memes that are designed to appear to come from average people writing about the issues. The narratives are designed to create or reinforce doubts about diversity and inclusion and about public policies that support these efforts. Facts, research, and historical practices are often ignored. Tactics are designed to embolden White working-class citizens in the belief that people of color and other group-based identity populations (e.g., LGBTQ, disabled, immigrants, millennials, the educated elite) are all working against their interests. Social media is used to amplify such grievances.

Destroying beliefs and values supportive of inclusion is a cornerstone of those who seek to distort, twist, and bend the truth about diversity. Perversity is a deliberate desire to behave in an unreasonable or unacceptable way grounded in contrariness. The following are some strategies that are being employed:

- False or misleading narratives, actions, and plans to distort and reframe the truth about people, public policy, and programs supporting inclusivity.
- Attacks on civil discourse and dialogue, which are often framed as getting in the way of truth and free speech and dismissed as political correctness.
- A focus on character assassination: discrediting people with little interest in listening to substantive ideas and recommendations.
- A disdain for systemic intervention focused on removing institutional bias and barriers to change.
- Stereotyping and characterizing group-based identities as designed to separate and divide rather than as a way for people to bring their full selves and backgrounds to the table.

### *Adversity*

*Adversity* focuses on the impact of socioeconomic change, drawing attention to conditions that affect individuals and their families negatively. Poverty, income inequality, natural disasters, the impact of war, and shifting job design (requiring more sophisticated skills) are taking a toll on those who have pursued semi-skilled jobs in industry and creating an economic divide between rural and urban residents.

This economic divide is growing between urban centers, which are increasingly young and diverse, and rural areas, which are older, whiter, and have more residents suffering from the impact of manufacturing job losses. Many White working-class people in these communities benefited from apprenticeship programs that led to permanent jobs in their communities. Many successfully worked most of their adult work life with one or two employers in these rural communities. As local employers introduced technological innovation in the production processes and as the cost of production became more competitive outside the United States, the skill requirements and type of work and where it was performed changed. These dynamics impacted many workers in these rural communities. These conditions have forced people in many parts of the country to migrate to other areas with more job opportunities. As these job losses in rural areas increased, White working-class people, particularly those with limited transferable skills, have become more hostile to difference and perceived economic inequality.

White working-class citizens in these communities are being faced with higher levels of unemployment, increased opioid addiction, and health care challenges. These issues, which historically were disproportionately concentrated in urban, minority neighborhoods, are finding their way into many rural communities. Many White working-class citizens do not attribute these job losses and resulting problems to technology, but rather to increased competition from minorities and immigrants. Increasingly, White working-class people are attacking diversity efforts as the cause of their conditions and portraying themselves as the victims (Metzl, 2019).

This sense of adversity has a number of important implications, most notably the following:

- Diversity efforts must consider the impact of fear and the perceived loss by working-class White citizens who feel that they are being left behind.
- With a growing number of White working-class members suffering from income inequality, they are not supporting programs and strategies to widen the opportunity net.
- As many of these individuals resent people of color, women, and immigrants taking roles that historically favored White men, they are increasingly hostile to affirmative action and inclusion.

Forward-looking diversity change efforts must consider these three disruptive platforms in the process of seeking to build more diverse and inclusive societies, communities, and organizations. The emerging environment includes a number of multidimensional and intersectional forces that must be considered. The new environment must incorporate dimensions of cultural adaptation and assimilation as religion, heritage, socioeconomic status, migration patterns, and the increasing number of first-generation immigrants shape the demographic landscape.

## A Guiding Framework for Change

Many diversity practitioners have focused on building more diverse workforces and inclusive workplaces and believe that valuing diversity and fostering inclusion are important dimensions on the personal, interpersonal, organizational, and structural levels. Best practices and emerging D&I work have focused on increasing representation of underrepresented women and people of color, educating the workforce on everyday bias and respectful behavior, and talent acquisition, development, and retention strategies (Ferdman & Deane, 2014; O'Mara & Richter, 2016). Another important dimension has been work devoted to strategic outreach to underserved communities. However, diversity, equity, and inclusion practices of the future must consider the three platforms that were mentioned in the prior section. Reversity, perversity, and adversity issues can be disruptive of the best efforts and therefore must be a part of the analysis of the context and strategy for building sustainable change efforts.

*Diversity* encompasses the many ways people differ, including gender, race, nationality, education, sexual orientation, style, functional expertise, and a wide array of other characteristics and backgrounds (especially social identities) and are typically what connects us to some people and not others (Ferdman, 1995, 2003, 2014). Diversity actions should be focused on ensuring equitable representation of all members of society in an organization, business, or community.

*Inclusion* describes the way an organization configures opportunity, interaction, communication, information, and decision-making to utilize the potential of diversity. It refers to the organization's culture or work environment (Miller & Katz, 2002). Achieving inclusion means creating the structures, policies, and practices in organizational life that recognize the existence of multiple perspectives and signal the importance of learning from those differences.

The practice of inclusion requires a carefully developed framework for change that aligns DEI efforts with the vision, mission, and strategic objectives of the organization. Such a framework begins with an assessment of the level of readiness by leadership, and an assessment of the current state of practices, policies, and behaviors within the organization using a diversity, equity, and inclusion lens. This assessment identifies major challenges, gaps, and opportunities for improvement and establishes clear accountability for implementation and measuring progress.

Such frameworks include a clear statement of commitment by organizational leaders, definitions for diversity, equity, accessibility, inclusion, and belonging, and other important terms; an action plan covering key objectives, actions to achieve the desired outputs and outcomes, and measures to monitor progress. Figure 22.2 provides a high-level description of the change process steps.

The development of a resilient change framework should begin with examining the "why" for the effort. It should assess the level of readiness by organizational leaders. The framework should include major pillars, which include specific objectives, activities, outputs, metrics, and longer-term outcomes. Major pillars for the change may include broad categories, such as talent management, culture at work, people management systems and processes, DEI-informed marketing and product development, DEI-informed supply chain management, and DEI-informed external relationships. Figure 22.3 provides a high-level overview of the key components of a successful change framework.

## Inclusive Leaders Must Navigate Positive and Negative Realities

Inclusive leaders must develop sustainable organizational change processes in a period that is marked by significant polarities, ideological differences, and citizens who question diversity initiatives in the workplace as well as in educational and community institutions. Leaders must understand that their efforts may be sabotaged or derailed by a segment of society that does not support such interventions. To address this, leaders of progressive diversity change efforts must communicate their

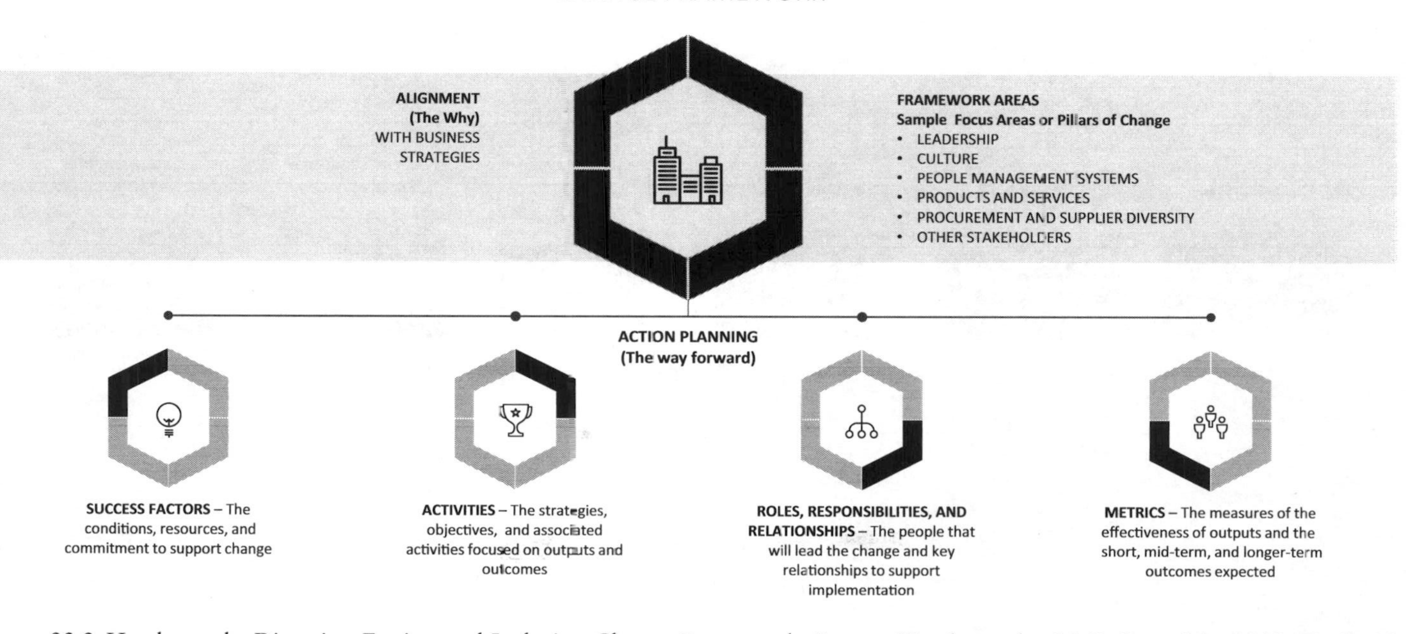


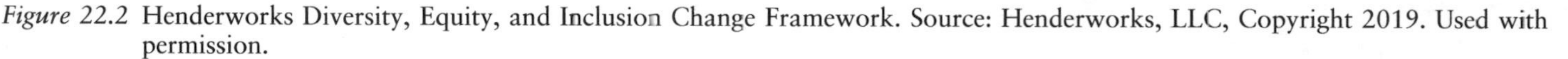

*Figure* 22.2 Henderworks Diversity, Equity, and Inclusion Change Framework. Source: Henderworks, LLC, Copyright 2019. Used with permission.

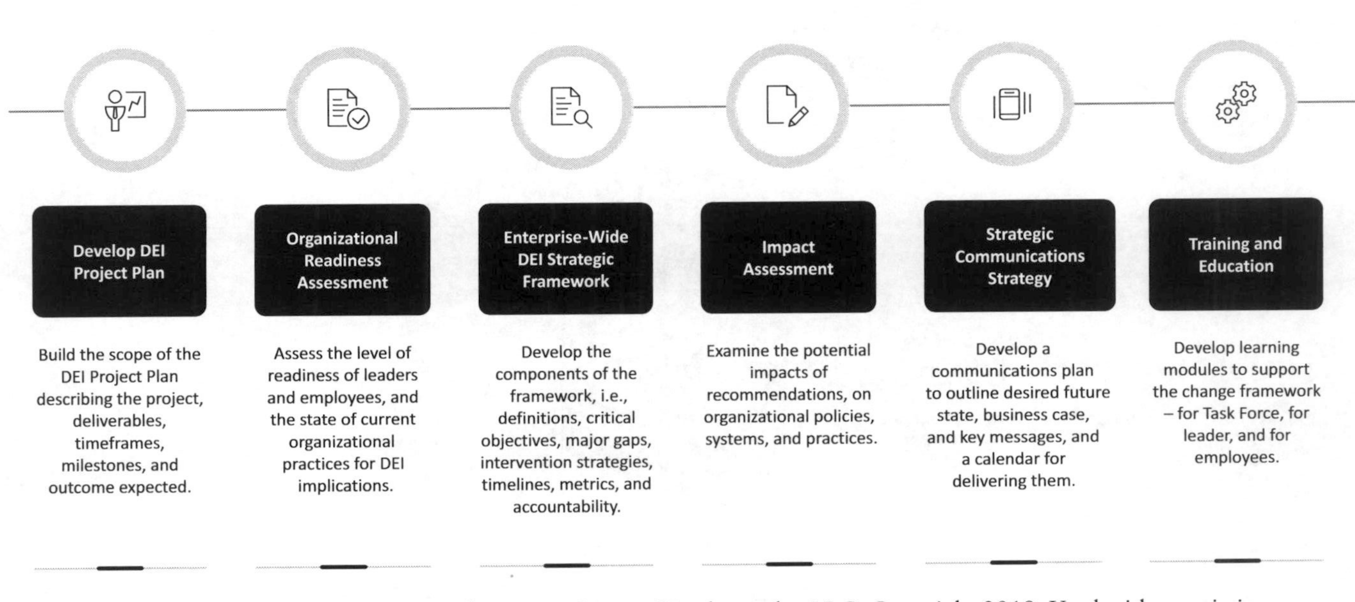


*Figure 22.3* Henderworks DEI Change Framework Process. Source: Henderworks, LLC, Copyright 2019. Used with permission.

commitment, define the strategic objectives of their initiatives, and share intentional and deliberate strategies that are tied to business outcomes and objectives. They must assess the opportunities for, challenges to, weaknesses of, as well as threats to building more diverse and inclusive organizations, communities, and civil society.

Organizational leaders are having to set direction for their organizations while concepts and values are changing. Identities and markers of difference in this emerging environment include a number of multidimensional and intersectional forces that overlap. Racial justice, oppression, privilege, and White fragility are topics that are top of mind for many advocates of change. These issues challenge leaders to demonstrate their personal and organizational commitment in their words and behavior and in work systems and practices.

Personal identity and a sense of belonging, in the context of a particular dominant culture, including level of assimilation and adaptation to the environment, are shaped by organizational values, creating a multidimensional and complex ecosystem of relationship and power. The leader is seen as the chief influencer of workplace practices (see Figure 22.4).

Success and sustainable change efforts are led by leaders who recognize they must own DEI work, set the expectations for others in the organization to support the work, and institute processes, practices, and systems for reporting progress. They must not tolerate those who resist and challenge these efforts.

Inclusive leaders understand that their obligation and responsibility as leaders is assuring that people are treated respectfully and fairly—that is, based on their unique characteristics rather than on stereotypes; that differences are valued—that is, understanding and valuing the uniqueness of others who are from diverse backgrounds, while also accepting them as members of the group; and that the thinking of diverse groups is leveraged for smarter ideation and decision making that reduces the risk of being blindsided (Bourke & Dillon, 2016). Inclusion is not limited to the way an organization deals with employees; it also refers to interactions with customers, clients, partners, vendors, suppliers, and subcontractors as well.

Inclusive leaders also understand that, at all organizational levels, company core values and beliefs shape views of diversity, equity, and inclusion. They must therefore build an environment where all employees have a strong sense of belonging. They create standards of professionalism that allow employees in general, and people of color and immigrants in particular, to bring more of their full selves and their cultural heritages to the workplace (Hofmans & Judge, 2019). Leaders must also understand the growing implication of technology. Social media, persuasion technology, artificial intelligence, and data science are powerful tools of persuasion. Such tools can change relationships,

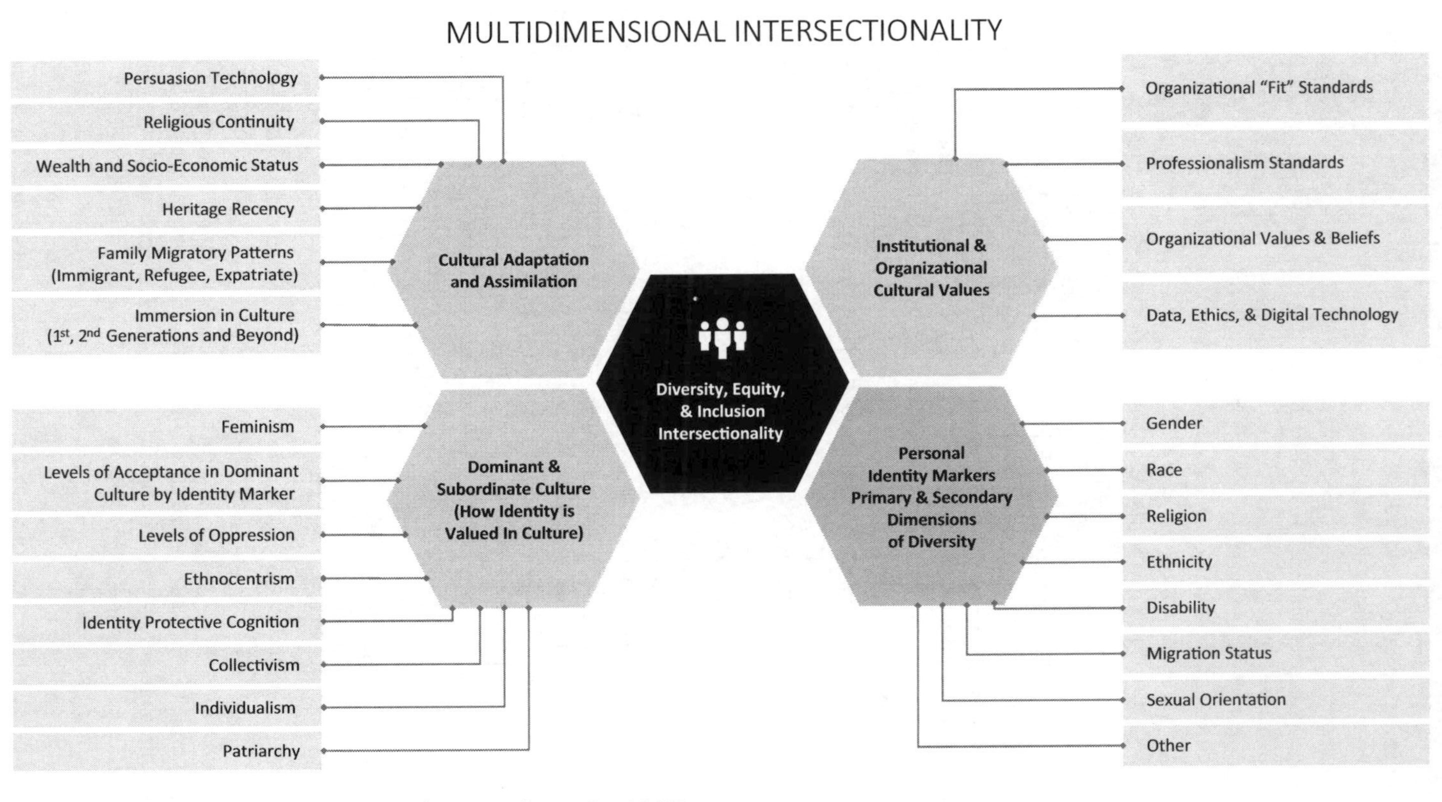


*Figure 22.4* Multidimensional intersectionality (Henderworks, 2019).

perspectives, and outcomes in both positive and negative ways. These tools can be used to instill fear and apprehension across an array of differences, including those based on gender, race, religion, ethnicity, disability, migration status, sexual orientation, and socio-economic status.

Inclusive leaders must learn to communicate more effectively across the cultural nuances of different identities and cultures in these polarizing times. Words and non-verbal communication matter. Cultures with Western European roots, such as the United States and Australia, are generally more low-context cultures while Asian, Arab, Central European, Latin American, and African cultures are high-context (Neese, 2016):

> A high-context culture relies on implicit communication and nonverbal cues. In high-context culture communications, a message cannot be understood without a great deal of background information. A low-context culture relies on explicit communication. In low-context communication, more of the information in a message is spelled out and defined.
>
> (Neese, 2016)

Inclusive leaders and diversity change agents must understand how to effectively navigate words, language, and nonverbal communication as growing ideological and political divides are finding their way into our workplaces. Expressions and behavior by leadership is telegraphic and can communicate messages with an unintended impact on people of color and those whose native language is not English.

Leaders need to monitor the culture at work and the lived experiences of people from diverse backgrounds. Employee satisfaction and engagement assessments, sponsorship of employee resource groups and inclusivity councils, regularly monitoring and assessing human resource practices, systems, and policies are important areas for regular assessment and reporting.

## Using Polarity Management Tools in Diversity and Inclusion Work

Growing ideological differences and pervasive right-wing strategies to reverse diversity initiatives compel progressive leaders to build their skills in conducting courageous conversations with those who have different perspectives about diversity and inclusion. Twenty-first-century inclusive leaders and change agents should consider the use of polarity management tools in managing these cultural clashes and in helping facilitate courageous dialogue in their organizations.

Polarities are powered by our values and by our fear of values we consider contrary to our own. These polarities create unavoidable conflicts that will occur in discussions about diversity and demographic changes impacting our workplaces.

Polarity management grew out of the work of Dr. Barry Johnson. In defining his concept of polarities, Johnson (1992) wrote:

> Polarities to manage are sets of opposites which can't function well independently. Because the two sides of a polarity are interdependent, you cannot choose one as a "solution" and neglect the other. The objective of the Polarity Management™ perspective is to get the best of both opposites while avoiding the limits of each.
>
> (p. xviii)

In any significant change initiative, there will always be tension between the status quo (tradition) and change. The critical question for diversity practitioners is this: how do we realize the full benefit of keeping what's important about our past and current diversity and inclusion experience, and innovate and learn new experiences so we can adapt to changing demographic realities? I believe we need to apply this thinking to our diversity, equity, and inclusion change efforts and practices. Based on Johnson (1992, 1998; see also https://assessmypolarities.com), I have adapted three key steps for leveraging the power of polarities in diversity and inclusion work:

1 **See it:** determine whether you have a diversity and inclusion problem to solve or a polarity to manage. Remember that there is a polarity behind every problem. Analyze statements such as "we need more women and minorities," "there is too much focus on numbers and representation, and not enough on qualifications," "White males are losing out on this strategy." Are we addressing a problem or trying to manage a polarity?
2 **Map it:** map the exclusion and inclusion polarity to see the whole picture, giving you critical insight into the upsides and downsides of both values. In any polarity people take on certain roles. Diversity and inclusion practitioners want change from the status quo. They are experiencing the downside of the pole that is overvalued by the group. Some citizens fear growing diversity and are therefore the protectors of the status quo. They want to keep the valuable upside benefits of the current dominant value or pole (exclusion) and they tend to fear the downsides of the pole that others are pushing for (inclusion). They fear they will lose out because of the growing diversity. Many organizations over-emphasize a single pole and increasingly experience its downside over time. Ironically, we get what we are afraid of by clinging to its apparent opposite (so we do things like set arbitrary diversity goals in the name of inclusion). This is a vicious cycle. This is where polarization occurs. The more

you push for diversity goals, the more working-class White males perceive this as threatening their personal situation (sense of exclusion or reverse discrimination), so they increasingly push back against your efforts.

3 **Leverage it:** define and monitor action steps and early warning signs to maximize the benefits and minimize the downsides of difference. There are many polarities and paradoxes in diversity, equity, and inclusion work. Bhatia et al. (2015) point out "that exclusively focusing on the representation of minority groups in an effort to create a diverse staff ... fails to accomplish that end" (p. 3). They go on to say that:

> Diversity strategies that overemphasize representation or are otherwise narrow in their approach may cause even well-intentioned organizations to stumble into one of several common pitfalls ... [including] the following: treating diversity as an HR or isolated function, defining diversity narrowly, failing to commit fully and authentically, expecting change without accountability, counting on minority groups to drive change, permitting an inhospitable environment, isolating minorities in their respective niche markets, [and] ignoring the human elements of diversity. Companies derailed by these pitfalls often have tense communications, higher turnover, and in extreme situations, may prematurely abandon their diversity efforts altogether.
>
> (Bhatia et al., 2015, p. 3)

## Operationalizing the Change Agenda

Building a resilient change agenda for diversity and inclusion is not a simple task. A question posed to me recently was: "A company commits to diversity, that's great! But is it reasonable to expect changes to how, when, where the work gets done to accommodate this growing diversity?"

Building an inclusive culture is not for the faint of heart, not for those with a short-term perspective, and not for those whose minds continue to be burdened by historic and often undisturbed bias. It takes a firm understanding of the context in which the change will occur, the needed resources (including a carefully developed and intentional strategy), as well as a clear focus on the systems, practices, and patterns of behavior that drive performance.

We must learn to coexist with all our differences and colors if our earthly home is to be sustainable. Learning to co-exist means measured speech, respectful behavior, and systems that are built on inclusivity amid growing differences.

Most importantly, leadership must move from acceptance of diversity as a necessary compliance requirement to a deeply held conviction that it must be part of the DNA of the organization to survive. Resilient and inclusive cultures are adaptive and agile and take time, commitment, and relentless energy to create. Is your organization up to the challenge?

Our world exists on many levels. Our relationships grow more interconnected and global. Survival cannot be achieved by one socioeconomic level, one ethnic group, or gender; it is intertwined in the destiny of us all. Climate change has a significant impact on the ecosystem of our relationships with one another as we run toward safety, stability, peace, and survival. Figure 22.5 graphically illustrates that culture and climate, the spirit of the times, the evolving practices, and the commitment of inclusive leaders are critical to sustainable and resilient outcomes over time.

Change must occur at multiple levels to be sustainable and to resist effort to reverse progress and policies. Four themes are important to consider during the development and implementation of a diversity, equity, and inclusion change strategy:

1 **Macro, Meso, and Micro Context for Change/Spirit of the Times.** This includes a clear understanding of the social context in which change will occur. It includes the degree of respectful versus hateful speech, progressive versus regressive leadership and governance, and the growing diversity of stakeholders. Change is in the context of many levels of power and privilege. Leaders must become students of context and resistance.
2 **Culture and Climate, and Organizational Support and Readiness for Change.** Successful outcomes depend on the degree to which leaders understand and embrace the business case and organizational imperative and demonstrate commitment to it and the degree to which there is a sense of belonging and inclusion in the organization and support for the effort by employees and other stakeholders.
3 **Inclusive Leadership Maturity—Setting the Right Tone.** Leadership readiness is key to getting it right and sustaining commitment. The level of commitment by senior leadership, the presence of inclusive change mechanisms (expectations, commitment, and governance of the strategy), and clear expectations and accountability that have been established and measured, including the consequences for noncompliance, are fundamental.
4 **Systemic Maturity—Evolving Practices, Policies, Systems.** Leaders must examine human resource systems to ensure that organizational policies, practices, and systems are bias-free, inclusive, and help to foster a sense of belonging and inclusion.

## In Summary: Implications for Practice

Diversity, equity, and inclusion initiatives are becoming significant gamechangers in twenty-first-century human capital management and

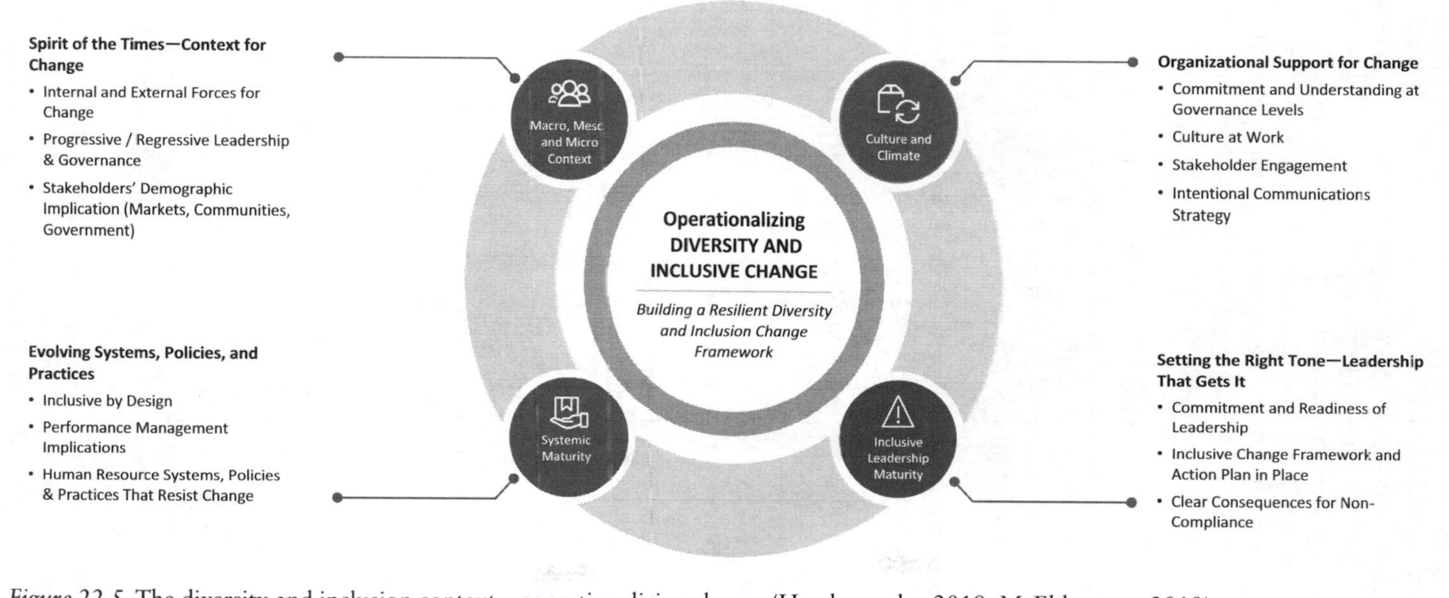


*Figure 22.5* The diversity and inclusion context—operationalizing change (Henderworks, 2019; McEldowney, 2018).

organization sustainability. They require committed leaders who get it. Corporate, government, NGO, and civil society leaders must deepen their understanding of the impact of demographic change and adapt their behaviors, processes, and institutional systems to become more inclusive of growing diversity. They must pay close attention to their offensive and defensive game to understand the forces supporting their efforts and those that resist inclusion. The following are 12 action-oriented strategies for inclusive leaders and change agents:

1 **Get in front of the past.** The U.S. is quickly becoming a "majority-minority" society; learn to embrace and value the differences that this diversity brings to us all. Do not dwell on the past but find ways to get out in front of this positive change. Create intentional and progressive strategies to defend against those who would oppose this inclusion.
2 **Reclaim your voice, become a provocateur.** Too many have been naively sitting on the sidelines in discussions and venues that are shaping public policy and diversity change strategies. Get involved. Offer alternatives. Share the impact of decisions in your organization, government, and community.
3 **Expose the truth.** Many leaders are using fake narratives and fear to heighten tensions between diverse groups. Call them out at all levels: social media, town hall meetings, team meetings, and with public commentary.
4 **Don't lie down when being attacked.** Clearly examine the intent of such attacks and share confidently the impact on you and your co-workers and community. Enlist others to fight against any repression and hate.
5 **Mobilize your resistance bloc.** Many of these anti-diversity leaders who are giving voice to hate and fear do so because many progressive leaders took this fringe movement for granted and did not resist their hate. Host discussion groups to share your knowledge and educate your family and community on what is at stake. Recognize that this bias and hate are finding their way into the workplace.
6 **Get out of your echo chamber.** Resistance to bigotry and hate has to be multifaceted, multicultural, and collaborative. Many anti-diversity leaders are trying to fracture relationships across group-based identities. Identify and strengthen relationships with allies in other identity groups (Armstrong & Stocking, 2016). Build a "fusion" strategy across difference, as Reverend William Barber (2016) mentions.
7 **Get educated on diversity, equity, and inclusion issues, and the implications of those who might resist change, and understand the impact on your identity group.** Seek to understand issues within

your workplace culture. Share what you have learned. It will take a village to address the forces that resist inclusive change.

8. **Understand what is behind disparaging words, expressions, and narratives.** Try to discern the underlying motives and behaviors. Seek to understand the root cause of such hate and bigotry. Share the real stories and the truth about such motives. Know that words matter.
9. **Assume that the vast majority of Americans, across ideology and socio-economic status, want the best for America.** Search for common ground, mutually beneficial outcomes, and ways to fight bigotry and hate, across demographic divides. As a leader, confront disrespectful and harassing behavior in the workplace.
10. **Challenge your organizational and corporate leaders to speak candidly about diversity and inclusion.** Support them in addressing issues that negatively impact relationships at work such as the Charlottesville incident (McEldowney, 2018), the Black Lives Matter movement (McKenna, 2018), and other polarizing topics. Remember that attitudes and opinions expressed by leadership help assure the organization that leaders are on top of these issues and that they are helping with healing during these trying times.
11. **Help others see how context shapes responses and emotional outbursts by fellow employees and members of the community who may be traumatized by current events.** Make visible how things get done in practice. Some may not see how a personal situation can be viewed as a barometer of larger societal ills. Many people examine events and behavior in the context of historical and group-based lens. Many others do not.
12. **Understand that sometimes personal pain, trauma, and loss can make some more sympathetic to larger, longer-term systemic racism and bias.** This is especially true when natural disasters like Hurricane Harvey strike. Adversity shapes the lens through which many respond to current issues. People are sometimes less sympathetic when their own lives and conditions have been severely and negatively impacted by disaster.

## References

Armstrong, J., & Stocking, B. (2016). *Collaborating with men: Changing workplace culture to be more inclusive for women.* Murray Edwards College, University of Cambridge. https:// www.murrayedwards.cam.ac.uk/sites/default/files/ Collaborating%20with%20Men%20-%20FINAL%20Report.pdf

Barber, W. J. (2016). *The third reconstruction: Moral Mondays, fusion politics, and the justice movement.* Boston, MA: Beacon.

Bhatia, A., Hay, B., Stellmaszek, F., Fraenkel, M., & Joshi, R. (2015, January). *The diversity paradox: Capturing the value of difference by looking beyond the numbers*. *The B Team*. https://bteam.org/assets/reports/B-Team-The-Diversity-Paradox.pdf

Bourke, J., & Dillon, B. (2016, April 14). *The six signature traits of inclusive leadership: Thriving in a diverse new world*. Deloitte Insights, Deloitte. https://www2.deloitte.com/us/en/insights/topics/talent/six-signature-traits-of-inclusive-leadership.html

Business Roundtable. (2019, August 19). *Business roundtable redefines the purpose of a corporation to promote an economy that serves all Americans*. https://www.businessroundtable.org/business-roundtable-redefines-the-purpose-of-a-corporation-to-promote-an-economy-that-serves-all-americans

Case, A., & Deaton, A. (2017). *Mortality and morbidity in the 21st century*. Brooking Papers on Economic Activity, BPEA Conference Drafts.

Dempsey, M., & Brafman, O. (2018). *Radical inclusion: What the post-9/11 world should have taught us about leadership*. Arlington, VA: Missionday Publishing.

Ferdman, B. M. (1995). Cultural identity and diversity in organizations: Bridging the gap between group differences and individual uniqueness. In M. M. Chemers, S. Oskamp, & M. A. Costanzo (Eds.), *Diversity in organizations: New perspectives for a changing workplace* (pp. 37–61). Thousand Oaks, CA: Sage. https://doi.org/10.4135/9781452243405.n3

Ferdman, B. M. (2003). Learning about our and others' selves: Multiple identities and their sources. In N. Boyacigiller, R. Goodman, & M. Phillips (Eds.), *Crossing cultures: Insights from master teachers* (pp. 49–61). London, UK: Routledge.

Ferdman, B. M. (2014). The practice of inclusion in diverse organizations: Toward a systemic and inclusive framework. In B. M. Ferdman & B. R. Deane (Eds.), *Diversity at work: The practice of inclusion* (pp. 3–54). San Francisco, CA: Jossey-Bass. https://doi.org/10.1002/9781118764282.ch1

Ferdman, B. M. & Deane, B. R. (Eds.) (2014). *Diversity at work: The practice of inclusion*. San Francisco, CA: Jossey-Bass.

Hassan, A. (2019, November 12). Hate crimes violence hits 16-year high, F.B.I. reports. *New York Times*. https://www.nytimes.com/2019/11/12/us/hate-crimes-fbi-report.html

Henderson, E. (2017, March 30). *Perversity: Actions and words to disparage and deceive people about the positive impact of America's diversity and inclusion imperative* [Post]. LinkedIn. https://www.linkedin.com/pulse/perversity-actions-words-disparage-deceive-people-impact-henderson

Henderson, E. (2019, October 7) *Fractionality — The political, economic and socially conservative response to diversity, equity, inclusion and intersectionality*. Medium. https://medium.com/@effenus.henderson/fractionality-the-political-economic-and-socially-conservative-response-to-diversity-equity-3704be9fa4c6

Hofmans, J., & Judge, T. A. (2019, September 18). Hiring for culture fit doesn't have to undermine diversity. *Harvard Business Review Digital Articles*. https://hbr.org/2019/09/hiring-for-culture-fit-doesnt-have-to-undermine-diversity

Hunt, V., Prince, S., Dixon-Fyle. S., & Yee, L. (2018, January). *Delivering through diversity*. McKinsey & Company. https://www.mckinsey.com/business-functions/organization/our-insights/delivering-through-diversity

Johnson, B. (1992). *Polarity management: Identifying and managing unsolvable problems*. Amherst, MA: HRD Press.

Johnson, B. (1998). *Polarity management: A summary introduction*. https://www.jpr.org.uk/documents/14-06-19.Barry_Johnson.Polarity_Management.pdf

Krupa, M. (2018, June 22). *America is changing. bigoted slurs, immigration bans and racist rallies can't change that*. CNN. https://www.cnn.com/2018/01/12/health/changing-face-of-america-trnd/index.html

McEldowney, M. (2018, August 12). *What Charlottesville changed*. Politico.com. https://www.politico.com/magazine/story/2018/08/12/charlottesville-anniversary-supremacists-protests-dc-virginia–219353

McKenna, C. (2018, June 7). *Black lives matter in conversation: Brooking panelists discuss race, state violence, and representation*. Brookings Institution. https://www.brookings.edu/blog/brookings-now/2018/06/27/black-lives-matter-in-conversation-brookings-panelists-discuss-race-state-violence-and-representation

Metzl, J. M. (2019). *Dying of Whiteness: How the politics of racial resentment is killing America's heartland*. New York, NY: Basic Books.

Miller, F. A., & Katz, J. H. (2002). *The inclusion breakthrough: Unleashing the real power of diversity*. San Francisco, CA: Berrett-Koehler.

Neese, B. (2016). *Intercultural communication: High- and low-context cultures*. Southeastern University. http://online.seu.edu/high-and-low-context-cultures

O'Mara, J., Richter, A., & 95 Expert Panelists (2016). *Global diversity and inclusion benchmarks: Standards for organizations around the world*. Centre for Global Inclusion. https://centreforglobalinclusion.org/gdib

Resnick, B. (2017). *White fear of demographic change is a powerful psychological force: Increasing diversity could make America a more hostile place*. Vox.com. www.vox.com/science-and-health/2017/1/26/14340542/white-fear-trump-psychology-minority-majority

Part V

# Approaches and Resources for Developing Inclusive Leadership

# 23 Accelerating the Development of Inclusive Leadership in a Global Materials Organization

*Judith H. Katz, Frederick A. Miller, and Monica E. Biggs*

## Case for Change

Many organizations today are focusing on the need for greater inclusion and how to leverage diversity as a lever for higher performance (Ferdman, 2014; Holvino et al., 2004; Katz & Miller, 2014; Katz & Miller, 2016; Miller & Katz, 2002). The challenge for many organizations is not only to develop inclusive leaders who learn the skills needed to model and practice inclusive interactions but also to ensure that the practice of those behaviors is sustainable and leads to organization-wide culture change (Hubbard, 2004; Katz & Miller, 2017).

With a history going back over 100 years, our client is a global leader in the production of specialty materials that are used in most major industries and consumer applications. It employs 7,500 people at manufacturing plants and operations centers around the world. The company has been successful by focusing on safety, innovation, and results. Its ability to execute and achieve business objectives, despite lean resources and competitive pressures, is a source of pride and a hallmark of its strong productivity culture.

Over the past few years, the company has been rolling out a new business model and strategy to drive additional value creation and be positioned to thrive in an increasingly uncertain global business climate. The CEO and the Senior Vice President of Human Resources understood that a diverse and inclusive work environment—which they described as "a winning culture where everyone's ideas are welcome and people feel they belong"—was a key enabler to successful business model execution. Greater inclusion and engagement were seen as market differentiators that could drive higher profitability, productivity, customer satisfaction, and reduce safety incidents.

## Inclusion as the *HOW*® Strategy

In our discussions with clients, we find it useful to position inclusion not as an endpoint but as the means to the organization getting the culture it needs to succeed. We see inclusion as a *HOW*—*how* the culture makes it safe for people to bring their different ideas, perspectives, and talents; *how* teams interact more effectively to drive greater collaboration and innovation; *how* an organization aligns its culture with its strategies for higher operational performance (Katz & Miller, 2010).

## Creating the Foundation for Inclusive Leadership

Our initial Inclusion as the *HOW*® Strategy focused on three key interventions over a 90-day period (see Figure 23.1):

1. A culture assessment to understand current state, identify areas for change, and provide a foundation for purposeful direction.
2. Education in inclusive mindsets and behaviors for Employee Resource Group (ERGs) members, the Advisory Council for Women, and other change leaders to prepare them to act as sounding boards, advocate for culture change, and start modeling the new desired behaviors.
3. Presence Consulting® to engage selected leaders in a "proof-of-concept" phase to test whether the use of inclusive mindsets and behaviors would enhance organizational effectiveness and project performance, improve the quality of the leaders' interactions with people, increase engagement, and reduce waste—outcomes that had all been achieved in other client systems.

The key question: was this organization ready for such a change in what leaders expect and how everyone interacts?

## Culture Assessment Process

We undertook a culture assessment that included face-to-face and phone interviews and an electronic survey with approximately 150 people, who were selected based on various criteria (e.g., level, function, gender, years of service, and geography) to represent a cross-section of the organization. In the interviews, individuals identified what they saw as the top

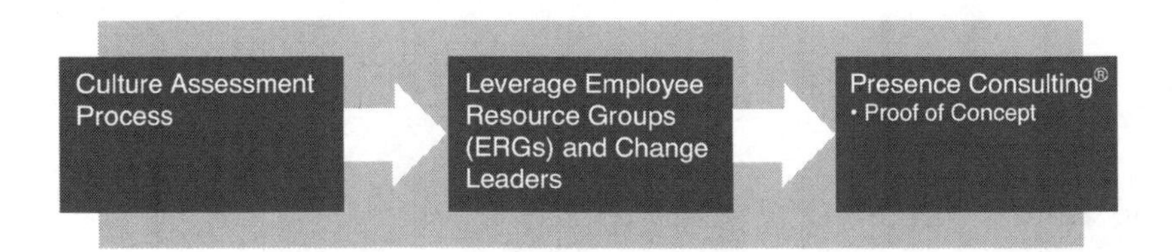


*Figure 23.1* Three key interventions.

five challenges and opportunities facing the company as well as key barriers to greater inclusion and engagement. The same electronic survey (without interviews) was administered to broaden the population surveyed.

The assessment showed that people were proud to work for the company and saw it as a place for smart, talented people to thrive. They liked the fast pace and constant change and had a strong willingness and ability to execute. They believed the new business model was transforming the organization. However, while people appreciated the efforts to create more inclusion and engagement, they also felt they were treated as costs rather than as assets to be nourished and invested in. This feeling, coupled with the fact that people were sought after by competitors and regularly scouted by headhunters, indicated the organization was facing significant risk of losing talent at all levels in the near future, including several of the top 100 leaders. This was of great concern to the senior leadership as they considered their pipeline and succession.

While many leaders believed that a diverse and inclusive culture would help drive growth and productivity, they struggled with making day-to-day interactions more inclusive. They lacked the skills and know-how to create such an environment. Few received direct feedback on their leadership styles. Little had been done to develop inclusive leadership capacity and capabilities, nor were inclusion-supportive behaviors made explicit as expectations for how leaders were to interact with others or be part of the criteria for performance feedback and evaluation.

At its most elemental level, an organization is only as productive as the interactions that take place among individuals, teams, and work groups. We have developed a set of standard interaction tools—Conscious Actions for Inclusion (see Figure 23.2)—that provide a common language and, when used consistently, increase "right first time" interactions and enable a culture in which people can join each other to do their best work (Katz & Miller, 2013). Conscious Actions for Inclusion were taught and modeled throughout the initiative to support the more rapid adoption of inclusive leadership mindsets and skills. These behaviors will be discussed in more detail in the sections following.

## Leveraging Change Advocates

Approximately 30 Employee Resource Group (ERG) members, the Advisory Council for Women, and others in the organization became early adopters and advocates for the culture change to accelerate the development of an inclusive and engaged work environment. Their role was to be the first to model the new ways of thinking and interacting. These individuals became valuable sounding boards, helped validate the Culture Assessment findings, and provided ideas and feedback as the

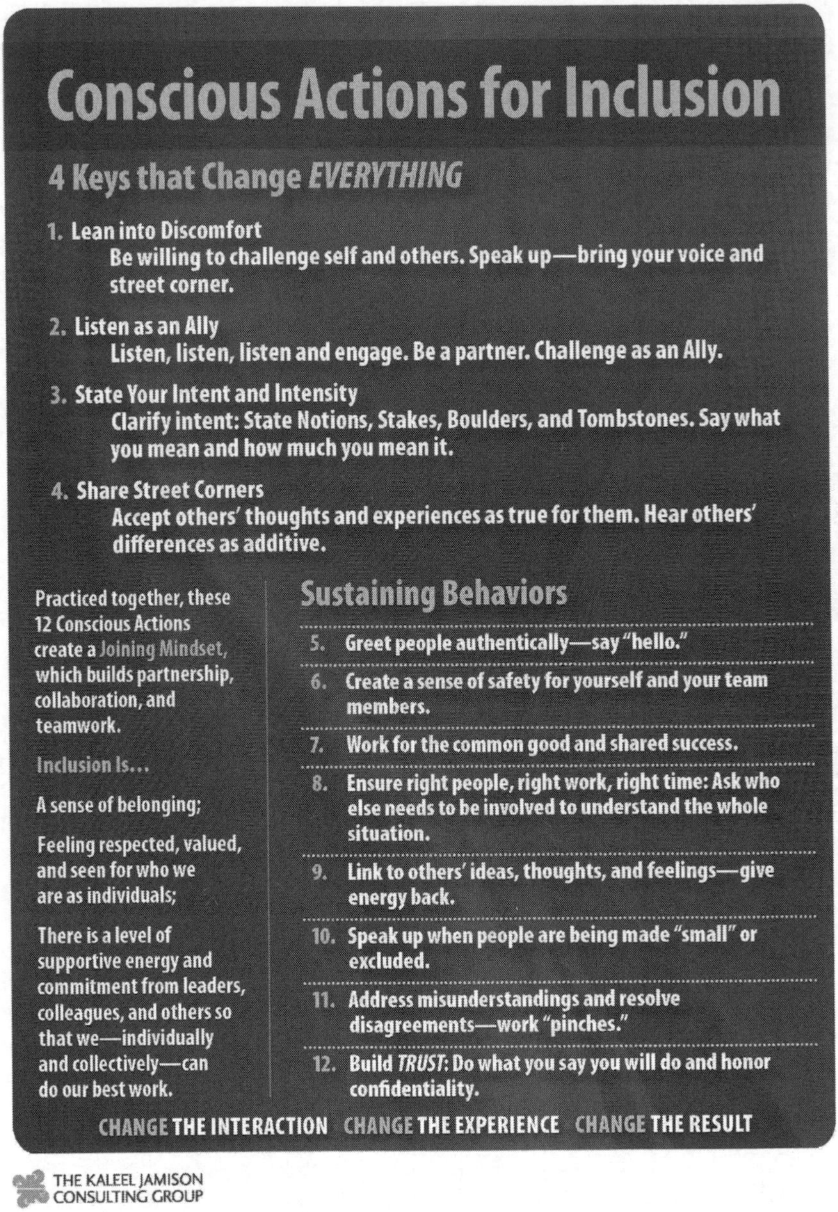

# Conscious Actions for Inclusion

## 4 Keys that Change *EVERYTHING*

1. **Lean into Discomfort**
   Be willing to challenge self and others. Speak up—bring your voice and street corner.
2. **Listen as an Ally**
   Listen, listen, listen and engage. Be a partner. Challenge as an Ally.
3. **State Your Intent and Intensity**
   Clarify intent: State Notions, Stakes, Boulders, and Tombstones. Say what you mean and how much you mean it.
4. **Share Street Corners**
   Accept others' thoughts and experiences as true for them. Hear others' differences as additive.

Practiced together, these 12 Conscious Actions create a Joining Mindset, which builds partnership, collaboration, and teamwork.

Inclusion Is...

A sense of belonging;

Feeling respected, valued, and seen for who we are as individuals;

There is a level of supportive energy and commitment from leaders, colleagues, and others so that we—individually and collectively—can do our best work.

## Sustaining Behaviors

5. Greet people authentically—say "hello."
6. Create a sense of safety for yourself and your team members.
7. Work for the common good and shared success.
8. Ensure right people, right work, right time: Ask who else needs to be involved to understand the whole situation.
9. Link to others' ideas, thoughts, and feelings—give energy back.
10. Speak up when people are being made "small" or excluded.
11. Address misunderstandings and resolve disagreements—work "pinches."
12. Build *TRUST*: Do what you say you will do and honor confidentiality.

CHANGE THE INTERACTION CHANGE THE EXPERIENCE CHANGE THE RESULT

THE KALEEL JAMISON CONSULTING GROUP

*Figure 23.2* Conscious actions for inclusion.

strategy was designed and implemented. They also shared their own examples of how applying inclusive behaviors improved collaboration and problem solving and reduced waste, which helped make the business case for culture change real for people.

## Presence Consulting® as Proof of Concept

Presence Consulting® was used to accelerate the coaching and feedback process as a proof-of-concept or pilot project to provide "evidence" that inclusive leadership changed the quality of people's interactions and, therefore, reduced waste and improved results. This approach pairs leaders who are leaning in and willing to at least try the new inclusive mindsets and behaviors on for size with Presence Consultants who support them in identifying opportunities to apply inclusive behaviors as they lead their teams. Three leaders were selected to participate based on their experience and level in the organization, their ability and willingness to influence and drive change, and representation of different parts of the business. Our expectation was that, after experiencing and demonstrating the differences made by practicing more inclusive leadership, these leaders would influence and support their peers to adopt new ways of thinking and interacting more rapidly. After being introduced to the concepts of Joining versus Judging Mindset (see Figure 23.3) and Conscious Actions for Inclusion (Figure 23.2), the leaders selected specific behaviors to practice.

A *joining mindset* is a fundamental component of inclusive leadership in that it sets the stage for how a person sees and interacts with others. Rather than *judging* others (i.e., withholding trust, expecting them to "prove" themselves, not giving the benefit of the doubt, focusing on blame rather than understanding and appreciation), individuals start from a focus on *joining* (i.e., assuming the other person has something of value to offer, being curious when differences arise, being open, truly listening, and seeking to find win/win solutions). In addition, the Conscious Actions for Inclusion provide specific language and behaviors to support and reinforce a joining mindset, as well as a common language to create greater understanding and partnership within teams and between team members.

Each Presence Consultant shadowed their leader in meetings—in person or virtually, one on one or with their teams. The consultant's role was to provide immediate feedback on the leader's verbal and nonverbal behaviors in handling the interactions, specifically about the use of the targeted inclusive behaviors. As the Presence Consultants came to understand the leader's style, they offered coaching about how to get unstuck from old routines and assisted the leader to see how changing the quality of interactions drives better results.

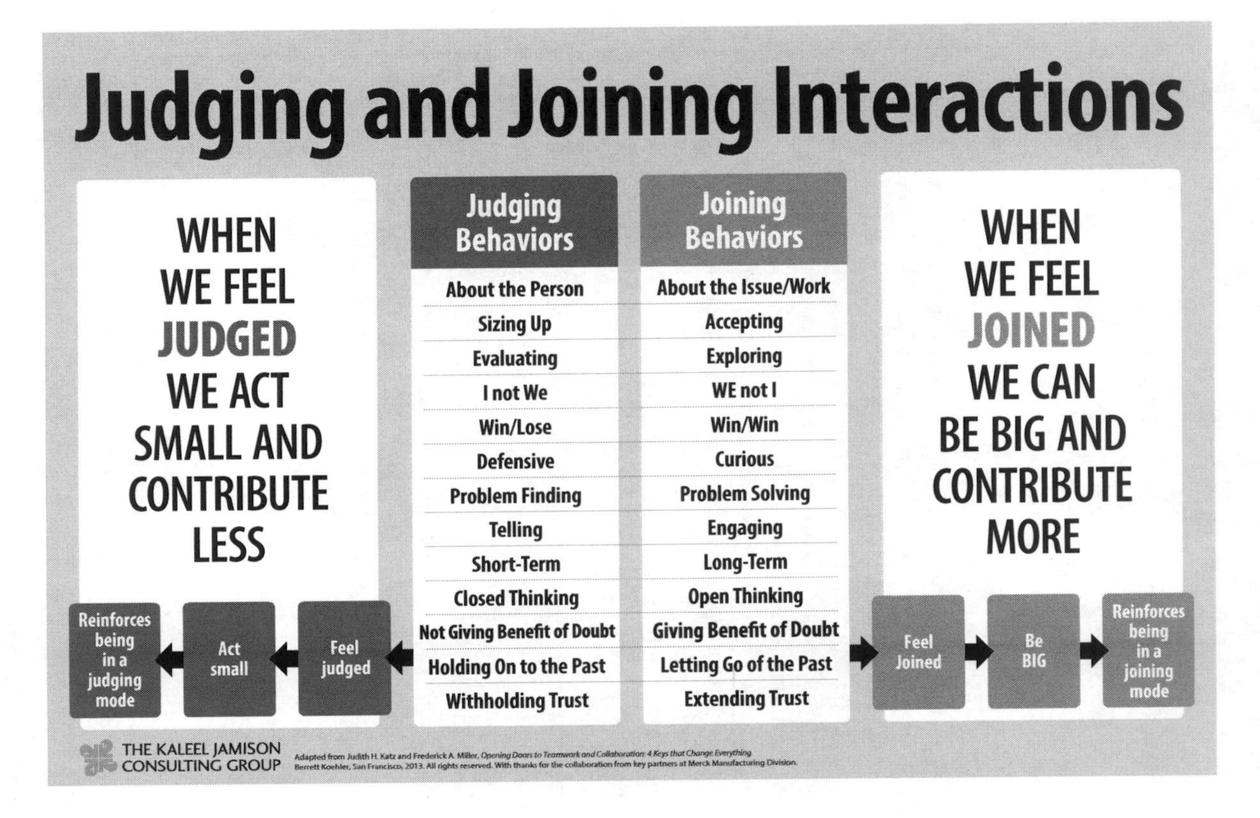


*Figure 23.3* Judging versus joining.

As the Presence Consulting process continued, leaders gained in their ability and consistency in demonstrating a *Joining Mindset* and practicing the *Conscious Actions for Inclusion*, which led to greater payoffs in their interactions with their team members and in achieving results. Payoffs included:

- **Less wasted effort and better solutions in meetings** as they used standard work agendas and ground rules to make meetings more effective and ensure the right people with the right information were "in the room" before final decisions were made.
- **Increased engagement and less waste in interactions** as they listened more, interrupted less, challenged others in a joining way, gave positive feedback when appropriate (giving energy back), and clarified the intent and intensity of their own communications—actions that enabled their team members to feel supported and appreciated and know that not only was it safe for them to give their thinking, but that their thinking was wanted, expected, and would be built upon.
- **Faster knowledge transfer and improved problem solving** by accessing a greater diversity of perspectives and skillsets as others were invited to share their different "street corners."
- **Improved team performance** as regular practice of a joining mindset and a common language of inclusion created an environment in which everyone in the room saw each other as part of the team and felt safe enough to speak up (Miller & Katz, 2018), resolve disagreements, and collaborate on tasks.

## Preparing for a "New" Annual Leadership Meeting

Based on the findings from the culture assessment, the voices of the early adopters, and the experience of the three leaders involved in the proof-of-concept process, the company decided that engaging the top 400 leaders in becoming more inclusive was critical for success. Like most, the company faced many competing demands on the business and its leaders. If the leadership meeting was going to be used as a vehicle for the senior leaders to accelerate adoption of a joining mindset and inclusive behaviors as a way to engage their team members and achieve results, it needed to be radically different from prior meetings, which tended to be top down, slide-deck-heavy, and consisting primarily of one-way communication. An overview of the preparations for the annual meeting is shown in Figure 23.4.

As shown in Figure 23.4, preparations for the meetings included a multi-part plan to position leaders to experience a new and different kind of annual meeting. The plans were developed to enable each leader to:

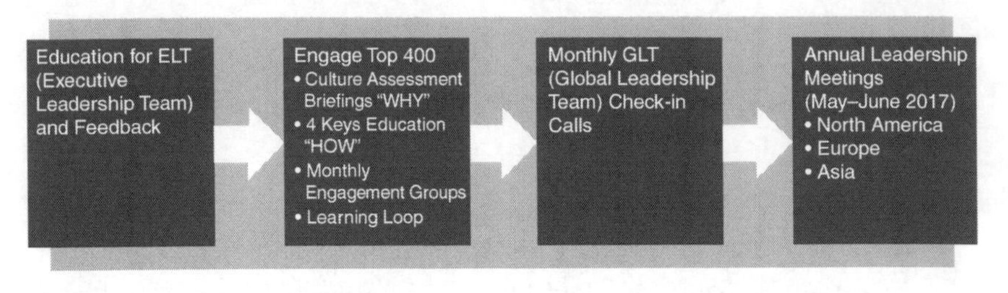


*Figure 23.4* Focus of interventions in preparation for annual leadership meetings.

- Prepare for the different format for the meeting through pre-readings and active participation with an engagement group prior to the meeting to help understand the culture assessment process and findings, read about and discuss what inclusion means and why it is important to the organization, and have a safe place to experiment with inclusive mindsets and behaviors.
- Actively contribute and take ownership of their experience.
- Have space and time to internalize why inclusion is important to the business and their area of responsibility.
- Model inclusion in their conversations and support their peers in new ways of thinking and interacting.
- Share examples of how inclusive behaviors have improved performance.
- Generate momentum and accountability for transferring knowledge back to their teams.
- Give leadership to the effort and enhance their actions regarding engagement and "Inclusion as the *HOW*®."

## Before the Annual Leadership Meetings: Connect and Educate Leaders

It was important to prepare leaders before the meeting to engage differently and to optimize their development of inclusive mindsets and behaviors. In the three months before the meeting, the 400 top leaders were organized regionally into Engagement Groups, each with ten people across the enterprise and the businesses, with varied functions, roles, tenure, etc. Each group was convened and facilitated by a member of the Global Leadership Team (GLT)—a group of 60 of the most senior leaders in the organization. As the organization's primary senior-level business and functional leadership team, the GLT's role in the overall change effort was to be a conduit both to the executive team and to the rest of the organization. The Engagement Groups met monthly in one-hour Skype calls, tasked to:

- Understand, discuss, and identify actions in response to the Culture Assessment findings.
- Learn about inclusion concepts and tools.
- Join peers in experimenting with new ways of interacting.
- Build momentum for participation in the annual meeting.

Monthly conference calls, led by a senior leader, also provided an opportunity for people to apply inclusive mindsets and behaviors in a virtual team setting. Inclusive meeting norms such as standard work agendas and check-ins (Miller & Katz, 2012) were put into practice, and Conscious Actions for Inclusion—such as slowing down to invite and listen to everyone's perspective or "street corner," leaning into discomfort to speak up or disagree, and being clear about intent and intensity—were encouraged by the senior leadership team (Katz & Miller, 2013).

Between the monthly calls, the groups leveraged the organization's internal social networking and collaboration platform, already in use across the organization, to stay engaged with each other, read articles, share links to webinars and videos, post questions and comments, and get assignments. Assignments helped individuals prepare for the monthly engagement group meetings and the leadership meeting itself as they were expected to take more ownership as leaders for the culture change effort. For example, in preparation for the leadership meeting, they were asked to gather additional perspectives by interviewing four or five people in the company (not direct reports) and a few people from outside the company to better understand barriers to doing their best work, what has slowed or impeded progress regarding leveraging diversity and/or greater inclusion in the workplace, and what leaders should be thinking about with respect to people. Eventually, they shared the insights gained as a result of hearing others' perspectives at the leadership meeting and used that as a foundation for developing action plans going forward.

The GLT members met monthly as a group with the Executive Team to compare notes on how their Engagement Groups were moving forward. Facilitated by one of the officers, who acted as Executive Sponsor, the check-ins were vital to sustain focus and energy, to clarify role expectations, and to ensure engagement by region.

## The Leadership Meetings: Using Inclusion to Accelerate Inclusive Leadership Development

When each of the meetings began, rather than asking attendees to take their seats inside the ballroom as was customary, the whole group gathered in the reception area where they were welcomed by the Executive Sponsor and invited to say "hello" to every person at the meeting (Miller & Katz, 2005).

On a fundamental level, people must be seen and acknowledged in order to do their best work. The very act of connecting via hellos is an initial invitation to join the discussion and make one's voice heard: it carries the message that "I see you, and I value you." Saying hello and making connections set the context for everyone to feel welcomed and invited to contribute. (Ideally, *every* team meeting should begin with "hellos" to model and reinforce the importance of inclusive practices.) Connecting, even briefly, with each person in the room energized the group and set the stage for "something different."

To create a more inclusive meeting environment, the meeting room was set up with circles of chairs (no tables). People sat with their Engagement Groups while two senior executives shared their expectations of what being a "good" meeting participant looked like. Making expectations explicit was a powerful way to contract with the group. It reinforced the behaviors that would increase inclusion, such as sharing your "street corner," listening and challenging as an ally, and being aware of—and adjusting for—style, culture, and language differences in the room. They made it clear that this was going to be a meeting of participation, not one of being silent spectators, which is one of the foundational principles of inclusive leadership and partnership. Critical to the success of the leadership meeting was creating and demonstrating an inclusive environment, not only in words but in all elements of its design and actions.

## Stories of Success

At several points during each of the sessions, leaders shared stories of how they had successfully used a joining mindset and inclusive behaviors in various work situations in the previous months. This proved to be a powerful way to energize people and build momentum. The success stories enabled people to rally together. They helped the group focus on what was working and how far the group had come, and they began to shift the narrative. The stories included examples about how using the Conscious Actions for Inclusion reduced waste, engaged people for better problem solving, improved collaboration, and moved the company toward operationalizing inclusion-building practices as key components of their proprietary Inclusive and Engaged Organization (IEO).

In the past, when business success stories had been presented, the focus was only on business results. Now, there was an emphasis not only on what was accomplished, but on *HOW* it was accomplished through the use of inclusive behaviors and a joining mindset. This addressed spoken and unspoken objections to inclusion as being "fluffy" or soft. The success stories demonstrated the critical role of inclusion as a key driver for performance and enhanced results, and as a business differentiator for the organization to move from at times being a short-term focused "results-at-any-cost organization" that treated its people as costs and replaceable cogs, to a forward-thinking organization that treated its people as true human resources—valuable resources that, if treated with care and respect, would appreciate in value and provide a handsome return on investment.

## Attendee (Not Facilitator)-Driven Content

The meeting design described above was radically different from those of past years in that most of the content was supplied by the attendees. The role of the facilitators, including the GLT, was to fully engage attendees, ensure that everyone had a voice in discussions, support experimentation and learning, and model inclusive ways of interacting. Aspects of the meeting that heightened inclusiveness and accelerated learning included:

- Use of real-time electronic polling to assess the degree of *Joining versus Judging* mindsets among the attendees.
- Open microphone at all sessions that encouraged a wider range of individuals to engage in the topic that was being discussed and share learning throughout the session.
- Utilizing participant-developed content throughout the meeting, including videos, "selfies" (short testimonials about personal learning journeys), success stories, and business cases highlighting what they had learned about the impact of inclusion on business results.
- Positioning *Engagement Groups* as a "touchstone" for attendees to connect with several times during the meeting. Within this peer group, attendees felt safe to share what they had learned, thought about, and experimented with related to engagement and inclusion in the months leading up to the leadership meeting. This output was consolidated and compared across the groups and provided the foundation for action and accountability planning.
- Presenting business updates with a focus not only on results, but also on how leaders had engaged their people to drive performance.
- Building in personal ownership for inclusive leadership. Every leader committed to one action they would take with their team and two behaviors they would personally demonstrate in the workplace. These commitments were recorded and shared as "I will" statements.

## Post Leadership Meetings: Support and Build Accountable Leaders

In a post-leadership-meeting communication, the Executive Sponsor said:

> Our time together allowed us to lean into discomfort to share our vulnerabilities and commit to be better leaders within our teams and

in working across the company. It's evident that we have a profound desire to create a positive culture as we execute for business success.

He asked for ongoing commitment and accountability to create what's next through several specific actions (see Figure 23.5 for an overview).

The post-meeting action plans implemented throughout the organization included:

1 **Continue Engagement Groups and monthly GLT check-in calls** to foster strong executive sponsorship and support leaders as they continued to experiment and transfer knowledge and skills to peers, key partners, and their teams. A workbook was provided at the leadership meeting that included discussion starters and skill-building activities for teams, as well as a monthly calendar of recommended things to read, do, watch, try and share.
2 **Begin a broader conversation** with the organization about putting an Inclusive and Engaged Organization into practice using *Inclusion as the HOW*, including the *Joining Mindset* and *Conscious Actions for Inclusion*.
3 **Share success stories** across the organization to accelerate a culture of inclusion and engagement to achieve results.

## Measurement of Impact

To begin to measure impact, a subset of the GLT was identified to develop and track accountability and progress. Quarterly reviews are being conducted to assess how inclusion is being demonstrated in

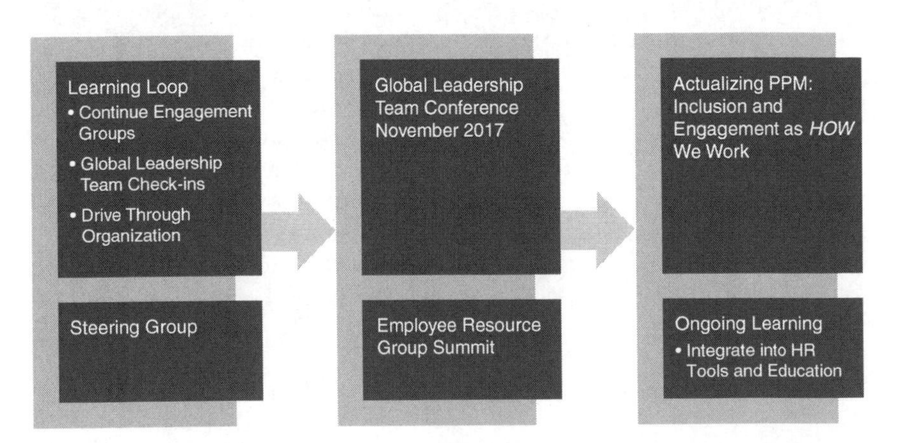


*Figure 23.5* Carrying inclusion and "engagement as the How" forward.

interactions and day-to-day operations: in how people join each other to achieve results, a greater focus on wellness, more volunteer hours, even better safety results, and ever-increasing levels of collaboration across businesses and functions. These measurements are being tracked alongside bottom-line productivity and profitability reports to maintain and cement the connection between the organization's people practices and its business practices.

## Insights and Suggested Actions for Inclusive Leadership

Although we are presenting the experience of a single company, we have seen similar strategies lead to similarly positive results in organizations of all sizes across a range of industries in countries on several continents. Organizations and change agents intent on pursuing sustainable success through building productively inclusive organizational cultures are offered the following suggestions for implementing their own culture-change efforts.

**1. Contract for an initial 90-day plan**
Leaders balance many competing demands on their time and resources, and often drive and measure initiatives quarter by quarter. A 90-day initial plan positions the client for success and creates a readiness to commit to a longer-term culture alignment strategy. Design the initial work to be "bite-size" with clear, achievable deliverables, and milestones.

**2. Use the culture assessment as a benchmark**
The initial culture assessment provided an important benchmark from which to build a global culture-alignment strategy. It highlighted the primary challenges the whole organization faced with respect to engaging people and addressing business needs while still acknowledging the differences across business units and location.

**3. Experiment with a proof-of-concept intervention**
Presence Consulting®, an accelerated coaching and feedback process, was used with three influential leaders as a proof-of-concept or pilot project to provide "evidence" that inclusive leadership changed the quality of people's interactions, reduced waste, and significantly improved results and people's commitment to doing their best work. After experiencing the differences that more inclusive leadership made, these leaders influenced and supported their peers to adopt new ways of thinking and interacting.

**4. Leverage allies to build momentum for change**
Leveraging the employee resource groups, leaders involved with the proof-of-concept and other change leaders enabled the effort to take root and

spread. ERG members and change leaders then could partner with leaders in their areas after the leadership meeting to accelerate change.

**5. Employ inclusive processes to build inclusive global leaders**

The meeting was not positioned as an event or a program, but as a new way of doing business and getting results in collaboration and partnership with people. The events before, during, and after the leadership meeting were designed to model inclusive practices and provided leaders with a safe space to learn, grow, experiment, and take ownership for the changes. To share the results of the culture assessment globally, webinars were developed so every leader could have an opportunity to deeply understand and discuss the current culture and what needed to shift. An inclusion-building webinar (based on our book, *Opening Doors to Teamwork and Collaboration*, Katz & Miller, 2013) introduced new inclusive mindsets and behaviors, and created a common language and gave leaders time and the structure needed to experiment with those behaviors before the global meeting.

## Conclusion

You can't build inclusion without practicing inclusion. To accelerate the development of a more inclusive leadership team, it is critical to use inclusive methodologies. The foundation provided by the cultural assessment helped to define why inclusion was critical to business success, and both leveraging internal advocates and having a "proof-of-concept" application by three key business leaders provided internal energy for making inclusion the *how* to achieve business results. All of this was fundamental to engaging leaders differently and enrolling them in the annual leadership meeting where—before, during, and after the meeting—the leaders themselves could learn about, practice, and then demonstrate in their own inclusion experience how to create a more inclusive and engaged environment. The impact of all of this was that leaders themselves felt more engaged and included—which has made it easier for them to then apply their learnings with their own teams and peer interactions. Moving to this more engaged and inclusive environment, coupled with their strength in achieving business results, is creating unforeseen opportunities and unleashing previously unappreciated skills and greater contributions of a talented and diverse workforce around the globe.

## References

Ferdman, B. M. (2014). The practice of inclusion in diverse organizations: Toward a systematic and inclusive framework. In B. M. Ferdman & B. R. Deane (Eds.), *Diversity at work: The practice of inclusion* (pp. 3–54). San Francisco, CA: Jossey-Bass. https://doi.org/10.1002/9781118764282.ch1

Holvino, E., Ferdman, B. M., & Merrill-Sands, D. (2004). Creating and sustaining diversity and inclusion in organizations: Strategies and approaches. In M. S. Stockdale & F. J. Crosby (Eds.), *The psychology and management of workplace diversity* (pp. 245–276). Malden, MA: Blackwell.

Hubbard, E. E. (2004). *The diversity scorecard: Evaluating the impact of diversity on organizational performance*. Burlington, MA: Elsevier Butterworth.

Katz, J. H., & Miller, F. A. (2010). Inclusion: The HOW for organizational breakthrough. In W. J. Rothwell, J. M. Stavros, R. L. Sullivan, & A. Sullivan (Eds.), *Practicing organization development: A guide for leading change* (3rd ed., pp. 436–445). San Francisco, CA: Pfeiffer.

Katz, J. H., & Miller, F. A. (2013). *Opening doors to teamwork and collaboration: 4 keys that change EVERYTHING*. San Francisco, CA: Berrett-Koehler.

Katz, J. H., & Miller, F. A. (2014). Leaders getting different: Collaboration, the new inclusive workplace, and OD's role. *The OD Practitioner*, *46*(3), 40–45.

Katz, J. H., & Miller, F. A. (2016). Leveraging diversity and inclusion for performance. In W. J. Rothwell, J. M. Stavros, & R. L. Sullivan (Eds.) *Practicing organization development: Leading transformation and change* (4th ed., pp. 366–375). Hoboken, NJ: Wiley. https://doi.org/10.1002/9781119176626.ch26

Katz, J. H., & Miller, F. A. (2017). Leveraging differences and inclusion pays off: Measuring the impact on profits and productivity. *OD Practitioner*, *49*(1), 56–61.

Miller, F. A., & Katz, J. H. (2002). *The inclusion breakthrough: Unleashing the real power of diversity*. San Francisco, CA: Berrett-Koehler.

Miller, F. A., & Katz, J. H. (2005). Hello: An exercise in building an inclusive community. In M. Morrow & K. Patenaude (Eds.), *The 2005 ASTD team and organization development sourcebook* (pp. 5–8). Alexandria, VA: ASTD Press.

Miller, F. A., & Katz, J. H. (2012). *Inclusive meeting norms: Eliminating waste in interactions*. Unpublished article, The Kaleel Jamison Consulting Group, Inc.

Miller, F. A., & Katz, J. H. (2018). *Safe enough to soar: Accelerating trust, inclusion and collaboration in the workplace*. Oakland, CA: Berrett-Koehler.

# 24 Developing Inclusive Ethical Leaders

## An Experiential Service-Learning Approach to Leadership Development Among Millennials

*Audrey J. Murrell, Ray Jones, and Jennifer Petrie-Wyman*

Defined as a leader's influence in shaping environments where belongingness and individual uniqueness are respected, inclusive leadership is often described as a form of relational leadership where the leader exhibits openness and accessibility, and values high-quality interactions among followers (Nembhard & Edmondson, 2006). This type of leadership invites and values diverse input from others who cut across boundaries such as demographics or social identity group membership. Psychological safety is based on individuals' perceptions that they can take interpersonal risks without fear or threat to their individual or social group identity and has been related to leadership style and to positive team and organizational outcomes (Randel et al., 2016).

Inclusive leadership builds trust and connectedness among others while valuing individual contribution and diverse perspectives. This type of leadership at the team, organizational, or societal levels sends a powerful signal to followers that belongingness, psychological safety, and identity are valued across different individuals. Inclusive leadership also incorporates a critical capacity to develop trust and embrace ethical behavior by allowing participants to acknowledge multiple identities in positive and productive ways. Thus, inclusive leadership helps to shape culture and climate of the work team and workplace to be more supportive, trusting, and ethical while modeling the sharing of power across and within diverse groups. Despite the substantial research on the importance of inclusive leadership, there is a need for more examples of how to apply this work to the effective development of inclusive leaders, especially for millennials. One such example is leadership development efforts that shift away from traditional hierarchical, power-focused, and competitive views of leadership toward collaborative, inter-connected, and values-based approaches (Bilimoria, 1995). Some evidence exists that relational and identity-based approaches are effective in leadership development programs that focus on women (Sugiyama et al., 2016).

Based on the changing demographics of the workforce, those within the millennial generation have received a great deal of attention from researchers and human resource professionals in terms of the need to move away from traditional approaches to leadership development (Harris-Boundy & Flatt, 2010). Millennials are often characterized as ambitious, as valuing personal development, as preferring meaning in their work, and as actively seeking personal fulfillment within the job (Chou, 2012). This work shows that millennials work well in team settings and prefer strong social interaction and peer-to-peer connections. In the context of leadership, millennials also place a high value on participative and inclusive leadership styles in the workplace.

This suggests that effective development of inclusive leaders will require a shift in our approach to leadership development—especially for millennials—to make it less focused on individual expert knowledge and more concentrated on situated learning as both a relational and a collaborative process. This is very similar to feminist models that posit that developing inclusive leaders requires providing a safe environment for critical "identity work" in which individuals are able to examine, challenge, redefine, and develop their own concept of effective leadership (Ely et al., 2011). From this perspective, developing inclusive leaders may require a diverse, interconnected social environment in which learning is both personal and reflective (Vinnicombe & Singh, 2002).

This chapter describes a model for developing inclusive leadership that provides a safe environment for situated learning and facilitates interpersonal connections as individuals engage with real-world issues such as social responsibility, equity, inclusion, ethics, and social justice. We describe our specific approach for developing millennials into inclusive ethical leaders by shifting the traditional social construction of leadership as grounded in power and dominance toward an inclusive, socially responsible, and relational leadership perspective. Given that the development of a leader's identity and leadership skills are inextricably linked, this approach leverages the well-demonstrated advantage of experiential learning approaches in order to create positive transformational outcomes for millennials. We also outline lessons learned for the ongoing development of inclusive leaders who are prepared for positive transformative work within teams, organizations, and society.

## Challenging Traditional Educational Approaches to Leadership Development

Over the past several decades, concern for business education has increased, particularly in the areas of ethics, socially responsibility, and inclusive leadership (Pless et al., 2011). Spurred by corporate scandals, social protests over inequities, and economic downturns, the public has demanded that business schools become more accountable for the training of business leaders in ways that focus more on creating socially responsible organizations and leaders (Gentile, 2010). For example, the increase in attention devoted to corporate social responsibility (CSR) and sustainability in businesses is encouraging the development of approaches to more directly focus on these critical and complex issues. This means the use of developmental integrative approaches that help individuals understand and apply theoretical concepts to complex decision-making such as ethical dilemmas in business (Seto-Pamies & Papaoikonomou, 2016).

Our approach supports the existing and compelling case that complex understanding is best achieved through experiential learning. This notion is rooted in Kolb's model of experiential learning, which identifies four learning processes: concrete experience, reflective observation, abstract conceptualization, and active exploration (Kolb & Kolb, 2005). Learning through active engagement and reflection can provide millennials (and others) with both personal space and collaborative practical experiences to address complex dilemmas while developing skills that can then be applied in real-world settings. One specific experiential approach is service learning, which provides individuals with real-world practical experience through exposure to socially responsible service projects or activities (Vega, 2007). We have developed a model of leadership development that focuses on inclusive leadership within an ethical framework and leverages experiential service-learning techniques, based on principles of social learning and situated learning (Lave & Wenger, 1991). We suggest that the development of inclusive leadership fits best with the use of experiential approaches. This approach provides individuals with a learning environment that shifts the focus away from traditional notions of expertise, power, and organizational hierarchy and toward collaborative, inclusive leadership perspectives. These newly developed leadership perspectives can then be applied via experiential learning methods such as service learning that develop leadership skills that address critical social problems and solutions in a manner well-suited for millennial learners.

## A Unique Leadership Development Program for Millennials

In 2004 the University of Pittsburgh's College of Business Administration implemented a unique 16-credit Certificate Program in Leadership and Ethics (CPLE). This program engages a cohort of 30 to 40 individuals who self-elect to pursue the program. Participants apply to the program and go through the curriculum as a cross-functional cohort (e.g., across finance, accounting, marketing, supply chain, human resource management, business information systems, and global management). The selection of each cohort focuses on ensuring diversity across multiple dimensions such as function, background, demographics, and career goals. The CPLE uses a competency-based approach focusing on leadership development across five critical competencies: ethical awareness and decision making, relational leadership, high impact communication, project team management, and civic/social engagement.

The explicit focus on socially responsible leadership is a distinctive content feature of the CPLE and each of the five required elements has an experience-based learning component. The model includes a variety of experiential projects that engage real-world clients from business and community organizations across a range of topics. The program also includes a global service-learning project as an elective option for all participants. The program is based on the assumption that an emphasis on leadership, without proper consideration of social responsibility, will not generate leaders who approach their roles with a sense of inclusion and accountability. By the same token, an emphasis on social responsibility, without proper consideration of leadership, will not produce leaders with the necessary skills to develop and impact their team, organization, or society. The CPLE offers millennial participants an integrated and sustained exploration into the importance of effective leadership that is both socially conscious and inclusive while contributing to their own unique development by providing hands-on experience into the nature of what it means to lead in complex business environments.

The program strategy reflects models of experiential learning that include both problem-based and service-learning approaches (Eyler, 2002). The use of experiential learning techniques has been cited as an effective tool for teaching complex issues such as social responsibility within a development-oriented curriculum (Laditka & Hauck, 2006). Thus, the CPLE curriculum is explicitly designed and marketed so that participants are aware that social responsibility is central for effective leadership throughout their career and their personal lives. This approach emphasizes not only socially responsible and ethical leadership, but also collaborative and inclusive leadership. Thus, a unique aspect of our approach is the explicit link between ethics and diversity, such that emerging leaders understand that inclusion is core to responsible leadership. In addition, our specific learning approach requires a series of hands-on experiences that place individuals in real-world, diverse, and complex settings. This allows participants to practice an inclusive and ethical leadership style while receiving immediate feedback from facilitators and from their peers. Our approach also leverages strong peer bonds and a team orientation, which are known to fit the unique needs of millennials and serve as powerful tools for inclusive leadership development.

One of the other key elements of this unique leadership development program is a required service-learning experience in which participants work in small teams on projects with real-world clients (local businesses, community organizations, etc.) who are willing to be engaged partners with our program. Participants first spend time in a traditional learning environment focusing on evidence-based knowledge related to ethics, social responsibility, and diversity. This component is important so that participants understand the evidence and knowledge basis underlying inclusive leadership practices. Following Kolb's model of experiential learning, participants are asked individually to reflect on their personal learning through written reflection work and case-based exercises. Once a base of knowledge has been established, participants work in peer teams on projects selected to present complex ethical and social challenges that often involve project clients who may hold values, expertise, and objectives that differ from those of our students. For example, one project involved ways to increase food access in poor and minoritized communities. Another project had participants work to increase recruitment efforts for teachers who had expertise and interest in working with urban school districts. One team of participants worked together with an alumnus of the program to assess the impact of a unique approach to financial literacy that had a significant impact on an increase in knowledge for high school students (Petrie et al., 2018). A global project examines issues related to financial sustainability for a non-profit organization that provides support for youth with developmental needs in the United Kingdom.

These real-world projects require participants to apply their business knowledge and at the same time to practice core principles of inclusive leadership (e.g., valuing diversity, social responsibility, inclusive communication, dignity, and respect), while simultaneously managing diverse team dynamics among their peers and project sponsors. The team focus helps to build critical leadership skills, including sense-making, issue-selling, high-impact communication, project team management, conflict resolution, agenda building, and collaboration (van Dierendonck, 2011). At the end of the project, participants receive feedback from the project sponsor and the project coach, as well as from their project peers. Their final assignment is to reflect on this feedback and what it means for their continued development as inclusive and ethical leaders.

## Developing Inclusive Leaders through Social Impact Learning

One of the most significant aspects of our approach is what we label *social impact learning*, which frequently occurs during the required service-learning experiences. Although there are many pedagogical tools and techniques available to promote the learning outcomes, we argue that effective and inclusive leadership must involve shared value in both process and outcomes across diverse stakeholder groups. We use service learning as a catalyst for social impact learning because it creates a natural tension between the importance of delivering value to key stakeholders and, at the same time, the need to meet the objectives of effective business processes and outcomes. Service-learning tools allow for the explicit acknowledgment of civic and social engagement on matters of social justice as a legitimate learning opportunity for leadership development (Morton & Bergbauer, 2015). Service learning also provides the opportunity for participants to rethink their own personal identities as leaders, to challenge their own personal assumptions, and to identify their limitations in working with people from different backgrounds and perspectives on their project teams.

Although participating in the projects provides a powerful leadership experience, the development of inclusive leadership is more than just placing people into settings with people from different backgrounds, experiences and demographic groups. Our use of self-reflection and identity work is important for personal leadership development, and especially for inclusive leadership development. The project team experience combined with required personal reflections and peer feedback often triggers the necessary identity work that challenges individuals' existing notions of leadership as they learn and apply inclusive leadership principles. Our model is unique because traditional approaches often focus only on functional skills or values-based development for inclusive leaders; in contrast, our model integrates both in the same learning context. We have found that the focus on social needs, team orientation, peer connections, and frequent feedback are essential learning tools for millennial leaders. The written personal reflections also provide evidence for the impact of their learning experience in the program and function as a necessary evaluation tool for what is working well and what aspects may need to be improved.

## Lessons Learned for Developing Inclusive Millennial Leaders

Our work across several program cohorts has yielded unique insight into the development of inclusive leadership and fits well with the growing population of millennials moving into leadership roles in organizations. A focus on the leadership development of millennials is important given their importance to the workforce, the aging population among leadership ranks in organizations, and the projections that millennials are rapidly becoming the largest portion of the workforce. In addition, the diversity within the millennial generation is increasing, with the Latino segment becoming the largest portion of the growing trend (Blancero et al., 2018). These trends will continue to challenge traditional approaches to leadership development, given that millennials are motivated by collaboration, innovation, social impact, and peer relationships. Our unique experience has yielded several key insights or lessons learned for inclusive leadership development for this important segment of the workforce.

One of the key insights is the importance of identity work for inclusive leadership developed across what Sugiyama et al. (2016) call the three levels of personal, relational, and collective. The explicit goal of the CPLE is the integration of these three levels toward a unified identity of inclusive ethical leadership while equipping leaders with skills necessary to take effective and impactful action. Using experiential, social, and situated learning tools such as service learning has provided us with the insight that social impact learning is both valuable and essential for identity work to occur. This means including experiences that trigger participants to examine their own views of leadership that are based on culture, unconscious biases, and limited personal experiences. This should be done in a safe and facilitated learning environment that simultaneously provides personal reflection on the value of shifting toward inclusive approaches to leadership. Our approach accomplishes this through an explicit endorsement of the impact of adding shared value while balancing individual, organizational, and societal well-being.

Using experiential tools coupled with social action learning provides an active demonstration of the benefits of inclusive leadership as a competitive advantage for the individual, business, and society. Our approach uses social action learning to help participants understand and apply principles that are fundamental to both inclusive and ethical leadership, such as "shared value" and values-based leadership. These complex concepts may first appear quite abstract or intangible, but being actively engaged in real-world social problem-solving helps to provide a context for learning and personal reflection.

Second, since millennials prefer to work with others and in collaborative or team-oriented environments, our approach leverages this tool to place individuals into diverse teams for social impact projects. These diverse teams fit well with a focus on team orientation and peer connections that are important to millennial leaders. In addition, the team projects help to strengthen necessary competencies that are related to inclusive leadership such as collaboration, effective communication, and team problem solving. These are both foundational skills for leadership and essential competencies for individuals who will lead an increasingly diverse workforce. The peer teams also simulate the real dynamics involved in working across diversity of people, thought, values, and expertise.

Lastly, our approach exposes individuals to real-world issues such as ethics, economic disparities, social justice, sustainability, and socially responsible business practices. Engaging participants in being part of the solutions to these complex issues reinforces the need for inclusive leaders to combine awareness with positive action. Our approach follows principles of "tempered radicalism" (Meyerson, 2001), which describes how involved individuals can be part of traditional culture while also trying to make fundamental changes to existing systems and structures. Our approach provides tools, techniques, and the connections among peers to reinforce the notion that inclusive leaders are most effective when they use their unique talents and skills to create positive change in organizations and society. Providing opportunities for participants to engage in social impact work as part of leadership development reinforces the learning that effective and inclusive leaders build capacity in their organization while caring about issues such as social justice, diversity, and equality. Our project experiences help them to learn how to be effective catalysts for organizational and social change. They also provide students with the tools for building inclusive teams, using persuasive issue-selling techniques, and engaging diverse stakeholders toward accomplishing shared values and mutually beneficial outcomes.

We are convinced that the use of action, problem-based, and collaborative learning approaches are keys to developing inclusive leaders. Our approach challenges traditional models that often honor materialism and reinforce mindsets that downplay the importance of differences in values and denounce the power of diverse communities. Our model provides a safe environment for millennial learners to engage in necessary personal identity work that is essential for developing ethical and inclusive leaders who will have positive and lasting impact on teams, organizations, and society, now and into the future.

## References


Bilimoria, D. (1995). Modernism, postmodernism, and contemporary grading practices. *Journal of Management Education*, *19*, 440–457. https://doi.org/10.1177/105256299501900403

Blancero, D. M., Mourino-Ruiz, E., & Padilla, A. M. (2018). Latino millennials – the new diverse workforce: Challenges and opportunities. *Hispanic Journal of Behavioral Science*, *40*(1), 3–21. https://doi.org/10.1177%2F0739986317754080

Chou, S. Y. (2012). Millennials in the workplace: A conceptual analysis of millennials' leadership and followership styles. *International Journal of Human Resource Studies*, *2*(2), 71–83. https://doi.org/10.5296/ijhrs.v2i2.1568

Ely, R. J., Ibarra, H., & Kolb, D. M. (2011). Taking gender into account: Theory and design for women's leadership development programs. *Academy of Management Learning & Education*, *10*, 474–493. https://doi.org/10.5465/amle.2010.0046

Eyler, J. (2002). Reflection: Linking service and learning—Linking students and communities. *Journal of Social Issues*, *58*(3), 517–534. https://doi.org/10.1111/1540-4560.00274

Gentile, M. C. (2010). *Giving voice to values: How to speak your mind when you know what's right*. New Haven, CT: Yale University Press.

Harris-Boundy, J., & Flatt, S. J. (2010). Cooperative performance of millennials in teams. *Review of Business Research*, *10*, 30–46.

Kolb, A. Y., & Kolb, D. A. (2005). Learning styles and learning spaces: Enhancing experiential learning in higher education. *Academy of Management Learning & Education*, *4*(2), 193–212. https://doi.org/10.5465/amle.2005.17268566

Laditka, S. B., & Hauck, M. (2006). Student-developed case studies: An experiential approach for teaching ethics management. *Journal of Business Ethics*, *64*, 157–167. https://doi.org/10.1007/s10551-005-0276-3

Lave, J., & Wenger, E. (1991). *Situated learning: Legitimate peripheral participation*. Cambridge, UK: Cambridge University Press.

Meyerson, D. (2001). *Tempered radicals: How people use difference to inspire change at work*. Boston, MA: Harvard Business School Press.

Morton, K., & Bergbauer, S. (2015). A case for community: Starting with relationships and prioritizing community as method in service-learning. *Michigan Journal of Community Service Learning*, *22*(1), 18–31, hdl.handle.net/2027/spo.3239521.0022.102

Nembhard, I. M., & Edmondson, A. C. (2006). Making it safe: The effects of leader inclusiveness and professional status on psychological safety and improvement efforts in health care teams. *Journal of Organizational Behavior*, *27*(7), 941–966. https://doi.org/10.1002/job.413

Petrie, J., Jones, R., & Murrell, A. J. (2018). Measuring impact while making a difference: A financial literacy service-learning project as participatory action research. *Journal of Service Learning in Higher Education*, *8*. https://journals.sfu.ca/jslhe/index.php/jslhe/article/view/169/62

Pless, N. M., Maak, T., & Stahl, G. K. (2011). Developing responsible global leaders through international service-learning programs: The Ulysses Experience. *Academy of Management Learning & Education*, *10*(2), 237–260. https://doi.org/10.5465/amle.10.2.zqr237

Randel, A. E., Dean, M. A., Ehrhart, K. H., Chung, B., & Shore, L. (2016). Leader inclusiveness, psychological diversity climate, and helping behaviors. *Journal of Managerial Psychology*, *31*(1), 216–234. https://doi.org/10.1108/JMP-04-2013-0123

Seto-Pamies, D., & Papaoikonomou, E. (2016). A multi-level perspective for the integration of ethics, corporate social responsibility and sustainability (ECSRS) in management education. *Journal of Business Ethics*, *136*, 523–538. https://doi.org/10.1007/s10551-014-2535-7

Sugiyama, K., Cavanagh, K. V., van Esch, C., Bilimoria, D., & Brown, C. (2016). Inclusive leadership development: Drawing from pedagogies of women's and general leadership development programs. *Journal of Management Education*, *40*(3), 253–292. https://doi.org/10.1177/1052562916632553

van Dierendonck, D. (2011). Servant leadership: A review and synthesis. *Journal of Management*, *37*(4), 1228–1261. https://doi.org/10.1177/0149206310380462

Vega, G. (2007). Teaching business ethics through service learning metaprojects. *Journal of Management Education*, *31*(5), 647–678. https://doi.org/10.1177/1052562906296573

Vinnicombe, S., & Singh, V. (2002). Women-only management training: An essential part of women's leadership development. *Journal of Change Management*, *3*, 294–306. https://doi.org/10.1080/714023846

# 25 The Role of White Male Culture in Engaging White Men to be Inclusive Leaders

*Michael Welp and Edgar H. Schein*

Many diversity and inclusion efforts fail because they don't know how to engage the majority group, which in many cases in the U.S., Europe, Australia, and beyond, is White men. Diversity efforts habitually simply don't speak to White men; in fact these efforts often either ignore them or blame them as the problem. This creates apathy, anger, and resentment among White men. Signs of this exist everyday in the media, as a growing critical mass of frustrated White men in organizations struggle with efforts to build greater inclusion. Or even worse, they create a recoil wave throughout a whole nation against the global shift toward greater diversity of groups represented at all levels of power. Yet, many in organizations and in society don't know how to respond in ways that transform this challenge into more passion for diversity and inclusion. This chapter is about the unique challenges along the path of White men becoming what we call "full diversity partners." This means being more actively engaged with White women, people of color, LGBT people, as well as supporting and challenging other White men to be better allies for diversity. Being the insider or dominant group in many organizations creates for White men unique challenges in discovering and overcoming our own biases in order to become inclusive leaders. This chapter looks at White men both at the individual and at the group or cultural level. Each level adds collectively to a more complete picture of what the White male leader who wishes to be more inclusive may be culturally up against.

One reason White men are left behind on diversity efforts is because of the mindsets commonly used to examine diversity. An exploration of race is usually focused on people of color, while an examination of gender often focuses on women. Similarly, an examination of sexual orientation or gender identity is focused on people who are gay, lesbian, bi-sexual, or transgender. Attention to race rarely focuses on exploring being White and gender explorations hardly ever examine men. Thus, heterosexual, cisgender White men are not focused on or examined. This leads White men to think diversity is not about them, and to think diversity is about helping other people with their issues. It is also assumed that those who are usually the focus, White women, people of color, and people who are GLBT, should be the leaders and teachers of diversity efforts. This mindset limits the role of White men to that of more passive supporters who don't see the crucial role they have of engaging their own group to grow their consciousness, competence, and courage to lead inclusively.

## The White Men's Caucus (Welp)

My (Welp's) dissertation research in the 1990s (Welp, 1997, 2002) found that most White men learn everything about diversity from women and people of color and don't look to each other for any learning. This places an enormous burden on others to educate White men, which is not sustainable, especially in the many organizations where a majority of senior level positions are held by White men. It is also inefficient because the very biases we are trying to learn about as White men can cause us to minimize the perspectives of people of color and White women. In addition, White men are less likely to project onto other White men that they have an "agenda" or a "chip on their shoulder" around gender or race. To create a more sustainable path, in 1997 Bill Proudman and I started regularly hosting four-day residential learning labs called White Men's Caucuses. The goal was to grow awareness around what it means to be White, male, and, for some of us, heterosexual, and then to use that awareness to build better partnerships and greater inclusion.

The idea of a White Men's Caucus is often disorienting and provocative for many White men—yet many have found it life-changing. On the first night, asking White men what it was like to tell others they were coming to a White Men's Caucus reveals experiences of awkwardness or avoidance. One man took a pair of scissors and cut the title out of his pre-reading on the plane so others next to him would not misinterpret and think he was part of an extremist group.

One aspect of the path to advocating diversity for White men is to become conscious of what it means to be White and male, and for some heterosexual and cisgender. I have found a multidisciplinary approach helpful by combining two group level viewpoints: a multicultural perspective and a power structure perspective. A power structure (or social justice) perspective, using the concepts of privilege or systemic advantage, helps contribute to an understanding of how White men are not having to navigate challenges that other groups deal with on a daily basis. The word *privilege* refers to not having to negotiate or navigate dynamics or challenges that other groups often have to deal with, at the same time assuming that others should recognize that we have worked hard for what we have. For example, having able-bodied privilege means I don't have to spend time navigating my way through buildings in a wheelchair or worrying about accessibility wherever I go, but I may also believe I have worked hard on taking good care of myself and staying out of harm's way.

The multicultural perspective looks through the lens of culture. Edgar Schein describes culture as the shared, tacit assumptions we take for granted as the way to perceive, think about, and act in a given situation (Schein, 1985; Schein & Schein, 2017). The multicultural perspective illuminates the possibility of the existence of a White male culture and we can then explore what its impact might be on inclusion and partnerships at work and beyond.

In cultures where White men are the dominant or insider group (North America, Europe, Australia, etc.) most White men do not, in fact, see themselves as a group. They see themselves as individuals. White men don't identify with the wide gamut of what is attributed to them, which can lead them to resist identifying with their group. This is partly because our White male culture emphasizes rugged individualism. It is also because we have never had to see ourselves as a group, which is common for any group that is the dominant group in any organization or system. We are like a fish in water. Because we have usually never had to leave the water, we have the least awareness of the water we are in.

Most White men who attend the White Men's Caucus talk about having new eyes and seeing themselves for the first time as a member of a group with a distinct culture and unique experience of the world that is different than the experience of White women, people of color, or other "outsider" groups. They learn about the individual-group paradox, that they are both unique individuals unlike anyone on the planet and at the same time part of a White male group that shapes how they see and experience the world.

In the White Men's Caucus we examine this idea of a White male culture before we explore the concept of systemic advantage or privilege. In this chapter we focus on this White male culture.[1] White men typically do not consciously focus on themselves and do not think they have their own culture. We think culture is something other people have. Many writings about American or U.S. culture don't identify the culture as White male, further confusing the issue. For example, Geert Hofstede's (1980) classic studies identifying U.S. culture were initially based on studying all White men who worked for IBM, which makes Whiteness and maleness an invisible part of the cultural literature as well. According to U.S. Census Bureau (www.census.gov/quickfacts/table/RHI705210/06) data on the racial composition of California, the largest state in the U.S., in July 2019 the White non-Hispanic population was only 36.8% of the total and not even a plurality, with Hispanic/Latinos making up 39.3%.

## White Male Culture and its Organizational/Managerial Impact (Welp/Schein)

When we attempt to identify White male culture, White men often assume we are going to critique it and say it is bad. This is, in part, because of their scar tissue from feeling blamed in the past for diversity problems. As we explore White male culture we have to remember that culture is neither good nor bad, but a response to historical events and what groups learned in adapting to their environment. It is helpful to simply explore what the culture is without initially attributing positive or negative value. Cultural traits that helped a group to adapt to one set of circumstances can become negative and maladaptive when circumstances change, a process that is sometimes called cultural lag. A White male culture that evolved when White men dominated the process of conquering the frontier and building a nation can become dysfunctional when historical circumstances create a more culturally diverse nation and new values around the role of women and gender. The problem of cultural lag is that the group that is still living by the old values does not realize it and, therefore, continues to behave in a dysfunctional manner. After initially describing White male culture one can reflect on how some of its assumptions impact White women, people of color, and other cultural groups.

It is nearly impossible to describe a whole culture. Culture describes the major shared characteristics of a group, but not every individual in the group has the same characteristics to the same degree. We find strong core themes that most White men identify with, but there is also considerable variance across regions of the U.S., and by age demographics, sexual orientation, industry, organizational function, religion, and class.[2] Let's look at seven characteristics.

### *Rugged Individualism and Competition*

Escaping the confines of being told what class and religion they were, many a White male pioneer took risks to come to the U.S. in order to "make a place for himself." They valued being able to "stand on their own two feet," and "pull themselves up by their bootstraps." This characteristic is symbolized by characters such as John Wayne and The Marlboro Man. In fact, the most common statue in Washington DC is of an individual on horseback.

In the U.S. we say "the squeaky wheel gets the grease," whereas in Japan (or some other Asian cultures) they say "the nail that sticks up gets hammered down" or "it is the tall poppy that gets cut." In many Asian cultures there is more of a focus on harmony. In the U.S., you are expected to speak up if you have something to say; in many Asian cultures you do not speak up until the higher-status members of the group have spoken. In the U.S., creative innovative out-of-the box thinking and proposing is valued as a source of inventiveness and entrepreneurship.

With individualism goes competition and the assumption that getting ahead means competing with others, the encouragement that "may the best man win," and the acceptance that one gains status by winning. This automatic assumption of competition in the economic system gets carried over into individual competition inside organizations and becomes dysfunctional as team work becomes more necessary. It is also easy to see how White men competing with other White men might bond together when they see a threat to the whole White male tribe from other cultural groups.

Individualism impacts our motivational theories as well, with the top of Maslow's (1943) hierarchy of needs being "self-actualization." Organizations build their entire career systems around individual potential and individual accountability. Harmony, teamwork, and collaboration, which might be central values in other cultures, tend to be dismissed as problem-solving mechanisms we occasionally need to get things done, but that are not intrinsically valued or developed. Asking for help or saying "I don't know" can be seen as a sign of weakness. Confidence is valued over humility, leading to a hierarchical form of organization in which power and rank become synonymous, sometimes resulting in what we might call "the divine rights of management" (Schein, 1989).

### *Low Tolerance of Uncertainty*

This characteristic can be traced back to Calvinistic thinking, emphasizing dichotomous "either/or" logic such as "you're either with us or against us." This can lead us to see the world in absolutes and miss the gray area in today's complex world. We tend to ask questions from an either/or logic such as: is male aggression caused by nature or nurture? This can prevent us from seeing the "both/and" answer.

This same desire to remove uncertainty has us wanting to know what the rules are around diversity. We may secretly wish for the wallet card that names the ten things to do or say to avoid mistakes in dealing with women or people of color. For example, one White male asked: "Should I open the door for women or not open the door for women, which is it? I've been chewed out for both." The complexity of today's diversity resists simplification and demands skills of accepting and even thriving in environments of ambiguity.

Our managerial culture that has evolved from linear, mechanistic, engineering-based logic has worked extremely well in building an industry and has led management to be dominated by the need to measure and control. Even the analysis of culture is viewed as "soft stuff" and avoided by line managers because they cannot see how to control a complex socio-technical system. This avoidance often leads to cultural issues like diversity being delegated to the human resource function, which then creates policy that, however, male White line managers only accept because some equal opportunity law requires it.

### *Action Over Reflection; Task Over Relationship*

Value is created by doing, by getting things done. We take pride in our problem-solving ability. We often try to fix something before we fully understand it. Our spouses may remind us they sometimes don't want us to fix their situation, they just want us to listen. Our identities come primarily from our work roles. A stranger meets someone new and asks, "What do you do?" Other cultures around the world would describe themselves not by their work role but by their family or where they grew up.

Our focus on action includes a can-do optimism that anything is possible, "the impossible just takes a little longer." We also take an ultimately pragmatic stance, "do whatever it takes," "leave no stone unturned." Our strong action/fix-it orientation leads us to the belief that we can dominate nature rather than be subservient to, or try to live in harmony with, nature.

Focusing on the task is also more important than focusing on relationships. We spend only enough time on relationships in order to get the task done. Doing is more important than being or relating. Other cultures would never step into a task without first building a strong relationship connection, exemplified best by the Asian need to precede work meetings with drinking and dinner in which personal relationships can be forged and trust built up. We end up not trusting each other, so we create contracts and written deals in place of handshakes and verbal promises. When we do spend "relational" time with each other, such as in golfing and fishing, it is notable how these activities are traditionally more male-oriented, much to the chagrin of women executives who are aware that important deals are made on the golf course from which they are often excluded.

In his book *Humble Inquiry*, Schein (2013) describes how "doing and telling and acting" are valued more than "reflection and inquiry" because that might reveal not knowing, uncertainty, and possibly weakness and vulnerability. White males don't realize how much of what they advocate as appropriate, especially in leadership positions, ensures their invulnerability and reinforces their sense of power.

### *Rationality over Emotion*

Technical rationality, often illustrated by quantitative measurement and the seeming objectivity of numbers, is often the source of our credibility, especially data that we can use to solve problems and get things done. The "either/or" mentality mentioned above and the low tolerance of uncertainty play out here. We assume we can be either rational or emotional but not both at the same time. Since rationality is more linked to our credibility we can leave our emotions behind for fear of being seen as irrational. We may have more permission to show anger as a sign of passion whereas compassion, sadness, or fear are seen as signs of weakness. Value is placed on having silent strength, as in the saying "run silent, run deep."

### *Time is Linear and Near-Future Focused*

Along with a focus on action is a sense that time is linear, and therefore limited: "Let's move—we are burning daylight." Our time is "monochronic" in that we assume we can only do one thing at a time, leading to appointments and careful scheduling. Hall (1959) points out that in many cultures time is "polychronic," in the sense that many things can be done at once and a unit of time is over when everything has been done, rather than by the clock. The leader holds council and deals with all the member issues in a single meeting. The nearest thing in White male culture is the dentist who works on four patients simultaneously.

Some say linear time is a survival mindset from the limited crop-growing season in northern Europe. Other cultures have more of a cyclical notion of time, including those who could grow crops year around. Time controls when our meetings start and stop, whereas in some other cultures it depends more on the energy and emotions that develop in an exchange.

We are focused on creating the future—"we are going to put a man on the Moon in ten years"—but our managerial culture is focused on the next quarter and we have designed some measures of economic health to be the *daily* stock price.

### *Status and Rank over Connection*

Historically many White men came to the U.S. to make a place for themselves and believed in the power of hard work to achieve their own status. Alongside this drive and our rugged individualism is a belief in healthy competition for rank, status, and power. There is also a resonance in the notions that everyone has a fair chance and that the playing field is level—anyone can make it who works hard, the Horatio Alger myth. This belief in meritocracy can make it hard for us to see when the playing field is, in fact, not level and that it is White male culture that has tilted it in its own favor.

Given our tendency to not show weakness or "show no chinks in the armor," we can use bantering as a way to connect. This is a way to playfully challenge each other with our status and rank, a behavior one executive team called *smacktalk*. According to linguist Debra Tannen (2001), women have more permission to be directly vulnerable with each other as a way to connect. In contrast, vulnerability for White men historically has been used by each other as an opening to tease through bantering or in some cases even to bully. The use of power in the hierarchy is an accepted way to coordinate tasks and achieve organizational efficiency.

### *Managerial Culture is Transactional (Level 1) rather than Personal (Level 2)*

The technically rational culture associated with organizations as machines led naturally to breaking work into separate roles, well defined by job descriptions, and designing organizations as hierarchies of connected roles that could be filled by anyone with the proper qualifications and training. With this design also came the assumed value that the organization would work best if people in their roles kept the appropriate social distance, often labeled as being "professional." Coordination would occur through the rules of design and personal relationships would be basically transactional—role to role. Schein (2016) called this a Level 1 culture to distinguish it clearly from what can be observed as work becomes more complex and interdependent even across hierarchical levels. Complexity and collaboration require that people have to get to know each other more personally in order to build openness and trust to deal with all the contingencies that the work situation creates. Getting to know the whole person, not just the role performance, is a Level 2 relationship, what many in the organization already have—the "old boy's network."

Schein and Schein (2018) argue in *Humble Leadership* that managerial culture will have to evolve to a much more personal level (Level 2), even between managers and their direct reports, to build the levels of openness and trust that will be required to do the ever-increasingly complex work that technological and cultural complexity are forcing on work systems. It is White male culture's individualism and competitiveness that might initially resist this change most, and that, in turn, raises the question of how this move from Level 1 to Level 2 impacts inclusion.

## Is Inclusion a Level 1 or Level 2 Issue? (Schein/Welp)

The identification of White male culture as primarily a Level 1 culture is a critical step in understanding how cross-cultural issues can both aid or hinder inclusion. In particular we need to understand the impact of White male culture on organizations and the whole concept of work relationships. As this chapter brings out, one could almost say that Western capitalist managerial culture has been basically a White male culture and it is only in the last few decades that we have begun to understand how many of the problems of product quality, safety, and lack of innovative capacity are the result of this same Level 1 culture, built on values of rugged individualism, competition, pragmatism, and "rules of the game" defined by those who were in power, that is, White men.

As described above, the industrialization of the U.S. has favored the machine model, the technical rationality that has created a Level 1 transactional culture built on the idea that organizations and hierarchies are structures of "roles" in which the people are interchangeable (Schein, 2016; Schein & Schein, 2017). Job descriptions and training programs define the competencies needed in the role occupant and the organization chart defines the connections to other roles to insure a smooth work flow.

This meritocratic, hierarchical, bureaucratic system of job descriptions, roles, and rules, organized around recruitment and training programs that would fit incumbents into these roles, also could easily lead to the implicit assumptions that the best employees would be people just like us; let's reproduce as best we can our successful culture by not allowing minorities with possibly different personal characteristics to enter even if they had the qualifications. This was correctly identified as *discrimination*, which became illegal. Various affirmative action programs were launched to ensure that minority applicants who had the formal Level 1 job qualifications had to be included and given a job.

However, when it came to internal movement in the organization, cultural norms that superseded norms of "job qualification" entered to form a different kind of discrimination, best exemplified by the "glass ceiling." For example, being very emotional was typically considered to be inappropriate for a manager, and especially so for a higher-level executive. No matter how competent a woman or minority might be, if she was someone who might cry or have an emotional outburst at work, that would make her suspect for a high-level executive role.

For example, Schein was present at a meeting of the personnel promotion committee of a corporate board of the Italian subsidiary of a big U.S. oil company and watched them disqualify the head of their Italian subsidiary for the job of European CEO on the grounds that "he is a good man, but much too emotional." Schein raised the question of what this meant and why it would be a problem, and found that this White male board politely but firmly told him that it was essential to be completely rational at all times at that level, so they could not risk appointing someone who showed evidence of occasionally becoming emotional at a meeting. At the same time, they admitted to being regretful because he was such a good performer and was so well qualified for the job! In the same vein, we have heard over and over again that a woman crying on the job would be inappropriate without ever hearing a job-related argument.

In other words, segregation and discrimination can only be partially dealt with by formal legal means because of the further exclusion that occurs within the work organization based on subtle subcultural criteria in the dominant subculture of White men. A further irony in the Italian case is that the company had done very well integrating different European cultures, had overcome some of their national stereotypes, yet was totally oblivious to the power of their assumptions about emotionality. It may well be that one conclusion is that the White male managerial culture has to evolve from being stuck in transactional bureaucratic relationships to a more personal "Level 2" set of relationships.

## Can Organizational and Managerial Culture Evolve to Level 2 *Personized* Relationships? (Schein)

The essential difference between Level 1 and Level 2 is that relationships in Level 1 are based on rules, job descriptions, and on formal norms of maintaining appropriate social distance between role occupants, whereas Level 2 implies that members of the organization treat each other as total human beings, above and beyond their formal roles. They *personize*, to introduce a new term, the relationship by seeing the whole human being who occupies the role.

When we *personize* a work relationship we are trying to see the other person, who may be a subordinate, a team member, or even the boss, as a colleague working with us in relation to our common goals of accomplishing something. We are not necessarily trying to build a friendship or get into issues that society's norms would define as deeply personal or intimate, (which we would think of as a Level 3 "intimate" relationship), but to get to know enough about each other to get the jointly shared goal accomplished.

We prefer the term *personize* because personalization is usually associated with identifying some customer characteristic in order to tailor our product or service to their needs, a kind of trying to figure out the unique characteristics of a customer or friend, client, or patient. What we want *personize* to mean is better conveyed by wanting to get to know the colleague in relation to our shared goals and our relative contributions to the process of accomplishing them. We are more likely to hear their perspective, broaden our view as we learn from them and come to appreciate their skills and resources. We are less likely to exclude, harass, or lie to a fellow employee whom we know personally.

If an organization can function well at Level 1, is it then enough to overcome the discriminatory forces with legislation and foundational diversity trainings operating within Level 1, or is it, in principle, necessary to define inclusion as *personal* knowing and acceptance of others from minority cultures (tribes)? Does inclusion mean accepting others with different cultural backgrounds, different ways of thinking and being, different values and goals? If we believe that inclusion has to occur at this more personal multicultural level, how will this play out in the White male culture we have described? We believe that Level 2 relationships are the minimum first condition for inclusion, even as institutional inequity and other social barriers prevail.

White men must then learn how to leverage Level 2 relationships to shift from the conscious or unconscious maintaining of exclusion to being a force for inclusion. White men can relate to each other at Level 2, seeing each other as human beings, and still reinforce an exclusive old boys club. We think this is more likely when the White male cultural traits such as viewing "emotions as negating rationality" and seeing "vulnerability as weakness" inhibit the learning necessary to shift this peer dynamic. In the White Men's Caucus, White men step *outside* these cultural norms by engaging head and heart and showing the vulnerability through exploring their blind spots around diversity. This normative re-education allows new Level 2 relationships to emerge, full of the challenge and support necessary to begin to see the blind spots and find the passion to become a peer network supporting inclusion. Transcending some of the White male cultural norms allows Level 2 relationships among White men to evolve attitudes and behavior that support inclusion rather than supporting denial of their biases in their exclusive clubs. This also removes the historical burden placed on women and people of color and other outsiders to be the sole educators of White men around their diversity blind spots.

Will White male culture consider it to be enough to provide opportunities to get jobs in formal work roles in Level 1 bureaucracies, be satisfied with meeting the legal affirmative action requirements, and remain blind to the fact that their unconscious biases and their tendencies to want to reproduce themselves will severely limit what we want inclusion to mean? Or, do we aspire to include members of minorities and all other cultures at Level 2, in which case we would need both institutional reform and the kind of program that the White Men's Caucus offers as minimal condition to make White men aware of their own culture and to teach them how to *personize* in deeper ways with each other and eventually with another culture or subculture.

Here, White men must also learn to transcend other White male cultural traits in order to partner more effectively with White women and people of color, and other outsider groups. White men generally lean toward engaging others from a problem-solving perspective, jumping directly to action without fully understanding another's world. We have observed White men often asking questions such as "What are the three things you want me to do differently to support diversity?" This reflects the White male cultural focus on doing, action, fixing, and the lack of emphasis on being, relating, and reflecting. We have observed that White men can create new Level 2 relationships with women and others when they first ask questions outside their cultural box such as "What's it like to be you in our organization?" We tell White men "you can't fix what you don't understand." Humble inquiry becomes a critical skill not emphasized by White male culture, yet is one of the keys to effective partnerships across differences. Inherent to humble inquiry is the building of Level 2 relationships. A Level 2 relationship across the gender subculture boundary, for example, immediately reveals that what things mean inside one subculture can mean something completely different in another subculture. The explosion of women speaking up about having been sexually harassed and molested by powerful White men is testament to the degree to which those same White men had huge blind spots around the implications of their own behavior and their conscious or unconscious use of power.

Inclusion, as an issue, reminds us forcibly that it is inevitable in all societies to form tribes within the main tribe (subcultures)—occupational groups, social groups, and eventually classes based on occupation, social background, and material accomplishments. Each of these groups, organizations, clubs, and often whole occupations think of themselves as wanting to include people like themselves and, at the same time, to set up conscious or unconscious mechanisms to exclude people not like themselves. When new members are to be selected, the insiders have learned through experience what the signals are to determine whether a newcomer is okay or not, but to describe those criteria accurately becomes almost impossible. For example, in many start-up organizations or companies that feel they have very distinctive strong cultures, newcomers are put through various kinds of tests to determine whether they fit or not. Google claims that some of their new employees have to go through as many as 20 interviews. But they often cannot tell you what they are looking for. As one executive recently stated, "We say we want the *best* employees but think about who was here when 'what is best' was defined?" White men running businesses and other kinds of organizations will not be aware that they have evolved complex criteria of who fits and who doesn't.

The White Men's Caucus program brings this to the fore by making White men aware that they are a club of sorts and that their privileged power position automatically makes it difficult for people to enter this club if not invited. Even if White women or people of color are allowed to enter, they remain visible for an indefinite time as special cases or tokens. The discomfort of being in the token role is sufficient to make them resist accepting the invitation. For example, in a retirement home that we visited recently we learned that there are no African Americans in the independent living complex because a couple who were thinking about coming there declined when they discovered that they would be the only African American couple there. They said they might come if there were two or more couples coming, but they did not want to be the lone stand out.

## Overcoming the White Male Cultural Blind Spot through the Caucus (Welp)

Most of us in organizations dominated by White men have learned how to operate in this White male culture, so we likely don't think of it as being unique only to White men. Similarly, since White men often don't think they have a culture, they equate their culture with simply being a good human or a good American. From that perspective, they hire and promote others who fit into their unknown-to-them cultural box and mentor others to be like them. They might even say we don't see color or gender, they just treat everyone the same. While their intent is equality, others often hear it as having to assimilate and fit into our cultural box. White men don't even realize they are forcing others to assimilate.

The four-day program creates a cultural island (see Schein and Schein, Chapter 5, this volume) in which a variety of experiential tasks and focused dialogues enable the participants to begin to see their own culture. With a growing awareness of their own culture through the four-day program, White men gain the ability to see how we may be unconsciously expecting others to act like us and choose new employees who fit our cultural box. We can start to see how others may be leaving part of themselves at the door to fit into our culture. At some point we can start to see how we have also left part of ourselves at the door to fit into the White male cultural box.

This is a tipping point that lights a fire under White men to show up as sustainable passionate advocates for diversity and inclusion. They shift a fundamental assumption. That assumption is that, as diversity advocates, White men are helping others (White women, people of color, LGBT people, etc.) with their issues. The wake-up call here is that we gain through this diversity learning just as much or even more so than other groups. By learning to see our culture, we become more choiceful about when we want to use our strengths as well as claim the freedom to step outside of our culture when it serves us more in our roles as leaders, parents, spouses, and friends and colleague of others, including other White men.

For example, we might want to step outside of the rugged individualism and ask for help or say "I don't know." Maybe we want to accept more ambiguity and not try to remove some of the uncertainty in the world. We can choose to stop fixing what we don't understand and shift from doing and telling to humble inquiry. We can also allow ourselves to be both rational and emotional at the same time, and be more in our hearts relating even deeper to those around us. We use these shifts to create more connection with ourselves and others. Most White men discover in their White Men's Caucus that they are learning a sense of freedom and liberation to be more themselves. This tipping point often fuels lifelong passion around diversity.

There are several mindset shifts that happen for White men in this process. Here are three (of 12) that I (Welp, 2016) initially referred to in my book *Four Days To Change*:

1. My view of the world is not wrong, more likely it is incomplete. Multiple views give me a more complete picture.
2. A strength overused can become a weakness. Stop overusing my cultural habits when they don't serve me.
3. Vulnerability is not a weakness; it's actually a form of courage and creates more connection than I imagined.

With these shifts in mindset we find that both White men and others improve their ability to listen, integrate their head and heart, and see accept the complexity of diversity through multiple mindsets and seeing systemically. This leads to more willingness to engage in difficult conversations to improve workplace partnerships and become agents of change for inclusion.

If you are a White man, what can you do immediately? Here are some suggestions:

1. *Realize* you are part of a group and have a culture.
2. Take time to *reflect on* your culture and its impacts.
3. Step outside your cultural norms when new behavior serves you better.
4. Try to *notice* when you unwittingly impose your culture on others.
5. *Notice* when your impact is not congruent with your intent and *learn from it.*
6. Use reflection and inquiry to identify ways the playing field is not always level.
7. Take a public and active learning stance regarding issues of inequality and oppression.
8. Accept the critical role you play in educating your White male colleagues so that White women and people of color and others don't carry that burden.
9. Use your privilege honorably to *intervene* with other White men to support a level playing field; don't be a bystander.
10. Look at reward systems, formal and informal, to see to what degree your organization is really walking the talk of inclusion and diversity.
11. Convene a group of White men, or a mixed group, and watch Michael Welp's TEDx talk *White Men: Time to Discover Your Cultural Blind Spots* (TEDxTalks, 2017). Then discuss your reactions. What surprised you? What made you curious? What new questions surfaced? What is one take away you can apply at work or in your whole life?

## Conclusion

We have explored in this chapter the unique challenges and critical role White men play in being inclusive leaders. Current mindsets place the burden of educating this insider group on outsiders. Elements of the White male culture itself make it hard for White men to understand the complex dynamics around inclusion and act on their awareness. We explored the White Men's Caucus as one current practice that creates the learning for White men to become change agents for diversity and inclusion. This includes learning how to create Level 2 relationships with each other to develop the insights and courage to grow together into positive change agents for inclusion. In doing this they experience many other benefits as they rely on the best of their cultural traits and gain the freedom to step into other ways of seeing and being when it better serves them and their organizations and families. New Level 2 collaborative partnerships with others become possible. This is critically important work that needs to expand across our society for inclusive organizations to thrive. It also serves as a strong example of the role insiders play across the globe in creating an inclusive space for those who find themselves as outsiders in any system.

## Notes

1 For an exploration that includes both, see Welp's TEDx talk *White Men: Time to Discover Your Cultural Blind Spots* (TEDxTalks, 2017), which provides an overview, or Welp's (2016) book *Four Days To Change*, which gives an in-depth "fly on the wall" experience of being inside the White Men's Caucus.

2 Based on patterns of immigration across U.S. history, Woodard (2011) identifies 11 different cultural patterns in different regions of the U.S. based on where immigrants landed, established themselves, and settled in. All are basically White-male-based.

## References

Hall, E. T. (1959). *The silent language*. Greenwich, CT: Fawcett.

Hofstede, G. (1980). *Cultures consequences: International differences in work related values* (abridged ed.). Newbury Park, CA: Sage.

Maslow, A. H. (1943). A theory of human motivation. *Psychological Review, 50*(4), 370-391. https://doi.org/10.1037/h0054346

Schein, E. H. (1985). *Organizational culture and leadership*. San Francisco, CA: Jossey-Bass.

Schein, E. H. (1989). Reassessing the "divine rights" of managers. *Sloan Management Review, 30*(2), 63–68.

Schein, E. H. (2013). *Humble inquiry: The gentle art of asking instead of telling*. Oakland, CA: Berrett-Koehler.

Schein, E. H. (2016). *Humble consulting: How to provide real help faster*. Oakland, CA: Berrett-Koehler.

Schein, E. H., & Schein, P. A. (2017). *Organizational culture and leadership* (5th ed.). San Francisco, CA: Wiley.

Schein, E. H., & Schein, P. A. (2018). *Humble leadership: The power of relationships, openness, and trust*. Oakland, CA: Berrett-Koehler.

Tannen, D. (2001). *Talking 9 to 5: Women and men at work*. New York, NY: William Morrow.

Welp, M. (1997). *Pathways to diversity for White males: A study of White males' learning experiences on the path toward advocating for inclusion and equity* [Unpublished doctoral dissertation]. The Fielding Institute.

Welp, M. (2001). Treasures and challenges of diversity for White men. In A. Arrien (Ed.), *Working together: Diversity as opportunity* (pp. 107–115). San Francisco, CA: Berrett-Koehler.

Welp, M. (2002, April). Vanilla voices: Researching White men's diversity learning journeys. *American Behavioral Scientist*, *45*(8), 1288–1296. https://doi.org/10.1177/0002764202045008012

Welp, M. (2016). *Four days to change: 12 radical habits to overcome bias and thrive in a diverse world*. Portland, OR: EqualVoice.

TEDxTalks (2017, July 6). *White men: Time to discover your cultural bias | Michael Welp* [Video]. YouTube. https://youtu.be/rR5zDIjUrfk.

Woodard, C. (2011). *American nations: A history of the eleven rival regional cultures of North America*. New York, NY: Viking.

# 26 Navigating Inclusion as a Leader

## Lessons from the Field

*Bernadette Dillon and Sandy Caspi Sable*

In an era characterized by rapid change and uncertainty, and influenced by deepening social fractures and tensions, organizational interest in diversity and inclusion has never been stronger. And for good reason.

A workplace that is inclusive of diversity can promote innovation and creativity. It can provide insight into the needs of diverse customers, improve decision-making, and reduce the risk of being blindsided. Critically, with many organizations increasingly purpose-driven and focused on their impact on people and society more broadly, an inclusive workplace can promote equality and connectedness, helping all employees to thrive and ensuring businesses are representative of the communities they serve.

Against this backdrop, there has been increased recognition of the critical role that leaders play in advancing diversity and inclusion. It is now well accepted that an inclusive culture starts at the top, with a critical mass of leaders role-modeling inclusion.

More pointedly, research shows that a leader's actions have a material impact on both an individual's feelings of inclusion and, in turn, business performance. For example, in their survey of 2,100 employees across five continents, Catalyst (Travis et al., 2019) found that almost a half of an employee's experience of inclusion can be explained by their manager's behaviors (see also, Van Bommel et al., Chapter 8, this volume). Similarly, and with respect to the link between inclusion and performance outcomes, Deloitte found that "teams with inclusive leaders are 17% more likely to report that they are high performing, 20% more likely to say they make high-quality decisions, and 29% more likely to report behaving collaboratively" (Bourke & Espedido, 2019, para 2).

Indeed, according to the Global Diversity & Inclusion Benchmarks: Standards for Organizations Around the World (O'Mara & Richter et al., 2017), developed by the Centre for Global Inclusion, inclusive leadership is a differentiating factor in best practice organizations, with leaders seen as "change agents and role models." In this context, the emergence of groups such as CEO Action for Diversity & Inclusion in the U.S. (https://ceoaction.org) and Male Champions of Change in Australia (https://malechampionsofchange.com) points to an increasing willingness by senior leaders to use their influence in the pursuit of more inclusive workplaces and societies.

Despite this positive recognition and intent, inclusive leadership is easier said than done. Inclusion is a deliberate and iterative practice requiring leaders to be alert to their actions, and the impact of these on different people, in varying workplace contexts (e.g., interpersonal, team, and organization). Yet research shows that many leaders lack fundamental knowledge about inclusive leadership and personal insight into their own effectiveness, which is needed for them to successfully adapt and to role-model inclusion.

For example, in their analysis of inclusive leadership across 450 leaders on behalf of Deloitte, Bourke and Espedido (2019) found that "rarely were leaders certain about the specific behaviors that actually have an impact on being rated as more or less inclusive" (para. 12). As such, we see many leaders reliant on trial and error and unable to be intentional in their efforts to be inclusive on a day-to-day basis.

Compounding this knowledge gap is the fact that many leaders find it difficult to accurately assess how inclusive they are. In Deloitte's study (reported by Bourke & Espedido, 2019), just one-third (36%) of leaders could accurately judge their inclusive capabilities as others saw them, with a third (32%) overestimating their effectiveness. Similar findings have been seen in research by leadership experts Zenger and Folkman (2017), who identified an inverse relationship between leaders' confidence in their inclusiveness and their actual competence. Most notably, they found that "many leaders assume they are better at valuing diversity than they actually are" (Zenger & Folkman, 2017, para. 5), with those leaders "who are the worst at valuing diversity ... more likely to overrate their effectiveness" (para. 7). While it is a miscalibration often seen in other leadership self-assessments, it is an effect potentially exacerbated because inclusion "is particularly in the eye of the beholder" (Zenger & Folkman, 2017, para. 9). That is, as Zenger and Folkman go on to point out, "you might *intend* to be inclusive, and even think you *are* inclusive, but your impact on others might be very different" (para. 9, italics in original).

Below we provide insights and strategies to address these two challenges. Drawing on our experience as practitioners, we offer a new framework of inclusive leadership—the Inclusive Leadership Compass—designed to provide *clarity of understanding*. We also offer some learning from our work with business leaders; in particular, helping them increase *personal insight* into their leadership shadow through our 360 Inclusive Leadership Compass feedback tool (the 360 ILC). We end with a sample of questions from the 360 ILC to help readers begin their own process of self-reflection and understand the practical actions they can take to strengthen their shadow.

## Increasing Clarity of Understanding—A Practical Framework of Inclusive Leadership

Inclusive leadership is an approach to leading that is unique in its application to the diversity context. In our view, it is demonstrated when individuals' belief in the social and economic importance of diversity motivates them to focus energy on adapting to and empowering diverse talent, as well as harnessing people's differences to create value. This conceptualization underpins the Inclusive Leadership Compass framework.

More specifically, our work shows that inclusive leaders exhibit four practices that span the distinct but reinforcing domains of self, others, team, and organization:

1 Embrace difference (Self)
2 Empower diverse talent (Others)
3 Enable diverse thinking teams (Teams)
4 Embed diversity and inclusion across the organization (Organization).

This comprehensive framework, shown in Figure 26.1, is grounded in literature and empirical research on inclusion, leadership, and high-performing teams. It encompasses 16 focus areas, which are each mapped to one of the domains. As its name suggests, the Inclusive Leadership Compass is designed to help orient leaders' attention toward the four critical sites of influence and to understand the specific actions they can take in different leadership contexts to be more inclusive of different people around them. The four domains are described in more detail in the following sections.

### *Embrace Difference (Self)*

The path to inclusive leadership starts with leaders themselves: the personal values, beliefs, and attributes that influence their motivation and ability to behave inclusively in an authentic and sustained way. These include strong egalitarian views and a belief in the value of difference, along with a willingness to move outside of their comfort zone (Ferdman, 2017) and to subordinate their self-interest for the benefit of others when required. They also include personal attributes such as an openness to different people, ideas, and change more broadly; a high degree of self-awareness enabling adaptation; and humility, with preparedness to be vulnerable, promoting connectivity, learning, and growth.

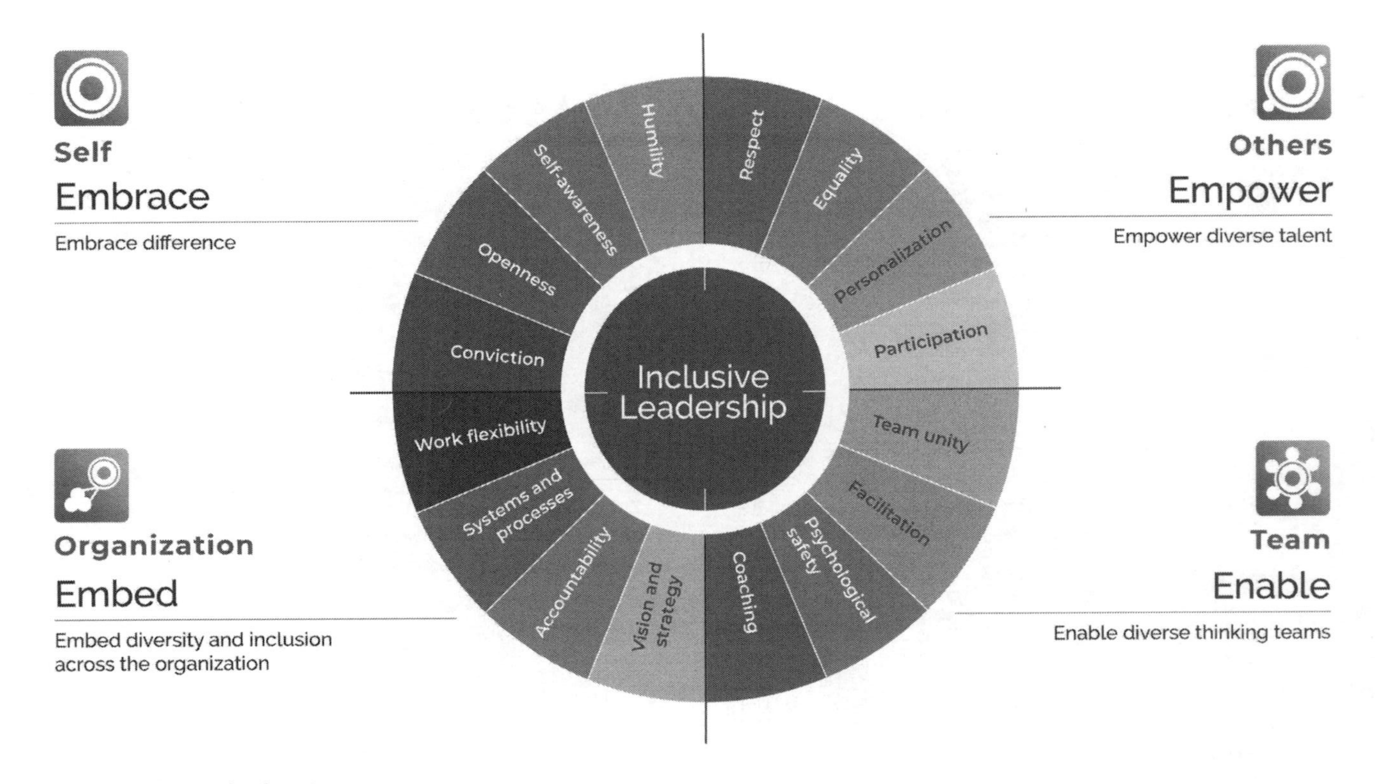


*Figure 26.1* Inclusive Leadership Compass.

The Inclusive Leadership Compass is a proprietary tool of Chalk & Cheese Consulting Pty Ltd ©2020 www.inclusiveleadershipcompass.com

### *Empower Diverse Talent (Others)*

The mounting expectation toward more human-centric leadership is deeply rooted in how inclusive leaders relate with others at an interpersonal level. Inclusive leaders treat all people with dignity and respect and exert considerable effort to self-regulate their own biases and treat others fairly. Inclusive leaders view people through a very human lens, understanding their individuality while promoting connectiveness and demonstrating empathy and genuine concern for their well-being.

Driven by the goal to help people thrive, inclusive leaders proactively throw their support behind diverse talent, clearing or creating new pathways to success. Similarly, they encourage autonomy and delegate decision-making authority to people, balancing this with their availability for consultation on problems when the need arises.

### *Enable Diverse Thinking Teams (Teams)*

Inclusive leadership is often thought of through an individual lens and with respect to equality and inclusion of diverse employees. As we describe above, this is a critical dimension. However, with the shift toward teams and the value inherent in harnessing their collective intelligence, a focus on leading diverse groups is also important.

Inclusive leaders recognize this and give attention to inspiring a sense of unity and shared purpose among different team members. They also lean into their personal attributes of humility and openness to create an environment of psychological safety in which members feel safe to speak up without fear of negative consequences. Inclusive leaders are skilled facilitators enabling the constructive exchange of different ideas. They manage dominant voices and encourage quieter ones, coaxing creative abrasion while avoiding unproductive conflicts.

Understanding their role as coach and the dynamic nature of leadership itself, inclusive leaders also proactively support team members in becoming more inclusive themselves. For example, they set clear standards of acceptable behavior, create opportunity for dialogue about differences, and facilitate capability development.

### *Embed Diversity and Inclusion across the Organization (Organization)*

To create a workplace that is truly inclusive, diversity and inclusion must run through the core of the organization, with business systems aligned to reinforce behaviors and enable the sustained cultural shifts required.

Knowing this, inclusive leaders step up and use their power to challenge the status quo, influencing the adaptation of systems and structures that reinforce the centrality of diversity and inclusion to the organization's purpose and business strategy. For example, they articulate a compelling vision, emphasizing inclusion as a fundamental organizational value. Similarly, they integrate diversity and inclusion into business reporting and accountability measures, and work to ensure these aspects are important considerations in talent-related processes. In addition, inclusive leaders are visible advocates for flexibility across the organization.

## Inclusive Leadership Compass

As we noted above, the Inclusive Leadership Compass is designed to help demystify inclusive leadership for both leaders and organizations more broadly. Importantly, when applied as a 360-feedback tool, the framework allows leaders to understand their inclusive leadership shadow, including any blind spots, which in turn enables them to adapt and make changes to their behaviors to become more inclusive of different people around them. In the next section we offer some learnings from our work with leaders who have used our 360-feedback tool.

## Increasing Personal Insight: Seeing Yourself Through the Eyes of Others

We noted earlier that a significant challenge for leaders in acting inclusively is the fact that inclusion is in the eyes of the beholder—that is, it is an experience on the part of each person with whom the leader interacts. As such, even the most well-intentioned leader may fall short of being experienced as inclusive by everyone. This is particularly so in the context of diversity, where a broader range of difference (e.g., identity, approach, and style) between the leader and the people they are intending to include may expose unintentional biases and exacerbate the "intent–impact gap," so that a leader's instinctive behaviors do not have the intended outcome. For example, to invite the contribution of others in team meetings, a more extroverted leader may put more introverted team members "on the spot," making them feel uncomfortable and unfairly singled out. Or, in an effort to strengthen team bonding, a leader may instigate weekly "Friday night drinks" at a nearby bar, leading some with caring responsibilities or who do not drink alcohol to feel excluded. In both cases, the leader was intending to be inclusive, yet was met with unexpected reactions (Ferdman, 2017) from different people.

The reality is that inclusion requires leaders to be much more attuned to the impact of their actions on others. Consequently, in the absence of feedback from others, leaders are operating by guesswork when it comes to navigating inclusion. Worse still, if the only feedback on their inclusiveness is from people like them, this will not provide an accurate guide and can even cause them to be overconfident on the assumption that they have got inclusion covered. As the Male Champions of Change (2014) put it, "If we want our leadership to make a difference, we must understand our own impact—the shadow we cast. The challenge is that it is hard to see our own shadow—its shape, clarity and reach" (p. 4).

This was a strong motivator for us in developing our multi-rater feedback tool, the 360 ILC. Designed for developmental purposes, the 360 ILC collects and contrasts feedback from multiple sources (i.e., the leader, their direct reports, manager(s), peers, and other colleagues) to help the leader understand how inclusive different people experience them to be, and the practical actions they can take to be more inclusive of those around them. The insights it has given leaders on their inclusive leadership shadow have been many and varied; we have selected two cases to share as they sit at opposite ends of the capability–confidence spectrum.

The first is the archetypal target for a 360-feedback process: the leader who has a misguided self-confidence in their capability. Here, the obvious value is the reality check provided by the contrasting evidence of how different people actually experience the leader. However, as we see below, there is a deeper value that comes from the nuanced understanding the leader receives about where and how they are falling short on inclusion, and the almost transformational impact detailed feedback on people's experience of a leader's (lack of) inclusiveness can have on that leader. Most importantly, the 360 feedback offers the leader practical guidance on what they can do to get back on course.

Our second example is almost the polar opposite: a leader with high capability who significantly underestimates themselves. While you would be forgiven for thinking that the 360 ILC process has less utility for this leader—after all, they're already impacting others in a positive way—our experience suggests otherwise. As we shall see below, there are two main benefits to this kind of leader from the 360 feedback. The first is to pinpoint and encourage them to continue with those behaviors that are working well. The second is to give them the confidence and platform to be more visible advocates of inclusion across the organization (if they are not already), as well as to take on the role of coaching others to build their own inclusive capability.

## Case Study 1

Dean is the Head of Sales for a medium-sized but high-profile entertainment organization. He carries himself with the ease that might be expected from an extroverted, 6 ft. 3 in. tall White man whose career progression has been both rapid and smooth. Dean participated in the 360 ILC as part of an initiative sponsored by his CEO.

When we sat down to debrief his feedback report, Dean spoke about his long hours and driving himself hard—neither of which was a sacrifice for him as he loved what he did. He joked that we probably thought he had "rigged" his raters, as his relationships with those around him were strong. He also emphasized that he was a keen supporter of diversity, especially women, and gave the example of how he promoted a woman to his former role.

Dean was in fact one of the lowest scoring leaders since the 360 ILC's inception, with an Inclusive Leadership Impact Score of 2.6 out of 5. As an overall measure of his effectiveness, this meant that others experienced him as role-modeling inclusion to a small extent only, with the feedback across the rater categories (i.e., manager, reports, and peers) consistently unfavorable. Digging deeper, his report showed scores of 3 or below (out of 5) for 12 of the 16 focus areas comprising the ILC, while the qualitative feedback he received left no doubt that his impact on others was far from inclusive.

All of this came as a shock to Dean as he had consistently rated himself higher than his feedback providers. Dean believed that, while not perfect, he was demonstrating many of the behaviors measured "to a large extent." However, through our debrief, a few key things became clear to Dean that helped him understand: (a) why he had some way to go before he would be the inclusive leader he wanted (and needed) to be; as well as (b) the apparent disconnect between that intention and his impact on others.

More specifically, our debrief revealed that Dean's all-in approach to his work was a major Achilles heel to his inclusive leadership. He operated at an extreme pace, focusing relentlessly on results, and expected others to do the same. High in intellectual confidence, he was quick to express his frustration when people did not meet his expectations or agree with his views or approach. He mistakenly thought that, because he spent at least two to three nights per week "socializing" with his team and peers, the bonds were strong and that this "balanced out" his directive, abrasive style at work.

Dean's 360 feedback allowed him to understand that people found him intimidating, making some reluctant to speak up with questions, ideas, and concerns. It revealed that what Dean thought was harmless "banter" was impacting many people negatively. He also learned that some people believed he played favorites in the team. Finally, Dean realized that he wasn't seen as a true D&I advocate, and that the messages and actions he thought demonstrated his commitment were not resonating with those around him. This last point hit especially hard as Dean had, as we noted earlier, prided himself on "helping women."

So, what to do with this insight? Cognizant of striking a balance between giving Dean time to process the data without becoming overwhelmed by introspection, we took a short break and then moved into action-planning mode. Our goal was to offer simple, actionable advice that would help him get on track and better align his desire to lead inclusively with his ability to do so, all the while being sensitive to his business context. Of course, this reorientation would take time, and our approach was to focus on the next three months before reconvening to discuss learnings and planning the next phase of actions together. So, together with Dean, we agreed to focus actions initially around the Self domain of the ILC framework, given this was an area with some of the lowest scores and largest blind spots. In particular, we targeted Self-Awareness, Humility, and Conviction. Below is a snapshot of where we landed in terms of actions Dean would try out:

1 In relation to Conviction: It was very important to Dean that others knew that he was personally committed to diversity and inclusion. To help demonstrate his intent toward becoming a more inclusive leader, it was agreed that Dean would email each of his raters to thank them for their candor and willingness to give their feedback. In a demonstration of real courage by Dean, this would also include him acknowledging his development areas and letting them know that he was committed to working on them.

2 In relation to Self-Awareness:

   a To better understand the different work styles and communication preferences of people in his team, and how they may differ from his own, Dean would integrate the use of a certified tool and debrief into his team's next offsite. The goal was to help him modify his own style and approach when interacting with different people (and to help other team members to do the same).
   b To help keep him on track, Dean would share his development areas and action plan with a trusted colleague and ask them to call him out when exhibiting a behavior he planned to change, including communicating in a non-inclusive way.

3 In relation to Humility: To help demonstrate greater intellectual humility and show team members that no one is perfect, Dean would find an opportunity to share a personal story of failure at the next team offsite, including lessons learned.

## Case Study 2

Angelo is a soft-spoken man in his mid-40s. Having grown up abroad, he is fluent in three languages and worked in several countries over the course of his career. Now based in the U.S., Angelo leads a large division in the technical area of a global manufacturer. He also sits on the region's senior leadership team.

In reviewing Angelo's 360 ILC report, we were genuinely perplexed. Here was a leader who rated himself at 3 or below for almost every focus area. Yet his raters' scores painted a very different picture. With an overall Inclusive Leadership Impact result of 4.3 out of 5, they saw him as someone who behaved inclusively "to a large extent." This was the most significant positive gap between self and other ratings we had ever seen. Puzzled, we tripled checked the data, but they were correct.

So, what lay behind this wildly inaccurate self-critique? Deep-seated insecurities seemed the obvious explanation. If correct, then a main purpose for our debrief would be to instill a sense of confidence in Angelo with respect to his inclusive leadership capability, so that he might see himself as others did. However, as we explored the data with him, it became clear this was not the case. In fact, Angelo was a quietly confident, deeply reflective leader. The positive gap was simply a reflection of his humility, cultural intelligence, and commitment to self-improvement. As he explained:

> I'm told that I'm too hard on myself. But, even if others think I'm doing alright, I know I can always do better. It doesn't matter how much experience you have, there are things you can improve on and learn when you're leading people. I've worked in enough different environments to know that what works for one won't necessarily work for another.

While this obviated the need for a pep talk, there were still key insights available to Angelo through a discussion of his feedback. And in a general sense, these hold true for any already-inclusive leader who is seeking to take their capability to the next level.

Perhaps most obviously, we homed in on the behaviors on which Angelo's raters scored him relatively lower. The majority of these were in the Organizational domain, although as we see below, there were also a handful in the Team domain.

With respect to those lower-scoring behaviors in the Organizational domain, the subtle message that these lesser (albeit still respectable) ratings conveyed was that Angelo could take more of a lead in championing diversity and inclusion across the organization: for example, by articulating his own compelling and relatable vision for diversity and inclusion, and being explicit about the business case for both, as well as proactively setting goals, measuring progress, and holding people to account. When we asked Angelo whether this rang true for him, and if so, what was holding him back from doing these things (to a greater extent), he gave this thoughtful explanation:

> I think it's two things really. I feel like people have been bombarded with the D&I rhetoric over the last ten years, so why add another voice to the noise? And I also think that I can better influence inclusion by my actions, not my words.

Both parts to Angelo's reflection offered a springboard for deeper insight. We started with his reference to the possible fatigue people may have around D&I messaging in his organization given its repetition over the years. And while "diversity fatigue" is a documented phenomenon (Catalyst, 2019), we also know that failing to talk about something is the surest way to see it fade into oblivion. What's more, given Angelo's genuine belief in the value of diversity and inclusion and his overall inclusive leadership competence, his voice was an important one to add to the mix. Coming from him, it would feel less like rhetoric and more like a reminder of why his colleagues needed to persist in building a more diverse and inclusive business.

The second part of his explanation—a preference to focus on his actions, rather than his words—provided the perfect segue into helping Angelo better understand the nature of his leadership shadow around inclusion. We agreed that a leader's actions—what they do—is critical to casting a strong shadow. However, we reminded Angelo that people also take note of what the leader says, measures, and prioritizes (Male Champions of Change, 2014). And they look for congruence between all four aspects in order to gauge the sincerity and depth of the leader's commitment.

With this, Angelo was convinced that he had to be a more vocal champion of D&I across his organization. It also enabled him to appreciate that he needed to create visible accountability measures for himself and others to solidify his shadow and boost his inclusive leadership impact. He therefore committed to the following actions:

1 To craft his elevator pitch around why D&I were important to him personally and plan for three organizational events in the next quarter where he would speak publicly to this.
2 To meet with the Chief Human Resources Officer to discuss what key D&I metrics were available currently, and how they could develop a diversity and inclusion dashboard that he could then use with his own team and his senior leadership team to track and report on progress.

There was one final insight from Angelo's data that enabled us to see how he could become even more inclusive—and it was not expected. As noted above, the other area where raters had marked Angelo slightly lower than their usual 4+ was the Team domain. In particular, there were three behaviors we decided to highlight as potential opportunities for small but impactful inclusive leadership uplifts based on the fact they all scored below 4:

- Works to build trust between team members;
- Addresses cliques that get in the way of team unity; and
- Facilitates constructive debate when team members present divergent views.

When we asked Angelo for his reaction to this feedback, he thought it fair. He didn't do these things consistently. However, in line with his considered approach to leading, he shared his reasoning. Angelo explained that he was conscious of respecting the maturity of his people to manage themselves, so tended to take a more "hands-off" approach. He went on to note that, having worked in many different cultures, he had learned to respect different ways of behaving so "when some people tackle a situation more assertively in team meetings, I usually just sit back and let the discussion run its course." He reflected further: "But maybe what I thought was being respectful is feeling too passive for some?"

And there he had it. As shown in his 360 ILC report, Angelo's paramount inclusive leadership strength was his respect for others. It was his highest rating focus area, with a score of 4.8 out of 5, and it was a repeated message in the qualitative feedback he received. It was also, it seemed, getting in the way of him reaching his full inclusive leadership potential in terms of helping team members from different cultural backgrounds to work effectively together—at least insofar as it stopped him from proactively managing conflict and in- and out-groups within his team, particularly in the context of how different ideas were being discussed. This somewhat surprising insight led to Angelo's last action item:

3 He would facilitate a team session to develop a set of simple ground rules for how the team wanted to engage on challenging issues given the various cultural or individual communication preferences at play for various team members. He would then commit to playing an active mediator role in all significant team meetings, ensuring those rules of engagement were adhered to. Finally, he would build into his fortnightly one-on-ones with direct reports an agenda item around "how well are we working as a team and what do we need to focus more on/do differently?"

For us, Angelo's experience reinforced the value to leaders of comprehensive and systematic feedback on their inclusive leadership shadow even where their capability is already strong. Both the richness of the data and the discussions it inevitably sparks enable leaders like Angelo to build on their considerable strengths and become true role models of inclusive leadership.

## For the Reader: Beginning Your Own Process of Self-Reflection

Here we provide a sample of eight questions (two from each domain) from the 360 ILC to help readers begin the process of self-reflection. Having read this chapter, it should be expected by readers that these are offered with a strong caveat: many leaders tend to over-estimate their capability and thus a self-assessment should not (and cannot) be used as an accurate measure of one's inclusive leadership effectiveness. However, the sample questions do have value in terms of helping readers get a sense of the behaviors that are important to leading inclusively and to start reflecting on where their strengths and gaps may lie. In this way, we also provide some examples of actions that readers can take where potential gaps have been identified. (For more information on the Inclusive Leadership Compass, readers can visit www.inclusiveleadershipcompass.com.)

### *Instructions*

For each question in Table 26.1, reflect on the extent to which you demonstrate the behavior, using a scale of 1 (not at all) to 5 (to a very large extent). For scores below 3, consider trying the action suggested. To provide a reality check on your own assessment, you may consider soliciting feedback from different people around you in relation to each question.

*Table 26.1* Inclusive leadership self-assessment: sample items from the 360 Inclusive Leadership Compass

| *On a scale of 1–5, to what extent do you . . .* | | *If you scored yourself a 3 or below, consider the following actions:* |
|---|---|---|
| Openness | Invite views that are different to my own. | Practice the Simon Sinek (Kovacs, 2017) approach of being "the last to speak." In meetings, ask for others' ideas and opinions before giving your own. |
| Self-Awareness | Regularly seek feedback to improve your interactions with others. | Try the fast-5 practice: at the end of each meeting, have team members use Post-It notes to rate your facilitation (on a scale of 1 to 5) based on how included they felt (entirely anonymously, if appropriate). If someone feels less than a 5, also ask them to write one suggestion on what you could do better next time to make them feel more included. |

(*Continued*)

*Table 26.1* (Cont.)

| *On a scale of 1–5, to what extent do you ...* | | *If you scored yourself a 3 or below, consider the following actions:* |
|---|---|---|
| Equality | Treat people fairly and without favoritism. | Keep a weekly record of team member achievements so you are more objective when making performance decisions. |
| Personalization | Take a personal interest in people. | Use people's names in conversations. If pronouncing them is difficult for you, politely ask for clarity or search guides online. Keep a record of the names of their important others (e.g., in your phone). |
| Facilitation | Manage dominant voices in team meetings. | In meetings, monitor who is and who is not contributing, particularly on calls (e.g., keep a list of names and mark when they have contributed). Invite others to participate (e.g., "We've heard Nick's view. It would be good to also hear what others think.") |
| Coaching | Provide opportunities for your team members to develop their own inclusive capability. | Use these questions as a guide to reflect on each of your team members' capability. Invest in or advocate for inclusive capability assessment and/or development. |
| Systems and Processes | Prioritize diversity as a recruitment objective. | Broaden your talent pool. For each new role, deconstruct what is actually required in terms of skills and experience and change unnecessary criteria that may narrow the list of potential candidates. |
| Work Flexibility | Support flexible work for all employees, regardless of their gender. | To help redefine societal norms, adopt the PepsiCo approach of "leaders leaving loudly" (Hilton, 2018, para. 10) whereby leaders (including men) make clear to their team members that they are leaving work to attend to a family commitment (e.g., child pick-up) rather than sneaking out. |

## References

Bourke, J., & Espedido, A. (2019, March 29). Why inclusive leaders are good for organizations, and how to become one. *Harvard Business Review Digital Articles*. https://hbr.org/2019/03/why-inclusive-leaders-are-good-for-organizations-and-how-to-become-one

Catalyst. (2019, August 7). *Diversity fatigue in the workplace: How to get unstuck*. https://www.catalyst.org/2019/08/07/diversity-fatigue

Ferdman, B. M. (2017). Paradoxes of inclusion: Understanding and managing the tensions of diversity and multiculturalism. *The Journal of Applied Behavioral Science*, *53*(2), 235–263. https://doi.org/10.1177/0021886317702608

Hilton, J. (2018, April 23). How PepsiCo is supporting gender diversity. *Human Resources Director*. https://www.hcamag.com/au/specialisation/corporate-wellness/how-pepsico-is-supporting-gender-diversity/152193

Kovacs, M. (2017, October 24). Simon Sinek on why leaders should hold their opinions and "be the last to speak." *Smart Company*. https://www.smartcompany.com.au/people-human-resources/leadership/mk-simon-sinek-on-why-leaders-should-hold-their-opinions-and-be-the-last-to-speak

Male Champions of Change. (2014). *It starts with us: The Leadership Shadow*. https://malechampionsofchange.com/wp-content/uploads/2015/02/20.-The-Leadership-Shadow.pdf

O'Mara, J., Richter, A., [and 95 Expert Panelists] (2017). *Global diversity and inclusion benchmarks: Standards for organizations around the world* (5th ed.). Centre for Global Inclusion. https://centreforglobalinclusion.org

Travis, D. J., Shaffer, E., & Thorpe-Moscon, J. (2019). *Getting real about inclusive leadership: Why change starts with you*. Catalyst. https://www.catalyst.org/research/inclusive-leadership-report

Zenger, J., & Folkman, J. (2017, October 26). Leaders aren't great at judging how inclusive they are. *Harvard Business Review Digital Articles*. https://hbr.org/2017/10/leaders-arent-great-at-judging-how-inclusive-they-are

# 27 Inspiring Inclusion with the Appreciative Leadership Lotus Model

*Tanya Cruz Teller*

## Introduction and Context

I chose to work in organization development (OD) creating healthy, inclusive organizations as a means to positively impact society. In our current volatile, uncertain, complex, and ambiguous (VUCA) world, I believe a thriving organization is necessarily an inclusive organization. It is the wealth of different points of view and experiences that make it possible to successfully navigate an emerging unknown future; accessing this diversity requires inclusion (Ferdman, 2014; Miller & Katz, 2002; Molefi, 2017).

In the workplace, inclusion is the big and small behaviors that create a sense of belonging and purpose, not in spite of but because of the diversity of experiences and contributions each employee brings. At Mandate Molefi, a company I work with that equips leaders to drive culture change and build an equitable, inclusive world, we explain that while diversity is a noun, inclusion is a verb—a call to action for people to engage, value, and amplify diversity in organizations (Molefi, 2017). Inclusive leaders are therefore people who use whatever agency they have to create this sense of belonging and purpose. This experience at work can be brought into employees' homes and communities and thereby have a positive ripple effect in society.

My OD practice and perspective are grounded in Appreciative Inquiry (AI), the strength-based approach to organizational change created by David Cooperrider and Diana Whitney (2005), and many others. The original AI model, summarized by discovering the best of what is, dreaming what might be, designing how it can be, and then delivering what will be, has been expanded and adapted over time by many practitioners (e.g., Kelm, 2005; Odell, 2000; Stavros & Hinrichs, 2009; Watkins & Mohr, 2011), reflecting the inherent generative nature of AI. My Appreciative Leadership Lotus Model is one such expansion; it applies a relational lens to AI and is the focus of this chapter.

This relational lens in my work is inherently informed by the South African concept of *Ubuntu*, we are who we are through one another, and our humanity is bound up in one another (Tutu, 1999). Nzimakwe (2014) furthers understanding of relational leadership when describing the principles of *Ubuntu* as sharing "ownership of opportunities, responsibilities and challenges" (p. 30) including participatory decision-making. These principles are also central to inclusive leadership, which is fundamentally relationship based and, at its best, multiplies participation and ownership.

## Theory of Change

"We know the problems. We know what's wrong. What we don't know is what's possible." Marlene Ogawa, Acting Country Director of the Synergos Institute in South Africa, shared this insight with me as her call to action in our work together. In this section I outline the roadmap or theory of how desired change comes about (how we move from one state to another) that guides my work. This is the approach I use to guide people, groups, and organizations to discover "what's possible."

### *Spaciousness*

My theory of change (see Figure 27.1 for a graphic representation) is seemingly quite straightforward:

> In an ever-growing environment of conflict, problems, and complexity, when we (humans) focus on the possibilities more than shortcomings, and do so in a manner that connects our curiosity (head) with our compassion (heart)—first within ourselves and then with each other—we experience spaciousness.

When feeling this sense of spaciousness, people report feeling included, and in turn act more inclusively with others, and are more inspired to generate exponential ideas leading to self-organizing action. If you have organizations that want to move from problems and conflict to innovation and inclusion, then design and facilitate meetings where people experience spaciousness.

It is important to note that I position my approach as a partner to and not a substitute for the important work of addressing conflict, unconscious bias, and structural inequality within institutions, which are also important components for laying the groundwork of inclusion. Conflict resolution expert and TEDx speaker on internalized oppression Ntombi-Zandile Xaba shared with me that:

> It's essential to understand that relationships tend to be combative because of the history. There is something very important about creating a platform where relationships can flourish and be nurtured

instead. This then allows for difficult conversations later because there would have been a place for relating and seeing each other as human beings.

Spaciousness, an appreciative approach to change and inclusion, is this platform for relationships to flourish and be nourished.

### *Appreciative Leadership and Inclusion*

In my diversity, equity, and inclusion practice, I focus on appreciative leadership as the way to create spaciousness, wherein people have a shared sense of connectedness and new possibilities rather than a sense of fatigue and hostility. Whitney et al. (2010) define appreciative leadership as "the relational capacity to mobilize creative potential into positive power" (p. 3). Most definitions of leadership imply individual behaviors or characteristics of a leader. Following Whitney et al., however, I define appreciative leadership as a relational process by which people—not just

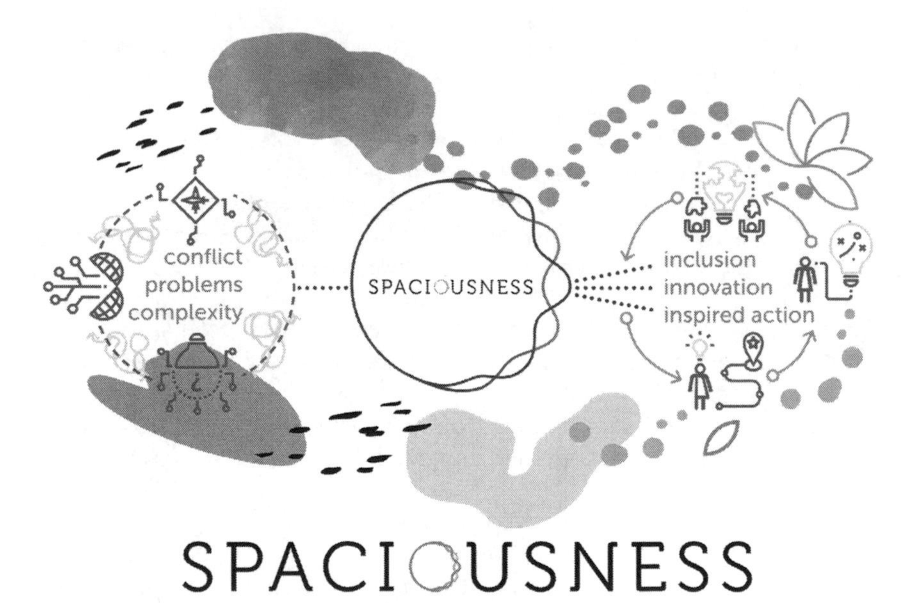


*Figure 27.1* The graphic illustrates that creating spaciousness within a context of conflict, problems, and complexity can result in increased inclusion, innovation, and inspired action.

the positional leader—emphasize appreciative relationships to themselves and each other, seek to build on that which is working well, and together innovate that which is possible into fruition. Appreciative leadership inherently inspires and facilitates inclusion because it is a relational process that addresses people's need "to know they belong and to feel valued for what they have to contribute" (Whitney et al., 2010, p. 23).

## The Work of Fostering Appreciative Leadership

My organization development work in South Africa spans across all sectors and focuses on strategic planning and culture change. It has included engagements with various types of organizations that were either in a culture transformation process, or, by the very nature of their mission, involved in contributing to a more diverse and inclusive society. For the purpose of using diverse examples to describe the approach and model in this chapter, the organizations I worked with include the following:

- A mining company listed in the top 50 companies in the world. When I worked with them, they had just stabilized internally after significant stress with several years of market downturn and a recent protracted strike; there was a desire to have all leadership stakeholders involved in creating a new inclusive culture. My work focused on several hundred corporate and union leaders engaging in re-building trust and relationships and co-creating the ideal culture away from a bargaining table.
- The National Labour & Economic Development Institute (NALEDI), a research institute whose policy-relevant work builds the capacity of the labor movement to effectively engage with the challenges of the new South African society. My work with them supported the new leadership's desire for a strategic planning process focused on defining a vision and including all staff.
- Genesis Analytics, a for-profit firm commited to making a positive impact in South Africa that has grown to be the largest economics-based consulting firm in Africa. My work with them included the development of a transformation vision to guide their transformation journey, particularly toward race and gender inclusion.
- The Conversation Africa, a non-profit digital news agency disrupting traditional media by partnering with universities to unlock academic knowledge for free use by the wider public. When I worked with them, this organization was in a vital stage of development and growth as a second-year start-up. The focus of the engagement was on developing and annually reviewing a pan-African growth vision and strategic plan.

As a key component of my work with these organizations and as a core method in applying my appreciative leadership model, I utilized appreciative interviews, asking generative questions that focus on peak moments of strength. The storytelling at the core of appreciative interviews helps to lay the foundation for the future that participants are co-creating. It is therefore congruent for me to give a sense of the appreciative leadership lotus model throughout this chapter using client interviews. These clients were Hameeda Deedat, Acting Executive Director, and Liesl Orr, Senior Researcher, NALEDI; Stephan Malherbe, Chair and Partner, Genesis Analytics; Pfungwa Nyamakachi, Strategic Partnerships and Stakeholder Manager, and Caroline Southey, Founder and Editor, The Conversation Africa. I quote their experiences here without specific attribution to be consistent with the method, which focuses on equally weighting the ideas generated rather than focusing on who originated them.

## The Appreciative Leadership Lotus Model

In reflecting on the central principles emerging from my practice, the lotus surfaced as a working metaphor and became the basis for my model of an appreciative leadership process that can create spaciousness. The remainder of this chapter explains the lotus model (illustrated in Figure 27.2) with its three key principles—a muddy birthplace, inherent wisdom, and emergence—that underpin a process of four iterative steps: (1) establish a positive relationship to self; (2) deepen one's compassion and connection to others; (3) imagine a shared future by co-creating it; and (4) commit to heartfelt actions, together.

### *The Lotus Model Principles*

There are three unique properties to the lotus that act as guiding principles for appreciative leadership:

1 *The Mud*: the lotus flower begins growing from a muddy, murky foundation.
2 *The Seed*: the lotus seed contains perfectly formed petals, miniatures of what they will become when the lotus blooms. They start with their full potential.
3 *The Flower*: the lotus flower has petals than unfold one at a time. The full bloom is emergent.

Each lotus principle inspires generative questions, the hallmark of appreciative and innovation processes.

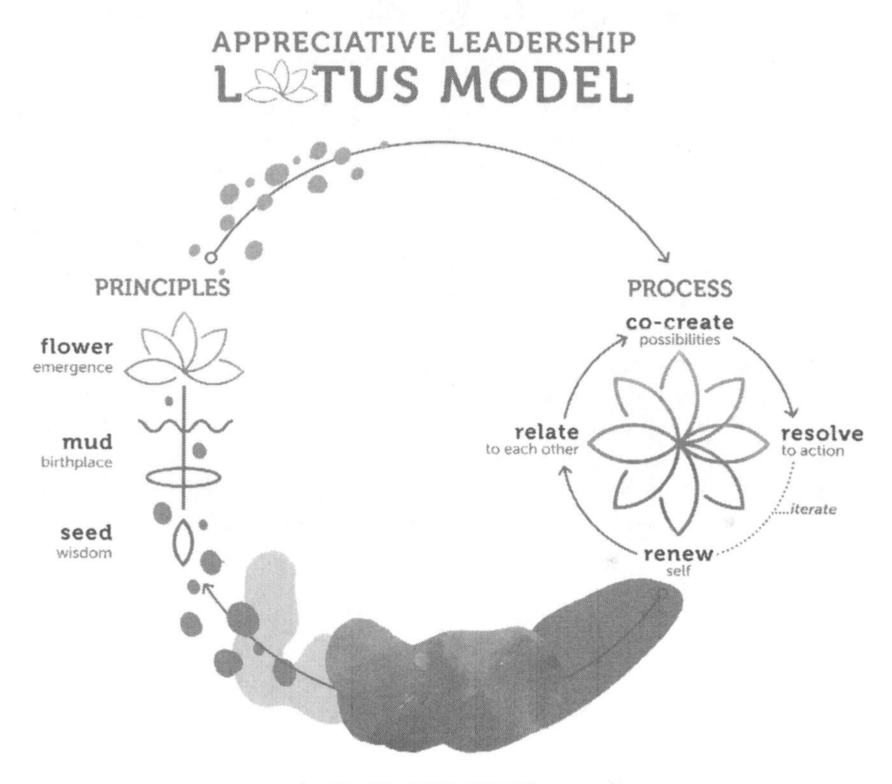


*Figure 27.2* The illustration shows the three principles underpinning the Appreciative Leadership Lotus Model and the four iterative steps in the process.

## *The Mud*

That a lotus flower can only grow in muddy ground can invite powerful reframing: What if we were aware that our "muck" is a necessary ground from which we can bloom? Would we feel hopeful in our capabilities and evolution? How could this perspective give us the resilience to persevere when feeling stuck in the muck? The mud principle is that conflict and complexity are contexts that have resources within and are not just deficit based; seeking out these strengths enables people to be in a resourceful state within the current reality.

Part of the muddy ground of transformation is creating opportunities for those who have been historically disadvantaged without triggering a scarcity mentality in those currently in power. What is possible when leaders spend less energy on defending what they have created and more on innovating a new future together? One client explained as follows:

> It's helpful to acknowledge that there's a great deal of anxiety where significant change is needed. As leaders ... it's change of what you're used to, but more importantly change of what you've built .... While we can pretend the process is all rational, there's actually quite a number of emotions related to significant change [that] can impact the work if not tended to. That's the reality. And if we stand for a process that humanizes everyone, we do mean everyone.

With appreciative leadership, leaders reported feeling they were also "rising out of the mud together" and began to exhibit more inclusive leadership behaviors, such as being aware of the impact of their own actions, listening to understand rather than with an agenda, and committing to having hard yet necessary conversations. They stated an openness to step into courageous conversations because they themselves felt included and invested.

### *The Seed*

What if each person knew that important new ideas for transforming teams, workplaces, and society is already within them and each other—that each person has the capacity to make a meaningful contribution and be a unique part of a whole solution?

The seed principle states that each person has valuable experiences and ideas to contribute; within a group the strongest solutions are generated when co-created by everyone. This principle can be quite liberating for leaders wanting to be more inclusive as it helps guide the ego, a common tripwire in leaders. One client explains it this way:

> Appreciative [leadership] ... works to appease [the ego], through the focus of what's gone well, what you've done well, what you value, and what you wish for. [I]t also creates an opportunity to [invite everyone to contribute]. As a leader it's important to understand what role ego plays, so you can put it aside and understand your role is one of many, and the power is in the collective. If ego is not managed, you'll never ... be able to tap into the knowledge, insight, and wisdom of the team.

### *The Flower*

An oft-quoted African proverb goes as follows: "Question: How do you eat a huge elephant? Answer: In pieces." The VUCA world has many people feeling overwhelmed. But what if we trusted that achieving our vision was a series of steps with an unfolding process, like that of lotus petals? The flower principle states that systems change is emergent, so that small steps when co-created and fully owned lead to desired outcomes.

An emergent approach can reduce anxiety and diffuse overwhelming urgency, often an obstacle to taking the time to be inclusive in teams. Additionally, a perspective that allows for considering what is working, as well as what is next, enables people to engage the change process differently. As stated by one client, "what was really powerful about the method was that it created an internal shift [to] 'okay we can do this.' Even when there's areas where we're not yet there, there's a great sense of agency that you can reach that." With fewer feelings of being overwhelmed and with a greater sense of agency, teams have a greater capacity to tap into in their diversity of opinions and experiences.

## The Lotus Model Process

The Lotus Model principles described above underpin an iterative process (illustrated in Figure 27.2) comprised of four components or "petals":

1 Renew: engendering a positive sense of self.
2 Relate: connecting with others.
3 Co-create: generatively visioning a desired future together.
4 Resolve: committing to heartfelt actions.

In this model I propose that if people can renew an authentic, positive view of themselves, they will be more open to relating to others. When in healthy relationship to others and feeling connected, group members are able to share more of their unique experience and expertise, to innovate solutions, and then move to action planning around bold new ideas.

### *Petal 1: Renew*

The focus of this step is to generate a renewed or new sense of self. This can be in the form of connecting to one's competence in the task at hand and a feeling that there is space for one's unique presence in the room, so one can bring one's experiences, identities, ideas, passion, and purpose to work. This accelerates an individual's feeling of inclusion and increases the diversity of ideas available for co-creating and critical for innovation.

Enablers for a positive sense of self include intentional communication and agreements reassuring people that the process will build upon their existing knowledge and experience. I have found that Harrison Owen's Open Space Technology principle, "Whoever comes is the right people" (2008, p. 92), and Ezelle Theunissen's AI principle of "Nothing Must

Be, Anything Can Be" (personal communication, 2017), to be effective agreements. They also invite inclusion and innovation.

Verbally inviting people to bring their whole selves is followed by a tangible experience of this principle, the Renew petal and the following Relate petal, using appreciative interviews.

The opportunity to be deeply listened to while focusing on a peak experience and one's core values refreshes one's sense of uniqueness and contribution to the topic, as noted in this comment:

> At a cultural level, traditional African culture, you're brought up to always be humble. So self-promotion is constantly discouraged. Appreciative interviews created [a space] to feel free to talk about what they've done well, and what they're proud of. It gave people permission ... not to be humble—without feeling guilty.

Being seen or witnessed in a successful, competent capacity contributes to the experience of inclusion and connection:

> Appreciative interviews become an equalizer. You're not asking me something that would be known better by another person. The questions about myself, what I'm proud of really empowers everyone to speak from the I. I can hold the conversation without worrying about someone differing with me. And when there's a culture where issues of rank and power are barriers to people expressing themselves, this is a good equalizer.

### *Petal 2: Relate*

Whether it is reconnecting within existing relationships or establishing new connections, the focus of this step is for people to increase positive regard and relationship to another. Just as they included more of themselves, they are then willing to extend that sense of inclusion to others.

Quite often I hear of positive relational shifts from appreciative interviews, along with recognition of unconscious biases, which can be barriers to acting inclusively: "I learned something about her that changed my whole notion of her. And dissolved a prejudice for me."

Following paired interviews there is group and ultimately plenary work. This flow enables people to continue to build relationships with an ever-growing number of people from a place of self and relational value. The unique ideas and experiences born of the diversity in the room flow unencumbered by power differentials. One participant described it this way: "I can be myself ... rather than wait for an advocate. This afforded me the opportunity to know I can speak up, show myself, share my ideas."

This self and other positive relational shift also positively impacts collaboration:

> It brought us closer to a willingness to engage around [issues]. And because of seeing the person in a different light—rather than opposite sides of a thing, we were able to see each other as part of a team and could see [each other's] perspective and [contributions].

When people build stronger, more inclusive relationships, they increase their generative capacity to co-create, the focus of petal 3.

### *Petal 3: Co-create*

The intention of this step is to envision an ideal future together in which the ideas are exponential because people feel and are valued for bringing their unique experiences and sharing them with others. This step also becomes an equalizer, as everyone, not just the most senior in the group, is tasked with contributing ideas. When people create something new with each other emanating from each person's contributions, inclusion is reinforced. One leader commented, "Solutions emerge that I could never have dreamt up. I only have one lens. [Appreciative leadership] allowed every single lens to come to play."

The method I use here is always creative, such as drawing or acting, and limits the use of words in the final product. This is intended to stretch most people's comfort zones in a work situation, which is exactly what is required to get out of "business-as-usual" thinking.

### *Petal 4: Resolve*

Once the vision of an ideal future emerges using petal 3, *co-create*, the focus moves to *resolve*, identifying heartfelt actions that will render this future into reality. The adjective *heartfelt* is specifically used to name the intentional head and heart connection in planning. The actions in this step are a combination of personal commitments and organizational solutions that can be brainstormed using a wide variety of planning tools, as time allows.

Because the lotus process generates ideas in an inclusive, connected way, people often continue to find inspiration in and affinity with the solutions they came up with personally and collectively. One client described this as follows: "It was clear that people who were there were committed … I remember walking out and thinking, 'wow, I think everyone wants to do this.' And I'm so clear on my part. That's so unique for a strategic plan."

Most importantly, I have found that the experience of inclusion in the lotus process can be reproduced, and people can step into leading inclusively. This is how one participant put it: "I hadn't felt [that] before, and that experience of non-judgment and collective solution finding I can and do re-create now that I know what's possible."

## Practice and Call to Action

Inclusion as a call to action for leaders requires perseverance and resilience. The hope generated with spaciousness helps to cultivate these virtues, as highlighted by one client:

> At the end . . . I am left hopeful. More connected than before, even if by a little bit, to another and my own self. This hope is the seed that carries stamina. While it may not be 100% of the shared sentiment, even just some feeling more hopeful, more connected, can make the difference between an initiative dead in the water and one that will be revisited another day.

There are a number of ways to put these insights into practice. Readers can practice inspiring inclusion with appreciative leadership by doing some or all of the following:

- Create a sense of spaciousness in the change process using appreciative approaches.
- Increase the time you, your team, and your organization spend focusing on what is working and what is possible. If you currently spend 100% of your time focused on the problem, try beginning the conversation to focus on what is working.
- Strengthen the human and relational aspect of strategic planning by introducing appreciative storytelling, asking how people are feeling at the opening and closing of meetings and workshops, and adding any of numerous ways to appreciate the colleagues in the room, starting with oneself.
- Use processes and methods that equalize power, including appreciative interviews, collective drawing, acting, and storytelling.
- Lean into creativity and play with relational intention. Use drawing, acting, and systems constellations (people physically moving and positioning themselves to represent their work or community or family system) as opportunities to connect people non-verbally and to co-create ideas.
- Intentionally name and frame the vulnerability of creativity as a tool to equalize power, connect people, and spark innovation as well as multiple modalities of thinking and feeling to connect the head and heart work necessary for authentic inclusion.
- Connect the lotus principles and experience of inclusion in workspaces to one's own agency in society. Using Ferdman's (2014) multilevel systems framework of inclusion (see also Chapter 1, this volume), for example, one can begin to identify opportunities to apply appreciative leadership on multiple levels.

## Conclusion

Inclusive leadership benefits from investing in what is working and what is possible and from leveraging human connection. Caroline Hopkins, an executive coach specializing in women and confidence in the workplace, framed this in our conversation as follows:

> Sometimes we need to break things down in order to understand or build them up better. But in our current climate, we are so disconnected already, if anything needs breaking down, it's what keeps us apart. People are longing to repair, rebuild, and create new connections in themselves and with others. Methodologies and processes that have that as an explicit aim are very needed in today's world.
>
> (personal communication, 2017)

The appreciative leadership lotus model, including its principles and process, provides a powerful way to create the spaciousness necessary to inspire and experience inclusion in a VUCA world. This workplace inclusion can change the transformation landscape of South Africa and the world.

## Acknowledgment

My writing was made possible by the generous wisdom of Einat and the Korman sisterhood, Marlene and Zed, Nene, Lauren P, Peter Lyons Design, and the sanctuary and support of Ben, Liz, Cruz, and Auggie.

## References

Cooperrider, D., & Whitney, D. (2005). *Appreciative inquiry: A positive revolution in change*. San Francisco, CA: Berrett-Koehler.

Ferdman, B. M. (2014). The practice of inclusion in diverse organizations: Toward a systemic and inclusive framework. In B. M. Ferdman & B. R. Deane (Eds.), *Diversity at work: The practice of inclusion* (pp. 3–54). San Francisco, CA: Jossey-Bass. https://doi.org/10.1002/9781118764282.ch1

Kelm, J. (2005). *Appreciative living: The principles of appreciative inquiry in personal life*. Wake Forest, NC: Venet Publishers.

Miller, F. A., & Katz, J. H. (2002). *The inclusion breakthrough: Unleashing the real power of diversity*. San Francisco, CA: Berrett-Koehler.

Molefi, N. (2017). *A journey of diversity & inclusion in South Africa: Guidelines for leading inclusively*. Randburg, South Africa: KR Publishing.

Nzimakwe, T. I. (2014). Practising Ubuntu and leadership for good governance: The South African and continental dialogue. *African Journal of Public Affairs*, 7(4), 30–41. https://hdl.handle.net/2263/58143

Odell, M. (2000). From conflict to cooperation: Approaches to building rural partnerships. *Global Social Innovations*, *1*(3), 16–22.

Owens, H. (2008). *Open space technology: A user's guide*. San Francisco, CA: Berrett-Koehler.

Stavros, J. M., & Hinrichs, G. (2009). *The thin book of SOAR: Building a strengths-based strategy*. Bend, OR: Thin Book Publishing.

Tutu, D. (1999). *No future without forgiveness*. New York, NY: Image.

Watkins, J. M., & Mohr, B. (2011). *Appreciative inquiry: Change at the speed of imagination*. San Francisco, CA: Pfeiffer.

Whitney, D., Trosten-Bloom, A., & Rader, K. (2010). *Appreciative leadership: Focus on what works to drive winning performance and build a thriving organization*. New York, NY: McGraw-Hill.

# 28 How to Develop and Support Leadership that Contributes to a More Equitable, Diverse, and Inclusive Society

*Leadership Learning Community Collaboration (Deborah Meehan, lead)*[1]

## Introduction

We live in a multiracial world, in which the nature and consequences of racism are in flux. Many people take pride in, and build on, the strengths of their racial and ethnic identities. Although many of the most egregious and overt examples of racism have been outlawed, it is still true that life chances and opportunities are heavily racialized—that is, determined by one's race or ethnicity. Differences by racial or ethnic identity remain, and in some instances are growing, in areas of well-being that include wealth, income, education, health, and even life expectancy. These differences are the result of historical and current practices that produce and reproduce racialized outcomes in a way that is not well revealed by looking through our old lens of race.

This chapter explores the ways in which our current thinking about leadership may contribute to producing and maintaining racialized dynamics, and identifies a set of core competencies associated with equity-focused leadership needed to advance an inclusive society. Recommendations are included for ways to develop and support these competencies. This chapter does not seek to address all positive leadership competencies, but rather to highlight some particular capacities and practices that can further equity, diversity, and inclusion in organizations, communities, and the broader society.

Leadership can play a critical role in either contributing to equity, diversity, and inclusion or reinforcing prevailing patterns of racial inequality and exclusion. In an ever-changing multicultural society, filled with racial complexities, the role that leadership plays requires continual re-examination and reshaping to contribute in positive ways toward creating an inclusive society in which opportunities and benefits are more equally shared.

## How Leadership Thinking and Practice Perpetuate Inequity

To a large extent, current thinking about leadership focuses on individualism, meritocracy, and equal opportunity, as described by the Aspen

Institute (2005) in a report titled Structural Racism and Youth Development: Issues, Challenges, and Implications:

- *Personal responsibility and individualism*: the belief that people control their fates regardless of social position, and that individual behaviors and choices determine material outcomes.
- *Meritocracy*: the belief that resources and opportunities are distributed according to talent and effort, and that social components of "merit"—such as access to inside information or powerful social networks—are of lesser importance or do not matter much.
- *Equal opportunity*: the belief that employment, education, and wealth accumulation arenas are "level playing fields" and that race is no longer a barrier to progress in these areas.

Issues of advantage and disadvantage are largely influenced by racialized structural arrangements and social group position (e.g., gender, sexual orientation, immigration status, religion, and class); however, the focus on individualism and equal opportunity fails to recognize that link. Current leadership thinking and practice are strongly influenced by values and beliefs that are part of the dominant culture of individualism in the United States. There are several ways of understanding how this plays out[2] in leadership work:

- *Meritocracy*: mainstream ideas about leadership carry the assumption that individuals have attained leadership positions based primarily on their talent, natural ability, or achievements. This thinking overlooks the many ways in which structural racism has created economic structures that create advantage, opportunities, and access (or lack of access) to leadership positions based on race. For example, focusing on supporting people's success and leadership without addressing structural racism that may undermine their achievements—such as telling a young person how to dress or behave in a job interview or leadership position without talking about racial barriers (prejudice, organizational culture, old-boy networks)—implies that they are fully responsible for their success or failure, in that if they work hard enough they have as much chance to succeed as the next person. Many organizations have demonstrated that this is not true and have statistically documented the disadvantage of race along a number of dimensions, including the likelihood of owning a home, of going to college, and of going to prison.
- *Systemic nature of inequity and racism*: focusing on the role of individuals in creating and solving problems does not look at the impact that systems have on the ways people behave, and tends to attribute racism and other forms of bias only to ignorance or hateful

behaviors. Based on this logic, it would follow that we could eliminate racism by changing people's attitudes; however, this is not entirely true. In her article, "Taking on Postracialism," Rinku Sen (2009) points out that while intrapersonal racism and bias are declining, incidents of structural racism are on the rise. This is because many of the policies and practices that produce disparities appear "race-neutral"—that is, they do not specify different actions by race—but their effect is to give Whites advantage over people of color. Funding education by property taxes is one example; requiring computer literacy or a valid driver's license for jobs that do not demand them is another. If we do not understand and address the consequences of structural racism, we help to maintain it.

- *Leadership exists within a context*: the focus on individuals in leadership thinking does not address differences in social contexts that are created by systems of structural advantage and disadvantage and that shape social and racial identity. These collective identities create a shared experience from which collective grievances and aspirations emerge to motivate collective action. The focus on individuals misses the influence of social identity as a context of collective leadership and action.
- *Leadership models*: leadership is often characterized by the heroic, directive, high-profile individual who exerts influence over others by virtue of authority, or position, or persuasion; this is, however, only one model of leadership. Leadership is not inherently individualistic. We often reward people whose leadership style is aligned with the individual model of the dominant culture, but not those who engage in more collective forms of leadership. This serves to render invisible the leadership of many women and people of different races/ethnicities.

## Core Competencies for Supporting Leadership that Advances Equity, Diversity, and Inclusion

Given the cultural influence of individualism, many leadership development programs assume that if you select individuals who have demonstrated leadership potential or ability and provide them with additional knowledge and skills, they will be able to contribute positively to a more inclusive society. Changing the behavior of individuals is not enough: it will not support a system intervention that addresses the root causes of structural racism and other forms of oppression. Having a systemic perspective and a focus on leadership as a process leads us to ask not only which individuals to support but also how to embed and cultivate equity, diversity, and inclusion competencies in the ongoing practice and culture of organizations, networks, and communities.

### *Meaning Making and Connecting*

Building alignment around an explicit and active commitment to equity, diversity, and inclusion requires a deep knowledge of oneself and others, and is core to working together to address equity and power in organizations and communities. This involves making meaning of one's own experience with issues of power. Understanding intersecting identities builds connection and shared commitment to racial equity work. Philanthropic Initiative for Racial Equity (PRE; https://racialequity.org) and mosaic consulting (https://web.archive.org/web/20110202185008/http://mosaicideas.com), in a report by Quiroz-Martínez et al. (2004), also link the meaning-making process to leadership development, explaining that the work of youth development organizations is to help youth analyze and comprehend the world around them at a critical stage in their development. As young people better understand how their lives and opportunities are influenced by racism, rather than individual strengths or challenges, they can become a collective voice and advocate for themselves.

For example, it is not uncommon for participants in leadership programs to talk about "connecting the dots." When a cohort of program participants see the common threads in their experiences they are able to move from personal and individual experience to understanding the social, economic, and political environments that have created these shared experiences. One program did this through study circles and other programs have used popular education and frameworks on structural oppression to help participants see that change needs to happen at the personal, interpersonal, and systemic levels.

### *Systems Thinking*

The Kirwan Institute (Menendian & Watt, 2008) helps us understand that racial disadvantage is primarily a product of opportunity structures within society:

> A systems perspective helps us understand how racial disadvantages manifest, accumulate, and resist efforts to address them by allowing us to see the world in terms of wholes, rather than in single event "snapshots" and how parts of a system work together to produce systems outcomes.
>
> ( Menendian & Watt, 2008, p. 12)

Systems thinking deepens understanding of how structural racism is perpetuated. This includes a commitment to assessing racial impacts of key plans and proposals before making final decisions, to maximize equitable systemic impacts.

For example, participants in a leadership program focused on creating health use systems thinking to identify the many issues like housing, transportation, access to recreation, jobs, and others that could impede opportunities to live the healthiest life possible. They were able to look at the pattern across these issues to understand the relationship between these issues and one's racial and social identity in determining who gets to be healthy. This analysis helps participants see the importance of working at the intersection of multiple issues.

### *Organizing*

Conscious attention should be paid to racial equity in all aspects of organizing, in a variety of contexts ranging from organizations to networks and coalitions. This means organizing the work such that equity and inclusion are paramount and the process and pursuits are fully aligned with outcomes that advance equity. It requires transparent conversations about power and privilege in decision-making and governance issues.

For example, in one leadership development program focused on supporting community organizing leaders, participants learned about the policies, practices, and structures that undergird systems of inequality and about grassroots approaches to changing these systems. By grounding theory in practice, participants learn to operationalize mechanisms of change. At its core, organizing involves individuals coalescing to build enough power to change the conditions that impact their lives. By applying an explicit racial equity lens, program participants learn to build collectives that avoid replicating the same inequities that engendered the problems they initially gathered together to fight.

### *Learning and Reflection*

Reflection on one's individual experience with institutional power and privilege, along with learning about racialized opportunity structures, is a continuous process that is integrated with action. It means being collectively accountable for how we are doing on our racial equity goals and mobilizing to do better, individually and as groups. This competency within organizations and communities includes understanding how to use data to diagnose an issue and track progress.

For example, some leadership programs introduce an equity/racial impact analysis tool that can be applied to projects and budgeting. The tool helps an individual or group analyze the impact a specific program or policy will have on different groups, because what may seem like a good policy for all might positively benefit some while having a negative impact on others. This kind of process could help people understand how a new transit stop that on the surface looked like a great thing for everyone was going to be built in a location that would displace community institutions and residents.

### *Bridging*

Understanding leadership as a process makes more visible the natural connections between many organizations and individuals in different parts of a system, and encourages leadership that builds strategic alignment around problem analysis and vision with a diverse array of stakeholders. To achieve racial and social justice, we need to move beyond the emphasis on the power of individuals to a philosophy of interdependence and building connections.

For example, a number of leadership programs are now cultivating network competency to help their graduates understand why and how to connect their efforts across different issues and organizations. They are able to use a social network map (a visual representation of relationships between people, organizations, and issues) to weave strategic connections because they can see more clearly the diverse set of stakeholders who need to be connected to tackle complex problems such as health inequities or disparities in education.

## Recommendations for Effectively Supporting Equity-Focused Leadership

### *Make Racial Equity an Explicit and Active Commitment*

Just as many programs have adopted an explicit commitment to diversity and anti-discrimination, organizations can be encouraged to adopt an explicit commitment to racial equity. It is helpful to see diversity as a tool to help us get to racial justice, rather than an end in itself. A survey of 122 leadership program staff about topics included in program curriculum, as reported by Potapchuk and Leiderman (2009), illustrates that a large number of leadership programs place a strong emphasis on diversity but more could be done to stress issues of structural racism and White privilege. (Although 90% reported that diversity was included in their curriculum, less than 60% reported that structural racism or White privilege were addressed.)

Racial equity leadership needs to express this commitment through concrete planning and, to make it a reality, through practice in terms of diverse staffing, inclusive policies, and power in making curriculum decisions. It is also important to understand how an organization's commitment to racial justice is reflected or inhibited in the structure of the institution and in relation to other institutions.

### *Be Accountable for Racial Equity Outcomes*

If we are going to hold ourselves accountable for transforming structural racism through our leadership work, then, according to Sally Leiderman of the Center for Assessment and Policy Development, we need to track all of the following: changes at organizational and community levels for different racial groups over the long term; the extent to which race becomes a less powerful predictor of how people fare; and progress toward a community's understanding of how privilege and oppression shape opportunities. And we must share our stories of success.

### *Provide Resources to Help Make Racial Justice a Core Leadership Focus*

Provide leadership with tools and resources that support making racial justice a conscious part of planning and decision-making in their leadership work. Leadership within organizations and communities needs to understand the racial impact of programs and policies.[3] This begins with developing the individual and institutional knowledge and the confidence to ask tough questions, such as: What aspects of our organizations actively work to create inequities? What are the power dynamics at play? Whose voices are at the table? Whose are not? Is there a single cultural lens through which policies, practices, and experiences are interpreted and determined? Who benefits from the way things are done? These leadership skills can be supported with the following types of tools and resources:

- **Issue framing guide.** Some organizations have learned new ways to highlight the racial dynamics of social issues they are addressing. For example, the board of directors of Citizen Action of New York enacted a policy that requires its chapters and issues committees to use a racial equity framing tool to assess whether to explicitly address racial inequities in its issue campaigns. If the chapters or committees decide not to address racism, they must provide an explanation to the board. Having this policy and tool provides leaders with a concrete way to consciously address race.
- **Policy and budget filter.** City officials in Seattle and county officials in King County, Washington, are using planning and budgetary guides to help them address racial disparities in making planning and budgetary decisions.
- **Racial Equity Impact Assessments.** Some government bodies and non-profits are beginning to use Racial Equity Impact Assessments (e.g., Keleher, 2009) during the planning and decision-making process to predict and prevent negative racial impacts. Legislators in Iowa and Connecticut have passed laws requiring the use of minority impact assessments when considering legislative proposals that could affect the racial population of state prisons, in order to help prevent further racial disparities.

### *Incorporate Racial Equity Training into Leadership Development Strategies*

Effective leadership development can be strengthened by racial equity trainings, which include an analysis of structural racism and support the development of skills and strategies for advancing racial equity and institutional change. These differ from diversity and cultural competency trainings, which often focus on interpersonal relations, prejudice reduction, and cultural awareness, and even from dismantling racism trainings. The latter, at their best, usually provide an institutional analysis and critique of racism and deeper awareness of racial privilege and oppression, but they tend to focus on organizational change and may fail to connect to strategies for external community and policy change.

### *Support the Development of Systems Thinking and Analysis*

Tackling structural racism as a system requires understanding how systems operate and perpetuate themselves—recognizing in particular the role of "leverage points" in altering a system's ability to maintain itself and resist efforts toward change.

Other considerations from a systems analysis approach include:

- **An understanding of the deep relational nature of systems.** It is important for leadership to understand resistance (whether implicit or explicit) to the goal of racial justice and how this goal aligns or conflicts with other institutional and inter-institutional goals and dynamics. Failure to understand and address such issues can undermine the effectiveness of leadership in general, but especially in matters of race.
- **A shift in the meaning of race and the grammar for race.** Instead of focusing on individual or group feelings and thoughts, it becomes necessary to consider what work the institutions are doing and how to influence them. It also becomes important to have an understanding of implicit racial messages and meaning.

### *Provide Time, Processes, and Conducive Space for Talking About Race and Racial/Ethnic Identity*

Conversations about race that deal honestly with conflict can give participants an opportunity to learn something new and transform their thoughts and feelings (Chan et al., 2009). Making meaning of individual and collective experiences in a safe environment for emotional exploration of racism can also support healing. It is important to address racial nuance in the course of business and to recognize and value the importance of giving needed time to these discussions in real time as racialized dynamics surface.

### *Promote Inclusive Models of Leadership That Recognize Leadership as a Collective Process Through Which Individuals and Groups Take Action on Racial Equity Goals*

Many programs promote the individual model of leadership, which is associated with leadership "over" others, creates relationships of dominance, and has historically applied coercion, force, or influence to reinforce power and privilege. Leadership needs to be reframed as the process by which individuals and groups align their values and mission, build relationships, organize and take action, and learn from their experiences to achieve their shared goals. Leadership programs should honor multiple approaches to leadership by inviting participants to share and learn from the different ways that they and their communities exercise collective, action-oriented leadership.

### *Provide Resources, Networks, and Skills to Groups That Have Been Historically Disadvantaged*

The kinds of support structures needed for people of color, especially those from low-income backgrounds, may differ considerably from those needed for middle-class Whites. Without paying attention to these differences, a typical program approach that assumes equal opportunity will not take the extra steps needed to address historical disadvantage. Examples of what to provide to program participants include:

- **Targeted resources**. Provide resources based on need; for example, cover child care costs, missed time from work, health care, and educational opportunities. Targeted efforts like these are critical to achieving more universal goals intended to benefit all, which, in the case of a leadership program, might be the intention to provide reflective time in a retreat-like environment, to help all participants align their mission and values.
- **Response to specific needs**. Provide a safe space in which people of color can examine their own internalized oppression, to avoid having others tokenize their experiences and to create effective multiracial coalitions for addressing ineffective policies and practices. White people may need different support structures to help them recognize their own White privilege and step out of their comfort zones to ask about and understand the effects of racism in order to become allies for racial equity.
- **Skills development**. Provide access to skills that facilitate participation of people of color at policy tables, to which they can bring a racial impact analysis, as well as access to planning, decision-making, and evaluation tools related to promoting racial equity outcomes.

- **Networks.** Provide strategies that connect people who have been marginalized to existing networks while building new networks for mentoring, intergenerational partnership, information exchange, and access to resources.

## Conclusion

We who are involved in leadership work have an opportunity to address disparities in how resources and opportunity are distributed in the U.S. Bringing a race-conscious lens to common assumptions about leadership raises an important question about the impact of our leadership work: "Are current approaches to leadership contributing to growing disparities or supporting a more equitable and just future for people of all races and ethnicities?" Leadership programs engage thousands of people every year and will make a difference. It is up to us to decide what that difference will be. A commitment to racial justice will require a new consciousness and new approaches to our leadership work. We developed this chapter to stimulate the conversation about needed changes in leadership work, offer suggestions about racial justice leadership strategies, and identify resources that can guide leadership programs in better supporting racial justice.

## Notes

1 In 2009, the Leadership Learning Community (LLC; https://leadershiplearning.org) launched a collaborative research project using a network strategy to explore the intersection of the racial equity and leadership development fields. Experts from these fields, listed below, wrote together on a public wiki, held a series of meetups around the country to test and develop ideas, and collaborated to edit the content of this chapter, which was first published in 2010 as "Leadership and Race: How to Develop and Support Leadership that Contributes to Racial Justice" (https://leadershiplearning.org/system/files/Leadership%20and%20Race%20FINAL_Electronic_072010.pdf) under a Creative Commons license. The authors of the report, in alphabetical order, are:

- Terry Keleher, Race Forward
- Sally Leiderman, www.arc.org/Development (CAPD)
- Deborah Meehan, Leadership Learning Community (LLC)
- Elissa Perry, Management Assistance Group
- Maggie Potapchuk, MP Associates
- Professor john a. powell, Haas Institute for a Fair and Inclusive Society
- Hanh Cao Yu, PhD, The California Endowment (TCE).

That report was adapted further by Deborah Meehan for publication in this book under the Creative Common Attribution 3.0 license.

2 How does structural racism play out? As an example of structural racism, the GI Bill disproportionately enabled White people to buy homes and create

wealth (Kirwan Institute for the Study of Race and Ethnicity). That wealth helped a generation of working middle-class White people to send their children to better schools and take care of their health needs more easily. Government policies also opened the doors to higher education for later generations, enabling those eligible for the GI Bill to finance their children's education as a consequence of wealth accumulated by home ownership. But these policies excluded certain groups of service people (nearly all people of color) and potential home buyers (also nearly all people of color). According to the website (https://www.pbs.org/race/000_General/000_00-Home.htm) for the PBS series *Race: The Power of an Illusion*:

> Today, 71% of whites own their own home, compared to 44% of African Americans. Black and Latino mortgage applicants are 60% more likely than whites to be turned down for loans. As housing gets more expensive and wealth gets passed down from generation to generation, the legacy of past discrimination persists, giving whites and nonwhites vastly different chances.

These factors, along with the fact that for many years the dominant culture accepted these differences as normal, are examples of structural racism with profound consequences.

3 Leadership development programs and strategies cannot undo structural racism, but they can provide increased opportunities for individuals and groups who, because of racialized systems of structural advantage, are less likely to have had equitable access to resources.

## References

Aspen Institute (2005, April 25). *Structural racism and youth development. Issues, challenges, and implications*. Aspen Institute. https://www.aspeninstitute.org/publications/structural-racism-youth-development-issues-challenges-implications

Chan, A., Pruitt, L. P., Allen, W., Johnson, J., Martinez, R., Moore, R., Moore, R., Poo, A., & Sebastien, C. (2009). *Taking back the work: A cooperative inquiry into the work of leaders of color in movement-building organizations*. Research Center for Leadership in Action, Robert F. Wagner Graduate School of Public Service, New York University. https://wagner.nyu.edu/leadership/reports/files/TakingBacktheWork.pdf

Keleher, T. (2009). *Racial equity impact assessment*. Race Forward, The Center for Racial Justice Innovation. https://www.raceforward.org/sites/default/files/RacialJusticeImpactAssessment_v5.pdf

Menendian, S. & Watt, C. (2008, December). *Systems primer: Systems thinking and race*. Kirwan Institute for the Study of Race and Ethnicity, The Ohio State University. http://kirwaninstitute.osu.edu/docs/systems_thinking_and_race_primer_july2009.pdf

Potapchuk, M. & Leiderman, S. (2009, April). *Transforming White privilege: A 21st century leadership capacity* [curriculum]. https://www.racialequitytools.org/module/overview/transforming-white-privilege

Quiroz-Martínez, J., HoSang, D., & Villarosa, L. (2004). *Changing the rules of the game: Youth development & structural racism*. Philanthropic Initiative for

Racial Equity, Washington, DC. https://www.racialequitytools.org/resourcefiles/quiroz-martinez.pdf

Sen, R. (2009, Fall). Taking on postracialism. *On the Issues Magazine*. https://www.ontheissuesmagazine.com/2009fall/2009fall_sen.php

# Part VI

# Reflections and Conclusion

# 29 Inclusive Leadership
## Insights and Implications

*Jeanine Prime, Bernardo M. Ferdman, and Ronald E. Riggio*

In compiling this volume, we set out to explore cutting-edge theory, research, practice, and experience on the pivotal role of leadership in fostering inclusion in diverse organizations and societies. Our goal was to draw from the collective wisdom of a diverse group of expert researchers and practitioners spanning disciplinary boundaries and grounded in scholarship, while highlighting clear applications. We sought from them both micro and macro perspectives to provide a multifaceted understanding of inclusive leadership, including what it is, how it can be cultivated and displayed, and how it helps to create positive and even transformational outcomes for people, organizations, and societies. Not surprisingly, the insights they have shared throughout the book are ultimately as much about the nature of inclusion as they are about the leadership practices that drive it. The collective wisdom accumulated here on the practice of inclusive leadership is thus aptly rooted in an analysis of inclusion itself.

From that analysis we learned that inclusion—at the individual level—requires the subjective experience of belonging—of sharing and being bound to others by important similarities—and the simultaneous experience of being unique—an experience derived from being valued for the attributes that *distinguish* us from others, as we engage together in collective work that is mutually beneficial. Inclusion is about engaging together with others—whether in a work group, an organizational system, a community, and a society, and yes—even the world—in ways that view and use differences as collectively valuable, that consider and provide for mutual benefit, and that strive to—and do—increase equity and social justice. In terms of objective indicators, authors described inclusion in terms of having equal access to valued resources and information, being able to fully participate and contribute to critical group processes, like decision-making, and having equitable opportunities to receive rewards.

Although our contributors had convergent views on inclusion in the abstract, the most salient differences in focus and perspective arose in their considerations of how inclusion is lived and operationalized. These insights offer a more practical view of what inclusive leadership requires and demonstrate why it is such a formidable challenge—especially when viewed as a relational process not tied to positional authority or status. In this concluding chapter, we outline and reflect on some of these key emerging insights about the nature of inclusion as well as their implications for the practice of inclusive leadership.

## What Did We Learn about Inclusion and the Practice of Inclusive Leadership?

Together, the chapters in this volume paint a multi-faceted and complex view of inclusion and its implications for the practice of inclusive leadership. Here we address four aspects of inclusion in this regard: it is person-centered and multi-layered, as well as intrapersonal and paradoxical.

### *Inclusion is Person-Centered*

Although authors commonly characterized inclusion as a combined sense of belonging and uniqueness, several acknowledged that the experience of inclusion is person-centered. In other words, the set of circumstances or interactions that create the experience of inclusion vary from person to person. As a result, inclusion exists in the eye of the beholder, and must be constructed anew in each relationship (Ferdman & Davidson, 2002). For this reason, Wasserman (Chapter 6) argues that inclusion must be understood from a phenomenological point of view. Similarly, Schein and Schein (Chapter 5) identify cultural orientation as a key factor that leaders must consider as they grapple with this variability in how people experience inclusion in different cultural contexts and from different cultural vantage points.

#### *What This Means for Inclusive Leaders*

If we cannot reliably cultivate inclusive interpersonal interactions with the same tactics and approaches across contexts, it means that inclusive leaders must be highly adaptive and flexible. A critical implication then is that leaders must let go of the notion of having all the answers and continually collaborate with others to co-create distinct practices and relationships that collectively engender shared experiences of inclusion—as Ferdman discussed in Chapter 1, and what Kegan and Lahey (2016) called an "everyone culture," in which all individuals feel included across identities or statuses. Doing so, argues Wasserman (Chapter 6), requires leaders to be vulnerable and to have integrity. This vulnerability is demonstrated by suspending their sense of certainty and knowing as they continually engage with differences and collaboratively derive meaning from those differences. It also means creating the conditions that foster voice and participation across diverse identities, as highlighted by Creary (Chapter 15) in her work on diversity workspaces and by Ferdman in Chapter 1. And it means building skills and practicing competencies for engaging across difficult and challenging differences, one relationship at a time, as illustrated by Winters (Chapter 16) in her work on "bold, inclusive conversations." Interestingly, these individualized relationships do not occur willy-nilly or randomly, but can (and, ideally, should) be fostered in the context of more systemic practices, as indicated by our next focal insight.

### *Inclusion is Multi-Layered*

As Ferdman (Chapter 1) laid out in the opening part of the book, inclusion is also a multi-layered construct—best understood and practiced simultaneously at the interpersonal, group, organizational, and societal levels (see also Ferdman & Deane, 2014). But since inclusion is often studied and addressed at the interpersonal or group level, we intentionally set out in this book to go further and offer a multilevel analysis of inclusion and the demands it places on inclusive leaders.

At the interpersonal level, we learned from Atewologun and Harman (Chapter 7) that experiences of inclusion and exclusion can be activated by micro-behaviors—small, subtle, often unconscious, interpersonal interactions. Inclusive micro behaviors affirm and legitimize *all* employees—irrespective of status. In contrast, exclusionary micro-behaviors tend to routinely affirm those from dominant groups and disaffirm those from nondominant ones.

At the group level, Nishii and Leroy (Chapter 12) conceptualize inclusion in terms of the workgroup climate—the shared expectations and behaviors that are rewarded within the group. When inclusive, affirming micro-behaviors, such as those Atewologun and Harman describe, become the shared norm that is practiced, recognized, and rewarded by all group members, we are more likely to achieve group-level inclusion.

By extension we realize organizational- and societal-level inclusion when institutional policies, practices, and resources normalize and reward inclusive interactions among constituent groups and their members, and when the values and processes of these larger systems serve to maximize the likelihood of both individual and collective experiences of inclusion, as well as equity and fairness. In this regard, Shyamsunder (Chapter 17) provided us with examples of such cross-level effects, and DiTomaso (Chapter 19), Lukensmeyer and Torres (Chapter 21), and Henderson (Chapter 22) described many of the challenges involved at this macro level and the ways in which inclusive leadership can address them.

### *What This Means for Inclusive Leaders*

The multi-level nature of inclusion poses unique challenges for inclusive leaders. At the individual level, it means leaders must work to identify and familiarize themselves with the range of micro-behaviors that both include and exclude. But they must also go further to act as what Nishii and Leroy (Chapter 12) call "engineers" of inclusive climates. In this role, inclusive leaders engage team members in creating a shared understanding of the benefits of inclusion to the team and of what it takes to realize those benefits by clarifying which behaviors are aligned and which are misaligned with the goal of inclusion. Role modeling inclusive behaviors is also important for leaders to be credible as climate engineers, yet Nishii and Leroy argue that it is insufficient. To ensure that inclusive behaviors are widely adopted, leaders should not assume that others will mindlessly follow their examples. Rather, to ensure widespread adoption of inclusive behaviors, leaders must co-create procedures and routines for group processes, such as decision-making and conflict resolution, that reinforce inclusive expectations and norms. Nishii and Leroy also contend that, to strengthen the climate, leaders must continually assess the extent to which there are gaps between the idealized climate and shared experiences of team members—continually working collaboratively to close these gaps through dialogue and collective problem-solving. We learn from Offermann and Lanzo (Chapter 13) that moving too slowly on these engineering tasks can be detrimental, as it is harder to establish inclusive norms later in a team's life cycle than during its formation. And we learn from Chrobot-Mason and Aramovich (Chapter 10) how important it is for leaders to have diverse networks that support connections, learning, and other types of exchange across multiple boundaries.

At an organizational level, inclusive leadership serves an important translator function. As Ferdman (Chapter 1) explains, inclusive leaders play an important role in giving visibility to inclusive behaviors and climates at the individual and group levels, so they gain significance at an organizational level where they can be institutionalized. At the same time, they are also translators of organizational-level priorities and values so they can be interpreted on the ground in practical terms. This function of bridging micro and macro levels of the organization is why Ferdman describes inclusive leadership as the "fulcrum of inclusion" in diverse organizations. Perhaps one of the most critical "fulcrum" functions, as Wasserman (Chapter 6) points out, is to create a meta-narrative that helps individuals "connect the dots" in terms of how inclusion is operationalized across micro and macro levels of the organization.

### *Inclusion is also Intrapersonal*

As noted above, the discourse on inclusion often centers around interpersonal and to a lesser extent intergroup and macro-level interactions. As a result, it can often neglect the *intrapersonal* processes that are essential to inclusion. As we noted earlier, a sense of uniqueness and authenticity are core to the subjective experience of inclusion. Davidson (Chapter 9) suggests that this sense of authenticity does not just come from the value that *others* place on our uniqueness—but rather also from the value that we place on it ourselves. Although people often try to conceal the differences that set them apart to gain a sense of inclusion, such measures ironically often have the opposite effect. Rather than increasing feelings of inclusion, covering or concealing one's atypical traits often paradoxically results in alienation and exclusion. Thus, embracing what makes one unique or "weird," as Davidson puts it, is a critical prerequisite for experiencing inclusion.

This intrapersonal aspect of inclusion can also extend to understanding how and where particular cultural influences may be reflected in our values, behavior, and expectations, as discussed, for example, by Welp and Schein (Chapter 25) in their work on engaging White men to be inclusive leaders. The process of self-development and insight (e.g., Dillon & Caspi Sable, Chapter 26) is certainly a key aspect of this as well.

#### *What This Means for Inclusive Leaders*

If inclusive leadership is about cultivating an "everyone culture" where differences are leveraged, it is easy to see how important it is for leaders to cultivate skill in embracing weirdness (Davidson, Chapter 9). When applied intrapersonally, it enhances the practice of inclusive leadership in two ways. First, by reflecting on their own weirdness, inclusive leaders gain greater comfort engaging with and learning from difference. Second, by understanding their own experiences of marginality—a byproduct of their weirdness—inclusive leaders gain greater empathy and insight into the experiences of *others* who are marginalized. In these ways, the ability to embrace weirdness intrapersonally is an asset that enables leaders to more effectively leverage difference at the interpersonal, group, and organizational levels.

We learn from several authors that self-awareness is also an accelerant of inclusive leadership. Clearly, it is impossible to embrace one's own weirdness without being fully aware of the qualities and attributes that contribute to that characterization. Yet even beyond this, self-awareness also helps inclusive leaders understand their own blind spots and specifically recognize how their memberships in multiple identity groups can impede their ability to leverage certain differences versus others.

### *Inclusion is Paradoxical*

Consistent with Ferdman's prior analysis (Ferdman, 2017), several authors also point to the paradoxical nature of inclusion. One key paradox is that inclusion results from opposing experiences—on the one hand, the sense of belonging that comes from the common ground that we share with others and from being an equal member of a collective, and on the other hand, the simultaneous sense of uniqueness gained from being valued for attributes that set us apart from others and from being able to express ourselves authentically.

According to Smith (Chapter 20), another key paradox stems from the nature of identity. Consider that identities are at the same time both personal and social. This reality creates an inherent tension. With respect to any specific identity, what an individual interprets as inclusive at a societal level may be at odds with what that person perceives as inclusive on an interpersonal level. For example, individuals from nondominant groups may perceive that affirmative action policies are needed to promote societal inclusion but may not wish to benefit from such policies individually. Further, because individuals have multiple, intersecting identities, the challenge of navigating the identity paradox becomes exponentially complex. Managing the identity paradox necessarily involves a continual negotiation of the norms of inclusion (Ferdman, 2017).

This reality itself presents yet another paradox: that we achieve inclusion when we establish norms that are both stable and consistent in their alignment to inclusive outcomes—yet at the same time are flexible, leaving room for reexamination and revision, as the context and people with whom we interact change (Ferdman, 2017).

#### *What This Means for Inclusive Leaders*

Inclusive leadership requires understanding and holding these and other complex paradoxes. Inclusive leaders cannot and should not seek to resolve these paradoxes, but they must become skilled in managing them. Henderson (Chapter 22) suggests that to manage such paradoxes and their underlying polarities, inclusive leaders must first work to clearly identify or "see" them. Then they must map the polarities, identifying the tradeoffs involved in prioritizing one over the other, and understand their respective impacts on stakeholders. Henderson advises inclusive leaders, once armed with these insights, to leverage polarities. Toward this end, leaders must define triggers and action steps to determine when they must rebalance efforts that might have gone too far in emphasizing one polarity over the other. Such practices can be viewed as an operationalization of what Van Bommel and colleagues (Chapter 8), as well as Booysen (Chapter 14), describe as a "both/and" mindset.

## Approaches for Cultivating Inclusive Leadership

Given its complexity, how can inclusive leadership be developed effectively? Although authors described a range of compelling approaches for cultivating inclusive leadership, these are generally rooted in common principles.

For example, across the board there was widespread acknowledgment that developing skills as complex as those needed for inclusive leadership requires the application of experiential learning frameworks. As such, the developmental path outlined in Kolb's (Kolb & Kolb, 2005) model of starting with (1) concrete experience (i.e., active engagement in an activity through which individuals can gain a fact base of knowledge that can be used to interpret and conceptualize inclusive leadership); followed by (2) reflection on this experience (i.e., assessing what one has learned from the previous step); then (3) abstract conceptualization (i.e., a process of development of new ideas and principles that can be applied to new experiences and situations); and finally (4) active exploration (i.e., where the learner tries to apply the ideas developed in stage three). Complementing this experiential approach to leadership development, several authors such as Murrell and colleagues (Chapter 24) also touted the importance of situation-based content (Lave & Wenger, 1991) and coaching to facilitate real-world application of the knowledge that learners developed.

Since intrapersonal work emerged as a critical prerequisite for inclusive leader effectiveness, we also observed a consistent emphasis on experiences and tools that would facilitate self-assessment. For example, Dillon and Caspi Sable (Chapter 26) described a compelling assessment process that enables leaders to measure and understand the underlying causes of the gap between their intent to lead inclusively and their actual impact in realizing this intent. This assessment process involves gathering 360-feedback from colleagues and forms the fact base for an introspective exercise enabling learners to explore the actions and underlying assumptions producing the intent–impact gap in their inclusive leadership profiles.

Another cornerstone of several of the approaches described is a reorientation of learners' mindsets about the nature and purpose of leadership itself. For example, Murrell and colleagues' program encourages learners to consider inclusive leadership as a means to achieving corporate social responsibility goals—rather than as a means of achieving short-term business performance goals—the typical measure of leadership effectiveness in a corporate context.

Similarly, the Leadership Learning Community Collaboration (Chapter 28) describes situational learning content that enables learners to rethink dominant heroic leadership models and instead consider a model of leadership that is not individualistic, but rather collective. Welp and

Schein's (Chapter 25) focus on helping White men reorient—aided in part by a physical removal from corporate contexts—from a transactional (level 1) model of leadership to a more personal (level 2) model, represents yet another example of this paradigm-shifting feature of inclusive leadership development.

Finally, we learned that inclusive leadership development is at its best when it enables learners to continually grow through generative questioning and connection with others across difference. Compelling examples of this come from Cruz Teller's description of an appreciative approach to organization development as a way to inspire inclusion (Chapter 27) and from Winters's description of bold, inclusive conversations (Chapter 16). Critical components of Winters's approach include (1) listening and questioning to learn and deepen understanding rather than to achieve closure, and (2) moving from mere exposure to difference to actively exploring it.

## A Call to Action

In an age of increasing globalization, extraordinary polarization, and growing economic inequality, the challenge of inclusive leadership is one we should accept—individually and collectively. It is unlikely that we will effectively succeed in meeting the myriad of complex and novel problems that we face today—from climate change to the threat of global pandemics—without doing so.

We hope and trust that this book has been successful in addressing key obstacles to the practice of inclusive leadership by filling gaps in our understanding of what inclusive leadership is and how to develop it. We acknowledge that while the insights we offer are necessary for advancing the practice of inclusive leadership, they are nonetheless insufficient to drive change. To realize the promise of inclusive leadership, we also need to change beliefs and mindsets about its power and impact so that we can motivate ourselves and each other to rise to the challenge and opportunity it represents. At the very least, we hope to have given advocates of inclusive leadership the knowledge, tools, and resources to change hearts and minds by their own examples, and to leverage small wins to create the momentum we need to achieve a tipping point in the practice of inclusive leadership.

## References

Ferdman, B. M. (2017). Paradoxes of inclusion: Understanding and managing the tensions of diversity and multiculturalism. *The Journal of Applied Behavioral Science*, *53*(2), 235–263. https://doi.org/10.1177/0021886317702608

Ferdman, B. M., & Davidson, M. N. (2002). A matter of difference—Inclusion: What can I and my organization do about it? *The Industrial-Organizational Psychologist*, *39*(4), 80–85.

Ferdman, B. M., & Deane, B. R. (Eds.). (2014). *Diversity at work: The practice of inclusion*. San Francisco, CA: Jossey-Bass.
Kegan, R., & Lahey, L. L. (2016). *An everyone culture: Becoming a deliberately developmental organization*. Boston, MA: Harvard Business Review Press.
Kolb, A. Y., & Kolb, D. A. (2005). Learning styles and learning spaces: Enhancing experiential learning in higher education. *Academy of Management Learning & Education*, *4*(2), 193–212. https://doi.org/10.5465/amle.2005.17268566
Lave, J., & Wenger, E. (1991). *Situated learning: Legitimate peripheral participation*. Cambridge, England: Cambridge University Press.

# Index